CROSSING

✶ THE ✶

RUBICON

THE DECLINE OF THE
AMERICAN EMPIRE
AT THE END OF
THE AGE OF OIL

D0004210

MICHAEL C. RUPPERT

foreword by Catherine Austin Fitts

NEW SOCIETY PUBLISHERS

Cataloging in Publication Data:
A catalog record for this publication is available from the National Library of Canada.

Copyright © 2004 by Michael C. Ruppert.
All rights reserved.

Cover design and illustration by Diane McIntosh.

Printed in Canada.

Paperback ISBN: 0-86571-540-8

Inquiries regarding requests to reprint all or part of *Crossing the Rubicon* should be addressed to New Society Publishers at the address below.

To order directly from the publishers, please add $4.50 shipping to the price of the first copy, and $1.00 for each additional copy (plus GST in Canada). Send check or money order to:

New Society Publishers
P.O. Box 189, Gabriola Island, BC V0R 1X0, Canada
1-800-567-6772

New Society Publishers' mission is to publish books that contribute in fundamental ways to building an ecologically sustainable and just society, and to do so with the least possible impact on the environment, in a manner that models this vision. We are committed to doing this not just through education, but through action. We are acting on our commitment to the world's remaining ancient forests by phasing out our paper supply from ancient forests worldwide. This book is one step towards ending global deforestation and climate change. It is printed on acid-free paper that is 100% old growth forest-free **(100% post-consumer recycled)**, processed chlorine free, and printed with vegetable based, low VOC inks. For further information, or to browse our full list of books and purchase securely, visit our website at: www.newsociety.com

NEW SOCIETY PUBLISHERS   www.newsociety.com

Advance Praise for
Crossing the Rubicon

Astounding! Alarming! ... And yet at last, with this — Mike Ruppert's beyond-courageous offering — we gain sight of the whole of corporate-managed, government-assisted, bank-laundered, drug-funded plunder. And a jolt to spur our movements to take back the world.

— Chellis Glendinning, PhD, author of
Chiva: A Village Takes on the Global Heroin Trade and
Off the Map: An Expedition Deep into Empire and the Global Economy

Mike Ruppert was one of the first journalists to understand the concept and importance of Peak Oil. What is more important, he has connected the dots: he understands the relationships between this historic watershed and the geopolitical events of our time. Mike still has the instincts of a cop (which he once was), but the criminals he is tracking these days are no small-time hoodlums; they are some of the most powerful people on the planet. If you want to understand the dynamics of the oil-money-drugs-and-war imperial system in which we are all embedded, start with this book.

— Richard Heinberg, author of *The Party's Over* and *Powerdown*

Mike Ruppert represents, from top to bottom, the best tradition of an independent thinking, open-minded, uncorruptable, humorous, prudent, American Cop. After running during his police career into conflicts with the drug dealing part of the CIA, Mike knows that government information seldom equals its disinformation. The doubt about the official 9/11 story brought us together. From the first day after 9/11, I could follow his scouting into the real world behind government propaganda. I firmly believe at the end of three years of conducting a really independent investigation, that Ruppert is not only heading in the right direction, but also touching the inner sanctum of the hidden government agenda.

— Andreas von Bülow, former German Cabinet Minister and Parliamentary Secretary, author of *The CIA and September 11*

Fasten your thinking caps! Something is clearly terribly wrong at the heart of American politics. The same is true of the mainstream media. Reporters just aren't asking enough difficult and dangerous questions. Michael Ruppert has been asking disconcerting but critical questions for more than two decades, even when it meant confronting unpleasant truths that challenge the very basis of industrial society. His unflinching reporting on the facts behind the coming decline of global petroleum has been an extraordinary service to the world. Whatever you think of Ruppert's bold hypotheses about the geopolitics of oil, this provocative book will force you to confront the contradictions of our increasingly unsustainable global economy.

— Julian Darley, author of *High Noon for Natural Gas: The New Energy Crisis,* founder and director of The Post Carbon Institute, and founder of www.globalpublicmedia.com

I'm proud Mike asked me to appear in his seminal film, *The Truth and Lies of 9/11*. Mike has traveled and studied the Peak Oil issue with world renowned experts, and he and I share an abiding shock at the rampant despoilment of our planet, through fake stoked resource wars that have real consequences in real lives. Mike has something to say and I'm going to listen.

— US Congresswoman Cynthia McKinney, Georgia

Mike Ruppert's work should be a household item for any American Muslim, Jew or Christian looking to understand the difference between authentic religious piety versus the criminality that occupies much of the headlines these days. He brings this home for every American by exposing the perpetrators here within our own government, most notably using 9-11 as a paradigm. All folk of religion must have the courage to expose the agendas that use 'religion' as a guise, be these agendas in the name of 'Islamic resurgence' or 'Securing the Jewish State.' Kudos to Mike, one of the last of the true-blooded Americans around.

— Faiz Khan M.D., Triage Emergency Physician on 9-11, Assistant Imam, New York

In a sector rife with disinformation and ill-informed comment, Michael Ruppert's work stands out as a conspicuous beacon of valuable well-informed analysis. His claims are bold and contrarian and have dramatic implications for the global oil price should the global economy experience a sustained recovery while Iraqi oil supplies are curtailed. Ruppert believes (with ample documentation to justify his view) that depletion dynamics will fuel energy price appreciation more in this cycle than any prior one. If he is anywhere near correct, as we believe, the oil market will begin an historic cyclical upmove with a tighter supply demand balance than at any prior cycle. For anyone wishing to understand the full ramifications of this for the energy markets and global economy, Ruppert's work is invaluable.

— Marshall Auerback, international portfolio strategist for David W. Tice & Associates, Inc., and weekly contributor to www.prudentbear.com

DEDICATION

For everyone who never gave up on me.

For every American and for every citizen of Germany, France, Britain, Canada, Australia, New Zealand, Indonesia, Malaysia, Japan, Russia, The Netherlands, Ireland, Scotland, Italy, Spain, Portugal, Egypt, Saudi Arabia, Lebanon, Israel, Iraq, India, Portugal, Greece, Sweden, Denmark, Norway, Poland, Belgium, Mexico, Panama, Cuba, Venezuela, Colombia, Peru, Argentina, Brazil – and every other country – who stood up after 9/11 and said "We do not accept this!" — and who stayed the course.

For every generation following mine from whom my generation and the ones before it have stolen so cruelly. For all life on this planet.

For every American government official, especially those from the State Department, the Department of Justice, and the Department of Defense who has resigned as a matter of conscience and principle since 9/11.

For every street cop, brick agent, and Air Force officer or enlisted person who did their damndest to prevent 9/11 and who fought for what was right – especially the ones who paid a price for it.

For every non-American press organization that pushed a well-understood envelope to its limits and beyond.

For Cynthia McKinney, Barbara Lee, Ron Paul, and Paul Wellstone. You are not Democrats or Republicans. You are Americans.

For Ellen and Louis Neil Mariani.

For John O'Neill

For every person who has died in the violence unleashed by 9/11, and for the ones who have yet to join them.

For a 27-year-old honest LAPD cop who thought he was acting just like any other cop would act, only to have his life taken away; and who was stupid enough to think that he had an obligation – as a matter of honor – to speak of what he had seen; long before he found out that it was a little bigger than he thought at first. The first bite was the hardest. You are free now. Get on with your life.

And for my ex-wife Mary who on September 11, 2001, sat for so many painful hours in her Battery Park apartment; trapped in front of a living TV screen she could not turn off; sending out e-mails from Hell reading, "My God, they're jumping …. I can see them when they hit …. Another plane just hit …. The buildings are coming down.

I don't know where to go."

May God grant all of you peace, a smile, and a good night's sleep.

We get answers that don't answer;

Explanations that don't explain;

And conclusions that don't conclude.

— Fred Hampton

In a ham and eggs breakfast, the chicken is involved
but the pig is committed.

— Unknown

CONTENTS

ACKNOWLEDGMENTS IX

FOREWORD by Catherine Austin Fitts XIII

INTRODUCTION 1

PART I — MOTIVE

CHAPTER 1: Petroleum Man 22

CHAPTER 2: Cheney Knew 41

CHAPTER 3: The CIA is Wall Street, and Drug Money is King 50

CHAPTER 4: Connecting Drugs and Oil 69

CHAPTER 5: A Criminal Meltdown 76

CHAPTER 6: Laying the Foundation: Destroy Russia,
Prepare the Battlefield 82

CHAPTER 7: Caspian Corruption 94

CHAPTER 8: Setting Up the War: Pakistan's ISI,
America's Agent for Protecting the Taliban and al Qaeda 103

CHAPTER 9: Business with the bin Ladens: The Real Saudi Arabia 123

PART II — MEANS

CHAPTER 10: PROMIS: Controlling the Data 152

CHAPTER 11: Vreeland I 175

CHAPTER 12: Executing a Conspiracy: Shame and Honor
in the FBI – An Air Force Colonel Blows the Whistle 203

CHAPTER 13: Penetration 225

CHAPTER 14: 9/11 Insider Trading, or "You Didn't Really
See That, Even Though We Saw It" 238

CHAPTER 15: Israel 254

CHAPTER 16: Silencing Congress 269

CHAPTER 17: Vreeland II: Silencing Me 291

PART III — OPPORTUNITY

CHAPTER 18: The Attacks 308

CHAPTER 19: Wargames and High Tech: Paralyzing the
System to Pull Off the Attacks 333

CHAPTER 20: Q&A: Many Asked, Some Answered
– and a Golden Moment 357

CHAPTER 21: The Last Hearing: *FTW* Confronts on the
Wargames; NORAD Runs 393

CHAPTER 22: Giuliani and TRIPOD II 404

CHAPTER 23: Dick Cheney, FEMA, and "Persons of Interest" 412

CHAPTER 24: The Secret Service and National Special
Security Events 427

CHAPTER 25: The Commission's Wild Blue Yonder 437

PART IV — EMPIRE AND DECLINE

CHAPTER 26: The Record 448

CHAPTER 27: "We Don't Need No Badges" 471

CHAPTER 28: Conquering the American People 482

CHAPTER 29: Biological Warfare 505

CHAPTER 30: The Order of Battle 527

CHAPTER 31: Peak Oil Revisited — The Bill Collector Calls 554

CHAPTER 32: Summation: Ladies and Gentlemen of the Jury 570

APPENDIX A: Joint Chiefs of Staff "Northwoods" Document 595

APPENDIX B: Vreeland Financial Document Sample 609

APPENDIX C: Iraqi/Saudi Oilfields Information 610

ENDNOTES 618

INDEX 658

Glossary of Acronyms 672

About the Author 675

Acknowledgments

This may be the most difficult part of the entire book to write. To borrow freely from Winston Churchill, I feel as if one man has never owed so much to so many.

My first and greatest thanks go to two men, without whose tireless work, their faith in me and in this project, this book would have died stillborn in the wreckage of a hundred obstacles over the last two years: Ken Levine; my indefatigable and masterful agent and publicist; and Jamey Hecht, PhD, my editor and fellow dreamer. Watching both of you gear up and show up, day after day, through numbing fatigue, endless frustrations, and myriad uncertainties, gave me the inspiration I needed to stay at it. Though I am sure that some critics will step forward and label me anti-Semitic for having criticized Israel's foreign policy, I will never forget, and the readership will not be able to ignore, the fact that two American Jews quite literally made this book happen. You believed because I believed. I believed because you believed.

I must also thank two of the world's most courageous, independent, and brilliant women: Catherine Austin Fitts, one of the greatest teachers I've ever had; and the most Honorable Cynthia McKinney, the former and next Representative of Georgia's Fourth District. I have watched both of you endure and persevere through obstacles, attacks, and challenges that would have defeated stronger people than me. We have stayed united through all of them. I can't tell either one of you of the number of times you have wordlessly instructed me about what strength is. You have told the truth where truth telling mattered most, and you have braved the retaliation from which others shrank. I would follow either one of you through flame and hail, and I know you have my back.

Special thanks are also due to New Society, the publishers of this book. Your entire team jumped on this project with commitment, and dedication. The way you stepped up to the plate and the enthusiasm you have shown has given me greater faith than you know. It just may help change this deeply troubled world.

No less important are the excellent writers who have made *From The Wilderness* a respected landmark over the last six and a half years, and especially the last three: Dale Allen Pfeiffer, *FTW's* Energy Prophet; Stan Goff, a soldier of honor and compassion on so many fronts whose passion and insights are second to none;

Michael Kane, whose independent journalism and Hip Hop are as intense as they are instructive; Tom Flocco, the bulldog who would not let go of the Kean Commission and some of the most important 9/11 stories; Nick Levis whose incisive thinking helped us all to find and crystallize our positions; Mike Davidson, who did such great reporting on the microbiology murders and biowarfare issues; and to Wayne Madsen in Washington, whose inside knowledge on intelligence issues and whose sense of humor kept our spirits high. To all the other writers who have graced the pages of *From The Wilderness* with your hard work and dedicated research, I offer my undying thanks.

Thanks also to *FTW's* office staff and all the others who kept us self-supporting, self-sustaining, and completely independent over the years so that I did not once have to look at any journalistic compass other than the truth. Without the compass, the map is nothing. I thank Secillia Sliffe, Jason Majik, Ryan Spiegl, Tim Barker, Andrea and C.J. Shepherd.

Equally important are all of *FTW's* subscribers and all of the donors who kept us afloat through countless emergencies, trials and challenges. Some of you have been with us from day one, and your loyalty has kept me strong in many difficult nights and days.

Special thanks to all of the donors who made it possible for *FTW* to run full-page newspaper ads in some of the nation's largest newspapers before they got wise and priced us out of the market. This especially includes true leaders like Jack Gubanc, Faiz Khan, Professor Francis Boyle, and so many others.

I thank also every event organizer, promoter, and sponsor who brought me to speak at more than 30 events in eight different countries since 9/11. I know there are many names I will forget here, and I ask your forgiveness in advance: Barry Zwicker, Duncan Roads, Nick Levis, Ronald Thoden, Heiner Buecker, Ian Woods, Michel Chossudovsky, Carol Brouillet, Terry Burrows, Dr. Faiz Khan, Pinnacle Quest International, and so many, many more.

Very special thanks to all of the Pacifica Radio Network supporters, listeners, and activists who fought messy wars against censorship and who kept my message going out over the airwaves, who countered the spinmeisters and who kept the debate focused on the important issues: Tracy Larkins, Eva Georgia, Gus Newport, Kellia Ramares, Larry Chin, Ian Johnston, and so many others. What a blessing it is for me to have enjoyed such loyalty and consistency.

Special thanks are due to Canada, its wonderful and decent people, its love of justice, its sense of fairness, and for all the moose you have promised to show me but which I have never seen. In particular I would like to thank two brave and forthright Canadian lawyers, Rocco Galati and Paul Slansky, who laid out the record of Delmart "Mike" Vreeland in a way that history cannot ignore. Hey, what are a few dead cats, smashed windows, and death threats anyway?

I thank all of my supporters in France, Britain, Latin America, and Australia, who have made me feel that I am a citizen of the world. I must also say a very special thanks to former German cabinet minister and parliamentary secretary Andreas von Bülow. Your generosity, your leadership, your courage, and your hospitality have meant more to me than you know. Cologne is indeed one of the most beautiful cities in the world. Without your hospitality, I would not have had the opportunity to see the house where Beethoven was born or hear such sublime chamber music.

Special thanks to all of the American Muslims who invited me to speak in their Mosques, and to all of the American Jews who took to this book and my work in the full recognition that we all worship the same God. This has been living brotherhood and spiritual integrity at its highest level. By your actions you have reminded a forgetful world that there are but two commandments: That thou shall love the Lord thy God with all thy heart, mind, and soul; and that thou shall love thy neighbor as thyself.

Thanks to Barbara Honegger, who kept hammering on the wargames until we all paid notice. Although I don't agree with every position you take and we have had our problems, I cannot deny that you showed me the most important lead I needed to put it all together. No one can take that away from you.

Thanks to my teachers on energy: Dale Allen Pfeiffer (again), Colin Campbell, Jean Laherrère, Richard Heinberg, Julian Darley, Kjell Aleklett, my newfound friend Ali Samsam Bakhtiari, and the candid Matthew Simmons.

Thanks to my teachers on writing and research; those who were both courageous pathfinders and who saved my life by having the courage to say that things were very, very wrong so many years ago: Peter Dale Scott, Fletcher Prouty, and Alfred McCoy. I have tried to emulate you wise men and, in that process, have become my truest and best self thus far. I wish the world had listened to you decades ago.

Thank you to my father Ed for lending me $500 to write a book 24 years ago. Although we saw three different books get close to life only to watch them mysteriously die, you stayed the course with me, and I am so proud to have placed a copy of this book in your hands before you "graduate" and leave this world.

Thanks to my mother, Madelyn, who never stopped believing in me until the moment of her death in December 2001. I can hear your cheers from beyond the grave.

Thanks to my God, who never left my side and asked only that I continue to show up, even when there was no hope and no energy, no vision and no money. Thanks to the God who taught me that faith the size of a mustard seed could indeed move mountains and who heard all of my prayers and who responded, perfectly and consistently, every time I put one foot in front of the other, believing that no matter what dark places I walked into and through, it was nothing more than the busting of the grandest illusion of all: fear – False Evidence Appearing Real.

Special thanks to Lois who came along late in the game, but at just the moment when I needed a stable, loving, supporting hand who could make God's reality accessible to my tired spirits. Thanks for making me laugh; for making me look at myself; and for making me find things in myself that gave me strength and a belief that I could reach the finish line. Thanks for making me believe there were some things to look forward to once I had crossed it.

Thanks to Richard Clarke who left so many great breadcrumbs. I don't know how you got away with it.

Thanks to Don Henley, Jackson Browne, and David Baerwald. Maybe I'll get to meet two of you someday.

But above all, I offer my deepest and most undying gratitude to all of the dedicated researchers who flooded my e-mail inbox (and many others) with as many as 400 e-mails a day. You gave me the stories, you caught the leads, you found the inconsistencies and the lies, you did the digging, and you asked the questions that made it possible for me to put this book together. I may have had the map before 9/11, but there were many uncharted areas on it. You charted some critical lands and seas.

Writing a major book like this is a process that cannot be fully described. No "one" just sits down and writes a good non-fiction book with more than 900 footnotes without help. It is a labor of love for all who participate. And if there is anything that gives me the slightest hope for the future, it is man's capacity to love life, to care for other men and women, and to undergo sacrifice for the sake of something other than their own well-being and comfort.

It is not over yet for mankind. Miracles can happen without our permission. This book is living proof of that.

Michael C. Ruppert
August 14, 2004

Foreword

A MATTER OF LIFE AND DEATH

By Catherine Austin Fitts

The real deal on corporate media

In 1990, a *New York Times* reporter writing about my work implementing financial transparency and controls as an Assistant Secretary in the first Bush administration resigned to prevent the *Times'* Washington Bureau Chief from intentionally falsifying the story. The bureau chief kept his job, a first rate investigative reporter left the news profession, and the story was buried. This manipulation protected 1980s black budget fraud at the US Department of Housing and Urban Development ("HUD"). It was one of my many lessons on the economic interests and political loyalties of corporate media.

Indeed, during the 1980s, the savings and loan industry and government insurance programs were stripped of an estimated $500 billion by syndicates of military, intelligence, and private financial interests. The profits were used to buy up banking, industrial, and media companies and to finance political campaigns. From a greater position of political, judicial, and economic power in the 1990s, these same syndicates then stripped an estimated $6 trillion of investors' value in pump and dump stock market and mortgage market schemes and an estimated $4 trillion of taxpayer money from the US federal government.

In 1997, the *Washington Post* killed a cover story on my efforts to help HUD insure the integrity of its mortgage programs, thus making possible the subsequent disappearance of $59 billion from HUD as a part of this orgy of "piratization" of government assets by private interests. Soon thereafter, when I attended a private invitation-only reception with colleagues at her home, Katherine Graham, the owner of the *Washington Post*, snubbed me by refusing to greet me in her receiving line.

Washington Post corporate interests profited from HUD programs used to gentrify Washington, DC neighborhoods. Check out the last few pages in Graham's autobiography — it's there in black and white. What's not to be found in the pages of the *Washington Post* or Graham's book is the "real deal" on who has profited from insider real estate development or narcotics trafficking in these same Washington neighborhoods — or from reinvestment of the resulting profits in stocks of local corporations like the *Washington Post*.

I do not mean to single out the *New York Times* or the *Washington Post*. I have had similar experiences with the *Washington Times,* the *Wall Street Journal, US News* and *World Report* and *Dow Jones Newswire,* to name a few. Trusted friends and colleagues have experienced similar situations with numerous newspapers, magazines, and networks owned and operated by corporate media interests.

George Orwell once said that omission is the greatest form of lie. That's the best description I know of corporate media today.

The growing power of real media

The cost to you of supporting corporate media is not just the subscription prices or the time lost to advertisements. It's the cost of omission — failing to tell you what you need to know. Consider that this cost includes:

— Your share of the $10 trillion that has been moved out of the US stock market and government without your having been informed by an alert and objective news media in time for you to take actions to protect yourself and your family.

— The dilution of your Constitutional freedoms and the vesting of power in a small group of individuals who defraud you (the public) of staggering sums of money and then use that money to buy up media and control your government and judiciary and to compromise your rights and the rights of people around the world.

— The impact on you and your children of having your streets and schools overwhelmed with dangerous narcotics and prescription drugs.

Our financial system depends on liquidity. In turn, liquidity depends on a popular faith in the system's "rule of law." Global leadership's power depends on the ability to combine criminal cash flows with liquid stock market and government securities. This is why Mike Ruppert's *From The Wilderness* and a growing global network of Internet media are accomplishing so much as we shift our readership and subscription dollars to them. The powers that be are highly motivated to protect the legitimacy of their financial system. If a little bit of well-placed illumination exposes some of this criminality, the criminals take notice. That little bit of illumination can also embarrass them a lot in front of their families and neighbors. Who wants to go to a PTA meeting after Mike Ruppert has explained that you are on the board of, or a lead investor in, a company complicit in slave trafficking or the torture of children?

David can defeat Goliath if we provide the resources to finance the stones — as you have helped to do by buying this book.

The record speaks for itself

The fact that America and many countries around the globe are being strip-mined in a manner that results in the destruction and "piratization" of our infrastructure

and natural resources, the reduction of the value of our personal assets and retirement and health care benefits and the abrogation of our civil liberties is not
something that the corporate media has made clear to you. Mike Ruppert has.

Allegations that the CIA and Department of Justice were complicit in the flow
of cocaine into South Central LA; that the Clintons were partnered with George
H. W. Bush and Oliver North through the offices of the National Security Council
in a little Iran-Contra arms and cocaine trafficking operation in Mena, Arkansas;
and that Hillary Clinton's law firm was helping launder the local share of the profits
through state housing agency securities and investments were never addressed objec-
tively by the corporate media. Mike Ruppert covered these stories and broke the story
of the possible connection between these allegations and the Clinton impeachment.

It is highly unlikely that you read or heard in the corporate media that the price
of gold was being manipulated to turn off our financial "smoke alarm," or to "pira-
tize" significant inventories of gold out of government and central banks globally
at suppressed values. It is highly unlikely that you read or heard that money was
allegedly being siphoned off from federal agencies using PROMIS-type software
programs and that important financial and securities investigation records were
destroyed in the Oklahoma City and 9/11 attacks. Mike Ruppert's subscribers
have read these stories.

You did not read or hear in the corporate media that the events of 9/11 "just
happened" to resolve the stalemate in the defense appropriations subcommittee
created when, in the face of the "disappearance" of $3.3 trillion from the
Department of Defense and a five-year refusal to produce audited financial statements, Congress was challenged with achieving a significant increase in defense
spending. Or that the events of 9/11 allowed the Federal Reserve to adopt highly
inflationary monetary policies that postponed dealing with serious financial system flaws. Mike Ruppert covered these stories.

You did not read or hear in the corporate media that our lives and economy
are entirely dependent on fossil fuel, that world oil and gas production will soon
decline, and what these facts have to do with the events of 9/11 and the subsequent invasions of Afghanistan and Iraq. Mike Ruppert covered these stories.

All these facts and allegations have been made abundantly clear by Mike and
his publication, *From The Wilderness*. While corporate media refines the art of
profitable omission, Mike Ruppert has risked his name, his financial security, and
his life to warn us — again and again.

An info cop's beat: Watching your back

Through his website, radio talk-show appearances, speeches, DVDs, monthly
newsletter, and e-mail updates, Mike has been telling us for years what he sees,
hears, and feels about "the real deal."

Mike Ruppert had to leave the Los Angeles Police Department because he tried to
prevent government-protected narcotics trafficking. After learning that the corporate

media would not tell the truth about this important story, Mike became a publisher. In the face of widespread public denial of the fact of our economic dependence on "narco-dollars" and warfare, Mike persisted. Mike is determined to help us face and recover from our financial addiction to an estimated $500 billion – $1 trillion of annual US money laundering.

In one sense, Mike is still a cop. He's publisher as "info-cop." His "info-beat" is the intelligence we need to protect ourselves — even if the lifting of the shades of denial means exposing our own complicity in the enjoyment of the fruits of the trickle down of dirty money.

Throughout the years, I have heard a lot of criticism of Mike and his work. For example:

Mike is too aggressive.

It's true that Mike is unbelievably aggressive. Mike's aggression is one of the reasons I am a subscriber to *From The Wilderness*. I want to hear about danger real loud, real clear, and on a real-time basis. I want Mike shouting "fire!" while I still have time to get out of the theater alive. It takes incredible aggression to stand up to the military banking complex and the academics, think tanks, not-for-profits, and corporate media they fund. All the money on the planet can, and does, buy a lot of attack poodles. It is full-time entertainment just watching them nip at Mike's heels and piddle on the fire hydrants when he's around.

Mike has a point of view.

It's true. Mike always expresses an opinion on matters covered in his stories. He is both commentator and activist in a new genre of what Al Giordano of Narco News calls "authentic journalism." This is another reason why I am a subscriber. A point of view is worth a heap of analytical power. Mike's job as "info-cop" is not to have an objective point of view. His job is to make sure we are safe by sharing the information we need. The only potential risk we can price, adjust for, or dismiss is the risk of which we are aware. If that kind of journalism comes with a vision and a perspective from the writer, I want that too.

Mike is "in your face."

Mike is not shy. You disagree? You have a problem? You got a question? You can take it to Mike, have it out with Mike, and speak your mind with Mike. Mike will say it to your face loud and clear. You can do the same. The only thing you can't do is to get him to agree with you when he does not. Mike's temper is big — but not as big as his heart.

Mike's courage and intelligence can save not just your time and your money, but your life.

This one's true, too. I'm a case in point.

A map of South Central Los Angeles

After a successful career on Wall Street, I moved to Washington, DC, to serve as Assistant Secretary of Housing in the first Bush administration. After I left the administration, I was invited to join the Federal Reserve as a governor. I declined the invitation in order to start my own investment bank, Hamilton Securities. Cleaning up Iran-Contra period fraud had persuaded me that democracy and markets depended on citizens having access to government financial disclosure contiguous to the political jurisdictions in which they elected officials. Owners of small businesses, farms, and real estate needed to finance privately with equity and stop depending on government credit programs that created a negative-return-on-investment economy in neighborhoods.

Hamilton was developing a software tool called "Community Wizard" that would have provided communities with their own access to rich databases and software tools that painted a clear picture of how government money works in each community. The first step to reengineering a negative-return-on-investment economy is to "see" it. In addition, we were designing a suite of software tools that would allow us to conform valuations of street-level land, housing, and real estate equity with valuations of outstanding mortgage and real estate securities. Such pricing data is essential for understanding how to reduce the harm done through the political and financial manipulation of neighborhood land and housing markets.

In March 1998, congressional hearings were held on one of two CIA Inspector General reports addressing allegations (especially those of Gary Webb in his stories for the *San Jose Mercury News,* which shaped his 1999 book *Dark Alliance: The CIA, The Contras, and the Crack-Cocaine Explosion*) about the role of the CIA and the Department of Justice in cocaine trafficking in South Central Los Angeles. Immediately prior to those hearings, Judge Stanley Sporkin approved the transfer of Hamilton's records to the control of a court-appointed "special master." As a result, Hamilton's offices were seized, our financial records manipulated in an attempt to falsely frame us, our computer systems ripped apart, and our digital records transferred to court control. During these same Congressional hearings, a 1982 memorandum of understanding between the Department of Justice and the CIA came to light. The memorandum effectively relieved the CIA of the legal obligation to report narcotics trafficking. The CIA General Counsel when that memorandum of understanding was negotiated and signed was Stanley Sporkin.

The transfer of control of Community Wizard and Hamilton's other programs and databases to the special master had the practical result of ensuring that the development of our software tools and the potential for public and private access to them came to an end. What was destroyed included the databases that supported maps of HUD mortgage defaults in South Central Los Angeles.

Hamilton had posted data maps on the Internet to show how the HUD money worked in select cities, one of which was Los Angeles. We hadn't understood all the implications when we posted them. The data for the Los Angeles map — specifically the South Central LA portion — show patterns of significant mortgage defaults contiguous to narcotics trafficking activity described in the *Dark Alliance* allegations. Such data has the potential to raise important questions regarding allegations that HUD mortgage insurance programs were being used to launder narcotics profits and that such profits were being magnified through the issuance of mortgage securities backed by fraudulent HUD-insured mortgage loans. Mike Ruppert had worked as a narcotics investigator for the Los Angeles Police Department, and his first words when I showed him the maps were "Holy Smokes!"

After the seizure of the Hamilton offices, I became for all intents and purposes a prisoner in my own home — a beautiful carriage house located in the Dupont Circle neighborhood of Washington, adjacent to the financial district and not far from the seat of national power. I was living with physical harassment and surveillance while various people around me were trying to persuade me that the dead animals on my doorstep, the break-ins, the people following me on foot or by car, and the clicking noises on my telephone were one ongoing coincidence. I determined that my life depended on learning as much as possible about who was really in charge.

I called a distributor of videos on government corruption and asked him to recommend films documenting government-sponsored narcotics trafficking and financial fraud. He sent me a copy of a tape of Mike Ruppert's confrontation of then-CIA Director John Deutsch at a town hall meeting. The confrontation was soon made famous by inclusion in an online video, *Crack the CIA,* which was made available on Guerrilla News Network and won an award at the Sundance Film Festival. I took one look at Mike making mincemeat of a very savvy CIA director on global TV and realized that this was a person who could help transform my situation.

I will never forget one of the first things Mike wrote to me by e-mail. "If they shoot at you [from the apartment building next to your house], remember to run toward the gunfire," he said. It was at that moment that the anxiety that came from living an Orwellian nightmare started to ease. The more I spoke with Mike, the more my cognitive dissonance disappeared. There was logic to the world. I could understand covert operations and narco-dollars. I was not alone. My pastor once said, *"If we can face it, God can fix it."* Mike made it possible for me to face what was happening, and as I faced it, God indeed went to work to fix it.

Early courage

Mike's extraordinary courage also spared me from a frightening loneliness in the darkest moments that descended upon those of us who tried to warn our loved ones during the events of 9/11. The official lies and profiteering by our leadership were met immediately and relentlessly by Mike Ruppert's outraged howl as he demanded answers to important questions. Thanks largely to Mike's initial stand and his ongoing support for key members in his media network — Michel Chossudovsky of Global Research, Alastair Thompson of Scoop Media, Al Giordano of Narco News, Tom Flocco of TomFlocco.com, and others — the 9/11 Truth Movement has staked out the moral high ground and is gathering strength every day. Thanks to Mike's courage, the questions regarding the possibility of insider responsibility or involvement and criminal gross negligence have remained on the table, right where they belong.

Since first meeting him in 1998, I have been "in cahoots" with Mike in various ways. Before leaving Washington, I had Mike come and speak to a group of Washington insiders at my home. Mike's speech was interrupted briefly by the appearance of two unmarked black helicopters hovering over my roof garden, an occurrence that inspired one of the guests — an influential reporter — to remark that Mike must be "the real deal" if he inspired such attention.

I have since published articles in *From The Wilderness* and had the opportunity to speak with Mike at public events and join him on radio talks shows. I enjoy the rich flow of "real deal" intelligence and the support I have received from Mike and the people I have met through him. I have emerged a more seasoned and knowledgeable investment banker with membership in a new and evolving global network. Litigation with the US government and its informant have helped me develop the skills required to survive and thrive in the midst of growing lawlessness and economic warfare.

If Mike can say "no" to going along with criminality, I can, too. And so can you.

On your side

Here, in a nutshell, is what I have learned about your consumer media choices.

If you want a good crossword puzzle and something safe to talk about at Sunday brunch, then subscribe and listen to the *New York Times,* the *Wall Street Journal,* the *Washington Post,* and network news.

If, instead, you want to know who is stealing your money and your freedoms and planning on drafting your children, and you'd like to find out in time to develop strategies to make sure your family has the health, the freedom, and the financial means necessary to enjoy a Sunday brunch, subscribe to *From The Wilderness* and listen to Mike Ruppert.

Mike Ruppert is an "info cop" who takes sides.

Mike is on your side.

If you are like me, having Mike and his global network of real deal media on your side could be a matter of life and death.

Catherine Austin Fitts
Former Assistant Secretary of Housing (Bush I)
Past Managing Director, Dillon Read.
August 19, 2004
Hickory Valley, Tennessee

Introduction

LADIES AND GENTLEMEN
OF THE JURY...

One thing that no one can dispute is that the attacks of September 11, 2001, were a homicide. Of all police investigations, none is more thoroughly and precisely investigated than the taking of human life as the result of the actions of another. As almost every text for homicide detectives has taught us, the certainty that murders will be thoroughly and fairly investigated according to uniform standards is among the core requirements of human civilization. While these attacks were arguably one of the most serious homicides ever committed, the investigation and "prosecution" of that case by means other than Dick Cheney's "war that will not end in our lifetimes" has never even approached the legal and logical standards governing all such investigations. No real case has ever been made that would pass first muster of even a junior assistant district attorney.

Without such a court process, we are forced to employ analogies and metaphors. But there remains to us the most successful, fundamental strategy for the prosecution of criminal behavior: demonstrating that a suspect did, or did not, have the means, motive, and opportunity to commit the crime.

With respect to al Qaeda and Osama bin Laden, that critical litmus test for any murder prosecution — means, motive, and opportunity — has never been fully applied. In a capital case each of these components would require demonstration "beyond a shadow of doubt." Regardless of whom the suspect(s) turns out to be, these are the basic questions every homicide investigator must seek to answer in the course of the investigation. This book will attempt to do that. In the end the only "suspects" found to meet all of these criteria will not be al Qaeda and Osama bin Laden. They will instead be a group of people operating within certain government agencies, including the White House, for the benefit of major financial interests within the United States and in other countries. This group will specifically include parts of the administration of George W. Bush and, before it, the administration of William Jefferson Clinton. However, the only possible unifying thread will be the intelligence community and, in particular, the United States Secret Service and the Central Intelligence Agency. I realize that this is a frightening statement. I submit that by the end of this book it will be the only statement that encompasses and reasonably explains the facts as documented.

A word about conspiracies

I am an investigator and a journalist. It is not my business to speculate, and my reasoning is not theoretical. As a detective it is my job to gather evidence, consider its authenticity, posit a hypothesis, and test that hypothesis against the larger pattern of facts. So much for "theory." As for the word "conspiracy," it's among the most common terms in the rigorous legal language of American jurisprudence. A conspiracy is generally defined as two or more people who plan to commit an illegal act and who then take one or more specific actions in furtherance of that plan. Conspiracy is a very real term for tens of thousands of minority men and women in the United States who are serving sentences of — in some cases — more than twenty years in federal penitentiaries like Leavenworth for "no-drug conspiracies." In many of those cases someone talked about acquiring drugs and someone else made a phone call asking if someone else had the drugs (in many cases only in very small amounts), and that's all it took to throw away the lives of these non-violent offenders.

One of the most trumpeted themes in the post-9/11 world has been a blanket assertion that such a large conspiracy (if conducted within the US government) could never be concealed from the American people or the people of the world before the crime was committed. It has been sounded by the likes of David Corn at *The Nation* and former National Security Counterterrorism Chief Richard Clarke. Clarke wrote in his 2004 bestseller *Against All Enemies*,

> Conspiracy theorists simultaneously hold two contrary beliefs: a) that the US government is so incompetent that it can miss explanations that the theorists can uncover, and b) that the US government can keep a big and juicy secret. The first belief has some validity. The second idea is pure fantasy.[1]

Richard Clarke misled you here. He also informed, in some very surprising ways. In fact, as I will show you later, he misled in many places in his book. From the Manhattan Project to the Stealth fighter, the US government has successfully kept secrets involving thousands of people. Secondly, in order to execute a conspiracy of the size and type I am suggesting, it is not necessary that thousands of people see the whole picture. The success of the US in maintaining the secrecy around the atom bomb and the Stealth fighter, or in any classified operation, lies in compartmentalization. A technician in Tennessee refining uranium ore in 1943 would have had no knowledge of its intended use, or any moral culpability in any deaths that occurred as a result of it. Another technician in Ohio, mixing a polymer resin in 1985, would have had no knowledge of what an F117A looked like or what it was intended to do.

The government routinely protects itself against disclosure by compelling millions of employees to sign security agreements and secrecy oaths which would make them subject to immediate incarceration or loss of benefits if they talked, even about criminal behavior. Perpetrating the murders of 9/11 required only a few people inside a small circle who did indeed "need to know" the entire plan, or most of the plan, in order to complete their tasks. For reasons of physical safety, freedom from legal sanction, and job security, participants would be motivated — and therefore, guaranteed — not to inform on one another.

This was one of many lessons I learned painfully with my first exposure to covert operations in 1976. In this book I will introduce you to several people who, I believe, had to have known enough to understand that the US government was planning for 9/11 to be successful ahead of time. I make no claim that these are the only ones involved at such a level, nor do I claim to know how many other such people might exist. My investigation will, however, demonstrate how easy it is in practice to conceal a broad conspiratorial agenda when the suspects control information flow and operational procedures inside the government. After two and a half years of investigation my estimate is that the number of people with complete foreknowledge of the attacks of September 11th would likely not exceed two dozen, all of them bound to silence by Draconian secrecy oaths. The actions of some I will name in connection with 9/11, however, certainly place them on a list of possible suspects who need to be thoroughly questioned in a public forum that includes consequences for dishonesty.

For many of you, the facts I present will be things you have never heard of or even considered. I guarantee that they will be fully documented in academic style footnotes so that you — members of the jury — may take them into your own rooms and evaluate them as you would "people's exhibits" in a murder trial. I ask you to accept nothing that I tell you at face value. Rather I demand of you that you make full use of the footnotes by examining the primary sources to which they refer. Examine them as you would a shell casing, a photo of a bloody footprint, a bank statement, or witness testimony. That is your obligation, your sacred duty.

Given that September 11th was a homicide, it was absurd that pronouncements of guilt were made within hours of the attacks, even before interrogation of material witnesses (including key members of the US government and the bin Laden family) or the collection and analysis of physical evidence could take place. Much of the physical evidence was destroyed without examination. That in itself is a key anomaly suggesting guilty knowledge on the part of whoever directed the destruction of evidence at a crime scene. In the case of the World Trade Center, a detective would demand an answer from the Department of Justice and the FBI.

To date, the case that 9/11 was perpetrated solely by Osama bin Laden and al Qaeda has never been proved, even to the most rudimentary standards. In fact, some 35 months after the attacks there has not been a single successful 9/11 prosecution anywhere in the world. The only conviction that had been secured, a German prosecution against Mounir el Motassadeq, charged with aiding the so-called Hamburg cell of Mohammed Atta, was overturned in 2004 because the US government refused to produce key witnesses and evidence relevant to the charges.[2] Every defendant in a Western criminal case has the right to examine the evidence used against him and to cross-examine witnesses.

That fact raises another set of critical questions.

The rules

Nothing changes the obligation to follow the investigative procedures used by any police detective, procedures which have been established by hundreds of years of precedent as the means of finding facts and then reconciling contradictory facts with each other in a way that establishes guilt or innocence. The law is also intended to remove, as thoroughly as possible, any personal interest on the part of witnesses giving testimony, or of persons involved in the prosecution of the case.

The fact that someone has what may be a prejudicial point of view is not disqualifying per se. In a trial these facts are presented to a jury who then weights the testimony according to their assessment of how much or how little the testimony is tainted. What is almost always unethical or disqualifying is a failure to disclose or conceal prejudice or a conflict of interest. The legal assumption is that concealment presumes that the material presented has been knowingly and unfairly biased toward one side or the other. Arguably, someone starting with an acknowledged bias who still claims that a case can be made according to proper evidentiary standards will have to meet an even higher standard than someone who can claim to have no bias at all.

With regard to 9/11, there are no unbiased parties anywhere. Some are psychologically fearful of admitting that the US, and especially the world economy, could possibly be as corrupt as I am going to establish. Some are afraid of losing jobs or suffering economically if what I present is true. Many will be afraid to look at their own complicity in the systemic corruption which helped to create the motive for 9/11 and which would prompt them instead to instantly believe in America's guilt, or Israeli guilt, or Muslim guilt without ever examining a single piece of evidence.

I will disclose and overcome my own bias by adhering to strict standards of investigation and presenting facts. I insist that each reader look inside and do the same with their own biases, fears and preconceptions and that they continue to do so with every page they turn.

Full disclosure

Everything I am about to tell you is abundantly documented at <www.fromthewilderness.com> in the section titled "About Michael C. Ruppert."

Many years ago, I was trained and worked as a police detective. Although my career as a detective with the Los Angeles Police Department was in its relative youth when it ended, I had been "loaned" into detective positions on a number of occasions. This was standard procedure to groom those who had demonstrated the ability and were going to follow that career path. I had spent a mere four weeks on loan to Wilshire Division's Team 5 homicide table to work with a seasoned detective named Mel Kissinger in 1976. I had previously also worked a combined total of about three months as a detective assigned to handle first auto theft and then burglary cases. Most importantly I had been loaned for a cumulative total of almost four months to work as a detective in Wilshire Division's narcotics unit and, aside from that, had been regularly pulled from uniformed field assignments to assist in narcotics investigations. I had shown such a knack for drug cases that in 1976 I was specially chosen and approved, over many senior candidates, to attend a two-week special narcotics investigation program run by the Drug Enforcement Administration. I had taken and passed the written civil service promotional examination for detective and had been given an oral examination score above 90 percent as evaluated by a panel of senior officers.

In July of 1977 I struggled to make sense of a world gone mad. In a last-ditch effort to salvage a relationship with my fiancée, a CIA contract agent named Nordica Theodora D'Orsay (Teddy), I had traveled to find her in New Orleans. Aside from having an enormous number of contacts in both law enforcement and organized crime, she was also a lifelong friend of a niece of the Shah of Iran (Minou Hagstrom) with whom she had attended grade school and junior high in California. Through Teddy I had met members of the royal family (Prince Shariar) and watched as letters came from and went to Tehran (where Minou was living) and Los Angeles. On a hastily arranged vacation, secured with the blessing of my Commanding Officer, Captain Jesse Brewer of LAPD, I had gone on my own, and unofficially, to avoid the scrutiny of LAPD's Organized Crime Intelligence Division (OCID).

Starting in the late spring of 1976 Teddy had wanted me to join her operations from within the ranks of LAPD. But her operations — from what little I had learned — always involved firearms leaving the country and drugs entering the country. Having specialized in drug cases, and looking forward to a career as a narcotics detective, I had steadfastly refused to get involved with drugs in any way. Everything she mentioned in her "terrorist" cases involved either heroin or cocaine, and firearms. Her stock response to my concerns was that "her people" were not interested in drugs. The director of the CIA at the time was George Herbert Walker Bush. I told her that I would never get involved in anything that overlooked narcotics.

Although officially on staff at the LAPD Academy, I had been unofficially loaned to OCID since shortly after January 1977 when Teddy, announcing the start of a new operation, had suddenly disappeared. She left many people, including me, baffled and twisting in the breeze. I became the regular recipient of harassing phone calls, burglaries, surveillances, and threats. The OCID detectives had been pressuring me hard for information about her and her activities. It was information I couldn't have given them even if I had known it. Hoping against hope that I would find some way to understand her involvement with the CIA, the LAPD, the royal family of Iran, the Mafia, and drugs, I set out alone into eight days of Dantean revelations that have determined the course of my life ever since.

Arriving in New Orleans I found her living in an apartment across the river in Gretna. Equipped with a scrambler phone and night vision devices, and working from sealed communiqués delivered by naval and air force personnel from nearby Belle Chasse Naval Air Station, she was involved in something truly ugly. She was arranging for large quantities of weapons to be loaded onto ships leaving for Iran. The ships were owned by a company that is today a subsidiary of Halliburton — Brown and Root. She was working with Mafia associates of New Orleans Mafia boss Carlos Marcello to coordinate the movement of service boats that were bringing large quantities of heroin into the city. The boats arrived regularly at Marcello-controlled docks, unmolested by the New Orleans police she introduced me to. Through her I also met hard-hat divers, military men, Brown and Root employees, former Green Berets, and CIA personnel.

The service boats were retrieving heroin from oil rigs in the Gulf of Mexico, and international waters, oil rigs built and serviced by Brown and Root. More than once during the eight days I spent in New Orleans, I met and ate at restaurants with Brown and Root employees who were boarding those ships and leaving for Iran within days. Once, while leaving a bar and apparently having asked the wrong question, I was shot at in an attempt to scare me off. It was not the last time I was to be shot at, nor was it the last punishment I would ever suffer for asking questions.

Disgusted and heartbroken at witnessing my fiancée and my government smuggling drugs, I ended the relationship. Then I returned to Los Angeles and reported all the activity I had seen — including the connections between Brown and Root and the CIA — to LAPD intelligence officers. They promptly told me that I was crazy and needed to see a psychiatrist they would gladly provide.

One of the smartest things I ever did was to avoid the offered "friendly" psychiatrist and find my own while securing a much needed rest at an LA-area psychiatric hospital. The psychiatrist there correctly diagnosed me with combat fatigue and reported that I was not crazy, just battered. Aside from a dozen tests which all showed that I was both sane and stable, the opinion of one psychiatrist was heavily influenced by a secret tape recording I had made of my fiancée discussing her operations. Upon learning of that tape, OCID promptly seized and destroyed it. Only the integrity of the psychiatrist in a written record saved me when he reported that I had played the tape for him.

I was returned to full duty, without restrictions, in the late fall of 1977. In my remaining fourteen months with LAPD I earned the highest rating reports possible, was certified for promotion to detective and assigned to a month-long school for those about to be promoted. As far as LAPD was concerned I could walk on water. More importantly, as a result of a meticulous paper trail I had compiled with the help of my attorney, Tim Callahan, the City of Los Angeles ultimately ruled that my hospital time had "Injured on Duty" status: it had arisen from what the

OCID detectives had subjected me to, and wh at they had asked me to do. I had been following orders and not acting on my own.

The impending fall of the Shah of Iran in the late autumn of 1978 prompted me to renew my efforts to find out what had happened to my life. Forced out of LAPD under threat of death at the end of 1978, with no pending disciplinary actions, and just days away from promotion, I resigned and made complaints to LAPD's Internal Affairs Division and to the LA office of the FBI. My decision to resign had been made for me when, after delivering a tape-recorded death threat to an aide to Chief Daryl F. Gates and asking for a meeting, I was told, "The Chief is busy. He can give you five or ten minutes in a week to ten days if you're still alive."

I, and my attorney, wrote to politicians; we wrote to the Department of Justice and the CIA; we contacted the *LA Times*. The result was less than satisfactory. Both the FBI's Los Angeles field office, then under the command of the Special Agent in Charge (SAC) Ted Gunderson, and the LAPD subsequently made official statements that I was crazy. History has come to my defense in spades.

According to a 1981 two-part feature story in the Los Angeles *Herald Examiner*, it was revealed that the FBI in New Orleans had taken my ex-fiancée into custody and then released her before classifying their investigation without further action. Former New Orleans Crime Commissioner Aaron Cohen told reporter Randall Sullivan that he found my description of events perfectly plausible after his 30 years of studying Louisiana's organized crime operations and their intelligence connections.

To this day a 1986 CIA report prepared as a result of my complaint remains classified and exempt from release, pursuant to Executive Order of the President in the interests of national security, and because it would reveal the identities of CIA agents. I filed a Freedom of Information Act appeal for its release, without success. A copy of the Agency's letter of refusal is posted on my website.

On October 26, 1981, while in the basement of the West Wing of the White House, I reported what I had seen in New Orleans to my then friend and UCLA classmate Craig Fuller, who was serving as Assistant to President Reagan for Cabinet Affairs. Again there was no substantive official response. Fuller went on to become chief of staff to Vice President Bush from 1981 to 1985.

In 1982, then UCLA political science professor Paul Jabber filled in many of the pieces in my quest. He was qualified to do so because he had served as a CIA and State Department consultant for the Carter administration. Jabber explained that, after a 1975 treaty between the Shah of Iran and Saddam Hussein (The Treaty of Algiers), the Shah had cut off all overt military support for Kurdish rebels fighting Saddam from the north of Iraq. In exchange the Shah had gained access to the Shat al-Arab waterway so that he could multiply his oil exports and income. Not wanting to lose a long-term valuable asset in the Kurds, the CIA had then used Brown and Root, which operated in both countries and maintained port facilities in the Persian Gulf and near Shat al-Arab, to rearm the Kurds. The whole operation had been financed with heroin, which the Kurdish partisans had smuggled for decades. Jabber was matter-of-fact about it. Brown and Root had also worked with the CIA for decades.

In 1983 Paul Jabber left UCLA to become a vice president of Banker's Trust and chairman of the Middle East Department of the Council on Foreign Relations.

Those wishing to learn more of this history may view the documentary record of events at <www.fromthewilderness.com/about.html>.

Bankers Trust Company
280 Park Avenue, New York, New York 10017

Paul Jabber
Vice President
Telephone: 212-850-2648

Mailing Address:
P.O. Box 318, Church Street Station
New York, New York 10015

December 21, 1984

To Whom It May Concern:

I first met Michael Ruppert several years ago, when he walked into my office at UCLA to seek my counsel on issues of Middle East politics for a writing project on the U.S. foreign policy tie-ins of the international drug traffic. Since then he has become a dear friend, and I have had multiple opportunities to appreciate his many sterling qualities, both personal and professional.

A sharp intellect, an alert and disciplined mind, and a wonderful ability to translate thoughts and feelings into the written word with seeming ease and much elegance are attributes that I quickly noticed in Mike. His blossoming journalistic career has therefore not come as a surprise to me. But on the subjects that intrigue him he also brings to bear an acute social conscience and a strong sense of ethics that flow naturally from his honest and upright character.

Mike's intelligence, determination and integrity provide in themselves a firm guarantee of success in any professional pursuits to which he may devote himself. He carries not only my vote of confidence, but also my best wishes.

Sincerely,

Paul Jabber

formerly,
Associate Professor
Political Science Department
University of California, Los Angeles

I have, then, a history of civic and personal frustration at the inaction of the United States government when confronted with ethically urgent constructive criticism. I forthrightly acknowledge that this history predisposes me to distrust my government, of which I am highly critical in these pages. But the grounds of my distrust are the same deeds of violence and deception I report here. To take civic issues personally is to take them seriously.

Edges of the foundation

Events in the five-year period that began on September 11, 2001 will determine the course of human history for several centuries to come. The fall of the World

Trade Center buildings and the Pentagon attack were not isolated events. They were one predictable outcome of an economic system whose pressures necessitated murder in the judgment of those who perpetrated it. As Alexander Solzhenitsyn once wrote, "Men, in order to do evil, must first believe that what they are doing is good." History is full of similar events, such as the attacks on Pearl Harbor, the sinking of the USS *Maine* in Havana Harbor, and the fictitious "attacks" by North Vietnamese torpedo boats on US ships off the Vietnamese coast in the Gulf of Tonkin in 1964. What have these events in common?

It's become increasingly clear that the Franklin Roosevelt administration had already broken the Japanese codes prior to the Pearl Harbor attacks and knew the attacks were coming. Yet the government took no precautions, other than to make sure that US aircraft carriers were safely out to sea on December 7, 1941. Roosevelt needed those attacks to stir a stridently isolationist American populace into frenzied support for entry into World War II and Britain's salvation.[3] History has also enshrined the notions that the sinking of the *Maine* and the Gulf of Tonkin incident were unprovoked attacks against innocent and noble Americans.[4] As a result the Vietnam War became an economic boondoggle for US defense contractors and resulted in an explosion in the heroin trade under CIA control from neighboring Laos.

For those who insist that such horrible actions on the part of the American government are inconceivable and dismiss them outright, I offer declassified top secret documents published by author James Bamford in his 2001 book *Body of Secrets* describing Operation Northwoods. (See Appendix A.) The Northwoods plan called for the downing of American aircraft and attacks on American facilities that were to then be blamed on the government of Fidel Castro as a pretext for war with Cuba.[5] Therefore it is not possible to dismiss the charges on the grounds that they are inconceivable. The Northwoods document constitutes a concrete historical precedent.

As I watched the second plane hit the World Trade Center on September 11th, I recognized that the biggest challenge was to prevent the enshrining of a "legend" that was completely unsupported by legal or academic standards, both of which require dispassionate, critical thinking. A detective's job is to first determine all available and relevant facts connected to a case, and then, through a process of elimination, reconcile those facts. It is a process of observation and deductive judgment.

The rule in homicide investigations is that if someone is lying, you have more work to do: figure out what the lie is and why it was told. This demands a logical winnowing of irreconcilable claims; when two apparent "facts" conflict, one of them is usually eliminated when you examine their relationships to the rest of the case. I've researched and investigated 9/11 since it happened. There are so many of these conflicts that a multi-volume encyclopedia would be needed just to catalogue them all. Consider the following two examples.

"No idea that planes could be used as weapons"

Shortly after September 11th both National Security Advisor Condoleezza Rice and Press Secretary Ari Fleischer stated unequivocally that no one in government had any idea that planes could be used as weapons to attack buildings. I'll discuss some of the many proofs that refute this claim. But for the moment we need only look at one piece of contradictory evidence to give our homicide detective a clue, something that his job requires that he reconcile before closing the case.

In his April 13, 2004 televised press conference, a disoriented President George W. Bush again made almost the exact same statement using the exact same words. "But there was a — nobody in our government, at least, and I don't think the prior government, could envision flying airplanes into buildings on such a massive scale." The words "massive scale" stood in contradiction to the earlier pronouncements. If Bush meant that he or others had indeed realized before the attacks that one airplane could be crashed into a building, but that nobody thought of four of them — then he had just, in effect, called his National Security Advisor a liar. Worse, in the same press conference Bush made fleeting reference to the G-8 Summit in Genoa, Italy. That summit required extraordinary security measures — closed airspace, anti-aircraft guns — precisely to defend George W. Bush from a possible airplane attack upon his own hotel.

Consider that on the website of the US Army's Military District of Washington (which labels itself "the Guardian of the Nation's Capital") a November 3, 2000, story reported on "Pentagon Mass Casualty Exercise," a contingency drill practicing for the crashing of a passenger plane into the Pentagon resulting in 341 deaths. A terrorism context was made clear by the following sentences in the story:

> The Pentagon Mass Casualty Exercise, as the crash was called, was just one of several scenarios that emergency response teams were exposed to Oct. 24-26 in the Office of the Secretaries of Defense conference room.
>
> On Oct. 24, there was a mock terrorist incident at the Pentagon Metro stop and a construction accident to name just some of the scenarios that were practiced to better prepare local agencies for real incidents.[6]

I chose to use this example, which was extant before 9/11, to illustrate the evidence that I and others worked with right after the attacks, rather than much more damning evidence which is available today. We were soundly criticized at the time for using this procedure although it has proved to be the same procedure used by the mainstream media since we literally led them, or in some cases, embarrassed them into it. For example, in July of 2003 the *Village Voice's* James Ridgeway documented 36 instances catalogued in the 2003 Joint House-Senate Intelligence Review of 9/11 where specific warnings had been received indicating that the designated suspects, Osama bin Laden and al Qaeda, had planned to crash aircraft into buildings. Many of these warnings included New York and Washington as targets.[7]

Before we move on, consider another salient demonstration that Condi Rice and the President were lying: On August 21, 2002, the Associated Press published the following story, so shocking in the context of the administration's claims that I'll quote it at length:

> (AP)-(Washington)-In what the government describes as a bizarre coincidence, one U.S. intelligence agency was planning an exercise last Sept. 11 in which an errant aircraft crashed into one of its buildings. But the cause wasn't terrorism — it was to be a simulated accident. Officials at the Chantilly, Va.-based National Reconnaissance Office had scheduled an exercise that morning in which a small corporate jet crashed into one of the four towers at the agency's headquarters building after experiencing a mechanical failure. The agency is about four miles from the runways of Washington-Dulles International Airport.
>
> Agency chiefs came up with the scenario to test employees' ability to respond to a disaster, said spokesman Art Haubold. To simulate the damage from the plane, some stairwells and exits were to be closed off, forcing employees to find other ways to evacuate the building. 'It was just an incredible coincidence that this happened to involve an aircraft crashing into our facility,' Haubold said. 'As soon as the real world events began, we canceled the exercise.'
>
> Adding to the coincidence, American Airlines Flight 77 — the Boeing 767 that was hijacked and crashed into the Pentagon — took off from Dulles at 8:10 a.m. on Sept. 11, 50 minutes before the exercise was to begin. It struck the Pentagon around 9:40 a.m., killing 64 aboard the plane and 125 on the ground. The National Reconnaissance Office operates many of the nation's spy satellites. It draws its personnel from the military and the CIA.
>
> An announcement for an upcoming homeland security conference in Chicago first noted the exercise: In a promotion for speaker John Fulton, a CIA officer assigned as chief of NRO's strategic gaming division, the announcement says, 'On the morning of September 11th 2001, Mr. Fulton and his team ... were running a pre-planned simulation to explore the emergency response issues that would be created if a plane were to strike a building. Little did they know that the scenario would come true in a dramatic way that day.'

The running of such an exercise is an excellent method of confusing emergency response personnel (for instance, pilots) who are trying to do their jobs. They expect a drill of a specific but utterly unlikely scenario; the scenario begins to unfold as expected, but then they're told it's not a drill — is it a drill, or not?

The intelligence/criminal wall

One of the hottest themes in the well-watched hearings of the so-called independent 9/11 commission in April of 2004 was that there was an alleged wall between law enforcement activities at the FBI and other agencies and the intelligence side of the FBI and the CIA which prohibited the sharing of information that might have prevented the attacks. This theme was sung like choir practice by virtually every witness who testified during the week from Condoleezza Rice, to Janet Reno, to John Ashcroft, to Louis Freeh, to Robert Mueller.

How does that reconcile with the following statement from a RAND Corporation study on terrorism from 2001? The RAND Corporation was formed as a think tank by the CIA and the US Air Force in the 1950s.

> Finally, it is important to note that efforts to prevent or disrupt terrorist action frequently are successful, and these activities have reduced the number of terrorist incidents that would have occurred in the absence of these activities:
>
> Disruption of terrorist events by working with foreign intelligence and law enforcement services has proved profitable; U.S. intelligence agencies prevented Osama bin Laden's organization from carrying out at least seven vehicle bomb attacks on U.S. facilities since August 1998 (Kelly, 1999, p.1A), and U.S. intelligence has conducted successful disruption operations in as many as 10 countries in the six months up to March 1999 (Associated Press, 1999).
>
> In actual operations and special events, agencies generally coordinated their activities. For example, we examined several overseas counterterrorist operations and found that agencies generally followed the draft interagency International Guidelines. DoD, the FBI, and the Central Intelligence Agency (CIA) performed their respective roles in military planning, law enforcement and intelligence gathering under the oversight of the State Department (e.g., the ambassador). Minor interagency tensions or conflicts during these operations were resolved and did not appear to have posed risk to the mission.
>
> In a similar vein, FBI data on terrorism in the United States suggest a reasonably high degree of success in terrorism prevention activities at home — only a small annual number of actual terrorist incidents occurred in recent years, and more preventions of terrorist incidents than actual incidents.[8]

A detective's strategy, a lawyer's thinking, a political war

At a crime scene the detective's job includes many tasks. He or she first determines that a crime has been committed. After that the priorities are to collect physical evidence and preserve it for scientific analysis, interview witnesses and evaluate possible suspects, attempt to reconstruct the crime and establish guilt.

Most of a detective's work involves the interviewing of witnesses and the interrogation of suspects. Anyone who has ever watched a crime drama has seen this (my favorite is Detective Andy Sipowicz of *NYPD Blue*). There's a reason why these dramatic dialogues are so important. Statements made by witnesses and suspects to detectives are considered direct evidence in court. Any other dialogue usually amounts to hearsay that is almost always inadmissible. Many 9/11 activists are still arguing with each other — as are JFK assassination researchers 40 years later — over pieces of physical evidence. Courts will not listen to such dialogue or debate between people who are not directly involved in the case. Absent a real court to control the debate, arguments about physical evidence stand an even smaller chance of compelling admissible revelations of guilt. They have done nothing to change the political landscape of the United States.

Let me say quite clearly that I have no other objective than to do just that: change the political landscape of the United States. In the matter of 9/11, I consider all other standards vain and irrelevant.

Another reason why the statements of suspects and witnesses are valuable is because they are usually verifiable without any reliance upon expert testimony or scientific analysis. For example, "I was at Joe's bar until 2 a.m." This statement can be checked quickly; if the check falsifies it, everyone can understand its significance.

Scientific evidence is more troublesome. It tends to make little or no sense to a layperson until it's explained by an expert. And that necessary mediation introduces a potential for distortion, misleading emphasis, or outright deception. Courts have procedures for deciding who may and who may not give expert testimony, and non-expert opinions count for very little. In most cases they are not even admissible.

So the investigation of statements from suspects and witnesses has been my steadfast approach to 9/11 and its greater context. It was through this strategy, I believed, that the trial in the public media might ultimately compel a real one.

I have testified as an expert 27 times in narcotics cases, sometimes in jury trials. After having been questioned by attorneys for both sides (and sometimes even the judge) I was permitted to offer an expert opinion under oath. What I observed was that, depending upon the amount of money the defendant had, the number of experts that could be called upon to refute me and contest the scientific/physical evidence was limitless. In many cases, experts with a half-dozen academic degrees literally prostituted themselves for generous fees. The case of 9/11, now being tried in our metaphorical court of the corporate media and public perception, leaves no doubt as to who could produce more expert witness testimony or present them in the most impressive manner.

Prosecutors and investigators usually want to avoid this kind of courtroom debate because of its numbing effect on the jury's mind and its ultimate lack of clarity. Fingerprints are one thing. It is something else to analyze the temperature at which steel is weakened and determining whether or not an unproven amount of burning jet fuel, in unspecified concentrations and unknown locations could have weakened steel supports in the World Trade Center to the point where an unspecified amount of weight might cause them to buckle. Backtracking that avenue of inquiry was also made impossible by the immediate removal and destruction of debris right after the attacks — before it had been examined by law enforcement personnel. Such a debate would be useless anyway, unless and until a legal proceeding — the second trial — had been initiated in a real courtroom. Experience has also taught me that in major cases the court system is extremely vulnerable to manipulation and corruption.

The quickest way to make the case of 9/11 would be to force the suspects, in this case the Bush administration and the intelligence community, to engage in a sort of proxy interrogation where their answers could be checked against a known record. That is, in effect, the strategy I chose to pursue from the day of the attacks. It would be much different, however, from television's Andy Sipowicz and a suspect sitting alone in an interrogation room. It would involve the publication of articles, activism, public and political pressure to the point where the suspects would have to say something in public in response. The 9/11 movement as a whole has been remarkably effective in making that happen.

Almost every major question about the government's activities before, during, and after 9/11 was first posed by my newsletter *From The Wilderness*. So this simple strategy has proven effective, and has met with considerable understanding and emulation. Many of these unanswered questions still reverberate in the pages of the *New York Times*, the *Washington Post*, the *Los Angeles Times*, the major TV networks, *TIME*, *Newsweek*, and CNN. Of necessity, then, the struggle to find the truth and lies of 9/11 has been a political and public relations struggle as well as an investigative one, requiring a completely different set of talents and skills from those needed by a detective. These were skills I acquired as a political activist and, among other things, as the Los Angeles County press spokesman for the 1992 Perot presidential campaign.[9]

Most homicides are solved within 72 hours of the crime. The bogus cover story appeared almost immediately.[10] But a huge collective effort has kept 9/11 in the public eye, expanding the window of opportunity for a real resolution. That window is now closing rapidly, and once the "official" inquiries into 9/11 are declared complete, it may be too late for any successful change in the American political landscape. Nor am I referring specifically to the particular portions of the political landscape directly affected by the attacks — say, aviation, intelligence reform, or greater accountability in agencies like the NSA. No, the entire continuum of public and private life in the United States has been transformed by 9/11, the lengthy preparations for it, the ensuing cover-up, and the massive consolidation of authoritarian policies and institutions achieved in its wake. In short, I maintain that unless this phenomenon is exposed at its roots, the fundamental changes it has wrought will become permanent. That would constitute the death of the American republic.

A context on the way to a motive

Benito Mussolini once said, "Fascism should more properly be called corporatism, since it is the merger of state and corporate power." In fact, during the 1920s and 1930s "fascism" and "corporatism" were often used interchangeably in public discourse. In his January 2003 State of the Union speech, George W. Bush referred to the evils of the twentieth century as "Hitlerism, Communism, and Militarism." He could not bring himself to say "fascism," because he is — by definition — a fascist.

The interchangeability of the terms "corporatism" and "fascism" has long been established by traditionally progressive critics who document the amazingly large scale of American corporate welfare and the impact of corporate lobbyists on public policy. This represents an institutionalized and ongoing attack on democracy, where the benefits of national wealth are privatized while the costs are socialized; the public pays for its own victimization through waste, fraud, and abuse; and the government sells to the highest bidder its capacity to protect the general population. That's been clear for a long time, and though it's a very important discourse, I am not repeating it here.

American fascism is something different now (and while I admire much of the work of these progressives, I am not one of them). It's not just private, elite control over the legal system, nor private evasion of the rule of law. It's a crisis-induced transition from a society with a deeply compromised legal system to a society where force and surveillance completely supplant that system. Although the apparent crisis is about terrorism, the real one is about energy scarcity. At the beginning of this book I document both the reality and the catastrophic implications of this epochal energy crisis. Because it's so central to the emergent new order of things in the United States (which determines US action abroad), an incisive account of the energy issue also explains the real functioning of the world's economy — and who controls it, and how this shapes so much of our daily lives. I begin the book with that story because without it, 9/11 seems like little more than a particularly horrible episode of mass murder (in a word, terrorism). But on this larger explanatory foundation, the evidence will inexorably prove our case: that the United States government not only had complete foreknowledge of the attacks of September 11, it also needed them and deliberately facilitated them, and even helped plan and execute them using techniques long understood in the world of covert operations. Once you understand the economic and financial forces governing the global economy, then the overwhelming evidence of the guilt of both the Bush and Clinton administrations, instead of being hard to believe, will suddenly appear to be unavoidable. That's a large statement, and nobody should take it on trust.

Knowing what we all now know about the deceptions used to "sell" the occupation of Iraq, can we afford to *not* question the multitude of contradictions, lies, falsehoods, and cover-ups surrounding the events of 9/11? It is in the examination of those lies that we uncover the real State of the Union. At this point in history no one can rationally say that the Bush administration is incapable of lying.

Since January 2001, my newsletter *From The Wilderness (FTW)* has correctly predicted or reported historical developments, sometimes as much as a year before they happened. Our working model has continually produced a navigable, accurate map of the near future. The methodology is like the protocols followed by a detective when developing a case. "Okay," one says to oneself, "if Bill's wife really did hire a hit man to kill him, there should be some record connecting a flow of money from her to the shooter." Finding the connection strengthens the working model. Failing to find it either doesn't help the model or weakens it. In more than 100 separate articles and all of my investigations since 9/11 I have found nothing to weaken my working model, only facts which have strengthened it. And I adhere to the same ethical standards a detective must adhere to. If I find something that exonerates my suspect then I must report it. For many detectives, the kind that I worked with and wanted to become, this is a matter of honor.

Sometimes, however, the problem is not with the facts.

We can look at a road map and say that if we are headed eastbound on Interstate 10 in southeastern New Mexico, then the next major city is El Paso. In the same way, we can look at a map of how the world works, determine our position and direction, and know what is likely to come next. One obstacle that must be overcome, however, is the inherent unwillingness of the human race to honestly admit where they really are. It is useless, while sitting in Chicago, to start driving east with a wishful expectation of getting to El Paso. And yet, millions of Americans are doing just that when they insist that the United States is a great and free nation; that it didn't do anything wrong; that its economy is the best, the healthiest, and the cleanest in the world; and that it never victimizes other nations.

2 + 2 = 4

In the classic dystopian novel *1984* George Orwell wrote, "Freedom is the freedom to say two plus two equals four. If that is granted, all else follows." The totalitarian power of Orwell's nightmare state couldn't be maintained without the successful eradication of precisely this freedom.

In May 1999 I had an experience that crystallized something I had known for a long time, but had never seen so clearly. At a sparsely attended and self-congratulatory "People's Tribunal," I witnessed the burial rite for an important issue that, had it been fully pursued, might have prevented the attacks of September 11, 2001. The subject of the tribunal, being held on a Saturday at the University of Southern California, was the drug war and the CIA's connections to the drug trade. Two and a half years earlier, the nation had been aflame after Pulitzer Prize-winning journalist Gary Webb reported on incendiary documents and witnesses linking the Agency directly to the crack cocaine epidemic that devastated America's inner cities during the 1980s.

What happened to Webb and his stories remains an object lesson for researchers and activists in the post-9/11 world. Members of Congress such as Maxine Waters of California, who had once vowed to make the issue her "life's work," presided over the demise of the story. Webb, pilloried by the media and punished by his employer the *San Jose Mercury News*, had in 1997 and 1998 been thoroughly vindicated by Congressional investigations. Webb's greatest vindication of all came in the form of a CIA Inspector General (IG) report released in a declassified version by CIA Director George Tenet on October 8, 1998 — one hour after Congressman Henry Hyde's House Judiciary Committee had voted out articles of impeachment against William Jefferson Clinton.[11]

Something got lost in the news that day. The cover letters and the summaries of the IG report, which is still on the CIA website, said that the exhaustive investigation had found no evidence that the CIA had done anything seriously wrong. Those who actually read the entire report, however, found devastating and damning admissions of criminal behavior on the part of the CIA and Vice President George Herbert Walker Bush. We have seen that pattern repeated over and over since 9/11.

Webb was an "Enemy of the State" in the minds of most Americans. He had challenged their sacred beliefs. Representative Waters, however, had seen her president safely through the impeachment and then gone strangely silent about a report that could have toppled a government and changed the world. The truth often gets traded too cheaply, and the victim of such trades is always the future.

I had been through similar experiences during the Iran-Contra scandal. I had read about, and later interviewed, others who had the same experiences in the case of POWs and MIAs abandoned in Southeast Asia after the Vietnam War. I had studied how the investigation into the murder of President John F. Kennedy had been controlled. I had also acquired personally painful and verifiable knowledge that the murder of John's brother Robert was a CIA operation. All the goodwill and energy of the researcher-activists in each of these cases was deliberately and meticulously sabotaged by interested parties and their allies in the dominant political class.[12]

By May of 1999 what should have been hundreds of thousands of people in the street and a massive government scandal had dwindled to about a hundred or so apparatchiks who would wave the *People's Tribunal* as evidence of their leadership. I laughed with pity as they returned to the beltway to ask for larger grants from their patrons, major foundations and other institutionally compromised entities. The people who ran the tribunals were ultimately beholden to the same powers that had created the problem in the first place. Experts with compromised wallets had staged a controlled burn of brief outrage, cooling rapidly to insouciance. The inconsistencies were soon forgotten.

There's an old saying that in a ham and eggs breakfast, the chicken is involved, but the pig is committed. None of us who were convinced of the urgency of the CIA-drug story and who were heartbroken by its burial doubted that unless people found the courage to deal with the problem, something much worse — something as bad as 9/11 — was certain to happen.

Yet one speaker at the USC event, retired San Jose Police Chief Joseph McNamara, gave me something powerful to take away. He said: "When Richard Nixon started the War on Drugs in 1972 the federal budget allocation for the war on drugs was $101 million. Today the federal budget allocation is $20 billion. And yet today there are more drugs in this country, they are less expensive, and they are of better quality than they were in 1972."

Pigs listen harder than chickens do. There were only two plausible ways to interpret that amazing fact. One could assume that a twenty-seven-year failure, despite a budget almost 200 times greater than when it began, and despite the application of the best minds in politics and law enforcement, was somehow the result of a collective and contagious stupidity. Not only had these people been negligent and incompetent, their budgets had been increased as a reward. This is exactly what we are being asked to accept about the attacks of September 11, 2001. Even in the arguably less urgent matter of illicit drug proliferation, a sane person should have demanded a total restructuring of the contaminated government entities, mass firings, and a serious strategy review. It was our money, the product of our labor, and our children's lives that these failures had wasted.

On the other hand, one could infer that this state of affairs — having been managed by the most educated and influential elite in the country — reflected exactly what was intended: a global drug economy that generated an estimated $600 - $700 billion a year in liquid cash profits from which someone was deriving great benefit. Who?

Occam's Razor (a principle of reasoning associated with medieval thinker William of Ockham, 1288 - 1327) recommends choosing the simplest workable explanation for a phenomenon. In that moment of clarity I had a vision of the degree of reality-twisting, pretzel-bending logic in which the "experts" had engaged. They had orchestrated the destruction and marginalization of people who held mirrors up to their irrationality. In the post-9/11 world, we live with the ultimate insanity that this thinking has produced.

When a flock of birds suddenly changes direction, simultaneously and uniformly, is it a conspiracy? Or is it just an instant recognition by every member of the flock where their collective interests lie?

It was at USC that I began to understand that the people shielding the system, and the knowingly guilty perpetrators within it, were hiding a truth that threatened all of them, the way psychologically sick families sometimes hide the sexual violation of their own children by a relative. I remembered the words of psychiatrist Carl Jung: "The foundation of all mental illness is the unwillingness to experience legitimate suffering."

2+2 = Oil

Today we have an empire that is defined by nothing but limits: limits on the available territory for occupation and expansion, limits on nonrenewable resources, and above all, limits on the one resource that has propelled the human race to over-expand and upon which the species is now dependent: hydrocarbon energy. Much more than any other industrialized society, contemporary America is an empire in deep trouble. Most of us know something about the colossal debt, the unprecedented trade imbalance, the dollar's precarious position, steep income polarization, endemic militarism, imperial overstretch, and a host of other woes that can still be repaired with sufficient resolve. But there is something waiting in the darkness, close enough that our civilization can already feel its presence, even if that feeling is only slowly forcing its way into conscious awareness. Just outside our ability to cope with upsetting information, an increasingly rapid stream of data and experience is ushering in what may be the most significant event in human history: the end of the age of oil.

In 100 years mankind has used up one-half (if not more) of all the oil on the planet.[13] The key is not the "half". Oil is not water in a glass. It's hard to get, and it gets harder to pump as reservoirs dry up; the biggest fields run dry, and newer fields are both smaller and harder to exploit. Once the midpoint is reached, oil production inevitably diminishes forever. If the midpoint is reached while demand soars, conflict is inevitable.

A simple exercise

Take a 20-dollar bill out of your wallet and set it in front of you. Now take a glass of water and set it next to the cash. Pretend that the glass represents a barrel of oil. Look at them both for second. Then ask yourself a question: What do they represent? If you keep distilling your answers down to their purest essence, you will see that the money and the oil both represent the same thing: the ability to do work. Both are useless if there is nothing to buy, drive or eat.

And yet our economic system, what we call capitalism but which is really something else, is predicated on debt, fractional reserve banking, derivative financing, and fiat currency. Therefore it requires that there must be limitless growth into infinity for it to survive. Growth is not possible without energy.

Now look at the barrel of oil and realize that the earth is a closed sphere, and that without the oil and natural gas, the financial system is doomed. There is nothing on our horizon — other than wishful thinking — that can completely replace hydrocarbon energy. The surest way to see this is to realize that, as the human race starts down the inevitable slope of shrinking oil and gas supplies, we have seen no hydrogen powered F 18 Hornets or M1 Abrams tanks. We have seen no vegetable oil-powered Bradley fighting vehicles or solar powered guided missile frigates.

There are many factors that the rulers of the American empire now have to manage as they read their own delusional map of the world. They have to:

• Apportion dwindling resources among competitors, some of whom possess nuclear weapons;

- Maintain and expand their control over enough of the oil and gas remaining to ensure their global dominance and maintain order among the citizens of the Empire;
- Simultaneously manage a global economic system, made possible by hydrocarbon energy, that is collapsing and in which the growing population is demanding more things that can only be supplied by using still more hydrocarbon energy;
- Acknowledge that they cannot save their own economy without selling more of these products;
- Control the exploding demand for oil and gas through engineered recessions and wars that break national economies;
- Hide the evidence that they are systematically looting the wealth of all the people on the planet — even their own people — in order to maintain control;
- Maintain a secret revenue stream to provide enough off-the-books capital for the purposes of providing themselves a distinct economic and military advantage, improving their technological posture, and funding covert operations;
- Repress any dissent and head off any exposure of their actions;
- Convince the population that they are honorable;
- Kill off enough of the world's population so that they can maintain control after oil supplies have dwindled to the point of energy starvation.

In the case of the War on Drugs, I infer that the result of some 30 years of effort, fueled by billions of dollars and managed by the "best and the brightest," is exactly what was intended. This is the premise from which I began looking at the events of September 11, 2001, as I watched the second airliner hit the World Trade Center.

I do not claim to have presented or reconciled every fact. That rarely happens in a complicated homicide investigation. The tasks of the investigator are to produce a reasonable explanation based upon evidence that establishes probability, and to eliminate reasonable doubt that a crime was committed and that the guilty have been successfully identified.

If I can make a case in this book that explains these events, identifies the suspects, and makes more sense than any other interpretation of the available and demonstrable facts; if I can then get it out in a way that further empowers our collective learning; if that helps to break down the destructively false paradigm that governs so much of our life today — then I have contributed something that is hope-giving for all of us. Otherwise, the future looks pretty grim.

This is a race against time.

Michael C. Ruppert
April 21, 2004

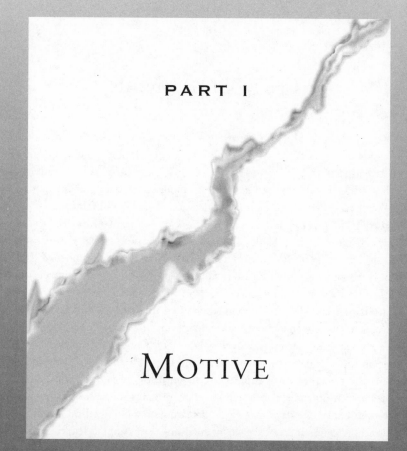

PART I

MOTIVE

CHAPTER 1

PETROLEUM MAN

G lobal demand for oil and natural gas is growing faster than new supplies are being found, and the world population is exploding. Currently the world uses between four and six barrels of oil for every new barrel that it finds, and the trend is getting worse.[1] Natural gas use is exploding while the rate of new gas discoveries (especially on the North American continent) is plunging.[2]

According to most experts — including Colin Campbell, one of the world's foremost oil experts with decades of experience in senior geologist, upper management, and executive positions with companies including BP, Amoco, FINA, and Texaco — there are only about one trillion barrels of accessible conventional oil remaining on the planet.[3] Presently the world uses approximately 82 mb/d (million barrels per day). Even if demand remained unchanged, which it clearly will not, that would mean that the world will run out of conventional oil within thirty-five years. Oil, however, does not flow like water from a bottle. Since the world's population and the demand for oil and natural gas are increasing rapidly, by reasonable estimates, the world supply of conventional oil is limited to perhaps 20 years. It's a common mistake to assume that oil will flow in a steady stream and then suddenly stop one day. Instead, the stream will gradually diminish in volume, with occasional small increases, even as the number of people "drinking" from that stream, and the amount they consume explodes.

Other issues compound the problem. As fields deplete, oil becomes increasingly expensive to produce. These costs must be passed on to consumers.

Not all oil in the ground is recoverable. *When it takes more energy to pump a barrel of oil than is obtained by burning it, the field is considered dead, regardless of how much oil remains.* Unconventional substitutes are extremely expensive and problematic to produce. Tar sands, oil shale, deep water, and polar oil sources have severe limitations. Canadian tar sands development is proving disappointing because it requires large quantities of fresh water and natural gas to make steam, which is a necessary part of the extraction process. Natural gas cost and fresh water shortages are already limiting production, and the material costs for the energy needed to make the energy have already begun to curtail production.

The same problems afflict the development of shale, deep water, and polar reserves. They are currently too expensive to develop in quantity, and when exceptions arise, they're too small to mitigate Peak Oil. Even the best-case "fantasy" scenarios for these energy sources don't change the picture much. To learn more about this I recommend two web sites: <www.peakoil.net>, and <www.hubbertpeak.com>.

I'm capitalizing the phrase "Peak Oil" to indicate that it's a historical event. It's an unavoidable, utterly transformative crisis, and an increasing body of evidence suggests two major consequences. I'll state them here in the starkest terms; later I'll add reassuring qualifiers and a few formulations that might be more palatable. But it comes to this: first, in order to prevent the extinction of the human race, the world's population must be reduced by as many as four billion people. Second, especially since 9/11, this reality has been secretly accepted and is being acted upon by world leaders. In this chapter I marshal the evidence for this disturbing pair of hypotheses which, taken together, constitute the ultimate motive for the attacks of September 11th, 2001.

What have hydrocarbons done for you lately?

Oil and natural gas are close cousins. In nature the two are often found very close together because they can originate from the same geologic processes, under conditions that have existed only rarely in the Earth's four-billion-year history. Oil and gas are hydrocarbons that come from dead algae and other plant life. There are biological traces in oil proving that it came from living matter.[4] Since the earth is a closed biosphere, oil and gas are finite, non-renewable resources. The world has used half (if not more) of all the hydrocarbons created over millions of years in just about one hundred years.[5]

According to Richard Duncan, PhD in 1999 approximately 95 percent of all transportation was powered by oil. And 50 percent of all oil produced is used for transportation purposes. No other energy source even comes close to oil's convenience, power, and efficiency.[6]

Oil pervades our civilization; it is all around you. The shell for your computer is made from it. Your food comes wrapped in it. You brush your hair and teeth with it. There's probably some in your shampoo, and most certainly its container. Your children's toys are made from it. You take your trash out in it. It makes your clothes soft in the dryer. As you change the channels with the TV remote you hold it in your hands. Some of your furniture is probably made with it. It is everywhere inside your car. It is used in both the asphalt you drive on and the tires that meet the road. It probably covers the windows in your home. When you have surgery, the anesthesiologist slides it down your esophagus. Your prescription medicine is contained in it. Your bartender sprays the mixer for your drink through it. Oh yes, and the healthy water you carry around with you comes packaged in it.

Be careful. If you decide that you want to throw this book out, your trashcan is probably made from it. And if you want to call and tell me what a scaremonger

I am, you will be holding it in your hands as you dial. And if you wear corrective lenses, you will probably be looking through it as you write down a number with a pen that is made from it. Plastic is a petroleum product, and its price is every bit as sensitive to supply shortages as gasoline. Oil companies do not charge a significantly different price for oil they sell to a plastics company than they charge a gas station owner. If the wellhead price goes up, then every downstream use is affected.

If you live in the United States and the power generating station that serves your community was built within the last 25 years, natural gas is probably providing you with the electricity that powers the bulb illuminating this book. According to figures supplied by the US government, some 90 percent of all new electrical generating stations will be gas powered. Vice President Cheney's "energy task force," the National Energy Policy Development Group (NEPDG), stated in summer 2001 that "to meet projected demand over the next two decades America must have in place between 1,300 and 1,900 new electric plants. Much of this new generation will be fueled by natural gas."[7]

Oil is also critical for our food supply. Quantitatively speaking, modern food production consumes ten calories of energy for every calorie contained in the food.[8] When the farmer (or more likely the "agribusiness employee") goes out to plant seeds, she drives a vehicle powered by oil. After planting she sprays the crop with fertilizers made from ammonia, which comes from natural gas. Then she sprays them several times with pesticides made from oil. She irrigates the crops with water that most likely has also been pumped by electricity generated by coal, oil, or gas. Oil powers the harvest, transportation to processing plant, processing, refrigeration, and transport to the grocery store (to which you, the consumer, drive an oil-powered vehicle).

You may pay for it with a piece of oil that you carry around in your wallet. Then you take it home, cook it by means of either electricity or natural gas, and eat it on a plate that may have been made from oil, after which you wash the plate with a synthetic sponge that is also made of oil.

Consider this: out of six and a half billion people, there are about four billion who don't have, and who want, all of the things I have just described. The current world economy is inherently committed to endless growth, and while physically impossible, this illusion is to be chased after by driving the poor countries into a globalized market for cheap goods. Haiti, for instance, has had its domestic rice farming ruined by American export dumping. When the Haitian farmers could no longer underbid the American rice in Haitian markets, they moved off the land and became urban unemployed. Then the Americans raised rice prices to crippling levels. So Haiti is a captive market, but it's a market nonetheless. Similar developing countries are slowly acquiring more purchasing power and the industrialized world is gaining a foothold in their domestic economies by targeting them for cheap exports. One way or another, the have-nots must become consumers.

Food

How important are hydrocarbons to food production? One recognized oil expert puts it this way: "If the fertilizers, partial irrigation, and pesticides were withdrawn, corn yields, for example, would drop from 130 bushels per acre to about 30 bushels."[9] That's bad news in more ways than you can think. The same applies in varying degrees to any crop: wheat, alfalfa, lettuce, celery, onions, tomatoes; anything that commercial agriculture produces. Oil and gas are irreplaceable if the world is to continue pumping out enough food to feed 6.5 billion people. And that says nothing about the additional 2.5 billion that are projected to be here before the middle of this century. Organic farming or permaculture is responsible and respectful of nature and may ultimately be nearly as productive as hydrocarbon-based agriculture. But the infrastructure is not in place to implement it. You could ask several billion people to stop eating for a year or two while we switch over and work out the bugs. Do you want to volunteer? Would you volunteer your children?

So what about all the beef cattle, pigs, and chickens that feed on grain and corn? Would you be prepared to pay $50 for a Big Mac if there were severe grain shortages? How about a $25 chicken breast? That would be a quality problem for an American, as opposed to someone in Africa or Asia who lived off of crops and food products sold by globalized agriculture in case there was nothing locally grown. You have always been told that these people just weren't as productive as we are. It's not true; they don't have the oil and the natural gas that we do. The United States contains 5 percent of the world's population and currently consumes 25 percent of the world's energy.[10]

Growth

Oil also powers more than 600 million vehicles worldwide.[11] Would you pay for a $50,000 car and pay $5 a gallon for gas? $10 per gallon? Could you? In the current financial paradigm, the stability of the world's economy depends upon *growing* revenues through the sale of more and more vehicles and other products that are useless without hydrocarbons. The revenues generated by current customers in developed countries won't be enough to sustain future growth, so cars and computers and air conditioners are beginning to flow into the new markets of China, Asia, and Africa. Those populations don't have these energy-guzzling machines (nor the myriad petroleum-derived plastic consumer goods enjoyed in the relatively high-wage countries), but they quite clearly desire them — especially the younger generation, whose purchasing power is growing at the fastest rate. As their economies grow more robust, wages rise and the consumers' desire becomes actual economic demand.

For the moment, much of the developing world remains ravaged by massive, artificially engineered debt to the World Bank and the IMF. But rising literacy rates and the correlative falling birthrates in many regions promise a massive expansion in consumer spending.[12] And this has already begun: Chinese auto sales are exploding. According to one report, 2002 Chinese auto sales jumped by more than 50 percent.[13] GM's auto sales in China jumped by 300 percent in 2002 alone.[14]

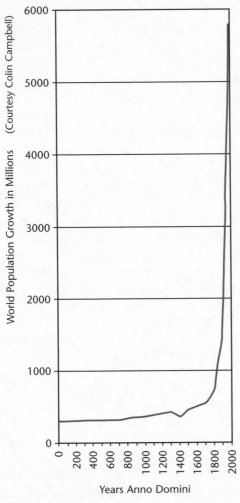

Years Anno Domini

If there is no growth in revenue for the corporations that make and sell these things, then what is left of your 401(k) plan will be worthless. And you might even be out of a job yourself.

Colin Campbell has rightly identified a subspecies of Homo sapiens that he calls Petroleum Man. He provided me with this population graph that shows the effect of hydrocarbons on the planet since their introduction. The little dip around 1400 was caused by the bubonic plague.[15]

A number of environmentalists have been sanely and prophetically decrying the destruction of the biosphere for decades. This is another key part of the equation. They have pointed to alternative energy supplies such as wind, solar, geothermal, and biomass as steps toward protecting the ecosystem. But very few understand the infrastructural problems that must be addressed if the crisis is to be solved in any rational manner. Peak Oil will likely turn human civilization inside out long before global warming does, unless — and there are signs that this is happening — oil and gas shortages elicit a tragically shortsighted return to coal.

Given the hundreds of thousands of non-combatant deaths in the resource wars of Afghanistan, Iraq, and so many other places; given the deaths in Europe and Asia from extreme weather conditions in both summer and winter months; given the murderous, smoldering conflict in Nigeria and other oil-rich countries where corporate power combines with the forces of local warlords; given all this, *Peak Oil is killing us now. That, and the argument that these are the merest hints of what Peak Oil is going to bring, is the message of this book.*

Making rational assessments

As I traveled throughout the US, Canada, and Australia in 2002 giving my lecture called "The Truth and Lies of 9/11," I was routinely asked by youthful activists about an immediate changeover to alternative energy sources. I first asked if they wanted to layoff tens of millions of people in the oil, shipping, and auto industries, in car dealerships, garages, and gas stations while all the factories and ancillary services were retooled. That process might take decades. Who, I asked, would pay the mortgages for the people thrown out of work? What would happen to the supermarkets, the banks (credit cards), the dry cleaners, et cetera, if all of these people suddenly stopped making payments? Who would make up the tax revenues that these people no longer paid? Who would finance all the capital investment needed to convert us over to alternative vehicles? And, in spite of recent promotions about hydrogen, as of October 2002 the federal government is still fighting tooth and nail to keep electric vehicles from becoming a commercially viable reality.[16] The myth of hydrogen salvation is a fantasy of the naive and a cruel hoax of the policy makers and business people who know better.

Remember also that electricity is not a primary energy source, but merely a carrier of energy produced by some other means. Although oil and gas are critical, it is electricity, as one scientist put it, that is "the indispensable end-use energy for industrial civilization."[17] Once you use an oil-powered vehicle to get to wherever you're going, think about what you would find there if there were no electricity. Refrigeration is only one of many essential services that come to mind. In 1999 an estimated 42 percent of the world's energy was used to produce electricity. Oil ate up 39 percent for non-electric uses; gas, 18 percent; and coal a measly 1 percent.[18] As this book goes to press, there are definite indications that the US is reverting to coal-fired plants as quietly as possible with some 94 new coal-fired electric plants planned across 36 states.[19] Even conservative Republicans who insist that global warming is a myth have acknowledged that burning coal is environmentally unsound. Although EPA regulations have made it economically difficult to bring new coal-fired plants online, strict retrofitting requirements passed by Congress to remove pollutants have been quietly skirted to keep America's electricity flowing.[20]

From a profit standpoint, this new coal rush can only be happening as a response to a shortage of the other fossil fuels. This is because the generating plants that are designed for oil and natural gas require less investment and regulatory oversight to construct, and have much shorter permit approval processes.

Electric vehicles are an illusory solution. I remember being on one of my 30 or so commercial flights (made possible by oil) in 2002 and reading an airline magazine article about a great new electric car. The author rightly commented that all the pollution the vehicle he test-drove was not putting out was, in fact, being spewed out by the coal-powered generating station that he had plugged into to charge it. In 2002 approximately 50 percent of all electricity in the US was generated by older, coal-burning power plants whose replacement is cost-prohibitive.[21] Until early 2002 it was officially anticipated that all new generating plants would be powered by natural gas. Then, America's energy planners encountered a separate problem hidden in plain sight: North American natural gas is running out faster than oil, and it can't be imported as easily without massive investment and time lags for the construction of Liquefied Natural Gas (LNG) tankers and terminals.

Understanding energy

In 1843 an American physicist named James Prescott Joule discovered a salient feature of the way energy behaves: the total inflow of energy into a system must equal the total outflow of energy from the system, plus the change in the energy contained within the system. That fascinating principle will become an important part of our story later on, but for now let's note that, in recognition of Joule's achievement, his name was adopted as the standard unit for energy. The measure of the energy produced by any system can always be expressed in joules, no matter what form of energy it is.

Suffice it to say that there is nothing on the immediate horizon that offers a realistic solution to humanity's dependence upon hydrocarbon energy.

Oil's bell curve

Every domain of oil production follows a general bell curve, whether it's a single oil field in Texas or Kuwait, or a country such as the US or Kazakhstan, or the planet as a whole. On a global scale, both oil and gas are nearing their peaks of production, at differing rates, and are in an inevitable and irreversible decline. The implications of this are staggering.

It was Dr. M. King Hubbert who, some 50 years ago, plotted the oil depletion curve that now bears his name. The Hubbert curve is not only descriptive of depletions that can be seen and measured in hindsight, it is strikingly predictive of resource outcomes that are still in the future. Indeed, Hubbert's fame is based on his successful calculation of the 1971 US domestic oil production peak some 14 years before the fact. Laughed to scorn at the time, his prediction eventually proved correct to within 12 months. Its effect on the astute portion of the geological public was like that of the ancient mathematician and philosopher, Thales, who once stopped a battle by stepping into the space between the two armies and successfully predicting a solar eclipse. The eclipse promptly happened, and the astonished soldiers all went home. Unfortunately, most of the profit-driven petroleum industry is still on the battlefield, only gradually realizing that they're fighting in the dark.

As *FTW's* Contributing Editor for Energy, geologist Dale Allen Pfeiffer wrote in late 2001:

> US oil production peaked in the early 1970s. To meet its rising energy
> needs after this point, the US became increasingly dependent on foreign
> oil. This paved the way for the Arab oil embargo. By the end of the
> decade, US oil production had begun to decrease irreversibly. Whatever
> anyone tries to say to the contrary, our dependence on foreign oil is

permanent and increasing all the time. Dr. Hubbert was vindicated, and
his methodology is now the standard for projecting oil production.[22]

Oil is getting more expensive to produce in almost every part of the world. As
oil fields get older, wells must be drilled deeper or in more hostile conditions, and
more frequently into reservoirs that either are emptying or are smaller than the
large fields that were tapped first. The oil thus obtained is also likely to be of inferior quality and thus more expensive to refine.[23] Almost all there is to be found has
been found.[24] There are not likely to be any major new discoveries that will make
a difference in this trend.

Confirming the last statement IHS, the world's foremost recognized consulting
firm cataloguing oil reserves and discoveries, announced that in 2003 — for the
first time since the 1920s — there was not a single discovery of a field in excess of
500 million barrels.[25] The significance of this becomes clear when one remembers
that the planet consumes a billion barrels of oil every 11.5 days. Although technological advances are improving extraction rates, the bottom line is that without
more discoveries, production cannot be increased indefinitely. And global oil discoveries peaked in the 1960s.[26]

New fields that are being discovered are much smaller than giant fields, and
they tend to be in less accessible environments, like deep sea or polar regions. New
discovery trends have been mathematically included in evaluations of the Peak Oil
model, and they make little difference in the scope or the timing of the outcome.

Pfeiffer provided *FTW* with the graphs below. One shows the bell curve for a
particular region, and the other shows Hubbert's Peak for the planet as a whole.
The third tracks population and per-capita production of hydrocarbon energy,
superimposed over energy production, showing that population will overshoot
production capacity by a large margin.

The catastrophe made inevitable by these limits is beginning now. This is the
canvass on which the post-9/11 world is being painted. Policy makers, economists,
the financial markets, and politicians are deceiving the world about how much oil
and gas are really left. They have to, in order to protect the markets and their jobs.
They are also misleading the population about what this means. The most
important of these events is the point in time when demand (need) for hydrocarbons outpaces the planet's ability to give them up.[27] The second is the fact that the
OPEC nations of the Middle East will peak last, many of them between now and
2010.[28] They will soon be supplying up to 40 percent of the world's oil.[29]

Whoever controls the oil in the Eurasian continent, which includes the Middle
East, the Caspian Basin, and Central Asia, will determine who lives and who dies,
who eats and who starves.

The demand for hydrocarbons

Clearly, short-term and mid-term increases in hydrocarbon energy will be supplied
by the so-called "swing" producers (countries able to vary production significantly

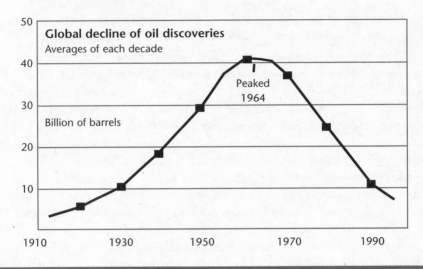

Global decline of oil discoveries
Averages of each decade

Peaked
1964

Billion of barrels

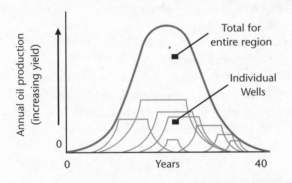

Annual oil production
(increasing yield)

Total for
entire region

Individual
Wells

Years

After Colin J. Campbell &
Jean H. Laherrère,
THE END OF CHEAP OIL,
Sci Am, March 1998.

Scenario of world's population and hydrocarbons (liquids + gas) production: 1900-2100

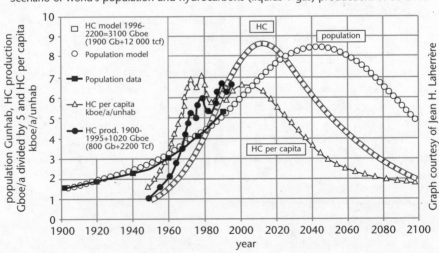

population Gunhab, HC production
Gboe/a divided by 5 and HC per capita
kboe/a/unhab

□ HC model 1996-
2200=3100 Gboe
(1900 Gb+12 000 tcf)

O Population model

■ Population data

△ HC per capita
kboe/a/unhab

● HC prod. 1900-
1995+1020 Gboe
(800 Gb+2200 Tcf)

HC

population

HC per capita

year

Graph courtesy of Jean H. Laherrère

enough to control price or meet demand) like Saudi Arabia, Iraq, Nigeria, and Venezuela. Saudi Arabia possesses 25 percent of the world's recoverable oil, and Iraq possesses 11 percent.[30] Yet even in Saudi Arabia, there is an awareness of the finite nature of oil. "They have a saying, My father rode a camel, I drive a car, my son rides in a jet airplane — his son will ride a camel."[31] In May of 2003 I attended an international conference on Peak Oil at the French Institute of Petroleum in Paris and was surprised to hear an expert from the Iranian National Oil Company describe data showing that Saudi Arabia is already at peak production. He had previously acknowledged that Iran passed its peak of production in the 1980s.[32] I reported this more than six months before the *New York Times* issued a report indicating that Saudi Arabian production had possibly peaked — which set off a subsequent round of reactive conferences in Washington, DC, and in certain New York financial circles.[33]

Another crucial factor: according to an oil industry executive I interviewed for this book, it takes about six weeks to get a drop of oil from the Persian Gulf into an American gas tank. If it comes from West Africa it takes about two weeks, and if from Venezuela, only four days.

What was known about Peak Oil and when

In April 2001 the Council on Foreign Relations and James A. Baker (Secretary of State for G.H.W. Bush) published a detailed study of world energy problems. Because it was not an official government document and not widely circulated, it could come closer to telling the truth without risking panic in the financial markets. It confirmed that key elites had been aware of Peak Oil for some time:

> Strong economic growth across the globe and new global demands for more energy have meant the end of sustained surplus capacity in hydrocarbon fuels and the beginning of capacity limitations. In fact, the world is currently precariously close to utilizing all of its available global oil production capacity, raising the chances of an oil supply crisis with more substantial consequences than seen in three decades.
>
> These choices will affect other US policy objectives: US policy toward the Middle East; US policy toward the former Soviet Union and China; the fight against international terrorism.
>
> Meanwhile, across much of the developing world, energy infrastructure is being severely tested by the expanding material demands of a growing middle class, especially in the high growth, high-population economies of Asia. As demand growth collided with supply and capacity limits at the end of the last century, prices rose across the energy spectrum, at home and abroad.[34]

The CFR report made clear another chilling point. "Oil price spikes since the 1940s have always been followed by a recession."[35] This fact has been acknowledged by financial media such as the *Wall Street Journal*, the *Financial Times*, and the *Asia Times*. A great many analysts understand, and have written, that one way to prolong inevitable decline is by the creation and management of recessions, which inevitably reduce demand for oil. People use less gas when they're unemployed.

In May 2001 a statement from the National Energy Policy produced by Vice President Cheney's National Energy Policy Development Group (NEPDG) hinted further at the pending crisis:

> America in the year 2001 faces the most serious energy shortage since the oil embargoes of the 1970s.
>
> Estimates indicate that over the next 20 years, US oil consumption will increase by 33 percent, natural gas consumption by well over 50 percent, and demand for electricity will rise by 45 percent.
>
> US energy consumption is expected to increase by about 32 percent by 2020.
>
> Between 2000 and 2020, US natural gas demand is projected by the Energy Information Administration to increase by more than 50 percent.
>
> Yet we produce 39 percent less oil today than we did in 1970 [the peak year of production in the US], leaving us ever more reliant on foreign suppliers. On our present course, America 20 years from now will import nearly two of every three barrels of oil — a condition of increased dependency on foreign powers that do not always have America's interests at heart.[36]

Lastly we look at an important quote from Zbigniew Brzezinski, former national security adviser to Jimmy Carter; intelligence adviser to Presidents Reagan and George H.W. Bush ; professor at Johns Hopkins; a co-founder of the Trilateral Commission with David Rockefeller; and a member of the CFR. In his 1997 book *The Grand Chessboard: America's Primacy and Its Geostrategic Imperatives*, Brzezinski wrote:

> The world's energy consumption is bound to vastly increase over the next two or three decades. Estimates by the US Department of Energy anticipate that world demand will rise by more than 50 percent between 1993 and 2015, with the most significant increase in consumption occurring in the Far East. The momentum of Asia's economic development is already generating massive pressures for the exploration and exploitation of new sources of energy, and the Central Asian region and the Caspian Sea basin are known to contain reserves of natural gas and oil that dwarf those of Kuwait, the Gulf of Mexico, or the North Sea.[37]

What "Zbig" didn't say was that the North Sea and the Gulf of Mexico have passed their production peaks. Kuwait, however, may not peak for about ten years. It is currently estimated to have about nine percent of all the oil on the planet.[38]

What Brzezinski should have said was that the oil (and gas) sources in the Central Asian Republics and the Caspian Sea Basin were — at the time he wrote the book — estimated to contain perhaps 200 billion barrels of oil. But according to Colin Campbell (citing actual drilling records), between October 2000 and October 2002 exploratory wells showed that there is not one deep pool of oil in Central Asia, but a series of separated pockets, which have produced revised estimates of only 40 billion barrels. There is however, in Qatar, a huge deposit of natural gas that could significantly soften the blow when natural gas supplies (which tend to fall off a cliff rather than politely declining down a bell curve) run out. Because of energy losses in conversion to liquefied natural gas (LNG) and in reversion back into gaseous form during and after extremely expensive shipping, those reserves will most likely benefit countries that can be reached by pipeline, or those which can afford the cost of LNG.

Regarding Caspian Basin oil, Campbell told *FTW* in an October, 2002, interview:

> There was talk of the place holding over 200 Gb [billion barrels] (I think emanating from the USGS [US Geological Survey]), but the results after ten years of work have been disappointing. The West came in with high hopes. The Soviets found Tengiz onshore in 1979 with about 6 Gb of very deep, high-sulfur oil in a reef. Chevron took over and is now producing it with difficulty. But offshore they found a huge prospect called Kashagan in a similar geological setting to Tengiz. If it had been full, it could have contained 200 Gb, but they have now drilled three deep wells at huge cost, finding that instead of being a single reservoir it, like Tengiz, is made up of reefs. Reserves are now quoted at 9-13 Gb. BP - Statoil has pulled out. Caspian production won't make any material difference to world supply. [39]

But to think merely in terms of numbers of barrels is to miss the point. Although, this is a virgin region, the oil is not as high quality as that found in other provinces. It has extremely high sulfur content. It will be little more than a diversified source of energy that gives an edge to whoever controls it. There are also very few ways to get that oil into the world's gas tanks without a heavy capital investment into pipelines threaded through some of the world's most deadly political geography.

Deceive the people, blame the people

The books on world oil reserves are as cooked as the books of Enron. As *FTW* continued to publish a series of articles throughout 2002 on the coming crisis, I was contacted by many people who insisted that the reserve projections were showing that more oil was somehow replacing that which had been pumped. They also said that government figures from the US Geological Survey showed that there was much more oil than we said there was.

First, it is critical to understand that if an oil company reports accurate reserves in a field promptly upon discovery of that field, they have to pay taxes on all of it at once. So they spread the tax burden out over several years — by reporting new finds in old fields. This practice maintains stock prices and investments for oil companies that haven't made any new finds. Oil in the ground is booked as a corporate asset on the balance sheet. Backdating oil discoveries to the date a field was opened is essential to understanding how quickly new discovery is really diminishing.

Patiently, Dale Pfeiffer responded to other misconceptions with hard science. What was being reported as new oil in old wells was sometimes the result of the seepage into spaces left by drilling from tiny deposits of oil that then filled the void. It was not much, and it would not make a difference.[40]

To the people who insisted that oil reserve figures for the Middle East showed that new oil was materializing, he pointed out that the OPEC nations, responding to the recession of the late 1980s, were faced with a problem. There had to be enough cheap oil to stimulate a recovery that would ensure the demand for oil. OPEC's control over that process was enhanced by a successful economic attack on the Soviet petroleum industry. By overproducing and price-cutting, OPEC rendered Soviet oil uncompetitive as its higher production costs began to approach its net revenues. Cutting Soviet oil revenue was a great way to bankrupt the Soviet Union. It worked.

All OPEC nations have production quotas to manage prices that are based upon stated reserves in the ground. When OPEC suddenly needed to increase production beyond their agreed- upon limits, they just broke out an eraser and changed the quantity of reserves on the books. Only one nation, Dubai, did not follow suit to match its neighbors. To believe that all this new oil suddenly appeared, one would have to argue that the oil somehow appeared under the ground in every Middle Eastern country except unlucky Dubai.

The following chart posted at <www.hubbertpeak.com> proves the point.

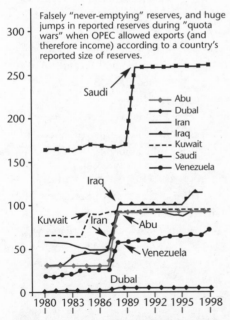

Falsely "never-emptying" reserves, and huge jumps in reported reserves during "quota wars" when OPEC allowed exports (and therefore income) according to a country's reported size of reserves.

Data is from Petroconsultants of Geneva, a consultancy whose database is the most comprehensive available for data on oil resources that exist outside of continental North America, and is used as a 'bible' by all international oil companies.

The US government, it turns out, is no less guilty of misrepresentation. Pfeiffer took on the magically self-adjusting reserves published by the US Energy Information Administration (EIA) and found evidence of cooked books:

> This [book cooking] is one of the major causes of disinformation regarding energy issues. The US government relies on the EIA for all of its energy information. Yet the EIA, a division of the Department of Energy, has admitted that it reverse- engineers its studies. "These adjustments to the USGS [US Geological Survey] and MMS [Minerals Management Service] estimates are based on *non-technical* [emphasis mine] considerations that support domestic supply growth to the levels necessary to meet projected demand levels," stated the EIA in a report titled *Annual Energy Outlook 1998 with Projections to 2020*. This means that the EIA first looks at projected figures for demand, then juggles reserve and production figures to meet that demand!
>
> Likewise, USGS reports can no longer be trusted either since the agency's about face in 2000. Prior to 2000, the USGS was talking about oil depletion and the crossover event between demand and supply. In 2000, however, the agency published a rosy report stating there would be abundant oil for many decades. Geologists working for the USGS have stated off the record that they do not trust USGS oil data.[41]

Further misleading the public are the following official statements. From the CFR report: "The reasons for the energy challenge have nothing to do with the global hydrocarbon resource base, which is still enormous."[42] The National Energy Policy blames everything on infrastructure and technology. In its opening page it denies all of the empirical evidence that it subsequently produces to the contrary. Referring time and again to the California energy crisis of 2001, it blames the problem on a lack of production capability. California was just the beginning of what the world can look forward to — and a mild version at that. Although it has since been disclosed that Enron and other companies worsened the crisis and took criminal advantage of it, they did not create the crisis in the first place.

While producing page after page of factual data establishing that this crisis is real and unavoidable, the NEDPG group also blamed everything on science and money. Dick Cheney signed off on a report that said, "we must use technology to reduce demand for energy, repair and maintain our energy infrastructure, and increase energy supply."[43] By similar logic, if you lock someone in a bank vault and give him enough money, technology, and incentive, he can materialize a ham sandwich.

Further compounding the problem, in late 2003, oil major Royal Dutch Shell announced that it had overstated its reserves (in order to maintain share prices) by as much as 20 percent. Shell actually cut its reserve estimates not just once, but three times.[44] Shell's fraudulent bookkeeping not only resulted in the resignations of its two co-chairmen; it also triggered a wave of reserve restatements throughout the energy industry that has yet to be fully played out. Shortly after Shell's announcement, US energy major El Paso announced that it had cut its stated natural gas reserves by 41 percent.[45] As a result, the *Los Angeles Times* reported that regulators had begun to examine the reserve statements of all major oil companies and that this might produce significant upward pressure on prices as reserves were revised downward. The *Times* reported, "For petroleum firms, reserves amount to nothing less than 'the value of the company,' says Ronald Harrell, chairman of Ryder Scott Co., a Houston petroleum engineering firm."[46]

In other words, the truth about diminishing reserves could destroy share prices, which could destroy financial markets and investments, which could lead to a collapse anyway. Such financial considerations are not irrelevant when one considers that, as the *Times of London* reported in January 2004, "The world's top ten energy companies are failing to find enough new crude to replenish their reserves, according to Wood Mackenzie, the oil consultancy, which sees exploration in the UK North Sea as the industry's biggest waste of money over the past five years."[47]

Alexander Solzhenitsyn said, "Men, in order to do evil, must first believe that what they are doing is good." Through all of this I see the same self-justification that has enabled all corrupt politicians and government apparatchiks to lie, to steal, to distort, to manipulate, to deceive, and to destroy: "I'm just doing what the people want." This is the rationale, I suspect, that George W. Bush and Dick Cheney use in their sleep and in their waking moments to justify the US aggression that has taken place since 9/11. George W. Bush did tell us that "the American way of life is not negotiable."

I found this attitude summed up again in a passage from the CFR report which read, "So we come to the report's central dilemma: the American people continue to demand plentiful and cheap energy without sacrifice or inconvenience."[48] Most of the American people don't have a clue as to what is really driving events. No matter what, leaders have an obligation to tell the people the truth. Recall the following quotation, attributed to Thomas Jefferson: "I believe that the people, when properly armed with the facts, will come to the right conclusion." As events have unfolded since 9/11, we have seen that we are being told anything but the truth.

Proving the crisis is here

> The earth is attempting to rid itself of an infection by the human parasite.
> — Richard Preston, 1994

Even the major oil companies understand the future. Both academics and former oil company executives have told me that the oil companies know exactly what is happening. They even produce figures confirming it. This explains why so many major oil companies have merged and are currently downsizing.[49] Even though reports from the White House and the CFR decry poor infrastructure as the problem, it is not likely that much new infrastructure will be built in the US. There won't be enough energy to power the plants and fill new pipelines. The undeveloped regions must be drilled and pipelines must be built to make the oil and gas useable. And still the new production from these regions will do little except to diversify supplies for a while and ease prices when necessary to avert an economic collapse before the inevitable physical one gets here. According to BP-Amoco, world oil production *per capita* peaked in 1979.[50] This figure is acknowledged by the International Energy Agency (IEA) and many other scientific journals. It is not going to get any better.

Dr. John Price, an economic analyst, pegged the heart of the problem in a May 2001 appraisal entitled "Oil and Global Recession."[51] He zeroed in on both the secretive Vice President's Energy Task Force (NEPDG) and the CFR report published only a month earlier. (Note the proximity of these reports to the attacks of 9/11). He used a quotation from CFR member Matthew Simmons, who had participated in both projects, to make his point:

> [Simmons] exhorted delegates to the recent Offshore Technology Conference to prepare for a 'World War II' scale operation to meet forecast energy demand. Only an operation of this scale could solve the 'energy crisis' - 'crisis' being defined as 'when a problem or series of problems turn from being troublesome to extremely severe' (or as some would say, when a problem suddenly becomes terminal).[52]

Price quoted Simmons as saying that the costs of the operation would be around $5 trillion dollars, not counting costs of infrastructure expansion. Then he observed,

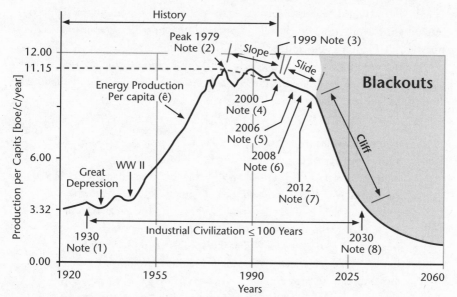

From Richard Duncan, *The Oil Crash and You*, August 2001.

"The CFR solution [political, manufacturing and economic restructuring] won't work. It's too big; it's too expensive; lead times are too long; and the return on investment is uncertain."

Returns on investment can only be uncertain if there is doubt about the availability of product. Demand (need plus purchasing power) is a given. Price then confirmed exactly what I have learned through many thousands of hours of research and interviews. This is exactly what Dale Allen Pfeiffer had told me when we first started talking, right after the World Trade Center attacks: "by way of confirmation, people in and close to the oil industry are reporting that increased drilling is not resulting as yet in significantly increased supply."

No doubt Price felt that Simmons was referring to a massive operation like the Manhattan Project that produced the first atomic bomb. However, I take the World War II operation suggestion a little more literally. So, it appears, did Richard Cheney and George W. Bush.

Where would the money in excess of $5 trillion come from? Well, our leaders have a habit of not telling people the truth. It's bad politics. They also have obligations to the people who put them in office (I did not use the word "elected"). But there is $600 billion a year in liquid cash from the drug trade. If invested well it could add several trillion to the pot while killing off "inferior" drug addicts (I have heard this attitude expressed by both intelligence operatives and political figures). What the heck — there are too many people anyway.

In this way, power and control could be maintained. Handsome profits could be passed out among those in the know. And why not? It's a zero-sum game. Individuals in power would be better prepared to deal with what follows when the peoples of the world begin to realize that the population is going to be reduced — one way or the other: relatively benign or absolutely horrific. The ultimate ethical question that is not being addressed openly is, which?

As Price wrote just 111 days before the World Trade Center ceased to exist, "The challenge of recession is immediate; the energy crisis is immediate. The immediate refuses to be ignored."

Sir Charles Galton Darwin wrote in 1952:

> The fifth revolution will come when we have spent the stores of coal and oil that have been accumulating in the earth during hundreds of millions of years .... It is to be hoped that before then other sources of energy will have been developed .... but without considering the detail [here], it is obvious that there will be a very great difference in ways of life .... Whether a convenient substitute for the present fuels is found or not, there can be no doubt that there will have to be a great change in ways of life. This change may justly be called a revolution, but it differs from all the preceding ones in that there is no likelihood of its leading to increases of population, but even perhaps to the reverse. [53]

Darwin's observations were reinforced by geologist Walter Youngquist in 1999. He wrote:

> World population will have to adjust to lesser food supplies by a reduction in population. Pimentel and Pimentel (1996) stated: "the nations of the world must develop a plan to reduce the global population from near 6 billion to about 2 billion. If humans do not control their numbers, nature will." Because stopping and then turning around the freight train of population growth can only be done gradually, this is a project that should be started now (Cohen, 1995).[54] If it is not done famine is likely to ensue.[55]

Geologist Jay Hanson, among the first to raise the issue of a global oil crisis resulting in population overshoot and collapse, came to the same conclusion in "The 'Longage of Critters' Problem":

> But when the above scenario seems inevitable, the elites will simply depopulate most of the planet with bioweapons. When the time comes, it will be the only logical solution to their problem. It's a first-strike tactic that leaves built-in infrastructure and other species in place and allows the elites to perpetuate their own genes into the foreseeable future.[56]

There is another highly significant test of whether or not what I have presented here is true. Think back to the statement about the results of the war on drugs after 30 years. Does my narrative scenario accord with the events since 9/11: the anthrax attacks (using spores developed by the CIA);[57] the new vaccination laws and programs; the erosion of civil liberties; all the inconsistencies in the government's statements about what happened on 9/11 and the bogus link between the attacks and Iraq; the sudden and nearly obsessive preoccupation with biological warfare; the invasion of Iraq itself; the creation of a Department of Homeland Security; and the deployment of US military personnel only in regions of the world connected to oil and gas production or transshipment.

As Colin Campbell, founder of the Association for the Study of Peak Oil (<www.peakoil.net>) has said, "The species Homo sapiens is not going to become extinct. But the subspecies 'Petroleum Man,' most certainly is."[58] Before that happens, there will, as we will demonstrate to you, the jury, inevitably be armed conflict to seize diminishing energy resources. *It doesn't have to be this way.* It shouldn't be this way. But the one thing that makes it inevitable is the operation of the world's economic system, a psychological and ultimately moral limitation that no political leaders and few human beings can see beyond.

I heard this reality confirmed by a major Dutch economist speaking at a Peak Oil conference in May of 2003 who said, "It may not be profitable to slow decline."[59] War is the most profitable business of all.

In this context five specific quotations from Zbigniew Brzezinski's 1997 book *The Grand Chessboard: America's Primacy and Its Geostrategic Imperatives* provide key landmarks in our investigation of 9/11:

- The attitude of the American public toward the external projection of American power has been much more ambivalent. The public supported America's engagement in World War II largely because of the shock effect of the Japanese attack on Pearl Harbor. (pp. 24-25)
- But the pursuit of power is not a goal that commands popular passion, except in conditions of a sudden threat or challenge to the public's sense of domestic well-being. The economic self-denial (that is, defense spending) and the human sacrifice (casualties, even among professional soldiers) required in the effort are uncongenial to democratic instincts. Democracy is inimical to imperial mobilization. (p. 35)
- To put it in a terminology that harkens back to the more brutal age of ancient empires, the three grand imperatives of imperial geostrategy are to prevent collusion and maintain security dependence among the vassals, to keep tributaries pliant and protected, and to keep the barbarians from coming together. (p. 40)
- That puts a premium on maneuver and manipulation in order to prevent the emergence of a hostile coalition that could eventually seek to challenge America's primacy. (p. 198)
- Moreover, as America becomes an increasingly multicultural society, it may find it more difficult to fashion a consensus on foreign policy issues, except in the circumstance of a truly massive and widely perceived direct external threat. (p. 211)

CHAPTER 2

CHENEY KNEW

The Cheney report is very guarded about the amount of foreign oil that will be required. The only clue provided by the [public] report is a chart of net US oil consumption and production over time. According to this illustration, domestic oil field production will decline from about 8.5 million barrels per day (mb/d) in 2002 to 7.0 mb/d in 2020, while consumption will jump from 19.5 mb/d to 25.5 mb/d. That suggests imports or other sources of petroleum ... will have to rise from 11 mb/d to 18.5 mb/d. Most of the recommendations of the NEP [National Energy Policy, May 2001] are aimed at procuring this 7.5 mb/d increment, equivalent to the total oil consumed by China and India.

— Professor Michael Klare, "Bush-Cheney Energy Strategy: Procuring the Rest of the World's Oil," Foreign Policy in Focus, January 2004

The White House Stonewall goes on, as the Bush administration continues to deny the non-partisan General Accounting Office's request for information on who the White House Energy Task Force met with while formulating national energy policy. For the first time in history, the GAO has sued the executive branch for access to the records. It has been 42 days since the GAO filed their suit against the Bush administration and 333 days since the White House first received the GAO request. Why is the White House going to such lengths? What are they trying to hide?

— Truthout, <www.truthout.org>, "White House Stonewall,"
April 5, 2002

The Supreme Court said Monday it will settle a fight over whether Vice President Dick Cheney must disclose details about secret contacts with energy industry officials as the Bush administration drafted its energy policy ....

The Supreme Court will hear the case sometime in the spring, with a ruling expected by July.

— Associated Press, December 15, 2003

Bush and Blair have been making plans for the day when oil production peaks, by seeking to secure the reserves of other nations.

— George Monbiot, "Bottom of the Barrel," The Guardian,
December 2, 2003

China and India are building superhighways and automobile factories. Energy demand is expected to rise by about 50 percent over the next 20 years, with about 40 percent of that demand to be supplied by petroleum ...

"Oil supplies are finite and will soon be controlled by a handful of nations; the invasion of Iraq and control of its supplies will do little to change that. One can only hope that an informed electorate and its principled representatives will realize that the facts do matter, and that nature — not military might — will soon dictate the ultimate availability of petroleum.

— Alfred Cavallo, "Oil: The Illusion Of Plenty," Bulletin of the
Atomic Scientists, Jan-Feb 2004

The 9/11 attacks gave the US an ideal pretext to use force to secure its global domination ....

The plan ["Rebuilding America's Defenses", Project for a New American Century - 2000] shows Bush's cabinet intended to take military control of the Gulf region whether or not Saddam Hussein was in power ....

The overriding motivation for this political smokescreen is that the US and the UK are beginning to run out of secure hydrocarbon energy supplies .... As demand is increasing, so supply is decreasing, continually since the 1960s.

— Michael Meacher MP, UK Environment Minister 1997-2003,
"The War on Terrorism is Bogus," The Guardian, September 6, 2003

How could the US government facilitate such attacks and launch aggression throughout the world? What would make America do such a thing?

I have said for two years that the deepest, darkest secrets of September 11th lie buried in the records of the US National Energy Policy Development Group (NEPDG) which began its work almost the same day the Bush administration took office and produced its final report in May of 2001, just four short months before the World Trade Center ceased to exist.

Part of the proof of this lies in the blatantly illegal and vehement manner in which the task force, headed by Vice President Dick Cheney, has failed to release its records for public scrutiny, in a clear and blatant violation of US constitutional law. This indicates that there is something to conceal.

When, in May 2001, the American conservative legal "watchdog" group Judicial Watch filed suit to see the NEPDG records, it was the first to protest the unheard of secrecy that had surrounded the task force's deliberations. As the White

House stonewalled, the Government Accounting Office (GAO) — the official investigative arm of the Congress — filed suit the following February. Congress had, after all, funded the project. Non-governmental officials had played major roles in its deliberations and under the Constitution, the GAO had an obligation to see how the money was spent and what was produced. White House refusals prompted media speculation about deals with Enron and big oil companies: a divvying of spoils, a rape of the environment. Judicial Watch was later joined in its suit by the progressive Sierra Club from the left. A scandal for everyone!

It's a sure bet that of all the plaintiffs from Congressman Henry Waxman (D — CA) and Comptroller General David Walker who fought for the GAO, to Judicial Watch's Larry Klayman, who had previously fought Bill Clinton, to the environmentalists, none had a clue as to what they were really asking for or why Dick Cheney fought them so ruthlessly and still does as of this writing.

The fight was, in fact, just beginning.

As reported in the congressional newspaper *The Hill* on February 19, 2003, the GAO dropped its suit after the administration made threats of heavy cuts to its budget. The offer GAO couldn't refuse was delivered by Republican Senator Ted Stevens of Alaska, where a lot of new drilling was expected to take place. Judicial Watch and the Sierra Club stood firm. Both had the money to see their suits through. The controversy boiled throughout 2001-2002. Were it not for the "war on terror," this might have been one of the biggest US constitutional crises of all time.

The Enron scandal seems like a pleasant diversion in retrospect. All these battles started *before* the first plane hit the Twin Towers. That's one reason why everyone was shocked at the blatantly illegal secrecy and the manner in which the administration fought. This was long before the Patriot Act, Homeland Security, Patriot Act II, and all the major lies of the Bush administration that have since been revealed. One of the administration's bets was that, in the wake of 9/11, the NEPDG records would be forgotten.

They lost that one.

Hints as to what was discussed in the secret task force are now on the table. They strongly suggest that inside the NEPDG records lay the deepest, darkest secrets of 9/11. The motive; the apocalyptic truth that would compel such carnage and a wrenching hairpin turn in the course of human history; the thing that no one ever wanted to know; the thing that makes it utterly believable that the US government could have deliberately facilitated the attacks of September 11th, stands on the brink of full disclosure — maybe.

Shortly after it was announced that the US Supreme Court would render a decision in the suits in July of 2004,[1] Dick Cheney found it convenient to go duck hunting with Justice Antonin Scalia who would hear arguments in the case in March and April. The vice president paid all expenses for the trip and even provided Justice Scalia with Secret Service protection and transportation.[2] In spite of widespread complaints and arguments that this posed a conflict of interest in the case, Scalia has refused to recuse himself and will cast what may be the deciding vote to keep the secrets of 9/11 from public view.[3]

A seven-page glimpse under the door

Last July, after appealing a Freedom of Information Act (FOIA) request for NEPDG documents, Judicial Watch won a small victory with the release of seven pages. They included:

- A detailed map of all Iraqi oil fields (11 percent of world supply);
- A two-page specific list of all nations with development contracts for Iraqi oil and gas projects and the companies involved;
- A detailed map of all Saudi Arabian oil fields (25 percent of world supply);
- A list of all major oil and gas development projects in Saudi Arabia;
- A detailed map of all the oil fields in the United Arab Emirates (8 percent of world supply);
- A list of all oil and gas development projects in the UAE.

The documents may be viewed online at:
<www.judicialwatch.org/071703.c_.shtml> .

In their austerity, the documents scream of what NEPDG was debating. If 7.5 mb/d of new oil production was to be secured, there was only one place to get it: the Persian Gulf. All told, including Qatar (firmly under US control and the home of headquarters for US Central Command) and Iran, the Gulf is home to 60 percent of all the recoverable oil on the planet. Not only would these oil fields have to be controlled, billions of dollars in new investment would be required to boost production to meet US needs, simultaneously denying that same production to the rest of the world where demand is also soaring.

Klare wrote:

> According to the Department of Energy, Saudi Arabia's net petroleum output must grow by 133 percent over the next 25 years, from 10.2 mb/d in 2001 to 23.8 mb/d in 2025, in order to meet anticipated world requirements at the end of that period. Expanding Saudi capacity by 13.6 mb/d, which is the equivalent of total current production by the United States and Mexico, will cost hundreds of billions of dollars .... The Cheney report calls for exactly that. However, any effort by Washington to apply pressure on Riyadh is likely to meet significant resistance from the royal family.

Not to mention from Muslim fundamentalists and ordinary Saudi citizens who oppose the corrupt and teetering regime.

Sixty per cent of all the recoverable oil on the planet is in an area no larger than the state of Kansas.

Herein lies the motive behind America's eagerness to quietly and wrongly implicate the Saudi government in 9/11. A closer look at the maps obtained by Judicial Watch explains why. When placed side by side the maps reveal that roughly 60 percent of the world's recoverable oil is in a "golden" triangle running from Mosul in northern Iraq, to the Straits of Hormuz, to an oil field in Saudi Arabia 75 miles in from the coast, just west of Qatar, then back up to Mosul. Almost all of Iran's oil lies near its western shoreline on the Gulf. This whole area would fit easily inside the northern portion of Texas, America's premier oil state. When the maps from Cheney's Energy Task Force are superimposed on a map of that state, the contrast in size is striking.

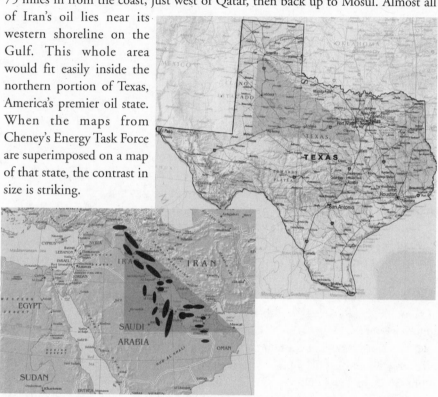

Maps obtained from the NEPDG showing the world's major oil fields and other documents show clearly what was of major concern in the secret proceedings. This map, prepared by the author, is a compilation of maps released in a bitter US lawsuit to release all of the Energy Task Force's records.

The US military already occupies part of this area and surrounds the remainder. So it's quite consistent with our stated motive to ask how easy it would be for American forces to occupy the entire oil-bearing region in the event that the Saudi monarchy should become unstable, as it surely will someday soon. I have been predicting such a US occupation for some time, and it's likely that the US government will begin the project with covert destabilization efforts. I will discuss the destabilization of Saudi Arabia later in the book.

The list of countries and companies already invested in new development projects in the region reads like the perfect answer to the question: "OK, whom do we have to deal with to get this done? Who will come with us if we offer them a piece, and who will refuse, no matter what, because they can't afford to have their share reduced?" Look at the documents and answer that question, and you have perfectly separated the investor nations into two camps: those nations who supported the Iraqi invasion and those who opposed it.[4]

As Michael Klare points out in this chapter's epigraph, the simple fact is, given that oil is peaking, to secure imports equivalent to the amounts consumed by China and India is to take that same oil away from China and India, or from some other mix of countries. The question is, from whom?

Other global battles for the oil that remains have already begun, albeit quietly for the time being. China has passed Japan as the world's second largest oil importer. A January 3, 2004, article by James Brooke in the *New York Times*, "Japan and China Battle for Russia's Oil and Gas," described the fierce high-stakes contest underway. Russia is going to build only one pipeline east from its Siberian fields. It is either going to terminate in the middle of China, or on Russia's Pacific coast where it can supply Japan, Korea, and the Philippines. Brooke wrote, "With the choice Russia faces, the political and economic dynamics of northeast Asia stand to be profoundly shaped for years to come."[5]

Russia has 60 billion barrels (Gb) of proven reserves, a 690-day supply for planet Earth, and there is no great likelihood that more significant quantities of oil will be discovered anywhere inside or outside of Russia.

West Africa, Latin America, Southeast Asia

The public NEPDG report also addresses (in oblique fashion) areas of the world that have increasingly become inflamed since 9/11: West Africa, South America, and Southeast Asia. For more than two years, FTW has paid close attention to a shift in US and NATO military presence in west Africa, Venezuela, Colombia, the Philippines, and Indonesia.[6]

Of particular interest here are the facts that on May 1, 2003, through the CIA's Voice of America, NATO commander James Jones announced that NATO was shifting its focus to west Africa; new US naval bases are being negotiated in the tiny west African island nations of Sao Tome and Principe (Klare); and the US gave six naval warships to Nigeria last summer (Reuters, CNN). Isn't it convenient that a US-friendly coup toppled the Sao Tome government last July?[7]

As detailed by Klare, the importance of these regions is that, while they contain far smaller reserves than the Gulf, they can be brought online (and drained) quickly to meet current demand without destabilizing the economies of the world in general and the US in particular. The tens and perhaps hundreds of billions of dollars needed to invest in infrastructure to increase production in the Gulf will come only when oil prices have soared enough to provide that capital. Don't expect Wall Street to drain their reserves. They aren't going to pay for it. You are.

Make no mistake, the oil companies and Wall Street are banking on severe oil price spikes to fund this short-lived development and, almost as importantly, to reduce consumption on an ad hoc basis as people in the US find they can't afford five- or six-dollar gasoline and businesses shut down. There are, at best, between 500 and 600 billion barrels in the Gulf, which can only be pumped at needed rates if the investment is begun immediately and sustained over the next ten years.

Do the math, and it's clear: when will the price spikes come? Within six months to a year after the 2004 election. Not before then, if the Bush group can prevent it.

I am not optimistic about the outcome. Nor am I optimistic about what will happen when the reality of Peak Oil sets in. Noted economist James Kenneth Galbraith has well described how current market forces really prevent any realistic addressing of the problem and only tend to exacerbate it by continuing to urge increased consumption.[8] Oil companies lie about reserves to protect share value and defray tax burdens. Financial markets deny there is a problem to avoid investor panic. Yet the first months of 2004 have seen an avalanche of stories in the major press organs of the world finally acknowledging, at least in some measure, the reality of Peak Oil. More such stories are appearing every day as this book goes to press. Shock waves rippled through the markets in 2004 as it was announced that Saudi Arabia, with 25 percent of the world's recoverable reserves may have passed its peak of production and could therefore never accommodate the production increases described by Michael Klare and mandated by NEPDG requirements.[9]

The United States has chosen to address the problem of Peak Oil in the most brutal, venal, and shortsighted way available: by using military force to commandeer what remains of the world's rapidly vanishing fossil fuels. The true attitude of American political leaders is that "the American way of life is not negotiable," especially if such negotiations would reduce their power or influence.

Cheney knew in 1999

In November 1999, then Halliburton Chairman Dick Cheney gave a speech to the London Institute of Petroleum. What he said in that speech was not widely known to researchers until a discussion of it appeared in the April 2004 issue of *Middle East* magazine. Professor Kjell Aleklett of the University of Uppsala in Sweden, who is also the 2004 president of the Association for the Study of Peak Oil and Gas, caught some key quotes and saw that it was apparent that Dick Cheney was aware of Peak Oil issues at the time. Aleklett reported that transcript of the remarks, previously available on the institute's website had been removed. [10]

A few days later Aleklett, having successfully located a transcript, forwarded it to me. Cheney's remarks speak for themselves:

> We as an industry have had to deal with the pesky problem that once you find oil and pump it out of the ground you've got to turn around and find more or go out of business ....

Every year you've got to find and develop reserves equal to your output just to stand still, just to stay even. This is true for companies as well in the broader economic sense as it is for the world. A new merged company like Exxon-Mobil will have to secure over a billion and a half barrels of new oil equivalent reserves every year just to replace existing production ....

...For the world as a whole, oil companies are expected to keep finding and developing enough oil to offset our 71 million-plus barrel a day of oil depletion, but also to meet new demand. By some estimates there will be an average of two percent annual growth in global oil demand over the years ahead along with conservatively a three percent natural decline in production from existing reserves. That means by 2010 we will need on the order of an additional 50 million barrels a day...

So where is the oil going to come from? ....

Looking back to the early 1990s, expectations were that significant amounts of the world's new resources would come from such areas as the former Soviet Union and from China ....

For most companies the majority of their profits come from core areas, that is areas where they have significant investments, economies of scale and large license areas locked up, but many of these core areas are now mature, and it can be difficult to replace the earnings from the high margin barrels there. Some of the oil being developed in new areas is obviously very high cost and low margin ....

Clearly the main driver behind the biggest mergers are the cost savings that are anticipated as a result of economies of scale .... There are also cases where difficulty in sustaining and growing the companies has led management to offer the firm to a bigger player. In the worldwide competition for capital, there are imperatives for size and scale. Larger companies tend to have the highest credit ratings and therefore the lowest borrowing costs, but they also tend to have higher multiples in the stock market. The share price premium becomes a valuable currency for takeovers ....

Oil is unique in that it is so strategic in nature. We are not talking about soapflakes or leisurewear here. Energy is truly fundamental to the world's economy. The Gulf War was a reflection of that reality .... It is the basic, fundamental building block of the world's economy .... Our constituency is not only oilmen from Louisiana and Texas, but software writers in Massachusetts and especially steel producers in Pennsylvania ....

Well, the end of the oil era is not here yet, but changes are afoot, and the industry must be ready to adapt to the new century and to the transformations that lie ahead ....[11]

Three Days of the Condor

There is a deeper part of human nature that covers the planet in a sickly, light-sweet-crude blanket of denial. It is perfectly epitomized by the closing lines of Sidney Pollack's extraordinary 1975 film, *Three Days of the Condor*. As *FTW* has shown in recent stories — using declassified CIA documents — the Agency was already well aware of Peak Oil in the mid 1970s.[12] Three Days of the Condor took that awful truth and said then, what few in the post-9/11 world have had the courage to say now. I can guarantee you that it is the overriding rationale in Dick Cheney's mind, in the mind of every senior member of the Bush administration, and in the mind of whomever it is that will be the next US president. Getting rid of George W. Bush will not address the underlying causative factors of energy and money, and any solution that does not address those issues will prove futile.

Turner (Robert Redford): Do we have plans to invade the Middle East?

Higgins (Cliff Robertson): Are you crazy?

Turner: Am I?

Higgins: Look, Turner…

Turner: Do we have plans?

Higgins: No. Absolutely not. We have games. That's all. We play games. What if? How many men? What would it take? Is there a cheaper way to destabilize a régime? That's what we're paid to do.

Turner: Go on. So Atwood just took the game too seriously. He was really going to do it, wasn't he?

Higgins: It was a renegade operation. Atwood knew 54-12 would never authorize it. There was no way, not with the heat on the Company.

Turner: What if there hadn't been any heat? Supposing I hadn't stumbled on a plan? Say nobody had?

Higgins: Different ball game. The fact is there was nothing wrong with the plan. Oh, the plan was all right. The plan would have worked.

Turner: Boy, what is it with you people? You think not getting caught in a lie is the same thing as telling the truth?

Higgins: No. It's simple economics. Today it's oil, right? In 10 or 15 years — food, plutonium. And maybe even sooner. Now what do you think the people are gonna want us to do then?

Turner: Ask them.

Higgins: Not now — then. Ask them when they're running out. Ask them when there's no heat in their homes and they're cold. Ask them when their engines stop. Ask them when people who've never known hunger start going hungry. Do you want to know something? They won't want us to ask them. They'll just want us to get it for them.

CHAPTER 3

THE CIA IS WALL STREET, AND DRUG MONEY IS KING

How is it that the economy could prevent finding solutions to Peak Oil? Answering that question not only corroborates motive and intent, it also allows us to examine the mindset of the suspects. It is a critical part of the foundation that must be laid in presenting my case for what happened on September 11, 2001. One of the biggest secrets of 9/11 is the connection between drug money and Wall Street.

Oil companies, banks, auto manufacturers, and computer companies all trade their stocks on Wall Street, whether on the New York Stock Exchange (NYSE), on the NASDAQ, or on the American Stock Exchange. They also trade bonds there. Shares of stock are fractions of ownership in companies, and they represent equity. Bonds are loans made to companies, and they represent debt. Companies raise capital to do such things as build refineries or drill for oil, either from their own profits or by selling shares of stock or issuing bonds. As we shall see, there are other ways that companies generate capital that aren't talked about in public.

The higher a company's stock price, the more capital it has available to buy raw materials, to build factories or refineries, to give to its investors in the form of dividends, or to split among the top executives and, in some cases, even the employees.

Another key component of trading in financial markets is the Chicago Board Options Exchange (CBOE). That's where futures derivatives like "put" and "call" options are traded. Derivatives are financial instruments that have no direct value in and of themselves but derive their value from other things that do. Puts and calls are basically bets that a stock price will either fall or rise at some future date. Members of the NYSE and the CBOE are in regular contact and watch each other's trading closely. The same applies for the American Stock Exchange and the relative newcomer, the NASDAQ, which is a privately owned trading exchange.

In a rapidly globalizing world economy, competitive edge is everything. In business, edge comes in several forms. First, there is intelligence. What does the market want? What is the competition doing? Can someone outbid us in our attempt to buy out XYZ Company? Is someone trying to make a run at our stock price? Does someone have a better or more efficient product or process? How close is the competition to getting its product to market? Can we invest $250 million in a refinery if Lukoil or Sibneft is going to get the rights to the oil field we're looking at? Who is going to build the pipeline to the refinery? How much will they have to charge to make it profitable? Does the competition have any weaknesses that we can exploit to give us an edge?

Then there is money itself. Catherine Austin Fitts knows money. She is a former managing director of the Wall Street investment bank Dillon Read, holds an MBA from the Wharton School of Business, and is a former Assistant Secretary of Housing.

Fitts expresses a key principle of competitive advantage thus: "Those who have the lowest cost of capital win." If you have financed a car or a home, you have probably had your credit checked. It is your credit rating and the down payment that determine what your monthly payments are. It is no different if, for example, ExxonMobil wants to finance a new refinery or if AOL wants to buy Time Warner and has to borrow money to do it. They call that a leveraged buyout or LBO.

If you finance a $24,000 car and make a $4,000 down payment then, assuming your credit is good, the dealership or your bank might finance your $20,000 loan at 5 percent interest over four years. In that case your payments would be $460.60 a month. If, however, your credit is not so good, then you might pay 10 percent, in which case your monthly payments would be $514.49.

Following this same premise let's say, for example, that you are ChevronTexaco (where National Security Advisor Condoleezza Rice used to sit on the board), and you want to finance a pipeline so that you can get your oil into people's cars, computers, and food. The cost of the pipeline is estimated at US$2 billion. You decide to put $300 million of Chevron's money into the deal. You form a consortium with other oil companies to share the costs. But none of you has all that money up front. That's not good business. The oil business is sometimes risky, and oil companies frequently keep large financial cushions to protect them in case there are international crises, oil prices drop, or a particular field they want to invest in is a dud.

An anecdote illustrates the point. The first well in Kazakhstan's Kashagan field, owned by a consortium involving Agip (Italy), British Gas, ExxonMobil, Shell, Total, BP, Phillips, and others, had cost $300 million by the time it was finished. What if that well and your next three proved to be dry holes? That would mean no income with continuing heavy capital expense.[1] Oil companies plan for these contingencies well in advance. They've been in the business for a hundred years now, and have had plenty of time to do accounting studies.

So, after doing all the analysis, you and your consortium find that you need to borrow $1 billion to finance and build your pipeline. You decide to amortize the payments over 20 years (the expected life of the field).[2] Now you have to go out and borrow the money. Let's see what various interest rates would do to the company's monthly payments. A major bank such as HSBC, Deutsche Bank, or

JPMorgan Chase might offer you an interest rate of, say, 9 percent. To pay back a billion dollars over 20 years at 9 percent interest, your monthly payments would be $917,000. But an interest rate of 6 percent would mean payments of $716,440 a month.

In other words, your company would have $200,560 extra profit each month merely by shaving 3 percent from the interest rate. This has a direct impact on net profits, which are defined as gross revenues minus the cost of doing business. And this is where *what the cost of capital can do* gets really interesting.

The pop

A price-to-earnings ratio (P/E or "the pop") for any given stock is calculated with two basic facts: the market capitalization of a company, and its net profits. Market capitalization is simply the total number of shares in circulation multiplied by the stock price at any given time. If someone has a company with 1,000 shares of stock, each selling at $100, then her market capitalization is $100,000.

Net profits are simply the gross revenues minus the cost of doing business. So if you have a company that brings in $100,000, and all of your costs to produce, advertise, sell, and pay your bills are $80,000, your net profits are $20,000. The important thing to note is that market capitalization cannot be lied about. It's there for everyone to see. Net profits, on the other hand, are something completely different. Enron, WorldCom, and a few other giant companies taught us that.

Now, if you had a company with a market capitalization of $300,000,000 and net profits of $10,000,000, your price to earnings ratio would be 30/1. Most sober financial analysts have long held that a healthy (i.e., rational from an investor's standpoint) P/E is about 15/1. That's why they shake their heads in disbelief when they look at companies like Enron, which had a P/E of 60 before it collapsed, or like Cisco Systems, which recently had a P/E of 90. That's also why many sober analysts believe that the Dow Jones average should properly be at around 5,000.

If the relationship were strictly mathematical then adding just one dollar to the "bottom line" would create 30 dollars in stock value.

$$\frac{30}{1} = \frac{60}{2}$$

It doesn't work that way in real life. What happens is that a market analyst will keep looking at the earnings reports of companies that he or she evaluates. When an analyst sees that a given company's earnings are rising quickly, the analyst will put out a "buy" or a "strong buy" recommendation. As people buy the stock, the share price will rise roughly to the point of the established P/E for that company.

Decreasing or increasing net profits thus has a multiplying impact on your stock value. So in our loan scenario evaluating different interest rates, a difference of $200,560 per month in profits means that with a P/E ratio of 60, over the course of a year the decrease in total stock value ($200,560 x 12 x 60) would be $144,403,200. With a P/E of 30 it would be $72,201,600. This is the main reason why Wall Street so closely watches what the Federal Reserve chairman does with interest rates.

A major tool for maintaining stock profits is to find the cheapest capital possible. This is especially true in a competitive bidding process where companies determine their bids based upon how much they can afford to pay back (in much the same way that most people buy cars). Thus, *those who have the lowest cost of capital win.* In the best-case scenario this would be capital on which you didn't have to pay any interest at all, or even raised — somehow — for free. Finding the cheap capital (just like the cheap oil) is the trick: knowing where the money is and how it works. But big money doesn't always broadcast its location.

The CIA is Wall Street

The CIA is Wall Street. Wall Street is the CIA. This is perhaps one of the easiest landmarks to establish on our map. We do it by looking at key players in the CIA's history and their relationships to America's financial engine.

Clark Clifford: The National Security Act of 1947 was written by Clark Clifford, a Democratic Party powerhouse, former secretary of defense, and one-time advisor to President Harry Truman. In the 1980s, as chairman of First American Bancshares, Clifford was instrumental in getting the corrupt CIA drug bank BCCI (founded by a Pakistani national) a license to operate on American shores. His profession: Wall Street lawyer and banker. BCCI and its particular web of characters have been a virtual cut-and-paste overlay linking up Osama bin Laden, al Qaeda, and terrorist financing.[3] It was Clark Clifford who was retained by former CIA Director Richard Helms when the latter was indicted and prosecuted for lying to Congress in 1976.[4]

Clifford and his banking partner Robert Altman were eventually indicted on criminal charges for their role in illegally helping BCCI purchase an American bank, First American Bancshares. At the time BCCI had been connected to both drug money laundering and financial support for Afghan rebels supported by the CIA through its director Bill Casey.[5]

John Foster and Allen Dulles: These two brothers "designed" the CIA for Clifford. Both were active in intelligence operations during World War II. Allen Dulles had been America's top Office of Strategic Services (OSS) spy in Switzerland, where he met frequently with Nazi leaders and looked after US investments in Germany. He also held an executive position with Standard Oil. John Foster went on to become secretary of state under Dwight Eisenhower, and Allen served as CIA director under Ike, only to be fired by JFK after the abortive 1961 US-led covert invasion of Cuba known as the Bay of Pigs. Their professions: partners in the most powerful — to this day — Wall Street law firm of Sullivan and Cromwell.

Enron is only one of Sullivan and Cromwell's current clients, and it employed a dozen "former" CIA officers before its fall from grace.[6] Other prominent Sullivan and Cromwell clients are AIG, Global Crossing, ImClone, Martha Stewart, and the Harvard Endowment.

After the assassination of JFK in 1963, Allen Dulles became the staff director and lead investigator of the Warren Commission, which asserted that Lee Harvey Oswald was a lone assassin who had fired a bullet that had caused JFK's throat wound, hung suspended in mid-air for several seconds, changed directions twice, then wounded Texas Governor John Connally in the chest, wrist, and thigh only to fall out of his body in nearly pristine condition on a stretcher at Parkland Hospital in Dallas about 30 minutes later. When asked about how he could have offered the Warren Report, full of inconsistencies, to the American people with a straight face, Dulles is reported to have said, "The American people don't read."

Bill Casey: Reagan's CIA director and the OSS veteran who served as chief covert wrangler during the Iran-Contra years was, under Richard Nixon, chairman of the Securities and Exchange Commission. His profession: Wall Street lawyer and stock trader.

In 1984 ABC News was devoting serious attention to a CIA scandal in Hawaii connected to the investment firm BBRDW (Bishop, Baldwin, Rewald, Dillingham, and Wong). The BBRDW story was lifting a veil connected to money laundering, drugs, and the failed CIA drug bank named Nugan-Hand. Bill Casey and the CIA's general counsel Stanley Sporkin put extreme pressure on both the network and anchor Peter Jennings to stop their coverage. During the semi-public battle, ABC's stock dropped from $67 to $59 a share, and by December, the firm Capital Cities was trying to buy the network. Capital Cities successfully completed the buyout of ABC in March of 1985, after which the CIA conveniently dropped a suit against the network.[7]

Bill Casey had helped to found Capital Cities and had served both as its lawyer and as a member of its board of directors in the years between his service as SEC chairman for Nixon and as director of Central Intelligence for Reagan. ABC became known thereafter as "the CIA network."

Other sources, including the family of the late Colonel Albert Vincent Carone — about whom I have written extensively — confirm that Casey was a lifelong resident of Long Island and that Carone, a "made" member of the Genovese crime family, retired NYPD detective, and CIA operative, routinely exchanged insider trading information with Casey. Multiple witnesses have confirmed that Casey attended the christening of Carone's grandson.

Stanley Sporkin: Sporkin served as the CIA's general counsel under Casey. But he had previously served for more than 20 years at the Securities and Exchange Commission, rising to the post of general counsel. Casey's right-hand man, he was one of the first people Casey brought with him to the CIA in 1981. Almost all of Sporkin's tenure at the SEC was spent in the enforcement division, charged with prosecuting corporate and stock fraud.

During the Iran-Contra investigations it was revealed that Sporkin had routine contact with Lt. Col. Oliver North, who was later convicted on several felony counts including lying to Congress.[8] At times the e-mails between the two men, alluding to the 1920s comedy team Laurel and Hardy, read "To Stanley from Ollie."

After retiring as CIA general counsel in 1986, Sporkin was soon appointed a US district court judge in Washington, DC, where he presided over some of the most important trials (including Microsoft's) in the country. He resigned from the bench in January of 2000 and joined the Wall Street law firm of Weill, Gotschall, and Manges, self-described as specializing in "Wall Street Management and Capital." Weill, Gotschall, and Manges is currently serving as Enron's bankruptcy counsel. Although Sporkin received praise for many of his decisions from anti-corporate critics such as Ralph Nader, he presided over a number of more nefarious cases, including that of former Federal Housing Commissioner Catherine Austin Fitts, whose firm Hamilton Securities had been targeted for malicious and unfounded harassment after uncovering evidence of covert operations that tied the Department of Housing and Urban Development (HUD) to drug operations, slush funds, "friendly" Wall Street interests, and political corruption.

Fitts was the target of a 1996 *qui tam* whistleblower lawsuit, which allows charges to be filed under seal for 60 days while the Department of Justice (DoJ) investigates whether there is merit to the case. As a result, Fitts was not allowed to know who had made allegations against her, or even what the allegations were. Sporkin extended that seal for five years, thereby turning a brief investigation period into a nightmare that prevented Fitts and her attorneys from being able to know, or even address, an accuser or his allegations. Sporkin was able to do this with no evidence of any wrongdoing, yet his decisions in the case routinely favored the unnamed parties seeking to discredit Fitts and upheld illegal actions by the federal government, including the seizure of her company offices (a clear violation of the Fourth Amendment).

During this period the government destroyed the company's proprietary software tools and databases that documented community financial flows, and kept the backup tapes under the control of Sporkin-appointed trustees. Fitts has subsequently been completely exonerated (no formal charges were ever filed), and it has been officially admitted that there was no basis for any action against her in the first place. Fitts has also documented several attempts by the Department of Justice investigators to falsify or destroy evidence. According to *Insight Magazine*, Department of Justice and HUD officials admitted off the record that it was a political vendetta.

After a *nine-year* herculean struggle, Fitts is still in court defending against the *qui tam* lawsuit (indirectly supported all this time by generous government payments and contracts to the government informant who originally brought the suit) and trying to recover an estimated $2.5 million in funds owed to her company,

Hamilton Securities. *A court of claims ruling in 2004 concluded that the government had breached its contract with Hamilton by refusing to pay Hamilton's outstanding invoices. DoJ has indicated that the government will not pay, but will appeal.*

Hamilton had successfully helped HUD auction defaulted home mortgages, saving the Federal Housing Administration Fund over $2.2 billion.[9] In 2001, after finally succeeding in getting the seal removed from the original lawsuit and obtaining some of the transcripts of sealed hearing — one crucial item was "missing" from court records, Fitts and her attorneys discovered that Sporkin, apparently frustrated at DoJ's inability to make anything stick, had actively coached DoJ attorneys on how best to keep the case going in spite of its transparent lack of merit *and that DoJ was taking contradictory positions in an unsealed case before a different judge in the same court.*

David Doherty, who replaced Sporkin as CIA general counsel in 1987, is now the executive vice president of the New York Stock Exchange, for Enforcement.

A. B. "Buzzy" Krongard: until he joined the CIA in 1998, Krongard was the CEO of the investment bank Alex Brown. In 1997 he sold his interest in Alex Brown to Banker's Trust, where he served as vice chairman until "joining" the CIA in 1998. A close friend of CIA Director George Tenet, the colorful, cigar-smoking former Marine specialized in private banking operations serving extremely wealthy clients. It has been heavily documented by official US government investigations into money laundering that private banking services are frequently used for the laundering of drug money and the proceeds of corporate crime.[10] Private banking services were especially criticized in investigations of money laundering connected to the looting of Russia throughout the 1990s.[11]

John Deutch: Deutch retired from the CIA as its director in December 1996. He immediately accepted an offer to join the board of directors of the nation's second largest bank, Citigroup, which has been repeatedly involved in the documented laundering of drug money. This includes Citigroup's 2001 purchase of a Mexican bank known to launder drug money, Banamex.[12] Deutch narrowly escaped criminal prosecution after it was learned that he had kept a large number of classified CIA documents on non-secure personal computers at his private residence.[13]

Maurice "Hank" Greenberg: The CEO of American International Group (AIG) insurance and manager of the third largest pool of investment capital in the world was floated as a possible CIA director by Bill Clinton in 1995.[14] *FTW* exposed Greenberg's and AIG's long connection to CIA drug trafficking and covert operations in a two-part series that was interrupted by the attacks of September 11. Under Greenberg's stewardship, an AIG subsidiary severely bent several laws in conjunction with the Arkansas Development Financial Authority (ADFA) to establish what many have alleged was a first-class money laundering operation for drug funds arising from CIA-connected cocaine smuggling into Mena, Arkansas, in the 1980s.

In that series *FTW* reported that AIG employed in its San Francisco legal offices the wife of Medellin Cartel co-founder Carlos Lehder. I actually went to San Francisco and had lunch with her in the summer of 2001. Our investigations later disclosed that AIG had been tied to US covert operations going back to the World War II and conclusively linked to the heroin trade.[15] We also reported that AIG owned and operated the largest private fleet of full-sized airliners and cargo planes on the planet.[16]

As an illustrative example of how the quiet connections operate behind the scenes to conceal criminal activity, it was an AIG subsidiary, Lexington Insurance, that was involved in the ADFA deal and that also acted as the errors and omissions carrier for Catherine Austin Fitts's Hamilton Securities. At the start of Fitts's harassment by DoJ, Lexington reneged on obligations to pay Fitts's attorneys, who then dropped out of the case. This effectively enabled the DoJ *with support from Judge Stanley Sporkin* to seize Hamilton's computers and data, destroy the computers and software, and tie up the backup tapes for years. Those tapes likely contain data — originally supplied to Fitts by HUD — that could expose many illegal covert government operations.

I was not surprised then when Greenberg — a staunch supporter of Israel — was chosen by the Council on Foreign Relations in 2002 to lead an investigation of terrorist financing. The CFR report, not surprisingly, was extremely critical of Saudi Arabia.[17]

Professor Peter Dale Scott of the University of California at Berkeley, author of many historically crucial books on covert operations and deep politics, observed in the early 1970s that six of the first seven CIA deputy directors were from the New York social register, and all seven deputy directors "under Walter Bedell Smith and Truman, came from New York legal and financial circles."[18] The headquarters of the CIA's World War II predecessor, the Office of Strategic Services, was in the New York financial district.

Drugs

In late June of 1999, NYSE Chairman Dick Grasso traveled to Colombia and met with the leader of the FARC rebels controlling the southern third of the country. His trip was reported in the Associate Press, and, remarkably, the AP openly stated that Grasso had asked the Colombian rebels to invest their profits in Wall Street. The FARC make their money by taxing the cocaine trade. Catherine Austin Fitts described the visit as "the ultimate cold call."[19]

The amount of profit generated annually by the drug trade, if it is known with any accuracy, is probably one of the most closely guarded secrets in the world. There are two kinds of money generated by the drug trade. First there is the money generated at all the stages from growth or manufacture, to processing, to perhaps two or three stages of wholesaling, to retail street sales. Then there is all the money generated by funding law enforcement, court systems, prisons, and all the construction, cars, radios, boats, guns, and airplanes that go into that. It has been estimated that the cost of prison construction and operation alone is around $30 billion a year.[20]

But all of that, as important as it is, is not what we are concerned with here. What we are concerned with is the cash generated from the growth or manufacture and sale of drugs — because that money is illegal. It needs to hide, and then it needs to be laundered before it can be used openly. It is not only cheap and secret capital; it is capital that must be put someplace legal before it can be used. The illegal-to-legal transition is where someone must know what is taking place. Ignorance there — especially when the laundering transactions are gigantic ones — is not a tenable position.

Among the many kinds of illegal activities in the world, the production and laundering of drug money is central because it establishes channels for the flow of other criminal profits. In 2001, according to the International Monetary Fund, money laundering processed $1.5 trillion, a figure that exceeded the gross domestic products of all but the world's five largest economies.[21] In 2000 *Le Monde Diplomatique*, a respected French publication, estimated total annual criminal revenues at $1 trillion: "The drug trade accounts for as much as $500 bbn and at least $1 bbn in criminal money is laundered every day."[22] In 1997 the United Nations estimated that, as of 1996, the drug trade represented 8 percent of all world trading activity as measured in dollars. It estimated then that the narcotics industry accounted for $440 billion in revenues.[23]

Looking at the cash flow in just one locality, PBS's "Frontline" tried to make the numbers a little easier to grasp. "Imagine a typical weekend in New York City. Experts estimate that at least one percent of the population (80,000 plus) spends $200 on illicit drugs. That alone would amount to $16 million dollars a week or $832 million a year. And that's just New York."[24]

Newer figures suggest that the drug trade generates $400-500 billion a year in cash. However, I once had a conversation with an expert on money laundering who held a very high-ranking position in a US government agency charged with monitoring global cash flows. On condition of anonymity, that expert told me, "It's much, much higher than that. Every conference I go to is attended by the CIA, and we all round the figure off to around $700 billion." Since the last real numbers I've been able to find date back a few years, and the drug trade is perpetually growing (along with the budgets to regulate it), I have settled on the figure of $600 billion a year for the purposes of my lectures and this book.

Six hundred billion dollars a year is too much money to hide under a pillow. In fact, that much cash turning up in one place could overwhelm the banking system of a small or medium-sized country. Of course the money is scattered all over the place, except in the cases of the major traffickers, and it has a way of moving by itself, electronically, always seeking the places where it will either earn the most profits or do the most good for its owners. Cash, either hard currency or the electronic kind, is a prized commodity on financial markets because it does things that other kinds of wealth cannot do — such as pay bills or investors. The money moves so quickly that, unless one were in control of the computer systems that handle it, or the software that manages it, it would be impossible to trace. (An excellent discussion of how illegal money moves according to a separate set of laws — having nothing to do with what we tend to think of as the law — is contained in *Hot Money* by R.T. Naylor [Black Rose Books, 1994].)

Second, of all the illegal drugs, from heroin to steroids to ecstasy to cocaine to marijuana, it is heroin and cocaine that are by far the most profitable and which make up the lion's share of that $600 billion figure. The mark-up for these drugs is substantially higher, especially when one considers the weight or volume involved per dollar of markup in price.

Almost all of the world's cocaine comes from Colombia, having been either grown or processed there. The heavy production of cocaine in the 1980s from Bolivia, Peru, and in smaller quantities from other Andean nations was largely eradicated by the early 1990s as most production moved north. However, it is important to understand that worldwide cocaine use has not seen a major drop since the 1980s. After having peaked at around 600 metric tons in 1987–1988, recent estimates and statements by the Department of Justice have placed US cocaine consumption at around 500 metric tons (a metric ton is 2,200 lbs) a year.[25] That's an interesting fact, since according to an interview I conducted with Dr. Sidney Cohen, a drug expert at UCLA, domestic cocaine consumption in 1979 was only around 80 metric tons.[26]

Somewhere between 400 and 500 metric tons of heroin is consumed worldwide each year. According to DEA and Department of Justice intelligence reports, about 60 percent of the heroin consumed in the US also comes from Colombia.[27] But almost all the heroin consumed elsewhere in the world comes from Afghanistan. Like the coca leaf, the opium poppy from which heroin is made grows mainly in the mountains and prefers altitudes above 5,000 feet. But unlike coca, opium is grown in several different regions of the world: South America; the so-called Golden Triangle of Laos, Burma, and Thailand; and Afghanistan, Pakistan, and central Asia in an area called the Golden Crescent. From 1997 to 2000 and again in 2002, the world's largest producer of opium was Afghanistan, responsible for about 70 percent of the world's supply.[28]

What happened in 2001? The Taliban banned opium production in the late summer of 2000 and destroyed almost all the opium that still remained planted; this was completed and confirmed in January of 2001.[29] According to the *Independent*, "The area of land given over to growing opium poppies in 2001 fell by 91 percent compared with the year before, according to the UN Drug Control Programme's (UNDCP) annual survey of Afghanistan. Production of fresh opium, the raw material for heroin, went down by an unprecedented 94 percent, from 3,276 tonnes to 185 tonnes."

Other sources placed the 2000 Afghan opium harvest (conducted from May to June, before the ban) at more than 3,600 metric tons. The planting season for opium in that region is November, and the harvest is in the spring. A kilogram (2.2 lbs) of Afghan heroin, refined at a 10:1 ratio from opium, was then fetching US$150,000 in Moscow.[30]

It is interesting to note that in 1996, according to the DEA, "Worldwide opium production was 4,157 metric tons" (an increase of 20 percent in a single year).[31] Contrast that with one report obtained from the UN Drug Control Program by the magazine *High Times* stating, "Production of raw opium in Afghanistan shot up from 2,600 tons in 1998 to a record 4,600 tons" in 2000.[32]

What is so significant about this is that if Afghanistan was producing 70 percent of the world's opium, and it produced a minimum of 3,600 tons in 2000, then global consumption increased from 4,100 tons to 5,100 tons (25 percent) in just four years. If, on the other hand, Afghanistan, as reported by the UN, produced 4,600 metric tons of opium in 2000 and retained a 70 percent market share, then world heroin use had risen 58 percent to 6,571 metric tons per year. Even Ken Lay of Enron would be jealous of that kind of growth.

It is not likely that opium use increased 60 percent worldwide in four years. Based on my years of experience, my estimate is that only 8–12 percent of the world's population is predisposed to addiction. The other conclusion available is that world opium production was being deliberately concentrated in Afghanistan. But by whom and for what purpose?

Drug money-steroids of the financial world

Now, if you were a corporate executive needing to borrow money for an LBO or to finance a pipeline, you could go borrow the money legally at 9 percent, or you could borrow drug money laundered once, looking to become legal, at 6 percent. The drug lord is only too happy to own the bonds of, for example, Halliburton or General Electric. But if you really wanted to make a killing, you would launder some drug money onto your bottom line and increase your net profits. You might do it by selling your products "off the books" and accepting cash for them. Then you would just inflate your net profits without any increased costs. Philip Morris has been charged with doing just that.[33] Or, if you made vehicles, you could sell large quantities for a check from an offshore bank, no questions asked, to a guy in South America who wanted to open a Chevy dealership. GM (below) has reportedly done that.

Enron's crimes all centered around the illegal overstatement of net profits. They cooked their books using an accounting system called Pro-Forma that allowed them to borrow money with one subsidiary and then book the deposits as earnings. They even created phony companies that could do business, using paper or electronic transactions, with other Enron companies. This was the purpose of Enron's so-called off-the-books partnerships known as Chewco, Raptor, and LMJ.

Enron also manipulated energy prices through a variety of methods to create or worsen shortages, raise prices, and rob Californians blind.[34] Enron engaged in a shockingly wide array of financial crimes, betraying their stockholders and employees. But all the creativity of Enron executives Andy Fastow or Jeff Skillings or Ken Lay could never produce the pure financial power that drug money offers.

Apparently Enron knew that. It ran about 2,000 subsidiary companies all over the world. About 700 of them were in the Cayman Islands.[35] There is no oil or gas in the Cayman Islands. There is, however, an awful lot of drug money.

Everything else Enron did had to pass through other companies, leaving records behind. Drug money is much, much simpler. Enron's trading company, Enron Online, was one of the largest money-moving operations in the world. It was just computers and wires in cities and to banks all over the globe. It was a bank. And it *was* there that the greatest criminal activity occurred. When Enron went bankrupt, the US government allowed Enron to sell Enron Online to the Union Bank of Switzerland.[36] That meant that all of the evidence of money laundering by Enron is now owned by a Swiss bank and out of reach for federal prosecutors. Neither the Congress nor any US enforcement agency did a thing to stop the sale or the transfer of the records. The evidence walked.

For banks also, drug money has a special allure. That is why major banks like Citigroup, Bank of America, Morgan Stanley, Deutsche Bank, and JPMorgan Chase all offer private client services for the very wealthy with very few questions asked. Yes, the US Treasury and the Department of Justice make a show of being tough under "Know Your Client" regulations. But the truth is that money does pretty much whatever it wants to. And for a bank, every dollar that it has on deposit allows it to lend between 9 and 15 or so dollars based upon the requirements set for it by the Federal Reserve System.

For a bank, a loan is the same thing an order is for a manufacturer. Loans show up on a bank's books as assets, and that's part of what helps determine a bank's stock value. Of course, if a bank takes an extra fee, no questions asked, as Citigroup did from Raul Salinas de Gortari, brother of the former Mexican president, for laundering $100 million in drug profits, who's to say how that money gets reported when it comes to net profits?[37]

Birds do it, bees do it — even GE does it

In 2000 the Department of Justice held a drug money laundering conference and invited some of the biggest names on Wall Street. The names were not chosen by accident. Their products had been tracked and linked to money laundering operations in Colombia. It had been noticed how much drug money was going into the bottom lines of certain major corporations. The companies asked to attend the conference were Hewlett Packard, Ford, Sony, General Motors, Whirlpool, General Electric, and Philip Morris.[38]

These companies, according to PBS and the Justice Department, were merely innocent victims of the trade. It's hard to understand how you are being victimized if your sales are great and people are paying with cash. But the case of Philip Morris perhaps exemplifies general corporate attitudes about drug money. Philip Morris has been sued by the government of Colombia for smuggling Marlboro cigarettes into that country (bypassing the tax man) and readily accepting large amounts of drug cash from traffickers, then smuggling the cash back into the United States.[39]

Just recently the tobacco giant RJ Reynolds (Nabisco) has been sued by the entire European Union for large-scale smuggling and money laundering.[40] The competitive edge provided by handling drug money is an instrumental factor in who can compete in a globalized, new-world, corporate order.

A final note before moving on: As Enron (an energy trading company) was failing, the energy giant Dynegy put up $1.5 billion in cash as part of a plan to bail Enron out. Enron got the money and Dynegy wound up getting nothing.[41] What is significant is that Chevron, which had vast investments in central Asian oil fields, had been a part owner of Dynegy since 1996. In 2001 Chevron added to its investment by giving Dynegy $1.5 billion just before Dynegy gave $1.5 billion to Enron.[42] So Chevron was either directly or indirectly bailing out Enron, without getting tarred by the unfolding scandal.

This takes on an added significance given Enron's drug money laundering connections and the fact that Enron, along with other energy companies like Halliburton, had deep financial commitments in the region that were tied both to the successful development of central Asian oil and gas and had ready access to drug cash.

Enron had the contracts to do feasibility studies for much of the pipeline construction that was desperately needed in the region, and it also had a $3 billion investment in a new "white elephant" natural gas-powered electrical-generating station in Dabhol, India, that had only one problem: it couldn't get access to cheap natural gas without a pipeline across Afghanistan. One former oil industry corporate attorney summed it up best when he said, "When big oil eats, everybody eats. When big oil doesn't eat, nobody eats."

The CIA's drug-dealing

This topic deserves an entire book. For 25 years I have researched it, studied it, and compiled documentary evidence proving it in the pages of *FTW*. In every one of my twenty-eight 2002 lectures the audience universally accepted that the Central Intelligence Agency of the United States deals drugs. But not everyone fully understood its significance.

In this section, rather than attempting to make the comprehensive case, what I want to do is merely present three or four key pieces of evidence demonstrating outright culpability on the Agency's part. They will all have a direct bearing on 9/11. My experience is that if three or four undeniable pieces of evidence don't convince people, the other 300 or 400 pieces will not make a difference.

A smoking gun

As the national controversy raged over the Gary Webb stories from 1996 through 1998, pieces of evidence started to leak into the public domain. One piece, a 1981 letter from then US Attorney General William French Smith to Director of Central Intelligence (DCI) Bill Casey, summarized the results of a long negotiation process that changed the CIA's obligations under the law when people who worked for it were caught dealing drugs.

It had previously been a requirement under Title 18 of the US Code that, whenever a manager or department of the executive branch discovered that an employee was breaking the law, an immediate notification to the US Department of Justice or one of its enforcement agencies had to be made. In 1981, at the start of the Contra War the CIA had a problem. It knew that the coming covert operations were going to witness a dramatic explosion in the volume of cocaine entering the States. It needed not only a cover for itself but also a legal way to circumvent what was sure to be a deluge of reports (which did occur) about US government personnel or contractors who were moving drugs.

In a two-stage negotiation process, the CIA and the Department of Justice first made an arbitrary decision that anyone who worked for the CIA (whether a full-time employee or contractor or employee of a CIA proprietary company)[43] who did not hold "officer" rank within the agency was deemed not to be an employee. In the next stage, it was decided that "no formal requirement" for the reporting of violations of drug laws was going to be required under the newly reached memorandum of understanding.

Proof of this surfaced when a copy of the letter formalizing the agreement was sent anonymously to the office of Congresswoman Maxine Waters when she was still championing the issue. A key sentence in the letter said, "In light of these provisions, and in view of the fine cooperation the Drug Enforcement Administration has received from CIA, no formal requirement regarding the reporting of narcotics violations has been included in these procedures."[44] With the stroke of a pen the CIA had been absolved from turning in its employees, its contractors, and the employees of its proprietary companies who were soon to be found smuggling cocaine, hand over fist, and airplane over cargo ship.

A copy of the letter was inserted in the CIA's final inspector general (IG) report in October 1998, long after the nation had forgotten the issue and become lost in Monika Lewinsky's dress. (See page 64)

The smoking airplanes

In the 1980s and 1990s the Central Intelligence Agency schemed to move a number of large C-130 Hercules transports from US government ownership into the hands of private contractors so that some of them could be used for covert operations that were "deniable" by the Agency. The C-130 is a military aircraft, and it is banned from export without State Department certifications. Under the CIA plan, some 28 of the giant transports were moved from the Department of Defense into the hands of the US Forest Service. From there, ostensibly for the humanitarian purpose of fighting forest fires, they were again transferred into the hands

Office of the Attorney General
Washington, D.C. 20530

February 11, 1982

Honorable William J. Casey
Director
Central Intelligence Agency
Washington, D.C. 20505

Dear Bill:

Thank you for your letter regarding the procedures governing the reporting and use of information concerning federal crimes. I have reviewed the draft of the procedures that accompanied your letter and, in particular, the minor changes made in the draft that I had previously sent to you. These proposed changes are acceptable and, therefore, I have signed the procedures.

I have been advised that a question arose regarding the need to add narcotics violations to the list of reportable non-employee crimes (Section IV). 21 U.S.C. §874(h) provides that "[w]hen requested by the Attorney General, it shall be the duty of any agency or instrumentality of the Federal Government to furnish assistance to him for carrying out his functions under [the Controlled Substances Act] . . . ." Section 1.8(b) of Executive Order 12333 tasks the Central Intelligence Agency to "collect, produce and disseminate intelligence on foreign aspects of narcotics production and trafficking." Moreover, authorization for the dissemination of information concerning narcotics violators to law enforcement agencies, including the Department of Justice, is provided by sections 2.3(c) and (j) and 2.6(b) of the Order. In light of these provisions, and in view of the fine cooperation the Drug Enforcement Administration has received from CIA, no formal requirement regarding the reporting of narcotics violations has been included in these procedures. We look forward to the CIA's continuing cooperation with the Department of Justice in this area.

In view of our agreement regarding the procedures, I have instructed my Counsel for Intelligence Policy to circulate a copy which I have executed to each of the other agencies covered by the procedures in order that they may be signed by the head of each such agency.

Sincerely,

William French Smith
Attorney General

of private contractors, many of whom were later revealed to have CIA connections or contracts, or established relationships with CIA proprietaries.[45]

The scheme started to come unraveled as a number of investigators, including Vietnam veteran Gary Eitel, himself a pilot, began turning up documents in court cases showing links to the Agency. The cases were extremely well covered by mainstream press; they prompted stories in the AP and a large series in the Riverside *Press Enterprise* by veteran reporter Dave Hendrix.[46] The problem was that many of the C-130s kept turning up in such remote locations as Panama, Mexico, Colombia, Angola, and the Middle East. In many cases, when they were examined, they were carrying anything but fire retardant. In fact, one of the C-130s, connected to CIA affiliate T&G Aviation of Arizona, was seized in 1994 with a billion dollars worth of cocaine on board. Eitel's investigation had established a connection between T&G, operated by Woody Grantham, and another company called Trans Latin Air.[47]

The Trans Latin Air investigation led to an investigation of Aero Postale de Mexico. In April 1998 stories in the Mexican paper *La*

Reforma reported that the Mexican Attorney General had indicted three officials of the private freight hauling company Aero Postale de Mexico which routinely delivered mail and other goods throughout Latin and Central America on charges that they had provided aircraft to the drug cartel headed by the Arellano Felix brothers. That investigation had commenced in 1997, and Aero Postale planes were reportedly hauling multi-thousand kilo loads of cocaine during the period. One of the C-130s was impounded at the Mexico City airport. Purchase of the aircraft was financed by Mexican banker Carlos Cabal, who was assured repayment of the loans by the US Import-Export Bank. It is impossible to believe CIA would not have noticed such a transaction. T&G sold the planes to Aero Postale in 1993 at the same time he sold planes to Trans Latin Air.[48]

Records of the massive cocaine bust, though suppressed by the major media, did get introduced into evidence in a major drug prosecution in Chicago that same year.[49]

The heat had started to fall on the Forest Service five years earlier when the planes first started getting caught with drugs aboard during Contra support

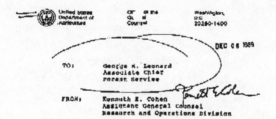

F 000133

operations. The Forest Service had their lawyers evaluate the situation in the perennial government game of CYA. As a result, one of the most chilling documents to ever reveal the depth of government cynicism emerged into public light. A 1989 memo from a Forest Service lawyer to Associate Chief George Leonard concluded, "Apparently, DoD [the Pentagon, CIA's name never appears on documents like this] thinks that by having the Forest Service as the intermediary, if any future aircraft are used in drug smuggling, the Forest Service and not DoD will suffer the adverse publicity."

The smoking Inspector General report

I could fill this book with excerpts from the CIA IG report, written by Frederick P. Hitz and released on October 8, 1998 — the same day that the impeachment of Bill Clinton began in the House. To demonstrate what kind of material is in that report, I will include just three brief quotations. The number in front of each paragraph refers to its location in the IG report.

> 490. On March 25, 1987, CIA questioned [Moises] Nunez about narcotics trafficking allegations against him. Nunez revealed that since 1985, he had engaged in a clandestine relationship with the National Security Council (NSC). Nunez refused to elaborate on the nature of these actions, but indicated it was difficult to answer questions relating to his involvement in narcotics trafficking because of the specific tasks he had performed at the direction of the NSC. Nunez refused to identify the NSC officials with whom he had been involved. [Note: Oliver North was the NSC point man for all Contra support activities.]
>
> 491. Headquarters cabled in April 1987 that a decision had been made to "debrief" Nunez regarding the revelations he had made. The next day however, a Headquarters cable stated that "Headquarters had decided against… debriefing Nunez." The cable offered no explanation for the decision.[50]

Another key passage discussing a Honduran airline documented to be moving as much as four tons of cocaine a month found that:

> 816. SETCO was chosen by NHAO [the Nicaraguan Humanitarian Assistance Office, at the time coordinated by current National Security Council staffer Elliot Abrams] to transport goods on behalf of the Contras from late 1985 through mid-1986. According to testimony by FDN leader Adolfo Calero before the Iran-Contra committees, SETCO received funds for Contra supply operations from the bank accounts that were established by Oliver North.[51]

And finally, the CIA acknowledged in its IG report that it had withheld information about drug trafficking by operatives involved in the Contra effort from

Congress, at the same time revealing that:

> 1074. The analyst who drafted a Memorandum for Vice President Bush in April 1986 that related to potential Contras' involvement in drug trafficking recalls that OGI analysts who worked on counternarcotics issues were not aware of those reports at the time — October to December 1984 — that they were first disseminated inside and outside the Agency. However, she says that CATF [Central American Task Force] Chief [Alan] Fiers did make the reporting available to her in April 1986, stipulating that it could be used only for the Memorandum she was preparing for Vice President Bush.
>
> 1084. 1986 Memorandum for Vice President Bush. On April 6, 1986, a Memorandum entitled "Contra Involvement in Drug Trafficking" was prepared by CIA at the request of Vice President Bush. The Memorandum provided a summary of information that had been received in late 1984 regarding the alleged agreement between Southern Front Contra leader Eden Pastora's associates and Miami-based drug trafficker Jorge Morales. Morales reportedly had offered financial and aircraft support for the Contras in exchange for FRS pilots to "transship" Colombian cocaine to the United States. CIA disseminated this memorandum only to the Vice President.[52]

The importance of this revelation is that it had been the official position of then Vice President Bush that he had no hands-on relationship with the Contras, was out of the loop, and knew nothing. That's the position he took with the press, with Congress, and with the American people.

Smoking history

The CIA has been dealing drugs since before it was the CIA; already in its first days, as the OSS during World War II it was facilitating and managing the trade, and directing its criminal proceeds to the places of its masters' choosing. For additional reading on the subject I recommend three excellent books: *The Politics of Heroin*, Alfred W. McCoy (Lawrence Hill Books, 1991); *Cocaine Politics*, Peter Dale Scott (University of California Press, 1991); and *Powderburns*, Celerino Castillo (Sundial, 1994). The use of the drug trade to secure economic advantage for an imperialist nation is at least as old as the British East India Company's first smuggling of opium from India into China in the late 1600s (the defense of that British practice, Scott points out, was John Stuart Mill's motivation for writing the tract "On Liberty"). They did that for 300 years. When something works that well, the ruling elites rarely let go of it.

An interesting end came to the investigations arising out of the Gary Webb stories that (re)started all the controversy about the CIA and drugs. Frederick P. Hitz, the CIA inspector general who oversaw the report's production, retired immediately afterward in March 1998. A graduate of the Harvard Law School, Hitz was rewarded with a teaching post at Princeton University funded by Goldman Sachs.[53] His retirement, seven months before a declassified version of the report was made public, was celebrated with an entry in the Congressional Record.

One question remains. Aside from the fact that from Afghanistan, to Pakistan, to Kazakhstan, to Colombia, oil and drugs always turn up in the same place, has there ever been any evidence connecting the oil industry to drugs directly? And what does that have to do with 9/11?

Afghanistan and opium post-9/11

In this context it is not surprising that the US completed its invasion of Afghanistan in November 2001 in the middle of the opium planting season. Among the first things the US forces and CIA did was to liberate a number of known opium warlords who, they said, would assist US forces.[54] Opium farmers rejoiced and, amidst reports that they were being encouraged to do so, began planting massive opium crops.[55] In December, former CIA asset and opium warlord Ayub Afridi was released from prison and recruited by the CIA to unify local leaders against the Taliban.[56]

When the harvest of June 2002 came, Afghanistan had again become the world's largest producer of the opium poppy and the world's largest heroin supplier. From a paltry 180 tons under the Taliban in 2001, according to the UN, the estimated 2002 harvest, under CIA protection, was close to 3,700 tons.[57] By March of 2003, World Bank President James Wolfensohn was reporting record levels of opium production and that drugs were a bigger earner for Afghanistan than foreign aid.[58]

The 2003 crop set new records, coming in at almost 4,000 tons.[59] And experts warned that the June, 2004 harvest might be 50 percent larger than that of 2003.[60] In November of 2003, Reuters reported that current Afghan opium cultivation was 36 times higher than under the last year of Taliban rule.[61]

When I learned in early 2001 that the Taliban had destroyed Afghanistan's opium crop, I wrote that it was a form of economic warfare that might take a whole lot of money out of the world's banking system and its cooked books. There is always a lag between planting, harvesting, and the cash flows that show up as the heroin moves from farm, to laboratory, through several layers of wholesaling to the streets. The positive cash flow generated by Afghanistan's first post-Taliban harvest would not have started to hit the banking system for maybe six to eight months after June of 2002. In the late summer and fall of 2002 the Dow Jones had sunk to nearly 7,200. As this book is written, and even as American jobs are disappearing, corporate profits and the so-called "non-job" recovery have seen the Dow again at 10,000 based upon massive consumer spending which is financed by credit that must be serviced with fractional amounts of cash by the lending agencies. The unprecedented 2004 harvest might be connected with the fact that it is an election year.

I don't mean to offer drugs as a complete explanation for the so-called economic recovery. But it helps to remember Occam's Razor.

CONNECTING DRUGS AND OIL

I wrote the following story for the October 24, 2000, issue of From *The Wilderness*. I have included excerpts here, and I thank author Kevin Phillips for quoting from it in his 2004 bestseller, *American Dynasty*.

Halliburton Corporation's Brown and Root is one of the major components of THE BUSH-CHENEY DRUG EMPIRE

FTW October 24, 2000 - The success of Bush vice-presidential running mate Richard Cheney at leading Halliburton, Inc. to a five-year $3.8-billion "pig-out" on federal contracts and taxpayer-insured loans is only a partial indicator of what may happen if the Bush ticket wins in two weeks. A closer look at available research, including an August 2, 2000, report by the Center for Public Integrity (CPI) at <www.public-i.org>, suggests that drug money has played a role in the successes achieved by Halliburton under Cheney's tenure as CEO from 1995 to 2000. This is especially true for Halliburton's most famous sub-sidiary, heavy construction and oil giant, Brown and Root. A deeper look into history reveals that Brown and Root's past as well as the past of Dick Cheney him-self, connect to the international drug trade on more than one occasion and in more than one way.

This June the lead Washington, DC attorney for a major Russian oil company, connected in law enforcement reports to heroin smuggling and also a beneficiary of US backed loans to pay for Brown and Root contracts in Russia, held a $2.2 million fund-raiser to fill the already bulging coffers of presidential candidate George W. Bush. This is not the first time that Brown and Root has been con-nected to drugs, and the fact is that this "poster child" of American industry may also be a key player in Wall Street's efforts to maintain domination of the half tril-lion dollar a year global drug trade and its profits. And Dick Cheney, who has also come closer to drugs than most people suspect, and who is also Halliburton's largest individual shareholder ($45.5 million), has a vested interest in seeing to it that Brown and Root's successes continue.

Of all American companies dealing directly with the US military and providing cover for CIA operations, few firms can match the global presence of this giant construction powerhouse which employs 20,000 people in more than 100 countries. Through its sister companies or joint ventures, Brown and Root can build offshore oil rigs, drill wells, construct and operate everything from harbors to pipelines to highways to nuclear reactors. It can train and arm security forces, and it can now also feed, supply, and house armies. One key beacon of Brown and Root's overwhelming appeal to agencies like the CIA is that, from its own corporate web page, it proudly announces that it has received the contract to dismantle aging Russian nuclear-tipped ICBMs in their silos.

Furthermore, the relationships between key institutions, players, and the Bushes themselves suggest that under a George "W" administration the Bush family and its allies may well be able, using Brown and Root as the operational interface, to control the drug trade all the way from Medellin to Moscow.

Originally formed as a heavy construction company to build dams, Brown and Root grew its operations via shrewd political contributions to Senate candidate Lyndon Johnson in 1948, Expanding into the building of oil platforms, military bases, ports, nuclear facilities, harbors, and tunnels, Brown and Root virtually underwrote LBJ's political career. It prospered as a result, making billions on US Government contracts during the Vietnam War. The *Austin Chronicle* in an August 28, Op-ed piece entitled "The Candidate From Brown and Root" labels Republican Cheney as the political dispenser of Brown and Root's largesse. According to political campaign records, during Cheney's five-year tenure at Halliburton the company's political contributions more than doubled to $1.2 million Not surprisingly, most of that money went to Republican candidates.

Independent news service, <www.newsmakingnews.com>, also describes how, in 1998, with Cheney as chairman, Halliburton spent $8.1 billion to purchase Dresser Industries, a supplier of oil industry equipment and drilling machinery. This made Halliburton a corporation that will have a presence in almost any future oil drilling operation anywhere in the world. And it also brought back into the family fold the company that had once sent a plane — also in 1948 — to fetch the new Yale Graduate George H.W. Bush, to begin his career in the Texas oil business. Bush the elder's father, Prescott, served as a managing director for the firm that once owned Dresser, Brown Bothers Harriman.

It is clear that everywhere there is oil there is Brown and Root. But increasingly, everywhere there is war or insurrection there is Brown and Root also. From Bosnia and Kosovo, to Chechnya, to Rwanda, to Burma, to Pakistan, to Laos, to Vietnam, to Indonesia, to Iran, to Libya, to Mexico, to Colombia, Brown and Root's traditional operations have expanded from heavy construction to include the provision of logistical support for the US military. Now, instead of US Army quartermasters, the world is likely to see Brown and Root warehouses storing and managing everything from uniforms to rations to vehicles.

Drugs

As described by the Associated Press, during "Iran-Contra" Congressman Dick Cheney of the House Intelligence Committee was a rabid supporter of Marine Lt. Col. Oliver North. This was in spite of the fact that North had lied to Cheney in a private 1986 White House briefing. Oliver North's own diaries and subsequent investigations by the CIA inspector general have irrevocably tied him directly to cocaine smuggling during the 1980s and the opening of bank accounts for one firm moving four tons of cocaine a month. This, however, did not stop Cheney from actively supporting North's 1994 unsuccessful run for the US Senate from Virginia just a year before he took over the reins at Brown and Root's parent company, Dallas-based Halliburton Incorporated in 1995.

As the Bush secretary of defense during Desert Shield/Desert Storm (1990–91), Cheney also directed special operations involving Kurdish rebels in northern Iraq. The Kurds' primary source of income for more than 50 years has been heroin smuggling from Afghanistan and Pakistan through Iran, Iraq, and Turkey. Having had some personal experience with Brown and Root, I took note when the *Los Angeles Times* observed that on March 22, 1991, a group of gunmen burst into the Ankara, Turkey, offices of the joint venture, Vinnell, Brown and Root and assassinated retired Air Force Chief Master Sergeant John Gandy.

In March of 1991, tens of thousands of Kurdish refugees, long-time assets of the CIA, were being massacred by Saddam Hussein in the wake of the Gulf War. Saddam, seeking to destroy any hopes of a successful Kurdish revolt, found it easy to kill thousands of the unwanted Kurds who had fled to the Turkish border seeking sanctuary. There, Turkish security forces, trained in part by the Vinnell, Brown and Root partnership, turned back thousands of Kurds into certain death. Today, the Vinnell Corporation (a TRW Company) is, along with the firms MPRI and DynCorp (*FTW* June, 2000), one of the three pre-eminent private mercenary corporations in the world. It is also the dominant entity for the training of security forces throughout the Middle East. Not surprisingly the Turkish border regions in question were the primary transshipment points for heroin grown in Afghanistan and Pakistan and destined for the markets of Europe.

A confidential source with intelligence experience in the region subsequently told me that the Kurds "got some payback against the folks that used to help them move their drugs." He openly acknowledged that Brown and Root and Vinnell both routinely provided NOC, or non-official cover, for CIA officers. No surprise there.

From 1994 to 1999, during US military intervention in the Balkans where, according to "The Christian Science Monitor" and "Jane's Intelligence Review," the Kosovo Liberation Army controls 70 percent of the heroin entering Western Europe, Cheney's Brown and Root made billions of dollars supplying US troops from vast facilities in the region. Brown and Root support operations continue in Bosnia, Kosovo, and Macedonia to this day.

Dick Cheney's footprints have come closer to drugs than is generally recognized. A Center for Public Integrity report from last August brought them even closer. It would be factually correct to say that there is a direct linkage of Brown and Root facilities (often in remote and hazardous regions) between every drug-producing region and every drug-consuming region in the world. These coincidences, in and of themselves, do not prove complicity in the trade. Other facts, however, lead inescapably in that direction.

A Direct Drug Link

The CPI report entitled "Cheney Led Halliburton To Feast at Federal Trough" written by veteran journalists Knut Royce and Nathaniel Heller describes how, under five years of Cheney's leadership, Halliburton, largely through subsidiary Brown and Root, enjoyed $3.8 billion in federal contracts and taxpayer insured loans. The loans had been granted by the Export-Import Bank (EXIM) and the Overseas Private Investment Corporation (OPIC). According to Ralph McGehee's "CIA Base ©," both institutions are heavily infiltrated by the CIA and routinely provide NOC to its officers.

One of those loans to Russian financial/banking conglomerate The Alfa Group of Companies contained $292 million to pay for Brown and Root's contract to refurbish a Siberian oil field owned by the Russian Tyumen Oil Company. The Alfa Group completed its 51 percent acquisition of Tyumen Oil in what was allegedly a rigged bidding process in 1998. An official Russian government report claimed that the Alfa Group's top executives, oligarchs Mikhail Fridman and Pyotr Aven "allegedly participated in the transit of drugs from Southeast Asia through Russia and into Europe."

Fridman and Aven, who reportedly smuggled the heroin in connection with Russia's Solntsevo mob family, were the same executives who applied for the EXIM loans that Halliburton's lobbying later safely secured. As a result, Brown and Root's work in Alfa Tyumen oil fields could continue — and expand.

The CPI story reports allegations that organized criminal interests in the Alfa Group had stolen the oil field by fraud. It then uses official reports from the FSB (the Russian equivalent of the FBI), oil companies such as BP-Amoco, former CIA and KGB officers, and press accounts to establish a solid link to Alfa Tyumen and the transportation of heroin.

In 1995, sacks of heroin disguised as sugar were stolen from a rail container leased by Alfa Echo and sold in the Siberian town of Khabarovsk. A problem arose when many residents of the town became "intoxicated" or "poisoned." The CPI story also stated, "The FSB report said that within days of the incident, Ministry of Internal Affairs (MVD) agents conducted raids of Alfa Eko buildings and found 'drugs and other compromising documentation.'"

Both reports claim that Alfa Bank has laundered drug funds from Russian and Colombian drug cartels.

The FSB document claims that at the end of 1993, a top Alfa official met with Gilberto Rodriguez Orejuela, the now imprisoned financial mastermind of Colombia's notorious Cali cartel, to conclude an agreement about the transfer of money into the Alfa Bank from offshore zones such as the Bahamas, Gibraltar, and others. The plan was to insert it back into the Russian economy through the purchase of stock in Russian companies "He [the former KGB agent] reported that there was evidence regarding [Alfa Bank's] involvement with the money laundering of Latin American drug cartels."

It would be difficult for Cheney and Halliburton to assert mere coincidence in all of this, as CPI reported that Tyumen's lead Washington attorney James C. Langdon Jr. at the firm of Aikin Gump "helped coordinate a $2.2 million fundraiser for Bush this June. He then agreed to help recruit 100 lawyers and lobbyists in the capital to raise $25,000 each for W's campaign."

The heroin mentioned in the CPI story originated in Laos, where longtime Bush allies and covert warriors Richard Armitage [Note: Richard Armitage is currently the US deputy secretary of state] and retired CIA ADDO (associate deputy director of operations) Ted Shackley have been repeatedly linked to the drug trade. It then made its way across Southeast Asia to Vietnam, probably the port of Haiphong. Then the heroin sailed to Russia's Pacific port of Valdivostok from whence it subsequently bounced across Siberia by rail and thence by truck or rail to Europe, passing through the hands of Russian Mafia leaders in Chechnya and Azerbaijan. Chechnya and Azerbaijan are hotbeds of both armed conflict and oil exploration; Brown and Root has operations all along this route.

This long, expensive, and tortured path was hastily established, as described by *FTW* in previous issues, after President George [Herbert Walker] Bush's personal envoy Richard Armitage, holding the rank of Ambassador, traveled to the former Soviet Union to assist it with its "economic development" in 1989. Trafficking heroin from the Golden Triangle (Burma, Laos, and Thailand), there was no way to deal with China and India but to go around them.

The Clinton administration took care of all that wasted travel for heroin with the 1998 destruction of Serbia and Kosovo and the installation of the KLA as a regional power. That opened a direct line from Afghanistan to Western Europe, and Brown and Root was right in the middle of that too. The Clinton skill at streamlining drug operations was described in detail in the May issue of *FTW* in a story entitled "The Democratic Party's Presidential Drug Money Pipeline." That article has since been reprinted in three countries. The essence of the drug economic lesson was that by growing opium in Colombia and by smuggling cocaine and heroin from Colombia to New York City through the Dominican Republic and Puerto Rico (a virtual straight line), traditional smuggling routes could be shortened or even eliminated. This lowered the level of risk, reduced operating costs, increased profits, and eliminated competition.

FTW suspects the hand of Medellin co-founder Carlos Lehder in this process and it is interesting to note that Lehder, released from prison under Clinton in 1995, is now reportedly active in both the Bahamas and South America. Lehder was known during the eighties as "the genius of transportation." I can well imagine a Dick Cheney, having witnessed the complete restructuring of the global drug trade in the last eight years, going to George W. and saying, "Look, I know how we can make it even better." One thing is certain. As quoted in the CPI article, a Halliburton vice president noted that if the Bush-Cheney ticket was elected, "the company's government contracts would obviously go through the roof."

Popstcript 2003

Some two years after this story was written, I note with irony that Brown and Root's (now Kellogg, Brown and Root, or KBR) government services continue to expand. This in spite of the fact that, along with about 25 other large companies Halliburton-KBR has been sued by stockholders and public interest groups for cooking its books to inflate stock values during Cheney's tenure. As in so many other instances, the administration has made it clear what their response is. On July 26, 2002 process servers, seeking to serve Vice President Cheney with a subpoena for his role in the allegedly criminal behavior, were turned away from the White House by armed guards.[1]

So much for the rule of law.

I also note with irony that, according to a November 2, 2002, Reuters story, a Colombian court has just ordered the release of Orejuela brothers, Miguel and Gilberto (arrested in 1995), from prison. Pro-American President Alvaro Uribe, a staunch opponent of the FARC guerillas who control most of southern Colombia with its oil and cocaine, has expressed shock and outrage. But I strongly suspect that the Orejuelas are back for a purpose, i.e., the control of narcotics cash flows once the FARC have been defeated, or as US control of the drug trade in the occupied territories of Afghanistan and Iraq requires special expertise.[2]

Gilberto Orejuela was, in fact, released from prison speedily and without interference by the Colombian government on November 7, 2002.[3]

Iraqi invasion validates the map

Shortly after the US occupation of Iraq in April 2003, a large no-bid contract was awarded to Halliburton subsidiary Kellogg, Brown and Root (KBR) to extinguish oil well fires.[4] There were not many such fires, and long-time critics of Halliburton were vocal about the apparent patronage shown to the company, once headed by Vice President Dick Cheney, by the no-bid process. Although Halliburton-KBR efforts to get further rebuilding contracts for hospitals and bridges were awarded to other major campaign donors like the Bechtel Group, KBR held on to the oil contract and also secured lucrative contracts to handle food and supplies for American troops. Just one such logistics contract had paid KBR $90 million by early May with little positive result and no apparent stimulation for the Iraqi economy.[5] This is the same company that I had personally seen involved in heroin smuggling with CIA personnel in 1977. KBR is always full of surprises.

But the biggest surprises were yet to come.

In mid-April the *New York Times* reported that the KBR oil well firefighting contract was worth up to $7 billion — which raised more eyebrows because the fires were out.[6] Further disclosures continued to arouse vocal public reaction, especially from California Congressman Henry Waxman, but none so much as the fact that the no-bid contract was ultimately found to have given Halliburton-KBR the authority to administer all of Iraq's oil fields and to distribute the oil. This striking development was the result of a decision awarded under an "extra work" clause in the firefighting contract. The original source of the contract was the US Army Corps of Engineers, under the supervision of then Army Secretary Thomas White, a former Enron executive.[7]

I could only laugh on May 11 when a story in Pakistan's the *Balochistan Post* reported that Baghdad, which had never had a drug problem and had never even seen heroin, had been suddenly "flooded with narcotics — including heroin." Citing reports from the UK's *Independent*, the story said that heroin was being traded in alleys, and that there had not been any drugs in the country until the US invasion. The story's headline read, "Where the CIA is in control, narcotics flourish — . After Afghanistan, Baghdad is flooded with heroin."[8] Oil pipelines reportedly make excellent vehicles for smuggling drugs. Oil-drilling equipment, sometimes arriving or departing by corporate jet, is rarely inspected for other priceless commodities.

[*For more about the interrelationship between drugs and oil, I strongly recommend the book,* Drugs, Oil and War: The United States in Afghanistan, Colombia and Indochina *by Professor Peter Dale Scott, Ph.D.; Rowman and Littlefield, 2003.*]

CHAPTER 5

A CRIMINAL MELTDOWN

Globalization, the World Trade Organization, NAFTA, the IMF, the World Bank, the Great Bull Market of the 1990s, and the economic adulthood of the Empire have all been nurtured by the controlled and directed use of criminal money streams. One of the other great contributors to America's economic growth has been its willingness to profit from the destruction of the life, health, safety, and happiness of its population. As I write, more than two million people are in prisons or jails in the United States.[1] Many of those prisons are run by private corporations. That the profits of crime and war, which are destructive of human life, of labor, of happy, healthy neighborhoods (whether in the US or in Afghanistan, Africa, and Iraq), are in effect a keystone of the global economy and a determinant of success in a ruthless competition, is a compass needle for human civilization. One cannot expect to follow the recipe for road-kill stew and produce a crème brûlée.

So obvious has the situation become that it was addressed in February 2001 by a five-volume US Senate investigation of money laundering by foreign banks through the US banking system. Senator Carl Levin (D-Michigan), the ranking minority member of the Senate's Permanent Subcommittee on Investigations, issued a particularly scathing minority report but seemed to miss the obvious:

> Through the Minority Staff's year-long investigation, its 450-page report, its close look at 10 high-risk foreign banks and its survey of 20 major US correspondent banks, and through the Subcommittee's two days of hearings last week with experts and correspondent banking participants, we are getting a good understanding of the role of US correspondent banking in money laundering. Drug traffickers, defrauders, bribe takers, and other perpetrators of crimes can do indirectly — through a foreign bank's correspondent account with a US bank — what they can't readily do directly — have access to a US bank account. The stability of the US dollar, the services our banks perform, and the safety and soundness of our banking system make

access to a US bank account an extremely attractive objective for money launderers. It is up to us — the Congress, the regulators, the banks — to try to stop money launderers from reaping the benefits of the prestigious banking system and stable economy we've worked so hard to achieve.[2]

Levin's statement missed the fact that the US economy was directly benefiting from this practice. Specifically named as offending banks, all too willing to do business with shell banks or banks known to lauder illegal money, were JPMorgan Chase, Citigroup, Bank of America, and First Union Bank.[3]

That report, and testimony during the hearings, acknowledged that approximately $500 billion to $1 trillion in criminal money was laundered annually through the US banking system. While acknowledging that correspondent banking had been a significant factor in the looting of Russia and in aiding terrorist and drug organizations, the report did not fully explore money laundering through US securities markets or by US banks directly. It did, however, acknowledge that probably half of all laundered money, anywhere, got washed in the United States.

Perhaps the best summation of how the global economy actually functioned just prior to the World Trade Center attacks was offered in a brilliant two-part series by *Le Monde Diplomatique* in the spring of 2000. In part, the series said:

Indeed the engine of capitalist expansion is now oiled by the profits of serious crime. From time to time something is done to give the impression of waging war on the rapidly expanding banking and tax havens. If governments really wanted to, they could right this overnight. But though there are calls for zero tolerance of petty crime and unemployment, nothing is being done about the big money crimes.

Financial crime is becoming less visible, periodically coming to light in one country or another in the guise of scandals involving companies, banks, political parties, leaders, cartels, mafias. This flood of illicit transactions — offences under national law or international agreements — has come to be portrayed just as accidental malfunctions of free market economics and democracy that can be put right by something called "good governance." But the reality is quite different. It is a coherent system closely linked to the expansion of modern capitalism and based on an association of three partners: governments, transnational corporations, and mafias. Business is business: financial crime is first and foremost a market, thriving and structured, ruled by supply and demand.

Big business complicity and political *laissez faire* is the only way that large-scale organized crime can launder and recycle the fabulous proceeds of its activities. And the transnationals need the support of governments and the neutrality of the regulatory authorities in order to consolidate their positions, increase their profits, withstand or crush the competition, pull off the "deal of the century" and finance their illicit operations. Politicians are directly involved, and their ability to intervene depends on the backing and the funding that keep them in power This collusion of interests is an essential part of the world economy, the oil that keeps the wheels of capitalism turning.

Better still, under the aegis of international financial crime's number one partner, the US, we are seeing a rationalization, or rather, Americanization, of corruption techniques, seeking to replace the somewhat archaic practices of palm-greasing and secret (or open) "commission" payments by lobbying, which is more effective and presentable. It is a service industry in which the Americans have a considerable lead over their competitors, not only in know-how, but also in the vast financial and logistical resources they are able to make available to their multinationals; these include the secret services of the world's most powerful state apparatus, which, with the cold war over, have moved into economic warfare.

The only objective of the anti-corruption campaigns taken up by international organizations (World Bank, IMF, and OECD) is the "good governance" of a financial crime that is now an integral part of market globalizations under the leadership of the American democracy, the most corrupt on the planet.

Countries have opened their borders wider to criminal trades more than to any other kind. Doubtless they had little choice, since the real pioneers of globalization, the 1960s drugs traffickers, obviously did not ask anyone's permission before organizing trade in the world's most expensive and profitable commodity on a global scale.[3]

Banamex

In May 2001 Citigroup paid more than $12 billion in cash to purchase Banco Nacional de Mexico, better known as Banamex.[4] Its owner, Roberto Hernandez, was widely known to be one of the largest drug money launderers in Mexico. Hernandez is also one of the largest landowners on the Yucatan Peninsula, home to the famous vacation resort of Cancun.[5] Because of the drug smuggling activity on Hernandez's land, the locals have come to call it "The Cocaine Peninsula."[6]

After buying Banamex, undoubtedly to gain control of its large cash flows, Citigroup placed Hernandez on their board of directors, right next to former CIA Director John Deutch and former US Treasury Secretary Robert Rubin. Hernandez is known for his political clout. Bill Clinton vacationed on his property in 2000.[7] Hernandez also shared a media consultant with Texas Governor

George W. Bush in 2000.[8] And the day after he was elected, Mexican President Vicente Fox paid a courtesy call to Hernandez, no doubt to express gratitude and ask for direction.[9]

So overt was Hernandez's drug activity that, when the Mexican paper *Por Esto* published a series with photographs, Hernandez lost his libel suit in a Mexican court. The reason: *Por Esto* had proved its case. Subsequently, American expatriate journalist Al Giordano, publisher of the wildly successful <www.narconews.com>, translated and expanded the *Por Esto* story in English. Hernandez sued again, this time in New York, in an attempt to quash Internet journalism by making journalists respond in a number of countries; the suit was again thrown out after many American journalists responded to Giordano's plight.

Pug Winokur and Enron

An outstanding homegrown example of *Realeconomik* is the career of Herbert "Pug" Winokur, Harvard man. Aside from playing a major role in the looting of Russia, Harvard University also seems to have deep connections into the domestic economy of crime. Catherine Austin Fitts connected the dots in a 2002 article which told us that not only had Winokur chaired the Enron finance committee and escaped federal scrutiny, he was also a lead investor in, and creator of, a company called DynCorp (now CSC-DynCorp) that has lucrative vaccine and biowarfare contracts. Through documentary videos, military investigations, and even its employees, DynCorp has been connected to a child prostitution/sex slavery ring in Bosnia.[10] So ubiquitous is DynCorp that we will see its hands all over the map in connection with 9/11 and the ruling of America. DynCorp is everywhere. It manages the Congressional telephone system. Along with Lockheed-Martin, it does the computerized bookkeeping for a dozen federal agencies including the DoD and HUD, which have lost (or allowed to be stolen) trillions of taxpayer dollars. It also has a contract to manage the police and court systems in US-occupied Iraq

Winokur's connections to Enron, DynCorp, and the Harvard Endowment (which, during the Clinton years, saw its assets increase from 3 to 19 billion dollars) demonstrate that quite often the key players escape mainstream scrutiny altogether. However, a group of diligent Harvard students did publish a series of investigative reports starting in October 2002 that shed unwanted light on Winokur's career and ultimately forced his resignation from the board of the Harvard Endowment.[11] Among other revelations were the facts that Harvard had made direct financial investments bailing out an ailing Harken Energy Corporation, then run by George W Bush, and that, through its investment arm, Highfields Capital, it had dumped large quantities of Enron stock just before it crashed: insider trading at its best.[12]

Conveniently, DynCorp's financial auditor until the company's merger with CSC in 2003 was Arthur Andersen, the same company that handled Enron's books. The new firm, CSC-DynCorp now has a sole source contract to provide police and court services in occupied Iraq.[13]

Europe vs RJReynolds

There has never been a spy novel or a political thriller that can compare with one remarkable battle that broke into public view in the fall of 2002. The combatants are the European economy and the American economy, and the fight is over dirty money.

On October 31, 2002, the European Union (EU), the official economic government for almost every nation on that continent, filed a Racketeering Influenced and Corrupt Organizations (RICO) lawsuit against the tobacco giant RJReynolds for knowingly laundering billions of dollars in criminal money derived from drug trafficking and other criminal enterprises. According to a press release issued by the EU, the RICO suit was filed after the technical dismissal of an original civil suit without prejudice, meaning that the dismissal had nothing to do with the merits of the case. The move to a RICO suit, which can lead to subsequent criminal prosecutions, indicates the threat that the EU sees to its economic survival. A press release from the EU tells more:

> In August 2001 the EC launched a tobacco smuggling complaint with the US District Court for the Eastern District of New York against three US cigarette manufacturers — Philip Morris, RJReynolds, and Japan Tobacco, together with the following Member States: Italy, Germany, France, Spain, Portugal, Greece, Belgium, The Netherlands, Finland, and Luxembourg. In February 2002, the US District Court in New York handed down a ruling which dealt separately with the smuggling and money laundering parts of the complaint.[14]

As critical as what the EU is alleging are the lengths to which the member nations have gone to in order to document RJR's criminal activity. A reading of the 100-plus-page complaint reveals that the intelligence and law enforcement agencies of the member agencies were involved in the investigation of RJR's criminal activities. The press release continued:

> The purpose of this new claim is to obtain injunctive relief to stop the laundering of the proceeds of illegal activities and to seek compensation for losses sustained. "Protecting the financial interests of the European Community and fighting against money laundering and fraud remains a top priority for the European Commission," said Commissioner Schreyer.[15]

Not surprisingly, the suit also takes us through the Balkans, the Middle East, and territories where Islamic fundamentalist groups linked to Osama bin Laden have been very active.[16] The kind of intelligence documented in the suit could only have been gathered by national intelligence services, which gives further credibility to the allegations of economic warfare raised in the chapter on PROMIS software.

For those in pathological denial

Now, some Americans will assert that the Bush administration is really trying to clean up the corporate corruption in the wake of the accounting scandals of 2002. They will point out that the president has appointed a White House staff member to oversee a crackdown on corporate corruption. They will contend that the SEC, under a new accounting law, is getting tough. And they will assert that the government itself, through the Treasury, is in ultimate control.

For the record: Larry Thompson, the deputy attorney general charged with leading the Bush anticorruption task force, has himself been sued by shareholders of Providian Bank Corp for participating in corrupt accounting practices and insider trading from 1997 to 2001. He sold almost $4 million in Providian stock just before the company's stock crashed after book-cooking was disclosed.[17] Harvey Pitt, the embattled SEC director and former board member of accounting firm Arthur Andersen, resigned his post at the SEC on November 5, 2002.[18] There are few who want the post, which, as many press reports later noted, may go unoccupied for some time.

And, after being asked by Senator Fritz Hollings to certify that the books of the United States government were as accurate as the government now expected corporate books to be, Budget Director Mitch Daniels refused to do it.[19] In an August 14, 2002 statement released on his Senate website, Hollings said, "I think Mr. Daniels's inaction also will make it more difficult for the Securities and Exchange Commission to come down on bad corporations. After all, how can the SEC throw the book at corporations, when the Administration fails to set a good example with its own accounting?"

CHAPTER 6

LAYING THE FOUNDATION: DESTROY RUSSIA, PREPARE THE BATTLEFIELD

Zbigniew Brzezinski's 1997 *The Grand Chessboard: American Primacy and Its Geostrategic Imperatives* laid a foundation for what became the 9/11 attacks. Some four years before the fact, the book articulated what purpose that disaster served in the creation and extension of an openly imperial new American order. But in doing so, Brzezinski gave us all a vivid glimpse of the remarkable foresight and planning that was brought to bear upon world events by the players who participated.

If what we find predicted in that book has been validated by events since September 11, 2001, we must infer that Peak Oil is no surprise to the Bush administration. And given the timing of the book, Brzezinski's background, and the patterns of strategic continuity that have dominated US foreign policy since the height of the Vietnam War, Peak Oil was never far from the minds of the Clinton administration, or the first Bush administration, or the Reagan administration, or the Carter administration. The Nixon administration faced the peak of US domestic oil production and the first massive OPEC-induced oil price shocks. To anyone whose head isn't totally submerged in the conventional wisdom, it's always been clear that a production cut must be either artificial or natural. Whether or not OPEC cuts oil production today, geology will be cutting it tomorrow.

When American oil production peaked in the early 1970s, there were hopes that oil discoveries — particularly in Central Asia — would mitigate the peak. Still, there was one major obstacle to US control of the Middle East: Russia.

Brzezinski is a member of the elite that presides above the American political system, which is frequently and accurately described as two factions comprising a single (corporate) party. He is best remembered as the National Security Advisor to President Jimmy Carter from 1977 to 1981. But his influence and power are better understood in light of his ongoing service as an intelligence advisor to both Presidents Reagan and Bush I. In 1988 he served as co-chairman of the Bush National Security Advisory Task Force. He is a Professor of American foreign policy at Johns Hopkins University. And perhaps most importantly, he's a colleague and friend of both David Rockefeller and Henry Kissinger. Brzezinski is a past member of the board of directors of the Council on Foreign Relations and a co-founder with Rockefeller of the Trilateral Commission (Jimmy Carter is also a member of both CFR and the Trilateral Commission). Brzezinski also served, as recently as 1998, as a paid consultant for BP-Amoco, one of the three largest investors in the Caspian basin.[1]

On December 24, 1979, the Soviet Army occupied Afghanistan and seized the capital, Kabul. It was the beginning of a decade-long, Vietnam-like conflict that debilitated the Soviet Union. Afghanistan was so much like Vietnam that it quickly developed a self-sustaining dynamic of massive heroin smuggling from a neighboring country, a dynamic that ran parallel to the war while remaining linked to it — not least by turning a percentage of the invading troops into addicts. In the case of Vietnam, the neighboring country was Laos, which then hosted the largest CIA station in history under the direction of legendary covert operative Ted Shackley. In Afghanistan, the neighboring country was Pakistan, where a massive CIA operation sprouted to support Mujahedeen freedom fighters.

In both wars heroin became the dominant note in the theme music behind the action. As noted by Professor Alfred McCoy, in 1975 none of the heroin entering the US came from Pakistan. By 1980 some 40 percent of the heroin in the US came from Pakistan, which had virtually become a CIA protectorate by that time.[2] Another striking similarity is that in both conflicts the CIA created powerful local warlords who were very well armed and who effectively prevented any national government from restoring stability. In both cases, the warlords derived their power from their direct involvement in the drug trade.

In Afghanistan Brzezinski demonstrated that he and his colleagues were capable of preparing the stage for a conflict long before the fighting — or the stakes — became visible to the world at large.

Just before the Soviet invasion, a Soviet-friendly regime had taken over Kabul in a coup and had instituted broad social reforms. But agitation believed to be backed by the regime of the Ayatollah Khomeini in Iran soon led to an uprising that prompted the first official request for limited Soviet military assistance to maintain control of key facilities in Herat.[3] In July, five months before the Russian invasion, President Carter, at the urging of Brzezinski, signed a secret directive for clandestine assistance to enemies of the pro-Soviet regime in Afghanistan (i.e., agents of our allegedly sworn enemy in Iran, the Ayatollah Khomeini).[4]

This was the first indication that a major conflict was being engineered behind the scenes. US assistance created more battles, threatening the Kabul regime and, ultimately, threatening the Soviet troops. That was what sucked the Russians into making a move that the United States immediately portrayed to the world as a massive and unprovoked invasion. An important question, asked frequently at the time, was, What in the world could the Russians possibly want with Afghanistan? There were very few good answers. Afghanistan wasn't producing much opium in those days.

Brzezinski admitted the setup and much more in 1998 to a French interviewer: "We didn't push the Russians to intervene, but we consciously increased the probability that they would... Regret what? That secret operation was an excellent idea. It had the effect of drawing the Russians into the Afghan trap. You want me to regret that?" When the interviewer asked if he regretted having supported the Islamic fundamentalists and giving arms and advice to future terrorists, Brzezinski replied: "What is more important to the history of the world ... the Taliban or the collapse of the Soviet empire? Some stirred-up Moslems or the liberation of Central Europe and the end of the cold war?"[5]

By 1997 the Soviet Union had been dead for six years. A new world had emerged in which the United States alone ranked as a superpower. Yet Russia still remained a threat — a potential block to the complete imposition of US economic and military will. So, to a lesser extent, did China, which, although it had a huge population, was technologically and militarily no match for the United States. China also represented the possibility of huge profits for American business. Another obstacle was the American people, who, as Brzezinski would note, were not psychologically built for the ways in which America would have to exercise dominion in the absence of a fair fight. It was to these and other issues — especially energy — that Brzezinski turned his attention in 1997 when he wrote *The Grand Chessboard*. Russia, as it turns out, is mentioned more frequently than any other country in the book.[6]

It was in Russia's backyard, the central Asian republics of the old Soviet Union, where Brzezinski saw that the move would have to be made. The history of mankind had always shown that controlling the heart of Eurasia was the key to controlling the entire globe. Though motives had changed over 20 centuries, this area's strategic importance remained essentially the same. Brzezinski spelled out the compelling issue driving American policy:

> A power that dominates Eurasia would control two of the world's three most advanced and economically productive regions. A mere glance at the map also suggests that control over Eurasia would almost automatically entail Africa's subordination, rendering the Western Hemisphere and Oceania [Australia] geopolitically peripheral to the world's central continent. About 75 percent of the world's people live in Eurasia, and most of the world's physical wealth is there as well, both in its enterprises and underneath its soil. Eurasia accounts for 60 percent of the world's GNP and about three-fourths of the world's known energy resources.[7]

The energy theme appeared again later.

> The world's energy consumption is bound to vastly increase over the next two or three decades. Estimates by the US Department of Energy

anticipate that world demand will rise by more than 50 percent between 1993 and 2015, with the most significant increase in consumption occurring in the Far East. The momentum of Asia's economic development is already generating massive pressures for the exploration and exploitation of new sources of energy.[8]

With the Middle East safely but quietly included in his dissertation, Brzezinski again stressed the energy importance of Eurasia, particularly for the critical goal of diversification of energy supplies:

> Moreover, they [the Central Asian Republics] are of importance from the standpoint of security and historical ambitions to at least three of their most immediate and more powerful neighbors, namely Russia, Turkey, and Iran, with China also signaling an increasing political interest in the region. But the Eurasian Balkans are infinitely more important as a potential economic prize: an enormous concentration of natural gas and oil reserves is located in the region, in addition to important minerals, including gold.[9]

As for Russia, the imperative was clear:

> Understandably, the immediate task has to be to reduce the probability of political anarchy or a reversion to a hostile dictatorship in a crumbling state still possessing a nuclear arsenal. But the long-range task remains: how to encourage Russia's democratic transformation and economic recovery while avoiding the reemergence of a Eurasian empire that could obstruct the American Geostrategic goal...[10]
>
> But in the meantime, it is imperative that no Eurasian challenger [i.e., Russia] emerges, capable of dominating Eurasia and thus of also challenging America. The formulation of a comprehensive and integrated Eurasian geostrategy is therefore the purpose of this book.[11]

Brzezinski gave one of several reasons why the US supported the Taliban and, indirectly, al Qaeda:

> In fact, an Islamic revival — already abetted from the outside not only by Iran but also by Saudi Arabia — is likely to become the mobilizing impulse for the increasingly pervasive new nationalisms, determined to oppose any reintegration under Russian — and hence infidel — control.[12]

This is a clear signal and admission that the United States had fostered and encouraged radical Islamic fundamentalist movements as a means to an end in Central Asia. Their usefulness to that end, as we shall see in subsequent chapters, certainly did not end with the fall of the Soviet Union.

Before going to the next Brzezinski quotation, consider the following ironic examples of how the United States created hatred and violence in Afghanistan. The first example concerns the actions of the US Agency for International Development (USAID), long known to be a progeny of the Central Intelligence Agency. I am indebted to the incredible work of researcher Paul Thompson for finding these illustrative and darkly humorous anecdotes. His entire timeline can be found at <www.cooperativeresearch.org>.

> 1984–1994: The US, through USAID and the University of Nebraska, spends millions of dollars developing and printing textbooks for Afghan schoolchildren. The textbooks are filled with violent images and militant Islamic teachings, part of covert attempts to spur resistance to the Soviet occupation. For instance, children are taught to count with illustrations showing tanks, missiles, and land mines. In the absence of any alternative, millions of these textbooks continue to be used long after 1994, and the Taliban were still using them in 2001. In 2002, the US has started making less violent versions of the same books, which Bush touts will have 'respect for human dignity, instead of indoctrinating students with fanaticism and bigotry.' Bush fails to mention who created those earlier books.[13] [*Washington Post*, 3/23/02, CBC, 5/6/02]

Just three years later Unocal, then fiercely motivated and fiercely frustrated by the Taliban in its efforts to build a trans-Afghani pipeline, hired the University of Nebraska to train 400 Afghani teachers, electricians, carpenters, and pipe fitters in anticipation of using them for their pipeline. They had 150 students attending classes in anticipation of successful negotiations.[14]

Brzezinski's maps

No doubt, Brzezinski had energy issues very much on his mind. He noted throughout the book that the region was becoming increasingly prone to violence. What he did not admit was that much of the violence was being initiated by US proxies. He placed two key maps in his book that would be of evidentiary value in the inconceivable scenario that the true 9/11 war-makers were ever brought to trial. One he labeled "The Global Zone of Percolating Violence."[15]

The second was a map labeled "The Eurasian Balkans" on which he placed a large circle indicating where he felt the next global conflict would emerge.[16]

Given that these maps were drawn and published a full four years before the first plane hit the World Trade Center, they would fall into a category of evidence I learned about at LAPD. We called them "clues."

As it turns out, *The Grand Chessboard* was a study prepared for the Council on Foreign Relations (CFR), also founded by the Rockefellers.[17]

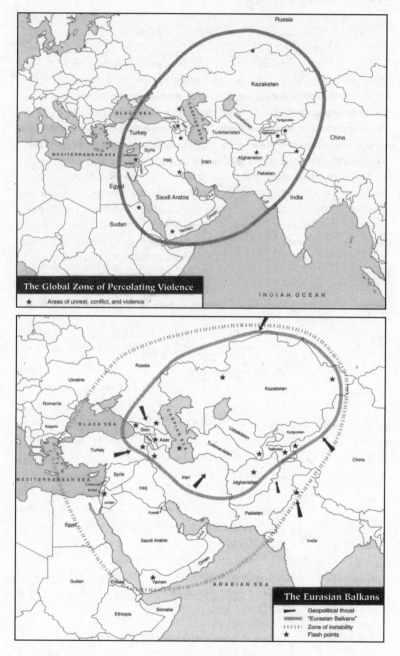

The Global Zone of Percolating Violence

★   Areas of unrest, conflict, and violence

The Eurasian Balkans

➤   Geopolitical thrust
▨▨▨ "Eurasian Balkans"
ꞮꞮꞮꞮꞮ Zone of instability
★   Flash points

Eliminating the competition

Two very important things happened immediately after the collapse of the Soviet Union in December 1991. The United States undertook a massive effort to help the FSU (Former Soviet Union), and in particular Russia, make a "successful transition" to capitalism, and the major oil companies stepped up their ongoing, oft-frustrated post-perestroika efforts to explore and establish joint ventures in the newly independent and oil-rich Central Asian republics of Kazakhstan, Turkmenistan, and Uzbekistan. Oil companies frequently had a number of CIA covert operatives on their payrolls posing as geologists and oil experts.[18]

As it turns out, both efforts were intended to remove large amounts of wealth from the region. Both may have had the equally important objective of preparing the way for the unopposed massive US military deployments in Central Asia that began in October of 2001 after the World Trade Center attacks.

Though the seeds had been planted by the outgoing first Bush administration, the US assistance program to facilitate Russia's transition to capitalism took off under the new Clinton administration in 1993. A task force headed by Vice President Al Gore, Treasury Secretary Lawrence Summers, Deputy Secretary of State Strobe Talbot[19] and involving exclusive US Treasury contracts with Goldman Sachs, the Harvard Institute for International Development, the IMF, and the World Bank worked in partnership with the government of Boris Yeltsin to remake the Russian economy. What happened was that Russia, in the words of Yeltsin himself, became a "mafiocracy" and was looted of more than $500 billion in assets; its economy was ruined, its currency destroyed, its population rendered desperate, and its ability to support a world-class military establishment smashed.

Journalist Anne Williamson was for many years a leading expert on Russian and Soviet affairs, writing for, among others, the *Wall Street Journal*, the *New York Times*, *Mother Jones*, and *SPY*. She lived in Russia, spoke the language, and saw first-hand what was done to Russia in the 1990s. In 1999 she completed a book on the subject, *Contagion: The Betrayal of Liberty, Russia, and the United States in the 1990s*, which despite a signed publishing contract has never been published, like so many other completed manuscripts that might have been vital to the world's understanding. According to Williamson, one publisher simply refused to read her first draft (October 1997), in which she explained the causes and mechanisms of the impending collapse of the Russian bond market that occurred in August 1998.

But Williamson did present her knowledge of what had happened in Russia to Congress in 1999, and that record is available. She pulled no punches in describing the rape of a country and of a people who had already been victimized by seven decades of Soviet communism:

> And there is no mistake as to who the victims are, i.e., Western, principally US, taxpayers and Russian citizens whose national legacy was stolen only to be squandered and/or invested in Western real estate and equities markets.
>
> Western assistance, IMF lending, and the targeted division of national assets are what provided Boris Yeltsin the initial wherewithal to

purchase his constituency of ex-Komsomol [Communist Youth League] bank chiefs, who were given the freedom and the mechanisms to plunder their own country in tandem with a resurgent and more economically competent criminal class. The new elite learned everything about the confiscation of wealth, but nothing about its creation.[20]

Brzezinski had made it a priority to identify the motivating factors that drove the political elites in a country that needed to be managed. What Williamson described is the creation and installation of a whole new set of elites, the oligarchs, whose motives — personal enrichment at any cost — were already known. The Empire loved the oligarchs because they were simple and could be easily controlled with money.

Williamson described two crucial mistakes made by the US fiscal experts who had exclusive contracts to manage the transition. First, they ignored the concept of private property (there had been none under Communism or under the Tsarist regimes). This gave the people no inherent rights to enormous physical equities such as real estate, manufacturing plants, oil refineries, mineral rights. Their only claim to ownership lay in the notion of post-Soviet assets as an abstract communal holding of "the Russian people." The West's experts found this communal holding established by the Soviet Constitution inconvenient. In the privatization program Harvard University and World Bank operatives devised and US taxpayers unknowingly financed, those constitutionally guaranteed communal ownership rights were transferred to the state, and only then parceled out to elected individuals in rigged auctions. Second, the good guys from the West turned loose monopoly markets, which caused prices to skyrocket. What little money individual Russians possessed was transferred quickly into the hands of the corrupt oligarchs — the "mafiya" with whom Boris Yeltsin had made his pact.[21]

Once all the assets had been transferred to the oligarchs, who were becoming fabulously wealthy, it was a simple matter for them to liquidate those assets by selling them to the US and other Western countries, and then laundering their money through US financial institutions such as the Bank of New York.[22] The money laundering and transfer of wealth made more than the Russian oligarchs rich. Billions of dollars accrued to Bank of New York executives and stockholders in 1999.[23] And during the years of the Clinton administration, as Al Gore worked in exclusive partnership with Russian Deputy Prime Minister Victor Chernomyrdin, the Harvard Endowment's value rose from 3 to 19-plus billion dollars.[24]

Compounding the pillage, a number of investment schemes sponsored by the Export-Import Bank of the United States, the Overseas Private Investment Corporation (OPIC), and a number of congressionally mandated "enterprise funds" were designed for individuals, Russian corporations, and banks. In essence, these initiatives wound up being huge money laundries. The domestic bond market's highly unjustified returns, paid with IMF loans, attracted many eager investors, and soon developed into a classic pyramid scheme. As quickly as the IMF, the World Bank, and other financial entities lent the money to Russia to realize mind-boggling returns for favored players, the money was taken right back out of Russia. Those huge sums, initially provided by taxpayers, returned to Wall Street, US banks, and Harvard.[25]

Russia was literally a free lunch for American institutions and non-profits. Williamson observed:

> Even the Ford Foundation's Moscow office sponsored its own internal Russian bond shop for which the unthinking Russian managers once asked this reporter to drum up US investors.[26]

It's interesting to note that the Ford Foundation is actively involved in the funding of "progressive" American media outlets, including Pacifica Radio, FAIR, Progressive Magazine, and is indirectly involved in several other well-known progressive media oracles and pundits.[27] At the same time, the Ford Foundation has been linked to the secret society Skull and Bones (through the late McGeorge Bundy), the Trilateral Commission, the Council on Foreign Relations, and the CIA.[28] Both George W. Bush and John Kerry are members of that secret society.

Remarkably, all that heavy Western investment in the Russian bond market was executed largely in defiance of Russian Federation legislation that limited foreign participation in that market. The Clinton administration and Harvard operatives looked the other way as major Clinton campaign donors employed corrupt Russian officials and financial notables to purchase bonds beyond the legal limits on foreign participation set by the Russian government. Williamson noted in her testimony, "The bread and butter of all equity markets are bonds. Wall Street wanted a debt market. You [USAID] build it and we'll come, they said."

Williamson's unpublished manuscript details how those firms that got in on the ground floor, such as Goldman Sachs, were able to work from the inside through alliances with personnel from Harvard's Russia Project.[29] Bonds represent debt. As with any debt, if it can't be paid, then the collateral used to secure it is forfeited. In this case, throughout the 1990s, what was forfeited was Russia's ability to function as a nation, to feed its people, and especially to support its military.

In the end, literally starved for cash, Russia sold much of its military equipment onto the black market. Some of it wound up in the hands of terrorist organizations from Bosnia to Chechnya and Russia's southern frontiers.[30] Again, when the time came for the US Empire to militarily occupy Central Asia and surround the oil fields of the Middle East, Russia had grave economic and military problems to deal with.

In describing how one particular looting scheme operated, Williamson testified:

> The CIA has determined that through Nordex, FPI [the International Foundation for Privatization and Private Investment] seized the export earnings from Russia's natural resource companies — oil, gas, platinum, gold, diamonds — and from industrial firms exporting items such as steel and aluminum, and then stashed the hefty profits

in Western bank accounts. And only now, eight years almost to the day later, do US taxpayers learn that the 'eager, young reformers' to whom their resources were sent for the purpose of building a new Russia were in league from day one with the exhausted Soviet *nomenklatura* in a scheme to loot Russia's wealth and park it in the West...[31]

Directors stashed profits abroad, withheld employees' wages, and after cash famine set in, used those wages, confiscated profits and state subsidies to 'buy' the workers' shares from them. The really good stuff — oil companies, metals plants, telecoms — was distributed to essentially seven individuals, 'the oligarchs,' on insider auctions whose results were agreed beforehand. Once effective control was established, directors — uncertain themselves of the durability of their claim to the newly acquired property — chose to asset strip with impunity instead of developing their new holdings.

Is all of this starting to sound a bit like Enron? Like WorldCom? Tyco? Halliburton? Like any of about 20 major US companies I could name? It is perhaps not by coincidence that we see some familiar names cropping up in the orchestration of this campaign to loot Russia that continued across two different presidential administrations. The US secretary of state who began the dialogues on privatization as well as the dismantling of Russia's nuclear weapons was James A. Baker. The James Baker Institute was the co-sponsor of the CFR report on energy in 2001, and James Baker was, in the words of one oil industry lawyer, "all over" the deals to get the major oil companies into Central Asia. The first official US envoy sent to aid Russia in its transition was our current Deputy Secretary of State, Richard Armitage.

Eventually, of course, the Russian economy collapsed so badly that it was necessary to secure an IMF bailout. That's the kiss of death for any country. Americans paid for that. Then in 1998 the Russian ruble inevitably collapsed because the debt couldn't be paid, and the people started starving in earnest. Consider these passages from a congressional investigation, the aforementioned Cox Report:

> The culmination of the Clinton administration's fatally flawed macroeconomic policy for Russia occurred in August 1998, when Russia's default on its debts and devaluation of the ruble led to the nation's total economic collapse. By all measurements, the disaster was worse than America's crash of 1929.
>
> The disaster that began on August 17, 1998, spread immediately throughout Russia. Millions of ordinary men and women who had deposited their money in Russian banks lost everything. ATM and debit cards ceased to work. Dozens of banks became insolvent and disappeared. Angry depositors besieged Russian banks, only to learn they had been wiped out.

Millions of senior citizens, whose meager pension income had been suspended for months, were cut off completely. When the dust finally settled in March 1999, the ruble — and with it, every Russian's life savings — had lost fully 75 percent of its value.

The devastation of Russia's economy was worse than what America experienced in the Great Depression. By 1932, the US gross national product had been cut by almost one-third. But within just six months of the 1998 crash, Russia's economy, measured in dollars, had fallen by more than two-thirds. From $422 billion in 1997 [the year when *The Grand Chessboard* was published], Russia's gross domestic product fell to only $132 billion by the end of 1998.

At the end of 1929, following America's disastrous stock market crash, unemployment in the United States reached 1.5 million, representing 1.2 percent of the total population. The 1998 collapse of the Russian economy was far worse: 11.3 million Russians were jobless at the end of 1998 — 7.7 percent of the nation's total population.

In the crash of 1929, stock prices fell 17 percent by year end — and 90 percent by the depth of the Great Depression four years later. By contrast, the Russian stock market lost 90 percent of its value in 1998 alone.

"Most fundamentally," said Sergei Markov, an analyst at the Institute of Political Studies, "it is a crisis of the real economy — Russia doesn't work"[32]

How much capital was looted out of Russia? Five hundred billion dollars, according to Congress.[33] And that $500 billion was not stockholder equity, a paper loss from some mutual fund. *It was cash.*

This congressional investigative report into what had happened in Russia came from the House Policy Committee under chairman Chris Cox (R-CA), a fierce Clinton opponent and supporter of the failed impeachment effort. It told some hard truths, but accomplished very little. Cox made the mistake of believing that what he had revealed — e.g., that the Clinton administration and Al Gore had openly gotten involved with criminals, and likely engaged in criminal behavior themselves — was something that would hurt his political opponents. Of course, it did not. What Cox failed to understand was that he was exposing an effort that was above partisan politics — one that represented the moneyed interests that fund and control both parties — an effort that was therefore protected. On the other hand, James Leach, Chairman of the House Committee on Banking and Financial Services, understood this reality perfectly. Once "instructed," Leach immediately buried the findings from his own committee's 1999 hearings into Russian money laundering.

Cox would not be the first experienced member of Congress to suffer for his own naiveté. As we will see, another Republican Congressman would make the same false assumption about the Clinton administration's activities, this time with respect to the Taliban.

Anne Williamson succinctly summed up what had been done to the people of Russia. She pointed out, "The Soviet Union was economically self-sufficient except for bananas, coffee, and coconuts."[34] By the dawning of the new century, except for small parts of Moscow, Saint Petersburg, and other cities where the oligarchs spent their money, it was as badly ruined as it had been at the worst part of World War II. It was a basket case that was self-sufficient in nothing except for its own oil that, incidentally, had already passed the peak of production.

In Moscow in March 2001, attending an international economic conference, I developed a liking for the Russian people, their hospitality, their endurance, and their sense of humor. I was saddened to hear Russian writers and business people in Moscow tell me that the population of Russia had shrunk from an estimated high of around 160 million people in 1991 to 145 million people in a decade; that the life expectancy of a male had dropped in 2000 to around 48 years; that the population was expected to drop to 130 million by 2030; and that, in the nearby Republic of Moldova, pieces of human cadavers were being sold in stores as meat. It was nothing, the Russian people joked. They recounted stories about the German siege of Leningrad, when people starved by the thousands every day. When times were at their very grimmest the people ate what they called "chicken." Nobody asked further than that, and I was jokingly told to avoid ordering chicken in any Russian restaurant outside the capital.

Moscow was a different story for an American male with a few hundred-dollar bills. I was amazed at the childless Americans I saw there adopting beautiful Russian children from families who could not feed them — another form of wealth transfer. I was stunned by the world-class opulence along Tverskaya, the street running out of Red Square; the casinos, the four-star hotels. An American was instantly recognizable on any street at any time. There was never any need to call a taxi. All one had to do was to step out from the curb and ever so slightly extend one's hand. In an instant two, three, and sometimes four private vehicles —in various states of repair — would pull to the curb. The owners would drive you anywhere, for any length of time, forgetting any other obligation they had, if you were willing to part with some rubles — or especially some US dollars.

Girls as young as 14 were available for sex on the same terms. Many American men went there for just that reason. One American businessman of Russian descent told me, "Prostitution is legal here, and the age of consent is 16. If a policeman catches you with a 14-year-old, all you have to say is that she looked 16."

Indeed, in Russia in 2001, the year of the World Trade Center attacks, if you were an American with hundred-dollar bills, you were God. And that is just the way the Empire wanted it.

Special thanks are due to Anne Williamson, who provided most of the research for the Cox Committee's report and received so little acknowledgment for it.

CHAPTER 7

CASPIAN CORRUPTION:

Enron, the Binladin Group, al Qaeda, oil companies, Dick Cheney, and John Ashcroft

Special acknowledgement is due to Paul Thompson and the Center for Cooperative Research (<www.cooperativeresearch.org>). Building on work pioneered by *From the Wilderness*, this group of researchers has compiled a timeline going back 20 years that undermines the credibility of the US government's position on the events of September 11, 2001. In this chapter, indented paragraphs beginning with a bold-faced date are quoted from that timeline, listing their references. The resulting view of the history of big oil's involvement in the Caspian Basin and Central Asia reveals more than the major media and the government would like you to know.

> **1991:** Future National Security Advisor Rice joins Chevron's board of directors, and works with Chevron until being picked as Bush's national security advisor in 2001. Chevron even names an oil tanker after her. She is reportedly hired for her expertise in Central Asia, and much of her job time is spent arranging oil deals in the Central Asian region. Chevron also has massive investments there, which grow through the 1990s. [*Salon*, 11/19/01] Other research indicates that Rice's specialty was Kazakhstan.[1]

> **1991–1997:** The Soviet Union collapses in 1991, creating many new nations in Central Asia. Major US oil companies, including ExxonMobil, Texaco, Unocal, BP Amoco, Shell, and Enron, directly invest billions in these Central Asian nations, bribing heads of state to secure equity rights in the huge oil reserves in these regions. The oil companies commit to future direct investments in Kazakhstan of $35 billion. But these companies face the problem of having to pay exorbitant prices to Russia for the use of Russian pipelines to get the oil out. These oil [and gas] fields have an estimated [in the early years of the decade] $6 trillion potential value. US companies own

approximately 75 percent of the rights. [*New Yorker*, 7/9/01, *Asia Times*, 1/26/02]

November 1993: *The Indian government gives approval for Enron's Dabhol power plant, located near Bombay on the west coast of India. Enron has invested $3 billion, the largest single foreign investment in India's history. Enron owns 65 percent of Dabhol. This liquefied natural gas powered plant is supposed to provide one-fifth of India's energy needs by 1997. [Asia Times, 1/81/01, Indian Express, 2/27/00]*

An initial Enron plan to secure natural gas from Qatar[2] fell apart in 1998, leaving Dabhol with only one hope, a gas pipeline across Afghanistan and Pakistan from Turkmenistan.[3] Earlier plans to secure natural gas supplies from Uzbekistan —which would have also required a trans-Afghan pipeline — were also failing as a result of Uzbekistan's concerns about the Taliban and failure to produce sufficient quantities of gas (see below).

October 21, 1995: Unocal signs a contract with Turkmenistan to export $8 billion worth of natural gas through a $3 billion pipeline which would go from Turkmenistan through Afghanistan to Pakistan. Political considerations and pressures allow Unocal to win out over a more experienced Argentine company [Bridas]. Henry Kissinger, a Unocal consultant, calls it "the triumph of hope over experience."[4] [*Washington Post*, 10/5/98]

[The Argentine company Bridas became uncompetitive after the implosion of the Argentine economy in December 2001. Was it coincidental?]

July 8, 1996: The US government agrees to give $400 million to help Enron and an Uzbek state company develop natural gas fields in the Central Asian nation of Uzbekistan. [*Oil and Gas Journal*, 7/8/96]

September 27, 1996: The Taliban conquer Kabul [AP, 8/19/02] and establish control over much of Afghanistan. Unocal is hopeful that the Taliban will stabilize Afghanistan, and allow their pipeline plans to go forward. In fact, "preliminary agreement [on the pipeline] was reached between [the Taliban and Unocal] long before the fall of Kabul."

October 11, 1996: The Telegraph has an interesting article about pipeline politics in Afghanistan. Some quotations: "Behind the tribal clashes that have scarred Afghanistan lies one of the great prizes of the 21st century, the fabulous energy reserves of Central Asia." "'The deposits are huge,' said a diplomat from the region. 'Kazakhstan alone may have more oil than Saudi Arabia. [Again, note that this is before any extensive drilling took place]. Turkmenistan is already known to have the fifth-largest gas reserves in the world.'" "Oil industry insiders say the dream of securing a pipeline across Afghanistan is the main reason why Pakistan, a close political ally of Americans, has been so supportive of the Taliban, and why America has quietly acquiesced in its conquest of Afghanistan." [*Telegraph*, 10/11/96]

By 2001 it was apparent that the results of drilling were lowering expectations. In December 2001 *Business Week* reported that the Caspian basin "holds an estimated 110 billion barrels of oil. Indeed, the Caspian's reserves rival those of Iraq, whose deposits of 113 billion barrels rank second in the world only to OPEC leader Saudi Arabia's [proven] 262 billion barrels."[5] Contrast that with the statement of oil expert Colin Campbell when I interviewed him in October 2002 that "reserves are now quoted at 9–13 Gb [billion barrels]. BP-Statoil has pulled out. Caspian production won't make any material difference to world supply. There is, however, a lot of gas in the vicinity." Indeed, the natural gas reserves in Turkmenistan have been proven to be as large as predicted. For this reason, the natural gas pipeline from Turkmenistan to Pakistan will probably be the first — and maybe the only — trans-Afghanistan pipeline ever built. However, uncontrolled guerilla resistance may prevent even that from being successful.

Brzezinski's *The Grand Chessboard* was published in 1997, when US relations with the Taliban were falling apart and al Qaeda terror activity was increasing. As many sources have told me, some of the first dry holes were being reported in the Tengiz fields and around what was hoped would be the larger Kashagan field in mid to late 1997. Although the degree to which estimates of Caspian and Central Asian reserves would have to be revised downward was not yet appreciated, every time the Caspian reserves got smaller, the importance of the reserves in Saudi Arabia and Iraq increased.

Officially, hope for a settlement with the Taliban that would have allowed pipeline projects to proceed continued almost up until the moment the first plane hit the World Trade Center. Yet, by September 2001 the majors had accumulated data showing that the Caspian Basin held far less oil than was originally thought. Had the geostrategic role of the Taliban thus been transformed from pipeline police into a much-needed enemy that would justify US military occupation in the region? The fact that the US had prepared invasion plans for Afghanistan while the talks continued to produce predictable and negative results suggests this.

It would be a mistake to believe that Brzezinski's book was motivated by a hope for reconciliation with the Taliban alone. In fact, a map he included in the book (see Chapter 6) indicating where the next conflict was likely to occur suggests otherwise.

US military deployments in 2001 and 2002 served the twofold purpose of blocking Russian moves into the region (protecting diversification of US supplies) and laying essential groundwork for the invasion and occupation of the Middle East as the US effectively surrounded it under the pretext of combating terrorism.

The Taliban were watching with oil reserves

As the Caspian and Central Asian reserve estimates grew smaller with each new well, both the proximity and severity of Peak Oil increased. An urgent question is whether or not there was a correlation between decreasing reserve estimates from the Caspian and increased terror activity from al Qaeda. There is reason to suspect such a linkage. It was, after all, al Qaeda that satisfied Brzezinski's stated requirement of a "direct external threat" that would trigger the support of the American people for an "imperial mobilization."

December 4, 1997: Representatives of the Taliban are invited guests to the Texas headquarters of Unocal to negotiate their support for the pipeline. Future President Bush Jr. is Governor of Texas at the time. The Taliban appear to agree to a $2 billion pipeline deal, but the Taliban will only do the deal if the US officially recognizes the Taliban regime... [*BBC*, 12/4/97; *Telegraph*, 12/14/97]

February 12, 1998: Unocal Vice President John J. Maresca — later to become a special ambassador to Afghanistan — testifies before the House of Representatives that until a single, unified, friendly government is in place in Afghanistan the trans-Afghan pipeline needed to monetize the oil [and gas] will not be built .... [House International Relations Committee testimony, 2/12/98]

December 5, 1998: In the wake of the al-Qaeda bombings on the US embassies in Kenya and Tanzania, the US gives up on putting a pipeline through Afghanistan. Unocal announces they are withdrawing from the CentGas pipeline consortium, and are closing three of their four offices in Central Asia. Worries that Clinton will lose support among women voters for upholding the Taliban also plays a role in the cancellation. [*New York Times*, 12/5/98]

Late 1998: During the investigation of the 1998 embassy bombings, FBI counter-terrorism expert John O'Neill finds a memo by al-Qaeda leader Mohammed Atef on a computer. The memo shows that bin Laden's group has a keen interest in and detailed knowledge of negotiations between the Taliban and the US over an oil and gas pipeline through Afghanistan. Atef's own analysis suggests that the Taliban are not sincere in wanting a pipeline, but are dragging out pipeline negotiations to keep Western powers at bay. [*Salon*, 6/5/02]

The Atef memo, discovered by O'Neill (who later resigned over continued interference with his investigations, only to perish in the attacks of 9/11 as the World Trade Center's chief of security) is particularly important. French authors Jean-Charles Brisard and Guillaume Dasquié, in their 2002 book *Forbidden Truth*, described the seven-page memo:

> Atef explains that the United States wants 'to take control of any region which has large quantities of oil reserves,' and 'the American government is keen on laying the oil and gas pipelines from Turkmenistan through Afghanistan to Pakistan.' Atef concludes that

al Qaeda's duty toward the movement [Taliban] is to stand behind it, support it materially and morally, especially because its regional and international enemies are working night and day to put an end to it and make it fail.

It seems clear the military chief didn't expect the pipeline negotiations to bear fruit. Referring to the Pakistani government as 'non-believers,' and noting that the pipeline 'will be under American control ... and it also goes through the territories of Pakistan which are allied to America,' Atef implies that the Taliban has no intention of ultimately cooperating with the project, but is trying to string along the Americans and Pakistanis to win some breathing space for its unpopular government.[6]

Who was stringing along whom? Oil industry sources who worked in the region, interviewed for this book, stated emphatically that Russian intelligence sources knew that Caspian drilling was producing disappointing results almost in real time. Obviously the oil companies doing the drilling knew it. However, the consensus was that rather than look at the long-term implications vis-à-vis Peak Oil, the Russians opted instead to focus only on the fact that Russian oil had thus become more important, while American planners simply asked, *Well, where do we go to get what we need?*

July 4, 1999: With ... a pipeline deal with the Taliban looking increasingly unlikely, the US government finally issues an executive order prohibiting commercial transactions with the Taliban. [Executive Order, 7/4/99]

May 2001: Vice President Cheney's national energy plan is publicly released. There are several interesting points, little noticed at the time. It suggests that the US cannot depend exclusively on traditional sources of supply to provide the growing amount of oil that it needs. It will also have to obtain substantial supplies from new sources, such as the Caspian states, Russia, and Africa. *It also notes that the US cannot rely on market forces alone to gain access to these added supplies, but will also require a significant effort on the part of government officials to overcome foreign resistance to the outward reach of American energy companies.* [Emphasis added. *Japan Today*, 4/30/02]

May 23, 2001: Zalmay Khalilzad is appointed to a position on the National Security Council as Special Assistant to the President and Senior Director for Gulf, Southwest Asia ,and Other Regional Issues. Khalilzad is a former official in the Reagan and Bush Sr. administrations. During the Clinton years, he worked for Unocal. [*Independent*; 1/10/02; State Department profile, 2001] [Note: Khalilzad is today the US proconsul in Afghanistan, but he also played a major US role in the US strategy towards Iraq.] [6a]

Mid-July, 2001: John O'Neill, FBI counter-terrorism expert, privately discusses White House obstruction in his bin Laden investigation. O'Neill says, "The main obstacles to investigate Islamic terrorism were US oil corporate interests and the role played by Saudi Arabia in it." He also states, "All the answers, everything needed to dismantle Osama bin Laden's organization, can be found in Saudi Arabia." He also believes the White House is obstructing his investigation of bin Laden because they are still keeping the idea of a pipeline deal with the Taliban open. [CNN, 1/8/02; CNN, 1/9/02; *Irish Times*, 11/19/01; the book *Bin Laden: The Forbidden Truth*, released 11/11/01]

Posturing to control energy

If it was clear by this time — especially in light of the 1998 Atef memo — that al Qaeda and the Taliban were never going to facilitate pipelines, why then would the US government have an interest in preventing the dismantling of al Qaeda and the destruction of Osama bin Laden? Only one explanation suffices: Bin Laden, al Qaeda, and the Taliban were being preserved — for the time being — to serve another purpose.

August 2, 2001: Christina Rocca, the Director of Asian Affairs at the State Department, secretly meets the Taliban ambassador in Islamabad, apparently in a last ditch attempt to secure a pipeline deal. Rocca was previously in charge of contacts with Islamic guerrilla groups at the CIA, and oversaw the delivery of Stinger missiles to Afghan Mujahedeen in the 1980s. [*Irish Times*; 11/19/01; *Salon*, 2/8/02; the book *Bin Laden: The Forbidden Truth*, released 11/11/01]

Sept. 11, 2001: The World Trade Center and Pentagon are attacked.

October 9, 2001: US Ambassador Wendy Chamberlain has a meeting with the Pakistani oil minister. She is briefed on the gas pipeline project from Turkmenistan, across Afghanistan, to Pakistan, which appears to be revived "in view of recent geopolitical developments." [*Frontier Post*, 10/10/01]

December 22, 2001: Prime Minister Hamid Karzai takes power in Afghanistan. It had been revealed a few weeks earlier that he had been a paid consultant for Unocal, as well as deputy foreign minister for the Taliban for a time. [*Le Monde*, 12/13/01; CNN, 11/22/01]

February 9, 2002: Pakistani President Musharraf and Afghan leader Hamid Karzai announce their agreement to "cooperate in all spheres of activity" including the proposed Central Asian pipeline, which they consider to be "in the interest of both countries." [*Irish Times*, 2/9/02]

February 14, 2002: The Israeli newspaper Ma'ariv astutely notes [in a column by Uri Averny]: "If one looks at the map of the big American bases created [in the Afghan war], one is struck by the fact that they are completely identical to the route of the projected oil pipeline to the Indian Ocean." The same article also states, "Osama bin Laden did not comprehend that his actions serve American interests .... If I were a believer in conspiracy theory, I would think that bin Laden is an American agent. Not being one I can only wonder at the coincidence." [*Chicago Tribune*, 3/18/02]

May 30, 2002: Afghanistan's interim leader, Hamid Karzai, Turkmenistan's President Niyazov, and Pakistani President Musharraf meet in Islamabad and sign a memorandum of understanding on the trans-Afghanistan gas pipeline project. [*Alexander's Gas and Oil Connections*, 6/8/02; *Dawn*, 5/31/02]

October 18, 2002: "The massive mothballed Dabhol power project that bankrupt US energy company Enron Corp. built in western India could be running within a year, with a long-standing dispute over power charges close to being renegotiated, a government official said." Dabhol is India's largest ever, foreign investment project. Despite reorganizing from a bankruptcy, Enron still holds a controlling 65 percent stake in the Dabhol Power Co., while General Electric Co. and Bechtel Corp. hold 10 percent each. The Maharastra State Electricity Board holds the remaining 15 percent. [*AP*, 10/18/02]

Before leaving this section it is important to note that Enron's Dabhol power plant was deemed so important both to Enron and to US economic and political interests that the National Security Council actually convened a Dabhol working group in the summer of 2001. E-mails obtained by both the *Washington Post* and the *New York Daily News* confirmed that the NSC had prepared talking points for and briefed Vice President Cheney and President Bush on Enron's difficulties with the Indian government as it attempted to sell its interest in the power plant for $2.3 billion and get its hands on payments which the Indian government felt it was not obligated to pay.[7] The stories confirm that Cheney did speak to an Indian official on Enron's behalf, but indicate that a subsequently planned discussion by President Bush did not take place because Enron's financial collapse had become front-page news.[8]

The fact that Enron is still alive and still retains control of the project appears to be a great deception — especially insofar as Enron's stockholders and the American people are concerned.

The deal with Iraq

By the time the United States publicly turned its gaze on Iraq, it was clear that the Caspian Basin and Central Asian oil prospects had become a serious disappointment.

What were once touted as oil reserves possibly as big as Saudi Arabia's, then possibly as big as Iraq's lesser but still massive reserves, had become, according to the *New York Times*, insignificant in their potential for ameliorating the coming crisis:

> The State Department is exploring the potential for post-Taliban energy projects in the region, which has more than 6 per cent of the world's proven oil reserves .... [9]

Iraq had 11 percent of the world's oil reserves; many of the wells were already drilled, there was infrastructure (albeit shabby after 12 years of sanctions) in place, and there was less need to invest in new pipelines or to wait for them to be built over long distances. It is inconceivable that the NEPDG did not know that Caspian reserves were inconsequential, and that this had somehow not been discussed inside the Task Force.

What also makes Iraq so spectacularly different from Central Asia is the degree to which nations that had been key US allies in the early war against terror had strategically invested in Iraq; such investments simply didn't exist in Central Asia. The US made it clear that the Iraq investments of these countries (especially France and Russia) might be forfeited in retaliation for their opposition to the war. In fact, during the most dramatic stages of US negotiations with the UN over the Iraqi invasion, the US, speaking through its puppet organization the Iraqi National Congress, made it clear that, absent full cooperation — nations with vested interests in Iraq might lose out completely after the US took control.[10] That position has been reaffirmed and even strengthened several times since.

In retrospect, the revelations in 2003-2004 that George W. Bush was fixated on an Iraqi invasion while the WTC rubble was still smoldering are consistent with all of this. Revelations that the Project for a New American Century (PNAC), contributor of so many Bush administration officeholders, planned for an Iraqi occupation as far back as September of 2000 coincide with the Caspian basin drilling results. The PNAC report mentioned Iraq in 24 places and stated:

> Indeed, the United States has for decades sought to play a more permanent role in Gulf regional security. While the unresolved conflict with Iraq provides the immediate justification, the need for a substantial American force presence in the Gulf transcends the issue of the regime of Saddam Hussein.[11]

Russia acted as a US partner in the post-9/11 world and derived some benefit from that role — but only until Iraq took center stage. Russian companies had already been heavily partnered with Western interests in many early explorations and pipeline contracts running from the Caspian basin, such as the Caspian Pipeline Consortium's (CPC) Novorossiysk pipeline, which opened in November, 2001.[12] A larger project, known as the Silk Road Energy Strategy, looked forward to the development of pipelines eastward, and Russia remained a key player in those projects. Russia benefited from post-9/11 US military operations in the region, that significantly weakened Islamic fundamentalist movements along its southern border, freeing it to address the oil and pipeline interests in Chechnya that were vital to ensuring the short-term stability of Russian exports — a necessary ingredient for a Russian economic recovery.

Iraq was different. It was a strategic interest, one that could make or break any economy. It seems clear that the regional issues of Central Asian and Caspian participation were tactical concessions that allowed the US to gain the strategic military position in the Middle East. In September 2002 the *Washington Post* reported that Russia, France, China, Italy, Spain, India, Algeria, the Netherlands, and Britain had massive investments all centered around the future development or refurbishing of Iraqi oilfields.[13] Russia, having already passed its peak of production and owed billions of dollars by the Iraqi government, had a special stake in seeing that agreements were honored and that the price of oil remained high.[14]

The Elephant in the Living Room

In perhaps one of *FTW's* most incriminating post 9/11 stories, "The Elephant in the Living Room," I built on leads provided to me by a former high-ranking attorney in the Justice Department and an incredible piece of investigative reporting done by Seymour Hersh.[15] That story revealed that major bribes totaling as much as $1 billion had been paid by ExxonMobil and BP-Amoco to Kazakh President Nursultan Nazarbayev in order to secure equity rights in Kazakh oil fields during the 1990s. My own investigation revealed that, even as three separate US grand juries were investigating the bribes, Attorney General John Ashcroft had accepted large campaign donations from both companies. In the case of ExxonMobil he had taken more money than he had from Enron.

This placed Ashcroft in a dilemma: although he had promptly recused himself from any participation in the Enron investigation, he had not recused himself from the grand juries. In fact, several inside sources told me that Ashcroft was, in fact, interfering with grand juries. I also disclosed that when the bribes were given and the equity rights transferred, Dick Cheney, then CEO of Halliburton, had also been a sitting member of the Kazakh state oil advisory board which had approved the sale on direction of Nazarbayev.[16] That made Cheney the principal target of a felonious bribery investigation. No wonder John Ashcroft needed to control the grand juries.

Both ExxonMobil and BP-Amoco were granted access to Dick Cheney's energy task force, a body that — as of this writing — is still illegally refusing to release its records to the American people. It now seems likely that the Caspian drilling failures were a major item on the discussion agenda of those secret meetings, further adding to the sense of urgency building before September 11th.

CHAPTER 8

Setting Up the War: Pakistan's ISI, America's Agent for Protecting the Taliban and al Qaeda

The US secret team exposed
Clues to election 2000

We have demonstrated that Saudi interests have, with US blessing and sanction, acted as the chief financial and in some cases strategic supporters of the Taliban and Osama bin Laden. In turn Pakistan, acting under US direction and guidance, has served as the logistical support arm for US geostrategic "imperatives" in Central Asia. In an examination of Pakistan's role we see evidence of an elite cadre of personnel, transcendent of either political party, which makes this kind of conspiracy function effectively and in secret without involving large numbers of people. In fact, this critical lesson will be demonstrated for us by an influential Republican member of the House International Relations Committee. In this chapter we meet one of many key witnesses who need a thorough interrogation about 9/11, Karl "Rick" Inderfurth.

I would like to express my deep gratitude and profound respect for the work of two scholars, Professor Michel Chossudovsky, PhD of the University of Ottawa and the Centre for Research on Globalization, and Nafeez Ahmed of the Institute for Policy Research and Development. Their work has laid enormously important foundations for all of us.

The ISI

Since 9/11 there has been little denial in the mainstream press or elsewhere that Pakistan's Inter Services Intelligence (ISI) has been a close ally of the CIA. The use of Pakistan by the CIA in the 1980s to conduct a clandestine war against the Soviet occupation of Afghanistan is well documented. Pakistan's leader at the time, Zia ul-Haq, intensified an already strong CIA-ISI relationship during covert operations planned by Brzezinski and others, and then executed by CIA

Director Bill Casey under Ronald Reagan. During the 1980s, the heroin trade in the region exploded, and Osama bin Laden, fighting alongside the likes of opium warlord and CIA protégé Gulbuddin Hekmatyar, got his first taste of guerilla warfare and terrorist tactics in Afghan and Pakistani mountains. Those mountains became riddled with reinforced caves, in many cases built by the Binladin Group and paid for by the CIA.

I was not surprised when Michel Chossudovsky told me in a 2001 conversation that by verbal agreement each new head of the ISI had to receive the personal blessing of the director of Central Intelligence in Langley, Virginia. The rise of the Taliban to assert control over fragmented tribal cultures in Afghanistan happened because the CIA and the ISI made it happen. According to the lingering cover story, the United States believed that in the Taliban it had found one group that could unify the country and provide a stable platform for the construction of pipelines. This may in fact have been the case at first, but as the Caspian oil bonanza went bust, things changed. Yet the CIA still protected the Taliban. Why?

In The *War on Freedom*, Ahmed wrote:

> Control of Afghanistan by the warlords of the Northern Alliance was
> ... increasingly curbed by Taliban forces backed by Pakistan and Saudi
> Arabia. When the Taliban took control of Kabul in 1996, signaling
> the faction's domination of Afghanistan, respected French observer
> Oliver Roy noted that: "When the Taliban took power in Afghanistan
> (1996), it was largely orchestrated by the Pakistani secret service [ISI]
> and the oil company Unocal, with its Saudi ally Delta."[1]

This was confirmed by additional research from Peter Dale Scott indicating that ISI support for the Taliban was facilitated — if not directed — by Saudi Arabia, the CIA, and Unocal.[2]

Ahmed continued:

> After a visit by the head of Saudi intelligence, Prince Turki [Saudi
> Arabia's liaison with bin Laden for more than 20 years], to Islamabad
> and Kandahar, US ally Saudi Arabia funded and equipped the Taliban
> march on Kabul. US Afghan experts, including Radha Kumar of the
> Council on Foreign Relations, now admit that the US supported the
> rise of the Taliban.[3]

Remember that in 1996 Osama bin Laden was already a wanted man. But it was also a logical move to have a scion of the family with experience in the oil business where he could be useful: owning the largest construction company in the region.

Although the Saudi-Taliban relationship was generally denied in the first months after 9/11 as many writers tried to bring it to light, we have generally won concession on this point in the mainstream press.

One wonders then about the real purpose of a series of secret meetings held by the so-called "6+2 Group" that culminated in July 2001 involving the six countries bordering Afghanistan, as well as Russia and the United States. Afghanistan's contiguous neighbors are Pakistan, China, Iran, Uzbekistan, Tajikistan, and Turkmenistan. US representatives included Tom Simmons, former US Ambassador to Pakistan; Lee Coldren, a former State Department expert on South Asian affairs; and Karl "Rick" Inderfurth, former Assistant Secretary of State for South Asian affairs. These meetings and the US participants are well documented in major European press outlets and in *Forbidden Truth*.[4]

Simmons, Coldren, and Inderfurth had only recently become "former" US officials. They had all been part of the Clinton administration, and they continued in the talks as private citizens, giving them a degree of deniability in what Brissard and Dasquié call Level Two diplomacy. It was, as a matter of fact, Rick Inderfurth who had made the first (January 2000) official US visit to Pakistani General Pervez Musharraf after the latter seized power in a 1999 coup. While there, Inderfurth met with two representatives of the Taliban.[5] It was reported in a number of news stories that the Pakistani representatives (including the ISI) attending these 6+2 meetings served as intermediaries with the Taliban during negotiations when the Taliban were not present.[6]

Although all press accounts offer the same basic description of the purpose of these meetings, they are nowhere explained in greater detail than by Brissard and Dasquié in *Forbidden Truth*. Having been created in 1997 under UN auspices and approved by Deputy Secretary of State Strobe Talbot, the group was intended to secure multinational agreements that would allow the development of Caspian oil and gas resources and the construction of pipelines. For two years the group's negotiations were hobbled by internal disputes. But by the end of 2000 it appeared as though an agreement was near. The Taliban often attended these meetings, and for a while it seemed there was no need for war. Even the surrender of Osama bin Laden himself was on the table:

> One month later, on October 18, 2000, the State Department recognized the work being done by 6+2, as well as the pursuit of negotiations with the Taliban in the name of pacifying Afghanistan. Two weeks later the negotiations seemed to be on the verge of conclusion. [UN special representative] Francesc Vendrell announced that for the first time the Taliban and the Northern Alliance were considering a peace process under the guidance of 6+2. The West's great hopes for Afghanistan's stability seemed, more than ever, on the verge of being realized, and Osama bin Laden would be driven out of his sanctuary. Yet suddenly, at the very end of the Clinton administration and after the US election debacle which saw George W. Bush emerge as the victor, everything changed, seemingly in cadence with the election.

In less than a month, the diplomatic equilibrium between the Taliban and the West had been broken. Negotiations were now out of the question, as were the discussions led by 6+2. Remarks on both sides were violent and full of suspicion, even anger ....

Most inflammatory — from the Taliban's perspective — was Russia's call to harden sanctions against the Taliban, and the UN Security Council resolution that the US and Russia were drafting that proposed banning sales of weaponry to the Taliban but not to the opposition.[7]

This was a 180-degree shift from secret positions taken by the US for the preceding four years. Previously, the US had been arming the Taliban and denying aid to its opponents. Of course, after four years and having achieved control of the country, one might well ask how many more weapons the Taliban needed.

In one of its last diplomatic initiatives the Clinton administration called for painful new sanctions on the Taliban.[8] Several questions merit discussion. First, *Forbidden Truth* is not clear as to what caused relations to worsen at a moment when the long-sought oil agreements were within reach. All we know is that this change coincided with the election. Second, the US and Russia acting jointly to sour relations and call for sanctions suggests something other than an embittered Democratic administration scorching the earth behind it. Russia would never act against its own interests, either in the region or globally, by irritating an incoming American president with whom it was going to have to live for at least four years. There had to have been some approval by the incoming administration for this antagonistic shift.

What is known is that the plans for an invasion of Afghanistan in a so-called "military option" had been in place for some time (they were initiated during the Clinton administration).[9] It is also known that India, Russia, Pakistan, Uzbekistan, and Tajikistan had been part of the preparations for what was reportedly joint US-Russian military action against Afghanistan scheduled for October 2001. It was even being openly discussed in regional newspapers in June 2001.[10] In the months following the 9/11 attacks a number of military websites contained references to US military personnel being quietly dispatched to Central Asia from as far back as 1997.

Even the *Washington Post* reported that a quiet US military buildup was taking place in Kazakhstan, Kyrgyzstan, and Uzbekistan for months before the Presidential election.[11] After having consulted with a number of military experts including retired West Point instructor Stan Goff, I find it difficult to believe that invasion plans could have been concocted and implemented from scratch in January 2001 in time to have become public knowledge by June. The military option was clearly initiated under Clinton.

Another historical landmark is important here. It was right after the 2000 spring harvest that the Taliban instituted its opium ban. With world opium production centered in Afghanistan, the result was a blow to the world's financial markets. I characterized the ban as a form of economic warfare.[12]

According to Paul Thompson's timeline,

> Accounts vary, but former Pakistani Foreign Secretary Niaz Naik later says he is told by senior American officials at the [July 2001 6+2] meeting that military action to overthrow the Taliban in Afghanistan is planned to "take place before the snows started falling in Afghanistan, by the middle of October at the latest." The goal is to kill or capture both bin Laden and Taliban leader Mullah Omar, topple the Taliban regime, and install a transitional government of moderate Afghans in its place. Uzbekistan and Russia would also participate. Naik also says "it was doubtful that Washington would drop its plan even if bin Laden were to be surrendered immediately by the Taliban." [*BBC*, 9/18/01][13]

That was a great way of ensuring that bin Laden would remain in Afghanistan, especially if the Taliban were sensing their impending doom. It is likely also a sign that the CIA had become desperate to restore the cash flow generated by the opium trade. The CIA was already well placed in the region; it had an infrastructure, and its mandate was to protect the drug cash flows for Wall Street's benefit.

An April 11, 2002, speech by CIA Deputy Director of Operations James Pavitt at Duke University Law School belied the myths that the CIA either lacked resources or was somehow not present in the region. The speech was posted on the CIA's website and later brilliantly analyzed by journalist Larry Chin of the *Online Journal* (<www.onlinejournal.com>). Key excerpts from the speech show the importance of the region and CIA's active presence in it:

> We had very, very good intelligence of the general structure and strategies of the al Qaeda terrorist organization. We knew, and we warned, that al Qaeda was planning a major strike. There need be no question about that .... If you hear somebody say, and I have, the CIA abandoned Afghanistan after the Soviets left and that we never paid any attention to that place until September 11th, I would implore you to ask those people how we were able to accomplish all we did since the Soviets departed. How we knew who [sic] to approach on the ground, which operations, which warlord to support, what information to collect. Quite simply, we were there well before the 11th of September .... In the Directorate of Operations alone, since just five or six years ago, we are training more than 10 times as many operations officers.[14]

The new Bush administration promptly engaged in what was to become a frenzy of renewed and hostile negotiations with the Taliban. The UN-appointed head of the 6+2 group, Francesc Vendrell, made five trips to Afghanistan between April and August of 2001 alone.[15]

The culmination of these last and secret negotiations held in July 2001 in Berlin was apparently triggered by discussions at the July 15 G8 summit in Genoa, Italy, where the focus of discussion comprised pipelines, oil issues, and Osama bin Laden.[16] It was immediately afterward that Inderfurth, Simmons, and Coldren started slamming the military option at the Taliban through messages relayed by the ISI.[17]

All of this would seem to indicate that another set of priorities — other than the pipelines — had taken over. And yet it was at this time that the American representatives delivered a reported ultimatum to the Taliban to surrender bin Laden, stabilize, and negotiate, or the choices would be between a carpet of gold and a carpet of bombs.[18] This ultimatum, widely reported in the European press, evoked a number of equivocal explanations from meeting participants. Pakistani Ambassador Niaz Naik, who attended the fateful meetings, agreed that the statement was made but denied that pipelines were the subject of the negotiations. This seems unlikely, because one is compelled to ask where the "gold" for the Taliban was going to come from if not from the pipelines.[19] So what were the urgent negotiations intended to accomplish? The more layered the deceptions, the more effort is required to understand them and reverse engineer the imperatives that brought them about.

Clues about the 2000 election

Certainly by the end of 2000 a true picture of the actual Caspian oil reserves was becoming visible to the major US oil companies and to BP-Amoco. It was also likely known by the Taliban and bin Laden, whose Islamic network was well established throughout the Muslim populations of Central Asia. It is not likely, given the damage such knowledge would cause on the financial markets, that this information would be widely shared. For a similar reason, sharing it with other nations would immediately signal that the US would be turning its sights on Iraq and Saudi Arabia. There was no place else to go. US oil consumption, depletion, and demand were an open book for all to read. So were the relevant data for every nation and region of the world. The need for oil was exploding, and there was less to obtain. The oil companies had already invested billions in Central Asia and had committed to spending billions more. Public knowledge of the Central Asian bust would lead to a frenzied worldwide repetition of the California gold rush in the Middle East, where the stakes would be much higher. American foreign policy had been focused on the isolation of Iraq through sanctions, and a unilateral decision, objected to by many of the major oil companies, to prohibit business with Iran. The US was faced with obstacles of its own making in getting to the remaining supplies of oil. That much is clear, no matter what view one takes as to the original intentions behind those American policies toward Iraq and Iran: whether they're seen as troublesome byproducts of older conflicts, or as cynically engineered facets of an eventual oil-seeking militarization whose hour had finally come.

Just four days after taking office, Vice President Cheney organized his energy task force in near total secrecy. But some scraps of information were allowed to fall from the table; for instance, the small revelation that the task force would examine the development of new partnerships in Central Asia.

Could it be that, with it known to only the elites that Central Asian oil (the terms "Central Asian" and "Caspian" are used interchangeably) was a bust, it was recognized before the 2000 election that perhaps the biggest crisis in human history was both nearer and more threatening than imagined? Could it be that a crisis management program was put into effect? If so, that crisis management program would have necessitated that an administration capable of ruthless covert and overt actions, friendly to the drug trade, and knowledgeable about oil and energy, be immediately installed in the White House. And if the election, rigged or stolen by whatever means necessary, were challenged, it would require that the Supreme Court render an illegal decision to achieve the desired results. This is exactly what happened.

This would require of course that other nations be kept in the dark about the true nature of the crisis. It would also require that the general business community and the markets be shielded from knowledge of the imminence of Peak Oil. It would likely require the violation of American law and custom, even perhaps the total violation of the Constitution not once, but repeatedly. If the crisis were that serious, and given the mindset of the powers behind globalization and the oil-gluttonous American Empire, what other options could they see? They put their "nasty" team, the one that had produced Iran-Contra, death squads, the Savings and Loan scandal, and the Gulf War, into office and gave them carte blanche.

Still, something would be required to justify Brzezinski's "imperial mobilization" and a massive deployment of US military forces into Central Asia and the Middle East on a war footing — an enemy capable of presenting a "massive and widely perceived direct external threat." Here we need to take a look at the man who, at the beginning of the Bush administration, became the Taliban's main antagonist. During the Clinton years he had been its patron saint. His change in position came as suddenly as the election of 2000 seemed endless. Having created and armed an enemy, the US government now had to make the enemy act like one on a broad enough scale to make the world believe that it could provide the planning and logistical support for the attacks of 9/11.

Deep politics and a secret team

Understanding how such a plan might have been enacted quietly, from behind the scenes, without causing undue political or economic alarm, is facilitated by looking more closely at Rick Inderfurth and a member of Congress who openly criticized him. Inderfurth's biography, obtained from the Internet, says:

Karl F. Inderfurth served as Assistant Secretary of State for South Asian Affairs from August, 1997 to January, 2001. In this capacity, Assistant Secretary Inderfurth had responsibility for the countries of India, Pakistan, Afghanistan, Nepal, Bhutan, Bangladesh, Sri Lanka, and Maldives. From October, 1997 to December, 1998 Assistant Secretary Inderfurth also served as the US Special Representative of the President and the Secretary of State for Global Humanitarian Demining. As the Special Representative he oversaw the President's "Demining 2010 Initiative."

Prior to his Presidential appointment as Assistant Secretary, Mr. Inderfurth served as the US Representative for Special Political Affairs to the United Nations, with the rank of Ambassador. His portfolio included UN peacekeeping, disarmament, and security affairs. Ambassador Inderfurth also served as Deputy US Representative on the UN Security Council.

Mr. Inderfurth departed government service in January of this year, at the end of the Clinton Administration. His activities now include Senior Advisor to the Nuclear Threat Reduction Campaign (an initiative of The Justice Project), Raymond and Juliet Bland Professorial Lecturer at George Washington University's Elliott School of International Affairs, Senior Associate at the Institute for Global Engagement, US participant in United Nations Track II diplomacy on Afghanistan [this is confirmation of the 6+2 effort] and member, Board of Directors of the Landmine Survivors Network.

Mr. Inderfurth was born in Charlotte, North Carolina, in 1946. He attended the University of North Carolina at Chapel Hill, majored in Political Science and received his BA in 1968. He was a Fulbright Scholar at the University of Strathclyde in Scotland in 1973 and earned his MA from the Department of Politics at Princeton University in 1975.

Subsequently, Mr. Inderfurth served in several government positions, including on the staffs of the National Security Council and US Senate Intelligence and Foreign Relations Committees. In 1981 he joined ABC News, first as a National Security Correspondent with a special focus on arms control for which he won several honors, including an Emmy Award. Mr. Inderfurth was Moscow Correspondent for ABC News from February 1989 to August 1991.

Mr. Inderfurth is a member of the Council on Foreign Relations in New York, the International Institute for Strategic Studies in London, the Fulbright Association, and the Council of American Ambassadors. Along with Dr. Loch K. Johnson of the University of Georgia, he co-authored an examination of the history and transformation of the

National Security Council entitled *Decisions of the Highest Order: Perspectives on the National Security Council.*[20]

Inderfurth also served on the staff of the 1975–1976 Church Committee, investigating CIA abuses (I suspect as part of a damage-control team) with fellow CFR member Zbigniew Brzezinski.[21]

A colorful Congressional figure who publicly criticized "Rick" Inderfurth and who spent a great deal of time in Congress attempting to blame the Clinton administration and the Democratic Party for the ascendancy and seeming invulnerability of the Taliban is Republican Congressman Dana Rohrabacher of Orange County, California. The biography on his Congressional website says,

> Prior to his election to Congress in 1988, Dana served as Special Assistant to President Reagan. For seven years he was one of the president's senior speechwriters. During his tenure at the White House, Rohrabacher played a pivotal role in the formulation of the Reagan Doctrine and in championing the cause of a strong national defense. He also helped formulate President Reagan's Economic Bill of Rights, a package of economic reforms that the president introduced in a historic speech before the Jefferson Memorial.[22]

Other websites reveal the special nature of Rohrabacher's connections to Afghanistan.

> A staunch supporter of the Afghan freedom fighters since his days as a White House speechwriter for President Reagan, Congressman Rohrabacher remains committed to bringing democracy and peace to Afghanistan. Rohrabacher has traveled inside Afghanistan with Afghan freedom fighters during the war with Soviet-backed forces. As a member of the Subcommittee on Asia and the Pacific House Committee on International Relations, he has played a leadership role in organizing Congressional hearings and fact-finding missions regarding Afghanistan.[23]

The website for the conservative *Human Events* magazine even displays a 1998 photograph of a bearded Rohrabacher, dressed in tribal garb and holding an AK-47 rifle as he posed with anti-Taliban rebels in the Afghan hillside.[24]

Rohrabacher has one other little-known claim to historical connectedness. On the night of June 5, 1968, as a 21-year-old activist, he was at the Ambassador Hotel in Los Angeles when Robert F. Kennedy was assassinated after winning the California primary and securing the Democratic Party's presidential nomination. His name turns up in LAPD interrogation records of the event.[25]

As a former LAPD investigator, I have noted how Rohrabacher's trips to Afghanistan in the 1980s had been facilitated by the CIA, and I know with certainty that the CIA was directly connected to RFK's assassination. In 1993 I consulted briefly on a BBC-funded documentary that brought many of those connections to light. I also knew it from first-hand experience with some of the people charged with framing Sirhan Sirhan.[26]

This is not to say that by implication Rohrabacher was part of the larger and secretive strategic planning that had, I believe, taken place regarding Afghanistan. On the contrary, it is to suggest that Rohrabacher, having reached a certain level, like Christopher Cox, in his attempts to damage the Clinton Administration for the criminality of its Russia policies, was not privy to or aware of the larger agendas that transcend political parties and that determine the course of world events. And when it came to Pakistan, US support for the Taliban, and "Rick" Inderfurth, Rohrabacher hit a brick wall that seemed to cause him a big headache. He had "exceeded his pay grade."

Perhaps one of the greatest post-9/11 research discoveries is reported by Nafeez Ahmed in *The War on Freedom*, a record of a 2000 Congressional hearing on Pakistan and Afghanistan that is more revealing and adds more to our case than any additional writing I could do on the subject.

From *Hearings on Global Terrorism and South Asia, held in the House Committee on International Relations*, Washington, DC, July 12, 2000:

> REP. DANA ROHRABACHER: After a year of requesting to see State Department documents on Afghan policy — and I would remind the committee that I have — I have stated that I believe that there is a covert policy by this administration, a shameful covert policy of supporting the Taliban — the State Department, after many, many months — actually, years — of prodding, finally began giving me documents, Mr. Chairman. And I have, in the assessment of those documents, I have found nothing to persuade me that I was wrong in my criticism. And I might add, however, that there has been no documents provided to me, even after all these years of requesting it, there have been no documents concerning the time period of the forming of the Taliban. And I would again, I would hope that the State Department gets the message that I expect to see all those documents...
>
> And although the administration has denied supporting the Taliban, it is clear that they discouraged all of the anti-Taliban supporters from supporting the efforts in Afghanistan to defeat the Taliban. Even so much as when the Taliban was ripe for being defeated on the ground in Afghanistan, Bill Richardson and "Rick" Inderfurth, high-ranking members of this administration, personally visited the region in order to discourage the Taliban's opposition from attacking the Taliban... and then going to neighboring countries to cut off any type of military assistance to the [opponents of the]

Taliban. This at a time when Pakistan was heavily resupplying and rearming the Taliban.

What did this lead to? It led to the defeat of all of the Taliban's major enemies except for one, Commander Massoud, in the north, and left the Taliban the supreme power in Afghanistan... [Massoud was assassinated by al Qaeda operatives posing as TV cameramen two days before the attacks in New York and Washington.]

One last note. Many people here understand that I have been in Afghanistan on numerous occasions and have close ties to people there. And let me just say that some of my sources of information informed me of where bin Laden was, they told me they knew and could tell people where bin Laden could be located. And it took me three times before this administration responded to someone who obviously has personal contacts in Afghanistan, to even investigate that there might be someone who could give them the information. And when my contact was actually contacted, they said that the people who contacted them were half-hearted, did not follow through, did not appear to be all that interested...

Later the subject of discussion between committee members turned to who had been supplying that Taliban with weapons.

REP. ROHRABACHER: (Laughing) This is a joke! I mean, you have to go to closed session to tell us where the weapons are coming from? Well, how about let's make a choice. There's Pakistan or Pakistan or Pakistan. (Laughs) Where do you think the Taliban — right as we speak — I haven't read any classified documents. Everybody in the region knows that Pakistan is involved with a massive supply of military weapons and has been since the beginning of the Taliban.

Let me just state for the record, here, before I get into my questions, that I think there's — and it's not just you, Mr. Ambassador [Michael Sheehan, State Department Coordinator For Counterterrorism], but it is this administration and, perhaps, other administrations as well. I do not believe that terrorism flows from a lack of state control .... Only the United States has given — and I again make this charge — the United States has been part and parcel to supporting the Taliban all along, and still is let me add ... We have been supporting the Taliban, because all our aid goes to the Taliban areas. And when people from the outside try to put aid into areas not controlled by the Taliban, they are thwarted by our own State Department...

Again, let me just — I am sorry Mr. Inderfurth is not here to defend himself — but let me state for the record: at a time when the

Taliban were vulnerable, the top person of this administration, Mr. Inderfurth and Bill Richardson [Clinton Energy Secretary and now Governor of New Mexico] went to Afghanistan and convinced the anti-Taliban forces not to go on the offensive and, furthermore convinced all of the anti-Taliban forces, their supporters, to disarm them and to cease their flow of support for anti-Taliban forces.

Rohrabacher's pique continued during an exchange with Deputy Assistant Secretary of State (Inderfurth's assistant) Alan Eastham.

REP. ROHRABACHER: But the Taliban were included; except what happened right after all of those other support systems that had been dismantled because of Mr. Inderfurth's and Mr. Richardson's appeal, and the State Department's appeal? What happened immediately — not only immediately after, even while you were making that appeal, what happened in Pakistan? Was there an airlift of supplies, military supplies, between Pakistan and Kabul and the forward elements of the Taliban forces?

REP. ROHRABACHER [answering his own question]: The answer is yes. I know.

MR. EASTHAM: The answer is —

REP. ROHRABACHER: You can't tell me because —

MR. EASTHAM: The answer is —

REP. ROHRABACHER: — it's secret information.

MR. EASTHAM: The answer is closed session. If you would like to dredge up that record.

REP ROHRABACHER: Well, I don't have to go into closed session because I didn't get that information from any classified document .... Mr. Inderfurth, Mr. Bill Richardson, a good friend of mine, doing the bidding of this administration, basically convinced the anti-Taliban mentors to quit providing them the weapons they needed, with some scheme the Taliban were then going to lay down their arms. And immediately thereafter, Pakistan started a massive shift of military supplies that resulted in the total defeat of the anti-Taliban forces .... Why haven't I been provided any documents about State Department analysis of — during the formation period of the Taliban, about whether or not the Taliban was a good force or a bad force? Why have none of those documents reached my desk after two years?

MR. EASTHAM: The effort was to stop the support for all the factions.

REP. ROHRABACHER: That's correct. You didn't deny that we disarmed their opponents, you just said we were doing it with the Taliban as well. But as I pointed out, which you did not deny, the

Taliban were immediately resupplied. Which means that we are part and parcel of disarming the victim, thinking that the aggressor was going to be disarmed as well, but it just didn't work out — at the moment when Pakistan was arming them I might add.

Pakistan's 9/11 smoking gun in the CIA's hand

One of the most important items *FTW* was to bring to light immediately after the attacks is listed as item 18 in our timeline "Oh Lucy, You Gotta Lotta 'Splainin' to do!"

> May 2001 — Deputy Secretary of State Richard Armitage, a career covert operative and [reported] former Navy Seal, travels to India on a publicized tour, while CIA Director George Tenet makes a quiet visit to Pakistan to meet with Pakistani leader Gen. Pervez Musharraf. Armitage has long and deep Pakistani intelligence connections. It would be reasonable to assume that while in Islamabad, Tenet, in what was described as "an unusually long meeting," also met with his Pakistani counterpart, Lt. Gen. Mahmud Ahmad, head of the ISI. [Source: The Indian *SAPRA* news agency, May 22, 2001][27]

One could argue that these meetings were essential in light of the deteriorating political situation. However the evidence suggests a different motive altogether — especially for Tenet's visit to Pakistan; that darker agenda is suggested by previous history and by the cover-up behavior of the White House and its pliant allies in the media.

[Special acknowledgement and thanks are given to Professor Michel Chossudovsky of the University of Ottawa who granted me permission to include lengthy excerpts from the following article that he published on June 20, 2002.]

> ### Political Deception: The Missing Link behind 9-11
> by Michel Chossudovsky [Reprinted with permission]
>
> A "Red Herring" is a fallacy of rhetoric, in which an irrelevant topic is presented in order to divert attention from the original issue.
>
> The foreknowledge issue is a Red Herring.
>
> On May 16th the *New York Post* dropped what appeared to be a bombshell: "Bush Knew." Hoping to score politically, the Democrats jumped on the bandwagon, pressuring the White House to come clean on two "top-secret documents" made available to President Bush prior to September 11, concerning "advance knowledge" of al Qaeda attacks. Meanwhile, the US media had already coined a new set of buzzwords: "Yes, there were warnings'" and "clues'" of possible terrorist attacks, but "there was no way President Bush could have known" what was going to happen. The Democrats agreed to *"keep the cat inside the*

bag" by saying: *"Osama is at war with the US,"* and the FBI and the CIA knew something was cooking but "failed to connect the dots." In the words of House Minority Leader, Richard Gephardt: *"This is not blame-placing .... We support the President on the war against terrorism. Have and will. But we've got to do better in preventing terrorist attacks."*

The media's spotlight on "foreknowledge' and so-called "FBI lapses" served to distract public attention from the broader issue of political deception. Not a word was mentioned concerning the role of the CIA, which throughout the entire post-cold war era, has aided and abetted Osama bin Laden's al Qaeda, as part of its covert operations.

Of course they knew! The foreknowledge issue is a red herring. The "Islamic Brigades" are a creation of the CIA. In standard CIA jargon, al Qaeda is categorized as an "intelligence asset." Support to terrorist organizations is an integral part of US foreign policy. Al Qaeda continues to this date (2002) to participate in CIA covert operations in different parts of the world. These "CIA-Osama links" do not belong to a bygone era, as suggested by the mainstream media.

The US Congress has documented in detail, the links of al Qaeda to agencies of the US government during the civil war in Bosnia-Herzegovina, as well as in Kosovo. More recently in Macedonia, barely a few months before September 11, US military advisers were mingling with Mujahideen mercenaries financed by al Qaeda. Both groups were fighting under the auspices of the Kosovo Liberation Army (KLA), within the same terrorist paramilitary formation.

The CIA keeps track of its "intelligence assets." Amply documented, Osama bin Laden's whereabouts were always known. Al Qaeda is infiltrated by the CIA. In other words, there were no "intelligence failures"! In the nature of a well-led intelligence operation, the "intelligence asset" operates (wittingly or unwittingly) with some degree of autonomy, in relation to its US government sponsors, but ultimately it acts consistently, in the interests of Uncle Sam.

While individual FBI agents are often unaware of the CIA's role, the relationship between the CIA and al Qaeda is known at the top levels of the FBI. Members of the Bush administration and the US Congress are fully cognizant of these links.

The foreknowledge issue focussing on "FBI lapses" is an obvious smokescreen. While the whistleblowers serve to underscore the weaknesses of the FBI, the role of successive US administrations (since the presidency of Jimmy Carter) in support of the "Islamic Militant Base." is simply not mentioned.

Fear and disinformation campaign

The Bush administration, through the personal initiative of Vice

President Dick Cheney, chose not only to foreclose the possibility of a public inquiry, but also to trigger a fear and disinformation campaign: "I think that the prospects of a future attack on the US are almost a certainty .... It could happen tomorrow, it could happen next week, it could happen next year, but they will keep trying. And we have to be prepared." What Cheney is really telling us is that our "intelligence asset." which we created, is going to strike again. Now, if this "CIA creature" were planning new terrorist attacks, you would expect that the CIA would be first to know about it. In all likelihood, the CIA also controls the so-called "warnings" emanating from CIA sources on "future terrorist attacks" on American soil.

Carefully planned intelligence operation

The 9/11 terrorists did not act on their own volition. The suicide hijackers were instruments in a carefully planned intelligence operation. The evidence confirms that al Qaeda is supported by Pakistan's military intelligence, the Inter-services Intelligence (ISI). Amply documented, the ISI owes its existence to the CIA: "With CIA backing and the funnelling of massive amounts of US military aid, the ISI developed [since the early 1980s] into a parallel structure wielding enormous power over all aspects of government .... The ISI had a staff composed of military and intelligence officers, bureaucrats, undercover agents, and informers estimated at 150,000."

The missing link

The FBI confirmed in late September 2001, in an interview with ABC News (which went virtually unnoticed) that the 9/11 ring leader, Mohammed Atta, had been financed from unnamed sources in Pakistan:

> As to September 11th, federal authorities have told ABC News they have now tracked more than $100,000 from banks in Pakistan, to two banks in Florida, to accounts held by suspected hijack ring leader, Mohammed Atta .... *Time Magazine* is reporting that some of that money came in the days just before the attack and can be traced directly to people connected to Osama bin Laden. It's all part of what has been a successful FBI effort so far to close in on the hijacker's high commander, the money men, the planners, and the mastermind.

The FBI had information on the money trail. They knew exactly who was financing the terrorists. Less than two weeks later, the findings of the FBI were confirmed by *Agence France Presse* (AFP) and the *Times of India*, quoting an official Indian intelligence report (which had been dispatched to Washington). According to these two reports, the money used to finance the 9/11 attacks had allegedly been "wired to WTC hijacker Mohammed Atta from Pakistan, by Ahmad Umar Sheikh, at the instance of [ISI Chief] General Mahmoud [Ahmad]." According to the AFP (quoting the intelligence source): "The evidence we have supplied to the US is of a much wider range and depth than just one piece of paper linking a rogue general to some misplaced act of terrorism."

Pakistan's chief spy visits Washington

Now, it just so happens that General Mahmoud Ahmad, the alleged "money man" behind 9/11, was in the US when the attacks occurred. He arrived on September 4th, one week before 9/11, on what was described as a routine visit of consultations with his US counterparts. According to Pakistani journalist, Amir Mateen (in a prophetic article published on September 10):

> ISI Chief Lt-Gen. Mahmoud's week-long presence in Washington has triggered speculation about the agenda of his mysterious meetings at the Pentagon and National Security Council. Officially, he is on a routine visit in return to CIA Director George Tenet's earlier visit to Islamabad. Official sources confirm that he met Tenet this week. He also held long parlays with unspecified officials at the White House and the Pentagon. But the most important meeting was with Marc Grossman, US Under Secretary of State for Political Affairs. One can safely guess that the discussions must have centred around Afghanistan …. and Osama bin Laden. What added interest to his visit is the history of such visits. Last time Ziauddin Butt, Mahmoud's predecessor, was here, during Nawaz Sharif's government, the domestic politics turned topsy-turvy within days.

Nawaz Sharif was overthrown by General Pervez Musharaf. General Mahmoud Ahmad, who became the head of the ISI, played a key role in the military coup.

Schedule of Pakistan's Chief of Military Intelligence Lt. Gen. Mahmoud Ahmad, Washington, September 4–13, 2001:

Summer 2001: ISI Chief Lt. Gen. Mahmoud Ahmad transfers $100,000 to 9/11 Ringleader Mohamed Atta.

September 4: Ahmad arrives in the US on an official visit.

September 4–9: He meets his US counterparts including CIA head George Tenet.

September 9: Assassination of General Massood, leader of the Northern Alliance. Official statement by Northern Alliance points to involvement of the ISI-Osama-Taliban axis.

September 11: Terrorist Attacks on the WTC and the Pentagon. At the time of the attacks, Lt. Gen. Ahmad was at a breakfast meeting at the Capitol with the chairmen of the House and Senate Intelligence Committees Sen. Bob Graham and Rep. Porter Goss. Also present at the meeting were Sen. John Kyl and the Pakistani Ambassador to the US, Maleeha Lodhi.

September 12–13: Meetings between Lt. Gen. Ahmad and Deputy Secretary of State Richard Armitage. Agreement on Pakistan's collaboration negotiated between Ahmad and Armitage. Meeting between General Ahmad and Secretary of State Colin Powell

September 13: Ahmad meets Senator Joseph Biden, Chairman of the Senate Foreign Relations Committee.

Condoleezza Rice's press conference

In the course of Condoleezza Rice's May 16 [2002] press conference (which took place barely a few hours after the publication of the "Bush Knew" headlines in the *New York Post*), an accredited Indian journalist asked a question on the role of General Mahmoud Ahmad:

Q: Dr. Rice?

Ms RICE: Yes?

Q: Are you aware of the reports at the time that the ISI chief was in Washington on September 11th, and on September 10th $100,000 was wired from Pakistan to these groups here in this area? And why was he here? Was he meeting with you or anybody in the administration?

Ms RICE: I have not seen that report, and he was certainly not meeting with me.

Although there is no official confirmation, in all likelihood General Mahmoud Ahmad met Rice during the course of his official visit. Moreover [as was the case with President Bush's 2003 dishonest statement about Iraqi attempts to purchase uranium from Niger] she must have been fully aware of the $100,000 transfer to Mohammed Atta, which had been confirmed by the FBI.

Mysterious 9/11 breakfast meeting on Capitol Hill

On the morning of September 11, General Mahmoud Ahmad, the alleged "money-man" behind the 9/11 hijackers was at a breakfast meeting on Capitol Hill hosted by Senator Bob Graham (Democrat) and Representative Porter Goss (Republican), respectively chairmen of the Senate and House Intelligence Committees. While trivialising the importance of the 9/11 breakfast meeting, the *Miami Herald* (September 16, 2001) confirms that General Ahmad also met Secretary of State Colin Powell in the wake of the 9/11 attacks. "Graham said the Pakistani intelligence official with whom he met, a top general in the government, was forced to stay all week in

Washington because of the shutdown of air traffic 'He was marooned here, and I think that gave Secretary of State Powell and others in the administration a chance to really talk with him,' Graham said."

With the exception of the Florida press (and <www.salon.com>, September 14), not a word was mentioned in the US media's September coverage of 9/11 concerning this mysterious breakfast reunion. While the *Washington Post* acknowledges the links between ISI Chief Mahmoud Ahmad and Osama bin Laden, it fails to dwell on the more important question: *What was Mahmoud doing on Capitol Hill on the morning of September 11, together with Rep. Porter Goss and Senator Bob Graham and other members of the Senate and House intelligence committees?*

The investigation and public hearings on "intelligence failures"

In a bitter irony, Rep. Porter Goss and Senator Bob Graham, — the men who hosted the mysterious September 11 breakfast meeting with the alleged *"hijacker's high commander"* (to use the FBI's expression), had been put in charge of the investigation and public hearings on so-called "intelligence failures."

Meanwhile, Vice President Dick Cheney had expressed anger on a so-called "leak" emanating from the intelligence committees regarding "the disclosure of National Security Agency intercepts of messages in Arabic on the eve of the attacks. The messages ... were in two separate conversations on September 10 and contained the phrases 'Tomorrow is zero hour' and 'The match is about to begin.' The messages were not translated until September 12."[28]

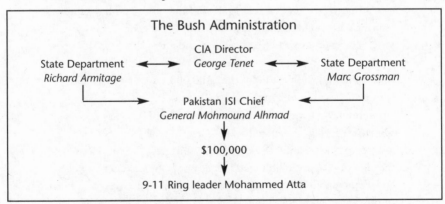

The media commits a crime

Below is a transcript of the same Rice press conference (obtained by Chossudovsky) from the *Federal News Service*. Both the CNN and White House transcripts reported that when Rice was questioned about Ahmed's presence in Washington the identity of the person being asked about was inaudible! Yet the *Federal News Service* got it right. In watching a tape of the press conference every word was crystal clear. There was not the slightest chance that any part was inaudible.

> Federal News Service May 16, 2002, Thursday,
> SECTION: WHITE HOUSE BRIEFING,
> HEADLINE: SPECIAL WHITE HOUSE BRIEFING
>
> Q: Are you aware of the reports at the time that ISI chief was in Washington on September 11th, and on September 10th, $100,000 was wired from Pakistan to these groups here in this area? And why he was here? Was he meeting with you or anybody in the administration?
>
> MS. RICE: I have not seen that report, and he was certainly not meeting with me.

Daniel Pearl

Wall Street Journal reporter Daniel Pearl was kidnapped in January of 2002 from Pakistani streets. His body was found in May, and at the same time the Pakistani police announced that they had a prime suspect in the case, Omar Saeed Sheikh.

He is variously known also by the names Ahmad Umar Sheik, Ahmad Omar Saeed Sheikh, and Umar Sheikh. He was raised and educated in London, and, by whatever name he is known, it has been acknowledged that he was an ISI agent. When the *Times of India* revealed that by examining his cell phone records (obtained through Indian intelligence services) they could prove that he was the leg man who had wired $100,000 to Mohammed Atta in Florida just days before the attacks, they did not know that he was going to be arrested and convicted for the murder of Pearl. It was the cell phone records, among other things, that tied Sheikh directly to the ISI.[29] And before his link to ISI Chief General Ahmad became known and corroborated by major US papers, the American press had been setting him up as the number one al Qaeda bag-man.

The ISI connection changed all that and became a liability for the US government. Paul Thompson's timeline contains a compelling entry on the case that could have proven devastating for the CIA had the dots been connected properly.

> September 8-11, 2001 (C): Saeed Sheikh transfers money from the United Arab Emirates to Atta in Florida on September 8 and 9 (the United Arab Emirates is known for lax banking laws and has no law against money laundering [State Department

briefing, 7/8/99]). On September 9, three hijackers, Atta, Walid Alshehri, and Marwan Alshehhi, transfer about $15,000 back to Saeed's account. [*Time*, 10/1/01; *Los Angeles Times*, 10/20/01] Apparently the hijackers are returning money meant for the 9/11 attacks that they didn't use. Saeed then flies from the United Arab Emirates to Karachi, Pakistan, on 9/11. These last minute transfers are touted as the "smoking gun" proving al-Qaeda involvement in the 9/11 attacks, since Saeed is a known financial manager for bin Laden. [*Guardian*, 10/1/01][30]

With so much damning evidence stacking up to suggest that the CIA had actually helped to finance the 9/11 attacks, there was nothing left for the mainstream press to do but engage in a game of confusion. Instead of asking the questions that should have been asked, the media confused the issue by describing the same man in his roles as ISI agent and bin Laden bagman under many different names and by attempting to insert another individual into the mix.

Researcher Chaim Kupferberg documented the major media's name game in trying to confuse Sheikh's identity with another man, bin Laden's brother-in-law. Kupferberg meticulously pulled apart about two dozen mainstream press reports and demonstrated deceptive reporting in attempts to conceal Sheik's identity by attributing acts originally been reported as Sheikh's to another person entirely.[31]

After Sheik's conviction for Pearl's murder in July 2002, other revelations showed that Pearl had maintained fairly close relationships with the CIA. One report indicated that Pearl was involved in passing a hard-drive from an al Qaeda laptop computer to the CIA. Another quoted former CIA case officer Robert Baer as saying, "I was working with Pearl." Baer stated in the story that he had been encouraging Pearl to investigate the CIA's top operational suspect in the attacks, Khalid Shaikh Mohammed.[32]

Abandoning the tortuous logic of trying to rationalize actions indicating guilty knowledge and cover-up, it is appropriate to ask if Pearl was really investigating the hottest 9/11 story around. Was Pearl investigating the ISI? At least two sources say yes. Kupferberg wrote"

> Tariq Ali of the *Guardian* reported on April 5, 2002: 'Those he [Pearl] was in touch with say he was working to uncover links between the intelligence services and terrorism. His newspaper has been remarkably coy, refusing to disclose the leads Pearl was pursuing.'[33]

And in the spring of 2002 I interviewed an international attorney just returning from several months of work in Pakistan. Because he has ongoing business in Pakistan I cannot name him here, but I can tell you what he said. "Oh, there's no doubt about it. It was common knowledge on the streets. Pearl was investigating the ISI."

CHAPTER 9

BUSINESS WITH THE BIN LADENS: THE REAL SAUDI ARABIA

The most important thing for us is to find Osama bin Laden. It's our number one priority, and we will not rest until we find him.

— George W. Bush, September 13, 2001

I don't know where he is. I have no idea, and I really don't care. It's not that important. It's not our priority.

— George W, Bush, March 13, 2002

Osama bin Laden is probably the last witness the United States would like to have interrogated. There is a compelling case to be made that Osama bin Laden has long been a well-cultivated, protected, and valued asset of US and British intelligence. It is also possible that he has been used.

The bin Laden family of Saudi Arabia is vastly different from what has been described in the American press. Much of its wealth, power, sophistication, and political and economic influence has been overlooked. A close examination leads directly to US economic and intelligence interests. And this does much to explain why American corporate media has avoided discussing it in detail.

To understand the deep connections and alliances between the bin Ladens and Western economic and political interests — including the Bush family — is to glimpse the overall fragmented nature of Saudi Arabia: at once extremely powerful and extremely fragile because of its own internal fault lines; under intense pressure and held together by extraordinary means; manipulated unceasingly by the United States and its own elites.

It is necessary to dispel one popular myth that has remained in the public consciousness since September 11: that of Osama bin Laden as an outcast, totally estranged from his family. This estrangement allegedly occurred after the 1991 Iraq War as the United States kept its military bases on Saudi soil and Osama, who had been a US ally and CIA protégé during the Soviet-Afghan conflict of the 1980s, turned towards terrorism.

Prodigal black sheep with an open door

Both the United States government and global business trumpeted a 1993 statement by Bakr bin Laden, the successor as family head after the 1988 death of Osama's older brother Salem. "The entire family regrets, denounces, and condemns all of the acts committed by Osama bin Laden."[1] That was a convenient statement serving many interests.

After he took a public stance opposing the Saudi regime's decision that allowed US troops to be housed on holy soil, Osama bin Laden's citizenship was revoked in 1994, giving the appearance of a total split with both his family and the monarchy. Whenever financial transactions between either the family or Saudi potentates and Osama have been disclosed, the explanation has been offered that these were extortion payments to keep him from making attacks inside Saudi Arabia. This position has been essential to the US's credibility in its business and diplomatic dealings. And, like so many other official US positions taken since 9/11, it is at least partially deceitful.

Not only did the bin Laden family continue to openly receive and visit Osama after 1994, members of the family have assisted in funding al Qaeda and its terrorist operations. That should not be taken to mean that they were acting in the interests of Saudi Arabia. It means that they were acting in the interests of the bin Ladens and their allies. This, at a time when they operated an enormous global financial empire that enjoyed large-scale joint business ventures with American oil companies including Enron, major financial institutions, and even the Bush family itself. The bin Ladens are major players in the new globalized financial order. For some companies, terrorism is good business.

In their book *The Forbidden Truth*, French authors Brisard and Dasquié wrote:

> Osama bin Laden's own sister recently admitted that it was inconceivable that 'none of the fifty-four family members kept ties with him.' But she also revealed the change in tone that has recently been adopted with regard to her brother. Since the September 11 attacks Osama bin Laden has become a 'half brother' to his siblings. But this word choice is arbitrary; in an Islamic country that practices polygamy, the children born of different wives are simply brothers and sisters.[2]

Of the more than 50 "brothers and sisters"[3] all fathered by Osama's father Mohammed, Osama is the only child to have also been born of a Saudi mother. In the Saudi culture and "in the eyes of the authorities, this 'Saudi' son would make a trustworthy representative, and he would eventually become a close confidant of Prince Turki, the head of Saudi intelligence."[4]

Brisard and Dasquié also quote an undated CNN interview with Peter Arnett in which Osama claimed that his "mother, uncle, and brothers" had visited him in Khartoum, Sudan. This presumably occurred in the mid 1990s, during the period in which Osama resided there after the reported rift.

There is much more information showing that the reported schism in the family is a convenient charade. From Paul Thompson's timeline:

> **Spring, 2000:** Sources who know bin Laden later claim that bin Laden's mother has a second meeting with her son in Afghanistan. The trip is approved by the Saudi royal family. The Saudis pass the message to him that 'they wouldn't crack down on his followers in Saudi Arabia' as long as he set his sights on targets outside the desert kingdom. In late 1999, the Saudi government had told the CIA about the trip, and suggested placing a homing beacon on her luggage. This doesn't happen — Saudis later claim they weren't taken seriously, and Americans claim they never received specific information on her travel plans. [*New Yorker*, 11/5/01, *Washington Post*, 12/19/01]."[5]

This also is one of the literally dozens of opportunities for bin Laden's capture which the US government chose to ignore. Sudanese officials had been keeping real-time surveillance of bin Laden's movements in the country while he lived there until 1995 and giving the results to US intelligence. The US government could have easily apprehended bin Laden with Sudanese assistance. The Sudanese would have gladly provided it in order to continue receiving US financial aid. Instead the US forced the Sudanese to expel bin Laden, driving him back into Afghanistan, where he became a pivotal influence in the growing power of al Qaeda and the Taliban.[6] In fact, the Sudanese government offered to take bin Laden into custody and was rebuffed. One is compelled to ask whether this is collective, contagious, and continuing stupidity or more evidence of desired outcomes being realized.

The *Washington Post* explicitly suggested that the real relationship between the United States government and Osama bin Laden may be quite the opposite of what it seems. "As early as March 1996, the government of Sudan offered to extradite bin Laden to the United States. US officials turned down the offer, perhaps preferring to use him 'as a combatant in an underground war.'"[7] In other words, as a US government agent.[8]

In a follow-up story, the *Village Voice* expanded further on the Sudanese fiasco:

> Nevertheless, one US intelligence source in the region called the lost opportunity a disgrace. "We kidnap minor drug czars and bring them back in burlap bags. Somebody didn't want this to happen." He added that the State Department may have blocked bin Laden's arrest to placate a part of the Saudi Arabian government that supported bin Laden. (Much of bin Laden's funding and some of his followers, including suicide bombers, come from Saudi Arabia, which was one of only three countries to recognize the Taliban. That changed after September 11. By then, the Saudis had fired their longtime intelligence

chief, Prince Turki al-Faisal, reportedly for his support of bin Laden.)
Another American intelligence official told the *Voice*, "I've never seen
a brick wall like this before."[9]

Not only did family connections continue after the "rift," there is evidence that
members of the family also supported terrorist activity. In reality, [the family's] ties
with Osama bin Laden had always existed and were never really broken. As one
Western intelligence agency noted, the bin Laden family had rigorously followed
'the principal of total family solidarity among all its members' since the 1980s.

> In this way, two of Osama bin Laden's brothers-in-law, Muhammad
> Jamal Khalifa and Saad Al Sharif, played a crucial role, according to
> American authorities, in the financing of al Qaeda. The first did so
> through a charity organization based in Jeddah that did work in the
> Philippines. He also financed bin Laden's activities in Malaysia,
> Singapore, and Mauritius.[10]

Khalifa was linked by former CIA official Vince Cannistraro to a Yemeni terrorist group that claimed responsibility for the 2001 bombing of the U.S.S. *Cole*.
After he had been detained in the US by immigration authorities when this was
known, instead of holding him for trial in the US, American officials deported him
to Jordan, where he was wanted but was soon released on a technicality.[11]

Two more compelling citations from Paul Thompson's timeline further give the
lie to the myth of Osama's ostracism:

> **February 2001:** A former CIA anti-terror expert tells the *New Yorker*
> that an allied intelligence agency sees "two of Osama's sisters appar-
> ently taking cash to an airport in Abu Dhabi, where they are suspected
> of handing it to a member of bin Laden's al Qaeda organization." This
> is cited as one of many incidents showing "interconnectedness" between
> Osama bin Laden and the rest of his family. [*New Yorker*, 11/5/01][12]

> **November 5, 2001:** A *New Yorker* article points to evidence that
> the bin Laden family has generally not ostracized ... bin Laden as is
> popularly believed (for instance, see [*Newsweek*, 10/15/01]), but
> retains close ties in some cases. The large bin Laden family owns and
> runs a $5 billion a year global corporation that includes the largest
> construction firm in the Islamic world. One counter-terrorism expert
> says, "There's obviously a lot of spin by the Saudi Binladin Group [the
> family corporation] to distinguish itself from Osama. I've been fol-
> lowing the bin Ladens for years, and it's easy to say, 'We disown him.'
> Many in the family have. But blood is usually thicker than water." The
> article notes that neither the bin Laden family nor the Saudi royal
> family have publicly denounced bin Laden since 9/11. [*New Yorker*,
> 11/5/01][13]

The family's continuing support for Osama bin Laden became a matter of public record in 1999. As Thompson's timeline observes:

> **April 1999:** A Saudi government audit shows that five of Saudi Arabia's billionaires have been giving tens of millions of dollars to al Qaeda. The audit shows that these businessmen transferred money from the National Commercial Bank to accounts of Islamic charities in London and New York banks that serve as fronts for bin Laden. $3 million was diverted from a Saudi pension fund. The only action taken is that Khalid bin Mahfouz, founder of National Commercial Bank, Saudi Arabia's biggest bank, is placed under house arrest. Bin Mahfouz had invested in George Bush Jr.'s businesses starting in 1989. The US has not frozen the accounts of bin Mahfouz, and he continues to engage in major oil deals with US corporations. [*USA Today*, 10/29/99, *Boston Herald*, 12/10/01]

Just what is the "Saudi Binladin Group" and what does it do?

The Saudi Binladin Group (SBG)

Perhaps the most comprehensive breakdown of the bin Laden family's operations was compiled by former French intelligence consultant Jean-Charles Brisard as a project commissioned by the French intelligence community entitled *The Economic Network of the bin Laden Family*. Much of that work was reproduced in *Forbidden Truth*.

With its headquarters in Jeddah, the parent company of SBG, Saudi Investment Company (SICO) operates four subsidiaries: SICO Curacao (Dutch Antilles), the Tropiville Corporation NV (Dutch Antilles), Falken Ltd. (Cayman Islands), and Islay Holdings (Isle d'Islay). Falken and Tropiville together own Russell Wood Holdings Ltd. (London) and Russell Wood Ltd. (London). An additional six subsidiaries, controlled by either Russell Wood or Islay Holdings, all with innocuous-sounding names starting with "Falcon," "Globe," "Turkey Rock," or "Saffron," are all located in Britain. In addition, one subsidiary, Falcon Properties Ltd., in conjunction with Saudi investor Ghaith Pharoan, owns the Attock Oil Company, also located in England.

Founded in 1931 at the same time as the nation of Saudi Arabia, the bin Laden family business is the largest construction company in the Middle East. But this easy observation leads to a tangled web of financial and political machinations. The holding companies are located on Caribbean islands frequently associated with money laundering. Obviously a great many financial and corporate entities can be concealed within tightly controlled holding companies. What else is known about the operations of this empire?

The Saudi Binladin Group owns orbiting satellites and has contracts with the US Department of Defense (DoD). Iridium Satellite, LLC is a privately held, bin

Laden Group company which owns a series of 73 low-orbit stationary satellites designed to provide satellite phone coverage across the surface of the Earth. Originally developed by Motorola, Iridium LLC was bankrupt in 1999 when the bin Laden group purchased it and renamed it Iridium Satellite, LLC. The company is based in Leesburg, VA, not far from the CIA and the National Reconnaissance Office. Since the bankruptcy takeover, the company has garnered a $72 million DoD contract and a $300,000 NSF grant to "gauge the magnetic characteristics of the energy fields caused by solar storms."

Apparently, 600 Iridium Satellite phones were en route to Florida on September 11 and were redirected to NYC to help with the tragedy. After September 11, there was some talk of using Iridium Satellite LLC's "low Earth orbiting satellites to provide real-time cockpit voice and flight data monitoring of commercial aircraft, replacing the on-board 'black boxes.'"[14]

SBG's construction arm was involved in the building of US military bases in Saudi Arabia, including the Khobar towers, destroyed by a terrorist bomb in June 1996 killing 19 US servicemen. SBG also had business ventures with US oil companies such as Unocal and Enron. In addition they built large portions of the holy sites at Mecca for the Saudi government as a result of a special relationship they have enjoyed with the royal family since the founding of the kingdom.[15]

As the exclusive contractor for the holy sites in Mecca, Medina, and Jerusalem (until 1967), SBG and the bin Laden family enjoyed virtually competition-free access to government contracts. The company even served as a tutor for members of the royal family on matters of business and international finance.[16] Even more significant, in an Islamic culture strictly opposed to the collection of interest, "the SBG is the only private Saudi institution able to issue bonds. In 2001 it had 35,000 employees with estimated revenues of $3 – 5 billion. In the 1980s it represented the likes of Porsche and Audi and developed Saudi partnerships with GE, Nortel, and Schweppes. All of these companies pretend to this day that SBG and Osama bin Laden are totally divorced."[17]

As for its banking relationships, SBG is known to favor the Saudi Commercial Bank,[18] Deutsche Bank's London office, and Citigroup.[19] It also has extensive financial relationships with Goldman Sachs and the Fremont Group, a San Francisco investment firm whose directorate includes former Secretary of State George P. Shultz. His connections to the SBG reach from the banking side to the construction side; Shultz is the former CEO of the Bechtel Group, a heavy construction firm with major interests in pipeline construction throughout the Middle East.[20] Just after the US occupation of Iraq in April 2003, Bechtel was awarded a contract worth up to $680 million to assist in the rebuilding of Iraqi infrastructure.

In 2001, the *Wall Street Journal* succinctly captured the importance of SBG in the operations of the Empire:

"If there were ever any company closely connected to the US and its presence in Saudi Arabia, it's the Saudi Binladin Group," says Charles Freeman, president of the Middle East Policy Council, a Washington nonprofit concern that receives tens of thousands of dollars a year from the bin Laden family.[21]

SBG also makes sizeable investments in foreign corporations, including many in the US. *FTW* was among the first, just after the attacks of 9/11, to bring public attention to the fact that the bin Ladens had a multimillion-dollar stake in the Carlyle Group, a privately held US company.

Carlyle

On October 9, 2001, I published a story in *FTW* on connections between the Bushes and the bin Ladens; it helped start an uproar that eventually led to the SBG divesting itself from Carlyle. Why is Carlyle so significant? As a holding company and investment bank, it is a major component of the US defense industry. Most people are unaware that on September 11, 2001, as the attacks were taking place, members of the bin Laden family (along with other key investors) were in Washington, DC meeting with the Carlyle Group at the Ritz Carlton Hotel, just blocks away from the White House.[22] Following are excerpts from that story.

The Carlyle Group, the Bushes, and bin Laden

The warnings about the Carlyle Group, the [at that time] nation's eleventh largest defense contractor, and the Bushes came long before the World Trade Center attacks. The Carlyle Group is a closely held corporation, exempt, for that reason, from reporting its affairs to the Securities and Exchange Commission. Little is known of what it actually does except that it buys and sells defense contractors. As of October 4, 2001, it has removed its corporate website from the World Wide Web, making further investigation through that channel impossible. Its Directors include Frank Carlucci, former Reagan Secretary of Defense; James Baker, former Bush Secretary of State; and Richard Darman, a former White House aide to Ronald Reagan and Republican Party operative.

On March 5, 2001, just weeks after George W. Bush's inauguration, the conservative Washington lobbying group Judicial Watch issued a press release. It said:

(Washington, DC) Judicial Watch, the public interest law firm that investigates and prosecutes government abuse and corruption, called on former President George Herbert Walker Bush to resign immediately from the Carlyle Group, a private investment firm, while his son President George W. Bush is in office. Today's *New York Times* reported that the elder Bush is an 'ambassador' for the $12 billion private investment firm and last year traveled to the Middle East on its behalf. The former president also helped the firm in South Korea.

The *New York Times* reported that as compensation, the elder Bush is allowed to buy a stake in the Carlyle Group's investments, which include ownership in at least 164 companies throughout the world (thereby by giving the current president an indirect benefit). James Baker, the former Secretary of State who served as President George W. Bush's point man in Florida's election dispute, is a partner in the firm. The firm also gave George W. Bush help in the early 1990s when it placed him on one of its subsidiary's board of directors.

"This is simply inappropriate. Former President Bush should immediately resign from the Carlyle Group because it is an obvious conflict of interest. Any foreign government or foreign investor trying to curry favor with the current Bush administration is sure to throw business to the Carlyle Group. And with the former President Bush promoting the firm's investments abroad, foreign nationals could understandably confuse the Carlyle Group's interests with the interests of the United States government," stated Larry Klayman, Judicial Watch Chairman and General Counsel.

"Questions are now bound to be raised if the recent Bush administration change in policy towards Iraq has the fingerprints of the Carlyle Group, which is trying to gain investments from other Arab countries who would presumably benefit from the new policy," stated Judicial Watch President Tom Fitton.

Judicial Watch noted that "even the Clinton administration called on the Rodham brothers to stop their business dealings in [the former Soviet Republic of] Georgia because those dealings started to destabilize that country."

Since the WTC attacks, the *Wall Street Journal* has reported (September 28, 2001) that, "George H. W. Bush, the father of President Bush, works for the bin Laden family business in Saudi Arabia through the Carlyle Group, an international consulting firm." The senior Bush had met with the bin Laden family at least twice in the last three years (1998 and 2000) as a representative of Carlyle, seeking to expand business dealings with one of the wealthiest Saudi families, which, some experts argue, has never fully severed its ties with black sheep Osama in spite of current reports in a mainstream press that is afraid of offending the current administration.

The *Nation,* on March 27, 2000 — in a story co-authored by David Corn and Paul Lashma — wrote, "In January former President George Bush and former British Prime Minister John Major paid a social call on Saudi Arabian Crown Prince Abdullah ...." This story confirms at least one meeting between the elder Bush and Saudi leaders, including the bin Ladens. That the bin Ladens attended this meeting was confirmed in a subsequent September 27, 2001, *Wall Street Journal* (WSJ) story. The January 2000 meeting with the bin Ladens was also later confirmed by Bush (the elder's) Chief of Staff Jean Becker, only after the WSJ presented her with a thank-you note sent by Bush to the bin Ladens after that meeting.

James Baker visited the bin Ladens in 1998 and 1999 with [then] Carlyle CEO Frank Carlucci.

The WSJ story went on to note, "A Carlyle executive said that the bin Laden family committed $2 million through a London investment arm in 1995 in Carlyle Partners II Fund, which raised $1.3 billion overall. The fund has purchased several aerospace companies among 29 deals. So far, the family has received $1.3 million back in completed investments and should ultimately realize a 40 percent annualized rate of return, the Carlyle executive said.

"But a foreign financier with ties to the bin Laden family says the family's overall investment with Carlyle is considerably larger ...." In other words, Osama bin Laden's attacks on the WTC and Pentagon, with the resulting massive increase in the US defense budget, have just made his family a great big pile of money.

More Bush connections appear in relation to the bin Ladens. The *WSJ* story also notes, "During the past several years, the [bin Laden] family's close ties to the Saudi royal family prompted executives and staff from closely held New York publisher Forbes, Inc. to make two trips to the family headquarters, according to Forbes Chairman Caspar Weinberger, a former US Secretary of Defense in the Reagan administration. 'We would call on them to get their view of the country and what would be of interest to investors.'"

President G. H. W. Bush pardoned Weinberger for his criminal conduct in the Iran-Contra scandal in 1989.

Our current President, George W. Bush, has also had — at minimum — indirect dealings with both Carlyle and the bin Ladens. In 1976 his firm Arbusto Energy was funded with $50,000 from Texas investment banker James R. Bath, who was also the US investment counselor for the bin Laden family. In his watershed 1992 book, *The Mafia, the CIA and George Bush,* award-winning Texas investigative journalist Pete Brewton dug deeply into Bath's background, revealing connections with the CIA and major fraudulent activities connected with the Savings & Loan scandal that took $500 billion out of the pockets of American taxpayers. A long-time friend of George W. Bush, Bath was connected to a number of covert financing operations in the Iran-Contra scandal, which also linked to bin Laden friend Adnan Khashoggi. One of the richest men in the world, Khashoggi was the arms merchant at the center of the whole Iran-Contra scandal. Khashoggi, whose connections to the bin Ladens is more than superficial, got his first business break by acting as middleman for a large truck purchase by Osama bin Laden's older brother, Salem.

Another key player in the Bush administration, Deputy Secretary of Defense Richard Armitage, left his post as an assistant secretary of defense in the Reagan administration after a series of scandals connected to CIA operatives Ed Wilson, Ted Shackley, Richard Secord, and Tom Clines placed him at the brink of criminal indictment and jail. Shackley and Secord are veterans of Vietnam operations and have long been linked to opium/heroin smuggling. The Armitage scandals all focused on the illegal provision of weapons and war materiel to potential or actual enemies of the US and to the Contras in Central America.

Armitage, [allegedly] a former Navy SEAL who reportedly enjoyed combat missions and killing during covert operations in Laos during the Vietnam War, has never been far from the Bush family's side. Throughout his career, both in and out of government, he has been perpetually connected to CIA drug smuggling operations. Secretary of State Colin Powell, in a 1995 Washington Post story, called Armitage, "my white son." In 1990, then President Bush dispatched Armitage to Russia to aid in its "transition" to capitalism. Armitage's Russian work for Bush has been frequently connected to the explosion of drug trafficking under the Russian Mafias who became virtual rulers of the nation afterwards. In the early 1990s Armitage had extensive involvement in Albania at the same time that the Albanian ally, Kosovo Liberation Army, was coming to power and consolidating its grip, according to the *Christian Science Monitor*, on 70 percent of the heroin entering Western Europe.[23]

Armitage and Carlucci are both board members of the influential Washington think-tank, the Middle East Policy Council. [This is the same Middle East Policy Council that receives funding from the bin Laden family.]

According to a 2000 story from *Harper's Magazine*, in 1990 our current president had additional connections to the bin Laden family through a position as a corporate director of Caterair, owned by the

Carlyle Group — at a time when the bin Ladens were invested in Carlyle. On March 1, 1995, when George W. Bush was Texas governor and a senior trustee of the University of Texas, its endowment voted to place $10 million in investments with the Carlyle Group. As to how much of that money went to the bin Ladens, we can only guess. But we do know that there is a long tradition in the Bush family of giving money to those who kill Americans.[24]

In January 2000 it was announced that Louis Gerstner, outgoing IBM chairman, had replaced Frank Carlucci as chairman of the Carlyle Group.

Bin Laden special services

Paul Thompson's timeline reveals what may be long-standing covert relationships between the bin Ladens and the Bushes.

Covert operations

October 1980: Salem bin Laden, Osama's eldest brother, is later described by a French secret intelligence report as one of the two closest friends of Saudi Arabia's King Fahd. As such, he often performs important missions for Saudi Arabia. The French report speculates that he is somehow involved in secret Paris meetings between US and Iranian emissaries this month. Frontline, which published the French report, notes that such meetings have never been confirmed. Rumors of these meetings have been called the "October Surprise" and some have speculated Bush Sr. negotiated in these meetings a delay of the release of the US hostages in Iran, thus helping Reagan and Bush win the presidency. All of this is highly speculative, but if the French report is correct, it points to a long-standing connection of highly illegal behavior between the Bush and bin Laden families. [PBS Frontline, 2001][25]

Salem, the same bin Laden who was to turn over US control of US bin Laden family finances to George W.'s friend and Air National Guard squadron-mate, James Bath, in the early 1980s, also turns up again in Iran-Contra.

Mid-1980s: It is later suggested that Salem bin Laden, Osama's eldest brother, is involved in the Iran-Contra affair. The *New Yorker* reports, "During the nineteen-eighties, when the Reagan administration secretly arranged for an estimated thirty-four million dollars to be funneled through Saudi Arabia to the Contras, in Nicaragua, Salem bin Laden aided in this cause, according to French intelligence." *New Yorker* is obviously quoting the same French report posted by Frontline (see October, 1980). [*New Yorker*, 11/5/01; Frontline, 2001][26]

George W.'s wallet

Several bin Ladens turn up in the business life of President George W. Bush.

> **1988:** Prior to this year, George Bush Jr. is a failed oil man. Three times friends and investors have bailed him out to keep him from going bankrupt. But in this year, the same year his father becomes president, some Saudis buy a portion of his small company, Harken, which has never worked outside of Texas. Later in the year, Harken wins a contract in the Persian Gulf and starts doing well financially. These transactions seem so suspicious that even the *Wall Street Journal* in 1991 states it "raises the question of ... an effort to cozy up to a presidential son." Two major investors into Bush's company during this time are Salem bin Laden, Osama bin Laden's father, and Khaled bin Mahfouz. [*Salon*, 11/19/01; *Intelligence Newsletter*, 3/2/00][27]

We could devote a whole chapter to Harken Energy. As the corporate scandals of 2002 rocked the American financial landscape, a number of stories surfaced showing that George W. Bush had knowingly participated in a huge "pump and dump" scheme with Harken stock just before its collapse in 1991. Apart from its smaller scale, this is strikingly similar to the Enron debacle of a decade later. But in light of the fact that none of the evidence that surfaced in 2002 (including SEC records and statements) had even the slightest impact on the course of American history or the election of 2002, I see no point in delving deeper into that episode here. Harken energy is just another little piece that fits nicely into the broader landscape of that map.

Kosovo and the Balkans

Osama bin Laden's connections to, and service for, the CIA did not end when the Russians departed Afghanistan prior to the collapse of the Soviet Union. In fact, a compelling trail of evidence shows that the US has maintained continuous ties to al Qaeda, bin Laden, and other Islamic terror organizations to this day. Much of this evidence is found in the recent history of the Balkans, especially in the robust American involvement with the Kosovo Liberation Army.

Since 9/11 few have accomplished as much as Professor Michel Chossudovsky of the University of Ottawa in exposing the deceitfulness of US government statements about Osama bin Laden. In 1998 the United States openly sided with the Kosovo Liberation Army (KLA), then responsible for 70 percent of the heroin smuggled into Western Europe, in a war against another useful US-manufactured bogeyman, Slobodan Milosevic. And it is there, Chossudovsky tells us, that bin Laden footprints appear again. After examining 21 different source records — including US congressional records and reports by the Republican Party — he found direct links between Osama and the CIA:

The evidence amply confirms that the CIA never severed its ties to the "Islamic Militant Network." Since the end of the Cold War, these covert intelligence links have not only been maintained, they have become increasingly sophisticated.

New undercover initiatives financed by the Golden Crescent drug trade were set in motion in Central Asia, the Caucasus, and the Balkans. Pakistan's military and intelligence apparatus (controlled by the CIA) essentially "served as a catalyst for the disintegration of the Soviet Union and the emergence of six new Muslim republics in Central Asia..."

The same pattern was used in the Balkans to arm and equip the Mujahideen fighting in the ranks of the Bosnian Muslim army against the Armed Forces of the Yugoslav Federation. Throughout the 1990s, the Pakistan Inter Services Intelligence (ISI) was used by the CIA as a go-between — to channel weapons and Mujahideen mercenaries to the Bosnian Muslim Army in the civil war in Yugoslavia. According to a report of the London based International Media Corporation: "Reliable sources report that the United States is now [1994] actively participating in the arming and training of the Muslim forces of Bosnia-Herzegovina in direct contravention of the United Nations accords."[28]

Chossudovsky next draws the handcuffs tighter around the wrists of both bin Laden and the CIA:

> During September and October [1994], there has been a stream of "Afghan" Mujahideen ...covertly landed in Ploce, Croatia .... Confirmed by British military sources, the task of arming and training of the KLA had been entrusted in 1998 to the US Defence Intelligence Agency (DIA) and Britain's secret intelligence service MI6 .... Bin Laden had visited Albania himself .... It is important to note that the KLA was basically an Albanian ethnic Army and that it has been documented that Albanian organized crime elements are both powerful and well respected in the region, even by their Italian counterparts. Also, remember that it was heroin grown in Afghanistan that was passing through the KLA's hands that was funding a great many Islamic terrorist organizations all over Europe and Asia.[29]

Chossudovsky documented that some of bin Laden's most trusted operatives even participated in the fighting. "Another link to bin Laden is the fact that the brother of a leader in an Egyptian jihad organization and also a military commander of Osama bin Laden, was leading an elite KLA unit during the Kosovo conflict."[30]

Further corroboration came in a May 1999 story in the *Washington Times*. Citing intelligence reports presumably obtained from US agencies, reporter Jerry Seper wrote:

> The intelligence reports document what is described as a "link" between bin Laden, the fugitive Saudi including a common staging area in Tropoje, Albania, a center for Islamic terrorists. The reports said bin Laden's organization, known as al Qaeda, has both trained and financially supported the KLA ....
>
> *Jane's International Defense Review,* a highly respected British Journal, reported in February that documents found last year on the body of a KLA member showed that he had escorted several volunteers into Kosovo, including more than a dozen Saudi Arabians.[31]

It is important to remember that the NATO commander in charge of all operations in the region was 2003-2004 Democratic presidential hopeful Wesley Clark at a time when NATO was supporting the KLA.

Chechnya

One 9/11 researcher drew compelling links between Osama bin Laden and Chechnya, where Muslim separatists remain a formidable thorn in the side of Russian President Vladimir Putin:

> In his 28 September interview [with a pro-Taliban newspaper], bin Laden is quoted as follows: "I can go from Indonesia to Algeria, Kabul to Chechnya, Bosnia to Sudan, and Burma to Kashmir," he said. "This is not a question of my survival. This is the question of the survival of jihad (holy war)."
>
> "Wherever required, I will be there."
>
> This amounts to a confession that bin Laden has been involved with the very terrorists that the US has sponsored, for example in Chechnya, Bosnia, Macedonia, Algeria, and Indonesia, and also with the KLA whom the US government has sponsored in attacking Serbia.[32]

Chossudovsky again expanded on and illuminated the secret and mutually beneficial relationship between Osama bin Laden and the CIA:

> With regard to Chechnya, the main rebel leaders Shamil Basayev and Al Khattab were trained and indoctrinated in CIA sponsored camps in Afghanistan and Pakistan. According to Yossef Bodansky, director of the US Congress's Task Force on Terrorism and Unconventional Warfare, the war in Chechnya had been planned during a secret summit of Hezbollah International held in 1996 in Mogadishu, Somalia.

The summit was attended by Osama bin Laden and high-ranking Iranian and Pakistani intelligence officers. In this regard, the involvement of Pakistan's ISI in Chechnya "goes far beyond supplying the Chechens with weapons and expertise: the ISI and its radical Islamic proxies are actually calling the shots in this war."

Russia's main pipeline route transits through Chechnya and Dagestan. Despite Washington's perfunctory condemnation of Islamic terrorism, the indirect beneficiaries of the Chechen war are the Anglo-American oil conglomerates which are vying for control over oil resources and pipeline corridors out of the Caspian Sea basin.

The two main Chechen rebel armies (respectively led by Commander Shamil Basayev and Emir Khattab) estimated at 35,000 strong were supported by Pakistan's ISI, which also played a key role in organizing and training the Chechen rebel army[emphasis added].[33]

On Her Majesty's Secret Service

Great Britain — one of the major players supporting the KLA in Kosovo — also maintained secret relationships with bin Laden and al Qaeda that served its interests. In 1996 Britain's exterior intelligence service, MI6, actually funded and worked with al Qaeda in a plot to assassinate and overthrow Libya's Muammar Qaddafy. Details of the relationship emerged after a British domestic intelligence (MI5) officer, David Shayler, went public with documents detailing the relationship between Britain and bin Laden.

In November, 2002 — and in the wake of 9/11 — as Shayler's trial brought the case to public attention, the British government invoked measures of the State Security Act to hide embarrassing information. The government's efforts even went so far as the issuance of a "D" notice by Prime Minister Tony Blair requiring that previously published news stories on the case be withdrawn and removed from public websites. A remaining story in Britain's *Observer* suggests the degree to which the British (and indeed, the US) government is exposed by the facts' emergence. It reported, "The Libyan al Qaeda cell included Anas al-Liby, who remains on the US government's most-wanted list with a reward of $25 million for his capture. He is wanted for his involvement in the African embassy bombings. Al-Liby was with bin Laden in Sudan before the latter returned to Afghanistan in 1996.

> Astonishingly, despite suspicions that he was a high-level al Qaeda operative, [Anas] al-Liby was given political asylum in Britain and lived in Manchester until May of 2000 when he eluded a police raid on his house and fled abroad. The raid discovered a 180-page al Qaeda "manual for jihad" containing instructions for terrorist attacks.[34]

Much of the information revealed by Shayler, who has reportedly been sentenced to six months for violating secrecy oaths, was confirmed by French authors Brisard and Dasquié, who noted in *Forbidden Truth* that the first real Interpol wanted notice for Osama bin Laden came not from the US but from another so-called terrorist leader, Muammar Qaddafy, in 1994. At the time, bin Laden was wanted for the murder of two German intelligence agents in Libya, and Qaddafy's actions suggested that he had found common ground with some Western governments on the issue of Saudi Arabia's most wanted son.

Since the attacks of 9/11 Libya has rarely been mentioned as a state sponsor of terrorism and has recently "cleaned up its act" as US oil companies have secured new Libyan contracts. Qaddafy, the terrorist *du jour* of the 1980s, is now respectable.

All this seemingly nonsensical behavior, rendering more incredible the now discredited US charges that Saddam Hussein was an ally of Osama bin Laden, is explained by information given to me by an influential investment banker shortly after the attacks of 9/11. That information indicated that Qaddafy had recently signed an oil lease with Texas oil magnates Nelson and Bunker Hunt, good friends of the Bush family.

Britain's dealings with Osama bin Laden have extended to allowing him to visit their country while he was a wanted man. As I noted in 1998, "the French Internet publication *Indigo* reported that bin Laden had been a London guest of British Intelligence as recently as 1996, and his treasurer recently defected to the Saudis as different factions shifted alliances for new campaigns in the Middle East. If Osama travels to London and has businesses in the Caymans and Geneva, how difficult can he be to find?"[35]

Unsurprisingly, a November 2002 UPI story by Arnaud de Borchgrave indicated not only that the Pakistani ISI had helped Osama bin Laden escape from Afghanistan but also that the American government had deliberately paid little attention to offers from an Afghan warlord to pinpoint and capture the alleged mastermind of 9/11. De Borchgrave reported that Deputy Secretary of Defense Paul Wolfowitz took down the name of the warlord — who had communicated directly with the reporter — and promised to look into the matter, and that nothing ever came of it. De Borchgrave became frustrated.

> Could it be that the intelligence community, already overburdened by
> the requirements of the coming war on Iraq and the war on terror, is
> not too interested in a 'we've got Osama alive' melodrama that might
> detract from the current 'get Hussein' priority objective?[36]

While de Borchgrave worried about terror attacks if bin Laden were captured, I chuckled at the thought of frightened officials in Washington worrying over the possibility that bin Laden might one day talk.

With this perspective it is possible to take a rational look at the actual state of affairs in Saudi Arabia in light of the controversy over the 28 censored pages of the

House-Senate 9/11 intelligence report that reportedly focus on it. George W. Bush refuses to declassify this section of the report while what are reported to be its contents are conveniently leaked throughout the mainstream American press. I tend to think that the 28 pages, as originally reported, have more to do with advance warnings of the attacks from foreign governments than they do with Saudi Arabia.

One must remember that Saudi Arabia is the ultimate prize in the war for oil. That's because, to paraphrase convicted bank robber Willie Horton, "It's where the oil is."

Excerpted and updated from the August 2002 issue of *From The Wilderness*:

Saudi Arabia: The Sarajevo of the 21st Century

- Is Iraq a Diversion from the Real Invasion or Will Bush Try to Occupy Both Countries at Once?
- A Saudi Sarajevo?

The global horrors of World War I ("the war to end all wars") began with the assassination of Archduke Francis Ferdinand in Sarajevo in 1914. The apocalyptic war of the 21st century may have begun with a $1 trillion lawsuit filed in the United States by 9/11 victims' families against Saudi Arabian banks and members of the Saudi royal family. In what may be the opening salvos of a financial and energy apocalypse, the *Financial Times* reported that wealthy Saudi investors had begun a run on their US banking deposits that may have taken as much as $200 billion out of US banks. These massive withdrawals — carved off of an estimated $750 billion total in Saudi US investments — occurred within days of the August 15 filing of the suit. Ironically, the principal attorneys in the suit are all political insiders; one of them is a member of the Council on Foreign Relations. You might think they would have thought of this beforehand.

There are two basic questions to ask about Saudi Arabia. Why was Saudi Arabia not a focus of US action and serious media attention in the immediate aftermath of September 11, even though there were so many obvious connections? And why is Saudi Arabia now so prominently a focus of what is apparently government-approved US animosity? One thing is obvious: the deployment of US military personnel in the region for the invasion of Iraq is also a convenient placement of resources for what may be a one-two punch to take over a tottering kingdom that owns 25 percent of all the oil on the planet at the same time that Saddam Hussein is removed from power in a country that controls another 11 percent. Together, the two countries — which appear not to have peaked in production capacity just yet, and which are the only two nations capable of an immediate increase in output — possess 36 percent of the world's known oil. [*FTW* became the first news service to report on the possibility of Saudi Arabia's having peaked in May 2003. This was more than a year before the possibility was raised in the *New York Times*.]

The Saudi situation is complicated by much of Saudi Arabia's wealth being invested in US financial markets; its sudden loss could devastate the US economy. But Bush brinksmanship — an understatement — is making possible a scenario where Saudis long loyal to the US markets cut off their own arm in a coyote-like effort to free themselves from a trap that threatens the stability both of their kingdom and of the global economy.

Osama bin Laden is a Saudi. Fifteen of the 9/11 hijackers [according to their passports] were Saudi. There has been an obvious and clear financial trail showing Saudi support for al Qaeda. In fact, as has recently been noted by French author and former intelligence officer Jean-Charles Brisard in his *Forbidden Truth*, the financial support network of al Qaeda is a virtual cut-and-paste reincarnation of BCCI, a Pakistani bank known for terrorist, drug, and CIA connections in the 1980s. One of BCCI's former executives, Khaled bin Mahfouz, remains the banker for the Saudi royal family today.

After months of strenuous and repeated assertions by the Bush administration that Saudi Arabia was a key ally in the war on terror, that they were loyal and trusted partners in US-led efforts, someone has suddenly turned on the tap for anti-Saudi propaganda, and the mainstream media outlets are eating it up.

On June 20 [2002] the Jang group of newspapers in Dubai reported that al Qaeda networks were active in Saudi Arabia. This followed a June 18 announcement that a group linked to al Qaeda had been arrested inside the kingdom and charged with planning attacks on Saudi government installations.

On July 18 the BBC reported that Saudi Prince Nayef bin Sultan bin Fawwaz Al-Shaalan had been indicted by a Miami court on charges of having smuggled 1,980 kilos of cocaine on his private jet in 1999.

On July 28, Britain's *Observer* released a story that quickly spread around the world. It was headlined, "Britons left in jail amid fears that Saudi Arabia could fall to al Qaeda." The lead paragraphs read, "Saudi Arabia is teetering on the brink of collapse, fuelling Foreign Office fears of an extremist takeover of one of the West's key allies in the war on terror."

> Anti-government demonstrations have swept the desert
> kingdom in the past months in protest at the pro-American
> stance of the de facto ruler, Prince Abdullah.

At the same time, Whitehall officials are concerned that Abdullah could face a palace coup from elements within the royal family sympathetic to al Qaeda.

Saudi sources said the Pentagon had recently sponsored a secret conference to look at options if the royal family fell ....

Anti-Abdullah elements within the Saudi government are also thought to have colluded in a wave of bomb attacks on Western targets by Islamic terrorists.[37]

After finally mentioning the apparently unimportant subject of the headline — the fact that several Britons had been jailed on bootlegging charges — the story concluded with the statement that feuding between factions in the Saudi court was going to increase with the death of King Fahd who was unstable in a Swiss hospital.

The story ended by quoting Saudi dissident Dr. Saad al-Fagih who declared, *"There is now an undeclared war between the factions in the Saudi royal family."*

On the same day a lengthy essay on Saudi Arabia in the *Asia Times* by Ehsan Ahrari observed, "It is interesting to note that [Prince] Sultan is believed to be a preferred US candidate for the Saudi throne." Abdullah is the crown prince, not Sultan.

On July 29 *Stratfor*, an intelligence reporting and analysis service, reported that a feud was brewing between Saudi Arabia and neighboring Qatar over Qatar's willingness to openly support the US invasion of Iraq. Qatar is nearly sinking under the weight of predeployed military equipment and has a brand new state-of-the-art US Air Force Base.

On July 30 the suggestions that internecine warfare had erupted in Saudi Arabia were given credence by an *Agence France Presse* report describing the recent deaths of three Saudi princes in eight days. Prince Fahd bin Turki died of thirst in the desert on July 30. Prince Sultan bin Faisal died in a car crash on July 23, and Prince Ahmed bin Salman died the day before of a heart attack.

On August 1 the *World Tribune* reported that Saudi Arabia, which has been acquiring long-range ballistic missiles had also, according to reports confirmed by US officials, been attempting to acquire nuclear weapons from Pakistan — which has been well documented to have heavy concentrations of al Qaeda supporters within all parts of its government.

On that same day, Saudi dissident Dr. al-Fagih appeared on the Australian Broadcasting Corporation program *Lateline* and offered some startling revelations:

Prince Abdullah who is supposed to be the next in charge, the next King, would not accept to appoint Prince Sultan as Crown Prince, and Prince Sultan insists that he should be the next in line for Abdullah to be [king].

Al-Fagih predicted the imminent death of the ailing King Fahd and noted, "That's why probably the foreign office have [sic] expected some major thing happening in the next few weeks ....

"I mean, Prince Abdullah is in charge of the national guard, and Prince Sultan is in charge of the army, and either one will use his own force to fight the other to fight for power. Now they will use all elements of the population, of the society ..." [including a large portion of the population that supports al Qaeda and radical Islamic fundamentalism].

Al-Fagih said that there was a psychological barrier in the country because all information is so thoroughly controlled, and the regime maintains the appearance of complete control. Almost all Saudis dislike the corrupt regime for a multitude of differing reasons. But, said the medical doctor who once served with Osama bin Laden in the Afghan war against Soviet occupation, "Once this psychological barrier is broken, either by a dispute of the royal family, or by a financial collapse, you would expect a major act by the people against the regime."

Al-Fagih also noted that in general the dislike of the Saudi people for the US was intense because of its unremitting support of Israel and also because the US had maintained a military presence on Saudi soil long after the end of the Gulf War.

Just five days later on August 6, the *Washington Post* reported that a month earlier on July 10, a top Pentagon advisory group had received a briefing from Rand Corp. analyst Laurent Murawiec describing Saudi Arabia as an enemy of the US and threatening seizure of its oil fields and financial assets if it did not stop supporting terrorism. The Pentagon group that received the briefing, the Defense Policy Board, is headed by renowned hawk Richard Perle. [Perle resigned from the board in February 2004 amidst growing controversy over his hawkish views and personal financial relations with firms seeking government contracts.] Although high-level Bush administration figures like Colin Powell downplayed the briefing's significance, it received heavy-handed media play for several days. Subsequent reports stated that Vice President Dick Cheney's staff had "embraced" the report.

On August 7 Saudi Arabia made clear and unequivocal public pronouncements that it would not allow its soil to be used for an invasion of Iraq.

On August 14 Reuters reported that King Fahd, who had just been moved to Spain, was in failing health and possibly near death.

On August 15 amid massive daylong publicity, a 15-count, $1 trillion lawsuit was filed against various Saudi interests for liability in the 9/11 attacks. Included among the defendants were the Saudi Binladin Group of companies (previously connected through the Carlyle Group to Bush family finances), three Saudi princes, seven banks, eight Islamic foundations, a number of charities, and the government of Sudan.

The three Saudi princes are Turki Faisal al Saud, Prince Sultan bin Abdul Aziz (same as above), and Prince Mohamed al-Faisal.

This new suit eclipsed three earlier suits, largely ignored by the major media, filed by victim families charging various degrees of liability and/or complicity by the US government. The key lawyers in the case have a history of close affiliation with the Republican Party, the Bush family, and/or the Council on Foreign Relations. Media coverage of the suits continued through the weekend ending August 18.

What gives?

Following The Money

The instability in Saudi Arabia may well be just the end result of internal decay and rot. But the consequences and implications of Saudi Arabia's current crisis are deeper once one examines the financial threat that Saudi chaos might unleash.

Like that of the United States, the Saudi economy is in tatters, and like the US economy it needs only one thing to keep it afloat — cash. Saudi Arabia, for all of its wealth, actually began borrowing money to meet budget deficits and finance economic development in 1993.[38] It says something about the level of corruption that a nation with as much wealth and income as Saudi Arabia found its treasury running low. Yes, oil prices change things. But the implication is that the Saudi elites are lining their own pockets to the detriment of the long-term financial stability of their country — as happens in the United States, it seems.

The Saudi government rightly fears US military success in Iraq. A first inevitable consequence would be serious anti-American protests from the Saudi population. The second inevitable consequence would be an almost immediate increase in Iraqi oil production, [Iraq's out-of-control insurgency and the continuing sabotage of infrastructure have prevented this], generating a price reduction that might break the back of OPEC and dramatically reduce oil income. Seeing that the US economy is on the brink of collapse, the Bush administration, facing a potentially disastrous 2004 presidential election, must do whatever it takes to keep itself in power. For this administration, so predominantly populated by oil men (and woman), cheap oil is the obvious first choice; in other words, oil is not only the actual issue, it's also the one to which the public relations and electioneering skills of this particular regime gravitate in the face of electoral trouble. By focusing their policy efforts on the energy issue — while pursuing a profligate, oil-dependent, war-driven future — they are addressing exactly the right thing in the most wrong way possible. Without significant capital investment in any alternatives, oil remains king. Where the oil is, there will be war.

Saudi Arabia seems to have seen this coming for some time. In April 2002 the Saudi government announced that it was considering privatizing parts of Aramco, the Saudi national oil company, and selling off some of Aramco's operations to Exxon, BP-Amoco, Shell, and other major companies. Though little has been disclosed since the early announcements, this move would benefit the Saudis in two big ways. First, it would give Western companies an equity stake in the stability of the monarchy, making it difficult for the US to consider bombing or imposing embargos upon operations owned by Western companies. Secondly, it would generate large amounts of cash to offset declining economic growth, rising unemployment, and declining per capita income, according to *Stratfor* on April 29, 2002.

The oil-based standoff is mirrored by what is effectively a much more successful financial deterrent — the Saudis' ability to wreck the US financial markets should they see their situation become utterly desperate.

Owning the American Dream

It is impossible to quantify exactly the Saudi holdings in the US economy. But anecdotal evidence is compelling. The *New York Times* reported on August 11, "An adviser to the Saudi royal family made a telling point about Saudi elites. He said an estimated $600 billion to $700 billion in Saudi money was invested outside the kingdom, a vast majority of it in the United States or in United States-related investments." The BBC has estimated Saudi US investment at $750 billion.

Adnan Khashoggi, perhaps the best-known Saudi billionaire, controls his investments through Ultimate Holdings Ltd. and in Genesis Intermedia, which was reported to have been connected to suspicious stock trades around the time of the September 11 attacks. (No linkage has been made between these trades and the attacks themselves). The rest of his private US holdings are administered through his daughter's name from offices in Tampa, Florida, not far from where many of the hijackers received flight training at both private schools and US military installations.

Khashoggi is a longtime financial player, deeply connected to the Iran-Contra scandal of the 1980s and also to BCCI. But Khashoggi doesn't even make the Forbes list of the richest people in the world. One Saudi who does is Prince Alwaleed Bin Talal, who ranks as the fourth richest man on the planet with an estimated net worth of $21.5 billion (Alwaleed is also an investor in and reported client of the Carlyle Group).[39]

Some of Alwaleed's holdings and recent acquisitions include:

- The single largest sharehold in Citigroup, the teetering US financial giant, which is reported to have a derivatives bubble of more than $12 trillion and has reportedly sought recent emergency assistance from the Federal Reserve. Alwaleed's shareholding in Citigroup remains near the $10 billion mark. The BCCI scandal was not the last instance where the prohibited foreign ownership of US banks was an issue that touched Saudi interests. Prince Alwaleed's heavy stake in Citigroup was concealed from 1991 until recently by the Carlyle group, which, acting as a virtual cutout, disguised Alwaleed's heavy investment in the bank.[40]

- Alwaleed also owns, according to an August 9, 2002 story in the *Guardian*, three percent of the total shares of Newscorp (FOX), making him the second-largest shareholder behind Rupert Murdoch.

- Alwaleed's other significant holdings include Apple Computer, Priceline, the Four Seasons Hotels, Planet Hollywood, Saks, and Euro Disney.

- Alwaleed also sits on the Carlyle Group's board of directors.

- Alwaleed alone is in a position to pull the plug on the US economy. But, of course, he would cost himself billions to do it, and this is not a likely scenario because he has long been a pro-democratic US supporter.

This applies to the rest of Saudi-held assets in the US, just as surely as it applies to Alwaleed's. Taken as a whole, the dollar-denominated wealth of the Saudi royals is so large that its sudden withdrawal from the American economy would be devastating to America. And it would entail very serious financial losses for the Saudi investors, who would find themselves with a mountain of dollars whose value they had just decimated, backed by the full faith and credit of the tooth fairy. So the dreaded Saudi money-withdrawal is in nobody's near-term interest and it does not happen. It keeps right on not happening, and will presumably continue to not happen for a long time to come.

But this assumes, of course, that the Saudi monarchy remains a stable political entity; that the US economy does not implode under its own debt-load; that no major, protracted regional conflict occurs; and that the US therefore remains the most profitable place for Saudi investment. But if the US economy fails? If the Euro becomes stronger than the dollar?

The Bush administration's unilateral and illegal commitment to an Iraqi invasion brings all three essentials into question. The August 20 [2002] report from the *Financial Times* suggests that the Saudis are, at minimum, firing a clear warning shot across the bow of the USS *"Bush"*...[41]

Only two points of my analysis have proven incorrect. The now obvious guerilla war in Iraq and the deterioration of Iraqi oil infrastructure have prevented any real surge in Iraqi oil production. This fact alone would make Saudi Arabia and smaller swing producers in West Africa more important to US short-term needs. Second, King Fahd remains on life support in Spain. I can only conclude that his death will come at a time more convenient to US objectives, perhaps after the inauguration of a new president.

According to an investment banker in the author's acquaintance who is well versed in Middle Eastern and oil finance, two capital streams emerged in the prelude to the invasion of Iraq. One was a stream of Saudi capital being returned to that country from the US. The second was a stream of Saudi flight capital fleeing to the US, being sent by an elite group who expected to soon be living here in exile, after the fall of the monarchy and the partition of the country.

Peter Dale Scott, reaching the same conclusions earlier, wrote:

> The kingdom is now a key battlefield in the conflict between America and its allies and the forces of extremist Islam. It is a conflict that is now threatening to tear Saudi Arabia apart. Revolution is in the air.
>
> The Western community [in Saudi Arabia] is living in fear. It has become the target of a series of bomb attacks, carried out by al Qaeda-linked terrorists who want to drive all non-Muslims out of the Arabian Peninsula. But the terrified Westerners have received little help from the Saudi authorities.
>
> The US may hope that it can weaken royal support for anti-American protests by its war preparations in the Middle East, including the timely regrouping of US forces from Saudi Arabia to neighboring Qatar. Alternatively, it may have to use them.[42]

Additional entries from the Thompson timeline add the necessary pieces to confirm that the movements and activities of Osama bin Laden and his family are desired outcomes rather than effects of collective stupidity.

1996: FBI investigators are prevented from carrying out an investigation into two relatives of bin Laden. The FBI wanted to learn more about Abdullah bin Laden, "because of his relationship with the World Assembly of Muslim Youth [WAMY] — a suspected terrorist organization." Abdullah was the US director of WAMY and lived with his brother Omar in Falls Church, a town just outside Washington. The coding on the document, marked secret, indicate the case involved espionage, murder, and national security. WAMY has their offices at 5613 Leesburg Pike. Remarkably, four of the 9/11 hijackers later are listed as having lived at 5913 Leesburg Pike, at the same time the two bin Laden brothers were there. WAMY has not been put on a list of terrorist organizations in the US, but it has been banned in Pakistan. A high-placed intelligence official tells the *Guardian*: "there were always constraints on investigating the Saudis. There were particular investigations that were effectively killed." An unnamed US source says to the BBC, "There is a hidden agenda at the very highest levels of our government." [BBC Newsnight, 11/6/01; *Guardian*, 11/7/01]

July 12, 2001: Bin Laden supposedly meets with CIA agent Larry Mitchell in the Dubai hospital on this day, possibly others. Mitchell reportedly lives in Dubai as an Arab specialist under the cover of being a consular agent. The CIA and the Dubai hospital deny the story; *Le Figaro* and Radio France International stand by it. [*Le Figaro*, 10/31/01; Radio France International, 11/1/01] The *Guardian* claims that the two organizations that broke the story, Le Figaro and Radio France International, got their information from French intelligence, "which is keen to reveal the ambiguous role of the CIA, and to restrain Washington from extending the war to Iraq and elsewhere." The *Guardian* adds that during his stay bin Laden is also visited by a second CIA officer, "several members of his family and Saudi personalities," including Prince Turki al Faisal, then head of Saudi intelligence. [*Guardian*, 11/1/01] At the very least, doesn't this show bin Laden was never estranged from much of his family?

The story in *Le Figaro* caused a great international uproar, including fierce personal attacks on me for having publicized it. If true, it establishes that just two months before 9/11, one of the most wanted men on the planet was exchanging information — personally — with CIA personnel. In light of what has been revealed in this chapter, one thing can safely be stated with confidence: The historical context of the relations between the bin Ladens, the Bushes, and US economic interests certainly makes the *Le Figaro* stories plausible.

September 13–19, 2001: Members of bin Laden's family and important Saudis are flown out of the US. The *New York Times* explains, "The young members of the bin Laden clan were driven or flown under FBI supervision to a secret assembly point in Texas and then to Washington from where they left the country on a private charter plane when airports reopened three days after the attacks." If you read carefully, note they are flown to Texas and Washington before the national air ban is lifted — the fact of flights during this ban is now unfortunately widely called an urban legend. [*New York Times*, 9/30/01] There have been conflicting reports as to whether the FBI interviewed them before they left the country. Osama bin Laden's half brother Abdullah bin Laden stated that even a month later his only contact with the FBI was a brief phone call. [*Boston Globe*, 9/21/01; *New Yorker*, 11/5/01]

It turns out that the flights did occur, and according to former National Security aide Richard Clarke, in his testimony before the Kean Commission, the orders possibly came from "The White House."[43]

Paul Thompson's timeline adds more details of the special flights:

September 13, 2001: Confirmation that bin Ladens and Saudis did fly during the no-fly ban and left the country before they could be properly questioned comes from a *Tampa Tribune* article. A Lear jet takes off from Tampa, Florida, while a ban on all non-military flights in the US is still in effect. It carries a Saudi Arabian prince, the son of the Saudi defense minister, as well as the son of a Saudi army commander, and flies to Lexington, Kentucky, where the Saudis own racehorses. They then fly a private 747 out of the country. Multiple 747s with Arabic lettering on their sides are already there, suggesting another secret assembly point. Intriguingly, the Tampa flight left from a private Raytheon hangar. [*Tampa Tribune*, 10/5/01]

October 27, 2001: The bin Laden family divests from the Carlyle Group around this time, in light of public controversy surrounding the family after the 9/11 attacks. [*Washington Post*, 10/27/01]

October 14, 2001: The *Boston Herald* reports: "Three banks allegedly used by Osama bin Laden to distribute money to his global terrorism network have well-established ties to a prince in Saudi Arabia's royal family, several billionaire Saudi bankers, and the governments of Kuwait and Dubai. One of the banks, Al-Shamal Islamic Bank in the Sudan, was controlled directly by Osama bin Laden, according to a 1996 US State Department report." A regional expert states, "I think we underestimate bin Laden. He comes from the highest levels of Saudi society and he has supporters at all levels of Saudi Arabia." [*Boston Herald*, 10/14/01]

Two of the three banks referred to above are not included in President George W. Bush's crackdown on terrorist financing after the attacks. Both of the banks had played financing roles in W.'s Harken energy deals in the region.[44]

A final note on the unwillingness of the US government to take advantage of numerous opportunities to neutralize bin Laden: Apparently several of the offers came directly from the Taliban. The *Village Voice's* James Ridgeway wrote:

> [Niece of former CIA Director Richard Helms and Taliban Lobbyist Laila] Helms described one incident after another in which, she claimed, the Taliban agreed to give up bin Laden to the US, only to be rebuffed by the State Department. On one occasion, she said, the Taliban agreed to give the US coordinates for his campsite, leaving enough time so the Yanks could whack al Qaeda's leader with a missile before he moved. The proposal, she claims, was nixed.[45]

Before going to Pakistan let's revisit one of the most important quotes in *The Grand Chessboard* by Zbigniew Brzezinski:

> Two basic steps are thus required: first, to identify the geostrategically dynamic Eurasian states that have the power to cause a potentially important shift in the international distribution of power and to decipher the central external goals of their respective political elites and the likely consequences of their seeking to attain them; second, to formulate specific US policies to offset, co-opt, and/or control the above.[46]

As with Russia, the political elites in Saudi Arabia are either created or defined by American money and influence. As the US used the Mafia in Russia to destabilize and neutralize that country, so too it appears it has done in Saudi Arabia with al Qaeda. That country, with 25 percent of the oil on the planet, has only existed since 1931. What arguable overriding loyalty to their country exists for those Saudis whose billions depend upon the Empire? If the performance of the Russian oligarchs is any standard, then the malignant Iraq war and the increasingly serious stirrings of Islamic protest might lead to a collapse in Saudi Arabia within a year or two that would play right into America's hands. Then the biggest prize of all will have been safely secured before the world even understands what has happened. That prize will be secured whether the Bush regime endures in power or not because all the pieces are in place. The only delays as of this writing are the 2004 presidential election and the US military posture that has been seriously weakened as a result of massive Iraqi uprisings and the withdrawal of troops by many nations of the Bush coalition who no longer have the stomach for the carnage and the animosity created by US policy in occupied Iraq.

Skeptics will point to the fact that on April 29, 2003, the Pentagon announced that it was beginning to remove American military personnel and aircraft from Saudi Arabia to nearby bases in Qatar, Kuwait, and Dubai. They might assert that this shows that the US has no intention of military action against Saudi Arabia. I would contend, on the other hand, that if the kingdom becomes unstable, having military resources out of the country, but close enough to launch immediate attacks, is a way of protecting them from sabotage or attack if the anti-American sentiment felt by most of the Saudi populace is unleashed. That eventuality arrived in 2004 as the state department ordered an evacuation of Saudi Arabia, and bombs blew apart Saudi police facilities.

As for Osama bin Laden, he will not be caught or killed until two things happen: He has outlived his usefulness as an enemy at a time when the United States need no longer fear economic reprisals; and Israel has emerged as the de facto global manager of all economic interests in the Middle East. Neither is a certainty.

As Caesar might say, "It's the way things work."

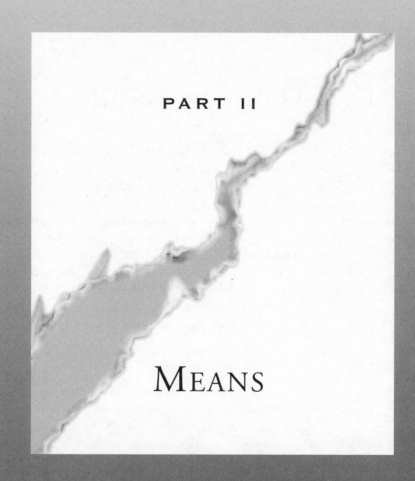

PART II

MEANS

CHAPTER

10

PROMIS: CONTROLLING THE DATA

A year before the attacks of 9/11 *FTW* completed a major investigation that had begun when I was contacted by two members of the Royal Canadian Mounted Police's National Security Staff. The focus of that investigation was on an almost mythical computer software program that was to later be a part of, and connected to, insider trading on 9/11; new US government programs peering into Americans' private lives; resource management; biological warfare, and also — as revealed by FOX news shortly after the attacks — in the hands of Osama bin Laden.

The following story appeared in the September, 2000 Special Edition of *From The Wilderness*, Vol. III, no. 7 — edited for length.

PROMIS
By
Michael C. Ruppert

US journalist Mike Ruppert, a former Los Angeles police officer who now runs a website that seeks to expose CIA covert operations, said he met with RCMP investigator McDade on Aug. 3 in L.A. Ruppert said the RCMP officer was anxious to see documents he received three years ago from a shadowy Green Beret named Bill Tyre [sic] detailing the sale of rigged PROMIS software to Canada. — *The Toronto Star*, September 4, 2000.

Only the legends of Excalibur, the sword of invincible power, and the Holy Grail, the chalice from which Christ took his wine at the Last Supper begin to approach the mysterious aura that has evolved in the world of secret intelligence around a computer software program named PROMIS. Created in the 1970s by former National Security Agency (NSA) programmer and engineer Bill Hamilton, now President of Washington, DC's Inslaw Corporation, PROMIS (Prosecutor's Management Information System) crossed a threshold in the evolution of computer programming. Working from either huge mainframe computer systems or smaller networks powered by the progenitors of today's PCs, PROMIS, from its first "test drive" a quarter-century ago, was able to do one thing that no other program had ever been able to do. It was able to simultaneously read and integrate any number of different computer programs or databases simultaneously, regardless of the language in which the original programs had been written or the operating system or platforms on which that database was then currently installed. [Note: This applied only when PROMIS had actually been physically installed on computer systems.]

In the mid 1970s, at least as far as computer programs were concerned, the "universal translator" of *Star Trek* had become a reality. And the realm of *Star Trek* is exactly where most of the major media would have the general public place the PROMIS story in their worldviews. But given the fact that the government of Canada has just spent millions of dollars investigating whether or not a special version of PROMIS, equipped with a so-called "back door" has compromised its national security, one must concede that perhaps the myths surrounding PROMIS and what has happened to it need to be re-evaluated. Myths, by definition, cannot be solved, but facts can be understood and integrated. Only a very few people realize how big the PROMIS story really is.

It is difficult to relegate PROMIS to the world of myth and fantasy when so many tangible things, like the recently acknowledged RCMP investigation, make it real. Canadians are not known for being wildly emotional types given to sprees. And one must also include the previous findings of congressional oversight committees and no less than six obvious dead bodies ranging from investigative journalist Danny Casolaro in 1991, to a government employee named Alan Standorf, to British publisher and lifelong Israeli agent Robert Maxwell also in 1991, to retired Army CID investigator Bill McCoy in 1997, to a father and son named Abernathy in a small northern California town named Hercules. The fact that commercial versions of PROMIS are now available for sale directly from Inslaw belies the fact that some major papers and news organizations instantly and laughably use the epithet "conspiracy theorist" to stigmatize anyone who discusses it. Fear may be the major obstacle or ingredient in the myth surrounding modified and "enhanced" versions of PROMIS that keeps researchers from fully pursuing leads rising in its wake. I was validated in this theory on September 23rd in a conversation with *FTW* Contributing Editor Peter Dale Scott, PhD, a professor emeritus at UC Berkeley and noted author. Scott, upon hearing of the details of my involvement, frankly told me that PROMIS frightened him. Casolaro, who was found dead in a West Virginia motel room in 1991, had Scott's name (Scott is also a Canadian) in a list of people to contact about his PROMIS findings. He never got that far.

A close examination of the PROMIS saga actually leads to more than a dozen deaths that may well be why so many people avoid it. And many of those deaths share in common a pattern where, within 48 hours of death, bodies are cremated, residences are sanitized, and all files disappear. This was certainly the case with my friend Bill McCoy, a legendary retired army CID investigator who was also the principal investigator for Hamilton in his quest to recover what may be hundreds of millions in lost royalties and to reunite him with the evolved progeny of his brainchild. Those progeny now have names like SMART (Self Managing Artificial Reasoning Technology) and TECH. I will never forget hearing of McCoy's death and his immediate cremation.

In researching this story I found a starkly recurring theme. It appeared first in a recent statement I tape-recorded from probably one of the three best-informed open sources on the story in the world, William Tyree. I also came across the same theme, almost verbatim, in a research paper that I discovered while following leads from other sources.

The information from Tyree, recorded in a phone conversation on August 28, 2000 and the research work on "block-modeling" social research theory uncovered while researching other leads both describe the same unique position or vantage point from hypothetical and actual perspectives. Tyree described an actual physical point in space, further out than ever thought possible and now used by US satellites. This distance is made possible by PROMIS progeny so evolved that they make the original software look primitive. The social research, which included pioneering mathematical work — apparently facilitating the creation of artificial intelligence — postulated that a similar remote hypothetical position would eliminate randomness from all human activity. Everything would be visible in terms of measurable and predictable patterns — the ultimate big picture. Just one of the key websites where I found this information is located at <http://web.syr.edu/~bvmarten/socialnet.html>.

One of *FTW's* guiding principles is our incessant drive to separate that which is important from that which is merely true.

What would you do if you possessed software that could think, understand every major language in the world, that provided peepholes into everyone else's computer "dressing rooms," that could insert data into computers without people's knowledge, that could fill in blanks beyond human reasoning, and also predict what people would do — before they did it? You would probably use it wouldn't you? But PROMIS is not a virus. It has to be installed as a program on the computer systems that you want to penetrate. Being as uniquely powerful as it is, this is usually not a problem. Once its power and advantages are demonstrated, most corporations, banks, or nations are eager to be a part of the "exclusive" club that has it. And, as is becoming increasingly confirmed by sources connected to this story, especially in the worldwide banking system, not having PROMIS — by whatever name it is offered — can exclude you from participating in the ever more complex world of money transfers and money laundering. As an example, look at any of the symbols on the back of your ATM card. Picture your bank refusing to accept the software that made it possible to transfer funds from LA to St. Louis, or from St. Louis to Rome.

The other thing to remember is that where mathematics has proved that every human being on Earth is connected to every other by only six degrees of separation, in covert operations the number shrinks to around three. In the PROMIS story it often shrinks to two. It really is a small world.

The first rip-off

Reagan confidant and overseer for domestic affairs from 1981 to 1985, Ed Meese loved PROMIS software. According to lawsuits and appeals filed by Hamilton, as well as the records of congressional hearings, the FBI, and dozens of news stories, the legend of PROMIS began in 1981–82. After a series of demonstrations showing how well PROMIS could integrate the computers of dozens of US attorneys' offices around the country, the Department of Justice (DoJ) ordered an application of the software under a tightly controlled and limited license. From there, however, Meese, along with cronies D. Lowell Jensen and Earl Brian allegedly engaged in a conspiracy to steal the software, modify it to include a "trap door" that would allow those who knew of it to access the program in other computers, and then sell it overseas to foreign intelligence agencies. Hamilton began to smell a rat when agencies from other countries, like Canada, started asking him for support services in French when he had never made sales to Canada.

The PROMIS-managed data could be anything from financial records of banking institutions to compilations of various records used to track the movement of terrorists. That made the program a natural for Israel that, according to Hamilton and many other sources, was one of the first countries to acquire the bootlegged software from Meese and company. As voluminously described by Inslaw attorney, the late Elliot Richardson, the Israeli Mossad under the direction of Rafi Eitan, allegedly modified the software yet again and sold it throughout the Middle East. It was Eitan, the legendary Mossad captor of Adolph Eichmann, according to Hamilton, who had masqueraded as an Israeli prosecutor to enter Inslaw's DC offices years earlier and obtain a firsthand demonstration of what PROMIS could do.

Not too many Arab nations would trust a friendly Mossad agent selling computer programs. So the Mossad provided their modified PROMIS to flamboyant British publishing magnate Robert Maxwell, a World War II Jewish resistance fighter who had assumed the Anglo name and British citizenship after the war. It was Maxwell, capable of traveling the world and with enormous marketing resources, who became the sales agent for PROMIS and then sold it to, among others, the Canadian government. Maxwell drowned mysteriously in late 1991, not long after investigative reporter Danny Casolaro was "suicided" in West Virginia. Maxwell may not have been the only one to send PROMIS north.

In the meantime, after winning some successes, including a resounding congressional finding that he had been cheated, Bill Hamilton hit his own buzz saw in a series of moves by the Reagan and Bush Justice Departments and rigged court decisions intended to bankrupt him and force him out of business. He survived and fought on. In the meantime hundreds of millions of dollars in royalties and sales fees were going into the wrong pockets. And, as was later revealed from a number of directions, this initial tampering with the software was far from the only game in town. Both the CIA, through GE Aerospace in Herndon Virginia (GAO Contract #82F624620), the FBI, and elements of the NSA were tinkering with PROMIS, not just to modify it with a trap door, but to enhance it with artificial intelligence or AI. It's worth noting that GE Aerospace was subsequently purchased by Martin-Marietta that then merged to become Lockheed-Martin the largest defense and aerospace contractor in the world…

Confidential documents obtained by *FTW* indicate that much of the AI development was done at the Los Alamos National Laboratory and Sandia Labs using research from other US universities, including Harvard, Cal-Tech, and the University of California. And it was not just Reagan Republicans who got their hands on it either. As we'll see shortly, PROMIS came to life years *before* the election of Ronald Reagan. It was also, according to Bill Tyree, an essential element in the espionage conducted by Jonathan Pollard against not only the US government but the Washington embassies of many nations targeted by Israel's Mossad.

The Last Circle

For more than a year and half, members of the National Security Section of the Royal Canadian Mounted Police (RCMP) have been traveling through the US, often in the company of a savvy female homicide detective named Sue Todd from the small California town of Hercules. Even now questions linger as to what the Canadians were really after. But there is absolutely no question that while surreptitiously in the US the Mounties spent more time with author and investigative reporter Cheri Seymour than with anyone else. And for good reason.

Seymour, under the pen name of Carol Marshall is the author of a meticulously researched e-book entitled *The Last Circle*, available at <www.lycaeum.org/books/books/last_circle/>.

Our fact-checker at *FTW* has found the book to be meticulously researched and documented, an opinion shared by Bill Hamilton and the RCMP, who have also told me of its precision.

I first met Cheri in person this spring after she had contacted me via the Internet. I traveled to her home, some three hours outside of Los Angeles and viewed acres of documentation for a saga that started with drug-related murders and police corruption around methamphetamine production in northern California in the 1980s. That investigation later connected to politicians like Tony Coelho and major corporations like MCA and eventually led to a shadowy scientist named Michael Riconosciuto. Familiar names like Ted Gunderson and relatively unknown names like Robert Booth Nichols weave throughout this detailed epic that takes us to the Cabazon Indian Reservation in the California Desert and into the deepest recesses of the 1980s Reagan/Bush security apparatus.

Gunderson, a retired FBI Special Agent in Charge (SAC) from Los Angeles, and Nichols, a mysterious Los Angeles man, exposed through court documents obtained by Seymour as being a career CIA operative, connected with scientist/ programmer Riconosciuto in a sinister, yet now very well-documented phase of PROMIS's development. In affidavits Riconosciuto claimed that one of the tasks he performed at the Cabazon reservation was to install a back door in the version of PROMIS that was sold to Canada. In August of this year the RCMP investigators told both Seymour and me that they had traveled to the reservation several times and had confirmed many details of Seymour's research. They had also interviewed Riconosciuto on more than one occasion. As with everyone else I have ever met who has spoken with him, both the Mounties and Seymour kept a reserved distance from him and always "counted their fingers after every handshake."

The Last Circle describes in detail how PROMIS software was modified by Riconosciuto to allegedly include the back door "eaves-dropping" capability but also enhanced with one form of AI and subsequently applied to the development of new weapons systems including "ethnospecific" biowarfare compounds capable of attacking specific races. Riconosciuto, now serving time in a federal prison in Pennsylvania has a cell a very short distance from fellow espionage inmates Edwin Wilson and Jonathan Pollard. While his tale is critical to understanding what has happened to PROMIS, the fact remains that Riconosciuto has been out of the loop and in legal trouble for eight years. He has been in a maximum-security prison for at least six. What was surprising was that in 1998 he contacted homicide detective Sue Todd in Hercules and told her that the murder of a father and son, execution style, was connected to the PROMIS story. One connection was obvious. Hercules is a "company town" connected to a weapons manufacturer described in Seymour's book that also connects to the Cabazon Indian Reservation.

The three Bills

I lived in Washington, DC from August 1994 until late October of 1995. It was during that time that I was a semi-regular visitor at the Fairfax, Virginia, home of Bill McCoy, a loveable 60-something giant, always adorned with a beret who complained ruthlessly about what had happened to the United States since "The Damned Yankee Army" had taken over. Writers were "scribblers." People who thought they knew something about covert operations without ever having seen one were "spooky-groupies." "Mac," as we called him, had his investigative fingers in almost everything, but he was most involved with PROMIS. McCoy was a retired chief warrant officer from the US Army's Criminal Investigation Division. He had broken some of the biggest cases in army history. It was Mac who first introduced me to both Bill Tyree and to Bill Hamilton in 1994. I recall scratching my head as I would be sitting at Mac's dinner table when a call would come in from Hamilton asking if there was any new information from Tyree. "Not yet," McCoy would answer, "I'll call as soon as I get something."

"How," I asked, "could a guy in a maximum security prison like Walpole State Penitentiary in Massachusetts be getting information of such quality that someone like Hamilton would be calling urgently to see what had come in?" "That," answered McCoy was the work of someone known only as "The Sergeant Major," and alternately as "His

Eminence" who fed the information to Tyree, who in turn fed it to McCoy, who then passed it on to Hamilton. Sometimes however, Tyree and Hamilton communicated directly. To this day the identity of the Sergeant Major remains a mystery and the puzzle piece most pursued by the RCMP when they visited me in August 2000.

It was also not by coincidence then that, in the same winter of 1994–95, McCoy revealed to me that he was using former Green Berets to conduct physical surveillance of the Washington, DC offices of Microsoft in connection with the PROMIS case. *FTW* has, within the last month, received information indicating that piracy of Microsoft products at the GE Aerospace Herndon facility were likely tied to larger objectives, possibly the total compromise of any Windows-based product. It is not by chance that most of the military and all of the intelligence agencies in the US now operate on UNIX or Macintosh systems.

In late 1996 Tyree mailed me a detailed set of diagrams and a lengthy narrative explaining the exact hows and whys of the murder of Danny Casolaro and an overall view of the PROMIS saga that is not only consistent with what is described by Seymour in *The Last Circle* but also provides many new details. Those documents, as later described to me by RCMP Investigator Sean McDade, proved to be "Awesome and right on the money."

The essence of those documents was that, not only had the Republicans under Meese exploited the software, but that the Democrats had also seen its potential and moved years earlier. Nowhere was this connection more clearly exposed than in understanding the relationship between three classmates from the US Naval Academy: Jimmy Carter, Stansfield Turner (Carter's CIA director), and billionaire banker and Presidential kingmaker (Carter's Annapolis roommate), Arkansas' Jackson Stephens. The Tyree diagrams laid out in detail how PROMIS, after improvement with AI, had allegedly been mated with the software of Jackson Stephens' firm Systematics (now Axciom). In the late 70s and early 80s, Systematics handled some 60–70 percent of all electronic banking transactions in the US. The goal, according to the diagrams that laid out (subsequently verified) relationships between Stephens, Worthen Bank, the Lippo Group, and the drug/intelligence bank BCCI, was to penetrate every banking system in the world. This "cabal" could then use PROMIS both to predict and to influence the movement of financial markets worldwide. Stephens, truly bipartisan in his approach to profits, has been a lifelong supporter of George Bush, and he was, at the same time, the source of the $3-million loan that rescued a faltering

Clinton Campaign in early 1992. There is a great photograph of Stephens with a younger George W. Bush in the excellent BCCI history, *False Profits*.

In the fall of 1997, Bill McCoy, having recently gone off his heart medication was found dead in his favorite chair. In the days and weeks before, he had been advised by Tyree that a Pakistani hit man, on an Israeli contract, had been in the states seeking to fulfill a hit on McCoy. There had been other hints that someone closer to McCoy might do the job. Tyree recently told *FTW* that just before his death, he had given McCoy information on Elbit flash memory chips, allegedly designed at Kir Yat-Gat south of Tel Aviv. The unique feature of the Elbit chips was that they worked on ambient electricity in a computer. In other words, they worked when the computer was turned off. When combined with another newly developed chip, the Petrie, which was capable of storing up to six months worth of key strokes, it was now possible to burst transmit all of a computer's activity in the middle of the night to a nearby receiver — say in a passing truck or even a low-flying SIGINT (Signals Intelligence) satellite. According to Tyree this was the methodology used by Jonathan Pollard and the Israeli Mossad to compromise many foreign embassies in Washington.

Within 48 hours of his death Bill McCoy had been cremated and in less than four days all of Mac's furniture, records, and personal belongings had been removed from his home by his son, a full colonel in the army. The house had been sanitized and repainted, and aside from the Zen garden in the back yard, there was no trace that McCoy had ever lived there.

Harvard and HUD
(Department of Housing and Urban Development)

Former Assistant Secretary of Housing, Catherine Austin Fitts has had about as much ink in *FTW* as anyone else.

One of the empires Fitts threatened was that of the Harvard Endowment. The Harvard Endowment is not really a benevolent university fund but an aggressive investment predator with $19 billion in assets, some from HUD-subsidized housing. Harvard also has a number of other investments in high-tech defense operations and had a big hand in investing George W. Bush's lackluster firm Harken Energy. "W" has a Harvard MBA. Fitts' chief nemesis at Harvard, Herbert "Pug" Winokur, head of Capricorn Investments, and member of the board of the Harvard Endowment is also a PhD mathematician from Harvard where the mathematical breakthroughs that gave rise to artificial intelligence using block-modeling research were discovered. In the 60s Winokur had done social science research for the Department of Defense on causes of inner city unrest in the wake of the 1967 Detroit riots.

The pioneering research at Harvard that allegedly gave rise to the artificial intelligence installed in PROMIS later moved north. According to a Harvard website, "Much of the effort of the Harvard group — no longer based solely at Harvard — was centered on the International Network for Social Network Analysis (INSNA) at Toronto..."[1] Things grew more suspicious as Fitts' research disclosed that Winokur, through Capricorn Investments, had a decisive role in the 1980s management of the intelligence/government outsourcing mega-firm DynCorp, of Reston, VA. Winokur served as DynCorp CEO from 1989 to 1997.

In juxtaposition, Harvard and HUD differ in one striking respect according to Fitts. The Harvard Endowment has enjoyed wildly uncharacteristic above-market tax-free returns for the last decade, (33 percent in 1999), while HUD, in the same year, was compelled to do a "manual adjustment" to reconcile a $59-billion shortfall between its accounts and the US Treasury account.

I was not surprised when Bill Hamilton confirmed to both Fitts and to me that Winokur's DynCorp had played a role in the evolution of PROMIS in the 1980s. One other surprise was to come out of Fitts's investigations that had months earlier led her to conclude that she was up against PROMIS-related interests. On the very day that DoJ and HUD shut her down she was discussing software development with a Canadian firm that is at the heart of the Canadian space program, Geomatics. The term Geomatics applies to a related group of sciences, all involving satellite imagery, used to develop geographic information systems, global positioning systems, and remote sensing from space that can actually determine the locations of natural resources such as oil, precious metals, and other commodities.

Apparently centered in Canada, the Geomatics industry offers consulting services throughout the world in English, German, Russian, French, Arabic, Spanish, and Chinese. Geomatics technology, launched aboard Canadian satellites via US, European, or Japanese boosters can help developing or industrialized nations inventory and manage all of their natural resources. There are also several Geomatics-related companies in the US including one not far from the Johnson Space center in Houston.

This situation is custom-made for enhanced PROMIS software with back-door technology. What better way to map and inventory all of the world's resources than by making each client nation pay for the work? By providing the client nation PROMIS-based software it would then be possible to compile a global database of every marketable natural resource. And it would not be necessary to even touch the resources because commodities and futures markets exist for all of them. An AI-enhanced, PROMIS-based program would then be the perfect setup to make billions of dollars in profits by watching and manipulating the world's political climate to trade in, let's say Tungsten futures. Such a worldwide database would be even more valuable if there were, for example, a sudden surge in the price of gold or platinum.

Bill Hamilton readily agreed that this was an ideal situation for the application of PROMIS technology. In furthering our research on Geomatics we discovered that almost everywhere Geomatics technology went we also found Lockheed-Martin.

Enter the Mounties

Thanks to a strong push in my direction from Cheri Seymour, the Mounties and Hercules PD Homicide Detective Sue Todd arrived at my door on August 3rd. They had already consumed most of the *FTW* website and were well familiar with my writings. I had let them know, through Cheri, that I did have information on PROMIS from Bill Tyree and that I would be happy to share it. Before getting into details we all went out for lunch at a nearby Chinese restaurant.

Over lunch the Mounties were quite candid about the fact that the RCMP had PROMIS software and that it even went by the name PROMIS. I think they may have also mentioned the name PIRS, which is an acknowledged system in the RCMP network. They stated that they had been given their version of PROMIS by the Canadian Security and Intelligence Service (CSIS).

CSIS was an intelligence breakaway from the Mounties in 1984, intended to be a pure [sic] intelligence agency. It was created largely with the expertise and assistance of the CIA. All of us understood two things about that arrangement, and we discussed them openly. First, there was a question as to whether or not any intelligence service created by the CIA could be completely loyal to its native country. Secondly, it was also understood that there was a rivalry between the two agencies similar to the one that existed between the FBI and the CIA, or in a larger context, the Clinton gang and the Bush gang in the US. The chief concern of the Mounties, clearly, was to ascertain whether or not their version of PROMIS was one that was compromised. McDade also described in detail how he knew that supposedly secure RCMP communications equipment had been compromised by the NSA. The Mounties acknowledged regular meetings with Cheri

Seymour but evinced none of the interest she said that they had previously shown in the Mossad. With me their single-minded focus was Bill Tyree and where and how he obtained his information.

Sue Todd, confirmed for me suspicions that there was an unspoken alliance between the RCMP investigators and the FBI. She said that during the course of her three years of efforts to solve the double murder in Hercules, she had routinely visited FBI offices and enjoyed access to FBI files relative to both the PROMIS investigation and anything connected to her victims. That information was obviously being shared with the Mounties, and that implied the blessings of the FBI. In short, a domestic law enforcement officer was sharing information with agents of a foreign government. In some cases that could provoke espionage charges, but in this case it was apparently sanctioned. The Hercules murder victims had no apparent connection to PROMIS software in any way except for the fact that Riconosciuto had possessed knowledge about the murders that he had provided to Todd from prison. The Hercules Armament Corporation, featured in *The Last Circle*, was an obvious link. I also noted that the father in Todd's case had been a computer engineer with passions for both geological research and hypnosis and no other visible connections to the PROMIS story.

As we copied Tyree's papers and went through other materials the next day, I was aware that the Canadians expressed special interest in Jackson Stephens and anything having to do with the manipulation of financial markets. They asked for copies of news reports I had showing that General Wesley Clark, the recently retired NATO commander, has just gone to work for Stephens, Inc. in Little Rock, Arkansas. (Undeclared Presidential candidate Wesley Clark maintains a relationship with Stephens and Axciom to this day.) I also provided documents showing that Stephens' financial firm Alltel, heir to Systematics, was moving heavily into the mortgage market. As the Mounties repeatedly pressed for information on the identity of the Sergeant Major I referred them to Tyree directly through his attorney Ray Kohlman and to Tyree's closest friend, the daughter of CIA bagman and paymaster Albert Carone, Dee Ferdinand.

McDade did eventually contact Ferdinand by phone, and shortly thereafter one of the most bizarre twists in the whole story took place.

About a week after meeting the Mounties I heard back from Sean that the Tyree documents and flow charts from 1996 had been right on the money. A special recurring theme in those documents that meshes with Seymour's research is the fact that modified versions of PROMIS software with both artificial intelligence and trap doors were being smuggled out of Los Alamos nuclear labs in containers labeled as radioactive waste. According to Tyree and other sources, after an Indian reservation, the safest place in the world that no one will ever break into is a nuclear waste dump. This also applies to containers in transit between countries. The radioactive warning label guarantees unmolested movement of virtually anything. PROMIS software is apparently no exception.

Bill Casey and Al Carone from the grave

Albert Vincent Carone has also been covered exhaustively in *FTW*, both in the newsletter and on the web site. A retired NYPD Detective, also a "made" member of the Genovese crime family, Carone spent his entire working career as a CIA operative. *FTW* has special reports on both Bill Tyree and Al Carone available from the web site. For more than 25 years before his mysterious death in 1990, Al Carone served as a bagman and liaison between George Bush, CIA Director Bill Casey, Oliver North, Richard Nixon and many other prominent figures including Robert Vesco, Manuel Noriega and Ferdinand Marcos. The Carone-Tyree connection, covered in detail in the Sept. 1998 issue (Vol. I, no. 7) goes back to operations in the mid 1970s when Tyree, serving with the Special Forces, engaged in CIA directed missions for which Carone was the paymaster.

Carone's death from "chemical toxicity of unknown etiology" in 1990 resulted in the sanitizing of all of his military and NYPD records as well as the theft and disappearance of nearly ten million dollars in bank accounts, insurance policies and investments. Virtually overnight, almost every record of Carone disappeared leaving his daughter and her family nearly bankrupt under the burden of tens of thousands of dollars in medical bills. In 1996, Carone's daughter, Dee Ferdinand, discovered that Tyree and Carone had known each other and that Tyree could prove instrumental in helping to restore Carone's lost fortune. Ferdinand filed suit in US district court this spring [Note: The suit has since been dismissed] seeking to recover pensions, insurance policies and benefits in a case which has no known connection to PROMIS. I have known Ferdinand and her family for more than seven years. Never once has she mentioned a connection between her father and PROMIS although she was well familiar with the case from Tyree and conversations with Bill Hamilton. I had referred the Mounties to her because of my belief that she could possibly help identify Tyree's source, the Sergeant Major.

On August 10th, exactly one week after the Mounties came to see me, the DoJ mailed Ferdinand a response to her suit seeking dismissal. Included in the paperwork was a bizarre document, now in *FTW's* possession, that, by the account of both Ferdinand and her lawyer, had absolutely nothing to do with her case. The document in question was a March 29, 1986 Declaration from CIA Director William Casey, a close friend of the Carone family. Paragraph 6 of that document (prepared for another case) stated, *"Two of the documents responsive to Plaintiffs' Request No 1, specifically the one-page letter dated 28 March 1979 and a one-page letter dated 8 January 1980, have been released in the same excised form as they were previously released by the Government of Canada. I independently and formally assert the state secrets privilege for the information excised from these two documents."*

Dee Ferdinand called me immediately. The letter had nothing to do with her suit. It mentioned Canada. Canada was not even mentioned in her suit. What was going on?" she asked. "It's blackmail," I answered. "CIA, which is monitoring everything the Canadians do, everything I do, everything you do, knows that I will tell the Mounties of these letters." McDade didn't grasp the concept at first. He was a straight-ahead street cop. But I had been through something similar when serving as the [L.A. County] press spokesman for the Perot Presidential campaign in 1992. I explained it to Sean, "Sean, you and I are just the messengers. But I guarantee that at some level of your government the CIA's reference to these letters will scare people to death. It is a reminder that CIA has them."

A week later McDade told me that the dates were indeed significant — very significant. That's all he would say…

Headlines

On August 25th the *Toronto Star* broke what was to become a series of stories by Valerie Lawson and Allan Thompson. The cat was out of the bag. Various figures known to have direct connections to Riconosciuto had been virtually dogging the Mounties' every move as they traveled in the US. One even contacted me just days after the Mounties left LA. It was a story that could not be kept under wraps forever. Most of the *Star* story was accurate. It was going to be difficult for the RCMP to move quietly now. A Reuters story the same day closed with the following paragraphs, *"Canada's national counterintelligence agency said in a June report that friendly nations were making concerted efforts to steal sensitive technology and information.*

"The Canadian Security Intelligence Service said outsiders were particularly interested in aerospace, biotechnology, chemicals, communications, information technology, mining and metallurgy, nuclear energy, oil and gas, and the environment." That was Geomatics, at the heart of Canada's space program, Canada's flagship space technology. I checked the *Star* story. There had been no mention of high

tech or space related issues. What did Reuters know? In mid September, after receiving confidential source documents related to the case telling me that one version of PROMIS, modified in Canada was handled through the Canadian firm I.P. Sharp, I got an answer. A quick search on the web revealed that Sharp, a well documented component of the case, had been bought by a Reuters company in the early 90s. Hamilton later told me that he had heard that Reuters possibly had the PROMIS software. That would explain how they knew about the aerospace connection.

Michael Dobbs of the *Washington Post* called and asked what I knew. I confirmed that I had met with the Mounties but didn't know much else other than giving them the Tyree flow charts. The *Post* was never going to tell the truth. Their business was keeping secrets, not revealing them. The Mounties had made waves.

On August 28 the phone rang and it was a collect call from Tyree. "Get a tape recorder and turn it on," he said. Over the course of the next half an hour Tyree, obviously reading from detailed and copious notes, named individuals and companies dealing with PROMIS software and its progeny. The tape was specific down to naming specific engineers in military and private corporations doing PROMIS research. Tyree described specific Congressional committees that had been infiltrated with "enhanced" PROMIS. Tyree described how PROMIS progeny, having inspired four new computer languages, had made possible the positioning of satellites so far out in space that they were untouchable. At the same time the progeny had improved video quality to the point where the same satellite could focus on a single human hair. The ultimate big picture.

PROMIS progeny had also evolved to the point where neural pads could be attached to plugs in the back of the human head and thought could be translated into electrical impulses that would be equally capable of flying a plane or wire transferring money. Names like Sandia, Cal-Tech, Micron, Tech University of Graz, Oded Leventer, and Massimo Grimaldi rolled from his lips as he tore through the pages of notes. Data, such as satellite reconnaissance, could also now be downloaded from a satellite directly into a human brain. The evolution of the artificial intelligence had progressed to a point where animal behavior and thought were being decoded. Mechanical humans were being tested. Animals were being controlled by computer.

Billy saved Canada for last.

"Here's how we fuck Canada," he started. He was laughing as he facetiously described what was coming as some sort of bizarre payback for the War of 1812. Then, placing the evolutions of PROMIS in context with the Canadian story Tyree asked a question as to why one would really now need to go to all the trouble of monitoring all of a foreign country's intelligence operations. "There's an easier way to get what I want," he said. "I access their banks. I access their banks and I know who does what and who's getting ready to do what," he said. He described how Canada had been provided with modified PROMIS software that Canada then modified, or thought they had modified, again to eliminate the trap door. That software, turned loose in the financial and scientific communities, then became Canada's means of believing that they were securing the trap door information from the entities to whom they provided *their* versions of PROMIS. But, unknown, to the Canadians the Elbit chips in the systems bypassed the trap doors and permitted the transmission of data when everyone thought the computers were turned off and secure. Tyree did not explain how the chips physically got into the Canadian computers.

"This," Tyree said "is how you cripple everything Canada does that you don't like. And if you want proof I offer you the fact that we toppled the government of Australia in 1980 [sic]." "[Prime Minister] Gough Whitlam and Nugan Hand [Bank]," I answered. Tyree affirmed. The Labor Government of Whitlam had been suddenly unseated after making nationalistic noise and questioning the role of US intelligence agencies in Australian affairs.

The issue of a coming feud between the dollar and the Euro came up. I suggested that rapidly vanishing support in South America and Europe both were threatening the military operations of "Plan Colombia" and the economic boost it would give the US economy. Tyree jumped in, "If I can put Canada in line and show the Eurodollar, the 'Eurotrash' what I have already done to my neighbor, whom I value to some degree — remember, these are not nice people — these are financial thugs at their worst. So what they are going to do is sit down discreetly and say, 'Look, this is what we did to Canada. Now, would you like us to do this to the European market as well?' Mike, they're not going to think twice about it. A weapon is only good if someone knows what its capability is. Prior to using the atomic bomb it was irrelevant." He continued, "They refer to it as the Nagasaki Syndrome."

…Then, chillingly, he described something familiar to any military strategist. The penetration and looting of HUD was the test bed, the proving ground, the "White Sands" of the PROMIS economic Atom bomb. Once the CIA and the economic powers-that-be had proven that, over a period of years, they could infiltrate and loot $59 billion dollars from HUD, they knew that they could do it anywhere. Said Tyree, "Then they knew they had what it took to go abroad and create mayhem. It was planned 20 years ago."

It took several days to reach Sean McDade who had been on vacation. I played the Tyree tape for him over an open phone line into RCMP headquarters. He asked me to make a physical copy right away and send it to him. After he had had time to listen to it he cautioned me against sending it anywhere else. I told him that as long as his investigation was active that I would do nothing more than make the standard copies I make of any sensitive documents as a precaution. I could tell that the tape had rattled him...

If keeping the tape quiet would give the Mounties an edge I would do it — but only as long as they had a case.

Sudden Death

Then it was over.

On September 16th the *Toronto Star* announced that the RCMP had suddenly closed its PROMIS investigation with the flat disclaimer that it did not have, and never did have, *any* version of Bill Hamilton's software. That was as shocking a statement as it was absurd. "The only way that you can identify PROMIS," said a perplexed Bill Hamilton, "is to compare the code. Sean McDade said that he was not an engineer and couldn't read code so how did he know?" Hamilton was as emphatic as I was that McDade had said that RCMP had PROMIS. So was Cheri Seymour. I offered a fleeting hope that the Mounties were playing a game, saying that they had terminated the investigation to shake some of the incessant probing that had been taking place around McDade's every move.

I was finally convinced when McDade e-mailed me and said that it was his view that the Mounties did not have *any* version of PROMIS and that he had no objections if I decided to write a story. I then agreed with Seymour that, whether they had said so or not, both the Mounties and Sue Todd had left enough visible footprints that it was their intention for us to go public. It might be the only protection they had...

Diplomacy

Just three days after the *Toronto Star* announced the abrupt termination of the RCMP investigation the Canada based International Network on Disarmament and Globalization (INDG) posted an electronic bulletin on a speech by former Canadian Ambassador to the US. In an address the night before, less than 48 hours after the termination of the RCMP investigation, Derek Burney, current president of CAE, a Canadian firm manufacturing flight simulators, criticized the US aerospace industry for being overly protectionist under the guise of national security. In addressing the Aerospace Industries Association of Canada, according to large stories that appeared in CP (Canadian Press) and Toronto's *Globe and Mail*, Burney was characterized as sounding unusually tough in his criticism of American policy that was freezing Canadian firms out of aerospace contracts. Both stories were ambivalent in that they alternately made Burney sound critical of the US while championing Canadian interests and at the same time weak as he noted that Mexico stood poised under NAFTA to replace Canada as the US's number one trading partner.

The CP story made two telling observations. It quoted Burney as saying that Canada needed to do more to "preserve and enhance its access to the American market." Then it closed it's story on Burney's speech, advocating a compromise agreement between the US and Canada, by saying that Burney's position "risks being perceived here at home as a sellout or worse."

A close examination of Burney's remarks, published in the INDG bulletin revealed something more like an obsequious surrender rather than a mere sellout. While there were a few tough-talking paragraphs that saved Canadian face, the essence of the speech was that Burney believed that American defense firms, the largest of which is Lockheed-Martin, were poised to transfer the bulk of their contracts to companies in Mexico. Citing Canada's dependence upon access to American avionics and "databases," Burney painted a picture that seemingly left Canada over a barrel. Without access to American technology the Canadian aerospace industry could not function.

Buried deep in the text of Burney's speech we found the following paragraph that is, we believe, the best place to end this story.

"That does not mean that we have to agree with everything Washington does or says or do things exactly as the Americans do. On the contrary, one of the advantages of being a good neighbor and close ally is that we can speak freely and forthrightly to the Americans - provided we have a solid case and are seeking to influence their position and not simply capture a quick headline. And, never forget, it is always more effective to be frank in private. Otherwise your motive can be somewhat suspect."

PROMIS postscripts

At 2:15 on the afternoon of November 10, 2000, I was called by Jan Belton, a Canadian accountant with many years of experience in the securities industry. He had read the previous story and he wanted me to know that I was right on the money. He had been one of the people interviewed on many occasions by the

Mounties during their investigation and he had been involved in its mysteries since the mid 1980s. Belton said that it was a given that PROMIS was used for a wide variety of purposes by intelligence agencies, including the real-time monitoring of stock transactions on all of the world's major financial markets.

He then confirmed for me that in April of 1991 Derek Burney, a close political ally of Canadian Prime Minister Brian Mulroney, received a personal briefing on PROMIS software. "Check it out," said Belton, "It's in [Israeli Mossad agent] Ari Ben-Menashe's book [*Profits of War*]." Ben-Menashe was one of Israel's top spies. In both congressional investigations and many reports, he was linked to the Iran-Contra scandal and the October Surprise in which Bush, Casey, and others, in order to win the 1980 presidential election, made a deal with the Iranian government not to release US hostages taken from the American embassy in Teheran until after Ronald Reagan had won the election. It was Ari Ben-Menashe, reportedly, who had tipped off the press to weapons shipments being handled by Oliver North which resulted in the breaking of the Iran-Contra scandal.[1] Belton stated that complaints had been filed with the RCMP from as far back as 1983 regarding both Robert Maxwell and Earl Brian who had actually sold the Mounties their doctored version of the software. Brian, a medical doctor who founded the company Hadron, had also been involved in shady dealings with firms connected to disease research, cytology (the study of cells), and biotechnology. This has significance in the post 9/11 world because, as we shall see, Hadron will turn up at the heart of secret US government operations involving biowarfare and vaccines.

PROMIS and whatever forms it has morphed into are incredibly powerful tools that can be used in any number of applications. It was not until a few months after the attacks of 9/11 that I even suspected that it might have been in the hands of Osama bin Laden.

FTW published the following story on November 16, 2001:[2]

Bin Laden's Magic Carpet: Secret US PROMIS Software
FBI/Justice Claims of Discontinued Use Leave Questions Unanswered
Britain and Germany in the Lurch?
Did bin Laden Use It To Break White House Codes
And Threaten Air Force One?

by

Michael C. Ruppert

FTW, October 26, 2001 — 1300 PDT (UPDATED November 16, 2001) — An October 16 FOX News report by correspondent Carl Cameron indicating that convicted spy, former FBI Agent Robert Hanssen, had provided a highly secret computer software program called PROMIS to Russian organized crime figures —who in turn reportedly sold it to Osama bin Laden — may signal a potential intelligence disaster for the United States. Admissions by the FBI and the Department of Justice in the FOX story that they have discontinued use of the software are most certainly a legal disaster for a government that has been engaged in a 16-year battle with the software's creator, William Hamilton, CEO of the Inslaw Corporation. Over those 16 years, in response to lawsuits filed by Hamilton charging that the government had stolen the software from Inslaw, the FBI, the CIA and the Department of Justice have denied, in court and under oath, ever using the software.

Bin Laden's reported possession of PROMIS software was clearly reported in a June 15, 2001 story by *Washington Times* reporter Jerry Seper. That story went unnoticed by the major media. In it Seper wrote, "The software delivered to the Russian handlers and later sent to bin Laden, according to sources, is believed to be an upgraded version of a program known as PROMIS — developed in the 1980s by a Washington firm, Inslaw, Inc., to give attorneys the ability to keep tabs on their caseloads. It would give bin Laden the ability to monitor US efforts to track him down, federal law-enforcement officials say. It also gives him access to databases on specific targets of his choosing and the ability to monitor electronic-banking transactions, easing money-laundering operations for himself or others, according to sources."

In a series of excellent stories by the Washington Times, and as confirmed by parts of the FOX broadcast, it appears that Hanssen, who was arrested in February, in order to escape the death penalty this summer, agreed to provide the FBI and other intelligence agencies with a full accounting of his sale of PROMIS overseas. Reports state that almost until the moment of his capture, Hanssen was charged with "repairing" and upgrading versions of the software used by Britain and Germany.

On October 17 two different spokespersons at the FBI's Office of Public Affairs told *FTW*, "The FBI has discontinued use of the PROMIS software." The spokespersons declined to give their names.

On October 24 Department of Justice spokesperson Loren Pfeifle declined to answer any questions about where, when, or how PROMIS had been used and would say only, "I can only confirm that the DoJ has discontinued use of the program ...."

"Numerous news stories, books and investigative reports including a September 2000 story in *FTW* (Vol. III, no.7), spanning nearly two decades, have established that PROMIS holds unique abilities to track terrorists. The software has also, according to numerous sources including Hamilton, been modified with artificial intelligence and developed in parallel for the world's banking systems to track money movements, stock trades and other financial dealings. Systematics — since purchased by Alltel — an Arkansas financial and technical firm headed by billionaire Jackson Stephens, has often been reported as the primary developer of PROMIS for financial intelligence use. Systematics through its various evolutions had been a primary supplier of software used in inter-bank and international money transfers for many years. Attorneys who have been connected to Systematics and PROMIS include Webster Hubbell, Hillary Clinton, and the late Vince Foster.

If true, and if claims by the FBI and the Department of Justice that they have "recently" discontinued the use of PROMIS are accurate, the likelihood than bin Laden may have compromised the systems the US government and its allies use to track him is high. Additional information in the FOX broadcast indicating that Britain stopped using the software just three months ago and that Germany stopped using the software just weeks ago are equally disturbing. These are mission-critical systems requiring years of development. What has replaced them? And even if the US government has replaced the software given to its allies with newer programs — several of which *FTW* knows to be in existence — the FOX report clearly implies that bin Laden and associates have had ample time to get highly secret intelligence data from both Britain and Germany. Those systems might, in turn, have compromised US systems. The WTC attacks had — by all reckoning — been in the works for years, and bin Laden would certainly have known that the US would be looking for him afterwards…"

"Approximately two weeks after the September 11 attacks on the World Trade Center and the Pentagon, the History Channel aired a documentary entitled "The History of Terrorism." In that documentary, a law enforcement officer described some of the methods used to track terrorist movements. He stated that "computers" were able to track such things as credit card purchases, entry and exits visas, telephone and utility usage etc. It was implied that these diverse database files could be integrated into one unified table. He gave an example that through the use of such a system it would be possible to determine that if a suspected terrorist entered the country and was going to hide out, that by monitoring the water and electrical consumption of all possible suspects in a given cell, it would be possible to determine where the terrorist was hiding out by seeing whose utility use increased. Conversely, it would be possible to determine if a terrorist was on the move if his utility consumption declined or his local shopping patterns were interrupted. Aren't those "club" cards from your supermarket handy?

This is but the barest glimpse of what PROMIS can do. Mated with artificial intelligence it is capable of analyzing not only an individual's, but also a community's entire life, in real time. It is also capable of issuing warnings when irregularities appear and of predicting future movements based upon past behavior.

In the financial arena PROMIS is even more formidable. Not only is it capable of predicting movements in financial markets and tracking trades in real time. It has been reported, on a number of occasions, to have been used, via the "back door" to enter secret bank accounts, including accounts in Switzerland and then remove the money in those accounts without being traced. Court documents filed in the various INSLAW trials include documentation of this ability as well as affidavits and declarations from Israeli intelligence officers and assets..."

"...A key question that lingered after the meetings with the RCMP was how many versions of the software had the CIA and the US government given out and might they not have been also using a back door against "friendly" nations for economic motives to give advantage to US companies. It was not a question that the RCMP dismissed as unlikely.

"In another mind-boggling development, on November 10 the *Calgary Sun* reported: 'US police said many of the suspected al Qaida terrorists were nabbed through the use of a state-of-the-art computer software program called PROMIS. The system interfaces with any database and can provide information on credit card, banking, pension, tax, criminal and immigration records. Police can input an alleged terrorist name or credit card and the software will provide details of the person's movements through purchases or phone records...

"The FOX story reported that Osama bin Laden once boasted that his youth 'knew the wrinkles of the world's financial markets like the back of their hands and that his money would never be frozen.' He may be right. And an administration so lost in covering up criminal conduct (no less than the conduct of the ones which preceded it) while trying to fight a war at the same time — might find itself doubly wounded by the software of Bill Hamilton and Inslaw."

And if you think that Bill Tyree's descriptions of the capabilities of enhanced PROMIS progeny are exaggerated then consider the following recent developments from official sources:

"At Wright-Patterson Air Force Base in Ohio, for example, the military's Alternative Control Technology Laboratory has experimented with systems that allow pilots to 'fly by thought.' By controlling their brain waves, human subjects at the laboratory can steer a flight simulator left or right, up or down, a skill that most people at the lab master in only an hour..."3

Caltech researchers have invented a "neurochip" that connects a network of living brain cells wired together to electrodes incorporated into a silicon chip. The neurochips were unveiled at the annual meeting of the Society for Neuroscience, held in New Orleans the week of October 25-30, 1997.4

11

VREELAND I

I'm sure you (and Mr. Taus) realize that the ideal "solution" for the dark forces is the gratuitous possibility that the target of discreditation, if subjected to the most personally embarrassing and socially reprehensible kind of (false) allegation, might self-destruct — thus reinforcing the concocted aura of suspicion and negating the necessity for further character assassination.

This is standard MO for the Agency's counter-intelligence operations and has become a blueprint for other Federal entities as a means of quieting the most threatening whistle-blowers. Lo be it if you have any kind of vulnerability (or skeleton in the closet)! This is particularly the case in matters of sex or moral turpitude. How many have been taken out by suicide, devastated mentally or emotionally and institutionalized, or sought some escape in drugs and alcohol? Lives destroyed in one way or another in the pursuit of truth — by false accusation.

Confirmed former CIA Agent Bradley Earl Ayers,
In a letter to the author — April 3, 2000

There is one man who spent a great deal of time and effort attempting to warn US and Canadian authorities of the attacks that occurred on September 11th, 2001. In spite of all the raging controversy that occurred around him, and around me for bringing him to light, there is one fact that cannot be denied. Both he and his Toronto attorneys Rocco Galati and Paul Slansky spent months in a well-documented, indisputable, and ultimately futile effort to prevent those attacks. That can be easily established. From the moment I made the fateful decision to get involved in his case, this fact — and this fact alone — is the only thing that I have ever considered important about it.

When one enters into the world of Delmart Edward Joseph Michael Vreeland one enters into a world where gravity seems to go up, and where red means go, and green means stop. It is not the *Twilight Zone*. It is a terribly real world, so unfamiliar and counterintuitive that most people can't tolerate information about it.

They tend to go temporarily numb, or they fend off the new information in a more aggressive way. This subject triggers people's defenses so easily because it carries threatening implications about what the United States has become, and about our place in this order of things, and about human nature.

Before proceeding it is necessary for you to meet some of the other people who live in this bizarre world. It is necessary because what is known about these men is documented, verifiable, and proven. Once you know a bit about them and their stories, Mike Vreeland will be just a little easier to take; his story just a little easier to understand. It is not necessary that you like these men. It is not necessary that you trust these men. What is necessary is that you accept that these men exist and that their stories are the interface between parallel universes, for the most part unseen in your life, but which determine much more of your reality than you are likely to suspect. Good or bad, these men have existed in the fault lines between the seemingly good and normal and the purely evil and deceptive. Almost all of them have been ground to dust for it.

Brad Ayers

It can never be asserted that Bradley Earl Ayers hasn't had anything to do with the Central Intelligence Agency. He has been interviewed by *60 Minutes*. He has testified before Congress, and he has been employed by the DEA as an expert covert operative and informant. A decorated army ranger, Ayers was seconded to the CIA's JM WAVE Miami station in the early 1960s, then run by one of the CIA's all time greatest spooks, Ted Shackley. Even Shackley himself acknowledged Ayers, a gifted writer, in his own very hard to find 1981 book, *The Third Option*. Shackley listed a 1976 book by Ayers (*The War That Never Was*) in his bibliography.[1]

During the Vietnam War a disillusioned Ayers, having completed his CIA missions, resigned his army commission and spoke out against the war but continued to serve as a contract operative for the government. During the 1980s, as a DEA asset, Ayers became heavily involved in investigations of CIA air operations in south Florida tied to the Contras that led him to personally recover cocaine residue from aircraft operating on CIA-sponsored programs. He has provided me with DEA and other law enforcement records demonstrating not only his disclosure of CIA drug connections but of the arrest and prosecution of a senior customs official in south Florida as a result of his work.

A man of honor, Ayers spoke out about the drugs and suffered the usual whistleblower punishments. Having committed no crimes of any kind and having few closet skeletons that could discredit him, Ayers was nonetheless subjected to 15 years of major harassments including burglaries, threats, intimidations, and interferences in his business life. What real events could not provide to destroy Ayers, innuendo and dirty tricks took care of.

In 1993 the US Marshals Service in Minneapolis issued a falsified caution notice with a photograph indicating that Ayers was possibly an armed and dangerous criminal suspect, apparently with the hopes that he would be shot. It nearly worked. At the time he was neither wanted, charged, or under investigation for anything except the fact that he was telling the truth.

I have lost contact with this eloquent and straightforward man who had taken to living quietly in the woods with his pets, apparently the only living things he can trust. Someday I would like to shake his hand.

Scott Barnes

If ever there was a prototype of the mold that created Delmart "Mike" Vreeland, it is Scott Barnes. In US covert operations throughout the 1980s and even into the presidential campaign of 1992 Scott Barnes turns up everywhere. Lacking the kind of background that might support him as Ayers was supported by a distinguished military record, Barnes was one of the ideal personalities for the dirtiest and ugliest secret missions — the kind the government can never afford to have exposed. There's a good reason why, and it has been best explained by authors Rodney Stich and T. Conan Russell in their expose of the BBRD&W affair that led to the CIA's takeover of ABC. It seems that Barnes was hired to assassinate Ronald Rewald, a financial player working for the CIA, who got a little too extravagant (a la Edwin Wilson below) and who wound up in jail in Hawaii.

> ... a CIA contract agent, Scott Barnes, had decided to visit Hawaii, for a break from his problems on the mainland. At the same time he could fulfill his latest assignment for the Agency.
>
> Barnes, the ultimate prototype contract agent because he could be so easily discredited by his checkered past, had become to a lesser degree a sensation on the mainland. This was primarily a result of his association with POW-MIA issues ....
>
> ... the disinformation specialists had been active. At the time of the collapse of BBRD&W, Gritz, Barnes, and others had been thoroughly trashed in a special edition of Soldier of Fortune Magazine .... [2]

In spite of prior criminal allegations, a serious trail of bad publicity, and a less than stable work record, Barnes was hired by the prison ministry where Rewald was being held without being fingerprinted, photographed, having a background check run, or being issued ID, and he was given direct access to the intended target. Barnes reportedly changed his mind about the hit but Hawaiian authorities, slightly suspicious, issued Barnes a subpoena that compromised the mission.[3] ABC News even reported that the CIA had hired Barnes to assassinate Rewald.[4]

Retired Army Special Forces Lt. Col. Bo Gritz, who had been involved with Barnes on an early POW search mission, did not have a high opinion of Barnes. Gritz wrote a rather disingenuous description of how Barnes became a part of one of his first POW missions.

ISA[5] had run a pre-launch security check and OK'd all but Barnes. They said he had been released from the army after the first few months for accusing the commanding general of Fort Lewis, Washington, of running drugs! Barnes, they said, had been a clerk in the post stockade. After leaving the army Barnes got a job as a reserve policeman in Southern California. During the prosecution of Hell's Angels in San Francisco, Barnes volunteered to say that he had planted dope on the Angels as an undercover biker .... I decided to send Barnes anyway.[6]

As we will see in the section on Gritz we have two men, demonstrably and unfairly discredited by the government, who also discredit each other. This is the surreal world of covert operations, and it is not a place for neophyte researchers whose thought processes are not yet adapted to the perversity of the intelligence business. They tend to get intellectually panicked, as I have seen many seasoned journalists do, when presented with contradictions of this kind. The only thing that works is patient, diligent research and a suspension of judgments based upon any one official document or published news report. The investigation of the men and women who surface in connection with covert operations is a painstaking, frustrating, groping-in-the-dark process that requires singular analytical skills and the ability to withhold any automatic acceptance of data that the normal world accepts instantly.

One woman who did a masterful job of walking these minefields with Barnes is Monika Jensen-Stevenson, a former Emmy Award-winning producer from CBS's *60 Minutes* and the author of *Kiss The Boys Goodbye*, one of the best books on covert operations I have ever read. Aside from being a nuts-and-bolts deconstruction of the US government's shameful abandonment of Vietnam-era POWs, it is also a blueprint of the ways in which the government neutralizes popular movements arising in response to government crimes that can no longer be hidden. I cannot recommend a better book for anyone trying to deal with the crimes of the US government connected to 9/11.

Jensen-Stevenson dealt extensively with Barnes. At her disposal she had the financial and research resources of CBS News plus a full-time assignment to find out what had happened to American servicemen left behind in Southeast Asia. It took her more than a year of full-time work. These were resources I was not to have when I decided to take on the case of Mike Vreeland. But with Vreeland, as it turns out, I was to have one advantage that she did not.

In *Kiss The Boys Goodbye*, Jensen-Stevenson concluded that Barnes had, in fact, been a US government operative. So, as she reported, had Texas billionaire Ross Perot who was deeply involved in POW rescue efforts. CBS News facilitated multiple polygraph examinations by the CIA's retired top polygraph examiner who was regarded as the best in the business. Barnes passed them all with flying colors. Later Barnes was submitted to videotaped questioning under heavy doses of "truth serum" by a psychiatrist and again passed with flying colors. Later, documents surfaced indicating that he had worked for the Defense Intelligence Agency (DIA), and it was confirmed that he had done undercover work, while these relationships existed, with the Hell's Angels.

Admirals, army officers, and intelligence operatives surfaced stating that Barnes was who he said he was and inside information he provided regularly proved accurate. He was questioned by congressional investigators looking into Iran-Contra, and he also testified before congress on POW issues. During the course of her investigations for *60 Minutes*, Jensen-Stevenson described how Barnes was nearly killed in a knife attack and how he had relayed details of the attack — before calling for medical assistance — to someone he thought he could trust. At the same time he was systematically trashed by the press, his name being blackened in media stories to the point where he could not find employment.

He always spoke to Jensen-Stevenson in strings of code words and jargon. He tape recorded almost everything he did, and after months of dealing with him and triple checking and verifying almost of all of his information, Monika described him thus:

> *What was worrisome was Barnes's ability to pick up so much detail. He reminded me of a certain kind of con artist. Perhaps his personality had seemed ideal for secret operations. He had a phenomenal memory to recreate reality. And he really believed what he said.*
>
> *Casino Man* [a code name for one of Jensen-Stevenson's military sources] *counterbalanced our skepticism by saying he had known Barnes in Vietnam. According to Casino Man, Barnes had worked with Command and Control North, the super-secret unconventional warfare group in Laos and North Vietnam. And Barnes himself talked knowingly about CCN.*[7]

I met Scott Barnes in 1992. In that fateful year I had served as the Los Angeles County press spokesman for the Perot presidential campaign. Though I was to be greatly disappointed by Perot's sudden withdrawal from the campaign (for reasons which I later concluded had to do with assuring a Clinton victory), I had been one of Perot's staunchest supporters. I was committed to serving the campaign of a man who had spoken out publicly about the CIA connection to drugs and the fate of the POWs. My non-stop dedication in the campaign resulted in a *People* magazine story about me in June of that year. It was only later that pieces fell together for me which suggested that Perot had led us all on a wild goose chase in a campaign that he had never intended to win.

At the time of Perot's abrupt withdrawal from the campaign in July — when he was ahead of both George Bush Sr. and Bill Clinton in the polls — it was widely reported that he had received information that his daughter was about to be "exposed" as a lesbian in a fabricated "smear." Other stories surfaced in the press that attempts had been, and were going to be, made on Perot's life.

Who was the person who took the information to Perot that ostensibly caused him to withdraw? It was none other than Scott Barnes. Perot himself vouched for many of Barnes's spook credentials as the American media went crazy.

After Perot's withdrawal I worked for a while with an experienced freelance journalist named Connie Benesch who had decided that she was going to write a book about what had really happened in the campaign. Barnes lived in the beach cities south of Los Angeles, and Connie and I drove down and had lunch with him.

Barnes was a fast talker, pleasant, decent looking and full of incredible tales, angles, and insights that came out faster than we could assimilate. At times empathetic, at times pathetic, at times not credible, and at times utterly convincing, Barnes let us have it for two hours. After the lunch was over, Connie, being the lead writer and financier of the book, was in an understandable sort of mental gridlock. So was I. There was no way to get to the bottom of Scott Barnes without the resources of CBS News, an unlimited budget, and the patience of Job.

Connie made the decision that most journalists make with people like Barnes, she decided not to "go there." Other less responsible journalists have in the past — and certainly since 9/11 — taken a worse approach: "destroy what you can't explain so that no one else can make you look bad later for not having done the work."

Gary Eitel

This decorated Vietnam helicopter pilot at one time flew courier missions for the CIA under orders. A skilled pilot in all types of aircraft, as well as a lawyer, Eitel is the man who single-handedly exposed the CIA's role in the C-130 Hercules scandal. He has been interviewed by *60 Minutes*, the US Congress, and as a whistleblower/attorney served as a federal prosecutor in the case. He was the principal source for my own reporting on the C-130 scandal.[8] After the Vietnam War, Eitel had been approached by a CIA officer named Branson in an attempt to recruit him for what Eitel quickly determined were illegal missions. Eitel refused. The CIA man told him, "We would have set you up and then burned you," Eitel recalls Branson saying. "And then we would have owned you for life." This is the way the CIA likes to work.

As a reward for his courageous efforts, Eitel was denied legal payment of monies due him as a result of the case and driven into bankruptcy. Because he had no criminal record and was a man of honor, a local smear campaign, including law enforcement threats and unwarranted actions against his family, was launched in an attempt to discredit and punish him. It resulted in a divorce and the loss of his home. Eitel remains a good friend and man for whom I have the greatest respect. A true survivor, he now travels the country in a motor home with two dogs.

John McCarthy

In 1967 US Army Special Forces Captain John McCarthy was detached to a secret CIA assassination team run out of Saigon known as Project Cherry. In 1968 he was framed and unjustly convicted in a secret trial for the assassination of a Cambodian double agent in what later evidence suggested was a "rogue" CIA operation intended to prolong the Vietnam War. In fact, within minutes of McCarthy's conviction, which suggested that the US had sabotaged and betrayed one of its own covert operations, the 1968 Tet offensive began.

Although it was later disclosed that the CIA, the army, and the government had withheld evidence that would have cleared McCarthy, his life has been plagued with the continuing reemergence of old and unfounded press stories at times when it was thought that he might be a threat. Even though the conviction was eventually set aside, McCarthy was subsequently denied employment as a police officer and in other careers.

Thirty-five years later, McCarthy is still pursuing legal remedies both to clear his name and to secure benefits to which he is entitled. Like Gary Eitel, John McCarthy is a man whose word I would take at face value any day, a warrior who has remained true to a warrior's code even as the rest of the world has forgotten the meaning of the word "honor."[9]

Terry Reed

Terry Reed was a fairly small-time player in the Iran-Contra scandal, but he was definitely involved. A pilot, air force veteran, and businessman, Reed became involved with Oliver North, Felix Rodriguez, Barry Seal, and several of the major players. His chief threat to the CIA and the American political establishment was that he could connect the Clintons, the CIA, Oliver North, Bill Casey, and drug-running through the Mena, Arkansas, Intermountain Airport all into one package.

Reed's fate was that both he and his wife were prosecuted and investigated for years on charges of insurance fraud in the alleged theft of their own airplane. This turned out to be connected to what is now a well-documented part of the Contra support operations run by Oliver North. These covert funding schemes involved widespread insurance "bust outs" and faked airplane thefts to provide airplanes, money, and supplies for an operation that Congress had prohibited. In several instances "friendly" insurance companies even participated in the schemes.[10] Reed fought back with the help of an honorable public defender named Marilyn Trubey and eventually beat all the criminal charges, but at great cost.

As Reed became a public figure toward the tail end of the Contra investigations, and as he decided to fight back against efforts to silence him, things got a bit stickier. His filing of a civil suit against the government that might have seriously hurt Bill Clinton right before the 1992 presidential election didn't help much either. On more than one occasion notices complete with photographs were placed in FBI computers stating that both he and his wife Janice were possibly armed and dangerous.[11]

To make matters worse, after putting his faith in *TIME* magazine and spending months with reporter Richard Behar, Reed's reputation and much of the truth of Iran-Contra were done away with as Reed was labeled a con man in 1992.

When *TIME* says it, your life is virtually over. I remember reading the story and wondering how any human being posing as a journalist could lie so obviously about many of the Iran-Contra truths that were even then well documented. Reed's book contains transcripts of tape-recorded interviews where Behar wore soft kid gloves with the likes of Oliver North and deliberately overlooked obvious leads and facts that Reed had documented beyond reproach.[12]

There is a disappointing endnote to the Reed affair. I have spoken to Reed several times and met with him in person here in Los Angeles. At that time he gave me some information about his relationship with the drug smuggler Barry Seal that investigative reporter Daniel Hopsicker and I later determined had been embellished by Reed. Reed even admitted the embellishment to Hopsicker later.

The truth is that while the government and the intelligence agencies can commit a million crimes, lie through their teeth, and still enjoy credibility, the slightest mistake by an otherwise innocent victim renders him "smelly." There are many portions of Reed's book that I, and others familiar with Iran-Contra, find implausible and difficult to accept. But much of what Reed said about Mena, the CIA, and Bill Clinton is dead-on accurate. It has been confirmed by other sources, other records, other court cases, and other investigations.

Bill Tyree

I have written extensively on the case of this former member of the US Army's 10th Special Forces Group. He was briefly mentioned in Chapter 8 on PROMIS software. Tyree has been incarcerated for 25 years on a life sentence for the murder of his wife who was also in the army and who had been documenting crimes at Fort Devens, Massachusetts, where both were based. The prosecution of the case was in itself unusual. The original trial judge, having reviewed a very weak prosecution case, dismissed all the charges, indicating clearly that the suspect was another member of the 10th Special Forces Group. However a young assistant D.A. from Middlesex County, Massachusetts, named John Kerry, reinstituted the prosecution under another judge.

Kerry is now, of course, the junior senator from Massachusetts and the Democratic Party presidential nominee in 2004.

Tyree's subsequent conviction could be described as falling well outside standard legal procedures in Massachusetts and, for 20 years, myriad attempts to challenge the conviction have been uniformly denied. Many of the evidentiary inconsistencies in the case were discussed in a 2000 episode of Bill Curtis's *Investigative Reports* titled "Murder at Fort Devens."

Another key aspect of Tyree's case was the now well-documented and systematic alteration of his military service records and continuing refusals to release official documents in the case. Many documents obtained by Tyree and his attorneys have been heavily redacted in the interests of national security.[13] *From The Wilderness* sells a comprehensive report on the Tyree case from its website containing many of these documents.

While Tyree has been consistently demonstrated to be a reliable source of information and someone in whom officials like members of the RCMP National Security Staff have expressed great interest, he has also proved himself capable of being deceptive and misleading. On more than one occasion I have found various pieces of information he provided to be self-serving and questionable. Like Barnes and Reed before him — and Mike Vreeland after him — Tyree demonstrated the ability to mix in "bullshit with the ice cream." Yet there remains no doubt that he has been severely victimized in a game that he himself chose to play.

Ed Wilson

In 1983 the trial of "former" CIA officer Ed Wilson was at a critical juncture. At the end of the trial Wilson's attorneys had made a good case that his activities in arming Moammar Qadaffy, the man who was then considered the world's number-one terrorist, had taken place at the direction of the CIA. The CIA, however, insisted that Wilson had stopped working for them in 1971. Wilson stood accused of shipping 42,000 pounds of the plastic explosive C-4 directly to Libyan dictator Qadaffy in 1977, and then hiring US experts — former US Army Green Berets — to teach Qaddafy's people how to make bombs shaped like lamps, ashtrays, and radios. Bombs were actually made, and foes of Qaddafy were actually murdered.

This was the ongoing crime that had made Wilson, and his still-missing (and believed dead) accomplice, former CIA employee Frank Terpil, the most infamous desperadoes in the world. C-4, according to some experts, was at the time the most powerful non-nuclear explosive made. Two pounds in the right places can bring down a jumbo jet. Hence, 42,000 pounds would be enough to bring down 21,000 jumbo jets. C-4 is highly prized on the world's black markets and is much in demand. It is supposedly very tightly controlled where it is manufactured: in the US.

At first the CIA hoped to kill the defense's well-documented argument of ongoing CIA relationships by having a CIA officer testifying under a pseudonym. But when it was learned that the trial judge would allow the witness to be cross-examined, the CIA took another tack. An affidavit prepared by the CIA's then Executive Director, Charles Briggs, stating that Wilson had had no official relationship with the Agency since 1971, was submitted under oath as a rebuttal document and given to the jury. Members of the jury later admitted that the affidavit had carried weight in their deliberations and subsequent guilty verdict. The problem was that the affidavit was itself an act of perjury.

In January of 2000, after reviewing more than 900 pages of newly submitted documents in the case and after assistance from Wilson's new lawyer David Adler — himself a former CIA case officer — *I was able to publish an internal CIA memorandum showing that the writer or writers of the affidavit had known it to be false* at the time the CIA presented it under penalty of perjury, and at the time when CIA General Counsel Stanley Sporkin affixed the CIA seal to it. The CIA internal memo indicated no less than "80 non-social contacts" between Wilson and the Agency after 1971, and some of those were very close in time to the Qadaffy deal. I published a copy of the relevant part of the affidavit in the January 2000 issue of *FTW*.[14] I did receive one letter from Wilson, then held at the maximum security Allenwood federal penitentiary, thanking me for my story, and that was it.

Ed Wilson's conviction was overturned in October of 2003. A probe of the DoJ officials involved with the perjurious memorandum was instituted in December, and the following February the DoJ announced that it would not retry Wilson on the charges.[15]

There are many other cases I am familiar with that I could include here to show that when it comes to criminal records, testimony, affidavits, official statements from prosecutors, or anything to do with the character of whistleblowers or leakers, nothing coming from an official source can be taken at face value. Every one of the people I have described in this chapter has been shown — after the controversies surrounding the person's case had subsided — to have had a real connection to covert operations. Finally, consider the case of John "Sparky" McLaughlin, an intrepid and honest Pennsylvania state narc who uncovered direct evidence linking the CIA to Dominican drug dealers operating on the Eastern seaboard.

As a reward for McLaughlin's integrity, in 1996 a major smear campaign was launched against him in print, on television, and inside the Pennsylvania government. Both McLaughlin and his straight-arrow squad have survived years of administrative punishment, bankruptcies, loss of pay and benefits, and they are still fighting the good fight to clear their names.[16] It took Sparky and his colleagues seven years to win a $1.5 million judgment against their tormentors.

Of the more than 20 cases I have investigated, in many instances having met or spoken with those involved, I can name only four men whom I consider to be totally trustworthy, honest, and straight-talkers: Brad Ayers, Gary Eitel, John McCarthy, and John McLaughlin.

It is now possible to take a look at the case of Mike Vreeland and try to judge its significance for 9/11.

Before I ever met Vreeland's attorneys or published a word about the case, Bill Tyree called me from his prison cell and warned, "They're going to turn Vreeland into a 'honey pot.'" A honey pot, in intelligence jargon, is a tempting source of information or "dangle" that is set out to lure intended victims into a trap. Ultimately the honey pot is violently and maliciously discredited so as to destroy the credibility of anything stuck to it by association. In some cases the honey pot is an innocent victim. But in many other cases he or she is a willing part of the plot, serving covert interests in order to cut a deal for themself.

Mike Vreeland

As early as November of 2001, I started getting e-mails about a case in Toronto concerning a man who was claiming to be an officer in what was traditionally called the Office of Naval Intelligence and who had forewarned of the attacks of 9/11. I had been sent a copy of an October 23 *Toronto Star* story, by a reporter named Nick Pron, that described the basics of the case. The man, Delmart "Mike" Vreeland, had been held in jail since December of 2000 and was fighting extradition to Michigan on charges of credit card fraud. According to Pron's story, Vreeland had written a sealed warning of the attacks a month before 9/11 and handed it to his jailers. The note had been opened on September 14.[17]

Pron's story was about a 35-year-old man who claimed to have been part of a special US Navy undercover unit investigating both organized crime and drug smuggling and who had recently returned from a secret mission to Moscow. Pron described what I took to be a cover story concerning Vreeland's claims that he had been dispatched to retrieve or examine documents concerning the Star Wars missile defense system. He returned from Russia only to be jailed, almost immediately, on the fugitive warrant from Michigan. Right off the bat I suspected that this was the tip of a tiny tail fin on the back of the Loch Ness monster. If Vreeland was for real he was making the most common mistake I have seen made in such cases. He was trying to serve two masters by simultaneously trying to prove his credentials while also attempting to prove his loyalty to a system that had written him off.

I had already amassed substantial information showing that foreign intelligence services had been sending the CIA, the FBI, and even the White House extremely specific warnings about the attacks for months before they happened. Taken together, warnings from French, German, and Russian intelligence alone showed that al Qaeda was intending to crash hijacked airliners into the World Trade Center in the week of September 9th, 2001. Not only had those warnings gone unheeded, no one in the government was acknowledging even their receipt. This was in spite of the fact that major European papers such as the *Guardian* and *Frankfurter Algemeine Zeitung*, as well as the British Broadcasting Corporation, were basing their reports on interviews and documents provided directly by the intelligence services themselves. Even Russian President Vladimir Putin, after leaving a live NPR radio broadcast in Manhattan on September 15, went on MS-NBC and stated clearly that in August of 2001, he had ordered Russian intelligence to send specific messages to the CIA including details of the attacks. Putin had also sent a warning to George W. Bush "in the strongest possible terms" about planes being crashed into buildings and other specifics. Russian news stories had proved even more revealing about how much the Russian government knew beforehand.

One story from *Izvestia* was to subsequently have a key paragraph removed but not until after my staff had archived the story for safekeeping. I made sure to obtain two different translations to make sure that the wording was correct. We have posted the original story in Russian on the *FTW* website.[18] Portions in bold were subsequently deleted from the *Izvestia* website:

September 12, 2001 (14:15) Yesterday at the headquarters of Central Intelligence Service in Langley a confidential meeting between one of the Deputy Directors of CIA and a special messenger of Russian Intelligence Service took place. According to NewsRu sources he delivered to his American colleagues some documents including audiotapes with telephone conversations directly relating to terrorist attacks on Washington and New York last Tuesday. According to these sources, Russian Intelligence agents know the organizers and executors of these terrorist attacks. More than that, Moscow warned Washington about preparation to these actions a couple of weeks before they happened.

Russian Intelligence Service states that behind the terrorist attacks on Washington and New York stands the organization of Usama ben Laden, Islamic movement of Uzbekistan and Taliban government. According to our intelligence agents among terrorists there were at least two Uzbeks, natives of Fergana, who arrived in the U.S.A. on forged documents about ten months ago. A terrorist group which realized actions against the U.S.A consisted of at least 25 people. All of them had a special training on the territories of Afghanistan and Pakistan including piloting of an aircraft.

The *Izvestia* mention of audiotapes of telephone conversations was one of about six different news stories and other records — some from the US government — indicating that all of al Qaeda's supposedly secure communications had been compromised well before the attacks.

My first inclination was to avoid Vreeland because I thought that I understood how messy a story like this could be. But several readers kept prodding me to look into it. I didn't know what "messy" meant.

Our *FTW* investigations of 9/11 were traveling the globe at the speed of light, and I was quickly being booked for eight months of speaking engagements that would see me traveling more than 90,000 air miles in 2002. One of the first lectures booked was at the University of Toronto for January 17th, followed by a repeat performance two nights later.

Readers who had noted the two or three limited mentions of Vreeland in the Canadian press pressured me to investigate while in Toronto. Being wary of tipping off my moves too far in advance I waited until I was in the boarding area at LAX on November 16th to call and leave a message for Rocco Galati, one of Vreeland's lawyers. Galati returned the call quickly. He was eager to meet me.

On January 17, I took a cab to the Toronto criminal courts building to observe a hearing in the case. Security was incredibly tight. Not only was I scanned with a hand-held metal detector, every item in my pockets and briefcase was individually inspected. Entering the almost empty courtroom I saw Vreeland sitting shackled at counsel table in jailhouse coveralls. Galati wore the black robes and wig that are de rigueur in Crown legal proceedings. The bailiffs were obviously on high alert.

Vreeland, gray, gaunt, fatigued, and jumpy, turned quickly to see who I was. He leaned over to Galati who turned, looked, recognized me from my picture on the website, and whispered in Vreeland's ear. I took out my notebook and listened.

The hearing had been in progress for some time, but the first thing I heard was the judge making a reference to having portions of certain documents deleted stating, "these items shall be deleted by means of scissors and once deleted, should be destroyed."

Having had no real access to information, I could only scribble notes of portions of the hearing that seemed pertinent. There was discussion by counsel from both sides indicating that Vreeland had, in fact, provided witness testimony against organized crime interests in Michigan in a case involving a Bobby Moore and that he was also a Crown witness in a continuing investigation and prosecution of a Nestor Fonseca who had been connected to a Canadian murder plot.

With that much confirmed, and through watching an animated Vreeland in his chair at counsel table, I was rapidly concluding that Vreeland's case was totally consistent with what prior experience had told me to expect.

The Crown Solicitor made a good point. Vreeland and his attorneys were alleging that he had been sent to Moscow in 2000 to retrieve extremely sophisticated scientific information connected to the Star Wars missile defense system that only he could evaluate. From my knowledge of covert operations this had to be a cover story. It was ludicrous to believe that the US government would ever send any person with the kind of technical knowledge required to evaluate top secret technology into a foreign land. In fact the travels of such people within the US intelligence and scientific community is closely monitored and restricted. This would be making a gift of the real secrets to the enemy.

Vreeland had allegedly returned from Moscow with several sealed pouches of intelligence data. Galati made a point of telling the court that he had not seen the pouches and had no first-hand knowledge of what they contained. The Crown Solicitor then referred to Vreeland's military record. I noticed that Vreeland's fair-complexioned lawyer Galati, who looked like a cherubic, playful pit bull, became animated any time Vreeland's military records were mentioned. It was immediately obvious that Galati did not suffer fools gladly, and he was not afraid to let the court see his emotions. This, I have found, is both a gift and a curse of anyone who is certain of his intellectual and factual foundations. I liked him immediately.

The Crown Solicitor asked why the US government would send someone who had been discharged from the navy after only a few months, with minimal education, and official training in the tool and die field to evaluate top secret scientific material in Russia. This was a good rhetorical question, given the Crown's position that Vreeland had only been in the navy for a few months. But Galati kept reminding the court that the records were inconsistent, that they had been altered, and that some of them indicated that Vreeland's service record was over 1,200 pages in length, not bad for someone who had only served for a few months before being discharged as unfit. Some were dated well after his supposed discharge date.

Then, just about 15 minutes later, I heard the Crown Solicitor step through the looking glass into the parallel universe.

He was rebutting the claim that Vreeland's other lawyer, Paul Slansky, had previously made a phone call from the (open) courtroom to the Pentagon switchboard. And in that phone call a Pentagon operator had confirmed Vreeland's rank as a naval lieutenant (impossible for someone who only served a few months) and provided Slansky with an office number and a direct dial phone number. To counter this claim the Crown Solicitor then suggested that Vreeland, who had been held without bail for more than a year on a non-capital offense, had somehow hacked into the Pentagon's computer system from his jail cell and altered the Pentagon's database.

Galati was vibrating with frustration from his chair as the Crown Solicitor also suggested that "Vreeland-the-Idiot" had somehow translated documents in Russian and Albanian and then had them posted on a secure and unknown website. Galati was quick to point out to the court that Vreeland didn't speak Russian or Albanian and he was wondering why the Crown Solicitor was so quick to have Vreeland be both a village idiot and a criminal mastermind at the same time.

This was all too familiar, but I was not making up my mind until after I had spoken to both Galati and Slansky. That was most definitely going to happen before I went anywhere near Vreeland personally. Looking at him in the courtroom, all I could see was a gigantic wriggling can of worms.

At one point the Crown Solicitor made a statement that I was careful to record exactly. "The inescapable inference [of Vreeland's allegations] is that US intelligence had that information as early as 2000 and made no effective use of it." Exactly, I thought. Exactly! That is why they must destroy him and anyone who makes him credible.

The hearing ended inconclusively on issues of bail, a safe house, and the very interesting issue of why Galati and Slansky were not being allowed to submit evidence supporting Vreeland's claims or the right to call US witnesses. I decided that there were only two litmus tests that would affect my decision to get involved. First, was there definitive proof that this so called warning note — which I had not yet seen — had been written prior to 9/11? And second, was it a certainty that Vreeland had been referring to the 9/11 attacks when the note was written? A "No" answer to either question would mean that I could happily brush my hands and walk away.

Galati and I left the courtroom together. We were joined in the cafeteria by his co-counsel Paul Slansky. Where Galati seemed brilliant and fiery, the bearded, dark-haired Slansky appeared by contrast methodical, good natured, conservative, and subdued. I was later to learn that Slansky also had exhibited moments of pique. Both men, who together had more than 30 years of legal experience, most of it as Canadian federal prosecutors — the US equivalent of assistant United States Attorneys — struck me as respectable and competent men. Neither one was making a fortune off the case, as Vreeland at that time was almost indigent. They believed in what they were doing.

I asked the two important questions right away. Both men were clear and unequivocal in their answers. They stated that they knew of a certainty that Vreeland had written the note in mid-August, a month before the attacks, that it could be proven, and that they were even then trying to get the court to do just that. They were also absolutely certain that Vreeland had been referring specifically to the attacks of 9/11 when the note was written.

They added that what was not acknowledged in the press was that they had spent months trying to alert Canadian and US officials about the attacks, and that the attempts had all been documented. In playing a cat-and-mouse game with US intelligence agencies they had declined post 9/11 invitations for meetings with US consular officials in the US or at the US consulate out of fear that they would be taken and held. One meeting involving Galati had actually been held in the same cafeteria where we then sat. Neither man had the slightest doubt that Vreeland had worked for the Office of Naval Intelligence or in some similar capacity, possibly for the CIA. And both men admitted what I already knew to be true. Mike Vreeland was an erratic, volatile, frightened, and sometimes inconsistent royal pain in the ass.

I also learned that both men had been seriously intimidated since taking on the case. Both had been followed. Galati had had a dead cat hung on his porch, and Slansky's car had been burglarized with a rear window smashed out. I was to ride in that car days later and see the broken window for myself. Both men believed that their offices were bugged and their telephones monitored.

Over the course of my four-day stay in Toronto I spent about ten hours with the two lawyers. They were, in my opinion, exactly what they presented themselves as, serious and ethical attorneys with solid professional reputations who were devastated by 9/11 and the fact that they knew that they had possibly been in a position to help prevent the attacks and yet had been systematically ignored.

Galati took me to his law office in the Italian district. It was piled high everywhere with case files and clothing he needed for court appearances. He readily opened his Vreeland files to me and showed me his notes. Page after page documented phone calls and letters to Canadian and US officials in the months prior to 9/11, especially in August. All he and Slansky had asked for was that Vreeland be taken to a safe place and thoroughly debriefed about what he knew. They had encountered nothing but resistance.

The note

One futile meeting where two junior RCMP officials traveled to interview Vreeland in his lock up had produced no results. Out of frustration and desperation a scheme had been concocted whereby Vreeland would write details of his warning, couched in terms better understood by intelligence officials at the Pentagon, and seal them in an envelope. As a means of proving that the note was written before the attacks Vreeland acquired two fine-point, light-blue ink pens, which were considered contraband by his jailers. All inmates were required to have only Bic medium-point blue pens, and their cells were regularly searched to remove any contraband. One reason for this is that other types of pens are preferred tattooing instruments, and if permitted they expose jails to medical liability issues.

Once the note was written with the forbidden pens it was sealed in an envelope, placed into Vreeland's personal property out of his reach, and there it remained until it was opened by Canadian officials on September 14, 2001. Contents of the letter were immediately forwarded to Ottawa while the letter itself was submitted as Exhibit "N" in Vreeland's case on October 7th. To my knowledge the original letter still remains in Vreeland's case files in Toronto.

Exhibit "M" in the case — a letter written by the Ministry of Correctional Services and dated September 17, 2001 — states that on August 13, 2001, Vreeland's cell was searched and that two "contraband" ink pens were confiscated. No record exists of them having been booked into his property and an August 14th written request by Vreeland to have them returned was subsequently denied.

The current status of those pens is unclear, and the court repeatedly refused to have the ink on Vreeland's letter tested and compared with the pens that could not have been in his possession after August 14th. I later asked Vreeland, Slansky, and Galati how often Vreeland's cell had been searched after mid-August, and they all indicated that it had been a regular occurrence. No other contraband had been found or seized since.

In an interview for this book conducted in late November 2002 I reaffirmed what had been told to me in a conversation with Slansky. Yes, he was absolutely certain that the note had been written a month before the attack. And as to whether he was certain that the note and Vreeland's near-panicked attempts to warn of attacks in August were about 9/11 — and nothing else — Slansky left no doubt. "I didn't know what was in the note when he wrote it. Right after September 11th I thought that the attacks were what Vreeland had been referring to. But when I saw the note I was absolutely certain."

The fact that the note had been sealed into evidence a month before the attacks was never officially disputed by Canadian officials until the summer of 2002. It had certainly never been disputed in a courtroom. And even then the denial was weak. Journalist and publisher Sander Hicks, after a six-month investigation into the case produced a lengthy and detailed investigation of the Vreeland saga for the Guerilla News Network (<www.guerrillanews.com/>), which had recently won an award at the Sundance Film Festival for a short documentary on CIA's involvement in the drug trade. In his story Hicks wrote,

> However, a [summer 2002] phone call to the Canadian prosecution team resulted in new, somewhat murky results. When I asked Assistant D.A. Dorette Hugins to confirm that the prosecution didn't dispute that the

*notes were handed to the jailers in mid-August 2001, she immediately
said, that "Yes, it is true." A minute later, she changed her answer to, "No,
the prosecution now thinks he got the notes to the jailers after 9/11."[19]*

By the time that story was published, Delmart "Mike" Vreeland was either a
fugitive from justice, the victim of a kidnapping, or something else.

This was a head of the hydra of covert operations sticking up out of a hole into
the parallel universe where "normal" people live. I was going to have very limited
time and no ability to investigate anywhere nearly as completely as Monika
Jensen-Stevenson had with Scott Barnes.

Once I looked at the note I saw that indeed it mentioned Osama bin Laden,
the World Trade Center, and the Pentagon. It also mentioned other things that
had been prominently in the news right after the attacks: Sears Towers, water supplies, the White House, the Navy Pier, and several Canadian targets.

Two chilling sentences appeared in the top half: "They will paint me crazy and
call me a liar"; and "let one happen — stop the rest!!!" The last phrase was the most
important item on the note. It directly implied that US intelligence services had
achieved complete penetration of al Qaeda cells involved in the attacks. This was
something I had suspected.

The lower half of the note was filled with a variety of names that had little
immediate significance. I did recognize the name "ulista petrovka" as being a street
or place in downtown Moscow not far from Red Square. Upon returning to L.A.,
I checked a few of the names to see what I could find quickly. One in particular
was Chalva Tchigirinsky, (Vreeland had misspelled it) who was connected somehow with money. It did not take long for me to confirm that Tchigirinski was a
Russian oil executive who had business relationships with BP and Gazprom, the
company that had been trying to build the trans-Afghan gas pipeline from
Turkmenistan. Tchigirinski's interests stretched into Central Asia and the Caspian.
He was also president of the Moscow Oil Company.

Later on a talented researcher named Nico Haupt was to forward me a detailed
background on Tchigirinski, which elaborated further on his oil, real estate, and
business ventures, including a deal signed in early 2002 with Halliburton.
Tchigirinski was an oligarch.

One other entry stood out, but there was little I could do with it at the moment.
It was significant because it was the second place where "World Trade Center" had
been written. The entry read "world trade center/in jail (Dr. Haider)?"

As luck would have it, a brave young woman named Greta Knutzen came to
both of my lectures in Toronto. A fresh college graduate, the British expatriate living in Toronto offered her services to me in any way I thought might help.
Knowing that Vreeland's case would require more local attention than I could possibly give, I immediately hired her as a part-time correspondent. This would have
been a daunting task for a seasoned journalist who knew something about intelligence. Yet Greta was willing, and she was very brave, and she would solve the

(197)

This is Exhibit ..."N"... referred to in the
afficavit of ...D.E.M.J. Vleeland...
sworn before me, this ...7th...
day of ...OCTOBER... 2007
19
A COMMISSIONER FOR TAKING AFFIDAVITS

Navy yard
Sears tower ? change
world trade center
White House —
pentagon ?
world bank Malasia —
water supplies —
Scotia buildey toronto —
Parloment Bldg. ottawa —
Royal Bank Toronto or Mont.

they will paint me crazy, and call me a liar —

lets one happen stop the rest !!!

NOTES:	Blockade	MKOSA — world Bank — Lian cHamker/malasia	Bilateral
Monkey —	CHALVA TcHABULDSKY	Zastra — Brown recluse —	arms/techn — epchange —
KGB —	OLES —	ulista petrovka	(satellite/ade —) wHY Bush ?
?	MARC	wall trade ctr (DR. HAIDER)?	2007 2009
V-Team	HENREY	in July	—ccu —Bio/ no Niton Parlyn one attack ?
Stuart	OTTAWA-EM. R./ Boston/	Need — decontam	BROWN RECLUSE
coninct of ALL V-Team	DOCKS FCR.	PRimorsky VLaDivostok/ KRay	WATER How ?
	VIPS mtg — M234 Rog Riewalt. E, paperate laundone	WHats his contacts —	

— No COMMENTS on LETTER — No THANKyou, No comment —
TRANSFER TO OTTAWA, NEW Custody, SAFE HOUSE or M. BASE — OR
my own PRIVATE APT MY EXPENSE — NEW JO

C/R :— Coop agreement 76-97

mystery of Dr. Haider. Here are some excerpts of her first story that I published in the February issue of *From The Wilderness*.

US and Canadian Governments' position crumbling in the case of a US intelligence officer with foreknowledge of 9/11 attacks

by

Greta Knutzen, *FTW* Staff Writer

TORONTO, February 29, 2002 — A man who claims to be a US intelligence officer accurately predicted the September 11 attacks on the World Trade Center and the Pentagon, recently unsealed court documents show.

Delmart Edward Mike Vreeland is currently incarcerated in a Toronto prison. His claims, however, are corroborated by evidence that has surfaced during his ongoing court battle in Canada. Court hearings in late February have only deepened the mystery and added to the list of questions, calling into question the integrity of the US government.

Vreeland has been subject to physical attacks while behind bars, indicating that the certain death he fears if he is returned to the US might become a reality behind the jailhouse walls in Toronto.

Yet, despite Vreeland's repeated attempts to inform them, both the American and Canadian governments have oddly and inexplicably refused to listen. Their argument goes something like this: Vreeland is not perceived to be trustworthy or credible. Therefore, nothing he says can be deemed trustworthy or credible. But they have never seen fit to ask how he knew of the attacks in the first place.

Vreeland's story does indeed resemble something that John Grisham might produce in the throes of a caffeine-induced frenzy. However, Vreeland's story begins to look less like the stuff of unadulterated fiction when one takes into account actions of US and Canadian authorities that seem equally bizarre.

It is becoming increasingly evident, as the case against him unfolds, that the documentation pertaining to Vreeland, supplied by the US Navy and Canadian law enforcement officials, is itself so contradictory and incomplete as to defy logic. As such, the validity of the charges against Vreeland and the position adopted by US and Canadian authorities raise more questions than they answer.

Vreeland, an American citizen who has been in jail since December 6, 2000, claims he is a US naval lieutenant who has worked for naval intelligence since 1986.

Justice Archie Campbell of the Superior Court of Justice, who briefly presided over the case, is in agreement with the Crown's assessment and has described Vreeland as nothing more than a petty fraudster with a vivid imagination.

Ostensibly, Vreeland's story begins in the fall of 2000. In a sworn affidavit filed in court documents on October 16, Vreeland claims that he was sent on assignment to Russia where he was in contact with Marc Bastien, a computer systems specialist working for Foreign Affairs at Canada's embassy in Moscow.

Vreeland acquired information vital to the national security of the US and Canada. Vreeland alleges he left Russia with the documents and arrived in Canada on December 2, 2000. According to his affidavit, he expected to meet Bastien two days later in Toronto to hand over the documents to a third party.

Bastien did not show up, however, so Vreeland hung onto the documents. Vreeland asserts that he proceeded to upload the documents onto a secure website, the location of which is unknown to anyone to the present day, including his attorneys, Paul Slansky and Rocco Galati.

Vreeland claims that Bastien had given him two telephone numbers at CSIS, the Canadian intelligence service, to contact in the event that anything went wrong. He was subsequently arrested in Toronto on December 6, 2000, on alleged fraud charges. At the time of his arrest Vreeland claims that he attempted to contact CSIS per Bastien's instructions, but he was unsuccessful.

Upon his arrest, Vreeland was placed in solitary confinement. The reason for this treatment was the difficulty Toronto police had in confirming his identity. FBI fingerprint records, requested by the Toronto police, were negative, indicating that Vreeland had no criminal record.

After he was removed from solitary confinement on January 15, 2001, he learned that six days after his arrest, on December 12, 2000, Bastien was found dead. The official explanation was that he died of natural causes. Vreeland stated in his affidavit that he believed Bastien was in fact murdered, a statement which later proved correct.

In May, the US government issued a formal request for the extradition of Vreeland on charges of credit card fraud. It was at this point that he hired Slansky, and later, Galati, to fight the extradition. *Vreeland's first objection was that the credit card in question was his own. In addition, his criminal record shows that he was detained in New York at the time the alleged offence was committed in Michigan...* [emphasis mine]

In June, Vreeland informed his counsel that he had information vital to US and Canadian national security... Between June and September, Vreeland's counsel made repeated requests to US and Canadian intelligence offices that they speak to their client. Their requests were ignored, except for one meeting with the Royal Canadian Mounted Police (RCMP) on August 8. The RCMP contacted the US Navy and was told that Vreeland had been unsatisfactorily discharged in 1986 after four months of basic training.

The position of the navy was contradicted by an attaché at the US embassy in Ottawa, who spoke with the RCMP and confirmed that Vreeland was a lieutenant in the US Navy. The navy refused to cooperate with the RCMP, and the attaché's statement has since been retracted. Because of this, the RCMP did not follow up on the meeting, and Vreeland was dismissed as a crank.

On October 5, Vreeland's counsel wrote to the Canadian government's intelligence and law enforcement agencies. The letter has been filed in court documents. The attorneys confirmed their head-bashing attempts at convincing the RCMP to deal with their client in a serious manner, repeatedly urging that they sought only an opportunity to *"place him in protective custody for 4-5 days so that you can satisfy yourselves as to the veracity of his national security information...."* [their emphasis]

In August, Vreeland wrote down information from the documents he acquired in Moscow. The information was fed to him in jail by telephone from a contact he had on the outside who had access to the secure website.

Vreeland requested that his guards seal the note and register it in his personal effects, which they did. The fact that the note was written and sealed a month prior to the violent attacks of September 11 has not been disputed. Another name on the note was "Dr. Haider," followed by the question, "Whats his contacts." [sic]

It may well be a coincidence, but, a man called Abu Doha, using the alias Dr. Haider, was arrested in London in early 2001. The sworn affidavit of an FBI special agent dated July 2 indicates that Doha was suspected of conspiring to bomb various US targets, including airports. Doha was allegedly a leader of an Algerian terrorist cell operating from Afghanistan, associated with Osama bin Laden's terrorist network, al Qaeda. Coincidence or not, it certainly begs the question of how a jailed man with limited access to computers could know such an obscure detail.[20]

Parliamentary Secretary Lynn Meyers granted Galati a meeting, the first of three, in Ottawa on September 20. They met again on

October 10 at Mr. Meyers's office in Waterloo in the presence of Slansky and another unidentified individual. During this meeting Meyers confirmed that Bastien, Vreeland's alleged contact in Moscow, had indeed been murdered. Vreeland was thus vindicated on this point. The coroner's report, which suggests Bastien was poisoned, was only made public three months later, on January 21.

On October 15, Galati traveled again to Ottawa to meet Meyers, this time under the impression he would also meet Solicitor General Lawrence MacAulay to voice his concerns about Vreeland's information. The Department of the Solicitor General oversees Canadian law enforcement and intelligence communities. But when Meyers and Galati met MacAulay, he refused to grant them even 15 minutes of his time.

Instead of being a reason to disbelieve Vreeland, the criminal records alleging fraud are entirely consistent with covert intelligence operations. Vreeland was allegedly allowed a per diem of $19,000, and his credit cards would likely have been underwritten by the US Navy or the CIA. As documented by the history of the Iran-Contra scandal, any number of intelligence operatives who had discretionary control of large sums of money were routinely controlled by this method.

Galati's response was that if Vreeland is the petty criminal they claim he is, his criminal record should take five minutes to produce. It would also settle the argument as to Vreeland's whereabouts at the time the alleged credit card fraud took place in Michigan. At present, records show him to be in two places at once, something surely even Vreeland is not capable of.

Although MacDonald acknowledged that the computerized records provided by US law enforcement officials regarding Vreeland's criminal convictions are terse, incomplete, and confusing, he rejected the request made by Vreeland's counsel that their client's asylum claim be permitted to proceed on constitutional grounds.

In other words, MacDonald's decision was based on a subjective assessment of degrees of probability, rather than proven fact. Galati, who intends to appeal the decision, said that MacDonald's judgment suspends reality and brings judicial proceedings into the realm of *Alice in Wonderland.*

As Vreeland's counsel has been denied access to their client's certified criminal record and the missing pages from his navy personnel record, they have opted for the next best thing — witnesses. Slansky requested that he be permitted to summon witnesses during the extradition hearing that could corroborate Vreeland's story. Among the witnesses they seek to question are individuals familiar with Pentagon computer security and personnel records, as well as Commander Nieusma, who forwarded Vreeland's inconsistent navy personnel record. The judge's decision on this matter is still pending.[21]

So why is the personal credibility of a man who has been right about the murder of a Foreign Affairs worker and who had fore-knowledge of the September 11 attacks an issue? Mike Vreeland's story raises the question of why the US and Canada insist on ignoring such an obvious investigative lead. If no stone is to be left unturned, why is Vreeland's Rock of Gibraltar being left alone?[22]

Greta's article was well done and well received.

Then another key fact was to later surface that would give Mike Vreeland an additional mark of credibility. Although I was not to catch it for some time, it would prove to be a link to something even more threatening to the US government. In October and November, long before I had had any real involvement in the Vreeland case, a Southern California man named Steve Tangherlini had made a number of persistent attempts to get me to investigate a major financial fraud that was taking trillions of dollars out of the US Treasury. It was beyond both my professional skill and resources to investigate.

On November 12 Tangherlini sent me a 23-page fax with legal documents and what looked like banking documents describing the transfer of hundreds of billions of dollars from various US government accounts and the Federal Reserve System (the Federal Reserve System is not a US government entity; it's a privately-owned banking syndicate). Frustrated at my inability to help Tangherlini in his repeated requests to cover his "Project Saving America," I forwarded copies of the documents to former Assistant Housing Secretary and Wall Street investment banker Catherine Austin Fitts. Both Fitts and another researcher, a former banking executive who prefers to remain anonymous, reached the same conclusion.

The documents looked real and could very well be real. However there was no known way to validate them, and thus there was no story. Fitts did offer one compelling observation: "Heck, I already knew, and it had been documented in the mainstream press that trillions of dollars were being stolen from the American people. That's a fact. So these documents didn't surprise me at all. Whether they are authentic or not doesn't matter; this is what is happening right now."

Imagine my surprise then, when I discovered that documents Mike Vreeland was to publish on his website in the spring turned out to be the same ones sent to me by Tangherlini. It was something I didn't catch for almost a year because, by the spring of 2002, I was receiving 400 emails a day and about 300 pages of unsolicited material and two books each week.

And I was to have a great many other distractions. After my first in-person meeting with Vreeland in jail in March, and especially after his release on bail, Mike Vreeland was to move into my life like an occupying army. I knew that I was dealing with someone who was using me and very likely trying to destroy me by having me pursue bad information that could have been used to discredit me. Very quickly after my first Vreeland story, "A White Knight Talking Backwards," published on January 25, Vreeland was hard at work throwing disinformation all over the place.[23] I had taken the story title from the 1960s Jefferson Airplane song called "White Rabbit" about drugs and Alice in Wonderland. Both were to become important pieces of the Vreeland story. The telling lyrics of that song fit well:

> When logic and proportion
> Have fallen softly dead,
> And the White Knight is talking backwards,
> And the Red Queen's *off with her head!*
> Remember what the dormouse said:
> *'Feed your head. Feed your head. Feed your head...'*

Almost immediately after my first story appeared, unprincipled and amateur journalists who talked to Vreeland were writing stories about red mercury, nuclear warheads, Iraq, China, and Russia based upon information I already knew was bogus. Some were trying to sell audiotapes of Vreeland's interviews. Others like the energetic radio talk-show host Alex Jones, who has a sizeable following, interviewed Vreeland on the air. Jones inadvertently helped to spread the inaccurate information, apparently with good intentions. But Jones's inability or unwillingness to thoroughly check Vreeland's material raised the risk that bad information might get put out to the public as fact. I alerted Jones to the possibility that Vreeland was a honey pot, and he backed off. I had made the decision that if anyone could ride the wave I could. I knew what the issue was, and I thought I knew what it would cost. What Vreeland had done with his note needed to be preserved for history.

There was much more to come from the world of Mike Vreeland and it was not going to be pleasant.

GALATI, RODRIGUES¹, AZEVEDO" & Associates
BARRISTERS & SOLICITORS

637 College Street, Suite 203
Toronto, Canada M6G 1B5

Direct Line (416) 536-7811 Fax (416) 536-6801

October 5ᵗʰ, 2001

¹ Rocco Galati
B.A. LL.B. LL.M.

Roger D. Rodrigues
LL.B.

Daniel A. Kleiman
LL.B.

Fay Fuerst
B.A. LL.B.

William E. M. Naylor
B.A. LL.B.
Counsel

In association

" Manuel A. Azevedo
LL.B. LL.M.

Harry C. Rankin
Q.C.
Counsel

Andrew A. Powell
B.A. LL.B.

Halldor K. Bjarnason
B.A. LL.B.

In association

Royal Canadian Mounted Police
2755 High Point Drive
Milton, Ontario
L9T 5E8

Fax No. (905) 876-9771

Dear Ms.   :

This is Exhibit .... " ✓ " referred to in the
affidavit of .D.E.??.M. Vreeland
sworn before me, this .7ᵉ
day of ... OCTOBER 2001,
.... A COMMISSIONER FOR TAKING AFFIDAVITS

RE: Delmart Edward Joseph Michael Vreeland II

This will confirm our head-bashing attempts at convincing, since June, 2001, the RCMP, upon CSIS referral and declining of involvement pending RCMP "investigation", to place Mr. Vreeland into police custody, on consensual Court order, so that he convey vital information to you of national security both to Canada and the U.S.A.

His attempts have fallen on deaf and incredulous ears of the RCMP notwithstanding my attempts with the Solicitor-General's office(s) in Ottawa following events of September 11ᵗʰ, 2001 in New York City.

Your position with respect to this simple and inconsequential request from Mr. Vreeland is beyond the pale for both Mr. Slansky and I, both former Crown Attorneys, as well as seasoned in extradition matters, in light of:

1. the clearly falsified and doctored criminal record and Navy record of Mr. Vreeland forwarded by his government;

2. the U.S.A. refusal, on your word, to co-operate with the RCMP notwithstanding that extradition is being ostensibly sought by them;

/...2

¹ Toronto Office
637 College Street
Suite 203
Toronto, Canada
M6G 1B5

" Vancouver Office
148 Alexander Street
Vancouver, Canada
V6A 1B5

2

3. the clear and incontrovertible remaining evidence that does remain in my clients' possession indicating that he was and is, as of August 21st, 2001, apparently a Lieutenant in the U.S. Navy (notwithstanding the three break-ins to his mother's business where most of his documents have been stolen since his incarceration in Canada);

4. the fact that the extradition case against Mr. Vreeland embarrassingly and insultingly much further lacks in credibility than any allegations of incredulity against Mr. Vreeland;

5. the fact that while Mr. Vreeland provided confirmed and credible information and is going to be the central witness in a criminal charge against Fonseca for counseling the murder of RCMP officers, Federal Crown Attorneys, a Canadian judge, FBI agents and U.S. witnesses;

6. that he provided credible information regarding the circumstances regarding the reason for what he states was the murder of a Canadian diplomat, Marc Bastien, and information regarding the risk to others flowing from those circumstances;

7. the fact that on or about August 11 – 12th he had sealed a list and notes containing possible targets of violent attacks, which was unsealed by senior jail officials on September 14th, 2001. On this list appear the World Trade Centre, Pentagon, and other cities, including Canadian cities, as well as several names, including Bin Laden.

All that was being sought was an opportunity to place him in protective custody for 4 – 5 days *so that you can satisfy yourselves as to the veracity of his national security information.* At that time, our client was willing to be subjected to polygraph examination, psychiatric examination and cross-examination by Naval intelligence and military experts. Yet, you have applied a ludicrous litmus test to pre-judge the credibility of his information. You have been told that additional information exists, including forensic testing to prove that the list/notes referred to in paragraph 7 was made prior to September 11, 2001. You tell us that you are not interested. In light of the statements made by our Government in the aftermath of September 11, we would have thought that you would be willing to at least check out this information. Your inaction reveals the stated intentions of the Government to be little more than rhetoric. We are being met with refusals by both his government and ours on the patently absurd conclusion and assertion(s) that Mr. Vreeland is a "nut-case" [sic] or lacks credibility when a sober review of the extradition proceedings against him, and what *little evidence* he has remaining and conveyed to us and to you and officials in Ottawa clearly indicate that your conclusion(s) are incomprehensible, irrational, and irresponsible.

/...3

3

This is to advise that we, as his counsel, despite our best and relentless efforts, take no responsibility, nor can we control our client, in his loss of patience and threats to have return what he claims to be documentation brought back from Russia "returned" to their rightful owners – the Russians. *Mr. Slansky* and I are *NOT privy to whatever it is Mr. Vreeland has been attempting to convey to his government and ours.* Mr. Vreeland does not wish to divulge matters of national security to Mr. Slansky or myself. He wishes to speak to his government or ours. He is frustrated and angered at being dismissed as a simple criminal, and his continued incarceration since December, 2000, on minor and dubious credit card charges.

The end conclusion of all of this is that neither Mr. Slansky nor I can hold Mr. Vreeland off in divulging whatever he wishes to divulge with whatever international reaction which may ensue, from other governments, and as such, the responsibility of the obstinate refusal by C.S.I.S., the RCMP, and the Solicitor-General to accede to such a simple request, is to be borne by the Government. The RCMP and CSIS are answerable to the Her Majesty's Minister of the Crown, the Solicitor-General. However, in practice they are operationally reacting as if they all three operate in different countries.

Lastly, neither Mr. Slansky nor I, as Mr. Vreeland's legal counsel, can refuse to follow the legal instructions of our client to pursue and defend his legal rights, in the context of the extradition proceeding on which he has been held in jail , and the upcoming Fonseca trial in which the Crown intends to have him testify. We are duty bound to defend his rights in accorance with his leagl instructions, within legal bounds.

Neither myself, nor Mr. Slansky, in the combined 30 years as Barristers, both as former Crown counsel, as well as private Barristers, have seen anything as incomprehensibly frustrating, inexplicable, and irresponsibly absurd given the context of events, as the R.C.M.P.'s position that they are not interested in reviewing Mr. Vreeland's information, evidence nor talking to any corroborating witnesses in Canada nor the U.S.A.

Lastly, it is incredible to us to be met with statements from both the R.C.M.P and C.S.I.S. that they are unwilling to share information, as between them, on the same investigation and in respect of national security concerns

/...4

4

All of which is respectfully submitted.

Yours very truly,
GALATI, RODRIGUES, AZEVEDO & Associates
Per:

Rocco Galati, B.A., LL.B, LL.M.
RG/PBS*cfc/pbs

Paul Slansky , B.A., LL.B, J.D.
RG/PBS*cfc/pbs

c.c.: CSIS
c.c.: ████████, Parliamentary Secretary to the Solicitor-General
c.c.: Solicitor-General
c.c.: Minister of Justice
c.c.: RCMP Commissioner

CHAPTER 12

EXECUTING A CONSPIRACY:
SHAME AND HONOR IN THE FBI —
AN AIR FORCE COLONEL
BLOWS THE WHISTLE

It doesn't take many people to execute a conspiracy, especially when the people involved are accustomed to dealing with compartmentalized information.

Few organizations are more familiar with compartmentalized information, and with what happens to whistleblowers who compromise intelligence operations, than the FBI. Indeed, the bureau is almost always the first place where people seek help when the inevitable retributions begin. It is the first place I went in 1978 after resigning from the LAPD with tape-recorded death threats when I knew that the CIA was dealing drugs. Who better to know and understand what whistleblowers face when they make their momentous decisions to come forward?

But what happens when FBI agents blow the whistle? The truth of the matter is that many FBI agents, employees, and even military personnel did speak out, both before and after 9/11. What they said is damning. And what has happened to them remains a continued warning (though not an excuse) for those who still function within the system and keep it going. The main reason why these whistleblowers have been so thoroughly smashed is because they all threatened to expose direct US connections to the attacks of 9/11 and those who carried them out.

White House orders

In a watershed moment two months after the World Trade Center attacks, the BBC's Greg Palast disclosed that shortly after taking office the Bush administration acted to prevent an FBI investigation into two of Osama bin Laden's brothers, Abdullah and Omar, living in a DC suburb near CIA headquarters. With the cooperation of veteran investigative journalist Joe Trento, Palast was actually able to produce a classified FBI national security report disclosing the damning evidence. The subject of the investigation was the World Assembly of Muslim Youth

(WAMY), a charity that had been repeatedly documented as having funneled money to terrorists.[1]

In the course of the broadcast Palast made these remarks:

> I received a phone call from a high-placed member of a US intelligence agency. He tells me that while there's [sic] always been constraints on investigating Saudis; under George Bush, it's gotten much worse. After the elections, the agencies were told to 'back off' investigating the bin Ladens and Saudi royals, and that angered agents. I'm told that since September 11th the policy has been reversed. FBI headquarters told us they could not comment on our findings. A spokesman said: 'There are lots of things that only the intelligence community knows and that no one else ought to know.'[2]

But the documents are more revealing, as Palast explains:

> This document is marked "Secret." Case ID — 199-Eye WF 213 589. 199 is FBI code for case type: 9 would be murder, 65 would be espionage, 199 means national security. WF indicates Washington field office special agents were investigating ABL — because of his relationship with the World Assembly of Muslim Youth, WAMY... ABL is Abdullah Bin Laden, president and treasurer of WAMY...
>
> The US Treasury has not frozen WAMY's assets, and when we talked to them, they insisted they are a charity. Yet, just weeks ago, Pakistan expelled WAMY operatives. And India claimed that WAMY was funding an organisation linked to bombings in Kashmir. And the Philippine military has accused WAMY of funding Muslim insurgency. The FBI did look into WAMY, but, for some reason, agents were pulled off the trail.
>
> TRENTO: The FBI wanted to investigate these guys. This is not something that they didn't want to do — they wanted to .... they weren't permitted to...
>
> MICHAEL WILDES (LAWYER): I would never be surprised with that. They're cut off at the hip sometimes by supervisors or given shots that are being called from Washington at the highest levels....[3]

Robert Wright

Twelve-year veteran FBI agent Robert Wright Jr. should be proud. Of all of the FBI "brick" agents who have come forward since 9/11 to describe the deliberate obstruction of investigations that could have prevented the attacks, no others have taken the risks or endured the punishment that Wright has. For good reason.

Wright is the only agent in the FBI's history to have conducted an investigation of terrorists that resulted in the seizure of financial assets. In 1998 he began an investigation — since terminated by the FBI — into terrorist money laundering in the United States. That investigation resulted in the seizure of bank accounts and other assets of Yassin Kadi, who has "since been identified as one of the 'chief money launderers' for Osama bin Laden." Kadi is reported to have provided as much as $3 billion to al Qaeda before Wright shut him down. [4] (Wright's investigations also put a major crimp in the funding for Hamas, another Palestinian-related support group that has been linked to terrorist activities in Israel).

Based in Chicago, home of the Chicago Board Options Exchange (CBOE) where a great deal of 9/11-related insider trading was to take place, Wright was in one of the three most important financial centers of the United States. Nobody moves $3 billion without using exchanges such as the NYSE or CBOE. It's just too much money and must move in financial streams where it would not stand out.

In the only real coverage of Wright's decision to come forward — which was coupled with a formal complaint against the FBI for its suppression of him — the *Congressional News Service* told a chilling tale as it reported on a press conference held by Wright and his legal team on May 30, 2002:

> In a memorandum written 91 days before the September 11 terrorist attacks, an FBI agent warned that Americans would die as a result of the bureau's failure to adequately pursue investigations of terrorists living in the country... Wright says that FBI management 'intentionally and repeatedly thwarted and obstructed' his attempts to expand the investigation to arrest other terrorists and seize their assets ....' As a direct result of the incompetence and, at times, intentional obstruction of justice by FBI management to prevent me from bringing the terrorists to justice, Americans have unknowingly been exposed to potential terrorists attacks for years,' he charged.[5]

FBI Director Robert Mueller held a May 29, 2002, press conference where he stated, "It is critically important that I hear criticisms of the organization including criticisms of me in order to improve the organization." Meanwhile the FBI was landing on Wright's chest with both feet. It had issued Wright written orders not to discuss what he knew and not to disclose, either in speech or writing, the contents of an unpublished manuscript entitled *Vulgar Betrayal* that he had written for Congress. Wright was threatened in writing with disciplinary action, civil suits, revocation of security clearances, and even criminal prosecution if he talked. That letter was received by Wright's attorney, David Schippers, at 5:00 pm *on the same day* Mueller lied to the American people about his pure intentions.[6]

The next day, Wright concluded his own press conference in tears: "To the families and victims of September 11th," he said, "on behalf of [FBI Special Agents] John Vincent, Barry Carmody, and myself — we're sorry."[7] But the real truth of what was done to this ethical law enforcement officer is contained in a May 22 letter written by Schippers to the FBI and in the words spoken at the press conference itself.

In writing to Wright's superior, Chicago Special Agent in Charge (SAC) Thomas Kneir, Schippers described how Wright had voluntarily given a heads-up about a *New York Times* investigation into what had happened with his investigations. Wright was subsequently ordered not to talk to the press. He complied. Schippers wrote,

> The FBI has failed seriously to address Robert Wright's work-related concerns regarding the FBI's terrorism responsibilities. In fact, we believe there has been a concerted effort by the FBI to discredit Agent Wright and minimize his concerns regarding the FBI's failures in connection with international terrorism matters prior to September 11th, 2001. In part, this effort includes providing false and misleading information to the New York Times regarding Agent Wright and his Vulgar Betrayal investigation. Even more disturbing is the fact that the FBI has prevented Agent Wright and Special Agent John Vincent from providing written responses to the New York Times to counter that false and misleading information .... Agent Wright has also filed two complaints with the US Department of Justice (DOJ) in an attempt to have his concerns addressed .... To our astonishment, the DOJ employee advised that, although the allegations were extremely serious, the Inspector General's Office did not have the resources to conduct an investigation of this anticipated size and scope.[8]

The sheer vindictiveness of a system that seeks to silence whistleblowers was most fully revealed in the press conference itself, in which it was disclosed that Wright, Schippers, and attorney Larry Klayman of Judicial Watch (a Washington, DC-based legal watchdog group) had actually met months before 9/11. They also disclosed that Wright had written most of his manuscript and decided to speak out about the repression well before the first plane hit the World Trade Center. Repeating allegations that Wright had been threatened and intimidated by the Bureau, Klayman stated that Wright's manuscript hits both Bush and Cheney "hard." That leaves little doubt about where the orders to crush Wright were coming from. Shippers added that Wright had even been ordered not to talk to Congress. John Ashcroft was not spared in the scathing statements. Klayman said that "Ashcroft very likely had all of this information" and didn't use Wright's investigative work to pull the financial plug on al Qaeda before the attacks.

The lawyers also described how Wright had, since voicing his concerns, been demoted to performing "innocuous tasks"; his office had been moved, computer equipment had been taken away from him, and he had been forced to purchase computers with his own money (which he did, out of sheer devotion to his work). Klayman stated that his office, aware of the direct connections between Wright's work and Osama bin Laden, had called Attorney General Ashcroft immediately after the attacks. The response was terse: "We're tired of conspiracy theories."

For a time C-SPAN carried a downloadable video file of the entire compelling press conference, which received no attention in the major media.[9] It has since been removed.

Kenneth Williams and the Phoenix memo: a CIA connection

On July 10, 2001, Kenneth Williams, the senior special agent from a Phoenix FBI terrorism task force, sent a memo to FBI headquarters. That memo, resulting from a seven-year investigation, alerted FBI headquarters that a number of Muslims, suspected of radical ties, were taking flight lessons in Arizona. It was later confirmed that Hani Hanjour, who was to be listed as the suspected pilot of the airliner the government says crashed into the Pentagon, had received his flight training in Arizona.

The memo specifically mentioned Osama bin Laden and warned that terrorists were possibly going to hijack aircraft or penetrate airport security. Williams requested that the FBI institute a nationwide survey of aviation schools to ascertain if there were large numbers of Middle Eastern students enrolled in them. The request was denied, reportedly for lack of resources.[10] The excuse seems weak. A list of flight schools is readily available through the Internet, and a telephone survey would have yielded fast results.

Williams was not the first FBI agent in Phoenix to complain about interference and obstruction by FBI headquarters. In 1994 Special Agent James Hauswirth complained about it after retiring and wrote a letter of complaint to FBI Director Mueller in December 2001. Hauswirth wrote, "The [international anti-terrorism] program ground to a halt a couple of years ago because of the micromanaging, constant indecision, and stonewalling."[11]

There was serious reason for the Phoenix "brick agents" to be concerned. They had watched some of their suspects who were taking flight training practicing at pistol ranges, and one of them was an associate of Sheik Omar Abdel Rahman, imprisoned for the 1993 World Trade Center bombing.[12]

After disclosure of the Phoenix memo's existence in May of 2002, FBI Director Mueller took the same tack as in the Wright case: he classified it and refused to show it to members of the Senate panel investigating 9/11. This outraged Senator Arlen Specter of Pennsylvania, who threatened a subpoena and a fight.[13] Unlike Wright, Williams — as a result of public pressure — was allowed to testify before the intelligence panel, and that panel has seen the memorandum that, however, *remains classified.*

Another person who saw the memo was *Fortune* reporter Richard Behar. This is the same Richard Behar who was instrumental in destroying the credibility of Iran-Contra figure Terry Reed in the previous chapter. It seems Mr. Behar is a trusted asset of intelligence agencies, who should not have disclosed anything the government didn't want known. But in his May 22 story on the Phoenix memo, he did. He described the Phoenix Field office's interest in a man named Zakaria Soubra: "Soubra, the memo said, was a student at Embry-Riddle Aeronautical University in

Prescott, Arizona (according to the *Los Angeles Times*, he was questioned by FBI agents in 2000, after he was observed at a shooting range with another Muslim, who was a veteran of Islamic jihads in the Balkans and the Middle East...). The organization named in the memo's title, the Islamic Army of the Caucasus, is based in Chechnya and was at one time headed by a man named Amir Khattab, who, according to news reports, is suspected of having ties to Osama bin Laden."[14]

We have previously documented that Chechen rebels were trained in camps funded and operated by the CIA, and that these operations were connected to Osama bin Laden, who was acting on behalf of the CIA in both the Balkans (Kosovo) and Chechnya. Khattab was one of the key players in those operations.

As reported in a previous chapter, Michel Chossudovsky told us why the Williams memo was so dangerous:

> With regard to Chechnya, the main rebel leaders Shamil Basayev and Al Khattab were trained and indoctrinated in CIA sponsored camps in Afghanistan and Pakistan. According to Yossef Bodansky, director of the US Congress' Task Force on Terrorism and Unconventional Warfare, the war in Chechnya had been planned during a secret summit of HizbAllah International held in 1996 in Mogadishu, Somalia.[15]

Williams's memo was sent to the desk of Supervisory Special Agent Dave Frasca at FBI headquarters in Washington, where Frasca sat on it with an anvil. We may never know what is in the rest of that memo and what Richard Behar kept hidden for the interests he apparently serves. What has been documented here, however, is yet another case of senior FBI personnel deliberately suppressing information that might have prevented the attacks of 9/11 in order to protect CIA assets who were subsequently connected to those same attacks.

Another major inconsistency in FBI operations is that, in 1995, after receiving warnings that al Qaeda operatives might be planning to crash hijacked airliners into CIA headquarters, the FBI "descended" immediately on flight schools all over the country.[16] Yet in 2001 it was too busy.

Colleen Rowley

On May 22, 2002, Minneapolis FBI Special Agent Colleen Rowley hand-delivered a 13-page memorandum to FBI Director Robert Mueller. In keeping with his customary practices, Mueller immediately classified the memorandum from the Minneapolis Field Office's top lawyer "Secret." That didn't help much, because Rowley, claiming protection under the federal whistleblower statute, had also delivered copies to the Senate Intelligence Committee and two of the Committee's members, Republican Richard Shelby and Democrat Diane Feinstein.[17]

The efforts of Rowley and her fellow brick agents in Minneapolis centered on the so-called twentieth hijacker, Zacarias Moussaoui, who had been in FBI custody since August 15 on immigration charges. It seems that for months before 9/11, FBI headquarters (FBIHQ) had systematically blocked every effort to investigate yet another case that — had it been supported — might have prevented the 9/11 attacks.

Rowley was irritated. It wasn't long before the memorandum — edited of course — was published by the likes of *TIME*, the *Associated Press*, and *Newsweek*. Rowley's move was supremely well considered and executed in such a way that there was little else for Congress to do but embrace it. And the best thing to do with Colleen Rowley is to get out of the way and let her speak for herself.

May 21, 2002
FBI Director Robert Mueller
FBI Headquarters
Washington, D.C.

Dear Director Mueller:

I feel at this point that I have to put my concerns in writing concerning the important topic of the FBI's response to evidence of terrorist activity in the United States prior to September 11th. The issues are fundamentally ones of INTEGRITY and go to the heart of the FBI's law enforcement mission and mandate ....

To get to the point, I have deep concerns that a delicate and subtle shading/skewing of facts by you and others at the highest levels of FBI management has occurred and is occurring. The term "cover up" would be too strong a characterization which is why I am attempting to carefully (and perhaps over laboriously) choose my words here. I base my concerns on my relatively small, peripheral but unique role in the Moussaoui investigation in the Minneapolis Division prior to, during and after September 11th ....

I feel that certain facts, including the following, have, up to now, been omitted, downplayed, glossed over, and/or mis-characterized in an effort to avoid or minimize personal and/or institutional embarrassment on the part of the FBI and/or perhaps even for improper political reasons:...

2) As the Minneapolis agents' reasonable suspicions quickly ripened into probable cause, which, at the latest, occurred within days of Moussaoui's arrest when the French Intelligence Service confirmed his affiliations with radical fundamentalist Islamic groups and activities connected to Osama Bin Laden, they became desperate to search the computer lap top that had been taken from Moussaoui as well as conduct a more thorough search of his personal effects. The agents in particular believed that Moussaoui signaled he had something to hide in the way he refused to allow them to search his computer....

3) The Minneapolis agents' initial thought was to obtain a criminal search warrant, but in order to do so, they needed to get FBI Headquarters' (FBIHQ's) approval in order to ask for DOJ … approval to contact the United States Attorney's Office in Minnesota. Prior to and even after receipt of information provided by the French, FBIHQ personnel disputed with the Minneapolis agents the existence of probable cause to believe that a criminal violation had occurred/was occurring. As such, FBIHQ personnel refused to contact [DoJ] to attempt to get the authority. While reasonable minds may differ as to whether probable cause existed prior to receipt of the French intelligence information, it was certainly established after that point and became even greater with successive, more detailed information from the French and other intelligence sources… [i.]

Notably also, the actual search warrant obtained on September 11th did not include the French intelligence information. Therefore, the only main difference between the information being submitted to FBIHQ from an early date which HQ personnel continued to deem insufficient and the actual criminal search warrant which a federal district judge signed and approved on September 11th, was the fact that, by the time the actual warrant was obtained, suspected terrorists were known to have highjacked [sic] planes which they then deliberately crashed into the World Trade Center and the Pentagon. To say then, as has been iterated numerous times, that probable cause did not exist until after the disastrous event occurred, is really to acknowledge that the missing piece of probable cause was only the FBI's (FBIHQ's) failure to appreciate that such an event could occur ....

It is obvious, from my firsthand knowledge of the events and the detailed documentation that exists, that the agents in Minneapolis who were closest to the action and in the best position to gauge the situation locally, did fully appreciate the terrorist risk/danger posed by Moussaoui and his possible co-conspirators even prior to September 11th. Even without knowledge of the Phoenix communication (and any number of other additional intelligence communications that FBIHQ personnel were privy to in their central coordination roles), the Minneapolis agents appreciated the risk. So I think it's very hard for the FBI to offer the "20-20 hindsight" justification for its failure to act! Also intertwined with my reluctance in this case to accept the "20-20 hindsight" rationale is first-hand knowledge that I have of statements made on September 11th, after the first attacks on the World Trade Center had already occurred, made telephonically by the FBI Supervisory Special Agent (SSA) who was the one most involved in the Moussaoui matter and who, up to that point, seemed to have been consistently, almost deliberately thwarting the Minneapolis FBI agents' efforts (see number 5). Even after the attacks had begun, the SSA in question was still attempting to block the search of Moussaoui's computer, characterizing the World Trade Center attacks as a mere coincidence with Minneapolis' prior suspicions about Moussaoui. [ii.] ...

5) The fact is that key FBIHQ personnel whose job it was to assist and coordinate with field division agents on terrorism investigations and the obtaining and use of FISA searches (and who theoretically were privy to many more sources of intelligence information than field division agents), continued to, almost inexplicably [v.] throw up roadblocks and undermine Minneapolis' by-now desperate efforts to obtain a FISA search warrant....

HQ personnel brought up almost ridiculous questions in their apparent efforts to undermine the probable cause. [vi.] In all of their conversations and correspondence, HQ personnel never disclosed to the Minneapolis agents that the Phoenix Division had, only approximately three weeks earlier, warned of al Qaeda operatives in flight schools seeking flight training for terrorist purposes! Nor did FBIHQ personnel do much to disseminate the information about Moussaoui to other appropriate intelligence/law enforcement authorities. When, in a desperate 11th hour measure to bypass the FBIHQ roadblock, the Minneapolis Division undertook to directly notify the CIA's Counter Terrorist Center (CTC), FBIHQ personnel actually chastised the Minneapolis agents for making the direct notification without their approval!

6) Eventually on August 28, 2001, after a series of e-mails between Minneapolis and FBIHQ, which suggest that the FBIHQ SSA deliberately further undercut the FISA effort by not adding the further intelligence information which he had promised to add that supported Moussaoui's foreign power connection and making several changes in the wording of the information that had been provided by the Minneapolis Agent, the Minneapolis agents were notified that the NSLU [National Security Law Unit] Unit Chief did not think there was sufficient evidence of Moussaoui's connection to a foreign power....

The e-mail communications between Minneapolis and FBIHQ, however, speak for themselves and there are far better witnesses than me who can provide their first hand knowledge of these events characterized in one Minneapolis agent's e-mail as FBIHQ is "setting this up for failure." My only comment is that the process of allowing the FBI supervisors to make changes in affidavits is itself fundamentally wrong .... understand that the failures of the FBIHQ personnel involved in the Moussaoui matter are also being officially excused because they were too busy with other investigations, the Cole bombing and other important terrorism matters, but the Supervisor's taking of the time to read each word of the information submitted by Minneapolis and then substitute his own choice of wording belies to some extent the notion that he was too busy. As an FBI division legal advisor for 12 years (and an FBI agent for over 21 years), I can state that an affidavit is better and will tend to be more accurate when the affiant has first hand information of all the information he/she must attest to.... but changes of some substance as apparently occurred with the Moussaoui information which had to be, for lack of a better term, "filtered" through FBIHQ before any action, whether to seek a criminal or a FISA warrant, could be taken .... Even after September 11th, the fear was great on the part of Minneapolis Division personnel that the same FBIHQ personnel would continue their "filtering" with respect to the Moussaoui investigation, and now with the added incentive of preventing their prior mistakes from coming to light. For this reason, for weeks, Minneapolis prefaced all outgoing communications (ECs) in the PENTTBOM investigation with a summary of the information about Moussaoui. We just wanted to make sure the information got to the proper prosecutive authorities and was not further suppressed!...

7) Although the last thing the FBI or the country needs now is a witch hunt, I do find it odd that (to my knowledge) no inquiry whatsoever was launched of the relevant FBIHQ personnel's actions a long time ago. Despite FBI leaders' full knowledge of all the items mentioned herein (and probably more that I'm unaware of), the SSA, his unit chief, and other involved HQ personnel were allowed to stay in their positions and, what's worse, occupy critical positions in the FBI's SIOC Command Center post September 11th. (The SSA in question actually received a promotion some months afterward!)...

8) The last official "fact" that I take issue with is not really a fact, but an opinion, and a completely unsupported opinion at that. In the day or two following September 11th, you, Director Mueller, made the statement to the effect that if the FBI had only had any advance warning of the attacks, we (meaning the FBI), may have been able to take some action to prevent the tragedy ....

The official statement is now to the effect that even if the FBI had followed up on the Phoenix lead to conduct checks of flight schools and the Minneapolis request to search Moussaoui's personal effects and laptop, nothing would have changed and such actions certainly could not have prevented the terrorist attacks and resulting loss of life. With all due respect, this statement is as bad as the first! Mr. Director... I think you have also not been completely honest about some of the true reasons for the FBI's pre-September 11th failures....

NOTES

...[v.] During the early aftermath of September 11th, when I happened to be recounting the pre-September 11th events concerning the Moussaoui investigation to other FBI personnel in other divisions or in FBIHQ, almost everyone's first question was "Why? — Why would an FBI agent(s) deliberately sabotage a case?" (I know I shouldn't be flippant about this, but jokes were actually made that the key FBIHQ personnel had to be spies or moles, like Robert Hansen, who were actually working for Osama bin Laden to have so undercut Minneapolis' effort.)...

Along these lines, let me ask the question, why has it suddenly become necessary for the Director to "handpick" the FBI management? It's quite conceivable that many of the HQ personnel who so vigorously disputed Moussaoui's ability/ predisposition to fly a plane into a building were simply unaware of all the various incidents and reports worldwide of al Qaeda terrorists attempting or plotting to do so....

[vi.] ...for the SSA continued to find new reasons to stall...

[viii.] For starters, if prevention rather than prosecution is to be our new main goal, (an objective I totally agree with), we need more guidance on when we can apply the Quarles "public safety" exception to Miranda's 5th Amendment requirements. We were prevented from even attempting to question Moussaoui on the day of the attacks when, in theory, he could have possessed further information about other co-conspirators. (Apparently no government attorney believes there is a "public safety" exception in a situation like this?!)[18]

Thus Moussaoui, who had paid the $7,000 for his flight lessons in cash; who was, according to press reports, not interested in learning how to take off or land; who wanted to know if the doors of an airliner could be opened in flight; and who was particularly interested in air traffic patterns around New York City, remained totally protected until after the attacks of 9/11 had taken place. And it was subsequently revealed that Zacarias Moussaoui had also fought in Chechnya where some of the players had been connected to CIA training camps.

> The French had been following Moussaoui for years. In the 1990s they tracked him to London where he learned militant Islam from radical clerics including Abu Qatada. French intelligence has linked Qatada to Osama bin Laden. Qatada preaches a particularly violent brand of Islam and encourages Muslims to take up jihad wherever they can. So Moussaoui took that advice and went to Chechnya to join Muslims in their fight against Russian troops. French intelligence was aware of that move and his later trip to Afghanistan.[19]

Zacaria Soubra from the Phoenix investigation and Zacarias Moussaoui in Minneapolis had something in common, other than allegiance to Osama bin Laden, which other members of al Qaeda did not. *They had both fought in Chechnya and both had met Amir al-Khattab who had been trained at CIA-operated and sponsored camps.* Conveniently, Khattab was reported killed in action in Chechnya in April 2002, just before the Williams and Rowley memos became news. Khattab's death was denied by Chechen rebel leaders.[20] Was a key witness being placed out of reach?

During my time as an LAPD officer and in the years since, I have met several FBI agents, including one former assistant director, who bragged about the FBI's ability to conduct "black bag" burglaries (surreptitious entries) during the 1960s and 1970s. Search warrants were never even a consideration. Keep this in mind as you reread the Rowley memo on the amazing refusal of FBI leadership to grant the field agents a FISA warrant. With Moussaoui's laptop in their possession for weeks before the attacks, it is very probable that they had already examined all of its contents. The reason why they needed the warrant was to make the evidence they had found admissible. Numerous press stories since 9/11 have indicated that the contents of that laptop will be used to convict Moussaoui of complicity in the attacks and most probably sentence him to death. I can only imagine the "off-the-record" conversations that took place between the brick agents in Minnesota and Washington as the brick agents — knowing of a certainty what was coming — tried in vain to get their search warrant.

And who was the supervisory special agent in Washington who brutalized the Minneapolis agents; who rewrote search warrants; who lied, obstructed, roadblocked, chastised, and suppressed? It was the same agent who received the Phoenix memo and sat on it: one Dave Frasca.

Carnivore

In March 2000 Denver FBI agents and other reviewing agents were "furious" after other agents in the bin Laden unit and at the International Terrorism Operations Center destroyed significant quantities of e-mail intercepts (received under authorization of a warrant) for a case connected to al Qaeda. The explanation given for the destruction of material of both evidentiary and intelligence value was that an e-mail surveillance system called Carnivore had errantly intercepted e-mails from additional innocent parties whose privacy had been violated. As a result, "'The FBI technical person was apparently so upset that he destroyed all the e-mail take, including the take on the suspect ....'"[21] "Take" means raw intelligence that has been collected but not yet analyzed.

This explanation is absurd, transparent, laughable, and offensive. It plainly contravenes 80 years of known FBI practice. Not only does it not make sense that the FBI wouldn't segregate the sought-after intelligence from that which was inadvertently collected; there was, in fact, a legal requirement that they not destroy anything at all. The Associated Press quoted Henry Perritt, the head of a review panel: "The collection is supposed to be retained for judicial review .... If an agent simply deleted a whole bunch of files without the court instructing, that's not the way it's supposed to work."[22]

Indeed, since a FISA (Foreign Intelligence Surveillance Act) warrant was involved in this case, the destruction of anything collected or seized as a result of that warrant is one of the most serious legal violations known. This would be true with any warrant. And yet it was confirmed that the decision to do so had been made within the UBL (bin Laden) unit, the same unit involved in the preceding cases. Here again we find Dave Frasca

A *Washington Post* story confirmed the above details but did not ask the obvious questions about why the entire take had been destroyed in direct violation of legal requirements calling for judicial review. It blamed the inappropriate collections on a problem with an Internet service provider. But even the *Post* story acknowledged — quoting an internal FBI memo — "To state that she [the memo's author] is unhappy with [the International Terrorist Operations Section] and the UBL Unit would be an understatement of incredible proportions."[23]

What was described here was not some frustrated, untrained agent knowingly destroying material out of an offended sense of dignity over a loss of privacy by victims who never even knew about it. What more likely happened was a deliberate destruction of intelligence information leading to Osama bin Laden that someone could not afford to have in any files where a dedicated agent might find it and start asking questions or putting people in jail. The use of the Carnivore program also suggests that whoever was running the unit had led field agents to believe that whatever they collected in this manner was legally admissible — and therefore protected from deletion. But in reality, both stories suggested that the program was still under evaluation and open to challenge. The field agents didn't know this. The result would be a built-in ability to destroy any prosecution using this material and allow the al Qaeda suspects to go free as a result of tainted evidence, while allowing gatekeepers at FBI headquarters to know how close agents were actually getting to sensitive covert operations.

Dave Frasca

Before concluding that Supervisory Special Agent Dave Frasca of the Radical Fundamentalist Unit at FBI headquarters was the primary agent responsible for the deliberate, willful, and arguably harmful suppression of evidence and of investigations that could well have prevented 9/11, a couple of key questions need to be addressed. Various press reports have described FBI units with oversight in these cases as the UBL (Osama bin Laden) Unit and as the Radical Fundamentalist Unit. Are they referring to the same thing? Secondly, is there any indication that any member of Congress or of any other oversight body has noticed at least some of these connections?

Dave Frasca was, until early 2002, the chief of the Radical Fundamentalist Unit within the FBI's Counterterrorism/Counterespionage branch. In that capacity, according to press reports, he oversaw the operations of several subunits, one of which apparently was the bin Laden or UBL unit. One ABC report said, "The Bureau's Radical Fundamentalist Unit, headed by Supervisory Special Agent Dave Frasca, and its Osama bin Laden Unit first got a memo that Phoenix FBI agent Ken Williams sent in early July."[24] The UBL unit was created, according to a statement by an FBI official, in 1999.[25]

A description of the duties of the RFU and its chief was found on the website of the high-technology, intelligence-connected SAIC Corporation, based in San Diego, which recently hired Frasca's predecessor, retired Supervisory Special Agent Robert Blitzer. SAIC's website gave a telling description of Frasca's duties, as he followed in Blitzer's footsteps.

> From 1993 to 1996, Blitzer served as chief of the Radical Fundamentalist Unit, Counterterrorism and Middle East Section at FBI Headquarters. As the leader of this unit, he was responsible for overall national coordination, oversight, and direction of all criminal and intelligence operations against the international terrorists who bombed the World Trade Center and who attempted to conduct a wave of bombings in and around New York City in early 1993.[26]

According to FBI spokesman Neal Schiff, Frasca's tenure in the RFU position lasted from 1999 until he was promoted in 2002. Frasca is currently the Assistant Section Chief of the International Terrorism Operations Section I. Schiff was ambiguous, at best, in describing the relationship between the RFU and the UBL units. While maintaining that the two were completely separate units, Schiff refused to confirm or deny that Frasca had supervisory responsibility for the UBL unit. At the same time he would not deny numerous press reports indicating that Frasca did work both units. The Phoenix memorandum was sent to the UBL unit, and Frasca apparently had a role in the decision not to follow up on it. As to the Wright case, and in contrast to statements given by Department of Justice officials on condition of anonymity confirming the RFU's role in squashing the Wright investigation, Schiff declined to confirm or deny any relationship. "That case is still pending and I can't comment," he said.

But the link between Robert Wright's oppressors and FBI headquarters was established only days after my office received the official statements from Schiff. On December 19, 2002, ABC News investigative reporter Brian Ross aired an interview with Wright and his partner John Vincent in which Wright stated, "The supervisor who was there from headquarters was right across from me and started yelling at me: 'You will not open criminal investigations. I forbid any of you. You will not open criminal investigations against any of these intelligence subjects.'"[27]

It was made clear in the story that the Wright/Vincent investigations had stemmed from the 1998 African embassy bombings and that the money trail led to Osama bin Laden. This would have placed the investigation within the UBL, Radical Fundamentalist Unit, and under the direct control of Dave Frasca. Schiff's assertion that the two units are separate and distinct entities is belied by Senate documents, press stories, and Frasca's own conduct post-9/11. A May 24, 2002, letter from Senator Patrick Leahy to FBI Director Mueller said:

> A press account on May 22 states that the Radical Fundamentalist Unit at FBI headquarters had decided not to pursue the recommendations in the Phoenix memorandum before September 11, 2001, since according to "officials... the FBI counterterrorism division was swamped with urgent matters." Another press account on May 23 contains a correction by "a senior FBI official" and [stated] that the FBI's "Osama bin Laden Unit was responsible" for the decision rejecting the recommendations ....[28]

Leahy's letter, in conformity with press stories, shows the interconnectedness of the two units, and Frasca's roles in cases involving both units is underscored by the fact that he was the agent (and in some cases, the only agent) who provided congressional testimony on all of these matters, whether they involved the RFU or the UBL unit. Schiff was unable to resolve these contradictions and went into "no comment" mode about press stories or congressional correspondence.

Knowing all this, it is now possible to state that Frasca almost certainly had direct oversight responsibility for all five of the previously described incidents. FBI sources I contacted confirmed, on condition of anonymity, that the RFU was the control point for all of these cases and that Frasca issued the orders thwarting investigations that could have prevented the 9/11 attacks. Looking at Frasca's actions, both in terms of their frequency and in terms of their consistency, it stretches the imagination to accept press accounts attributing FBI "screw-ups" relevant to 9/11 to incompetence, lack of resources, or overwork. There is a pattern here, rationally explained in only one way. Someone at the FBI, or elsewhere in government, needed to make sure that al Qaeda members were left in place — either to perpetrate the attacks or to take the blame for them afterwards. And the

Frasca connections — at least insofar as Minneapolis and Phoenix are concerned — were noticed. Frasca testified before both the Senate Judiciary and Intelligence committees, and many problems followed. First, Frasca told the Judiciary committee that he didn't see the Phoenix memo until after the 9/11 attacks. Later his statement was corrected to indicate that had seen the Phoenix memo before 9/11, but that the UBL unit had rejected the request for a survey of flight schools. His statement was different from press accounts which indicated that because the memo was marked routine, the deadline for response to it was 60 days, which would have been after 9/11 — so Frasca had taken no action.

Senators Patrick Leahy, Charles Grassley, and Arlen Specter were understandably miffed, especially when Leahy disclosed that he had acquiesced to a special request from Mueller to hold the secret hearing where Frasca testified without a stenographer or a transcript. Mueller didn't seem to have minded, however, when the Intelligence Committee was allowed to make a transcript of Frasca's statements for its members.

On May 24, 2002, Leahy closed a terse and eloquent letter to Mueller on the subject, signed also by Grassley and Specter:

> Finally, it has been noted that Supervisory Special Agent Dave Frasca in the Radical Fundamentalist Unit (RFU) may have been involved in handling the Phoenix memorandum and the Moussaoui investigation at FBI headquarters. [This had been previously confirmed in a number of press stories. The FBI only started changing their position after people started asking questions. - MCR] Please explain his role and the role of the RFU in evaluating the requests from the Minneapolis field office in the Moussaoui case; what connection, if any, he or others drew between the two ongoing investigations; and whether he or others brought such a connection to the attention of higher level FBI officials.
>
> If a briefing rather than a written answer would facilitate your response to the questions regarding agent Frasca, please let us know ....[29]

Some senators were a bit less polite in their remarks. Senator Richard Shelby, the Republican ranking member of the intelligence committee, was quoted as saying, "The information coming from Phoenix and the information coming from Minneapolis was stifled here at FBI headquarters." Senator Grassley of Iowa decried "sabotage" by FBI officials.[30]

A secret team

To understand how someone like Dave Frasca functioned inside the FBI, one needs to understand how the CIA and other intelligence agencies place their people throughout the government. Frasca fits that pattern perfectly. For those unfamiliar with the way covert operations function within the United States government, I cannot emphasize enough the importance of two books: *The Secret*

Team by the late Air Force Colonel L. Fletcher Prouty (the Pentagon's liaison with the CIA during the 1960s), and *CIA Diary* by former CIA Case Officer Philip Agee. Other excellent case studies in this area are found in *The CIA and the Cult of Intelligence* by Victor Marchetti and John D. Marks. Operational patterns described by all of these men are confirmed by hundreds of declassified documents that have surfaced in investigations like those conducted by the Senate's Church committee in the 1970s.

To sum up the lessons clearly explained in both books, all one needs to understand is that the CIA routinely places its deep cover agents in every branch of the US government, especially within the FBI, the DEA, and federal law enforcement agencies. They even do it with municipal police departments such as LAPD, NYPD, or the Chicago PD. The CIA attempted to recruit me in 1973 as a college senior, and the proposition was made that I become a case officer with CIA and then return to LAPD, go through their Academy, and use the LAPD position as a cover. Although I declined that offer and have never taken a penny from the CIA, I was able to find out years later that the CIA, because of my family connections to the Agency and the NSA, had actually steered several of my assignments as an LAPD intern while I was an undergraduate at UCLA. When the CIA places its agents inside the US military, the process is routinely called "sheep dipping."

Why would the CIA do this? Frasca's behavior is right out of the textbook. At LAPD I saw CIA assets and contractors with access to narcotics investigations making deliberate decisions as to who got arrested and who got away. Gary Webb documented one such instance in *Dark Alliance: The CIA, The Contras, and the Crack Cocaine Explosion* when he looked at massive CIA-connected cocaine shipments into Los Angeles. CIA assets doing CIA's bidding are always protected. There is no way to conclusively state that Dave Frasca either worked or works for the CIA, either as a case officer or as an asset. But the role he played before 9/11 clearly served interests other than those of the FBI or the innocent Americans killed or bereaved by the attacks. The power of this secret team is that they are always able to protect their assets, no matter how badly they are exposed. And, as Colleen Rowley noted, Frasca was actually promoted right after 9/11.

Tyrone Powers

On May 19, 2002, retired FBI Special Agent Tyrone Powers, currently the director of the Institute of Criminal Justice/Legal Studies and Public Service, also an assistant professor of law enforcement and criminal justice, was a guest on New York City's radio station 98.7 KIIS. He had some interesting things to say about 9/11. According to an Internet report by Dennis Shipman based upon a transcript of the broadcast, Powers made statements that are consistent with what we have just described.

> Tyrone Powers, a former African American FBI special agent, announced
> on NYC's … 98.7 KIIS FM … hosted by news director and morning

personality Bob Slade, that he had credible evidence strongly suggesting the Bush administration did in fact allow the September 11th attacks to further a hidden agenda ....

Like [sic] Pearl Harbor, the US government needed a substantive excuse to enter World War II and end German hegemony over Europe generally and England particularly .... So an environment had to be created causing an anticipated furor enabling the Roosevelt administration to declare war against this "axis of evil ...."

Does this scenario sound familiar? It ought to, because Powers argues persuasively that the Bush administration has taken a page from history in its endeavor to maintain control over rapidly dwindling oil reserves in the world generally and in the Middle East particularly ....

Powers claims that the Bush administration superciliously perceives itself to be the last world super power; an Empire and, by some misguided albeit self-serving divine right, has to sometimes make appalling decisions to further its imperialistic aim, which is the total, unequivocal domination of the world and, more tellingly, its mineral resources.[31]

During my post-9/11 investigations I verified that Powers had indeed appeared on the broadcast. I also verified his credentials, both as former FBI agent and current professor at Anne Arundel Community College in Maryland. He did not return several calls asking for further comment.

Sibel Edmonds

Initially it was bureaucratic infighting for more funding that derailed important security investigations and questions about contacts of a co-worker with targets of an FBI anti-terror investigation that prompted 33-year-old Sibel Edmonds to blow the whistle inside the FBI in 2002. Hired on an emergency basis and given a Top Secret clearance immediately after 9/11 because of her ability to speak fluent Turkish, Farsi, and Azerbaijani, Edmonds was promptly put to work translating mountains of audio recordings, videotapes, and written communications. By 2004 her complaints were to become much more serious.

At first she heard her supervisors telling her to slow down and not rush important translations. The ostensible purpose for this foot-dragging at a time of great danger was to allow FBI managers to ask for additional funding because they were so far behind. Then she saw civilian translators leaving FBI headquarters with classified material against regulations. The last straw was when a Turkish-American colleague, married to a Major in the US Air Force, disclosed that she had ongoing relationships with a Turkish organization that was an active FBI target. The colleague, Melek Dickerson, suggested that Edmonds should meet people in the organization and get involved. It got worse when Edmonds allegedly discovered that Dickerson had attempted to arrange it so that all translations concerning the Turkish organization would be done by Dickerson exclusively. However, it was also an organization covered in the "take" given to Edmonds, and she became suspicious.

Acting on those suspicions, Edmonds ordered files previously translated by Dickerson, checked them, and found that material information relating to terrorist investigations and espionage had been deleted, left un-translated, or marked as irrelevant.[32]

Edmonds — a neophyte with no prior intelligence training — assumed the worst but failed to comprehend the possibility that she was being "pitched" to spy on an organization that may have already been penetrated. In that eventuality an intelligence operation could be used to plant false information or perhaps even to manipulate other assets who might believe they were receiving orders from Islamic fundamentalist terrorists. Sanitized translations would prevent FBI agents from compromising a CIA operation in Turkey.

Published photos depict Edmonds as strikingly attractive; people like her are often prime subjects for recruitment as intelligence assets while being given as little information as possible as to how they are being used. In very sensitive operations if the "asset" has no knowledge that he or she is being "run," so much the better. One term used to refer to such assets in the intelligence community is "Dixie cups" because they are often used once and thrown away. Such "assets" are expendable.

The likelihood that Edmonds was being "pitched" was confirmed by a Senate intelligence staffer.[33] Yet if she was being pitched over an operation that had to do with identifying real terrorist threats, whoever was doing it was going about it the wrong way. Following the rulebook she had been given, Edmonds did exactly what would have been expected of a loyal employee. She complained first to her immediate supervisors and finally, in March of 2002, to the FBI's Office of Professional Responsibility (OPR) and then to the FBI's Inspector General.[34]

Her contract was terminated for the convenience of the government in March 2002 but not until after she had received threats, both direct and implied, from FBI supervisors and from Dickerson.[35] Her next stops were Congress and *60 Minutes* where she got a much better reception as she sought to find out what had happened and correct what she felt were genuine problems. Senator Charles Grassley found her convincing and credible.[36] In stories throughout 2002 Edmonds' plight was discussed in the press but there was no discussion of advance warnings of attacks known to the FBI or the White House. Edmonds filed suit against the FBI over its refusal to respond to her Freedom of Information Act request and against the Department of Justice for an improper termination. She was followed routinely, especially to court appearances. Attorney General John Ashcroft, in response to a request from FBI Director Mueller, sought and obtained a gag order restricting what Edmonds could say about her case. The authority invoked to secure the order was the rarely used "State Secrets" privilege.[37] The same privilege was invoked again by the Justice Department in April 2004 as Edmonds was subpoenaed to give a deposition in a $100 trillion civil suit against

Saudi interests for their alleged connections to the 9/11 attacks. A massive public response, including activist challenges to US Marshals and the clerk in US District court over an attempt to hold a closed hearing on the motion to quash Edmonds's subpoena, apparently caught the government by surprise. One of those who challenged the Marshal's move to close the hearing was African-American former 26-year CIA counterterror case officer Leutrell Osborne. Osborne is also the source from whom I received the unedited *Izvestia* story which went into great detail about an explicit warning sent (including targets and dates) directly from Russian President Vladimir Putin just days before the attacks.[38]

After the confrontation and an apparent huddle in chambers, Judge Reggie Walton decided to open the hearing. It was decided that he would issue a temporary order to quash the subpoena but would not render a final decision until sometime in June. As this book goes to press, the issue has not been decided.

As Edmonds's various legal matters continued into 2004 the 9/11 Commission chaired by former New Jersey Governor Thomas Kean came in to the spotlight as pressure from victim families, activists, and the mounting pile of documentation flatly contradicting the Bush administration's statements collided with the scheduled testimony of many key witnesses including Richard Clarke, John Ashcroft, Robert Mueller, George Tenet, Donald Rumsfeld, and National Security Advisor Condoleezza Rice.

At the same time that pressure was building for Rice to testify in public, Edmonds gave testimony to the commission. According to *Salon*, she told the commissioners that "the FBI had detailed information prior to September 11, 2001, that a terrorist attack involving airplanes was being plotted."[39] In a number of press interviews after Rice's testimony, and after the publication of an op-ed in which Rice stated that the administration had no specific information of a domestic threat or that airplanes might be used as weapons, Edmonds said, "That's an outrageous lie. And documents can prove it's a lie."[40]

Unfortunately in the same interview, Edmonds also expressed the view that when George W. Bush said that "they had" no specific information about September 11, he was telling the truth. Perhaps if Edmonds had been permitted to speak with some of her other colleagues she might feel differently; the system does an equally good job of isolating whistleblowers from the media and from each other. Alternatively, she may have been confining her criticism to the FBI out of a desire to choose her battles, or perhaps to protect some ally elsewhere in the administration whose responsibility included alerting the president. But all this is far less likely than a genuine ignorance on Edmonds's part; she knew enough to discredit Rice, then gave Bush the benefit of the doubt in the absence of better information about the president's knowledge — information other whistleblowers had.

Steve Butler

Air Force Lieutenant Colonel Steve Butler was yet another person with inside knowledge who spilled the beans about US government complicity in the attacks of 9/11. While Vice Chancellor of the Defense Language Institute in Monterey, California, Butler wrote a chilling May 26 letter to his local paper. It read:

A contemptible offense

It's about time conservative idiots like Steve Kelly and Rod Musgrove got a dose of reality. Of course President Bush knew about the impending attacks on America. He did nothing to warn the American people because he needed this war on terrorism. His daddy had Saddam and he needed Osama.

His presidency was going nowhere. He wasn't elected by the American people, but placed into the Oval Office by the conservative Supreme Court. The economy was sliding into the usual Republican pits and he needed something on which to hang his presidency.

For them to accuse Democrats of being "sleazy" is laughable. Isn't it ironic that Kelly begins his inane babble with a reference to Monica Lewinsky? How many people died because of Monica Lewinsky? And for Musgrove to call the assertions "contemptible" is another joke. Funny how he manages to make disparaging remarks about President Clinton, as well.

Face it people, Bill Clinton was a great president. This guy is a joke.

What is sleazy and contemptible is the President of the United States not telling the American people what he knows for political gain. The Democrats asking pertinent questions is their duty as public servants.

Steve Butler
Monterey.[41]

Butler's letter was startling when I learned of it by reading mainstream stories that Butler had been suspended for it — and was facing a court martial.[42]

In fact a multitude of press reports, including stories from the *New York Times*, the *Washington Post*, and *Newsweek*, all published between September 15 and 17, 2001, disclosed that at least five of the hijackers had received US military training at bases in the US, including flight lessons. Among the latter was Mohammed Atta, who apparently received his training while wanted for terrorist activities. Atta's US military training was confirmed by a separate story published by Knight Ridder at a time when many of the military training connections were causing the military to engage in some disingenuous doubletalk. Several subsequent stories indicated that while the five names matched up with 9/11 hijackers, it was apparently a case of more than one person having the same name. Yet the Department of Defense has not to this date disclosed the identities of the five people whose names matched those of 9/11 hijackers. Even more compelling is the fact that *Newsweek* reported three of the hijackers had received flight training at the Pensacola Naval Air Station.[43]

All told, 14 of the 19 9/11 hijackers lived and studied for a considerable period in southern Florida. No one has done a better job of investigating the connections of these hijackers to military and intelligence operations than investigative journalist Dan Hopsicker. His investigations have also produced compelling evidence linking Rudi Dekkers, the operator of the flight school attended by Atta and others, to US intelligence operations and the destruction and/or immediate confiscation of incriminating records immediately after the attacks *with the hands-on involvement of Florida Governor Jeb Bush.*[44] Hopsicker, a former broadcast news producer for MS-NBC, has produced a compelling video called *Mohammed Atta and the Venice Flying Circus* that details many of these links. He maintains a detailed website at: <www.madcowprod.com> [inexplicably, in the summer of 2004, Hopsicker performed a startling flip-flop by choosing to agree with most of the Kean Commission's highly questionable findings.]

How did Steve Butler fare? In June the Air Force announced that it had concluded its investigation and that Butler was going to face nonjudicial punishment likely to consist of a letter of reprimand. Had he chosen, Butler could have insisted on a court martial and public trial wherein he could have, and most likely would have, exposed direct links between the military and the hijackers. I finally located Butler in the summer of 2004. He confirmed having written the letter, but denied any contact with or knowledge of the hijackers. His school, the DLI, was only responsible for foreign language training. English language training was conducted at other facilities.

In spite of the US government's position that there was no compelling case that an attack on the US by al Qaeda was imminent, there was apparently one person who was paying very close attention to the information coming in from the brick agents in the field. In July 2001 Attorney General John Ashcroft stopped flying on commercial airlines altogether, opting instead for a chartered government jet. This, according to one story, was because of threat assessments from the FBI.[45]

CHAPTER 13

PENETRATION

9/11 Families Outraged Hijacker-In-Training Was Let Go

WASHINGTON — Relatives of 9/11 victims are expressing outrage that the government didn't pursue a lead offered by a man who said he'd been trained as a hijacker for Osama bin Laden.

Some of the families are reacting angrily to new details about the incident. Others are just learning about it for the first time.

In April 2000, a British Muslim went to the FBI's Newark, N.J., office and told agents of plans to hijack US airliners. The visit is according to the report of a Senate-House committee that studied the attacks.

The 30-year-old Khan said he was taught hijacking basics along with about 30 others in Pakistan, and learned how to smuggle weapons through airport security and techniques to overpower passengers and crew.

The FBI was unable to verify any aspect of Khan's story or identify his contacts in the United States.

But after his claims were investigated, he was turned over to British authorities and eventually freed.

The man was identified Thursday by The Wall Street Journal and "NBC Nightly News" as Niaz Khan, a Briton of Pakistani descent.

The families want to know why Khan's warnings were ignored.

A woman whose husband died in the World Trade Center calls the episode "another brand of negligence."

Associated Press — June 4, 2004

Chairman Graham, Chairman Goss, before I proceed with my statement, I want to make clear to you and the members of these two committees that the information I am going to present has been cleared for public release. As you know, much of the information the Joint Inquiry Staff has been examining is highly classified. Over the last two months, we have been working with the intelligence community in a long and arduous process to declassify information we believe is important to the public's understanding of why the

Intelligence Community did not know of the September 11 attacks in advance. By late last night we were able to resolve all but two issues.

The Director of Central Intelligence has declined to declassify two issues of particular importance to this inquiry.

- *Any references to the Intelligence Community providing information to the President or White House; and*
- *The identity of and key information on a key al Qa'ida leader involved in the September 11 attacks...*
- *The Joint Inquiry Staff disagrees with the DCI's position on both issues.*

— Eleanor Hill, Joint Staff Director of the Senate and House Intelligence Committees investigating 9/11, sworn testimony, September 18, 2002

Finally, it is important to note that efforts to prevent or disrupt terrorist action frequently are successful, and these activities have reduced the number of terrorist incidents that would have occurred in the absence of these activities: disruption of terrorist events by working with foreign intelligence and law enforcement services has proved profitable; US intelligence agencies prevented Osama bin Laden's organization from carrying out at least seven vehicle bomb attacks on US facilities since August 1998 (Kelly, 1999, p. 1A), and US intelligence has conducted successful disruption operations in as many as 10 countries in the six months up to March 1999 (Associated Press, 1999)...

In actual operations and special events, agencies generally coordinated their activities. For example, we examined several overseas counterterrorist operations and found that agencies generally followed the draft interagency International Guidelines. DoD, the FBI, and the Central Intelligence Agency (CIA) performed their respective roles in military planning, law enforcement and intelligence gathering under the oversight of the State Department (e.g., the Ambassador). Minor interagency tensions or conflicts during these operations were resolved and did not appear to have posed risk to the mission...

In a similar vein, FBI data on terrorism in the United States suggest a reasonably high degree of success in terrorism prevention activities at home — only a small annual number of actual terrorist incidents occurred in recent years, and more preventions of terrorist incidents than actual incidents.

— 2001 RAND Corporation Study on Preparation of the US Army for Homeland Security.[1]

There goes the excuse that there was incapacitating tension between the FBI and the CIA and that appropriate mechanisms were not in place to have prevented 9/11.

In fact, continuing assertions by law enforcement and intelligence executives and managers that they lacked the intelligence capabilities (both technical and legal) to have known of the attacks before they occurred are demonstrably false, as are the other positions we have thus far examined. Notwithstanding that the mainstream media have inexcusably tried to hammer this belief into the consciousness of the public, available evidence — most of it undisputed by the government — also reveals that al Qaeda and its operatives were under minute scrutiny years before the attacks. The open source material I present here suggests that the penetration of al Qaeda was complete to the point where Delmart "Mike" Vreeland's statement, "Let one happen, stop the rest" was not only operationally possible but very likely carried out just as he had predicted; the agencies concerned could pick and choose which terrorist actions to prevent or allow. The evidence also demonstrates that the Bush administration knew a great deal of specific information before the attacks.

Intelligence is broken down into three basic categories: HUMINT (human intelligence, gathered by people); SIGINT (signals intelligence, gathered by eavesdropping on land lines, cell phones, radios, and e-mail); and ELINT (electronic intelligence, gathered by such direct electronic surveillance as, for example, the use of parabolic microphones to overhear a distant conversation, or a body wire to record person-to-person conversations). Long before 9/11, US and foreign intelligence had achieved penetrations of al Qaeda by all three methods and in many differing circumstances in a manner that suggests there was very little that al Qaeda did that the Bush administration and many other governments were not aware of.

Within the SIGINT category lies an exceptionally powerful eavesdropping program called Echelon. Echelon's existence has been acknowledged by the Australian government since 1988, when it was exposed by whistleblowers who charged that it had been misused for political purposes. Building on an original post-World War II alliance between the US, Britain, Australia, New Zealand, and Canada, Echelon had by the late 1980s been expanded to include joint operations with Germany, Japan, and China. It was initiated on the legal premise that while it is not permissible for the US government to monitor the conversations of its citizens without a warrant, it is not *illegal* for British intelligence to monitor American citizens, etc. Once the "take" has been pooled, the respective agencies can have safe access to their own domestic intelligence, because the Britons, Australians, or Germans did it, and not the home government.

> Echelon's surveillance power resides in its ability "to tap all international and some domestic communications circuits, and sift out messages which sound interesting. Computers automatically analyze every telex message or data signal, and can also identify calls to, say, a target telephone number in London, no matter from which country they originate."[2]

Echelon has also been mated with computing programs and secret spy-satellite technology, including voice and "keyword" recognition that is remarkably effective in bringing critical messages to the attention of analysts on short notice. None of this, of course, diminishes the unlimited ability — which has existed since the first telephone number was issued — to intercept all communications to or from a known point. The primary operating agency for all Echelon activities worldwide is the US National Security Agency.[3]

Even as the US government has continued to officially deny Echelon's existence, the BBC discussed it at length in 1999, saying:

> Every international telephone call, fax, e-mail, or radio transmission can be listened to by powerful computers capable of voice recognition. They home in on a long list of key words, or patterns of messages. They are looking for evidence of international crime, like terrorism.[4]

So pervasive has Echelon become that in February 2000 the European Parliament was holding hearings on allegations that Echelon had been used to give unfair advantage to American and British companies. The French, the apparent targets, were quite upset, and the hearings made headlines across Europe for days.

Author James Bamford, a former NSA employee, has been justly praised for unearthing declassified Top Secret records — most significantly, Bamford publicized documents from Operation Northwoods, a 1960 program which the US military had approved but which President Kennedy prevented. Northwoods was a detailed plan to shoot down American aircraft and attack American military bases in the guise of Cuban forces, and then blame Fidel Castro as a pretext for a full-scale invasion of Cuba. Bamford observed, "The NSA's targets are on the front pages of the newspaper every day: Osama bin Laden, North Korea, missile transfers to Iran, nuclear weapons in Pakistan and India .... They don't care about [European consortium] Airbus, they don't care about Boeing, they don't care about the Acme Shoe Co. in Des Moines."[5] I happen to disagree on Bamford's last point, but notice that Osama bin Laden was the first item on his list.

By April of 2001 it had been documented that Echelon was particularly effective against cell phones, and had even been improved to the point where it would recognize the unique sound made by each individual key on a computer keyboard. This enabled the sound of keystrokes to be picked up remotely and translated into text.[6] And by May 2001, just months before the attacks of 9/11, the European Parliament was advising all member nations and their citizens to encrypt every e-mail they sent, even though there was good reason to believe that even all commercial encryption programs had crumbled under Echelon's might.[7] Consider the significance of this in light of the Indian government's having tied the $100,000 wire transfer from ISI Chief General Ahmad to Mohammed Atta via the cell phone records of Omar Saeed Sheikh. There is no question that, given a known reception point such as Mohammad Atta's cell phone, or any of the known residences used by the hijackers and their support cells, every call from any location would have been monitored.[8] Since 1988 Echelon had been continually refined and upgraded to intercept virtually every electronic communication on the planet, including satellite communications, e-mails (transmitted by fiber-optic cables, microwaves, and satellites), and banking wire transfers. And in spite of near total secrecy about the working of these "sources and methods," there is a compelling record of dots to connect that — in a rational world — would be very embarrassing to the US government and have not been addressed in the declassified Congressional intelligence report on 9/11.

The record

Consider these known al Qaeda penetrations broken down by category. All of them constitute advance warnings of the attacks.

HUMINT/ELINT: US officials have admitted that American agents had infiltrated al Qaeda cells. Electronically recorded conversations obtained from these agents on September 10 contained messages including "Watch the news" and "Tomorrow will be a great day for us." It was not disclosed how long these penetrations had been in place, and official spokespersons categorized these statements as "needles in a haystack."[9]

SIGINT: NSA Director Michael Hayden testified before Congress in October 2002 that the NSA had no indications that al Qaeda was planning attacks on US soil, let alone against New York or Washington.[10] This directly contradicts the fact that in the summer of 2001 the NSA had intercepted communications between the alleged tactical mastermind of the attacks, Khalid Shaikh Mohammed and Mohammed Atta. The NSA did not share the information with any other agencies even at a time when Mohammed was on the FBI's most-wanted terror list. The NSA also failed to translate some messages and later offered the nonsensical excuse that they had no way to separate these calls from millions of others.[11]

HUMINT/SIGINT/ELINT: Two of the 9/11 hijackers, Nawaf Alhazmi and Khalid Almidhar, share the distinction of having been active al Qaeda members connected to multiple terrorist attacks and also having been among the most closely watched, yet completely free to travel even while they were wanted men. A multitude of press accounts from AP, the *New York Times*, the *Los Angeles Times*, *Newsweek*, and perhaps two dozen major international press organizations have documented not only that the CIA, the FBI, and the NSA had been watching these two since at least 1999, but also that these agencies at times acted in ways to conceal or protect the pair's movements from law enforcement agents who had shown interest in them.[12] The press accounts have been corroborated in large measure by congressional testimony.

The pair traveled to Malaysia in January 2000, where they met with the highest-level al Qaeda officials, including Mohammed Atta and Khalid Shaikh Mohammad. All those attending the meeting were surveilled at every moment, and every activity, from e-mails at Internet cafes to private outdoor meetings to cell phone calls, was apparently recorded by both US and Malaysian intelligence. Both men had previously been traveling freely even after they had been connected to the African embassy bombings of 1998. Nor was their traveling liberty impaired, even after connections were later made to an al Qaeda operations center in Yemen and the October 2000 bombing of the USS *Cole*. Phone calls to and from a Yemeni safe house involving the pair were routinely monitored, and it was known that Osama bin Laden himself frequently used the house as a logistics center.

Even after the two had been listed as possible terror suspects, they were allowed to re-enter the US after the Malaysia meeting — their visas unchallenged — and to live openly in San Diego. They lived first in an apartment where as many as five of the 9/11 hijackers came to visit in 2001, then later in the private home of Abudssattar Shaikh, who was subsequently revealed to be a "tested asset" of the FBI.[13] They stayed with the FBI informant until just before the attacks.

In the months before the attacks the pair traveled (either separately or together) to Phoenix, where they met with the group being actively surveilled by FBI Agent Ken Williams. Papers later recovered from Zacarias Moussaoui mentioned Alhazmi and Almidhar as having facilitated his flight training. In spite of an extensive record of continuing surveillance of the two, and even after they had finally been placed on an FBI watch list and a priority CIA alert labeled "immediate" issued in August of 2001, they traveled openly and unmolested until the day of the attacks, making no attempts to conceal their identities.[14]

Apparently these urgent warnings of FBI Headquarters and the CIA were relayed neither to local field offices nor to local police agencies. It's easy to understand why. A rookie police officer could have found the two before breakfast. Both men had California driver's licenses, car registrations, Social Security numbers, credit cards in their own names, and even listings in the phone book. They were taking flying lessons near San Diego. They traveled under their own names, and one of them even booked his 9/11 ticket on the American Airlines website using his own credit card.[15]

An analysis of press stories shows that while Alhazmi and Almidhar were wanted for connections to the embassy bombings and the *Cole* attack — and were living with an FBI informant — no one except the other hijackers and the ringleaders was able to find them. At the same time, other press stories indicate that all of their communications and movements were being monitored. In fact, during his congressional testimony, NSA Chief Michael Hayden admitted that the agency had been watching the two and knew of their al Qaeda associations. Even though Hayden said that the information had been shared with other intelligence agencies, a congressional investigation subsequently disclosed that it had not.[16]

The strange behavior of US intelligence puzzled at least two foreign intelligence services who were also following the pair very closely. The Malaysian intelligence service had done an outstanding job of monitoring the January 2000 meeting of al Qaeda leaders as well as two visits to the same Kuala Lumpur condominium by Zacarias Moussaoui in September and October of 2000. "The Malaysians said they were surprised by the CIA's lack of interest following the January meeting. "'We couldn't fathom it, really,' Rais Yatim, Malaysia's Legal Affairs minister, told *Newsweek*. 'There was no show of concern,' he said."[17]

On August 23, 2001, the Israeli Mossad, which had been operating a large spy ring inside the United States following al Qaeda, provided the United States with a list of 19 terrorists who were planning to carry out an attack in the near future. Four of the names on the list are known, and they include Alhazmi, Almidhar, Marwan Alshehhi, and Mohammed Atta. In fact, according to multiple news sources, Mossad agents had rented an apartment in Hollywood, Florida, near where Atta and Alshehhi were then living and taking flight lessons. It may have been the specific Israeli warning that finally prompted the CIA to issue its urgent warning just weeks before the attacks, a warning which somehow never got circulated.[18]

Alhazmi and Almidhar also share one additional critical distinction. They both fought in Chechnya and Bosnia, where the CIA was actively working, with and supplying, al Qaeda elements. The pair's Chechen adventure was even acknowledged by DCI George Tenet in his unclassified testimony before the 9/11 congressional intelligence panels.[19]

SIGINT: For more than 18 months Italian authorities wiretapped an al Qaeda cell in Milan.[20] Starting in October 2000, FBI agents assisted Italian authorities in analyzing the tapes, and this resulted in a direct warning to the US from Italy that planes might be used as weapons against US targets.[21]

SIGINT: Intercepted communications from Afghanistan indicated that al Qaeda could be planning an attack in late June or July.[22]

SIGINT/ELINT/HUMINT: Italian authorities obtained information from wiretaps of al Qaeda cells that a possible attack was planned to kill President Bush at the G8 Summit in Genoa scheduled for July by crashing aircraft into the summit or his hotel. Additional information suggested that Egyptian intelligence had achieved HUMINT penetrations of al Qaeda cells that confirmed information from the wiretaps and surveillance. Some conversations were recorded as a result of the bugging of a Citroen automobile used by Egyptian terrorists in Italy who are close to bin Laden. As a result the airspace around Genoa was closed and the conference was ringed with anti-aircraft weapons.[23]

SIGINT: In early September 2001 the NSA intercepted multiple phone calls into the United States from Abu Zubaida, the man who is reported to be bin Laden's operations chief. No details of what was intercepted have been released, but it is obvious that the parties receiving the calls would have been identified.[24]

SIGINT: British sources disclosed that telephone conversations between Osama bin Laden and associates in Pakistan and Afghanistan in the weeks prior to 9/11 were monitored and that the attacks were generally discussed in those conversations.[25]

SIGINT: On September 9, 2001, Osama bin Laden reportedly called his mother to tell her, "In two days you're going to hear big news and you're not going to hear from me for a while." In making this revelation, US officials acknowledged that they had been able to monitor "some" of bin Laden's telephone communications. At the time bin Laden was using a satellite telephone, and the signals were intercepted and "sometimes" recorded.[26] Remember that the bin Laden family owns a commercial satellite company. Realizing that perhaps this self-serving revelation might later point to negligence or culpability and so backfire, officials downplayed the story on CNN, saying they doubted that this actually happened.[27]

SIGINT/HUMINT: In a major post-9/11 speech wherein British Prime Minister Tony Blair disclosed the "evidence" against bin Laden, it was revealed that the British government had both intercepts and interrogation summaries showing that bin Laden had sent out orders for al Qaeda operatives to return to Afghanistan by September 10.[28]

SIGINT: At least 30 additional electronic communications were later disclosed to have been intercepted by the NSA, including two placed the day before the attacks. One stated "the match begins tomorrow" and the other included the statement, "Tomorrow is zero hour." It was the disclosure of these intercepts by members of the Senate intelligence committee that prompted the FBI and the White House to threaten senators with polygraph examinations and office searches for disclosing classified information. The NSA later claimed that the messages weren't translated until after the attacks and that the agency had no way to separate them from thousands of other messages.[29] Again, utter nonsense. In fact the translation excuse is belied by the fact that American scientific journals have described how translation software possessed by intelligence agencies turns many of the world's spoken languages into substantively reliable English automatically.[30]

SIGINT: Senator Orrin Hatch (R - Utah), later to be chastised by Defense Secretary Donald Rumsfeld for making an unauthorized disclosure of classified information, stated to the Associated Press that the US government was monitoring bin Laden's communications electronically and overheard two of bin Laden's aides celebrating the attacks. Said Hatch, "They have an intercept of some information that included people associated with bin Laden who acknowledged a couple of targets were hit."[31] The administration's dilemma was obvious. While needing to make the case that bin Laden and associates had perpetrated the attacks, they could not afford to have it known that they knew everything that was being said in advance. It is preposterous to think that somehow US intelligence was able to intercept conversations on the day of the attacks but not before.

SIGINT: As reported in the German daily *Frankfurter Algemeine Zeitung* (FAZ) on September 14, the German intelligence service BND warned both the CIA and Israel in June that Middle Eastern terrorists were "planning to hijack commercial aircraft to use as weapons to attack important symbols of American and Israeli culture." The story specifically referred to Echelon. The BND warnings were also passed to the United Kingdom.[32] No known denial by the BND of the accuracy of this story exists, and the FAZ report indicates that the information was received directly from BND sources.

SIGINT: According to a September 14 report in the Internet newswire online, i.e., German police, monitoring the phone calls of a jailed Iranian man, learned the man was telephoning US intelligence agencies last summer to warn of an imminent attack on the World Trade Center in the week of September 9. German officials confirmed the calls to the US government for the story but refused to discuss additional details.[33]

SIGINT/ELINT?/HUMINT?: Russian intelligence warned the US weeks before the attacks that as many as 25 al Qaeda pilots had been training for an attack mission in the United States. On the day of the attacks a special Russian intelligence emissary delivered *audiotapes with telephone conversations directly relating to the attacks* to a deputy director of the CIA at Langley. In an MSNBC interview on September 15, Russian President Putin stated that he had ordered Russian intelligence to warn the US government "in the strongest possible terms" of imminent assaults on airports and government buildings before the attacks on September 11. No credible information has emerged from any source indicating that Putin omitted the above information when issuing the warning. Why would he?[34]

As noted by Peter Dale Scott in *Drugs, Oil and War* (Rowman & Littlefield) bin Laden had for years established close working relationships with the Russian Mafias. This has been acknowledged by US government officials. Part of this relationship centered on Afghani heroin. From this, there is good reason to infer, especially by virtue of the well-documented relationships between former KGB officers and the Mafias, that Russian intelligence had also achieved a degree of human penetration as well.[35]

SIGINT: On February 13, *United Press International* terrorism correspondent Richard Sale, while covering a Manhattan trial of one of Osama bin Laden's followers, Khalid al Fawaaz, reported that the National Security Agency had broken bin Laden's encrypted communications. The story said,

> The US case unfolding against him in United States District Court in Manhattan is based mainly on National Security Agency intercepts of phone calls between bin Laden and his operatives around the world - Afghanistan to London, from Kenya to the United States ....
>
> On August 11, two days after the bombings were completed, bin Laden's satellite number phone was used to contact network operatives in Yemen, at a number frequently called by perpetrators of the bombing from their safe house in Nairobi.
>
> Since 1995, bin Laden has tried to protect his communications with "a full suite of tools," according to Ben Venzke, Director of Intelligence, Special Projects for Defense ....

Since bin Laden started to encrypt certain calls in 1995, why would they now be part of a court record? "Codes were broken," US officials said.[36]

Even if that revelation prompted an immediate change in bin Laden's methods of communication, just six months before the attacks, the administration has consistently maintained — and military and covert experience dictates — that the attacks were planned for at least several years.

One press account described a related Sale story: "[the] story noted not that the US government had gained the capacity to eavesdrop on bin Laden at will but that it had 'gone into foreign bank accounts .... and deleted or transferred funds, and jammed or blocked the group's cell or satellite phones.'"[37]

This story, which was not evaluating the same Richard Sale story cited above confirmed that the penetrations of al Qaeda had been successful to the point of interfering with its finances. That, along with what is known of the Robert Wright FBI investigations in Chicago, is proof that al Qaeda financing could have been seriously disrupted.

Researcher Tom Flocco, who wrote a series on 9/11-related insider trading for *FTW*, looked more deeply into this point. Flocco observed:

> In the trial of former Deutsche Bank executive Kevin Ingram, who pled guilty to laundering drug money to finance terrorist operations linked to al Qaeda just two weeks before the 9/11 attacks, indications surfaced that the Justice Department had penetrated the terrorists' financial network. A November 16 [2001] Associated Press story by Catherine Wilson stated, 'Numerous promised wire transfers never arrived, but there were discussions of foreign bankers taking payoffs to move the money to purchase weapons into the United States,' said prosecutor Rolando Garcia. Two questions are invited but unanswered. How were the wire transfers blocked, and how was the Justice Department able to monitor the money flows without alerting either the bankers or the suspects?[38]

These are the footprints of PROMIS software. One is now compelled to ask if the $100,000 wired to Mohammed Atta by Pakistani ISI Chief and CIA asset Mahmud Ahmad was one transfer that the CIA wanted to go through successfully.

HUMINT/SIGINT: Jordanian intelligence had for years done a masterful job of infiltrating al Qaeda. A May 2002, story from *The International Herald Tribune* reported, "Since the early 1990s, the kingdom's well-organized and efficient intelligence service, the General Intelligence Division (GID), has carefully tracked the CIA-trained or Pakistani-trained guerillas or terrorists, or freedom fighters, or whatever you choose to call them — who survived their victorious 1979–89 war to expel the Soviet invaders from Afghanistan .... Jordan's GID hunted the returned fighters, capturing and bringing to justice several who became active terrorists. The

GID aided the US government in countless ways, even helping US law enforcement officers to apprehend Al Qaeda and other operatives who had formed cells in the United States or Canada."[39]

Author John K. Cooley, a veteran of ABC News and widely respected commentator on terrorism issues, described how in the summer of 2001 the GID made an intercept deemed so important that it was relayed to the US government not only officially, most likely through the CIA station in Amman, but also personally through an Iranian-born German intelligence agent. From my experience this was a form of insurance for the Jordanian government in case the US ever denied that Jordan had delivered the message or asserted that the Jordanian government had been less than a staunch ally. Such is the fear of the Empire's wrath around the world. The message clearly indicated that a major attack had been planned inside the continental United States and that aircraft would be used. The code name for the operation was "Al Ourush," or "The Big Wedding." When this information subsequently became embarrassing to the Bush administration, Jordanian officials backed away from their earlier confirmations.[40] The administration had been insisting since the day of the attacks that it had received no specific forewarnings.

Cooley's story told of a French magazine and a Moroccan newspaper (names not given) simultaneously reporting that a Moroccan agent named Hassan Dabou had penetrated al Qaeda to the point of getting close to bin Laden, who was "very disappointed" that the 1993 bombing had not toppled the World Trade Center. The agent remained in place until weeks before the attacks. He successfully delivered a message to Moroccan intelligence that al Qaeda was planning "large-scale operations in New York in the summer or autumn of 2001."

Then Cooley dropped a bombshell.

> Though Dabou won bin Laden's confidence at first, according to an unnamed French intelligence agent cited in the reports, after he was invited to the United States to tell his story he lost contact with al Qaeda, curtailing his ability to prevent September 11. Nonetheless, the story goes, he was given asylum and a new identity in the United States and is said to be helping out in the 'war on terror.'[41]

Judiciously, Cooley added the caveat that he had not been able to confirm the Moroccan story as he had the one from Jordan. However, a story from the *Times of London* a month later did just that, and even interviewed a recently surfaced Dabou in the process. The lead sentence stated that Dabou had successfully infiltrated al Qaeda for more than two years. In addition to confirming Cooley's story, the *Times* disclosed that, acting upon Moroccan intelligence information, the intelligence services of Britain, France, Italy, Spain, and the Netherlands successfully rounded up Moroccan suspects in Europe with ties to al Qaeda immediately after the attacks. It also confirmed that bin Laden had extensive operations in Morocco and that bin Laden's personal pilot L'Houssaine Kerchtou was a Moroccan national.[42]

It seems that someone in the intelligence community decided to make Dabou available for the *Times* interview — an extremely risky move for someone with the kind of knowledge about bin Laden and al Qaeda that Dabou reportedly possessed. And Dabou's statement in the *Times* story that he had broken cover on his own to warn of the attacks — a seeming attempt to put spin on Cooley's story — is not credible. Breaking cover means that one has exposed oneself as an agent and can never go back. No deep-cover agent is left without means of communication, and there is nothing to suggest that Dabou learned complete details of the attacks moments before they occurred and had to "run for it." The only thing that would have justified such a break in cover would have been Dabou's possession of enough information to actually prevent the attacks. Otherwise, the number-one imperative of the agent-in-place is to remain there until that knowledge is secured.

Judging from years of study of covert operations, talking to those who either were undercover or who "ran" assets that were, this episode means only one thing. It means that the CIA, knowing that there was an agent-in-place who could have compromised the Agency's role in facilitating rather than preventing the attacks, knowingly compromised an invaluable operation, extracted someone who could not be replaced, brought him to the United States, and hid him from the world in order to prevent him from preventing the attacks.

In light of these revelations about known penetrations of al Qaeda, the words of a former Egyptian foreign minister might seem just a little more credible to a skeptical American audience and are worth examining closely.

HUMINT/SIGINT: Egyptian journalist Mohammed Heikal, a former Egyptian foreign minister who has been described as "the Arab world's foremost political commentator," expressed disbelief that bin Laden and al Qaeda could have conducted the 9/11 attack without the US knowing. "Bin Laden has been under surveillance for years: every telephone call was monitored and al Qaeda has been penetrated by American intelligence, Pakistani intelligence, Saudi intelligence, Egyptian intelligence. They could not have kept secret an operation that required such a degree of organization and sophistication."[43]

Somebody knew

Throughout the world the independent media organizations have done an outstanding job of picking up and reporting on independently published stories that the major media overlooked. One of the most outstanding examples of this was a July 16, 2002, piece posted at the website of Portland *Indymedia* (<www.portland.indymedia.org>) that reproduced the following short article originally found at *The Memory Hole*.[44]

NPR interview on 9/11 confirmed attack was 'not entirely unexpected.'
It's certainly one of the most disturbing and important indications
that the government knew the attacks of September 11, 2001, were

coming. On that morning, National Public Radio (NPR) was presenting live coverage of the attacks on its show *Morning Edition*. Host Bob Edwards went to a reporter in the field — David Welna, NPR's congressional correspondent — who was in the Capitol building as it was being evacuated. Here is the crucial portion of Welna's report:

"'I spoke with Congressman Ike Skelton — a Democrat from Missouri and a member of the Armed Services Committee — who said that just recently the Director of the CIA warned that there could be an attack — an imminent attack — on the United States of this nature. So this is not entirely unexpected.'

(Audio links for this interview are located at The Memory Hole and NPR websites) <www.thememoryhole.org/tenet-911.htm>

This one story is in diametric opposition to all officially stated US government positions about US government foreknowledge of 9/11. In the fall of 2002 I placed several calls to the office of Congressman Skelton asking for comment. I had hoped to be able to interview him during a pending trip to the Capital. None of my calls was returned.

The bottom line is that, based upon what is known about successful intelligence penetrations for years prior to the attacks of 9/11, Osama bin Laden and al Qaeda could not have sneezed without the CIA or the NSA knowing about it.

CHAPTER 14

9/11 INSIDER TRADING, OR:
"YOU DIDN'T REALLY SEE THAT,
EVEN THOUGH WE SAW IT"

A "put" option is a leveraged bet that a stock price is going to fall precipitously (a "call" option is the opposite bet). One option covers 100 shares of a given stock and usually has an expiration date of four months. For a very small investment — sometimes a dollar a share — a speculator can purchase the right to sell a stock at a fixed price during the contract period even though he doesn't have to own the stock when the option is placed. So if one were to place a single put option contract on American airlines at $30 per share and the stock fell to $18 dollars a few days or weeks later, one could go out and purchase one hundred shares at $18 and then immediately exercise the option and sell them immediately at $30 netting a $12 per share profit or $1,200. This is what happened on a far larger scale and with many companies around the world on 9/11.

Outrage and a clear mission

> Sources tell CBS News that the afternoon before the attack, alarm bells were sounding over unusual trading in the US stock options market
> — CBS News, September 19, 2001.[1]

- A jump in UAL put options 90 times (not 90 percent) above normal between September 6 and September 10, and 285 times higher than average on the Thursday before the attack.
  — CBS News, September 26

- A jump in American Airlines put options 60 times (not 60 percent) above normal on the day before the attacks.
  — CBS News, September 26

- No similar trading occurred on any other airlines.
  — Bloomberg Business Report;[2] the Institute for Counterterrorism (ICT), Herzliyya, Israel[3] [citing data from the CBOE]

238

- Morgan Stanley saw, between September 7 and September 10, an increase of 27 times (not 27 percent) in the purchase of put options on its shares.[4]
- Merrill-Lynch saw a jump of more than 12 times the normal level of put options in the four trading days before the attacks.[5]

'It's not that farfetched,' said former SEC enforcement director William McLucas, now with the Wilmer, Cutler & Pickering law firm. *'This collection of terrorist acts has created a serious problem for our markets and a number of industry sectors. It is not as whacky or as Tom Clancy-ish as one might like to wish.'*

'This could very well be insider trading at the worst, most horrific, most evil use you've ever seen in your entire life.... It's absolutely unprecedented to see cases of insider trading covering the entire world from Japan to the United States to North America to Europe.'
— Dylan Ratigan of Bloomberg News, ABC World News Tonight, September 20, 2001.[6]

'I saw put-call numbers higher than I've ever seen in 10 years of following the markets, particularly the options markets,' said John Kinnucan, principal of Broadband Research, as quoted in the *San Francisco Chronicle*.
— *Montreal Gazette*, September 19 2001

'When I saw the volume of trading going up at other exchanges, I thought it was a little peculiar,' said [Bill] Kennedy, of ING Group NV's ING TT&S (US) Securities Inc, explaining that most trading that day was on other markets. *'There had not been a lot of volume in American the previous week. You hope there was a reasonable explanation, and there may very well be, but it leaves a very bad taste in your mouth.'*[7]

'It's a matter of great interest to intelligence. To the extent we find this evidence, we shouldn't just focus on it as proof of insider trading but as evidence of a desire to commit murder and terrorism,' said Columbia University law professor John Coffee.[8]

Germany's Bundesbank chief, Ernst Weltke, said on the sidelines of the meeting that a report of the investigation showed 'bizarre' fiscal transactions prior to the attacks that could not have been chalked up to coincidence.... Weltke said the transactions *'could not have been planned and carried out without a certain knowledge,'* particularly citing heavy trading in gold and oil futures.[9]

'It's absolutely unprecedented to see cases of insider trading covering the entire world from Japan to the US to North America to Europe.'
— ABC News Consultant Jonathan Winer, World News Tonight, September 20, 2001

'AMR [the parent company of American Airlines] *now represents just a tiny piece of what has become a giant international paper chase.'*
— *National Post*, September 22, 2001

'From my perspective, it is very clear that there was highly unusual and suspicious activity in airline and hotel stocks in the days and weeks leading up to this attack.' — Phil Erlanger, former senior technical analyst, Fidelity investments, writing in his newsletter *Erlanger Squeeze Play*, November 13, 2001. Erlanger added that the inside traders might well have made off with billions of dollars from 9/11.

The Chicago Board Options Exchange, the biggest US options market, said yesterday that it is investigating trading that happened before the terrorist attacks that flattened New York's World Trade Center and damaged the Pentagon.
— *Montreal Gazette*, September 19, 2001

'[Investigators will] certainly be able to track down every trade, where the trade cleared, where the trade was directed from.'
— Former SEC enforcement chief William McLucas in an interview with Bloomberg News.[10]

'If these clowns really bought puts on airline stocks and financial companies the day before the attacks, then they left another incriminating paper trail that may help provide proof of who masterminded the evil.'
— Bloomberg[11]

Backpedaling like crazy

Despite all the evidence to the contrary, the FBI's Dennis Lormel[12] said on October 3, 2001 before Congress that there were *'no flags or indicators'* referring to mere *'rumors'* about the pre-attack insider trading.[13]

However Treasury Secretary O'Neill downplayed hopes for a successful investigation by pointing out the challenge of penetrating veils of secrecy before a name can be attached to a suspicious trade. *'You've got to go through ten veils before you get to the real source.'* [14]
— Associated Press, September 20, 2001

After almost two weeks of investigation, financial regulators around the world have found no hard evidence that people with advance knowledge of the terrorist attacks in New York and Washington used that information to profit in the international securities markets. And a number of officials are beginning to express doubt that such a plan existed.

While the investigations are continuing and additional evidence is still to be reviewed, many leads that initially seemed to indicate a conspiracy to profit from the terrorist attacks have been found to have less sinister explanations.

— *New York Times,* September 28, 2001, *International Herald Tribune,* September 29-30, 2001[15]

There has been a great deal of talk about alleged insider trading of airline stocks by associates of Osama bin Laden prior to the September 11 attacks on the World Trade Center and the Pentagon .... In fact, based on financial information almost immediately available to investigators, even the most febrile conspiracy theorists would have to agree that this dog don't hunt .... such suspicions deserve nothing more than a curt 'So what?'

— *Insight Magazine* [16]

The only specific explanation offered for the unusual airline trades was, to say the least, a two-legged dog. The *New York Times* suggested that a smaller airline — reported by other sources to be Lufthansa — had placed London puts on either American or United. The *Times* did not specify how many trades were made, nor relate them to the puts placed through investment bank Alex. Brown (see below). Nor did it state how the "smaller airline's" actions translated into abnormal trading at 26 other companies, in oil, or in T-Bills, or in gold.

The most common explanation offered by nay-saying journalists was a vague assertion that airline stocks were weak and the economy had been going into a downturn. However, even these assertions were flatly contradicted by a Reuters story from September 10th, headlined "Airline stocks may be poised for take off."[17] The story reported, "Goldman Sachs, for example, said the firm is now an aggressive buyer of airline stocks because they are trading at four-year lows and valuations are compelling. The firm's top picks are Continental Airlines Inc., AMR Corp.'s American Airlines and Delta Airlines Inc."[18]

We don't see any elephant

A great many people knew that the attacks of September 11th were coming. Some of those people made a great deal of money from them. They knew exactly which stocks were going to plummet as a result of the attacks, and they knew that the attacks were going to succeed. Otherwise they would not have risked the sums of money that they did. That knowledge alone demonstrates — as we shall soon see — a degree of specific knowledge about the attacks that has not yet been revealed. And if the world views the attacks themselves as evil, then the insider trading connected to them — financial transactions made before the attacks happened and which could only be successful with the death of thousands of people — require a new word to describe them. I can't find it.

No rational mind, free of medication, can fail to see that the levels of insider trading that occurred before 9/11 were beyond aberrant behavior.

And the fact that a *single* $2.5 million put option trade on United Airlines went unclaimed after the attacks is appallingly clear evidence of criminal insider knowledge. News accounts speculated that those responsible for that particular trade did not act quickly enough to claim their profits and did not anticipate that the financial markets would be closed for four days after the attacks.[19] Perhaps a group of people with access to the knowledge got the idea to make trades at the same time and didn't realize it was going to be a stampede that would leave a huge dust cloud behind it. In spite of FBI statements calling such trades *rumors*, and *New York Times* assertions that there were benign explanations for the bizarre trading before the attacks, I can think of no reasonable explanation for someone leaving $2.5 million in profits unclaimed, except one: They would be arrested if they showed up and asked for it. That, as I learned when I was with LAPD, is another clue.

The massive insider trading that occurred proximal to the events of September 11th was not localized. It was, in fact, a worldwide event, and there is no chance that all or even most of the trades were made by Osama bin Laden or al Qaeda. With a high-caliber networking software program derived from PROMIS, anyone with basic knowledge of the transactions (the volume of shares, the prices paid, the times of the trades, and the financial firms that handled them) could go on to identify the traders as well as their degrees of connection. That at least one intelligence agency has already done this, must be clear from the deep political relationship between intelligence and high finance explored in Chapter 3, The CIA is Wall Street. But Langley may not require any retrospective scrutiny of these insider trades, having tracked them in real time as they happened.

Insider trading, or suspicious trades indicating possible 9/11 foreknowledge, were reported in the USA, Germany, Britain, Canada, Japan (8 times above normal levels on the Osaka Exchange), Switzerland, Hong Kong, France, Italy, Spain, Belgium, Luxembourg, and Singapore. Official investigations were announced in eight of those countries. Details of these international trades have not been disclosed, but shares of American companies are routinely purchased through foreign exchanges.

Nor was the trading limited to American and United Airlines. Shortly after 9/11 the SEC issued a sensitive list of some 38 companies whose shares had been traded suspiciously. SEC announced that it had quietly established relationships with brokerage firms to conduct its investigation. In publishing the list — which was quickly withdrawn from public circulation — the *Cleveland Plain Dealer* noted that all of these firms had seen unusual levels of put option purchases right before 9/11 and almost every company's shares had fallen sharply right after the attacks. The story quoted *Morningstar's* airline analyst Jonathan Schrader:

> While trading fluctuations happen all of the time for no apparent reason, it seems there's certainly something here. It's interesting that they thought they could get away with it.[20]

Indeed, no one could hope to get away with it unless they controlled all the enforcement mechanisms that would be called in afterward.

This expansion of the SEC probe was later confirmed by the *San Francisco Chronicle* which reported that the SEC's action in establishing "relationships" with private brokerage houses "effectively deputizes hundreds, if not thousands, of key players in the private sector."[21] What happens when you deputize someone in a national security or criminal investigation is that you make it illegal for them to disclose publicly what they know. Smart move. In effect, they become government agents and are controlled by government regulations rather than their own conscience. In fact, they can be thrown in jail without a hearing if they talk publicly. I have seen this implied threat time and again with federal investigators, intelligence agents, and even members of the United States Congress who are bound so tightly by secrecy oaths and agreements that they are not even able to disclose criminal activities inside the government for fear of incarceration. Even members of Congress fear that kind of retaliation and punishment. That restraint is much worse for members of congressional intelligence committees who sign even more draconian secrecy agreements in order to get their assignments.

As the *Chronicle* story emphasized, the SEC was looking for people it could *trust*. "In a two-page statement issued to 'all securities-related entities' nationwide, the SEC asked companies to designate senior personnel who appreciate 'the sensitive nature' of the case and can be relied upon to 'exercise appropriate discretion' as 'point' people linking government investigators and the industry."[22] Of course, such trust was meant to preclude precisely the sort of whistleblowing that might have led to a genuine investigation.

As mentioned above, not only did the insider trading involve oil and gold, it also involved heavy volumes in US T-Bills. The *Wall Street Journal* reported that there was an unusually high volume in the purchase of five-year Treasury notes just prior to the attacks and that these included one $5 billion trade.[23] Treasury notes are highly valued as safe havens for investors when the markets are in trouble and T-Bill prices rose immediately after the attacks.

More evidence appeared and had to be thoroughly ignored because it could not be explained with spin or ridicule. Convar, a German firm hired to retrieve data from damaged computer systems left in the rubble of the World Trade Center, found that there was a deluge of electronic trading just minutes *before* the first plane struck. Quoting a December 16 report from Reuters, writer Kyle Hence (of <www.911citizenswatch.org>) found a compelling quotation from one of Convar's directors:

> Peter Henschel, director of Convar … said, 'not only the volume, but the size of the transactions was far higher than usual for a day like that.' Richard Wagner, a data retrieval expert, estimated that more than $100 million in *illegal* transactions appeared to have rushed through the WTC computers before and during the disaster.[24]

The Reuters story was partially confirmed for me when I was contacted by a Deutsche Bank employee who had survived the attacks by fleeing the WTC after the first plane hit. According to the employee, about five minutes before the attack the entire Deutsche Bank computer system had been taken over by something external that no one in the office recognized and every file was downloaded at lightning speed to an unknown location. The employee, afraid for his life, lost many of his friends on September 11, and he was well aware of the role that the Deutsche Bank subsidiary Alex. Brown had played in insider trading. He also volunteered something that was being increasingly recognized around the world. Mohammed Atta and many of the 9/11 hijackers who had lived and planned for months with al Qaeda leaders in Frankfurt, Germany had kept accounts with Deutsche Bank.

How much money was made overall? Only those inside government agencies in the US and abroad know and they can't or won't talk. But outside the United States, there are some exceptions: "Andreas von Bülow, a former member of the German Parliament, once responsible for the oversight of the German secret services, estimated that profits by inside traders were $15 billion. CBS offered a far more conservative figure when it reported (September 26) that 'at least seven countries are dissecting suspicious trades that may have netted more than $100 million in profits.'"[25]

Revealing the secrets

Of all the stories I've written, the one that seems to have caused the most uproar was published one month after the attacks. Since publication of that story the entire United States government — as well as the entire world financial system — has gone completely silent about the insider trading. Why?

Answering that question is not so difficult; it requires a modicum of intellectual courage and some acquaintance with the scope and nature of insider trading prior to 9/11. Before we answer some of the more deeply disturbing questions about the insider trades, I want to put the October 2001 *FTW* story in front of you — so you can see the monkey wrench that ground the propaganda machine to halt.[26]

SUPPRESSED DETAILS OF CRIMINAL INSIDER TRADING LEAD DIRECTLY INTO THE CIA's HIGHEST RANKS CIA EXECUTIVE DIRECTOR "BUZZY" KRONGARD MANAGED FIRM THAT HANDLED "PUT" OPTIONS ON UNITED AIRLINES

by
Michael C. Ruppert

FTW, October 9, 2001 — Although uniformly ignored by the mainstream US media, there is abundant and clear evidence that a number of transactions in financial markets indicated specific (criminal) fore-knowledge of the September 11 attacks on the World Trade Center and the Pentagon. In the case of at least one of these trades — which has left a $2.5 million prize unclaimed — the firm used to place the "put options" on United Airlines stock was, until 1998, managed by the man who is now in the number three Executive Director position at the Central Intelligence Agency. Until 1997 A.B. "Buzzy" Krongard had been Chairman of the investment bank A.B. Brown (or Alex. Brown). A.B. Brown was acquired by Banker's Trust in 1997. As part of the merger, Krongard then became Vice Chairman of Banker's Trust Alex. Brown, one of 20 major US banks named by Senator Carl Levin this year as being connected to money laundering. Krongard's last position at Banker's Trust (BT) was to oversee "private client relations." In this capacity he had direct hands-on relationships with some of the wealthiest people in the world, in a kind of specialized banking operation that has been identified by the US Senate and other investigators as being closely connected to the laundering of drug money.

Krongard joined (or perhaps, rejoined) the CIA in 1998 as counsel to CIA Director George Tenet. He was promoted to CIA Executive Director by President Bush in March of this year. BT was acquired by Deutsche Bank in 1999. The combined firm is the single largest bank in Europe. And, as we shall see, Deutsche Bank played several key roles in events connected to the September 11 attacks.

The Scope of Known Insider Trading

Before looking further into these relationships it is necessary to look at the insider trading information that is being ignored by *Reuters,* the *New York Times,* and other mass media. It is well documented that the CIA has long monitored such trades in real time, as potential warnings of terrorist attacks and other economic moves contrary to US interests. Previous stories in *FTW* have specifically highlighted the use of PROMIS software to monitor such trades.

It is necessary to understand only two key financial terms to understand the significance of these trades: "selling short" and "put options."

"Selling short" is the borrowing of stock, selling it at current market prices, but not being required to actually produce the stock for some time. If the stock falls precipitously after the short contract is entered, the seller can then fulfill the contract by buying the stock after the price has fallen and complete the contract at the pre-crash price. These contracts often have a window of as long as four months.

"Put options," [See above]

A September 21 story by the Israeli Herzliya International Policy Institute for Counterterrorism, entitled "Black Tuesday: The World's Largest Insider Trading Scam?" documented the following trades connected to the September 11 attacks:[27]

- Between September 6 and 7, the Chicago Board Options Exchange saw purchases of 4,744 put options on United Airlines, but only 396 call options. Assuming that 4,000 of the options were bought by people with advance knowledge of the imminent attacks, these "insiders" would have profited by almost $5 million.

- On September 10, 4,516 put options on American Airlines were bought on the Chicago exchange, compared to only 748 calls. There was no news at that point to justify this imbalance. Assuming that 4,000 of these options trades represent "insiders," they would represent a gain of about $4 million.

- The levels of put options purchased above were more than six times higher than normal.

- No similar trading in other airlines occurred on the Chicago exchange in the days immediately preceding Black Tuesday.

- Morgan Stanley Dean Witter & Co., which occupied 22 floors of the World Trade Center, saw 2,157 of its October $45 put options bought in the three trading days before Black Tuesday; this compares to an average of 27 contracts per day before September 6. Morgan Stanley's share price fell from $48.90 to $42.50 in the aftermath of the attacks. Assuming that 2,000 of these options contracts were bought based upon knowledge of the approaching attacks, their purchasers could have profited by at least $1.2 million.

- Merrill Lynch & Co., with headquarters near the Twin Towers, saw 12,215 October $45 put options bought in the four trading days before the attacks; the previous average volume in those shares had been 252 contracts per day [a 1,200 percent increase!]. When trading resumed, Merrill's shares fell from $46.88 to $41.50; assuming that 11,000 option contracts were bought by "insiders," their profit would have been about $5.5 million.

- European regulators are examining trades in Germany's Munich Re, Switzerland's Swiss Re, and AXA of France, all major reinsurers with exposure to the Black Tuesday disaster. [FTW Note: AXA also owns more than 25 percent of American Airlines stock making the attacks a "double whammy" for them.]

- "October series options for UAL Corp. were purchased in highly unusual volumes three trading days before the terrorist attacks for a total outlay of $2,070; investors bought the option contracts, each representing 100 shares, for 90 cents each. [This represents 230,000 shares]. Those options are now selling at more than $12 each. There are still 2,313 so-called 'put' options outstanding [valued at $2.77 million and representing 231,300 shares] according to the Options Clearinghouse Corp."

- The source familiar with the United trades identified Deutsche Bank Alex. Brown, the American investment banking arm of German giant Deutsche Bank, as the investment bank used to purchase at least some of these options. This was the operation managed by Krongard until as recently as 1998.

- As reported in other news stories, Deutsche Bank was also the hub of insider trading activity connected to Munich Re that took place just before the attacks.

- The thoroughly unconstitutional power of the CIA can be measured by its impunity. In the face of overwhelming proof that the Agency knew about the attacks and did not stop them, its leadership remains totally silent on the issue. Whatever our government is doing, whatever the CIA is doing, it is clearly NOT in the interests of the American people, especially those who died on September 11.[28]

The hornets swarm

That was it. From the moment I broke that one story and made a single appearance on Pacifica radio's "Guns and Butter" show produced and hosted by Bonnie Faulkner and Kellia Ramares on October 12, the government never uttered another affirming public word about the insider trades as an avenue of post-9/11 investigation. And the major media, being unwilling to look at anything that pointed at the CIA, went dead silent.

A barrage of critics appeared, and for weeks they tried to spin my revelations away. No one, they said, would risk insider trading on so small an amount of money as $2.5 million dollars. But this, of course, proved nothing. They were either lying or mistaken, because they ignored all the well-discussed reports of perhaps billions of dollars in profits in many other countries.

Some critics like *Insight Magazine's* Kelly O'Meara wrote that trading levels of put options had been higher earlier in 2001 so there was therefore no proof that anyone had advance knowledge.[29] A generally outstanding investigative reporter (who has written excellent stories I cite elsewhere in this book), O'Meara missed the boat on this one. Insider trading is not measured solely by the number of put options purchased and whether they spike or not. It is measured, as noted above, by a marked imbalance between the number of put options as compared to the number of call options *in conjunction* with a spike in purchases and several other factors. While the first two quarters of 2001 did see larger numbers of put options purchased on both UAL and American Airlines, the fact is that almost as many call options were placed in the same period. And the *Insight* story didn't even mention the reports from CBS, Bloomberg, and ABC or the opinions of financial experts charged with monitoring such activity right after the attacks which screamed insider trading all over the place.

During the first two quarters of 2001, with the Dow above 10,000 and in a very flat market with no precipitous ups and downs, trading volumes were on average about 30 percent to 50 percent higher than they were before the Dow started its dramatic decline in the late summer of 2001. So were the numbers of puts and calls. As one experienced trader explained to me, "In a flat market, the serious traders place large numbers of put and call options at the same time. It's a way to generate cash flow if the market is only moving a few points one way or the other. But insider trading is a certainty if you see the two way out of balance, especially by many orders of magnitude. That's about the clearest warning there is."

Both CBS News and the Associated Press agreed with this clear description of what constitutes insider trading:

> The trades are called "puts" and they involved at least 450,000 shares of American [Airlines] .... But what raised the red flag is more than 80 percent of the orders were "puts," far outnumbering "call" options, those betting that the stock would rise .... Sources say they have never seen that kind of imbalance before, reports CBS News correspondent Sharyl Attkisson. Normally the numbers are fairly even .... An extremely unbalanced number of trades betting [that] United's stock price would fall also transformed into huge profits when it did [fall] after the hijackings.[30]

The Herzliya Institute for Counterterrorism — whose initial comprehensive analysis of the known patterns of trading alerted me to the scandal — also agreed on the imbalance issue overlooked by O'Meara. And it was their analysis that was the first to start asking the real hard questions that so much of the American media has been eager to sidestep.[31]

I can only speculate that O'Meara, like so many Americans since 9/11, did not want to recognize (or perhaps, admit) that the trading led right to the heart of the US intelligence community. As this chapter is intended to show, the trading story also has grave implications for the character of intelligence agencies around the world. It therefore casts the legitimacy of their sponsoring governments into doubt — and leaves little room for the more comforting idea of nation-states as world citizens whose international competition can offset their national excesses. Intelligence agencies can't be loyal to the national interest when their national governments have been quietly replaced by multinational corporations and/or organized crime syndicates.

Putting the trades in context

No one has disclosed exactly how many insider trades were made through so many different countries. Many trades were probably made through shell corporations, entities that the CIA has a special expertise in creating. So, of course, do organized criminal enterprises. And it is possible that some trades on US markets were placed through overseas brokerages. While former SEC enforcement chief McLucas was correct in his statement about being able to track the trades, he did not state that the trail would lead, through normal channels, to the original purchaser. In many cases the trail, still closely guarded as a state secret, will stop at the water's edge. PROMIS software and its progeny can leap off from that point and track a trade anywhere on Earth, but the US government does not acknowledge its own use of PROMIS in financial investigations. In the previous chapter I noted however that official USG records indicate that international wire transfers of terrorist groups had been blocked and bank accounts monitored. So why couldn't it be done with the put options?

Any statement by the US government that it lacks the ability to trace the trades is the dog that *can't* hunt.

Investigative journalist Tom Flocco wrote a subsequent three-part series on insider trading for *FTW*. Flocco obtained a revealing partial denial from the CIA on the issue:

> In a returned phone call from the Central Intelligence Agency, press spokesman Tom Crispell denied that the CIA was monitoring "real-time," pre-September 11, stock option trading activity within United States borders using such software as the Prosecutor's Management Information System (PROMIS).
>
> "That would be illegal. We only operate outside the United States," the intelligence official said. However, when asked whether the CIA had been using PROMIS beyond American borders to scrutinize world financial markets for national security purposes, Crispell replied, "I have no way of knowing what operations are [being affected by our assets] outside the country." [32]

When Flocco obtained this statement, the use of PROMIS by the Department of Justice and the FBI had already been exposed by FOX News and confirmed by my own investigations. The CIA knew that, as a result of my previous investigation into PROMIS involving the RCMP, I was in possession of a paper trail showing that CIA had the software as well.

Unfortunately it is impossible, because of banking secrecy and privacy laws, for a journalist to obtain trading records. The few trades that have been documented here are only the tip of the very large iceberg that German Central Bank chairman Weltke referred to in his candid initial statements.

Following up on some of the many unanswered questions Flocco tried to put the heat on some of the government agencies charged with investigating the trades:

Wide reports — including a 9/28/01 story in the Asian *Wall Street Journal* and a 10/1/01 story in the *Guardian* — indicate that investigators are checking Deutsche Bank's alleged links to Saudi "private banking," terrorist bank accounts, and $2.5 million in unclaimed United Airlines (UAL) put options profits; however, no government acknowledgement had ever been given of CIA's alleged use of PROMIS software prior to the attacks.

In a recent phone conversation, when asked about alleged terrorist ties to Deutsche Bank and potential pre-attack CIA trade monitoring via PROMIS, Treasury Department spokesman Rob Nichols remarked, "This is clearly an interesting line of questioning regarding conflicts of interest."[33]

Flocco then took his *FTW* investigation to the New York Stock Exchange. The results were less than satisfying.

And after pressing for information about what the NYSE is actually doing to investigate the suspicious trades on behalf of thousands of victims' families who may be concerned about the 'prior-knowledge' issue, [NYSE Communications Director Ray] Pellecchia still declined to confirm that Doherty's enforcement office had even sent a report to the SEC.

When asked why so many former key CIA executives currently hold, or have held in the past, top-level executive management positions connected in some way to the stock market via either the SEC, NYSE, or other investment banking entities, Pellecchia replied tersely, 'I am quite aware of Mr. Doherty's background and experience.'

As noted in Chapter 5, Doherty is the NYSE's executive vice president for enforcement. He is a former general counsel of the CIA.

Pellecchia also declined to discuss anything related to current CIA Executive Director A.B. "Buzzy" Krongard and his past relationship with Alex. Brown.[34]

Flocco's subsequent investigations disclosed that a former Banker's Trust Deutsche Bank executive, Kevin Ingram, had — just before the attacks — pled guilty to laundering drug money to finance terrorist operations for groups linked to Osama bin Laden. He also found that Deutsche Bank, long a favorite of the bin Laden family, turns up all throughout the post-9/11 financial investigations of the hijackers and their support network. Flocco discovered also that Deutsche Bank had correspondent relationships with banks in Bahrain and Kuwait that had served George W. Bush when he was engaging in his own illegal insider trading of the shares of his company Harken Energy just prior to the first Iraqi war.

Not surprisingly, both of those banks — Kuwait Finance House and Faysal Islamic Bank of Bahrain — had dealt with Al Qaeda and bin Laden, and both had been uncooperative with the US government's "all-out" hunt for terrorist money. What was surprising is that when the Bush administration released its worldwide list of suspect financial organizations and vowed to track down and eliminate terrorist financing, these two banks didn't even make the list.[35]

Mayo Shattuck III — another clue

Mayo Shattuck III is an extremely powerful and influential mover and shaker in the financial world. As head of the Alex. Brown unit of Deutsche Bank on 9/11, he had previously been involved in deals with Russian ruble trading, Microsoft, the Bronfman dynasty, Enron (where he assisted in deceptively concealing Enron's debts[36]), and with a massive insider trading scandal involving Adnan Khashoggi's Genesis Intermedia right before 9/11.[37] He was midway through a three-year, 30-million dollar contract as the head of the Alex. Brown unit of Deutsche Bank when the attacks came. Shattuck (who knows Buzzy Krongard well) took over Alex. Brown operations after Krongard had officially gone to the CIA in 1998. It was under Shattuck's management that some of the criminal trades on United Air Lines were placed right before 9/11.

Mayo Shattuck resigned suddenly on September 12th, the day after the attacks.[38]

A close associate of CFR powerhouses like Peter G. Petersen and Steven Bechtel of the Bechtel Corporation, Shattuck is today the President and CEO of Constellation Energy Group, one of the firms that gained access to Vice President's Dick Cheney's energy task force, the one from which the Bush administration is unconstitutionally refusing to release the records.

Alex. Brown also played a key role in refinancing the Carlyle Group for its acquisition of United Defense technologies in 2000.[39] This close connection to Bush family business ventures is not a surprise because Alex. Brown's connections to the Bush family stretch back for at least seven decades. The Alex. Brown investment bank helped to finance and organize the firm managed in the first half of the 20th century by George W. Bush's grandfather, Prescott Bush: Brown Brothers, Harriman. [40]

When all else has been eliminated

Sir Arthur Conan Doyle, through his creation Sherlock Holmes, once said that whenever you have eliminated all the explanations that are not possible, whatever remains — no matter how unlikely — must be the truth.

There is only one explanation of the 9/11 insider trades that fits with the known facts. And strangely enough it is my critics who have helped to make the case. The *Insight Magazine* story offered one critical piece by confirming that it was not difficult at all to establish in short order who made the trades.

> Lynne Howard, a spokeswoman for the Chicago Board Options Exchange (CBOE), tells *Insight* that information about who made the trades was available immediately. "We would have been aware of any

unusual activity right away. It would have been triggered by any unusual volume. There is an automated system called 'blue sheeting,' or the CBOE Market Surveillance System, that everyone in the business knows about. It provides information on the trades — the name and even the Social Security number on an account — and these surveillance systems are set up specifically to look into insider trading. The system would look at the volume, and then a real person would take over and review it, going back in time and looking at other unusual activity."

Howard continues, "The system is so smart that even if there is a news event that triggers a market event it can go back in time, and even the parameters can be changed depending on what is being looked at. It's a very clever system and it is instantaneous. Even with the system, though, we have very experienced and savvy staff in our market-regulations area who are always looking for things that might be unusual. They're trained to put the pieces of the puzzle together. Even if it's offshore, it might take a little longer, but all offshore accounts have to go through US member firms — members of the CBOE — and it is easily and quickly identifiable who made the trades. The member firm who made the trades has to have identifiable information about the client under the 'Know Your Customer' regulations (see 'Snoops and Spies,' Feb. 22, 1999), and we share all information with the Securities and Exchange Commission."

Given all of this, at a minimum the CBOE and government regulators who are conducting the secret investigations have known for some time who made the options puts on United and American airlincs. The silence from the investigating camps could mean any of several things: terrorists are responsible for the puts on the airline stocks; others besides terrorists had foreknowledge; or, the puts were just lucky bets by credible investors. [41]

While not acknowledging the reality of multiple shell corporations set up to conceal the identity of traders, or the fact that some countries don't cooperate fully with US investigations and routinely — as admitted by Senator Carl Levin's report on correspondent banking — slip transactions through the cracks, Howard not only confirmed that the trades could be tracked, she flatly contradicted the sworn testimony of the Secretary of the Treasury, Paul O'Neill.

The *New York Times* and Bloomberg dropped the biggest bombshells of all by admitting something we discussed in the chapter on PROMIS software. Although I was not aware of these reports at the time, I had been saying for months in my lectures (during 2001-2002) throughout the US, Canada, and Australia that neither Osama bin Laden nor al Qaeda would have been so foolish as to telegraph their intentions in an environment they damn well knew was watched more closely than grizzly bear cubs by Mama Bear.

Scott Keller, president of DealAnalytics told Bloomberg News,

> It would seem almost incredible to me that anyone would take the
> risk of trying to front-run the market on something like this. It would
> be a life sentence if they got caught.[42]

At the *New York Times*, spinmeisters Eichenwald and Andrews reported,

> A law enforcement official, speaking on condition of anonymity, also
> expressed doubt that a trading conspiracy existed. The official said it
> was unlikely that a terrorist group that had worked for months, if not
> years, to orchestrate its attack would be reckless enough to create even
> a subtle signal of its plans by engaging in the high-profile trading of
> public securities.[43]

The trades could only have been made by people high enough in the US,
Israeli, and European intelligence communities (including Russia) to know about
the attacks and — more importantly — which of many planned attacks were
going to be successful. This circle could, of course, have included key world financial and political figures who were implementing a global agenda. As we have
already seen, these two camps are one and the same. There is no other explanation
that encompasses all the known data, and takes notice of the incredible veil of
secrecy that has fallen over the issue.

Evidently, almost all the foreign intelligence services that had penetrated al
Qaeda ultimately realized that the US government was going to facilitate the
attacks. That knowledge migrated to certain investors who promptly capitalized on
it. To have brought these figures to justice would have revealed how much was
known about the attacks in so many places before they happened.

Nine agencies — SEC, NYSE, CBOE, Department of Justice, FBI, Secret
Service, CIA, Treasury, and the National Security Agency — opened investigations
into insider trading immediately after 9/11 based upon initially admitted and
obvious evidence that it had, in fact, taken place. Much of the major press immediately recognized the importance of the story and then shirked its obligation to
follow up. Not one of the agencies involved has to this day divulged any information to the public.

All the insanity and depravity suggested by 9/11 insider trading was made clear
when the Pentagon announced, and then immediately scrapped, plans for a futures
market on terrorist attacks called the Policy Analysis Market. This official program
constituted a frank admission that people with advance knowledge of terror attacks
would always seek to capitalize on that knowledge.[44] Although the outrage over the
program forced the resignation of convicted Iran-Contra felon John Poindexter, not
a single press story made any connection between the Pentagon's plans and the
trades of September 11th. The CIA is Wall Street. Wall Street is the CIA.

CHAPTER 15

ISRAEL

No discussion of the events before, during, and after 9/11 is either complete or intellectually honest without looking at Israel. Since 9/11, three nations — the United States, the United Kingdom, and Israel — have stood virtually alone as a tripartite alliance in complete support of the Empire's actions. One of the best questions to ask after any major event is *Cui bono*? "Who benefits?" And here, Israel, the largest recipient of US military and economic aid, has ranked at, or near, the top of the list in almost every world development. There is some good, and much that is bad, to be said about Israel and its actions. But almost every attempt at rational discourse on the question of the use of Israeli power has been hobbled by emotional, almost hysterical preconceptions — either pro or con — that miss some very important pieces of the new, accurate map I have been trying to draw for you.

Many of the top members of the Bush administration have exceptionally close ties with the Israeli government. These include the former Chairman of the Pentagon's Defense Policy Board, Richard Perle; Deputy Defense Secretary Paul Wolfowitz; Undersecretary of Defense Douglas Feith; Edward Luttwak of the National Security Study Group; Dov Zakheim, the Pentagon's Chief Financial Officer on 9/11; Elliot Abrams at the National Security Council, and Press Secretary Ari Fleischer. Some have even worked on joint planning projects with Israeli ministries. These relationships alone make Israel a subject worthy of discussion. These and many other Israeli-connected experts formed the core group at the Project for a New American Century that had drafted plans for the invasion of Iraq long before 9/11.

This chapter is a brief effort to put some very important pieces into place. And I should say at the outset that none of my research has found any compelling data to suggest that Israel was the architect or mastermind of the attacks of September 11, as is obvious from the preceding chapters. It would have been impossible for the Israeli government to have so compromised US intelligence, military, economic, and political systems as to have had control of the operation, not to mention the full and unquestioning cooperation of the American mid-level functionaries needed to execute it.

I'm repeating that statement here because it's so important to prevent the very common shaming, diversionary behavior illustrated by the following vignette: A colleague of mine who has been tireless in his efforts to distribute evidence of US government complicity in the attacks approached FOX News commentator Chris Matthews at a post-9/11 book signing. After he waited in line and then tried to place some of the evidence I've described in this book in Matthews's hands — a Quixotic effort in my opinion — Matthews asked him, "This isn't one of those 'The Israelis did it' things, is it?"

This shows how little real analysis is being done by the media, but it also shows the way valid questions are deflected or intentionally ignored by shame-based, propagandistic rhetoric. Any criticism of Israel tends to get dishonestly recast as anti-Semitism. So let's get a couple of things straight. Israel is not Judaism.

One is a state and the other is a religion. For centuries, Muslims and Jews lived side by side in relative tranquility in the Middle East. And during the Middle Ages it was the Muslims who gave Jews fleeing European Christian persecution safe haven in the Holy Land, where each group generally practiced its own religion in peace. A single day's reading in the Torah, the New Testament, and the Koran is enough to show that within each monotheist sacred text are passages of exclusivity and intolerance and other passages urging accord and acceptance. Islam is typical here; and while it takes a dim view of polytheist cultures like Hinduism, much of the Koran teaches that Jews should be good Jews and that Christians should be good Christians.

The term "anti-Semitism" refers to a European social and political phenomenon (which, like much of European pre-World War II ideology, still lingers in some places, e.g., Japan). Anti-Jewish feeling, thought, and behavior are as old as monotheism itself and have undergone almost as many transformations. There's the anti-Judaism of late antiquity; the massacres against Jews in the Crusades and the Inquisition, the murderous pogroms by rural European peasants in the 18th and 19th centuries, the middle-class resentment, mythologizing, and persecution that led to the Dreyfuss Affair in 1890s France, and a massive wave of hatred toward Jews that came upward from European folk ideology and downward from fascist and rightist parties and governments in the first half of the 20th century. Like all forms of bigotry, "Anti-Semitism" remains a serious problem all over the world. But the phrase itself has no real anthropological basis; it dates from the 1870s, when most European writers still divided up the world's peoples according to Biblical categories — "Semites" were thought to be descended from Noah's son Shem, while everybody else came from either Ham or Japhet. In fact, *Antisemitismus* was invented as part of an effort by German racist authors to replace the religion-based Jew-hatred (*Judenhass*) of the past with a more modern, ethnicity-driven contempt. Of course, this apparently intellectual construct barely masked a deep reservoir of anti-rational, virulent hatred. It formed the basis for the pseudo-scientific racism of the Nazi movement.

So the term shouldn't be used to refer to the attitudes of either side in the Arab-Israeli conflict, where it's misleading and inapt. As is often pointed out, Arabs and Jews are both called "Semitic" peoples. More importantly, "Anti-Semitism" is worse than useless in any discussion of Israeli domestic and international affairs. To talk about Israel as if its every citizen thought, felt, and acted as a unit in some giant monolithic crowd is as unfair as assuming that every American supports all of the US government's actions, its economic policies, and its militarism with exactly the same degree of feeling and for exactly the same reasons. Clearly, within Israel there are hugely divergent opinions on everything including the occupied territories and settlements, Palestinian history and politics, the conduct of Israel's foreign and domestic policies, and the vexing issue of compulsory military service. And Israel has a sizeable antiwar movement opposing the invasion of Iraq by the US. So what is important (indeed, essential) to examine are the actions of the Israeli government, in exactly the same way that we have examined the actions of the US government. Supporters of the state of Israel are often hysterically unable to tolerate that kind of critique, as though they know (all-too consciously in some cases, perhaps unconsciously in others) that a clear examination of Israel's national conduct reveals a pattern of stark horrors. This sort of denial is best maintained by ad hominem attacks, the most effective being the easy slander of anti-Semitism; if you're having any trouble preventing criticism of Israel, call the critic a bigot and it's all over.

Sometimes those reactions are triggered by the genuine anxiety that remains a permanent feature of Jewish life since the Holocaust. But it's very common for journalists (say, Chris Matthews), politicians, officials, and disinformationists to squander, sabotage, or abort an exceedingly important debate by turning on the red megaphone that warns against what isn't there.

To say that Israel did not perpetrate the attacks of 9/11 is not to deny that the Israeli government was very close to those attacks and may have played a role in them. There is evidence that points both ways. On the one hand it is clear that Mossad made several attempts to warn the US government that the attacks were coming — in one case even providing the US government with a list that included the names of four of the 9/11 hijackers, including Mohammed Atta and that charmed pair, Nawaf Alhazmi and Khalid Almidhar.[1] Everybody knew the attacks were coming. Yet even after this information was in American hands, various agencies of the US government allowed Alhazmi and Almidhar to roam free and unmolested.

The analysis of insider trading by the Herzliya Institute for Counterterrorism (ICT) is another example of Israeli action pointing toward, rather than away from, evidence that the CIA knew what was going on and allowed the attacks to happen.

But perhaps the most compelling reason to discount assertions that Israel was the primary executor of the attacks is the following UPI story, which is one of the most overlooked bombshells in the whole 9/11 saga:

A leaked Federal Aviation Administration memo written on the evening of September 11 contains disturbing revelations about American Airlines Flight 11, the first to hit the World Trade Center. The "Executive Summary," based on information relayed by a flight attendant to the American Airlines Operation Center, stated "that a passenger located in seat 10B shot and killed a passenger in seat 9B at 9:20 a.m. The passenger killed was Daniel Lewin, shot by passenger Satam Al Suqami." The FAA has claimed that the document is a "first draft," declining to release the final draft, as it is "protected information," noting the inaccuracies in reported times, etc. The final draft omits all mention of gunfire. Lewin, a 31-year-old American-Israeli citizen was a graduate of MIT and Israel's Technion. Lewin had immigrated to Israel with his parents at age 14 and had worked at IBM's research lab in Haifa, Israel. Lewin was a co-founder and chief technology officer of Akamai Technologies and lived in Boston with his family. A report in Ha'aretz on September 17 identified Lewin as a former member of the Israel Defense Force Sayeret Matkal, a top-secret counter-terrorist unit, whose Unit 269 specializes in counter-terrorism activities outside of Israel.[2]

This particular story raises a multitude of questions. Guns were on the hijacked flights? How did they get there? Why have they not been mentioned? What was someone with Lewin's background doing sitting in front of one of the hijackers on the day of the hijackings? Was he still active? Mere coincidence is nearly impossible here. So the question becomes: did the hijackers — all nineteen of them — plan their activities to kill Lewin, or was Lewin following the hijackers even into the gates of death? Did they have to kill him to complete their mission? Who had penetrated whom, and who had compromised Lewin's presence on the plane hijacked by Mohammed Atta? One thing is absolutely clear from my vantage point: someone at the highest levels of the Israeli government deemed Lewin expendable.

Behind the fragile logic and the false rumors that thousands of Jews didn't show up for work at the World Trade Center on 9/11 lie deeper truths that raise darker questions. As a classic piece of disinformation, the rumor about Jews not showing up for work — latched onto by prejudiced and undisciplined minds — made it impossible to rationally discuss such things as the Zim Israeli-American shipping lines having vacated their offices in the World Trade Center just a week before the attacks and moving to Norfolk, Virginia. Two sources told me on condition of anonymity that Zim broke its lease to make the move.

The disinformation worked like a charm. Here's one example: an African-American poet, Amiri Baraka, nearly lost his post as Poet Laureate of New Jersey in an apparent reprisal for his embrace of this particular rumor. Just a month after 9/11, Baraka published "Somebody Blew Up America," a passionately internationalist poem against fascism in all its forms. But he didn't do enough homework, and a single line, "Who told 4000 Israeli workers at the Twin Towers / To stay home that day?" touched off a small storm of boring controversy that clogged much of the Black press, the Jewish press, and the regional mainstream press for weeks. It's unfortunately true (and rarely noted) that Baraka has written some very bigoted poems in the past 35 years, but "Somebody Blew Up America" is not one of them.

Yet it's the one that got all the noise, and the whole episode helped to shut down any legitimate discussion of Israeli foreknowledge and possible involvement in 9/11. Those who believed the rumor think they needn't look further, and those who rejected it think the same, for opposite reasons.

So let's take a critical and rational look at Israel based upon facts. Let's stop to examine the truth behind an Israeli spy ring that was operating all over the United States before 9/11 and documented by the DEA, the FBI, and the CIA. And then, let's try to place Israel within the context of 21st century transnational fascism and the new order evolving at the end of the age of oil.

The record

Let's compare the violation of UN resolutions by Israel and by Iraq.

IRAQ:
- UN Resolutions violated, ignored: 16
- Countries attacked, invaded, violated: Iran, Kuwait
- Countries occupied for years: None
- Countries currently occupying: None
- Territory illegally annexed: None
- Wars started: 1980, 1990
- Possesses weapons of mass destruction: Unverified as of this writing. (However, evidence has surfaced this year showing that the United States provided Iraq with bioweapons material for, among other things, anthrax, plague, smallpox, and West Nile virus, as well as materials for the manufacture of chemical weapons during the 1980s. Iraq also likely possesses small quantities of nerve agents such as CS, GB (Sarin), and VX gasses. But these are not legally or intuitively weapons of mass destruction. These gases dissipate and become harmless roughly 30 minutes after being deployed on the battlefield.)
- Possesses nuclear weapons: No.
- Most notable atrocity against civilians: Mass killings of Kurds and Shi'ite Muslims numbered at less than 5,000 per incident. (New information from CIA records and testimony this year shows that Iraq — as widely reported — was not guilty of gassing as many as 100,000 Kurds in the early 1990s. It was Iran, concerned about separatist sentiments in its own Kurdish population.)[3]
- Currently under a regime of UN sanctions: Yes

ISRAEL:
- UN resolutions violated, ignored: 68
- Countries attacked, invaded, violated: Egypt, Jordan, Iraq, Lebanon, Syria, Tunisia.

- Countries occupied for years: Egypt, Lebanon, Syria
- Countries currently occupying: Syria
- Territory illegally annexed: Golan Heights, Jerusalem, Palestinian Territories
- Wars started: 1956, 1967, 1982
- Possesses weapons of mass destruction: Yes
- Possesses nuclear weapons: Yes
- Most notable atrocity against civilians: 17,500 Lebanese civilians killed in the 1982 invasion of Lebanon
- Currently under a regime of UN sanctions: No

Most of this material was compiled by Richard B. Du Boff of Bryn Mawr University and published by al Jazeera in September of 2002. The parenthetical comments are mine.[4]

Ariel Sharon

Having narrowly escaped (on a technicality) prosecution in Belgium for a 1982 three-day orgy of killing and rape at the Sabra and Shatilla refugee camps that occurred when he led an invasion of Lebanon and controlled the area as Israeli defense minister, Prime Minister Ariel Sharon was also charged with brutal 2001 and 2002 human rights violations in the Jenin and Nablus townships of the occupied territories in Palestine. In post-9/11 Israeli incursions, many innocent civilians were killed, houses were bulldozed, and people were left homeless and without food, water, or medical supplies in areas totally surrounded by Israeli Defense Forces (IDF).[5]

Covert operations and 9/11 connections

An Israeli owned company, ICTS, had a contract to provide security at Boston's Logan airport, from which 9/11 Flights 11 and 175 originated. And either directly or through subsidiaries it had contracts at every other airport where planes were hijacked on 9/11. The same company was apparently well aware that alleged shoe bomber Richard Reid was connected to al Qaeda, and yet they still allowed him to board the Paris-US flight he tried to blow up. If the UPI story about a gun on Flight 11 is correct, then this might help explain how it got through screening.[6]

FBI sources were quoted in an ABC News story indicating that five employees of an Israeli-owned moving company were on the roof of their truck in New York City with photographic equipment as the attacks were occurring on 9/11. A former CIA official confirmed that the names of several had turned up in an intelligence database, and the men were subsequently deported.[7]

In December of 2002 Palestinian security forces arrested a group of Palestinians for acting as *agents provocateurs* in collaboration with Israel. Those arrested had been posing as al Qaeda operatives in attempts to discredit Palestinians in the eyes of the US and the world and to buttress Sharon's claims that al Qaeda cells were operating in regions where the IDF has been engaging in brutal operations. A follow-up story in Israel's Ha'aretz confirmed some details of the Palestinian allegations and disputed others.[8] Historically, there has been no connection between al Qaeda and the Palestinian cause.

In June of 2002 six men carrying Israeli passports who had been previously detained by the INS later became the subjects of a manhunt after US authorities feared that they might be plotting terror attacks, possibly on the Alaska pipeline or a Florida nuclear reactor. Release of the men — after confirming that their passports were valid — by the INS before contacting the FBI reportedly made FBI Director Mueller "furious."[9]

In the fall of 2002 a well-financed ring of Israeli computer hackers began a sabotage and eavesdropping campaign against interests in America that had been critical of Israel and supportive of Palestinian interests. One of the targets was University of Illinois international law professor Francis Boyle. The tactics used included the rewriting of text on certain websites, the sending of phony emails intended to create animosity or discredit the victim, and deluging targets with tens of thousands of messages. The ring, operating from Israeli occupied territory, was eventually tracked down and exposed.[10]

In August of 2002 a Zim Antwerp ship, operated by Israel, was seized in Germany. It was filled with weapons and munitions headed for Iran. The firm, closely connected to the Israeli government, had been licensed to export the cargo to Thailand, but German intelligence had apparently determined that the final destination was Iran.[11]

In another backfired covert operation, what was originally heralded as a dramatic January 2002 Red Sea interception of an Iranian ship filled with weapons headed for Palestine turned out to be a major embarrassment for the Israeli government. The *Karine A*, contrary to what the Israelis had asserted, was not a Palestinian or Iranian vessel, and the whole affair was likely manipulated to provide a propaganda edge for Ariel Sharon as US envoys met with Palestinian officials. Lloyd's of London produced documents proving certain parts of the Israeli story false and disproving Israeli claims that the weapons had been bought in Iran by Palestinian interests.[12]

In 2000, after a protracted court battle, the Anti-Defamation League of B'nai Brith (ADL) lost a civil suit in California federal court after it was found that the ADL had engaged, in cooperation with Israeli and South African intelligence agencies, in a massive domestic spying operation against American citizens and organizations such as Green Peace and groups opposed to US involvement in the Contra war. American officials who cooperated with the ADL were sometimes given all-expenses-paid trips to Israel, where they were introduced to representatives from the Mossad and Shin Bet intelligence services. It was found that the ADL had broken many laws by storing illegal intelligence records from local, state, and federal law enforcement agencies. In ruling in favor of the plaintiffs a US District Court judge permanently enjoined the ADL from engaging in any further illegal spying against "Arab-American and other civil rights groups." Several members of the House of Representatives were plaintiffs in the suit.[13]

On April 25, 2002, former Congressman Pete McCloskey of California was awarded a $150,000 judgment against the ADL in a related case. McCloskey's suit was prompted by FBI and San Francisco police raids on ADL offices which discovered that the ADL had files on almost 10,000 people across the US, and that about 75 percent of the material had been illegally obtained. Two of the three victims in the case who won awards were Jewish. This ruling followed a March 31, 2001, ruling in a Denver court upholding a $10.5 million defamation judgment against the Anti-Defamation League for falsely labeling two Colorado residents as anti-Semitic.[14]

To think of the ADL affair as something that originated solely with Israeli impetus is to overlook some key historical data. In the wake of myriad violations of US law committed by the FBI, the military, the CIA, and other government agencies in the 1960s and 1970s, and especially after the damning revelations of the Frank Church (D-ID) and Otis Pike (D-NY) congressional investigations in the mid 1970s, American agencies were forced to divest themselves of illegal records and to cease domestic spying operations. The problem, from their point of view, was how to hold on to data they deemed irreplaceable. The ADL, a non-governmental organization connected with a foreign government, seemed an ideal solution. The solution was not without its costs.

In the 1980s the Los Angeles Police Department's Public Disorder Intelligence Division (PDID) was found to have been doing what was accomplished by other agencies directly through the ADL. Ultimately some ADL connections surfaced in the PDID case. Tens of thousands of illegal intelligence records were disclosed as having been stored in the private residence and storage facilities rented and maintained by LAPD Detective Jay Paul. Paul, who was later revealed to have ties to Israeli interests, maintained many of the records on computers provided by an ultra-right-wing group, Western Goals. Sitting at the time on the board of directors of Western Goals was Iran-Contra figure and retired Army General John Singlaub, a virulent anti-Communist and CIA-connected covert operative.

As the LAPD scandal was unfolding I served as one of the unnamed sources for the *Los Angeles Times'* reporting of the scandal. Although the *Times* stopped well short of stating that US intelligence agencies had supported this intelligence gathering, two decades later the pattern is very clear. The ADL was there when it was needed. Yet in using the ADL as a plausibly deniable cutout, American intelligence agencies at the state and federal level paid a price. They gave the ADL license to use the data for its own purposes and created a monster that ultimately became a liability in its own right.

The art students

A DEA report from 2001 firmly establishes that in 2000 and 2001 the United States was entered by at least 120 Israeli intelligence operatives posing as art students.[15] The M.O. of the ring was to have its members conduct street and door-to-door sales of artwork in specific areas of interest. Some of those areas were in Hollywood, Florida, San Diego, and Phoenix, where many of the 9/11 hijackers had lived and trained. The investigation revealed that the areas of interest at one level were offices of the DEA and other federal agencies and the homes of those who worked there.

Initial reports by FOX News's Brit Hume and Carl Cameron caused great national interest and international reaction in December 2001 by revealing active government investigations into the ring before and especially after 9/11. The report disclosed that many of the ring's activities seemed to run parallel with the movements of several of the 9/11 hijackers. Sources have told me that the information breaking the story was leaked to Hume by Vice President Dick Cheney at a DC-area a cocktail party about two months after the attacks.

The FOX stories raised interesting questions about two Israeli-owned companies in the US. One of them, Amdocs, handles almost all telephone billing records in the United States and thus was in a position to provide invaluable intelligence information about who was being called from what phones anywhere in the country. The second company, Comverse, has multiple contracts to handle sensitive wiretap operations for government agencies, and FOX reported that the Comverse systems included a "back door" for outside parties with access to it to overhear monitored conversations.[16] This is reminiscent of the back door in PROMIS software.

Cameron's story made it clear that federal investigators were highly concerned about indications that suspects in the spy ring and — by implication — some of the 9/11 hijackers were able to avoid detection and capture as a result of information derived from these two companies. This was a bit of disinformation that yielded great payoffs for the administration. The FOX and other stories from the same period revealed that some 60 Israelis had been detained and deported just after 9/11 for passport and visa violations.[17]

Comverse becomes especially interesting because of its relationship with the Israeli instant-messaging firm Odigo. On September 11 employees of Odigo in Israel received specific instant messages warning them of the attacks two hours before they happened. Although the story received intense attention briefly, little follow-up was done in the major press, and whatever was learned was subsequently hidden behind veils of secrecy.[18]

One breathtaking connection that was overlooked by the mainstream press, however, was that in January 2001, Comverse, along with Lazard Technology Partners and another venture capital group, purchased a $15 million stake in Odigo, giving it access to Odigo's operations, accounting, and technologies.[19]

The FOX stories clearly implied that the Israeli operatives had not done all they could have to help prevent the attacks and suggested that the Israelis had more knowledge about the attacks than had been publicly disclosed. At one point Hume asked Cameron,

Carl, I want to take you back to your report last night on those 60 Israelis who were detained in the anti-terror investigation, and the suspicion that some investigators have that they may have picked up information on the 9/11 attacks ahead of time and not passed it on. There was a report, you'll recall, that the Mossad, the Israeli intelligence agency, did indeed send representatives to the US to warn, just before 9/11, that a major terrorist attack was imminent. How does that leave room for the lack of a warning?

To which Cameron replied:

I remember the report, Brit. We did it first internationally right here on your show on the 14th. What investigators are saying is that that warning from the Mossad was nonspecific and general, and they believe that it may have had something to do with the desire to protect what are called sources and methods in the intelligence community. The suspicion being, perhaps those sources and methods were taking place right here in the United States.[20]

As previously noted, the Mossad warning was specific enough to have named four of the hijackers. Again, a bit of deception by FOX, whose news director is former Reagan and Republican Party advisor Roger Ailes. Though subtle and vague, Hume's implication was that Israeli operatives were assisting the terrorists. And it was enough to spark an Internet avalanche of speculation by biased covert operations dilettantes claiming that Israel had masterminded and executed the attacks. Once that had started, then the question about Israel, which had apparently begun with a leak from Dick Cheney, was misdirected and distorted into something that the media, e.g., Chris Matthews, could effectively dismiss out of hand. And yet the incident had cost Israel dearly in terms of prestige and credibility. Also, as we shall see below, it had served to hide some darker truths.

Shortly after the FOX News stories, investigative journalist and former naval and NSA intelligence officer Wayne Madsen secured a copy of the DEA report that had started it all. It revealed a great deal more than FOX let on.

Most of the targets for walk-in sales by members of the ring were DEA offices. The DEA did not play any central role in 9/11.

- Members of the ring also made cold-calls at the private residences of DEA employees, federal judges, Secret Service agents, and other federal law enforcement and military personnel. This indicates that the ring had acquired the home addresses — quite possibly through telephone records — of DEA employees all over the country and was quietly making that fact known for reasons I will discuss below.
- On December 12, 2000, one Israeli named Shay Ashkenazi, when stopped for an INS screening after entering the US, *volunteered*

information about the art students to authorities indicating that it was a fraud ring and actually named one of participants. Ashkenazi told the INS officers that he was a "former Israeli intelligence officer who was now traveling to 'enjoy life.'" This means that one Israeli intelligence operative tipped off the US government to the work of other Israeli intelligence operatives.

- The ring did have very heavy operations in some areas connected with 9/11, especially the area around Hollywood, Florida, where Mohammed Atta and other hijackers lived and trained, San Diego, where Alhazmi and Almidhar lived; and Phoenix, Arizona. In fact, a group of these agents were later confirmed to have been living virtually next door to Atta's Florida post office box and had been surveilling him for some time. Some of these agents had entered the US from Frankfurt, Germany, where Atta had also lived and planned for the attacks.

- The CIA is mentioned in only one place in the report — San Diego — where Alhazmi and Almidhar lived. The report said, "The San Diego [DEA] Division is currently working with the FBI, Department of State, and CIA personnel on advancing the investigation."[21]

Espionage 101

Those with experience in intelligence operations will recognize some patterns to this widespread operation. First of all, when mounting an operation of wide scope, governments usually allow the operation to be used for multiple purposes. Within the Israeli government there might be three or four different intelligence units that could benefit from a large-scale deployment of covert operatives. We have already seen how closely intertwined narcotics and intelligence operations are worldwide. Not only does drug dealing provide, in some cases, the necessary covert funding for the operations themselves, it is also a means of generating income for national economies. With the United States and the CIA as the "Alpha dog" in the world-wide drug trade, there are few areas of competition left to generate large cash flows. One area in which Israeli organized crime has excelled, however, is in controlling the largest market share of trafficking in the drug MDMA (Ecstasy). And the interfaces between intelligence agencies and organized crime are well documented.

Secondly, to have a multiplicity of purposes often throws counterintelligence personnel off the scent of the real purposes of covert operations. It is common to have covert operations that resemble Chinese boxes — one inside the other. Not every member of the art student ring would have known of deeper operations intended to track the 9/11 hijackers, and for good reason. And the fact that one Israeli intelligence operative actually tipped US authorities off to the operation might well have been a plausibly deniable heads-up to US intelligence that the ring was here and on the move.

A close reading of the DEA report suggests that on one level it was a direct intimidation effort aimed at various elements of the federal government. Nothing more disrupts criminal investigations than any hint that suspects have acquired the home addresses of investigating officers and know how to find their families. In dozens of cases, members of the ring showed up at private residences when only wives or other relatives were at home. Some of those relatives, their suspicions aroused, followed the art students and their canvases only to see that they had not called on any neighboring homes. It would have been nothing for Israeli intelligence to later hand over the addresses of these investigators to Israeli organized crime members, who are not known for their congeniality.

Yet on a deeper level this story reveals that Israeli intelligence services were operating as an accomplice of the US government to see that certain of the attacks would be successful, and that, if the need arose, other attacks could be prevented. Israeli agents compromised in the operation would not have led directly to the US government, and ultra-sensitive missions are often subcontracted between governments. As history shows, Israel has benefited enormously since the attacks, using the wave of emotion to brutally consolidate its positions — often to the point of embarrassing the United States. And, when two people are both guilty of murder, they can usually be counted on to keep their mouths shut.

An interesting side note to the art student spy scandal is the fact that after receiving the DEA report and authenticating it, Madsen wrote a story for the newsletter *Intelligence Online* published by Guillaume Dasquié, author of *Forbidden Truth*. From there it was picked up by *Le Monde* and reignited as a story of worldwide interest. But in early March, Madsen also took the DEA report to TV news reporter Dale Solly at Washington's ABC affiliate WJLA. On March 5, at the top of the 5 PM report, Solly aired an interview with Madsen. In that report Solly asked, *"But what, if anything did they learn? At worst, Madsen says,"* Solly continued, *"they had advance knowledge of the attacks and either didn't share all of it with US intelligence or were ignored if they did…. Late today, the FBI and DEA confirmed the arrests. The French newspaper Le Monde called this the biggest Israeli spy case in this country since the Jonathan Pollard case in 1986."* [22]

Solly, then 53, a nonsmoker and dedicated runner, died of a sudden heart attack on April 27. Anonymous sources who knew him stated that there was a considerable delay in securing a statement from the coroner that the cause of death was natural. What is harder to dismiss is the fact that one of WJLA's newsroom directors, Phil Smith, also died of a sudden cardiac arrest within three weeks of Solly. [23]

Before looking at deeper reasons why Dick Cheney would have wanted to bring the whole matter to light, it's necessary to look at the role of Israel in American politics.

AIPAC and Israeli political influence

Few Washington insiders will deny that the American Israeli Public Affairs Committee (AIPAC) is probably the most influential lobby in Washington. It is not difficult to find press stories about Israeli politicians boasting that the American

Congress is "controlled" by Israeli interests. Again, it is critical to find the truths and the untruths in statements like this.

I have witnessed the power of AIPAC. In mid December 2001, while in Washington, I happened to sit in on the mark-up of a House resolution in the International Relations Committee. The resolution was one condemning Iraq for its role in terrorism and its repeated violation of human rights. I walked into the hearing room in the Rayburn office building and sat in the crowded spectator area, which was occupied primarily by staff of the various members debating and voting on the measure. They had come to watch an important political event in the wake of 9/11. It proved to be more enlightening listening to the staff members — who worked in the offices of members with whom I don't usually do business — than to the members themselves.

The vote started slowly, with many of the votes going against the resolution. It seemed as though the harsh anti-Iraq resolution might fail. There had, after all, been no evidence released that Iraq had had anything to do with the 9/11 attacks. But then, from side doors in the rear of the hearing room, various representatives started sticking their heads in the door long enough to say "Aye." These were some of the most powerful members of the committee including among others, Henry Hyde, Ben Gilman, and Tom Lantos. As the members who were all voting in favor of the resolution stuck their heads in the door to vote, I overhead staff members all around me saying, "Here comes the AIPAC vote." The staffers were cynical, even fatalistic about the outcome. The measure passed by a wide margin, and it was not long afterwards that I reached the conclusion that we were going to go to war with Iraq.

Further evidence of Israeli influence over the US Congress was seen in November 2001, when 89 out of 100 US senators signed a letter urging President Bush not to hamper Israel's activities in retaliation for a wave of Palestinian suicide bombings that helped to turn Israel and Palestine into sausage factories. Justly playing on the point that no act of terror against innocent non-combatants is justified, the letter neglected to mention anything about the way Israel was using its massive military might to dislocate hundreds and thousands of Palestinian citizens who had nothing to do with the attacks.[24]

On August 26, as if the wishes of the Israeli government were not already known, an aide to Prime Minister Ariel Sharon formally urged the US to begin the invasion of Iraq as soon as possible, saying, "Any postponement of an attack on Iraq at this stage will serve no purpose."[25]

The 2002 midterm elections

Two African American members of the House fell, in large measure, as a result of being targeted by AIPAC and pro-Israeli American Jewish organizations in their 2002 primaries before the November election. The chief crimes of Earl F. Hilliard of Alabama and Cynthia McKinney of Georgia seem to be that they had openly supported Palestinian rights and had openly questioned the conduct of the Israeli government. A fact that aided in McKinney's demise was that she had long been a vocal critic of the CIA, covert operations, and globalization under both Presidents Clinton and Bush. And she had dared to make a public statement questioning how much the administration knew about the attacks of 9/11 before they happened. Shortly after this, a series of stories appeared suggesting that McKinney actually supported terrorism because less than a half dozen campaign donors had previously expressed support for Hamas and Hezbollah. I strongly suspect that at least some of those donations were planted in her campaign to discredit her.

McKinney's courageous stance made her a target of Republican interests as well as AIPAC, and the two combined in a serious effort, using heavy crossover (and possibly illegal) voting by Republicans and very large campaign donations from pro-Israel organizations and interests outside of Georgia into the coffers of her pro-Israel, pro-war, African American rival, former state judge Denise Majette. McKinney, a five-term member of the House, lost her primary. A lawsuit challenging the legality of the crossover vote is currently under appeal.

McKinney actually won the Democratic Party vote. Nevertheless the *Washington Post*, Reuters, CNN, and the *Congressional News Service* all acknowledged that she was targeted by AIPAC and out-of-state, pro-Israel funding, and that this made the difference in her defeat.[26]

Just days after the 2002 midterm elections, the *Jerusalem Post* published a celebratory story about how the 108th Congress would remain strongly pro-Israel, tallying up the Jewish members of both Houses. While there is an ample, but by no means uniform, correlation between Jewish identity and support for the state of Israel among American Jews, that correlation is almost absolute among Jewish members of Congress. The *Jerusalem Post* story noted how the 108th Congress would bolster President Bush's agenda for regime change in Iraq. Ironically, it cited the strongly pro-Israel stance of the new senator from Minnesota, Norm Coleman, as he replaced the late Senator Paul Wellstone — perhaps the only Jewish American legislator to take a position substantively critical of Israeli policy in the occupied territories. The *Post* didn't discuss that aspect of Senator Wellstone's legacy.[27]

Reaching an understanding

Israel has always spied on the US. Perhaps the most famous Israeli spy is an American Jew named Jonathan Pollard, who compromised secret US communications technology in the 1970s and 1980s and remains in maximum security lock-up. Former CIA officials have categorized Pollard as perhaps the most damaging spy ever to have betrayed his country. And in December 2001 American physicist Richard Smyth pled guilty to illegally providing Israel with nuclear triggers in 1982. He then spent 16 years on the run until he was captured.[28] What happened in these cases and in the case of the art students is nothing new. For decades the Israeli desk at the CIA was the only national intelligence desk at the agency kept within the Counterintelligence Directorate. The portfolio was handled for most of that time by the legendary alcoholic and paranoid James Jesus Angleton, who — even today — many believe was an Israeli mole.

In short, the mutually beneficial but mutually compromising relationship between America and Israel is the source of both geopolitical cooperation and domestic political sabotage. When an international institution like the UN threatens to take a position against human rights violations or aggressive warfare, Israel and the US can generally be found opposing it together. While the US maintains its permanent military outpost in the most oil-rich region on the planet, Israel fends off the legitimate claims of displaced Arabs without worrying over its own strategic encirclement. But those needs require continual surveillance and penetration of each country by the other.

There is a compelling case that Israel acted as a partner with US intelligence and financial interests in seeing to it that the attacks of 9/11 were carried out. Israel had the unique HUMINT and the ELINT capabilities to track, and even quietly protect, the 9/11 hijackers from capture without the hijackers knowing it. It also had PROMIS software. In that role they served as a cutout for US interests and afforded the CIA with a layer of protection. Neither the US nor Israel can afford to have these secrets come out, and each has a blackmail option against the other. If the claim that Dick Cheney leaked the art student story to Brit Hume is true, then what we witnessed was the American giant disciplining its headstrong junior partner.

And what might be Israel's future role? Consider the moneyed interests behind the neo-cons as a kind of corporate board. In the new world order that is emerging after 9/11, Israel is positioning itself to occupy the position of executive vice president in charge of Middle Eastern affairs. As it does so, the financial and military powers of what has become an almost openly fascist world order continue to drive humanity toward the brink of destruction.

However, as we shall soon see, there will be more very compelling evidence to show that Israel acted as a junior partner to key US leaders to actually carry out the attacks of 9/11.

CHAPTER 16

SILENCING CONGRESS

In the post-9/11 world of its own making, imperial America demonstrated an impressive new level of ruthlessness. Congress was the first and most important arena for a spectacular melodrama of political brutality. Starting within a week of September 11th the imperial power moved quickly and aggressively to silence those who threatened its interests. While some efforts were successful, others were not.

Believing that Congress will save the day is a trap. After more than 20 years of study and interaction with it, I reached the familiar conclusion that Congress is ineffective because its power is concentrated among a very few profoundly compromised legislators. Only the committee chairpersons and the party leadership can either promote or prevent serious change. On 9/11, the major senators in this category were former Senate Majority Leader Tom Daschle, and the Chairman of the Senate Judiciary Committee, Pat Leahy.

Because of their charismatic appeal and outspokenness, some members of the House of Representatives are threats to the Empire. These members take serious risks when they speak out. They pose greater dangers because they can spark popular sentiment and break (or redirect) the mass media's hypnotic hold on the public. In this category one finds Representatives Ron Paul of Texas, John Conyers of Michigan and Henry Waxman of California; former Representatives Cynthia McKinney and Bob Barr; and, in the Senate, Russ Feingold and the late Paul Wellstone. Conyers and Waxman have fought diligently in defense of civil liberties and executive branch accountability; if they are able to persist, they may yet succeed in restoring a degree of sanity to our political culture. Ron Paul, a feisty libertarian M.D., has been an eloquent champion of fiscal responsibility and an opponent of draconian moves toward compulsory vaccinations in the post-9/11 world.

Tom Daschle and Pat Leahy

Tom Daschle was in a position of enough power to derail all of the Empire's new legislative imperatives. Though his public stance vocally supported the administration's agenda, there were indications that, in the ultra-nationalistic fervor that followed the attacks, he was having quiet reservations about the new authoritarian onslaught. Daschle is by no means a crusader. Yet by October 10th his leadership had allowed Russ Feingold of Wisconsin to block passage of the undebated (and largely unread!) US Patriot Act — a monstrosity whose immediate passage the White House demanded.[1]

Getting Daschle (and his presidential ambitions) into line was a critical task for the Empire, because major pieces of legislation like Homeland Security, various bioterrorism measures, and a multitude of investigations were soon going to fall within his grasp. Prior to 9/11 he had not been a vocal critic of Washington's ways, but as events would show, it was imperative to make sure that he would not find his voice.

On October 15 it was disclosed that Daschle's office had received an anthrax letter, and that several members of his staff had been exposed.[2] By the 18th of October it was disclosed that as many as 31 senate staff members had tested positive for anthrax.[3]

The Patriot Act that eviscerated the Constitution was passed without debate on October 24th, 2001. Politically and physically frightened, a chamber full of pragmatists adapted to the new world by trading the Bill of Rights for their own political and physical security. In other words, Congress had gotten the message. The few opposition voices that remained, having been rendered ineffective, could be left in place as symbols to show that debate still existed. On January 29, 2002, CNN announced that both the president and vice president had asked Daschle to limit any congressional investigations into the attacks, arguing that they might take resources away from the war against terror.[4] Not only did Daschle comply, he delayed public investigations until revelations from other sources, particularly rank-and-file FBI agents, dictated that they had to be held in order to maintain the credibility of American government.

Senator Pat Leahy of Vermont was also in a position to derail many of the unconstitutional actions and the legislation coming out of the White House. As chair of the Senate Judiciary Committee he apparently had the power, the obligation, and the willingness to do so. He did it eloquently and with great fire until it was his turn to suffer. Throughout September, October, and November, Leahy was an open critic of the Bush administration and particularly of Attorney General John Ashcroft's moves to wiretap attorney-client conversations, to detain foreign nationals in secret and without trial, and to conduct secret military tribunals with the power of life and death where constitutional concerns had been tossed out the window.

Leahy was especially irritated at Ashcroft's imperial refusals to come and answer questions before his committee. He sent several terse letters to Ashcroft and ultimately *demanded* that Ashcroft appear. When that failed, Leahy demanded a *written* response to important questions from the committee. Ashcroft ignored Leahy, but only up to a point.

On November 16 Senator Leahy received his own anthrax letter. And the anthrax sent to Leahy's office was incredibly powerful, concentrated at a trillion spores per gram.[5] When, on December 6, Ashcroft finally made an appearance before the Judiciary Committee he was treated with kid gloves in an utterly appalling display of total surrender. I found it hard to keep from screaming as I watched Ashcroft enjoy his dog-and-pony show on C-SPAN.

It was not for some months that the American public and the world were to learn that the Ames strain of anthrax, which was identified as the strain sent to Congress, was solely and exclusively the product of a CIA weapons research program involving the US Army Medical Research Institute of Infectious Diseases (USAMRIID), the Dugway Proving Ground, and the Batelle Memorial Institute. All of the anthrax sent post-9/11 had come from within the United States and had originated in CIA-run covert research programs.[6]

Cynthia McKinney and Bob Barr

There is no question that of these two brave former members of Congress, who are as ideologically different as night and day, Cynthia McKinney stirred the most domestic and international reaction by asking questions that needed to be asked and by directly challenging the administration on its obvious deceptions. Bob Barr had also been extremely vocal in his criticism of the administration's assault on the Bill of Rights. McKinney and Barr represented neighboring districts in Georgia until January of 2003. Both were defeated in their primary election campaigns in August of 2002.

Barr, a Republican, had been one of the most outspoken critics of Bill Clinton and a leader of the Clinton impeachment effort in 1998-1999. He was one of the most conservative members of the House, and he supported the war on terror. Yet in defending the Constitution he crossed a line. An Associated Press story in November of 2001 opened with the lead:

> Georgia Rep. Bob Barr, a harsh critic of President Clinton in the previous administration, now has become the most outspoken Republican opponent of President Bush's efforts to expand law enforcement powers to combat terrorism .... there are parts [of the war on terror] the former federal prosecutor doesn't like, such as more wiretaps and possible military tribunals. He has gone on television, written newspaper columns, and issued statements to draw attention to what he, as well as more liberal lawmakers and groups, sees as infringements on privacy rights.[7]

The demise of McKinney and Barr was, at least in part, a bipartisan operation. There is a message in this. And because McKinney had asked tougher questions, she received a special kind of treatment reserved for no other. With the exception of Paul Wellstone, she was the ultimate congressional object lesson presented by the Empire after 9/11.

McKinney's crime

On March 25, 2002, McKinney appeared on a Berkeley, California, radio program on the Pacifica network, hosted by Dennis Bernstein. There she made the following statements:

> Moreover, persons close to this administration are poised to make huge profits off America's new war. Former President Bush sits on the board of the Carlyle Group. The *Los Angeles Times* reports that on a single day last month, Carlyle earned $237 million selling shares in United Defense Industries, the Army's fifth-largest contractor. The stock offering was well timed: Carlyle officials say they decided to take the company public only after the September 11 attacks. The stock sale cashed in on increased congressional support for hefty defense spending, including one of United Defense's cornerstone weapons programs.
>
> Now is the time for our elected officials to be held accountable. Now is the time for the media to be held accountable. Why aren't the hard questions being asked? We know there were numerous warnings of the events to come on September 11. Vladimir Putin, President of Russia, delivered one such warning. Those engaged in unusual stock trades immediately before September 11 knew enough to make millions of dollars from United and American airlines, certain insurance and brokerage firms' stocks. What did this administration know, and when did it know it about the events of September 11? Who else knew and why did they not warn the innocent people of New York who were needlessly murdered?
>
> We know that there were several warnings that were given prior to the events of September 11th. From people in Germany to people in the Cayman Islands to people who ... even, now we learn about the owners of the pilot schools. People were calling in to the CIA and the FBI, and they were giving information that was critical. Even prior to these warnings, we had the trial itself from the 1993 World Trade Center bombing. And we had the trial from the American Embassy bombings. So we know that the World Trade Center bombing trial gave us a lead on the fact that U.S. embassies were being targeted. And now the United States government is being sued by survivors of the embassy bombings because it is clear that America had warning and did nothing, did nothing, to protect the lives of the people who served in our foreign service, and who serve us in other ways in our embassies around the world. Now the United States government is being sued and we're going to have to pay for that, as those families are now paying every day with the loss of their loved ones ....

There was adequate warning. There were people who failed to act on the warnings. And THAT'S what ought to be investigated. But instead of requesting that Congress investigate what went wrong and why, we had President Bush, painful for me to say that, but, we had President Bush place a phone call to Majority leader Senator Tom Daschle, asking him NOT to investigate the events of September 11th. And then, hot on the heels of the president's phone call was another phone call from the vice president asking that Tom, that Tom Daschle also NOT investigate the events that led to September 11th.

My question is: What do they have to hide? And why is it that the American people are being asked to make tremendous sacrifices now in our civil liberties, in the fact that we got this request for an unprecedented hike in … in … the hike alone, of $48.1 billion, is more than any one of our allies spend TOTAL in their defense.

Then, the other issue that saddens me is the fact that the former president, President Bush's daddy, sits on the board of the Carlyle Group. And so we get this presidency of questionable legitimacy requesting a nearly unprecedented amount of money to go into a defense budget for defense spending that would directly benefit his father! Where is the … where are the brakes on transparency [sic] and corruption that I see happening as a result of the fact that the president's father stands to make money off of the very request that the president has made on what I would call a specious argument, saying that we needed to increase defense spending because of September 11th, when we now know that there were enough warnings to September 11th that we didn't even have to experience September 11th at all, at least that's the way it is now beginning to appear.[8]

For just a moment the earth stood still. People around the world held their breath waiting for a reaction that was not long in coming. All over the major media the reaction was brutal. McKinney had lost it. She was a pushy, arrogant bitch who had lost her mind at a time of great crisis. How could anyone suggest such things about America's great president?

She got the worst treatment from FOX News, run by former GOP political strategist and Bush ally Roger Ailes. FOX stooped to less-than-covert racial slurs; it seemed to me as if they stopped just short of calling McKinney an "uppity Negro" on the air.

Of course, as time revealed, she was absolutely right. And had she made her comments just a few months later, after the revelations had come from the Phoenix and Minneapolis FBI offices, she might have held her seat. There are strong signs that she will be back in office after 2004. Yet she had been a thorn in the Empire's side for a long time, and her criticisms had not begun with the Bush presidency. She had been a vocal and daring critic of covert operations and human rights violations in the name of profit all throughout the Clinton period. She was fierce-ly critical of Israel's conduct. She had been a vocal supporter of Palestinian rights. She was the biggest walking bull's-eye in Washington.

Both McKinney and Barr had to be removed before the general elections. Both occupied "safe" seats for their respective parties. If they won their primaries they would be re-elected. Not long before the August 20th primary, stories surfaced in Washington, Atlanta, and all around the country disclosing that McKinney had received donations from four men and one company that had expressed support for the Hamas and Hezbollah organizations. Both had been linked to support for organizations that supported terrorism but not to al Qaeda.[9] The largest contri-bution was $2,500; one was $1,000 and the rest were either $500 or $250.[10] Just prior to the election, several stories reported that some of the donations were reported on September 11th 2001.[11]

The national press had a field day making innuendos that McKinney sup-ported terrorism, and that the donations reported on September 11th had been celebratory rewards made by terrorist groups on that day. Only veterans of the civil rights movement and historians recalled that during COINTELPRO opera-tions in the 1960s the FBI and other entities had attempted to discredit the Reverend Dr. Martin Luther King Jr. by making donations later to be exposed as having come from Communist organizations. It was not until the 1980s that the world learned that King never received a penny from Communists, and that the FBI had never been able to find a shred of evidence suggesting that King had Communist affiliations.

Missing from the reports was the fact that the donations had been received at a fundraiser on the Friday before the attacks, and that they were simply reported the following week in compliance with Federal Election Commission regulations. McKinney's staff confirmed this to me when I visited Washington later in the year. There was no fundraising activity on September 11th, and though her staff admit-ted that the FEC regulations called for donations to be reported on the date received, they admitted to clerical tardiness in filing the paperwork. The forms had been completed on Monday September 10th and filed in the early morning of the 11th. Think about it. Congress was in panic, disarray, and flight on September 11th. Nobody was making or receiving any donations with Washington under attack. Nobody was even working!

Also omitted from the press stories was the fact that no politician does a background check on every single donor to his or her campaign, especially the smaller donors. Because of her pro-Palestinian advocacy McKinney had received broad support from Arabs and Muslims all over the country. But it was not until after McKinney had been defeated that any major press paid seri-ous attention to the fact that her opponent, Denise Majette — a Republican African American former state judge and former supporter of Republican Allan Keyes — had received enormous campaign funding from pro-Israeli groups. Yet the *Atlanta Journal Constitution* found it necessary to go through McKinney's list of donors and report how many (less than 25 percent) had "Arab-sounding" names.[12]

The most glaring and offensive aspect of the coverage was that none of the press, which was so eager to imply that Cynthia McKinney supported or was linked to terrorism, bothered to report on the case of the Safa Trust and its direct connections to the Republican Party and the Bush White House. Safa Trust is a Saudi-backed charity that gave large amounts of money to the Republican Party and supported the Bush administration. The FBI, who described it as a money laundering operation for terrorist groups, raided it in March 2002. Safa actually shared office space with Republican Party activist Grover Norquist. The sums involved in Safa's activities were in the tens of thousands of dollars, and this money apparently opened doors directly into the Bush White House.[13]

But when the Empire is out to discredit the people's elected Representatives, a genuine conflict of interest like the Republican-Safa Trust connection isn't required. And as Wayne Madsen showed in an article we republished on the *FTW* website, it used one stone to kill more than one bird.

Wither Congress, Wither America?
Crushing Congressional Dissent:
The Fall of Hilliard, Barr and McKinney

by
Wayne Madsen

Historians will one day write that the 107th Congress was the last to stand up to the constitutional encroachment by the military and monarchist policies of the Bush II administration. Just like its ancient Roman predecessor, the Congress of the United States is becoming an elite club of pathetic assenters and global elitists. Once the domain of great orators and dissenters like Cato and Cicero, the power of the Roman Senate was eventually subsumed by the Roman Army when the Emperor took on dictatorial powers. The Roman Senate could say nothing as the military dictatorship annexed Macedonia, Spain, Greece, the Middle East, and North Africa. By the time Emperors Tiberius and Septimius Severus took power, the Senate, which had grown to an elite club of 600, was a rubber stamp body that had no choice but to go along with the military's continued usurpation of power.

The United States Congress stands on the same precipice where its Roman ancestor once fell. If Bush pulls another electoral coup in 2004 and we see the presidential election thrown into the House of Representatives, the future for the country appears very dim.

The August 20 defeat of two Georgia Representatives, one a Democrat, the other a Republican, is a bellwether event that bodes ill for this November's elections. Rep. Cynthia McKinney was successfully challenged by a Republican- turned-Democrat for her Fourth District seat. Before a cleverly contrived political operation was launched under the aegis of Georgia's other quasi-Republican, Senator Zell Miller, no one outside of Georgia had ever heard of former state judge Denise Majette, a self-described supporter of lunatic fringe GOP presidential candidate Alan Keyes in 2000.

Majette will join in Congress fellow Ivy Leaguer Arthur Davis, who beat Alabama Democratic Representative Earl Hilliard in that state's primary because of the latter's outspoken support for a more even-handed Middle East policy. Hilliard and McKinney join a long list of politicians who were defeated after advocating an independent US foreign policy in the Middle East: Senators Charles Percy, James Abourezk, James Abdnor, and J. William Fulbright, and Representatives Paul Findley and Paul McCloskey. The careers of Adlai Stevenson and William Scranton were similarly ended after they supported a Middle East policy less tied to the interests of Israel. Only Michigan's veteran Representative John Dingell was able to stave off a recent assault from the powerful American Israel Public Affairs Committee (AIPAC) in a match off with fellow Representative Lynn Rivers in a redrawn congressional district.

However, Dingell's National Rifle Association ally, Georgia Representative Bob Barr, was not as fortunate. Barr was also a target of Miller's political operation. An opponent of the more draconian elements in Bush's and John Ashcroft's U.S.A.-PATRIOT Act and Homeland Security Department bill, Barr was a target of opportunity for the extreme right that favors turning the United States into a version of East Germany or North Korea. Moreover, Barr's chairmanship of the House Subcommittee on Commercial and Administrative Law gave him real gavel power to block Bush and Ashcroft on critical civil liberties and privacy infringements, a power Barr has not hesitated to wield. And after supporting Steve Forbes in the 2000 GOP primary, Barr did not fit into Bush's binary and simplistic world: "If you're not with me, you're against me."

Therefore Miller, who, according to a former aide, is targeting fellow Senator Max Cleland and Georgia Governor Roy Barnes for defeat by conservative Republicans, figured out that if Barr supporters in Gwinnett County, which straddles McKinney's Fourth District and Barr's Seventh District, could be coaxed into crossing over party lines and voting for Majette, it would kill two birds with one stone.

Barr would lose votes to his opponent John Linder and McKinney would get trounced by Majette in a low turnout (25 percent) election with a high GOP crossover vote. The gambit paid off. McKinney and Barr were both defeated handily, McKinney with the help of 25,000 crossover votes. Of course, the fact that people not authorized to vote in the Fourth District may have voted anyway would fall into the category of election fraud. But after the Florida debacle, the Ashcroft Justice Department sees such electoral machinations as an acceptable way to remain in power — like any totalitarian regime parading before the world as an exemplary democracy.

That McKinney and Barr were on the same neo-conservative hit list was exemplified on August 21 by a second-tier conservative radio talk show host in Washington, DC. Speaking on WTNT-AM, Oral Roberts University graduate, Pat Buchanan political adviser, and Tom DeLay-style Republican talk show host Michael Graham said it was great news that two "kooks" had been beaten in Georgia. He then stated he was talking about "Cynthia McKinney and her photo negative twin, Bob Barr." The statement was clearly racist in nature and a not-so-veiled reference, through a warped attempt at humor, to Barr's long-rumored African-American heritage. But for the extreme right that dominates the GOP, such incendiary xenophobic comments are the rule and not the exception.

McKinney had incurred the wrath of the White House by her question about what George W. Bush knew in advance about the September 11 terrorist attacks. But that was only the tip of the iceberg for the Republicans and their major campaign contributors. While it is true that McKinney has championed the cause of Palestinian statehood and self-determination, thus inviting the enmity of major Zionist organizations in the United States, it was her long-time opposition to the trade of blood diamonds and other strategic minerals in Africa that earned her a major challenge from multinational corporations, including Barrick Gold, on whose board President Bush's father serves as an international adviser. Among its other misdeeds, Barrick has been accused of helping to cover up the 1996 burying alive by one of its subsidiaries of over 50 Tanzanian gold miners in Bulyanhulu, in the northwest part of the country. Of course, when it comes to the lives and welfare of non-white people, the Bushes have never really held any soft spot, whether they are blacks in Africa or America's inner cities, Afghan or Iraqi children, or even a troubled half-Hispanic daughter/niece/granddaughter in Florida.

McKinney long advocated a halt in the pilferage of blood diamonds out of African war zones. She cited, on numerous occasions, the result of such commerce: the hacked off limbs, hands, and ears of small children in Sierra Leone; the permanent crippling from land mines of children in Angola and the Democratic Republic of Congo (DRC), and over 2.5 million deaths from civil wars in the DRC, Rwanda, Uganda, and Burundi. The diamond profiteers from this mayhem and death are largely the Hasidic diamond dealers of Antwerp, Amsterdam, New York, and Tel Aviv. These dealers and their lobbyists often circled in and out of House hearing rooms and McKinney's office when issues relating to stemming the flow of ill-gotten African diamonds came up for discussion. These diamond merchants also have a powerful ally in long-time Democratic Party fundraiser and diamond cartel magnate Maurice Tempelsman.

Without the robust conscience of Cynthia McKinney and the keen skepticism of Bob Barr, the 108th Congress will be a far more dangerous place. I have had the pleasure of knowing and working with both of them over the years: fighting battles alongside McKinney against US human rights offenses in Africa and elsewhere, and alongside Barr against rampant US government surveillance of the private lives and activities of American citizens. The next Congress will be full of complacent African-American opportunists like Majette and Davis; dangerous extreme rightists like former cockroach exterminator [Tom] DeLay and former sportscaster J. D. Hayworth of Arizona; pitiful morons like Florida's former Secretary of State and chief election rigger Katherine Harris; Republican moles and sleepers like Zell Miller and Joe Lieberman; and Democratic spineless amoebas like Richard Gephardt and Tom Daschle. They will stand ready to back Bush's military campaigns into Iraq, Iran, Venezuela, Colombia, or wherever Bush's economic interests are at stake. The country stands on the brink of disaster. But we cannot count on the future Congress to save us. Lacking a spine or any guts, it will surely help to bury us.[14]

Cynthia McKinney's loss did not remove her spirit, nor did it remove her from the public consciousness. Since the primary elections and the devastating performance of the Democratic Party in what I believe were rigged general elections the following November, McKinney has absorbed and redirected the energies directed at her — like a lightning rod. She is a skilled organizer and a veteran advisor for alliances that waited patiently for the Empire to stumble, as it did over its criminal representation of the threat posed by Iraq. Throughout 2003 and 2004 she remained one of the most sought-after speakers on the planet. And she will be back.

In May of 2002, after the public relations damage had been done, McKinney received her vindication as news of the Phoenix and Minneapolis FBI investigations became public. It was too late to make a difference in her campaign. Her comments then were, I believe, prophetic.

If committed and patriotic people had not been pushing for disclosure, today's revelations would have been hidden by the White House. Ever since I came to Congress in 1992, there are those who have been trying to silence my voice. I've been told to 'sit down and shut up' over and over again. Well I won't sit down and I won't shut up until the full and unvarnished truth is placed before the American people.[15]

Paul Wellstone

If Cynthia McKinney was loudmouthed and pushy, then Paul Wellstone was ten times worse. That might be why George Bush Sr. once referred to him as a "chickenshit."

I am convinced that Paul Wellstone was murdered. The following two *FTW* stories explain why. There is a lingering question as to why the American press never picked up on the fact that one of the victims of that tragedy had a direct connection to the so-called 20th hijacker, Zacarias Moussaoui. Here are excerpts of what *FTW* published on the crash which took his life.

Was Paul Wellstone Murdered?

- History Suggests It
- Crash Inconsistencies Suggest It
- Many, Including Some Members of Congress, Believe It

by
Michael C. Ruppert

Nov. 1, 2002, 15:00 PST (*FTW*) — The air crash deaths of Sen. Paul Wellstone, his wife, daughter, three staff members, and two pilots at approximately 10:25 a.m. on October 25 in Eveleth, Minnesota have given rise to the widespread belief — shared by at least two members of the House of Representatives who spoke on condition of anonymity — that the crash was a murder.

Almost as important as the known details of the crash, which often contradict mainstream press reports, is the fact that the belief is so widely held. It says something about America that cannot and should not be ignored.

A HISTORY TOO FULL OF COINCIDENCES

From a historical standpoint Democrats are twice as likely to die in air crashes as Republicans. Frequently, those who have died were known to have been either involved in the investigation of covert operations or to have taken highly controversial positions in opposition to vested government interests.

Sam Smith of the Progressive Review (<www.prorev.com>) published an October 25 story titled "Politicians Killed In Plane Crashes."

For his source he used a wonderful database found at <http://politi-calgraveyard.com>. Of 22 air crashes involving state and federal officials, including one ambassador (Arnold Raphael) and one cab-inet official (Ron Brown), *FTW* found that 14 (64 percent) were members of the Democratic Party and 8 (36 percent) were mem-bers of the Republican Party. If the list was limited to only elected members of Congress, the total was eight Democrats and four Republicans....

THE WELLSTONE CRASH

Perhaps no member of the Senate ranked higher on the Bush admin-istration's enemies list than Minnesota Democrat Paul Wellstone. And the enmity goes back years to when Bush's father was president. The November 4 issue of *TIME* recounts an encounter between Wellstone and the elder Bush after which he referred to Wellstone as "this chick-enshit." And it is known that there has been at least one prior reported attempt on Wellstone's life.

In the months before his death Wellstone had voted against sever-al key Bush agendas including Homeland Security, the Iraqi use of force resolution, and many of Bush's judicial nominees. In a Senate controlled 50-49 by the Democrats, Wellstone was perhaps the biggest one-man obstacle to Bush's fervent and stated desire to secure passage of the Homeland Security measure prior to a US invasion of Iraq...

So what happened to Paul Wellstone?

A check of more than 50 of the world's leading news organizations three days after the Wellstone crash left one clear impression: the crash had been caused by "freezing rain and snow," limited visibility, and likely icing of the wings. One CNN report on October 24 described the plane as flying in "snowy, frozen rain."

None of these conditions, which did **not** exist as just described, had anything to do with the crash.

Icing can be ruled out for a number of reasons. First, as reported in the *St. Paul Pioneer Press* on October 29, "Another pilot who land-ed a slightly larger twin engine plane at the airport on Friday, a couple of hours before Wellstone's plane crashed, said in an interview that he experienced no significant problems.

"Veteran pilot Ray Juntunen said there was very light ice, 'but nothing to be alarmed about. It shouldn't have been a problem.'

"He said he ran into moderate icing conditions at 10,000 feet and requested permission to drop to 5,000. At that altitude, he had only light icing. When he dropped to 3,400 feet, to begin his approach, 'the ice slid off the windshield,' he said.

"According to the NTSB [National Transportation Safety Board], Wellstone's pilots received warnings of icing at 9,000 to 11,000 feet and were allowed to descend to 4,000 feet. Juntunen said he was able to see the airport from five miles out, and another pilot landed a half-hour later and told him the clouds were a little lower, but still not bad."

Various local press reports state that the weather conditions at the time of the crash were overcast, with visibility of three miles and a ceiling of 700 feet.

An argument that the weather worsened immediately after these two pilots landed and before Wellstone crashed is belied by the fact that a contemporaneous Doppler weather radar map of the region obtained by *FTW* from the National Weather Service shows no major storm activity and the same basic conditions as reported previously.

To further clarify this, *FTW* interviewed a retired commercial airline pilot who still maintains full current FAA certifications. The pilot, who asked not to be identified by name, provided *FTW* with copies of his pilot's license, his current FAA medical certificate, and his gold membership card in the Airline Pilot's Association.

Upon reviewing the radar map he stated that there was nothing inherently dangerous in what he saw depending upon what additional conditions might be prevalent at the time, like ceiling and visibility. When advised that the reported visibility was three miles with a ceiling of 700 feet he stated, "That shouldn't be any problem, especially if you have planes taking off right before and even at the time of the crash."

In various press reports the King Air was described as a powerful aircraft, and that de-icing equipment was standard.

And *The Pioneer Press* reported on October 26 that Gary Ulman, the assistant manager of the Eveleth-Virginia Municipal Airport, "jumped into his own private plane and took off in search of the missing aircraft" after noting Wellstone's delayed arrival. Therefore, the icing conditions could not have been a contributing factor in the crash, or else the airport manager would not have taken off.

What has been disclosed by various local press sources, including stories in the October 28 and 29 *Pioneer Press*, is the following:

- The plane, although it was required to have only one, had two fully licensed commercial pilots. The lead pilot had 5,200 hours of flying time and the highest possible certification. No physical problems had been reported with either pilot;
- The plane was not required to and did not have either a flight data recorder or a cockpit voice recorder;

- Wellstone's plane had notified the Federal Aviation Administration (FAA) that it was on approach to the airport and had activated the runway lights;
- The time from the last radio contact with the FAA when everything was normal until the crash was approximately 60 seconds;
- The pilots — as is standard procedure for unmanned airports — had sent a radio signal from their airplane to equipment at the airport which turned on the runway lights and activated a directional beacon that would align the plane with the runway. [Note: The Eveleth airport was not equipped with a more sophisticated remotely activated instrument landing system that would have provided feedback to the pilots on speed, rate of descent and above ground altitude];
- The FAA found that "an airport landing beacon, owned and maintained by the state ...[was] out of tolerance Saturday and was retesting Sunday." This was later confirmed by the acting chairwoman of the NTSB, Carol Carmody [Note: According to the NTSB website, Carmody formerly worked for the Central Intelligence Agency];
- The runway selected ran directly east to west and Wellstone's plane was on final approach from the east;
- According to FAA records as reported October 29 in the *Workers' Daily*, at 10:19 a.m. at an altitude of 3,500 feet the plane began to drift away from the runway toward the south;
- According to the same source, the plane was last sighted at 10:21 a.m. flying at 1,800 feet;
- Paul Wellstone's plane was found approximately two miles south of the eastern half of the runway, facing south. [Early press reports placed the crash site at between 2-7 miles east of the runway. Subsequent television reports, accompanied by maps, placed the crash site at this location. *FTW* is continuing to investigate the exact location of the crash site.];
- The propellers were turning at the time of the crash;
- The angle of impact was 30 degrees (extremely steep), indicating the plane was out of control;
- The wing flaps, which should have been fully extended for landing, were only extended to 15 degrees (a setting used for initial approach descent);
- The plane had been traveling at approximately 85 knots.

One quotation from the *Pioneer Press* is interesting. "Radar tapes indicate the plane had descended to about 400 feet and was traveling at only 85 knots near the end of its flight. It then turned south, dove at an unusually steep angle and crashed."

Aside from the aircraft's sudden change in direction and the setting of the flaps, the airspeed is perhaps the most intriguing known element in the crash. A number of factors, if the data which had been released by the NTSB is to be believed, indicate that the Wellstone plane stalled just before crashing. A stall usually occurs when an aircraft's nose is raised too steeply for the throttle setting of the engine.

One account of a King Air's stall characteristics can be found at <http://www.ainonline.com/Features/Pilotreports2000/AIN_pr_kingair.html.>

This text described a case where the stall warning horn (an alert that warns if airspeed is too low) was activated under landing conditions (gear down with full flaps) at 85 knots. It is intentionally loud, distracting, and unmistakable. The account stated that the actual stall did not occur until the aircraft being tested reached 69 knots. That's 16 knots slower than what was reported.

Other factors like the plane's total weight and center of gravity might have changed these outcomes. The FAA lists the standard approach speed for a King Air B 100 (the type carrying Wellstone) as 111 knots. Therefore the crash speed was significantly below the recommended approach speed, which is generally estimated at 1.3 times the manufacturer's listed stall speed.

The fact that the plane's flaps were extended only 15 degrees would have raised the stall speed.

SPECULATION

This writer has spoken to several pilots who have flown high-risk covert missions for the CIA or the Department of Defense. One of them related to me that it would be easy to cause an aircraft to fly right into the ground by recalibrating the airport's IFR approach equipment and resetting the altitude (in fact, such a scenario was used in the fictional movie *Die Hard II*).

But the Eveleth airport was equipped with only a directional beacon to line the plane up with the runway. It has already been established that this equipment was not "properly calibrated" and yet there are no reports of any deviations by either of the two pilots who landed safely shortly before the crash. That might have been what caused Wellstone's plane to veer off to the south.

Mechanical sabotage of flight controls that would only be triggered under certain conditions or an incapacitating gas might also offer explanations as to why a stall warning horn was not responded to. King Airs have pressurized cabins.

There are many questions, but the circumstances of the crash, as known thus far, do not lead to conclusions of pilot error, mechanical failure or bad weather. What does that leave? It leaves us with three dead Democratic senatorial candidates (Litton — 1976, Carnahan — 2000, and Wellstone — 2002) who all died in small private airplanes just days before critical elections.

ARGUING WITH BLITZER OVER THE DEATH OF A KNOWN TARGET

Many experienced Internet researchers, especially post-9/11, understand the importance of immediately securing local press reports and eyewitness statements to pivotal events in the moments after they occur. Several keen observers were able to transcribe the following live dialogue between an on-the-scene reporter and CNN's Wolf Blitzer.

Reporter: There is no evidence that weather had anything to do with the crash.

Blitzer: But the plane was flying into some sort of ice storm, was it not?

Reporter: There is no evidence that the weather had anything to do with the crash.

According to these observers CNN immediately cut away from the on-scene reporter who was not heard from again. Other watchers noted a crawl along the bottom of the screen, which, they said, ran only one time, "Weather not a factor in crash."

Yet the stories currently posted on the CNN site still suggest that the crash was caused by bad weather and icing.

Paul Wellstone had been a target of an assassin once before. He was a strident opponent of Plan Colombia, a US military aid package which involves massive aerial spraying of lands believed to be growing cocaine and the use of private military contractors employed by companies like DynCorp. Wellstone had traveled to Colombia to evaluate the program.

Shortly after his arrival on December 1, 2000, as reported by a number of news sources including the AP, a bomb was found along his route from the airport. Although the State Department later downplayed the incident, the general opinion was, and remains, that as an outspoken critic of CIA and covert operations, Wellstone had indeed been a target.

Those suspicions gained credibility the next day when Wellstone and his staff were sprayed with glyphosate, a chemical that has been routinely documented as the cause of a variety of illnesses in the local population. It has left certain regions of Colombia, as one native put it, "Without butterflies or birds."

One anonymous author, using the pen name Voxfux, actually predicted Wellstone's assassination in spring 2001. The story can be read at <www.voxnyc.com.> In that missive the author predicted, "If the death occurs just prior to the midterm senatorial elections, expect it to be in a state with a close race. Expect a 'Mel Carnahan' style hit."

INSIDE SOURCES

FTW was able to receive comments on the crash from two Democratic members of the House of Representatives. Both, who spoke on condition of anonymity, stated that they believed that Wellstone had been murdered.

One said, "I don't think there's anyone on the Hill who doesn't suspect it. It's too convenient, too coincidental, too damned obvious. My guess is that some of the less courageous members of the party are thinking about becoming Republicans right now."

It is a rare occurrence when this writer refers to a quotation from an unnamed CIA source. I have demonstrated in at least four interviews with the staffs of both the Senate and House Intelligence committees established that I know sources who have worked for the CIA in some very nasty covert operations.

The day after the crash I received a message from a former CIA operative who has proven extremely reliable in the past and who is personally familiar with these kinds of assassinations. The message read, "As I said earlier, having played ball (and still playing in some respects) with this current crop of reinvigorated old white men, these clowns are nobody to screw around with. There will be a few more strategic accidents. You can be certain of that."

Quo Vadis?[16]

Dissatisfied with what was being disclosed in the press, we continued our investigation of Wellstone's death as our resources permitted. In the weeks that followed, we unearthed information that led me to suspect that the directional beacon's "miscalibration" had been only a part of the crime. What seemed clear, as we reached the end of our investigative string, was that something had caused everything in the airplane to turn off all at once, and the plane had stalled too close to the ground to recover. That is a perfect description of what the Pentagon's Electromagnetic Pulse (EMP) weapons are designed to do. We stayed on the story.

Wellstone Updates: FAA, FBI, Local Officials Evasive on Key Details
New Data Confirms Weather Not a Factor in Crash
Co-Pilot Knew Zacarias Moussaoui

by
Joe Taglieri and Michael C. Ruppert

November 27, 2002, 20:00 PST (*FTW*) [Updated Jan. 21, 2003] — The National Transportation Safety Board has said the investigation into the October 25 air disaster that killed Senator Paul Wellstone, his wife, daughter, three campaign staffers, and two pilots could take six months. In the meantime, as icy weather is trumpeted throughout the news media as the leading suspected cause, the following is a list of information about the crash that is known at this time. This report is an update of known information developed through *FTW's* investigation in advance of the NTSB's report on the crash.

FLIGHT'S FINAL MOMENTS

Citing NTSB chief Carol Carmody who referred to "air traffic control records," an October 27 *New York Times* story recounted the plane's final flight: "It took off at 9:37 a.m. from Minneapolis-St. Paul and at 9:48 was issued instructions to climb to 13,000 feet. At 10:01, air traffic control issued a clearance to land at Eveleth, and the pilot was given permission to descend to 4,000 feet. The pilot was also told that there was icing from 9,000 to 11,000 feet. At 10:10, the pilot began his descent. At 10:18, he was cleared for an east-west approach to the runway, and, according to radar, the plane was lined up with the runway.

"'That was the last transmission conversation with the pilot,'" Ms. Carmody, a former CIA employee, said.

"'Everything had been completely normal up until that time, and there was no evidence on the controller's part or from the pilot's voice that there was any difficulty, no reported problems, no expressed concern.'"

"At 10:19, according to radar, the plane was descending through 3,500 feet and began to drift southward, away from the runway. Two minutes later, radar recorded the last sighting of the plane at 1,800 feet and a speed of 85 knots just northeast of the accident site.

"'We don't know why the turn was occurring,' Ms. Carmody said. 'That's what we hope to find out.'"

A pilot who works at the airport discovered the crash site from the air at approximately 11 a.m., when he saw a cloud of "bluish gray" smoke rising from the ground. At that point he notified the control tower at the Duluth airport 60 miles away. The Duluth tower covers Eveleth, and it gave the Wellstone aircraft clearance to begin a landing approach at 10:18. This was the pilots' last radio communication, about two minutes later.

Local fire and rescue personnel arrived at the scene shortly thereafter, said Steve Shykes, the nearby town of Fayal's volunteer fire chief who was in charge of fire and ambulance personnel at the scene.

Shykes said he arrived at 11:45 that morning to set up his command post on the road about a half mile from the crash site.

CRASH SITE

The wreckage was found 2.1 miles southeast of the east end of Eveleth-Virginia Municipal Airport's (EVM) Runway 27, which is 3 miles southeast of Eveleth, Minnesota. The site's swampy, wooded terrain is 30 yards north of Bodas Road, according to a police and fire dispatcher who was at the site. Rescue workers had to use all-terrain vehicles equipped with tracks to access the downed aircraft. In some areas of the site, the mud was waist-deep.

According to investigators and photographs, the wings and tail section broke off as the plane descended into the trees at a steep 25-degree angle and a slow airspeed of 85 knots, compared to the normal 115-knot approach speed....

Press accounts reported that after impact, a massive fire consumed the rest of the plane, which was facing south, away from the east-west runway. This resulted in the near total disintegration of the fuselage and severe damage to the victims' bodies.

FTW has obtained two Associated Press photos of the crash site. No evidence of fire, charring, or smoke damage was visible on the wreckage shown in those photographs.

INVESTIGATORS

According to Frank Hilldrup and Paul Schlamm of the NTSB, the investigation is in the analytical phase. No conclusions will be drawn and a report will not be issued for several months.

Dr. Thomas Uncini, St. Louis County medical examiner, determined both pilots died from impact, not smoke inhalation, health issues such as a heart attack or stroke, nor a gunshot wound. The doctor told reporters he looked for gunshot wounds on all eight victims and found none.

Uncini could not be reached for comment, but according to the *St. Paul Pioneer Press* on November 21, he listed the cause of death for all eight victims as 'traumatic injury due to, or as a consequence of, an aviation crash with fire.'

The day of the crash, local fire and police investigators said personnel from their departments were on the scene shortly after 11.

Then in the afternoon between noon and 2 p.m., FBI agents from the Duluth and Bemiji office arrived at the crash site, according to Paul McCabe, a special agent and spokesman for the FBI office in Minneapolis. At approximately 3 o'clock, McCabe said, agents from Minneapolis arrived.

Throughout the afternoon, the FBI's Evidence Recovery Team searched the crash site for indications that foul play might have been involved. Agents found no evidence to warrant a criminal investigation, "pretty early on," said McCabe, and the NTSB took the lead on the investigation that evening when Carmody and her team arrived at about 8 p.m.

There are many unresolved questions as to the points of origin and assignments of the first FBI agents at the scene. Special agents from the Minneapolis office are known to have been at the scene approximately 2.5 hours after the crash, but the exact time of their arrival is a question that neither the FBI or incident commanders at the scene seem able to answer definitively.

McCabe's explanation contradicts reporter Christopher Bollyn of the *American Free Press*, who said he spoke to a female employee of the FBI Duluth office who said agents from Minneapolis — not Duluth — were the first to arrive at the crash site.

And Bollyn quoted St. Louis County Sheriff Rick Wahlberg as saying that he first saw FBI agents at the crash site 'early in the afternoon, about noon.'

When *FTW* contacted Wahlberg, he said he arrived at the crash site "around 1:30" and saw that FBI agents from Minneapolis who he knows personally were already on the scene. Minneapolis is about 175 miles from Eveleth, and driving time between the two cities is about 2.5 hours, according to local residents familiar with the route — a large portion of which is two-lane highway.

McCabe said agents from Duluth and Bemiji could have easily responded to the scene around noon, but he wasn't sure of agents' exact arrival times. When asked if logs were kept with such arrival times, McCabe said, "We don't really keep log time, per se, like that …. Like when I write reports on whatever investigation I do, you don't put times in there. It's a day, it shows the investigation was conducted on such-and-such a day."

Lt. Tim Harkenen of the St. Louis County Sheriffs Department was the law enforcement incident commander at the scene. Harkenen said on November 25 he would retrieve his files and look up the logged arrival times of various personnel who were at the crash site, but since that initial contact, he has not taken or returned *FTW's* calls.

FTW also requested from the FAA the maintenance and certification "337" documents for the aircraft in question. The order for a Federal Express overnight shipment was placed November 13 with the administration's Aircraft Registration Branch in Oklahoma City, but as of this story's publication, no documents have been delivered. Calls to the FAA have failed to yield an explanation as to why the documents have not arrived as promised. FAA form 337's are public

records and by law must be made available to anyone who requests
them.

WITNESSES

Gary Ulman, who co-owns Taconite Aviation based out of the Eveleth
airport, took his plane up after receiving word from the Duluth tower
that the Wellstone plane failed to land on EVM's Runway 27.

"Approach called up here to me on the telephone and asked if the
airplane was on the ground. And I told them no, it wasn't," said
Ulman. When he went outside to double check the tarmac, he phoned
the Duluth tower back to confirm that the Wellstone plane had not
landed. The controller called rescue personnel, said Ulman, and he
took his plane up to search for the missing flight.

Ulman and other local pilots who flew into Eveleth's airport that day
said icing was not at a dangerous level and have characterized the weather conditions at the time of the crash as not dangerous flying weather.

"I don't think icing had an effect," said Ulman, who took his plane
up twice after the crash — first to find the wreckage, then with Chief
Shykes to help direct the fire and rescue personnel to the site.

Local residents Rodney Allen, Megen Hill, and Kim Hill were
reported to have seen or heard the plane as it flew over their homes
moments before it crashed.

THE AIRCRAFT

The Beech King Air A-100 was built in 1979 and seated eight passengers and two pilots, though only one pilot was required for standard
operation. Wellstone traveled with two pilots as a safety precaution.
The plane was a Pratt/Whitney dual engine turbo-prop, registered as
N41BE, serial no. B-245....

The King Air is very widely used for charter services. It has a fatal
accident rate 25 percent lower than all privately owned and chartered
turbo props, according to the Associated Press citing Robert Breiling,
a Florida-based aviation consultant who studies business aviation accident rates....

WEATHER CONDITIONS

Automated instruments at the Eveleth airport at 10:14 a.m. CDT indicated the wind was calm and the visibility was three miles in light snow.
There were scattered clouds at 400 feet and overcast skies at 700 feet.

The temperature was 33 Fahrenheit, and the dew point was 32
Fahrenheit.

The altimeter, which measures a plane's height based on baromet-
ric pressure, was at 30.06 inches of mercury.

EVELETH-VIRGINIA MUNICIPAL AIRPORT

The airport has no control tower and is equipped with a VOR/DME landing guidance system. The minimum altitude for a landing approach is 371 feet from less than 2 miles out. If a pilot does not have visual sight of the runway at this altitude, he or she is required to call in a 'missed approach' and go around the airport for another landing attempt.

In the case of this crash, there is no reason to doubt that the pilots could see the runway, because the cloud ceiling was 700 feet. Ulman also doubted a missed approach was happening, because there was no contact from the pilots indicating this.

PILOTS

Richard Conry, an experienced pilot with more than 5,000 hours of flying time, was the doomed flight's captain. Conry, 55, had reportedly flown into the Eveleth airport many times prior to October 25, and Wellstone often requested Conry.

The *Minneapolis Star Tribune* reported that Conry served federal time because of a 1990 conviction for mail fraud, and he apparently exaggerated his level of experience flying large passenger aircraft for the airline American Eagle before being hired to fly Executive Aviation charters.

It has also been reported that Conry worked as dialysis nurse, and he completed a shift at a Minneapolis hospital at 9 o'clock the night before his scheduled flight with Wellstone on the morning of October 25.

Michael Guess, 30, had 650 hours of flying time and was employed as a pilot by Executive Aviation in April 2001.

Moussaoui

In a chilling footnote, the *Minneapolis Star Tribune* reported on October 26th that Guess had performed administrative work at the Pan Am Flight School in Minneapolis where Zacarias Moussaoui had been taking flight lessons.[17] Not only had Guess and Moussaoui known each other, but Guess had 'inadvertently given Moussaoui access to a computer program on flying a 747 jumbo jet.' The FBI later found the proprietary program copied on his laptop computer — the one which Supervisory Special Agent David Frasca had prevented the Minneapolis field agents from searching.[18]

CHAPTER 17

VREELAND II: SILENCING ME

I believe that, from the information I have seen, "Mike" Vreeland tried to pass information to the Canadian government that should have been passed to the US government. That information had to do with the attacks of September 11. Whatever other attempts were made by Vreeland and his attorneys to alert US and Canadian officials of the attacks, it is clear that he did pass information about the pending attacks to his guards in August. I am willing to go to the Secretary of the Navy to determine whether or not he was actually a Navy officer.

I know that there have been other US citizens with a similar background used on missions similar to what has been alleged by Vreeland. This man fits a pattern. I would like for the Secret Service to put him on a polygraph.

— Leutrell "Mike" Osborne, veteran former CIA case officer with
26 years of experience in counter-terrorism.

In some tough investigations when leads are sparse there are times when it becomes necessary for a detective to "shake the trees" and see what falls out. Rarely do the reactions of the suspect focus on the detective personally. When they do, however, the repercussions are always serious, sometimes even life threatening.

During 2002, *FTW's* investigations were beginning to resonate with some influential people. It was inevitable, and I knew it, that attempts would be made to diminish our effectiveness on Capitol Hill and elsewhere.

Bill Tyree had been absolutely right; Delmart "Mike" Vreeland was a "honey pot" — an intelligence asset who is sent out with material that proves to be legitimate but which subsequently turns on any bear that sticks his nose too close. The difference with Vreeland was that he did not become a honey pot until I decided to report on his case. He needed something to trade with those who were trying to silence him. Up until that time he had been like the other men described in Chapter 10, a guy who had exceeded his warrant, gotten too careless, or too cocky, or who had come to possess information that was way above his "pay grade." He was in fear for his life, and when I showed up he saw something that might buy his way into another round in the game. That was and is Mike Vreeland's ultimate addiction — if he is still alive.

I knew that Vreeland was going to try to discredit me almost immediately after Greta Knutzen and I traveled to the Peterborough jail outside of Toronto to interview him on March 6, 2002. Greta had become invaluable over time as she suffered through many frustrating encounters with Vreeland and painstakingly documented new developments in his case.

Vreeland was the subject of many conversations I had with Leutrell "Mike" Osborne, who also gave me a written, on-the-record statement about the case. Osborne had been a CIA counter-terrorist case officer for 26 years, and the only African-American case officer to have served in that capacity. "He's a dangle," Osborne kept saying. "I know, Mike, I know," I would respond. "But I have to keep him out of the hole and keep him talking about the note." A "dangle" in intelligence parlance is the same thing as piece of bait in a trap. Leu was telling me that I had taken the bait, and I was telling Leu that I knew it was bait when I took it.

So, if I knew that Vreeland was going to be used to discredit me, why did I report on him? That answer is simple. I did it because I knew, and his attorneys knew, and the record clearly showed that he had written a warning note, specifically about 9/11, a month before 9/11, and he had been chillingly accurate, not only in many of the big details, but also in some of the subtler nuances about oil and Russian organized crime. He had accurately told officials of the Canadian government that one of their operatives, Marc Bastien, had been murdered in Moscow and exactly how it had been done before those facts were acknowledged or even known in Ottawa. As Vreeland's attorney Rocco Galati pointed out later, "When have you ever heard of a case of a Canadian government employee being murdered in a foreign capital and his government never follows up on it?" There was more to learn.

I have never dealt with a bigger pain in the ass in my entire life than Mike Vreeland. He was admittedly an alcoholic. He also abused prescription medications and, I suspect, packed his nose from time to time with cocaine, called in the trade "Peruvian marching powder." I never saw him with any. He was not the first alky or addict I have known in the business. Vreeland also had a temper that was about as controllable as a first-generation Russian nuclear submarine reactor, and he could turn a tiny pimple of a problem or dispute into a gangrenous limb in need of amputation. He could piss off a dead man. This was how he did me the most damage.

On the very remote possibility that Vreeland did not deliberately try to discredit me, his handlers must have been laughing themselves silly knowing what I would have to deal with.

As people around the world read Vreeland stories they reached out to him. Released on bail in March 2002, after all Canadian charges against him had been dropped, he was granted temporary asylum until his extradition hearings in September of 2002. He was quickly online with at least one website and probably

20 e-mail addresses as hundreds of discussion groups and scores of pro and con websites briefly turned him into a 9/11 icon. And his computer skills, now that he had access to a computer, were truly amazing.

Vreeland started to contradict himself with many of these people and with statements he had made to me in an interview that I had published in April. But he never changed his story about the note. Nothing *could* change the record on the note, and this was the only place I had ever hung my journalistic hat in this matter. But soon bits and pieces of his criminal record started conveniently appearing in the hands of people who were unable to post anything under their own names. Some of the information contradicted what he had told me and also, apparently, what he had told his attorneys. Of course that proved nothing; we have seen how easily criminal and military records can be manipulated by the government. But it didn't help me.

One very interesting bit of history did turn up. It seems that in February 2000 a drunken Mike Vreeland was arrested by the Mishawaka, Indiana, police department for burglary, auto theft, and a particularly nasty assault on several officers and a police car. Having been a police officer I know that very close attention is paid to people who assault and cause injuries to cops. Yet in a very small town, where news of these events travels quick, like dye in a glass of water, Vreeland, who had given at least four different names to the police, was later released without identification and allowed to walk out of jail without even a hearing.[1] At the time, according to him, he was just about to embark on his mission to Russia, and strings were clearly pulled to get him out of jail. The police report chalked it up to a paperwork error. This fits our pattern perfectly.

When people started asking Vreeland about the many arrests that they felt were not becoming for an *officer and a gentleman*, and when some of his family members, not very credible themselves, utterly inconsistent and sometimes apparently as intoxicated as he was, started throwing gasoline on the fire, Vreeland lashed out with a particularly nasty brand of invective. His critics responded in kind. He tape-recorded every phone conversation. His threats against any who offended him were as numerous as locusts. Vreeland had attracted all kinds: a few serious researchers who focused on the critical details; lonely women who wanted to fall in love or rescue him; utterly naïve and gullible "wannabes" who could never get past the dear old notion that covert operatives were to be sexy, urbane, articulate gentlemen; and, undoubtedly, a large cadre of CIA/Pentagon-connected psychological operations personnel.

When Vreeland pissed people off they immediately turned on me, especially if they had been naive enough to buy into his disinformation. It was only because of me, they said, that they had reached out to him. Most of the offended ones who were not connected to government operations were oblivious to their own unresolved issues. People like that are not hard to find, and they are very easy to manipulate. All told, I received probably 2,000 very unpleasant e-mails from these people throughout 2002.

I knew exactly what he was doing, and he knew that I knew. The unspoken deal between us was that I was going to let him try to trash me by feeding me bad information so that he could uphold his end of his deal with his handlers and maybe get out of Canada alive. It was a chess game that only John Le Carré might understand. Vreeland was one of "Smiley's people" who had been inbred for way too many generations. I steadfastly held to my one interest: the only thing that mattered was how he had learned about 9/11, and the fact that his note and the irrefutable records of two Canadian lawyers and a court proceeding might someday become 9/11's biggest smoking gun.

After I published the first stories that brought Vreeland to world attention he started referring to me as me "Pops" and he called me three to five times a day. He followed those with five or six e-mails. He constantly fed me disinformation about red mercury, space-based missile-defense shields, China, Saddam Hussein, the Kursk (a sunken Russian nuclear submarine), the death of US Navy Admiral Jeremy Boorda, and a hundred other things. Over time he learned that I wouldn't bite on any of them. But there was to be a final irony, in his claims of having helped create an impenetrable missile defense shield that had been perfected by the Russians.

I understood his predicament. Like so many of the other men I had known in similar positions, he had run afoul of his keepers. A young, street-wise, undisciplined, and ignorant young man had evolved from his early days as a police informant to become a skilled government operative who had, over the years, been arrested many times and always found himself sharing a cell with a major criminal or intelligence target with whom he quickly became "friends." Then he joined the navy. He had become a criminal in order to work with criminals. This has never disqualified anyone from service as a covert operative. It is, rather, a prized job skill. Vreeland's conduct over the years shows what happens when so much license is given to an over-bright, undereducated street kid, who never developed enough social consciousness or a moral compass to separate his own life from the world in which he operated. His navy rank of Lieutenant had been nothing more than a reason for him to be at certain places and to access certain information.

I could see his hatred of the hypocrisy of the system that had created him and used him in every sip of rum and coke. I could hear it with every rattle of the ice in his glass and discern it in every one of the thousands of e-mails he sent out to his attackers and to his supporters alike. Yet because he possessed so many secrets and had developed his tradecraft so well, he had hidden the necessary evidence of his covert life as insurance policies in places where it could serve him. This was his game, and he was an excellent survivor. He was an intelligence junkyard dog, and the black world had given him a leash that allowed him to run out and do things that civilians could never do. Yet even the owners of junkyard dogs are careful about how they approach them. What Mike Vreeland ultimately revealed himself to be was a con-wise snitch, a street-wise intelligence courier, and a killer.

Not everything that Vreeland put out was disinformation. A disinformation source that releases nothing but disinformation soon has no audience and is useless. Vreeland had other cards to play, and he wanted the powers that be to know he had them.

On July 8, 2002, I participated in a five-way satellite, secure network phone conversation with Mike Vreeland, journalist Sander Hicks, former Ambassador Leo Wanta, and former Assistant United States Attorney Tom Henry who was acting as Wanta's lawyer. The subject was Vreeland's exposure of credible documents showing that trillions of dollars had been stolen out of the United States Treasury over a period of years and that some of the biggest names in American politics had been involved. These included the Bushes, the Clintons, Federal Reserve Chairman Alan Greenspan, and the heads of many major banks and government agencies. What I didn't catch until much later was that the documents posted on the web by Vreeland were the same ones that had been sent to me in November 2001 by Steven Tangherlini before I had ever met Vreeland. (See Appendix B and Chapter 11.)

It is absolutely correct that more than $3 trillion is currently missing from the US Treasury, and this has been reported by *CBS News,* the *Washington Times,* and other news outlets. The Pentagon and the Department of Housing and Urban Development have admitted as much. Vreeland had brought forward more than 100 credible pages of banking transaction records and was acting as a go-between for Wanta, who was trying to expose the thefts and recover the money — for a fee, of course.

Wanta, a former high-roller in the Bush I, Regan, and Clinton eras, had suffered the same fate as all the rest of the men in Chapter 11. He had been arrested on state income tax charges in Wisconsin and sentenced to imprisonment for decades for misdemeanor violations. Later, due to poor health, he had been confined to his home. His net worth had been officially estimated once at more than $400 billion. His credentials had been verified through several mainstream press stories and also by credible eyewitnesses who credited him with engineering a Russian ruble collapse which helped bring down the Soviet government in 1991. Hicks was also able to confirm Wanta's previous government positions and the fact that he had been appointed as Somali Ambassador to Canada as a means of providing him with diplomatic immunity. There was no way to say that Wanta had not been a player.[2]

Hicks had also obtained on-the-record statements from navy personnel confirming that Vreeland had held the rank of lieutenant and had been on active duty from 1986 until late 2000 before his detention in Canada.[3]

The FINs (financial documents) were discussed at length in the phone conversation with the five of us, and then Vreeland — apparently with Wanta's foreknowledge — turned the discussion to Switzerland in 1993. On that trip Vreeland had shadowed Wanta to a rendezvous where Vreeland's mission was to assassinate Wanta's contact, Marc Rich, who had allegedly crossed Bill Clinton. Wanta confirmed all of Vreeland's account, and both men agreed that the reason Rich was not killed was because the only shot Vreeland had at Rich was through

Wanta's head. Vreeland had radioed his handler, asked for direction, and he was told to stand down; don't shoot. Former Assistant US Attorney Tom Henry listened without comment as his client repeatedly confirmed Vreeland's account.

Henry wrote a letter addressed to Vreeland on his official stationary dated February 13, 2002. (See next page.) It said in part:

> I conversed with one of your attorneys and advised my clients that you would be contacting me. When you contacted me I was to ask certain questions and be as accurate as possible on reporting your responses. I was somewhat familiar with what questions were to be asked. I had been privy to various faxes, letters, and other communications sent by clients to the White House and other USG agencies over the past three or more months. Communications written by my clients referenced information similar to the information provided in your hand written note. For your and my future conversations they asked that I reference certain passwords or security code names and note your response. I can assure you that the responses you provided are the same as I have seen on correspondence from my clients to the White House, NSA, and other USG entities. On best information and belief I am of the opinion that my clients would endorse that you gathered the information that you have shared with my client while acting in the capacity of an "intel op" agent of the USG.
>
> I am available to clarify or respond to any questions regarding this letter. If you need additional information please do not hesitate contacting me."[4]

The attempted assassination of Rich intrigued me. It fit my assessment of Vreeland's skills and personality. Having once been a manager at what was then the largest gun store in the state of California, where I dealt with law enforcement and military customers, I asked Vreeland what kind of rifle and scope he had been using in 1993. His answer convinced me that he knew what he was talking about.

He described what is called a special "necked down" rifle and cartridge that is custom made. In that process a large caliber casing is specially manufactured to shoot a small caliber bullet at extremely high speed, oftentimes over 5,000 feet per second. The trajectory of the bullet is extremely flat with little drop due to gravity over long ranges. For example a 30.06 cartridge might be necked down to shoot a .223 bullet. This, of course, also requires a special, custom-built rifle that can chamber the casing but also has a barrel bore that matches the projectile. These are not off-the-shelf items, and they are extremely expensive to make. Only those with unlimited budgets and the need for pinpoint accuracy can afford to have them made. Vreeland's knowledge of scopes was also first rate. I concluded that among his other "skills" he was likely also a killer, as I had suspected from our first meeting.

THOMAS E. HENRY
Legal assistant to the offices of Jan Morton Heger

1125 South 79ᵗʰ Street
Omaha, Nebraska 68124
Phone: 402-933-6421
E-mail: agprochina@cox.net

February 13, 2002

Mr. "Mike" Vreeland
Toronto Ontario, Canada
VIA FACSIMILE: 1-888-771-5360

Dear Mr. Vreeland:

Please be advised that I have consulted with clients and have been authorized to provide the information outlined in this letter. Although I am a former Assistant United States Attorney I am no longer working in such a capacity. I am not an agent or employee of the United States Government. The information contained in this letter is based on best information and belief derived from discussions and consultation with clients.

Current clients consist of corporate entities organized as 18 United States Code Section 6 (USG Proprietary) companies. On best information and belief I am of the opinion that one or more of the individuals associated with the 18 USC 6 companies is and/or are employed by the USG and he or they implement their duties and responsibilities under the National Security Act of 1947. For the purpose of this letter and for reasons of confidentiality I will refer to the individuals collectively as Jack.

Approximately two weeks ago Jack asked that I contact the Canadian attorney's representing you. My clients had learned of your hand written note published on the internet concerning the 9/11 terrorists acts and asked that I attempt to contact you regarding names, places, dates and other apparent "intel-op" references in the hand written note. I conversed with one of your attorney's and advised my clients that you would be contacting me. When you contacted me I was to ask certain questions and be as accurate as possible on reporting your responses. I was somewhat familiar with what questions were to be asked. I had been privy to various faxes, letters and other communications sent by clients to the White House and other USG agencies over the past three or more months. Communications written by my clients referenced similar to the information provided in your hand written note. For your and my future conversations they asked that I reference certain passwords or security code names and note your response. I can assure you that the responses you provided are the same as I have seen on correspondence from my clients to White House, NSA and other USG entities. On best information and belief I am of the opinion that my clients would endorse that you gathered the information that you have shared with my client while acting in the capacity of an "intel op" agent of the USG.

I am available to clarify or respond to any questions regarding this letter. If you need additional information please do not hesitate contacting me.

Sincerely yours

Thomas E. Henry

Not long after the five-way conversation I received a postcard sealed in an envelope. The envelope had been postmarked in Venice, Italy. On the face of the postcard was a print from a European fairy tale, *The Queen and the Trolls*. The picture showed the Queen. The message read,

> Attn to Michael Ruppert Good Work! — To Mr. Vreeland for SSST… Change lawyer not in Canada, not in USA is his place — Help Him — by Casanova from PIOMBI.

If Vreeland was a con man he certainly had influence. He had never left Canada. He was under virtual house arrest and regularly checked on by his attorneys and the police. He had no passport in his possession. I had called him in Canada at the time the postcard was sent. His lawyers said that it was out of the question that he had left the country.

So who mailed the postcard? This is one of the many mysteries left behind by Mike Vreeland.

The hearing to determine Mike Vreeland's fate was scheduled for September 9th, 2002. He called me in New York on September 7th and said that he had discussed it with his lawyer, Paul Slanksy, and he had decided to produce some of the diplomatic pouches he had had brought back from Moscow. They were still sealed. I told him that if that was the case and he was talking to me over a cell phone that there was little chance he would ever be allowed to get to court.

Vreeland never showed up for the hearing. A provisional bench warrant was issued as Slanksy rushed to Vreeland's residence with the police. They found the apartment completely ransacked. The computer had been demolished, yet there was no blood or sign of foul play. All of Vreeland's clothing, his Canadian ID and papers, even his toothbrush were all left behind. To my knowledge he has not been heard from since, with one exception.

Vreeland contacted me about a week later to say that he was on the run and in the US. He said that he had been forced to leave Canada and that one of his two sons was being held under an assumed name somewhere in a Florida jail. His son's life was in danger. His number one priority, Vreeland said, was to save his son. The tale could have been another cover story, or perhaps Vreeland was sitting somewhere with a gun to his head. I called Slansky and told him of the call. Even now I still get an occasional call from an intelligence junkie trying to play in waters he or she knows nothing about, or an e-mail from a jilted would-be lover. Paul Slansky and Rocco Galati — who was on the hook for a $5,000 bond — still maintain that Vreeland has quite likely been abducted.

The Canadian government has never asked Galati to pay the promissory note attached to Vreeland's bond.

Silencing me

Each of my 9/11 stories had a big impact from the start. It was as if I had struck an inner chord by talking about deeper, fundamental issues and asking questions which had to be asked. My October 12th appearance on the Guns and Butter show at Pacifica's KPFA in Berkeley, where I broke the first key connections in the insider trading stories leading to Buzzy Krongard and the CIA, had reverberated throughout the network. The interview was rebroadcast again two weeks later due to listener demand. Some voices inside KPFA began circulating hostile critiques that had nothing to do with the factual information I had disclosed.

In November I taped a three-hour monologue for Pacifica's New York station WBAI. It aired during their fall fundraising drive, and we offered my video *Wall Street's War for Drug Money* as a premium. It raised more than $30,000 for the station, breaking several records in the process.

Following a series of successful lectures in Canada, Texas, Oregon, and California, Guns and Butter aired an interview with me during the station's fundraising drive on February 25, 2002. The Guns and Butter broadcast pre-empted a show hosted by Steve Rendell of FAIR (Fairness and Accuracy in Reporting). Rendell is a close associate of self-proclaimed media critic Norman Solomon of the Institute for Public Accuracy who later traveled to Iraq with Congressman Nick Rahall.[5] Guns and Butter offered The Truth and Lies of 9/11 as a premium and it raised $17,000 in one hour, placing it third on a list of the top 25 most successful public affairs fundraising hours in KPFA's history. Total orders for the tape surpassed $20,000 before the night was over.

At around the same time, Solomon contacted KPFA programmer and morning show host Philip Maldari. Solomon complained that my material should not be offered at the station because I was "not credible." He followed this with an internal memo stating the same thing — which was forwarded quietly to me. The memo was circulated through KPFA's senior programming and management staff, and embraced by most of the programmers.

By February 28 I was notified that I had been denied a spot on Pacifica's national fundraising day because, according to what KPFK Public Affairs Director Dan Pavlish told one of my supporters, I had provided "factually inaccurate information." Pavlish, since removed from his position for unknown reasons, had joined a small choir of voices in Pacifica including Larry Bensky, Kris Welch, and Sonali Kolhatkar who, from my perspective, were turning out to be supportive of the Empire and its positions.

On March 3, I was invited to be a guest on a prime fundraising slot at LA's Pacifica station, KPFK. Instead of being the sole guest I was confronted at the last minute before going on the air by station manager Steven Starr and pressured into accepting a live debate with Solomon. This was an extremely unusual format. In the debate Solomon offered the weak arguments that because I had quoted Iran-Contra figure Oliver North in one of my stories I was not to be trusted. He was implying that I liked Oliver North. He made the same innuendo about the fact that I had noted that Matt Drudge's website was useful because, from its home page, it provided more than 50 links to every major press organization in the world. I rarely read Drudge and find him to be extremely partisan. I just use the links on his website. Solomon also stated that Vreeland was a con man, and that I had rested most of my 9/11 credibility on the Vreeland case. It was classic "ambush" journalism. I won the debate whenever I could focus on the facts, which was not very often.

On March 3, 2002, an internal KPFK memorandum signed by Barbara Osborn, Suzi Weissman, Terrence McNally, Jon Wiener, and Marc Cooper was sent to station manager Starr and two other KPFK executives. It read in part:

Ruppert was dismissed from the LAPD with a psychological discharge. For years he has been peddling conspiracy theories about CIA in South L.A., Jeb and George W. Bush, and the drug trade, and now apparently, the CIA's involvement in the World Trade center attacks. Ruppert has been repudiated by everyone but the naïve, the unwitting, the psychotic, and those willing to exploit him....

Are we to assume that such an implied endorsement of Ruppert is done in the name of KPFK's mission and "free speech?" The central question at KPFK is not about "free speech" but about what kind of speech KPFK will make room for. As difficult as they are to draw, lines need to be drawn. Sources need to be vetted. What is credible and/or important, versus what is trivial or delusional needs, to the best of KPFK's ability, to be discerned.

It is a tragedy that KPFK would jeopardize its overall credibility by lending credence to perspectives that are not credible. Offering premiums like Mike Ruppert's 9/11 videotape can destroy KPFK as a credible information source for important news stories that are both controversial and credible. We can't have it both ways. Either we are a credible forum or we are an open mic for every delusional knucklehead who can talk his way onto the air.

The signatories attached the first of what was to be many spiteful and inaccurate articles by *Nation* Editor and FOX News commentator David Corn that labeled me as an unstable, mercenary, conspiracy theorist.

The statement that I was fired from LAPD with a psychological discharge was maliciously false. When I resigned from LAPD in December 1978, I was earning the highest rating reports possible, I had been certified for promotion to detective, and had no pending disciplinary actions of any kind. After learning of the memo and acquiring a copy I immediately posted all of my LAPD records proving the libelous assertions false on my website. They are still there. Later, after Corn had said in another major smear in the *LA Weekly* that I had never mentioned the CIA at the time of my resignation, I posted many pages of letters and correspondence from both me and my attorney proving that statement to be also inaccurate and dishonest. Then I posted a final CIA response to my Freedom of Information Act appeals which stated that their records on me were exempt from FOIA on the grounds of national security and because they would identify CIA employees.

I was told by friends at KPFK that the "Cooper Memo," as they called it, had been authored by recently ousted KPFK figure Marc Cooper. Cooper was part of a group who had lost a suit initiated by KPFK listeners, angry at the dictatorial manner in which the network had been "occupied" by people interested in censoring its airwaves and purging its staff of dissenters. There was good reason to suspect Cooper's authorship. In addition to his connections at KPFK, Cooper is also the news features editor at the *LA Weekly* and a contributing editor at *The Nation* with Corn.

Cooper's footprints showed up again in the March 22 issue of the *LA Weekly*. In another hit piece that called me a conspiracy theorist, writer Ella Taylor described me as a *"defrocked"* ex-cop.

The internal memo had not only been libelous; it was also a gross invasion of privacy. Many encouraged me to file suit. But I recognized another trap common in psychological warfare operations like this. A suit would have eaten up most of my available time and money. One of the main functions of psychological warfare is to distract opponents from fighting battles that might change the outcome of the war by making them fight smaller battles that don't ultimately matter.

Two days after the *Weekly* story, on March 24, 2002, the Sunday edition of the *Los Angeles Times* ran a huge editorial by Gale Holland titled, "Have You Heard About Osama's Cheez-It Stash?" The piece featured a picture of bin Laden next to one of Elvis Presley. The caption read, "Like Elvis Presley, Osama bin Laden keeps popping up all over, though typically in Utah where he is often seen devouring a Big Mac." Holland called me a conspiracy theorist who strung together unsubstantiated facts and then went on to quote Corn about how frustrating it was to deal with all of the mentally unbalanced conspiracy theorists who had bombarded him with information (including, no doubt, many of the facts presented in this book). Corn suggested that dealing with conspiracy theorists was a futile endeavor for the sane.

On May 30 the *Nation* published a huge hit piece by Corn which started out first with shots at Cynthia McKinney and then once again suggested that I had been fired from LAPD for psychiatric reasons. In that story, aside from misrepresenting my research Corn wrote, "he misrepresents his source material."[6] Corn referred to a previously cited UPI story by Richard Sale in which I accurately quoted Sale showing that the US government had been eavesdropping on bin Laden's cell phone calls for some time. Corn said I had made up the quotations. The *Nation* had to let me respond. They printed my rebuttal to Corn in which I accurately quoted the Sale piece and proved its existence. Corn's subsequent response was that, Gee, he couldn't find the story.

That makes an illustrative point. Once the damage has been done in a headline story, the corrections appearing afterwards are noted by only a few.

The crescendo of attacks continued throughout the late summer of 2002. A Lexis-Nexis search revealed 23 stories mentioning me between March and August of 2002. Of those, 19 were negative and 12 were either written by, or quoted, Corn. Many appeared in local newspapers just days before I lectured in Edmonton, Calgary, Vancouver, and Toronto. They had titles like "Mike Ruppert vs. the Space Lizards" or "The Sublime and the Stupid." It was not until the Colleen Rowley and Phoenix FBI fiascoes became front-page news and other damning revelations began leaking from within the joint Senate/House Intelligence Committee that the critics fell silent.

There had, however, been a particularly nasty and personal tone to Corn's attacks, which neatly managed to avoid any discussion of the facts. He had also reported on Vreeland's background in a particularly biased manner. If Vreeland burped on Monday, Corn was writing about it on Friday.

However, a rising cadre of talented and fearless independent journalists had been watching Solomon, Corn, Pacifica radio, *Z Magazine*, and the *Nation* as they continued to deny that there was any reason to suspect US government fore-knowledge of (let alone involvement in) 9/11. This new generation of truth tellers successfully waged a war of logic and documentation that was hurting the Elite Left's credibility with its own readership.[7] I was not alone on the battlefield.

Corn reserved his nastiest bits of invective for his huge article that appeared in the *LA Weekly* just a day after he had played out his own little conspiracy by ambushing me on a radio segment hosted by KPFK morning show host Sonali Kolhatkar. On June 13, Kolhatkar had invited me to appear as a solo guest on the show with an opportunity to discuss the evidence I had been gathering about US complicity in 9/11. At the time I had not developed all of the evidence presented in this book but I was convinced at least that the US government had allowed the attacks to occur to further their own needs. Kolhatkar repeatedly attempted to turn the discussion to statements I had never made and then injected David Corn into the discussion. Corn had been listening to the broadcast and had apparently made prior arrangements to call in. Sources who were inside the station's control room later confirmed this to me.

There were two issues. One of course was Vreeland, and the second was the fact that in a previous interview with the Portland Indymedia Group I had expressed my opinion that Corn was a paid government disinformation agent. I had never published a word to that effect in *From The Wilderness*. About halfway through the broadcast Kolhatkar went off the air for an unscheduled break. She came on the line with me off-the-air and advised that Corn was on the line and wanted to par-ticipate in the broadcast. Knowing that she would unfairly spin a refusal by me, I acquiesced. When Corn got on the air he wasted no time in attacking. He started on Vreeland first and then on my stated belief that he worked for the government. Corn lost control and ended the show screaming that I was delusional. Once again, information that was to be confirmed by the government in the summer and fall of 2003 was blocked.

One former CIA employee wrote to me that it was one of the worst cases of "ambush" journalism he had ever seen.

The very next day the *Weekly* published Corn's newest piece titled "To Protect and to Spin." A cartoon image of me appearing as a semi-adolescent crybaby took a whole page of the paper. I was again urged to sue but wisely chose to focus on the needs of my subscribers and listeners.

In spite of all this, audience attendance at my lectures in the US, Canada, and Australia remained at near capacity. Every time a new attack piece appeared I picked up several hundred more subscribers.

I laughed at the irony when, two months later, I read the following statement by *Nation* publisher Victor Navasky: *"I'm not a conspiracy theorist. I believe Oswald killed Kennedy and probably did it by himself, but I think it's important to raise questions."* 8 Navasky made the statement in a story discussing how his magazine's book publishing imprint, The Nation Books, had deliberately softened or weakened some of the more damning evidence disclosed by authors Brisard and Dasquié in their book *Bin Laden: The Forbidden Truth* on translating and releasing the US edition. Only the "sanitized" version of the book is available in the US.9

Fitting the mold

In 1977 the *Rolling Stone* published a watershed article by Watergate journalist Carl Bernstein titled, "The CIA and the Media."10 In that story Bernstein dissected the documentary evidence showing that more than 400 US journalists in the preceding 25 years had carried out assignments for the CIA. Bernstein later spelled out that this figure included only those journalists who had been "tasked" by the Agency and not those who had served as conduits for Agency propaganda. He used CIA documents and interviews with CIA personnel and members of the Senate's Church Committee to make his case. While making it clear that the CIA's primary and most important relationships had been with the *New York Times,* CBS, and *TIME* magazine, he also revealed that throughout a so-called free press, both at home and abroad, the CIA often recruited journalists, planted stories with them, and gave the cooperative ones access to "better" sources which ensured their career success. Bernstein even got one CIA official to acknowledge that at one time the *New York Times* had "provided cover for ten CIA operatives."11

Other publications that played ball with the Agency included the *Los Angeles Times,* the *Colombia Journalism Review, Newsweek,* the *Washington Star,* the *Miami News,* the *New York Herald Tribune,* the *Saturday Evening Post,* Scripps-Howard Newspapers, Hearst Newspapers, Copley Press, the Associated Press, United Press International, NBC, and ABC. One US senator who had been the target of CIA lobbying and smear campaign told Bernstein, "From the CIA point of view this was the highest, most sensitive covert program of all… It was a much larger part of the operational system than has been indicated."12

The relationships described by Bernstein have not changed. In January of 2003 journalist Alan Wolper revealed that *New York Times* national security reporter James Risen was permitting the CIA to review and edit the content of his new book *The Main Enemy.* Risen is one of the journalists charged with being a watchdog on the CIA, and he has, as correctly noted by Wolper, allowed a source under scrutiny to edit his content. That is a violation of one of the cardinal rules of journalism.13

I will go to my grave believing that David Corn and Marc Cooper are paid assets of the US government, rewarded with power and prestige (such as it is) for loyalty as wolves in sheep's clothing. Those, like Norman Solomon, may be motivated by more pedestrian hungers, but I doubt it. Solomon did have a book-signing party scheduled around the time when KPFA pre-empted a show hosted by his colleague, and the popularity of my work was likely cutting into his sales. Solomon's most effective criticism of me had been that in one story I had described Vreeland's note as a *detailed warning letter* and therefore anything that I said should be disregarded.

All of these people — the ones who attack not on grounds of investigative method nor on grounds of factual truth; who attempt to keep important information from the people; who loudly proclaim that they should be the gatekeepers of the public arena — whether they do it intentionally or not, are part of a political and social ecosystem which works to support the Empire.

Getting physical

In March of 2002 a locked outside storage area at our office containing business records and a computer was burglarized and cleaned out. In May while I was in Sydney, Australia, my hotel room was burglarized, and my laptop computer was stolen. Throughout the first seven months of 2002 extremely sophisticated attempts were repeatedly made to hack into our website and office computers. Many of the attempts were successful, and we were ultimately forced to transfer our hosting services to a highly secure commercial company charging almost $1,000 a month. This was not until after our site had been down for days. Viruses, unrecognized by our virus protection company, also destroyed the hard drives on three of our office computers and sent out thousands of e-mails in our name, some containing pornography. Through all of this we were able to protect the integrity of our databases, but it was extremely expensive. One of the things that came to our rescue was a worldwide outpouring of technical support and advice.

Finally, for several months in mid-2002 our L.A. office was bombarded with microwave weapons that turned off our computers and caused physical discomfort, disorientation, and nausea in the staff. Our general manager at the time was able to verify this. He had a scientific background and was an amateur hard-rock miner. When the symptoms started hitting, he brought a portable Geiger counter into the office and noted that the Gamma radiation, on the first floor of a three-story building, was peaking in noticeably lengthy spikes of between .16 and .24 Microsieverts and sometimes as high as .42 Microsieverts. Normal ambient Gamma radiation outdoors at our elevation is about .02 to .06 Microsieverts per hour, and although spikes can occur, prolonged peaks cannot be natural occurrences.

We contacted the manager of the building and had her come in and view the readings. She agreed with what we had seen. Then we made a big show of touring the building, even its roof, with a camera, other detection devices, and the Geiger counter. We sent out messages documenting our findings and let it be widely known what we were doing. After a week of this the interior Gamma radiation levels returned to normal.

Not long afterwards we found a story which disclosed that in the 1950s and 60s the US Embassy in Moscow believed that it was being bombarded by Gamma radiation which had resulted in the deaths of two ambassadors, the sickening of another, and a declaration that the embassy was a hazardous-duty zone. As it turned out the embassy was being bombarded by high-intensity microwave beams as part of an eavesdropping program. The microwaves had been detected by a Geiger counter brought in by security personnel.[14]

The question I am asked most frequently at my lectures is why I haven't been killed yet. I have two answers. First, it is not cost-effective, and the response would cause more problems that it would solve. I am not important enough to kill.

Secondly, I will not die one minute before God has decided.

Vreeland's final irony

Mike Vreeland went to great lengths to talk about and document his involvement with a new Russian weapon-neutralizing missile defense shields being developed in the US. This, he insisted, was the impetus for his trip to Moscow. He filled his website and phone conversations with details of how the system worked. The legal records maintained by his former attorneys are filled with references to it. I never reported on it because I had no ability to verify any of his claims. Quite frankly, I never really believed him.

In 2004, long after his disappearance, as his memory faded from the minds of all but the most dedicated 9/11 investigators, the following story appeared in the Associated Press.[15]

> MOSCOW (AP) — Russia has designed a "revolutionary" weapon that would make the prospective American missile defence useless, Russian news agencies reported Monday, quoting a senior Defence Ministry official.
>
> The official, who was not identified by name, said tests conducted during last month's military manoeuvres would dramatically change the philosophy behind development of Russia's nuclear forces, the Interfax and ITAR-Tass news agencies reported. If deployed, the new weapon would take the value of any US missile shield to "zero," the news agencies quoted the official as saying.
>
> The official said the new weapon would be inexpensive, providing an "asymmetric answer" to US missile defences, which are proving extremely costly to develop.
>
> Russia, meanwhile, also has continued research in prospective missile defences and has an edge in some areas compared to other countries, the official said.
>
> The statement reported Monday was in line with claims by President Vladimir Putin's that experiments performed during last

month's manoeuvres proved that Russia could soon build strategic weapons that could puncture any missile-defence system.

At the time, Col.Gen. Yuri Baluyevsky, the first deputy chief of the General Staff of the Russian armed forces, explained that the military tested a "hypersonic flying vehicle" that was able to manoeuvre between space and the earth's atmosphere.

Military analysts said that the mysterious new weapons could be a maneuverable ballistic missile warhead or a hypersonic cruise missile.

While Putin said the development of such new weapons wasn't aimed against the United States, most observers viewed the move as Moscow's retaliation to the US missile defence plans.

After years of vociferous protests, Russia reacted calmly when Washington withdrew from the Anti-Ballistic Missile Treaty in 2002 in order to develop a countrywide missile shield. But US-Russian relations have soured again lately, and Moscow has complained about Washington's plans to build new low-yield nuclear weapons.

PART III

OPPORTUNITY

CHAPTER 18

THE ATTACKS

Special thanks are given in this chapter to author/researcher Barbara Honegger who first drew my attention to several of the war game exercises being conducted on 9/11. She provided me with a few articles that were invaluable starting points for this part of my investigation of 9/11. By the time I was done I understood how the attacks were executed; that is, I understood how the perpetrators were able to effectively neutralize the most powerful and effective air defense system on the planet. After receiving those first articles from Honegger it was a fairly simple task to put the pieces together in a way that corresponded perfectly with the other evidence which had already been gathered.

> Washington Air Traffic Control Center knew about the first plane before it hit the World Trade Center. Yet the third plane was able to fly 'loop-de-loops' over Washington, DC one hour and 45 minutes after Washington Center first knew about the hijackings. After circling in this restricted airspace, controlled and protected by the Secret Service who had an open phone line to the FAA, how was it possible that that plane was then able to crash into the Pentagon? Why was the Pentagon not evacuated? Why was our Air Force so late in its response? What, if anything, did our nation do in a defensive military posture that morning?
> — Testimony of 9/11 widow Kristen Breitweiser before the Joint Senate House Select Intelligence Committee, Sept. 18, 2001

> b. Support. When notified that military assistance is needed in conjunction with an aircraft piracy (hijacking) emergency, the DDO [Deputy Director of Operations], NMCC [National Military Command Center], will:
> > (1) Determine whether or not the assistance needed is reasonably available from police or commercial sources. If not the DDO, NMCC, will notify the appropriate unified command or NORAD to determine if suitable assets are available and will forward the request

*to the Secretary of Defense for approval in accordance with DODD
3025.15, paragraph D.7 (Reference D).*

*(2) If suitable assets from a unified command or NORAD are not rea-
sonably available, the DDO, NMCC, will coordinate with the
appropriate Military Service operations center to provide military
assistance.*

— Chairman of the Joint Chiefs Instruction, CJCSI 3610.01A
Aircraft Piracy (Hijacking) and Destruction
of Derelict Airborne Objects, 1 June 2001

*The first hijacking was suspected at not later than 8.20 am, and the last
hijacked aircraft crashed in Pennsylvania at 10.06 am. Not a single fighter plane was scrambled to investigate from the US Andrews air force base,
just 10 miles from Washington DC, until after the third plane had hit the
Pentagon at 9.38 am. Why not? There were standard FAA intercept procedures for hijacked aircraft before 9/11. Between September 2000 and
June 2001 the US military launched fighter aircraft on 67 occasions to
chase suspicious aircraft (AP, August 13 2002). It is a US legal requirement that once an aircraft has moved significantly off its flight plan,
fighter planes are sent up to investigate.*

*Was this inaction simply the result of key people disregarding, or being
ignorant of, the evidence? Or could US air security operations have been
deliberately stood down on September 11? If so, why, and on whose
authority?*

Former British Environmental Minister and MP Michael Meacher
"The War on Terrorism is Bogus", The *Guardian*, September 6, 2003

Normal FAA procedures for responding to even minor deviations from air traffic control protocols were followed routinely and without complication 67 times
between September 2000 and June 2001 before a new convoluted order was
released by the Pentagon on June 1, 2001. That order inserted the Secretary of
Defense into a decision-making and action protocol, normally the domain of senior military commanders. Why?

Who can forget that scrambled fighter aircraft were flying beside the chartered
Learjet occupied by golfer Payne Stewart and his entourage on October 25, 1999,
after all had succumbed to explosive decompression at high altitude? It took only
minutes for the fighters to get there after Stewart's plane had missed only one turn
and failed to respond to radio transmissions for just a few minutes.

Why the enormous difference in responses between 1999 and 2001 when an
obviously greater emergency existed and was widely recognized?

Only part of the explanation lies in the dramatic, illogical, and possibly even
illegal change in what had been routine and effective operating procedures prior

to June 1, 2001. The other part lies in a deliberately superimposed overlay of war game exercises being conducted by several governmental agencies on September 11th that inserted false blips into radar screens in the Northeast Air Defense Sector (NEADS), involved live-fly exercises with aircraft posing as hijacked airliners, and effectively confused and paralyzed all response by loyal interceptor pilots who would have seized the initiative that day, regardless of protocol had they known where to go.

The enormous significance of the war games is confirmed by the fact that any detailed discussion of them and their relationship to 9/11 emergency response has been neglected by the press, avoided by the government, and ignored by the so-called independent commission looking into the attacks.

Ladies and gentlemen of the jury, it is here that we find more concrete evidence of willful and criminal behavior on the part of high-ranking US government officials. It is here that we find evidence of guilty knowledge, obstruction of justice, and gross dishonesty on the part of military and civilian officials whose obligation has always been to tell the truth.

The enormity of the crime committed by the Bush administration on September 11, 2001, is easily overlooked in the intentionally overcrowded morass of press reports, changing official positions, and self-contradictory statements made since the attacks. Timelines released after 9/11 by the North American Aerospace Defense Command (NORAD), the Federal Aviation Administration (FAA), and the Pentagon (DoD) do not agree as to actual events, who was notified about those events at what times, what orders were given, and the responses to those orders.

In spite of this, compelling evidence suggests that some aircraft were indeed scrambled, probably in time to shoot down Flight 93 over Pennsylvania when passengers aboard had apparently successfully regained control of it and might have landed the airliner, exposing a plot which had been orchestrated within the highest levels of the military and intelligence command structure.

Deconstruction Part I — If it ain't broke, don't fix it!

How did the air traffic control system operate in possible hijack scenarios before 9/11? The simple answer is, "Very well."

In examining the system as it stood until June 1, 2001, we will dispel some false notions that were deliberately lodged in the public mind after 9/11; for instance, the false assertion that once a commercial aircraft turns off its transponder it becomes invisible to air traffic control radar, or that military radars can no longer determine its altitude.

Transponders and radar

All commercial airliners are equipped with transponders — devices that emit radio signals at frequencies selected by air traffic controllers (ATCs) and pilots so that each aircraft can be easily identified on radar screens that are often very crowded. I have flown in small private planes many times and watched as the pilots responded to an ATC instruction to "squawk" on a designated frequency. This involves the pilot setting the frequency in the cockpit and pushing a button that emits a signal on that frequency. Failure to do so in a timely manner results in an immediate inquiry from the ATC and a repeated instruction.

When a transponder is turned off, several things happen to civilian (FAA) radar screens that do not affect military radar. First, a small identifying symbol on the blip on the controller's radar screen goes out. Second, although the civilian ATC still has the ability to track the aircraft in two dimensions, he or she is no longer able to pinpoint its altitude. Third, as reported in an on-the-record statement by a veteran pilot (and confirmed by at least a dozen others), when an aircraft under ATC control goes silent, the blip for that aircraft is instantaneously inserted in a conspicuous manner on the screens of every other ATC in the region. Everybody sees it.

> Michael Guillaume
> [In re:] scrambling
> Sun Jun 9 13:11:30 2002
>
> I am a pilot and I know what happens to me when I lose my transponder. The controller's console immediately alerts him to the fact, since he no longer has my transponder code and altitude. This causes him a great deal of trouble, and very shortly I get trouble also. I am usually instructed to stay below 3,500 feet and return to the airport. The reason for the concern is that I am a hazard to navigation. Now imagine the situation in the Air Route Traffic Control Center (commonly abbreviated to 'center'). This is in the northeast corner of the US, the busiest airspace on the planet. Each controller has a wedge shaped sector that he is responsible for. His airspace is also bounded by altitude limits. Commercial flights, referred to as heavies, are always under positive control.
>
> They must constantly be in communication with the controllers in order to maintain legal separation. If one of these heavies loses its transponder, it causes instant problems for more than one controller since altitude information is lost. The controllers still have a skin paint, or passive echo from the airframe, but the blip now shows up on all consoles for that sector, not just the original one that was handling the altitude range of the flight. If that same flight loses communication with the controllers as well, the controller workload takes another giant step upward. Keep in mind that this is in an area that is normally stretched to the breaking point with controller overload. This flight is now a hazard to air navigation, and the controllers' primary function of separating the planes is in jeopardy. The procedure for lost communication emergencies is simple: follow your last

clearance. If the flight under discussion follows its last clearance, the controllers can predict where it will go and can still keep other flights out of harm's way. If in addition to losing communication and transponder the flight starts to deviate from its last clearance, the whole system is in an emergency condition. Alarms all over the country would be going off. One interesting piece of information is the recording of controller and pilot conversations. These tapes are a matter of public record and are written over after a few days unless something interesting happens. These tapes would show the response of the system. Where are they?

So we know that the traffic control system would be in panic mode within two to three minutes of the initial events. We know that Otis Air Force Base is only five minutes from Manhattan by F15. We know that the controllers always had a passive return from the planes and could vector an intercept. The last *Airman's Information Manual* I bought has a date of 1989 and it describes intercept procedures. So we know that intercepts have been routine low-level events since at least that time. We know that there is an Air Defense Intercept Zone just offshore for the entire Atlantic Coast. This zone is constantly being patrolled. In general fast movers [fighter aircraft] would not need to be scrambled. They can be diverted from routine patrol and training flights for the intercept. I know from experience that early morning flights are every pilot's favorite. You preflight the plane in the dark and take off. Even in a Cessna, breaking out into the bright clear sunshine from the dark earth below is a kick. In an F15, doing Mach 1 straight up would make it impossible to stop grinning. The odds are that many flights would be on patrol just offshore. It would be most improbable that even one commercial flight could go [astray] more than ten minutes without being intercepted. The intercepting plane would slowly close from the left and take station slightly above and ahead of the errant heavy. At this point he would rock his wings and expect the other plane to do the same as a form of non-verbal communication. After this he would perform a gentle turn to the left and the intercepted plane is required to follow. If this does not occur, there are many actions, short of firing, the fighter can take to prevent the commercial jet from harming either itself, any other plane, or any ground structure.

Interceptions are routine daily occurrences. The fact that they didn't happen under extreme provocation raises some serious questions. I hope [former FAA Inspector General] Mary Schiavo will ask them.[1]

What is lacking in civilian radar is more than compensated for by US military radar. The major media have failed to disclose or discuss the fact that military radars — which are capable of determining the altitude of targets without transponders — are always tracking all commercial traffic inside the country as well. Investigative reports that became public after the equally suspicious 2000 crash of Egypt Air 990 off the Eastern seaboard establish this.[2]

Several commercial airline pilots also confirmed to me that all commercial airlines are equipped with Identify Friend or Foe (IFF) buttons on the control yoke which emit special frequencies to silently alert the FAA and military to specific emergencies: 7700 indicates emergency, 7600 confirms communications failure, and 7500 confirms a hijack. Once tripped, these transponder codes activate an SSR radar system that directly and continuously transmits the airplane's altitude above sea level. At least one press report from 9/11 confirmed that one or more of the hijacked pilots had pressed his button (see below). What about the other pilots?

I have received innumerable messages from commercial pilots, military personnel, and researchers describing a wealth of fighter aircraft routinely available at many bases in the area. There is also compelling evidence of scramble-ready fighters having been available at Andrews Air Force Base, just ten miles outside of Washington. What happened to them?

I received one message from a highly credible source expressing the outrage and horror felt by many government employees over the dog-ate-my-homework story offered on 9/11. Yet, like so many of these people, the writer, afraid for his pension and his family's welfare, denied me permission to publish his name.

> Something has bothered me since 9/11 and it just occurred to me what it is! What were they thinking when they sent an F-16 from Otis ANG [Air National Guard] base to NY? I worked as a general aviation pilot based in [deleted]. I flew for an FBO [Fixed Base Operator], a company that does charter flying. We used to take a group of gamblers to Atlantic City frequently. I did many trips to Atlantic City, and on almost every trip we landed in front of or behind NJ ANG F-16s. Atlantic City is an Air National Guard Base! Atlantic City is half the distance from NYC as compared to Cape Cod. Furthermore NAS [Naval Air Station] Willow Grove ... has a Marine Fighter/Attack Group flying F-18s. NAS Willow Grove is considerably closer to NYC. I don't know what it means to you, but to me it seems that someone did not want fighter protection to arrive too soon.
>
> XXXXX X. XXXXX
> FAA, Aviation Safety Inspector
> XXXX Flight Standards District Office

The rules before June 2001

One of the first analyses of how the system worked before 9/11 was offered by Jared Israel at <www.tenc.net>. Some of his work will be cited later in this chapter. But the analysis and presentation offered by Nafeez Ahmed in *The War on Freedom* does the best job of revealing how the system worked.

Ahmed wrote:

> Air traffic controllers routinely request fighter craft to intercept commercial planes for various reasons when problems faced cannot be solved through radio contact, e.g., to inform commercial pilots when their plane is off course, or simply to assess the situation directly.
>
> The deviation of commercial planes from their designated flight paths is a common problem solved via interception. As a matter of mandatory Standard Operating Procedures, no approval from the White House [or Secretary of Defense] is required for interception. On the contrary, interception occurs on the basis of established flight and emergency response rules....
>
> Detailed FAA and Department of Defense manuals are available online, clarifying that these instructions are exceedingly comprehensive, including issues from minor emergencies to full-blown hijackings. According to these instructions, serious problems are handed over to the National Military Command Center in the Pentagon, if necessary.
>
> Commercial flights must adhere to Instrument Flight Rules (IFR). According to IFR, before takeoff pilots must file a flight plan with the FAA.
>
> Each route consists of a sequence of geographic points, or fixes, which, when connected, form a trajectory from the point of departure to the point of arrival.
>
> As soon as a plane diverts from its flight plan for instance by making a wrong turn at a "fix" — an Air Traffic Controller contacts the pilot. If the controller fails to make contact or routine communication becomes impossible, established rules dictate that an aircraft will be requested to scramble and assess the situation by "interception."
>
> A clear example of this routine procedure is the FAA's response when the Learjet chartered by golf professional Payne Stewart deviated from its flight path while the pilot failed to reply by radio. MS-NBC reported that:
>
> "Pilots are supposed to hit each fix with pinpoint accuracy. If a plane deviates by 15 degrees, or two miles from that course, the flight controllers will hit the panic button. They'll call the plane, saying 'American 11, you're deviating from course.' It's considered a real emergency, like a police car screeching down a highway at 100 miles an hour. When golfer Payne Stewart's incapacitated Learjet missed a turn at a fix, heading north instead of west to Texas, F-16 interceptors were quickly dispatched."

The FAA, in other words, immediately contacted the military when it was confirmed that the plane was off course, and communication with the plane was blocked. As CNN reported:

"Several Air Force and Air National Guard fighter jets, plus an AWACS radar control plane, helped the Federal Aviation Administration track the runaway Learjet and estimate when it would run out of fuel."

Once a plane is intercepted by military jets, daytime communications with a plane that fails to respond properly to radio contact are described by the FAA manual as follows: "...[The interceptor military craft communicates by] rocking its wings from a position slightly above and ahead of, normally to the left of, the intercepted aircraft..." This action conveys the message "You have been intercepted." The commercial jet is then supposed to respond by rocking its wings to indicate compliance, upon which the interceptor performs a "slow level turn, normally to the left, on to the desired heading [direction]." The commercial plane then responds by following the escort.

The deviation of a plane from its designated flight path obviously creates a hazard in the form of a potential collision with another plane. The FAA thus has a clear definition of what constituted an emergency situation: "Consider that an aircraft emergency exists ... when: ... There is unexpected loss of radar contact and radio communications with any ... aircraft." Elsewhere the FAA states: "EMERGENCY DETERMINATIONS: If ... you are in doubt that a situation constitutes an emergency or potential emergency, handle it as though it were an emergency."

An FAA Air Defense Liaison Officer stationed in the headquarters of the North American Aerospace Defense Command (NORAD) plays the role of coordinating the FAA with the US military to handle emergencies as efficiently as possible. While NORAD normally scrambles fighter jets, if necessary, other military jets can be scrambled as well: 'Normally, NORAD escort aircraft will take the required action. However, for the purpose of these procedures, the term "escort aircraft" applies to any military aircraft assigned to the escort mission."

Again, the response to the deviation of Payne Stewart's jet from its flight path provides an example. ABC reported that:

"First a fighter jet from Tyndall, Fla., was diverted from a routine training flight to check out the Learjet. Two F-16s from another Florida base then picked up the chase, later handing it over to two F-16s from Fargo, North Dakota."

As a matter of mandatory routine, the established instructions for a serious emergency are followed, and this includes emergencies involving the possibility of a hijacking. "In the event of a serious emergency, or if a possible hijacking has occurred: The escort service will be requested by the FAA hijack coordinator by direct contact with the National Military Command Center (NMCC)."

The Department of Defense affirms the same, adding that once military planes are scrambled in accordance with immediate responses, the Department of Defense will be contacted for approval of special measures: "In the event of a hijacking, the NMCC will be notified by the most expeditious means by the FAA. The NMCC will, **with the exception of immediate responses** ... forward requests for DoD assistance to the Secretary of Defense for approval."

It should be reiterated that procedures also require controllers to immediately alert the military to scramble fighter craft, if a plane deviates from its flight path and communication between the plane and controllers is blocked....

Indeed, "The US military has its own radar network .... (NORAD) ... They are tied into the FAA computer in order to get information on incoming flights." If a target is discovered "without flight plan information," or in violation of the same, "they will call on the 'shout' line to the appropriate [Air Traffic Control] Center sector for an ID." If the Center sector "has no datablock or other information on it, the military will usually scramble an intercept flight .... and they will likely find two F-18s on their tail within 10 or so minutes."[3]

A critical distinction between the pre-9/11 procedure and that established in June of 2001 appears to be that the FAA and NMCC were free to initiate "immediate responses" without waiting for approval from the Secretary of Defense. Certain immediate response options were allowed in the 2001 order. However, they appear to be much more restrictive.

Historical context

Several civil suits have been filed against the US government since 9/11. One of those suits is being handled by attorney Mary Schiavo, a former inspector general of the FAA. Its primary targets are the airlines and the FAA, for their failures to provide paying customers with any credible advance warning of the attacks. Not far beneath this surface, however, there may well lie a more radical motive for the litigation, since both the evidence and the tone imply that FAA failures were perverse successes in a larger criminal conspiracy. Yet the Schiavo suit (out of strategic choice, ignorance, or mere timidity) does little to confront and develop its own implications; most importantly, it does not pursue issues of intelligence or military activities. As of May 2004, many victim families in this suit have expressed displeasure over what they perceive as Schiavo's willingness to yield to the government's efforts to keep critical records out of public view.

Schiavo made a formal statement at a June 10, 2002, press conference held at the National Press Club in Washington, DC, and sponsored by the 9/11 activist organization Unanswered Questions on the initiative of organizer Kyle Hence. While Schiavo has self-limited her public remarks, she raised some interesting questions at this press conference about whether the airlines, at a corporate level, might also have had some foreknowledge of the attacks. Both former Assistant Secretary of Housing Catherine Austin Fitts and I participated in that press conference, and I was astonished at what I heard. Here is some of what Schiavo had to say:

> First of all, the question is not what they should have known. And I believe I can show you in just a few seconds the question is what did they know? And believe me, they knew a lot. The second thing to emphasize is that in every single aviation disaster, whether there was intervening criminal activity or not, in every single one in the course of modern aviation history it has been followed by, not only were it necessary [sic], a criminal investigation, but also a National Transportation Safety investigation into what went wrong in the aviation system ....
>
> Because on a September day four planes were hijacked in an Islamic Jihad. It shocked the world and would forever change the law under which we act. It would set new laws. It would change the world as we knew it, and it should have forever changed the world of aviation. You think I'm talking about September 11th. I'm not. I'm talking about September 12, 1970. Yes we had an Islamic Jihad. Four airplanes were hijacked; actually it was supposed to be five. They were taken to Jordan. They were blown up on September 12, 1970 ....
>
> The date was 1970. So in the wake of September 11, 2001, when we heard the carriers and governments alike saying, "Oh, no one could have foreseen this. No one knew that this was coming. No one knew that there was any risk like this in the world," [it was] absolutely false. And we knew that before Condoleezza Rice made the shocking announcement a couple weeks ago about not only was there a great amount of information known, but that the carriers and the FAA were warned repeatedly. In fact, in that very speech the admission said that they were warned at least five times including specifically. I love this language that it wasn't a "specific warning." Let me tell you, "Middle Eastern terrorists hell bent on a hijacking" is pretty darn specific. And in fact there are cases in law in the history of — of aviation history, that say that airlines are responsible for that whether or not they follow the law. They should have, as necessary, even hired armed personnel to guard their passengers. Why? Because passengers had a contract. And in addition here, of course, you had a horrible, horrible tragedy on the ground as well.

Let me give you a little "for instance" of what was known out there in the aviation industry. Thirty-three years after the first attack on US aviation we had September 11th. But there were many, many other warnings in between.

I, for one, believe that you should leave no stone unturned in the search for justice. But you have to do what you do best. So I am personally looking at every single terrorist attack and hijacking against modern aviation. And I even gave the carriers a break. I didn't start in 1970 with the big four airplane Islamic Jihad. I started thirty years ago from September 11, 1972. You want to see what kind of numbers are out there when the carriers said, "Oh, we couldn't possibly have known this" and "We didn't know that airlines are subject to this kind of attack?" Here's what we're looking at folks. This is the unknown and unforeseeable. That's what we've got. That's what the airline industry really looks like. [*At this point Schiavo puts down on the podium a tall stack of documents several thousand pages in length*]. Here, I have some extras if you want to send them around. In the last 30 years we have had 682 hijackings — 682. Here's an interesting statistic. When we had the United States saying, "Oh, we couldn't have known this." And even when passengers were getting calls out to their family, what information went back to them? Guess what, of those 682 hijackings in the last 30 years, 101 times passengers fought to defend themselves and took down the hijackers, including, of course, El Al which successfully foiled the hijacking on September 12, 1970 in the ... original four-plane Islamic Jihad [hijacking].

How many bombings do you suppose there have been? That's what we say we were busy looking for on September 11th. They said, "We were looking for bombers. We were still looking for Pan Am 103." Well we had 682 hijackings, and we had 31 bombings. How about shoot downs? We think that's even rarer — 59. So the thing that we were all out there searching for, the Pan Am 103 bomber, among hijackings, shoot downs and bombings, was actually the least number of things that we had suffered ....

What about the information from the air traffic control? They had information that happened at the beginning. One of the other speakers has already mentioned the scrambling of the planes, and yet no warnings were given to the pilots about specific events that were going on or of warnings of [sic] "Don't open the door," what's going on, "Don't open that door under any circumstances." Already there's a federal aviation regulation about not opening the door. We need to know why. Why didn't that information go out? And finally, it was well known before September 11th not one, not two, not three, and even more than four federal investigations showed that security could be breached at will.[4]

Alhazmi and Almidhar

Chapter 9 discussed the charmed lives of two of the 9/11 hijackers, Nawaf Alhazmi and Khalid Almidhar. Before 9/11 they had been tracked by eavesdropping and electronic surveillance, and they had even lived for months in the private home of a trusted FBI informant. This was at a time when they were on several watch lists and had been directly connected to terror attacks for which they could have been immediately arrested. Yet no one in law enforcement seemed to be able to find them. Their "luck" held on September 11. While 9 of the 19 hijackers were reportedly selected for special screening before they boarded their flights, these two, who were on a CIA alert watch list and wanted by the FBI in an equivalent of an all points bulletin, were not even questioned.[5]

The following table, compiled mostly from Paul Thompson's timeline <www.cooperativeresearch.org>, is a partial comparison of key events during the attacks of September 11, 2001.

TIME	AIRLINE	FAA	MILITARY	BUSH & ADMIN.
8:13	Last routine contact with FLT 11 immediately thereafter the pilot fails to respond to a call to climb to a new altitude FLT 11 took off at 7:59. [1] FLT 11 hijacked. [2]			
8:14	FLT 175 takes off from Boston.[3] FLT 11 Pilot activates talk back button. Controllers can hear conversation in cockpit.[4]	UNEXPLAINED 11 MINUTE DELAY	FLT 11 hijacking confirmed — UNEXPLAINED 32 MINUTE DELAY — UNEXPLAINED 26 MINUTE DELAY	
8:20	FLT 11 stops transmitting IFF ("Identity Friend or Foe" — hijack alarm) beacon (confirming that it had been activated).[5]	<NORAD should have been notified here>	<Scramble order should have been issued by this point>	

TIME	AIRLINE	FAA	MILITARY		BUSH & ADMIN.
8:20	FLT 11 veers dramatically off course.[6] Boston ATC decides FLT 11 is a hijack. Official timeline shows other ATCs are not notified for 5 minutes. NORAD is not notified for 20 minutes.[7] FLT 77 departs Dulles Airport in Virginia.[8]	<FAA should have been notified here>			
8:21	FLT 11 Turns off transponder.[9]				
8:24	Pilot of FLT 11 activates talk button. Boston ATC overhears hijackers. Transponder has been off for 10 minutes.[10] Boston ATC sees FLT 11 make a 100 degree turn to the south. ATCs confirm they never lost sight of FLT 11.[11] Press accounts confirm that FLT 11's radar dot had been "tagged" for easy visibility even that the plane was being watched by American Airlines headquarters.[12] These stories contradict a Washington Post story saying that Boston Authorities had lost contact.[13]	UNEXPLAINED 11 MINUTE DELAY	UNEXPLAINED 32 MINUTE DELAY	UNEXPLAINED 26 MINUTE DELAY	
8:25	Boston ATC notifies other ATCs that FLT 11 is a hijacking.				

TIME	AIRLINE	FAA	MILITARY	BUSH & ADMIN.
8:25	They don't notify NORAD for another 13 minutes.[14]			
8:30-8:39			UNEXPLAINED 32 MINUTE DELAY / UNEXPLAINED 26 MINUTE DELAY	President Bush's motorcade leaves his Florida hotel for the Emma Booker Elementary School 9 miles away. The journey takes an incredible 25 minutes.[15]
8:37		Sector ATC asks pilot on FLT 175 to look for lost plane. Pilot of 175 says they can see FLT 11 and are told to keep away.[16]	8:37:53 Boston Center reaches NEADS and advises that FLT 11 is a confirmed hijack [17]	
8:40		Boston ATC notifies NORAD of FLT 11 hijacking.[18]	Two pilots at Otis AFB on Cape Cod in MA are told of the hijack. Yet no scramble order is given. Why?[19] NORAD, in its first official timeline, admits it was notified of hijack.[20] This time is changed in the final 9/11 Commission report.	
8:42	FLT 93 takes off from Newark after a 40 minute delay.[21] FLT 175 veers off course, "within 90 seconds of 8:41."[22]		UNEXPLAINED 16 MINUTE DELAY	

TIME	AIRLINE	FAA	MILITARY	BUSH & ADMIN.
8:42	FLT 175 reports hearing FLT 11's radio keyed. FLT 175 flight crew hears: "Everyone stay in your seats."[23]	FLT 175 hijacking confirmed		
8:43		NORAD notified of FLT 175 hijack. ATC reports that an emergency locator transmitter has been activated.[24]	*UNEXPLAINED 32 MINUTE DELAY* *UNEXPLAINED 16 MINUTE DELAY*	
8:46	**FLT 11 hits the World Trade Center** FLT 175 stops emitting transponder signal 50 miles north of NY City. [28] Other reports state that 175 had turned its transponder off, then back on again to an unassigned frequency.[29]		Scramble orders are issued at Otis AFB to go after FLT 11, 190 miles away. Fighters from closer bases like Atlantic City are not scrambled.[25] Acting chair of the Joint Chiefs, Richard Myers, claims that he sees a TV report about a plane hitting the WTC. He will later state that he was oblivious to any other events until the Pentagon is hit. [26] He will contradict himself in sworn testimony later saying that he made a decision to start launching after the 2nd tower was hit. [27] Three F-16s assigned to Andrews AFB are flying an air-to-ground strike training mission 207 miles from DC. Instead of	

TIME	AIRLINE	FAA	MILITARY	BUSH & ADMIN.
8:46			being ordered to DC at supersonic speeds, they return slowly, landing only after FLT 77 hits Pentagon. They could have been in DC airspace in 10 minutes.[31]	
After 8:46		FAA has open line to Secret Service. This is later confirmed by VP Cheney.[32]	NORAD and NMCC have open phone lines.[33]	
8:46-9:00				Navy Captain Deborah Loewer in the Bush motorcade receives a message from a deputy in the White House Situation Room about the first WTC impact. This is before Bush gets to Booker and while it is known that three airliners have been hijacked. [34] Bush will later state that he saw video of the first crash before he started speaking. This is a blatant lie. Video of the first crash will not be shown for hours.[35]
8:46 - 8:55	Barbara Olsen, wife of US Solicitor General, Ted Olsen calls her husband at the Justice Dept. from FLT 77. He calls the Justice Dept. Command Center and advises of hijacking. [36]	FLT 77 hijacking confirmed		
8:48	First TV and news reports of plane crashing into World Trade Center. [37]	UNEXPLAINED 29 MINUTE DELAY	UNEXPLAINED 32 MINUTE DELAY	

TIME	AIRLINE	FAA	MILITARY	BUSH & ADMIN.
8:50	Last radio contact with FLT 77. Pilot asks for clearance to a higher altitude then does not respond to a routine instruction.[38]			
8:52			Otis Air Natl. Guard pilots take off, 12 minutes after receiving notification. Flying F-15s their top speed is 1875 mph with a supersonic cruise of 1600 mph. [39]	
8:54	FLT 77 begins to go off course over Ohio.[30] FLT 77 turns around and heads east over east Kentucky indicating a target in Washington. [40]			
8:55		UNEXPLAINED 29 MINUTE DELAY	UNEXPLAINED 32 MINUTE DELAY	President Bush's motorcade arrives at Booker Elementary School. At this time there are 3 confirmed hijacks and one WTC tower has been hit. [41]
8:56	FLT 77 transponder is deactivated. This is 6 minutes before FLT 175 hits the WTC. [42]			
After 8:56			NMCC officials in the western part of the Pentagon are talking to law enforcement officials about possible responses.[43] This is 45 minutes before the Pentagon is hit.	
Before 8:58				A news photographer traveling with the Bush

TIME	AIRLINE	FAA	MILITARY	BUSH & ADMIN.
Before 8:58				entourage overhears a radio transmission that Press Secretary Ari Fleischer would be needed on arrival at the school to discuss reports of the crash. [44]
8:58				Latest confirmed arrival of Bush at the Booker Elementary School. At this time there are three confirmed hijackings. [45]
9:00		UNEXPLAINED 29 MINUTE DELAY	Pentagon moves its alert status up one level to Alpha, three levels below maximum. [49] UNEXPLAINED 32 MINUTE DELAY	Chief of Staff Andy Card officially notifies Bush about the 1st WTC impact. This is 12 minutes after the rest of the world has heard about it on TV and well after the staff knows. [46] Bush is taken to a holding room and briefed by National Security Advisor Condoleezza Rice. Yet he decided to go ahead and read to the children. [47]
9:01	The Pilots of FLT 93 reportedly acknowledge a general FAA warning about cockpit intrusion and request to barricade doors. The pilots are not told of the WTC crash or that another plane is missing. [50]			At this time, according to his own statement, Bush says that he was sitting outside a class room structure to go in and he saw an airplane hit the WTC. He thought it was a terrible pilot. This was hours before any footage of the fist impact had been broadcast. [48]
9:03	**FLT 175 hits South Tower, WTC**		The Otis AFB F-15s are still 71 miles away. Calculations indicated that they had been flying at	The Secret Service reportedly calls Andrews AFB and tells them to get F-16s ready to fly. Yet they have not rushed

TIME	AIRLINE	FAA	MILITARY	BUSH & ADMIN.
9:03			less than 700 mph.[51] The F-15's top speed is 1850 mph. [52]	Bush out of the school. The official story says planes still being loaded when Pentagon hit.[53]
9:03-9:06				Chief of Staff Andrew Card informs Bush of second impact.[54] Secret Service agents reportedly storm into the Vice President's office and carry him to the (PEOC) emergency bunker.[55] Bush continues to read to the children. Conflicting reports delivered later place the time of this 30 minutes later. All these reports came well after initial statements, as discrepancies started appearing in various records.
9:03-9:16 approx				At this time, Bush cannot be approached for shoot down discussions. Chief of Staff Andrew Card is the gatekeeper. Bush read to 2nd graders about a pet goat. This at a time when he should have been making decisions to shoot down airliners.[56]
9:05		West Virginia ATCs notice an eastbound plane with no transponder entering their airspace. It is FLT 77.[57]		
9:06		All ATC facilities nationwide are		

UNEXPLAINED 29 MINUTE DELAY

UNEXPLAINED 32 MINUTE DELAY

TIME	AIRLINE	FAA	MILITARY	BUSH & ADMIN.
9:06		notified that the FLT 11 crash a WTYC was probably a hijacking, yet the West Virginia ATCs do not notify NORAD for 18 more minutes.[58]	UNEXPLAINED 32 MINUTE DELAY	
9:09		UNEXPLAINED 29 MINUTE DELAY	NORAD orders F-16s at Langley AFB, 110 miles from D.C. to battle stations. This is **not** a scramble order. At this point, 11 aircraft nationwide are reported not in communication with ATCs or are off-course. [59]	
9:16		FAA informs NORAD that FLT 93 may have been hijacked. [60]	<ALL NEADS FIGHTER AIRCRAFT SHOULD HAVE BEEN SCRAMBLED>	
9:22			A US fighter aircraft passes near FLT 93 well before its crash in PA. The sonic boom is picked up by a seismic monitoring station in southern PA. That means that this same fighter could have reached Washington well before FLT 77 hit the Pentagon. [61]	
9:24		FAA notifies NORAD that FLT 77 may be hijacked and	One Air Force Pilot code named "Honey", who piloted an F-16 from	

TIME	AIRLINE	FAA	MILITARY	BUSH & ADMIN.
9:24		headed towards DC. [62]	Langley, disputes the official version. He says that the call to battle stations was not sounded until 9:24. [63]	
9:27			NORAD orders three F-16s to intercept FLT 77. They are 129 miles from DC. Available aircraft from Andrews AFB are not scrambled. [64]	Bush talks to Cheney at White House but there is no discussion of shooting down FLT 77 or 93. Why? [65]
9:29				Bush leaves Booker Elementary and stops to make a press announcement. He is keeping to his publicly announced schedule starting his announcement at the exact time that had been scheduled before the attacks. He is making himself a target. Why?[66]
9:33- 9:38	FLT 77 executes a 270 degree point turn over the Pentagon coupled with a sharp dive to take it to the west side which is under construction and largely unoccupied.[67] This is a feat of piloting skill.			
9:36	FLT 93 files a new flight plan, indicates it is going to Washington, DC and turns around 130 degrees. [68]	FLT 93 hijacking confirmed		
9:38	**FLT 77 hits the Pentagon.**		The Langley fighters are still 105 miles away. Simple math indicates that they have been flying at	Secretary of Defense Donald Rumsfeld is sitting in his office watching TV.

TIME	AIRLINE	FAA	MILITARY	BUSH & ADMIN.
9:38			a speed of 200 mph. [69]	This contradicts Richard Clark.[70]
9:40	Transponder contact on FLT 93 is lost. [71]			
9:41			The three F-16s already airborne from Andrews and on a training mission, return to base. [72]	The Secret Service orders fighters from Andrews into the air "now". The White House declares Washington DC a free fire zone. Is this a breach of chain of command by frustrated agents or the execution of a legitimate order? It is not delivered in the appropriate manner. [73]
9:43				Bush arrives at the Sarasota airport. As of this moment, it is confirmed that he is in the communication loop and capable of ordering a shoot down. [74]
9:49- 10:10			The F-16s from Langley reach the Pentagon. Basic computations indicate they were flying at 300-450 mph.[75]	
9:55				The Secret Service orders all pilots to protect the White House at all costs. [76] An aide advises VP Cheney that FLT 93 is 80 miles out of DC and that US fighters are close to it. Cheney is asked, "Should we

TIME	AIRLINE	FAA	MILITARY	BUSH & ADMIN.
9:55				engage" Cheney says "Yes" then confirms the order twice. [77]
10:01			Fighters are ordered to scramble from Toledo, Ohio. Though it has no "standby" fighters it has planes in the air in 18 minutes. [78]	
10:03	FLT 93 crashes in southern Pennsylvania. [79]			
Before 10:06	FLT 93 leaves a huge debris field over many square miles. This is inconsistent with a crash of an intact airliner. One half-ton piece of an engine is found more than a mile away. This is consistent with the impact of a missile at altitude. There are a dozen witness reports of events consistent with a shoot down plus smaller debris fields two, three and eight miles away. [83] Multiple witnesses also report a small unmarked white civilian jet circling FLT 93 and around the crash site. [84]	One ATC ignores the ban on public statements and states that an F-16 closely pursued FLT 93, making 360 degree turns to stay close.[81]	CBS reports that two F-16s are tailing Flight 93. [80] The mayor of Shanksville, PA states that he knows two people who heard a missile. [82]	

Special acknowledgement is given to Paul Thompson and the Center for Cooperative Research (<www.cooperativeresearch.org>), without whose incredible research timeline this chart would not have been possible. All endnotes for this section are accessible at: <www.cooperative research.org/comletetimeline.index.html>. Select the option for Sept. 11, minute by minute.

On September 11 and in the days that followed, both Vice President Dick Cheney and acting Chairman of the Joint Chiefs of Staff Richard Meyers deliberately misled the American press, the Congress, and the American people about what happened that day. An excellent deconstruction of their testimony was presented not long after 9/11 by researcher Jared Israel.

Mr. Israel reported, "Richard Cheney on *Meet the Press* [Sept 16, 2001, said,] 'Well, the — I suppose the toughest decision was this question of whether or not we would intercept incoming commercial aircraft.'" This is a clearly misleading statement intended to confuse listeners about the lack of effective, dutiful response by the National Command Authority. Cheney's deception was paralleled by two contradictory statements offered by Air Force Chief of Staff General Richard Myers, who was confirmed as Chairman of the Joint Chiefs just days after the attacks. Myers in his initial statements said that there were no fighters available to intercept any of the flights and then later testified that the fighters had in actuality been deployed according to the above timeline.[6]

Perhaps most compellingly, it has been shown that the website of Andrews Air Force Base, the home of Air Force One, was modified around the time of the attacks to hide the fact that it has always maintained scramble-ready fighters. This readiness is no secret to anyone who lives (as I did in 1994) near the sprawling air base near Upper Marlboro, Maryland. It is impossible to count the number of sorties involving F-15s, F-16s, F-18s, and other military aircraft originating from the base. It also defies logic to think that the home of the president's personal airplane and the closest airbase to Washington, DC — in the most intensely guarded airspace on the planet — would not have scramble-ready jets.

In fact, that's just what the Andrews website said it had — until sometime in 2001. Until April 19, 2001, the DC Air National Guard (DCANG) web page on the Andrews AFB website described the unit's mission thus: "To provide combat units in the highest possible state of readiness."

Another portion of a linked website dealing with the 113th Fighter wing based at Andrews said, "As part of its dual mission, the 113th provides capable and ready response forces for the District of Columbia in the event of a natural disaster or civil emergency. Members also assist local and federal law enforcement agencies in combating drug trafficking in the District of Colombia. [They] are full partners with the active Air Force."

And yet another Marine fighter squadron at Andrews described itself as follows: "Marine Fighter Attack Squadron (VMFA) 321, a Marine Corps Reserve squadron, flies the sophisticated F/A-18 Hornet. Marine Aviation Logistics Squadron 49, Detachment A, provides maintenance and supply functions necessary to maintain a force in readiness."[7]

Careful research showed that the Andrews AFB website and the page for the DCANG had been modified sometime between April 2001 and September 13, 2001, when it was discovered that the phrase "in the highest possible state of readiness" had been removed. The alteration was only discovered because an earlier version of the web page had been archived on April 19.[8]

Notwithstanding this evidence of guilty knowledge and evidence tampering, at least four major press organizations did report that Andrews-based fighter aircraft had scrambled immediately on 9/11.[9] All of these stories were published within five days of the attacks and before the revised official spin had percolated through the media mix.

Let one happen. Stop the rest!!

There is considerable evidence that Delmart "Mike" Vreeland's prediction became a reality on 9/11.

In a story headlined "FBI Investigates Possible Hijackers on 5th Flight, *Tribune* Says," Bloomberg News reported that the FBI had started an urgent investigation of an unspecified number of passengers booked on American Airlines Flight 43 from Boston to an unnamed West Coast city on the morning of September 11. The flight, scheduled to depart at around the same time as the others, had been cancelled because of an unspecified mechanical difficulty. The problem was that the passengers in question never came back for a rescheduled flight, nor continued their travels when air service was restored two days later. Other passengers with "Arabic-sounding" names, also on flight 43, were being sought by authorities.[10]

Canadian General Ken Pennie, Deputy NORAD Commander, reported the likelihood that more than four aircraft were involved on 9/11. He cited an instance where suspicious passengers left a grounded airplane somewhere in North America. A press report disclosed that Pennie had been alluding to a Los Angeles-bound flight grounded in New York from which three Middle-Eastern passengers had been kicked off after demanding that the plane take off. The plane, United Airlines Flight 23, was destined for the West Coast and full of fuel.[11]

And in Toronto an interesting discovery was made on a plane that never took off on September 11. Two box-cutter knives, like the ones reportedly used by the hijackers, were found in their original packaging in an overhead storage bin on an Air Canada flight that had been scheduled to fly from Toronto to New York. The discovery was made as the plane was prepped for its first post-9/11 flight on September 14. Canadian officials offered the explanation that they thought the box cutters had just fallen out of someone's luggage.[12]

CHAPTER 19

WARGAMES AND HIGH TECH: PARALYZING THE SYSTEM TO PULL OFF THE ATTACKS

C heney to Oversee Domestic Counterterrorism Efforts
President announces new homeland defense initiative
President Bush May 8 directed Vice President Dick Cheney to coordinate develop-
ment of US government initiatives to combat terrorist attacks on the United States...
— White House Press Release, May 8, 2001

Therefore, I have asked Vice President Cheney to oversee the development of a coor-
dinated national effort so that we may do the very best possible job of protecting our
people from catastrophic harm. I have also asked Joe Allbaugh, the Director of the
Federal Emergency Management Agency, to create an Office of National Preparedness.
This office will be responsible for implementing the results of those parts of the nation-
al effort overseen by Vice President Cheney that deal with consequence management.
Specifically it will coordinate all federal programs dealing with weapons of mass
destruction consequence management within the Departments of Defense, Health and
Human Services, Justice, and Energy, the Environmental Protection Agency, and other
federal agencies....

— Official Statement of President George W. Bush, May 8, 2001
Office of the Press Secretary, The White House

What wasn't addressed by any of the constructs previously posed by 9/11 investigators was an assumption that pilots and commanders would just sit passively by
and watch their country be attacked — no matter what the orders were — if Dick
Cheney, Donald Rumsfeld, or acting Joint Chiefs Chairman Richard Myers failed
to issue a scramble order or actually issued a (very risky) direct stand-down order.
That assumption had people looking for a single "stand down" directive originating from one hidden source. I never felt comfortable with that. A detective learns
to be vigilant against the temptation to cut corners; otherwise, the explanation
that requires the least investigative work is the one that gets all the attention. In a

sound investigation, the simplest explanation must also encompass the known facts without any of those facts being discarded as a measure of expedience.

Military discipline can be severe, but the absence of orders to scramble would never have provided our suspects with a guarantee that pilots and commanders would not respond on 9/11 and stop the attacks anyway. For an event like 9/11, where the American homeland was under attack and American citizens were dying, that would be the equivalent of asking a prizefighter who had trained his entire life not to enter the ring for his first-ever title fight — a championship match — when the opportunity presented itself and his or her name was called. My father flew in air force interceptors towards the end of the Korean War. I was a toddler then. We were stationed in Maine and I still remember the cold. I also remember the brava-do and the esprit de corps of men who believed in their mission.

Air Force flyers are a proud and assertive lot. They are trained to be aggressive and to show initiative. The lack of an order to scramble in the confusion of 9/11 was no guarantee that enough pilots wouldn't scramble to prevent the second and third attacks, especially after CNN had shown the World Trade Center burning. Clearly NORAD and the FAA knew that multiple hijackings were in progress by the time of the *first* impact. Strong initiative was demonstrated by NORAD's sec-ond-in-command, Lieutenant General Larry Arnold, from his command center at Tyndall Air Force Base in Florida (CONR). This was before the first impact. In a 2002 interview with *Aviation Week and Space Technology*, Arnold described his reaction when contacted by NEADS commander Col. Robert Marr who advised that American 11 had been hijacked and that he had gone as far as he could by getting F15 fighters battle-ready at Otis in Massachusetts. He had the pilots in the cockpits and the planes ready. That was as far as he could go.

> "I told him to scramble; we'll get clearances later," Arnold said. His instincts to act first and get permission later were typical of US and Canadian commanders that day. [1]

The same *Aviation Week* article which contained Arnold's quote contradicted itself a mere six paragraphs later by quoting Canadian Navy Captain Michael Jellinek, who was acting as NORAD's command director on 9/11 at Cheyenne Mountain. "NEADS instantly ordered the scramble, then called me to get Cinc [NORAD com-mander-in-chief] approval for it…"[2] That would have been General Ralph Eberhart.

There were so many conflicting statements flying around that it was reminis-cent of a search warrant I once participated in where, among four suspects, we had five different explanations of how six kilos of Mexican brown heroin had found its way into the same room with them. By the time we got to ten different versions from only four people, the lead detectives got confessions.

Whether the scramble was ordered by Arnold at Tyndall Air Force Base in Florida, or by Col. Marr at NEADS, it is clear that no one was going to wait for orders from Donald Rumsfeld. Press accounts and his own statements indicate that

Rumsfeld had not even been advised of the hijacking as he was pontificating to Representative Christopher Cox in his office at the Pentagon that another terrorist attack was imminent at 8:44 AM, just two minutes before the WTC was hit by Flight 11. This was at least 23 minutes after it had been confirmed that Flight 11 had been hijacked.[3] Still no fighters had left the ground, and according to FAA reports, Flight 175 had been off course with no transponder for at least two minutes — a second confirmed emergency. Before June 1, 2001, fighters had been off the ground in what I estimate to be about six to eight minutes on average, based upon the few available reports I could find.

Both Arnold's and Jellinek's statements demonstrate that the existing official policy laid out in the Joint Chiefs' instruction of June 1, 2001, was ignored on 9/11.

Something else must have been in place to paralyze fighter response on 9/11 and still offer the plausibly deniable excuse that the tragic outcome was unintended.

In April and May of 2004 I found it after author Barbara Honegger, a senior military affairs journalist with the Department of Defense, and a talented, if erratic, 9/11 researcher named Nico Haupt had again started asking questions in a 9/11 Internet discussion group about the role of a war game exercise on that day. Only one — Vigilant Guardian — was known or had been publicly mentioned at that time.

Starting in August of 2002 Honegger had mentioned Vigilant Guardian and had suggested that the hijackers and/or their controllers had to have somehow learned the date of a wargame to piggyback their attacks on top of it. That story was widely interpreted as suggesting that al Qaeda had penetrated US intelligence or the military with inside help — a conclusion Honegger disputes but which nonetheless was widely held and discussed by those who read her first and second articles on the subject.

A second article by Honegger in May 2003 did not clear up the confusion.

This writer did not become aware of Honegger's wargame research until she refined her original story into a May 2003 story title "The Ides of March."[4] After reading that article I too walked away believing that Honegger was arguing that there had been some kind of defection from within the government.

Honegger's stories posed two serious problems for researchers. First, a literal reading led most people to believe that she was asserting that al Qaeda had quietly penetrated classified operations. Second, she appeared to be willingly accepting the allegation that the 19 hijackers perpetrated the attacks all by themselves, were all aboard the hijacked airliners, and actually did all the flying themselves. As we will see, all of these assumptions are in serious doubt.

In May of 2003 I checked my reading of "The Ides of May" with a long list of 9/11 researchers, and we all drew the same conclusions. After much subsequent dialogue with Honegger I believe that her intent was to suggest that the US government had deliberately leaked the information to the al Qaeda "hijackers" so that the attacks could be carried out effectively. Unfortunately, that message was not clear, and much time had been lost.

In 2004 when Honegger and Haupt began compiling and posting research about previously undisclosed 9/11 wargames, it was immediately clear to me that they were on to something big. In the spring of 2004 I asked Honegger for, and received, a fairly complete list of every known wargame article (especially the newest). Honegger sent a shocking body of mainstream press stories.

It was then up to me to analyze those stories in detail and see how all the wargames worked together. Honegger's material was good and I was only able to find one or two small stories that she and Haupt had missed. What they revealed, however, has become — in my opinion — the Holy Grail of 9/11 research.

As we will see, the assertion that al Qaeda had somehow penetrated (in an active sense) the military may become an eventual fallback position for the planners of September 11th. In light of what has been unearthed, that assertion falls apart if you but breathe on it.

My answers came as they so often do for detectives working on a tough case: as a result of going back to the files and starting over one more time to look for something I had missed.

As it turns out, on September 11th, various agencies including NORAD, the FAA, the Canadian Air Force, the National Reconnaissance Office, and possibly the Pentagon were conducting as many as five wargame drills — in some cases involving hijacked airliners; in some cases also involving blips deliberately inserted onto FAA and military radar screens which were present during (at least) the first attacks; and which in some cases had pulled significant fighter resources away from the northeast US on September 11. In addition, a close reading of key news stories published in the spring of 2004 revealed for the first time that some of these drills were "live-fly" exercises where actual aircraft were simulating the behavior of hijacked airliners in real life; all of this as the real attacks began. The fact that these exercises had never been systematically and thoroughly explored in the mainstream press, or publicly by Congress, or at least publicly in any detail by the so-called Independent 9/11 Commission made me think that they might be the Grail.

That's exactly what they turned out to be.

For two and a half years after 9/11 the dominant question among skeptics of the official version was why fighters had not been scrambled in time to prevent at least one of the three "successful" attacks. We now know that there was ample time, under normal circumstances, and sufficient resources to have prevented at least two and probably all three of them.

At best I could only come up with questions and a list of people who needed to be interrogated looking searching for answers. Like many others, I concluded only that, if the system had worked perfectly so many times before with so much less provocation, it stood to reason that something must have willfully intervened on 9/11. That was the easy part. Internet stories had reported anecdotal evidence in the form of hearsay from someone who heard it from another person who said that they heard Dick Cheney make a cryptic statement that "the order still stands" and argued that this was "proof" that Cheney had issued a stand-down order. By any standard such claims do not constitute admissible evidence, and they would never be allowed in a court of law. They certainly do not constitute proof for a trained investigator. It only takes one good embarrassment under cross-examination in court over an overlooked avenue or missed step for a detective to say, "That's never going to happen to me again." It happens to most good detectives at least once.

Starting in April of 2004 it all fell into place. First, the June 2001 Joint Chiefs of Staff Instruction quoted at the beginning of this chapter surfaced on the website of the Defense Department's Defense Technical Information Center.[4] That demonstrated a willful intent to centralize decision-making authority away from field commanders prior to the attacks. As it turns out, the change in procedure had already been indirectly confirmed in a June 3, 2002, story in *Aviation Week and Space Technology*, and almost everyone missed it. That story quoted the order without disclosing that it had been put in place just ten weeks before 9/11. The wording was a near verbatim quote of the Joint Chief's Instruction. One exception in that order (Reference D) did leave some decision making in the hands of field commanders in certain exigent circumstances, but the thrust was a radical shift away from long-standing NORAD policy.

Further research into this change would disclose more evidence showing that, just a month before that, all counter-terror response planning and organization (with a focus on weapons of mass destruction) had been placed under the control of Dick Cheney.[5]

Then there were the exercises themselves.

Vigilant Guardian was named or referred to in several news stories including *Aviation Week*, Newhouse News Service,[6] and on two official web sites.[7] The official websites indicated — and this was later confirmed to me in my own queries with NORAD — that details of Vigilant Guardian were classified and not available for release. A Vigilant Guardian exercise focusing on cold war-era threats was, according to an official site, conducted by NORAD once a year. But a close look at what NORAD told the press described a Vigilant Guardian that was vastly different from an exercise preparing for a Russian attack. In their post-9/11 statements, NORAD officials described details of Vigilant Guardian that seemed to be describing something else altogether.

Aviation Week reported, "Senior officers involved in Vigilant Guardian were manning NORAD command centers throughout the US and Canada, available to make immediate decisions."[8] This confirmed the geographic scope of the exercise. Vigilant Guardian was played up in the press as though it had facilitated a quicker response. It did anything but that.

That Vigilant Guardian had a direct impact on the Northeast Air Defense Sector in which all four hijackings occurred was confirmed in a December 2003 original story by NJ.com, a New Jersey-based service also summarizing all major stories published by New Jersey press outlets.

> NORAD also has confirmed it was running two mock drills on
> September 11 at various radar sites and command centers in the United
> States and Canada, including air force bases in upstate New York,
> Florida, Washington, and Alaska. One drill, Operation Vigilant
> Guardian, began a week before September 11 and reflected a cold war
> mind-set: Participants practiced for an attack across the North Pole by
> Russian forces.[9]

The story never named the second drill, and the assertion that it was strictly a cold war-type exercise is belied by direct statements of many of the principals involved that day. The NJ.com story also raised another chilling issue.

> Investigators at the September 11 commission confirm they are inves-
> tigating whether NORAD's attention was drawn in one direction —
> toward the North Pole — while the hijackings came from an entirely
> different direction.[10]

Vigilant Warrior was specifically mentioned by former White House counterterrorism advisor Richard Clarke in his 2004 bestseller *Against All Enemies*. At the beginning of the book Clarke describes a series of conversations with key officials that occurred after the second tower had been hit as he chaired the White House's Crisis Strategy Group (CSG) during the first minutes of the attacks.

> "[FAA Administrator] Jane [Garvey] where's Norm?" I asked. They were
> frantically looking for Norman Mineta, the Secretary of Transportation,
> and, like me, a rare holdover from the Clinton administration. At first
> FAA could not find him. "Well, Jane, can you order aircraft down? We're
> going to have to clear the airspace around Washington and New York."
>
> "We may have to do a lot more than that, Dick. I already put a
> hold on all take-offs and landings in New York and Washington, *but
> we have reports of eleven aircraft off course or out of communications,
> maybe hijacked.*" [Emphasis added]...
>
> I turned to the radar screen. "JCS, JCS. I assume NORAD has
> scrambled fighters and AWACS. How many? Where?"
>
> "Not a pretty picture Dick." Dick Myers, himself a fighter pilot,
> knew that the days when we had scores of fighters on strip alert had
> ended with the cold war. "We are in the middle of Vigilant Warrior, a
> NORAD exercise, but ... Otis has launched two birds toward New
> York. Langley [Air Force Base] is trying to get two up now...
>
> It was now 9:28 [emphasis added][11]

[NOTE: Clarke's book was edited by the White House for some months prior to publication. The ellipsis (three dots) after the word "but" in Clarke's paragraph above are a direct quotation from the book suggesting the possibility that the White House had deleted whatever Clarke had written here.]

As the chart in the preceding chapter shows, according to data provided by the FAA, NORAD, and many press accounts, by 9:28 it was known that all four flights had been hijacked and that flight 77 had been headed towards Washington for some time.

This was the only reference to Vigilant Warrior I was able to find. Earlier references stored on the Web disclosed a 1996 exercise in the Persian Gulf with the same name, but nothing since. I knew that the names assigned to exercises had significance but did not know how names were allocated. Why would Myers indicate that a Persian Gulf exercise, not reported on anywhere else, had any bearing on domestic response on 9/11?

But if Clarke's account is accurate, the name was confirmed directly to him by the acting chairman of the Joint Chiefs of Staff. Military exercises are often linked, and according to several sources, when names are partially shared during simultaneous exercises this indicates a connection between them. The juxtaposition of the words "Guardian" and "Warrior" suggest opposing forces in a wargame exercise with one side playing the aggressor and another side playing the defender.

The fact that Jane Garvey indicated that as many as 11 aircraft were out of radio contact or off course was the most startling revelation. Was it an indication that one or more of them could be connected with the war games?

Northern Vigilance was an exercise being conducted on September 11th as reported only by Canada's *Toronto Star* in a story dated December 9, 2001. The story had a great deal to say about how 9/11 unfolded.

> Northern Vigilance, planned months in advance, involves deploying fighter jets to locations in Alaska and northern Canada. *Part of the exercise is pure simulation, but part is real world.* NORAD is keeping a close eye on the Russians, who have dispatched long-range bombers to their own high north on a similar exercise....
>
> The Federal Aviation Administration has evidence of a hijacking and is asking for NORAD support. *This is not part of the exercise.*
>
> In a flash, Operation Northern Vigilance is called off. *Any simulated information, what's known as an "inject" is purged from the screens...*
>
> "Lots of other reports were starting to come in," [Major General Rick] Findley [Director of NORAD operations] recalls. "And now you're not too sure. *If they're that clever to co-ordinate that kind of attack, what else is taking place across North America?"...* [emphasis added][12]

The reference to "injects" was chilling. No other mainstream press (especially in the US) had mentioned that false radar blips had been inserted onto radar screens on September 11th. But on whose screens? Where? A major anomaly in official 9/11 accounts had been officially ignored.

The only brief response I received from NORAD's public affairs office when I tried to sort out the various names and identities of the wargames contained the statement, "To help clarify, NORAD did issue a news release entitled "NORAD Maintains Northern Vigilance" on 9 SEP 01." The e-mail response directed me to a NORAD web page where I found the following:

> The North American Aerospace Defense Command *shall deploy fighter aircraft as necessary to Forward Operating Locations (FOLS) in Alaska and Northern Canada* to monitor a Russian air force exercise in the Russian arctic and North Pacific Ocean. [emphasis added][13]

So the fighters had been pulled north and west, away from New York and Washington.

Other press stories referred to Vigilant Guardian as the exercise focused on a simulated Russian attack. Which one was it? The official statements said that Northern Vigilance was the Cold War exercise. So what was Vigilant Guardian? And what were the other exercises all about? As I focused on these discrepancies it became much easier to find answers. They weren't pretty.

Northern Guardian was an exercise that was mentioned only once in a headline for an early version of the same *Toronto Star* story described above; and then, only in the headline. Being a journalist it appeared to me as though references to Northern Guardian had been removed from the text of the story by an editor while the headline reference had been overlooked. What appeared to be a later version of the same story, posted in the online business section the same day had the reference to Northern Guardian deleted. Otherwise, the stories were the same.[14]

The National Reconnaissance Office, a joint creation of the CIA and the air force that operates US spy satellites, was also running an exercise on September 11th. This one happened to involve a plane crashing into the headquarters of the ultra-secret agency in the Washington, DC suburb of Chantilly, Virginia, just outside Dulles International airport, the origin of Flight 77.

An Associated Press story dated September of 2002 was headlined "Agency planned exercise on September 11 built around a plane crashing into a building."

> WASHINGTON — In what the government describes as a bizarre coincidence, one US intelligence agency was planning an exercise last September 11 in which an errant aircraft would crash into one of its buildings. But the cause wasn't terrorism — it was to be a simulated accident.
>
> Officials at the Chantilly, Virginia-based National Reconnaissance Office had scheduled an exercise that morning in which a small corporate jet would crash into one of the four towers at the agency's headquarters building after experiencing a mechanical failure.
>
> The agency is about 4 miles (6 kilometers) from the runways of Washington Dulles International Airport.
>
> Agency chiefs came up with the scenario to test employees' ability to respond to a disaster, said spokesman Art Haubold...

The National Reconnaissance Office operates many of the nation's spy satellites. It draws its personnel from the military and the CIA (news - websites).

After the September 11 attacks, most of the 3,000 people who work at agency headquarters were sent home, save for some essential personnel, Haubold said.

An announcement for an upcoming homeland security conference in Chicago first noted the exercise.

In a promotion for speaker John Fulton, a CIA officer assigned as chief of NRO's strategic gaming division, the announcement says, *"On the morning of September 11th 2001, Mr. Fulton and his team ... were running a pre-planned simulation to explore the emergency response issues that would be created if a plane were to strike a building.* Little did they know that the scenario would come true in a dramatic way that day." [Emphasis added][15]

Strategic gaming, indeed.

A second confirmation of the CIA-run NRO exercise was stored at www.memoryhole.org.[16] It was clear that the CIA was in charge of the NRO drill. This corresponded perfectly with my experience which says that the CIA, when involved in any training exercise involving other agencies, or the military, is always the Alpha dog. How many others? Who was coordinating all these drills anyway? Somebody had to make sure that American pilots didn't start shooting down Canadian airliners or thinking that friendly planes simulating hijacked airliners were Russian bombers or worse, real hijacks.

Vigilant Guardian was a hijacking drill, not a cold war exercise

There were a number of direct quotes from participants in Vigilant Guardian indicating that the drill involved hijacked airliners rather than Russian bombers.

General Arnold had been quoted by ABC news as saying, "The first thing that went through my mind [after receiving the hijacking alert for Flight 11] was, *is this part of the exercise? Is this some kind of a screw-up?"* [emphasis added][17]

The *Aviation Week* article reported:

"Tech. Sgt. Jeremy W. Powell of ... Northeast Air Defense Sector (NEADS) in Rome, N.Y., took the first call from Boston Center. He notified NEADS Commander Col. Robert K. Marr Jr. of a possible hijacked airliner, American Airlines Flight 11.

'Part of the exercise?' the Colonel wondered. No, this is a real world event, he was told. Several days into a semi-annual exercise known as Vigilant Guardian....' [emphasis added][18]

The *Newhouse* story had opened with a reference to hijackings and also confirmed a hijack scenario being linked to Vigilant Guardian.

"Lt. Col. Dawne Deskins figured it would be a long day ....

September 11 was Day II of *'Vigilant Guardian,' an exercise that would pose an imaginary crisis to North American Air defense outposts nationwide....*

At 8:40, Deskins noticed senior technician Jeremy Powell waving his hand. Boston Center was on the line, he said. It had a hijacked airliner.

'It must be part of the exercise,' Deskins thought." [emphasis added][19]

For those unfamiliar with cold war-type air force exercises, for more than 50 years they have involved the simulated interception of Soviet (or Russian) strategic bombers or missiles coming directly over the North Pole. Simulated, in this case, means that interceptors are launched to intercept points. That's what my father's job was in Maine as radar operator/weapons officer in an F89D Scorpion from late 1952 through 1953. The intercepts occurred either in polar regions or in the far northern part of Canada, long before hostile forces could threaten the continental United States or CONUS as it is called. That's a long way from Boston, New York, Washington, and Pennsylvania. There is no way that NORAD officers in Rome, New York, or a Lieutenant General in Florida could possibly mistake a reported hijacking out of Massachusetts as part of that kind of exercise. Such a question could only arise if hijackings were a part of the scenario in one or more wargames being played inside the US, especially Vigilant Guardian.

Northern Vigilance pulled fighter aircraft away from NEADS and CONUS

I found two confirmations of this and a little more information about how extensive the deployment had been. The first, indirect and incomplete, was from NJ.com.

> NORAD confirmed it had only eight fighters on the East Coast for emergency scrambles on September 11. Throughout Canada and the United States, including Alaska, NORAD had 20 fighters on alert — armed, fueled up, and ready to fly in minutes.[20]

A more specific confirmation had already come from NORAD itself from the Northern Vigilance website.

> The North American Aerospace Defense Command shall deploy fighter aircraft as necessary to Forward Operating Locations (FOLS) in Alaska and Northern Canada to monitor a Russian air force exercise in the Russian arctic and North Pacific Ocean.[21]

The pieces were falling together rapidly. I remembered a story that the National Security Agency (NSA) had intercepted a message on September 10th between two al Qaeda members. CNN reported:

A message intercepted by US intelligence officials September 10 declared "The match begins tomorrow," and another declared "Tomorrow is zero hour" — but the messages were not translated until one day after the devastating terrorist attacks.[22]

That conversation was between Khalid Shaikh Muhammad, the so-called mastermind of 9/11, and Mohammed Atta, the reported lead hijacker.[23] Could "match" have referred to a wargame? Honegger had suggested this in 2002. The new wargame information now made that conclusion much more attractive.

It certainly appeared that someone in authority had deliberately interfered with FAA/NORAD operations on September 11th to make sure that some of the attacks succeeded. Richard Clarke's book, previously edited by the White House, had FAA administrator Garvey referring to as many as 11 off-course/out-of-contact aircraft. Was she saying that she couldn't tell the wargame inserts from the real thing?

It would take only a day or two more to find damning evidence that this is probably what she meant. The fact that the CIA had been running a plane-into-building exercise simultaneously with all the military exercises made me very suspicious. The first question that leapt at me was, with all these related exercises running at the same time, who or what was coordinating them? Someone at DoD had to have a regular job of knowing all the exercises being carried out everywhere to avoid SNAFUs. That question and others would require interviews.

"Live Fly" — Pogo bounces toward truth

On Monday, April 12, the Project on Government Oversight (www.pogo.org) released a copy of an e-mail that had been written in frustration on September 18, 2001, by former NORAD "member" Terry Ropes. In the wake of a multitude of contradictory statements by suspects Rice, Bush, Ashcroft, Tenet, and Mueller about how much had been known of "planes as weapons" warnings, a wave of indignation and journalistic embarrassment had swept the country. All who testified or answered questions, it seemed, had been saying that there had not been enough information about "planes as weapons" to institute any kind of preparatory responses. Ropes's email proved them wrong.

Some of the major media finally mentioned Project Bojinka, a plan to hijack a number of US-bound airliners over the Pacific and blow them up. Bojinka plans also called for the crashing of a hijacked, explosives-laden airliner into CIA headquarters. The FBI and CIA had learned of Bojinka in 1995 when they arrested Ramzi Yousef in the Philippines. An April 17, 2004, *New York Times* Op-Ed headlined, "Why Didn't We Stop 9/11?", finally — finally — mentioned Bojinka, the mother of all advance warnings.[24] We crazy, flaky, risible conspiracy theorists had been screaming about it for 31 months.

The US government found out about Bojinka when they seized Ramzi Youssef's personal computer and then brought him to the US and tried him for the first World Trade Center bombing. In 2001 Minneapolis FBI agents, eventually "adopted" by Colleen Rowley were apoplectically trying to get into Zacarias Moussaoui's laptop and receiving nothing but refusals. I wonder why? The agents were also speculating about a hijacked airliner being crashed into the World Trade Center after getting details of Moussaoui's flight training.

Ropes' e-mail, written a week after the attacks, expressed the frustration that we now know was felt throughout the military and law enforcement community. It did not take NORAD long to confirm the e-mail's authenticity for the *Boston Globe*.

> Subject: Exercise Scenario
> In defense of my last unit, NORAD.
>
> For POSITIVE FORCE/RSOI in Apr 01, the NORAD exercise developers wanted an event having a terrorist group hijack a commercial airliner (foreign carrier) and fly it into the Pentagon. PACOM [Pacific Command] didn't want it because it would take attention from their exercise objectives, and Joint Staff action officers rejected it as too unrealistic.
>
> Terry[25]

The media machine kicked into high gear to control the damage. But as is always the case in criminal investigations where the detective gets suspects to talk — just a little — the amount of information learned is directly proportional to the length of time the suspects (or his agents) keep talking.

April 14, 2004, stories in the *New York Times*, the *Boston Herald*, the *Boston Globe*, and the *Washington Post*, all took the same line, emphasizing that the simulation suggested in the POGO email was rejected as being "unrealistic."

The *Boston Globe*, however, added:

> Concerns that terrorists might use hijacked airliners as missiles date back to the 1996 Olympic games in Atlanta, when jets were placed on patrol to guard against such a threat.[26]

In the *same story*, retired FBI Director Louis Freeh (who had been FBI Director in 1996) stated regarding 9/11: "I was never aware of a plan that contemplated airliners being used as weapons after a hijacking." I suppose a really rich terrorist could buy a Boeing 757 for such a mission. Osama had lots of money.

Days later, simultaneous with the appearances of top Bush and Clinton officials in the theatrical environment of the so-called Independent 9/11 Commission, further stories revealed shocking information — including the fact that the government had itself been flying actual aircraft during simulated hijack exercises, possibly even on September 11th.

Two new pieces of crucial evidence were that the exercise envisioned in the POGO e-mail had, in fact, been conducted sometime after April of 2001, and that several hijack exercises involved actual aircraft posing as hijacked airliners in "live-fly" operations.

On April 18 *USA Today* spilled some of the beans. Headlined, "NORAD had drills of jets as weapons" it offered never-before reported details of 9/11.

> WASHINGTON — In the two years before the Sept 11 attacks, the North American Aerospace Command conducted exercises simulating what the White House says was unimaginable at the time: hijacked airliners used as weapons to crash into targets and cause mass casualties.
>
> *One of the imagined targets was The World Trade Center. In another exercise, jets performed a mock shootdown over the Atlantic Ocean of a jet supposedly laden with chemical poisons headed toward a target in the United States.* In a third scenario, the target was the Pentagon — but that drill was not run after defense officials said it was unrealistic, NORAD and Defense officials say....
>
> *"Numerous types of civilian and military aircraft were used as mock hijacked aircraft,"* the statement said. *"These exercises tested track detection and identification; scramble and interception; hijack procedures;* internal and external agency coordination and operational security and communications security procedures....
>
> *A White House spokesman said Sunday that the Bush administration was unaware of the exercises. But the exercises using real aircraft* show that at least one part of the government thought the possibility of such attacks, though unlikely, merited scrutiny....
>
> Until Sept 11, *NORAD was expected to defend the United States and Canada from aircraft based elsewhere.* After the attacks that responsibility broadened to include flights that originated in the two countries.

In the very next paragraph the story contradicted itself.

> But there were exceptions in early drills, including one operation, planned in July 2001 and conducted later, that *involved planes from airports in Utah and Washington State that were "hijacked."* Those planes were *escorted by US and Canadian aircraft to airfields in British Columbia and Alaska* [emphasis added][27]

The following day, April 19, CNN added fuel to the fire. For a moment — just a moment — I had a hope that 9/11 might be broken, and that some treasonous Americans might go to jail. The headline read, "NORAD exercise had jet crashing into building."

> WASHINGTON (CNN) — Sometime between 1991 and 2001, a regional sector of the North American Aerospace Defense Command simulated a foreign hijacked airliner crashing into a building in the United States as part of a training exercise scenario, a NORAD spokesman said Monday....

Military officials said the exercise involved simulating a crash into a building that would be recognizable if identified, but was not the World Trade Center or the Pentagon....

The identity of the building named in the exercise is classified....

This sector exercise *involved some flying of military aircraft* as well as a command post exercise in which communications procedures were practiced in an office environment....

NORAD has the ongoing mission of defense of US air space....

According to a statement from NORAD, "Before September 11th, 01, NORAD regularly conducted a variety of exercises that included hijack scenarios. These exercises tested track detection and identification; *scramble and interception; hijack procedures....* [emphasis added][28]

NORAD's own statement confirmed that real military and civilian aircraft had posed as hijacked airliners. Fighter pilots can't intercept thin air. They can't fly above and slightly to the left of thin air and rock their wings and wait for a response. They can't practice dodging sudden, unexpected movements, maneuver or lock missiles unless there's a real airplane to do it with.

The NORAD statement was quoted further in the story:

NORAD did not plan and execute these types of exercises because we thought the scenarios were probable. These exercises were artificial simulations that provided us the opportunity to test and validate our process and rules of engagement with the *appropriate coordination between NORAD's command headquarters, its subordinate regions and sectors and National Command authorities* in Canada and the United States.

Any assertion that the White House didn't know of such drills was pure bullshit.

The National Command Authority is the White House. It starts with the president and descends through the vice president (in the president's absence as was the case on 9/11), to the secretary of defense. Such exercises, when played in real life, usually involve White House staff standing in for the president. But since they are carried out using either the Presidential Emergency Operations Center or the Situation Room, how could the president, vice president, and national security advisor not know about drills that, of necessity, had taken place inside the White House?[29]

Note the fact that one particular hijacked airliner drill, conducted most likely between July 2001 and September 2001, had the hijacked plane crashing into a building. September 11th was the best possible "drill" of all; the real thing. Was the same exercise that had been rejected in April then carried out as an actual event *on* September 11th? Was the intended game target the World Trade Center? The Pentagon? Both had been mentioned as targets previously, and one of them had actually been bombed before. Was the White House a target? Was the CIA headquarters at Langley? It had been mentioned as a target in the Bojinka documents. The CIA then certainly had an interest in knowing about and participating in all such wargames.

The *USA Today* story quoted a NORAD spokesman as saying "No exercise matched the specific events of September 11th."[30] So there must have been a major salient difference between this particular drill and the events of 9/11 …. maybe they used an airplane with Delta markings instead of United and American, or maybe the number of peanuts on board was completely different. No match.

Other significant similarities to 9/11 jumped out. The one admitted domestic hijack drill involved both the Canadian and US Air Forces, exactly like the drills being conducted on 9/11. Importantly, at least one exercise involved the shoot-down of a simulated hijack that must have been remotely piloted. It would have been difficult to find volunteers for the role of doomed airline pilot in a drill like that.

My understanding of the air force, acquired through my father's career in the military and with Martin-Marietta, reminded me of two things. There are many old airliners lying around, and the air force likes to blow up the real thing rather than a Cessna with an American Airlines logo. The equipment involved on September 11th, Boeing 757s and 767s, were newer models. There might not have been any older ones serviceable lying in the "bone yards." Might the airlines, very close with the US Air Force, have conveniently loaned some to the air force for use in hijack drills? It's a great tax write-off. If they did, were they remotely piloted to avoid injury to airline personnel in case of an accident? The technology certainly existed. Intelligence agencies and the military have long disguised special combat aircraft as harmless commercial planes. I believe that one such plane, the white business jet from the chart in the previous chapter, shot down flight 93. We couldn't have a plane full of witnesses and live "hijacker/patsies" land and start talking; especially if the plane had been flying all by itself, now could we? We will see shortly that at least one of Flight 93's alleged hijackers, Saeed Alghamdi, had received English language training from the military. If he was on that plane and it was successfully landed, he would have some interesting things to say. If he wasn't — if only a few of the alleged hijackers had been on the plane, it would have raised an entirely different set of questions.

History remembers

A 1976 NORAD procedural memorandum established that NORAD was absolutely responsible for all air defense in wartime or "limited war" or an "air defense emergency" inside the US. The attacks of 9/11 would seem to qualify as a limited war.[31] There was no determinate country to attack that day, no invasion by foreign troops. The memorandum, called SCATANA (Security Control of Air Traffic and Air Navigation Aids), was partially implemented on 9/11. It had not been superceded by any later orders. The *Aviation Week* article contained three chilling paragraphs:

By 9:26 a.m., the FAA command center stopped all departures nationwide. At 9:41, American Flight 77 crashed into the Pentagon, elevating tension levels even further. NEADS' Sr. Airman Stacia Rountree, an identification technician, said, 'We had three aircraft down and the possibility of others hijacked. We had to think outside the box,' making up procedures on the fly. *Before the day ended, 21 aircraft across the US had been handled as 'tracks of interest.'*

'We didn't know how many more there were ... Are there five? Six? The only way we could tell was to implement Scatana — sanitize the airspace. Get everybody down,' said Lt. Col. William E. Glover Jr., chief of Norad's air defense operations.

Gen. Ralph E. Eberhart, NORAD commander-in-chief, was in the Cheyenne Mountain battle center by then. He and his staff suggested, via an open command link, *implementing a limited version of Scatana — a federal plan designed to take emergency control of all domestic air traffic and navigation aids.* Transportation Secretary Norman Y. Mineta immediately concurred and gave the order to get all aircraft on the ground as soon as possible. That action probably saved many lives, but without unnecessary, paralyzing restrictions of a full Scatana order.[32]

Many press stories, including some excellent reports in *USA Today*, painted a clear picture of the biggest problem facing NORAD and air force units as the attacks began. Many stories confirmed Jane Garvey's number of 11 possible hijacks. Some indicated that there were up to 21. How could a NORAD commander have known where to send fighters at that time? There were clearly many possible hijackings underway. No one knew the exact number. No one knew which were real.

Sending fighters to a "possible" hijacking was not acceptable. There weren't enough to go around.[33] And if they were sent to an intercept that turned out not to have been a hijacking, they would have been in the wrong place to respond to a real one. This was exactly the kind of uncertainty that would paralyze eager and loyal pilots and commanders until uncertainty had been eliminated. By that time of course, it was too late. Mission accomplished.

So who was flying those things anyway?

Especially with the case of Flight 77, which was, as 9/11-widow Kristen Breitweiser testified, "performing loop de loops" over the Pentagon, some serious flying was done on September 11th. Flight 77 not only flew straight towards the Pentagon from near the Ohio-West Virginia border, it made a sudden U-turn over Washington so that it could hit the Pentagon in a virtually unoccupied wing on the navy side. It also descended several thousand feet in a sharp dive and was able to pull out and approach the Pentagon just feet above the ground, without colliding with anything other than some trees and a streetlight.[34]

So who was piloting Flight 77? According to ABC you have your choice between our charmed lucky friends, Khalid Almidhar and Nawaf AlHazmi, or Wail Alshehri.[35] According to multiple sources all three were poor and inexperienced pilots. Someone made great progress in the summer of 2001. Or maybe it wasn't necessary.

Training provided by Uncle Sam

There are differences between intelligence "assets" who are expendable and those who are not. Usually, the non-expendable ones are people in whom an agency has invested a lot of time and money. According to *Newsweek,* as many as five of the 9/11 hijackers received training at US military installations.

> September 15 — US military sources have given the FBI information that suggests five of the alleged hijackers of the planes that were used in Tuesday's terror attacks received training at secure US military installations in the 1990s.
> *Three of the alleged hijackers listed their address on driver's licenses and car registrations as the Naval Air Station in Pensacola, Fla.* — known as the "Cradle of US Navy Aviation," according to a high-ranking US Navy source.
> *Another of the alleged hijackers [Atta] may have been trained in strategy and tactics at the Air War College in Montgomery, Ala., said another high-ranking Pentagon official. The fifth man may have received language instruction at Lackland Air Force Base in San Antonio,* Tex. Both were former Saudi Air Force pilots who had come to the United States, according to the Pentagon source.
> But there are slight discrepancies between the military training records and the official FBI list of suspected hijackers — either in the spellings of their names or with their birthdates. One military source said it is possible that the hijackers may have stolen the identities of the foreign nationals who studied at the US installations.[36]

Independent journalist and filmmaker Daniel Hopsicker moved to the Venice, Florida, area shortly after the attacks. In the *Washington Post* and the *Knight-Ridder* syndicate, Hopsicker found news stories confirming that some of the hijackers had received US military training. Those stories had Mohammed Atta pretty well nailed down. He had extensive US military training. He also spent a lot of time in bars and strip clubs — behaviors that are completely inconsistent with those of a devout Muslim about to meet Allah as a pure martyr.[37]

Credible press stories citing military sources and records also reported that some of the alleged 9/11 hijackers had received English language training at the military installations. The hijackers reported to have received such training here were Saeed Alghamdi and unnamed others; "more than one," according the Associated Press. Alghamdi was allegedly one of the hijackers of Flight 93.[38]

Again, a little familiarity with the military proved helpful. Military language instruction is a specialized, very elite school. Its primary providers of students have always been military and civilian intelligence agencies. As one former Special Forces soldier who attended the school told me, attendance is exclusively reserved for the most highly qualified applicants making a career in intelligence or the military. "It costs too damn much money for them to train you to be fluent in another language. It's a highly marketable skill. They won't just let you walk away after that," he said. The same thinking, he added, applied to foreign students receiving English language training.

But the assumption that the military had somehow trained some of the hijackers up to incredible skill levels didn't hold water. Venice, Florida, was where several of the hijackers received flight training in small, private aircraft. None received training on Boeing airliners. Only one or two of the 19 had an instrument rating. Over the course of two years Hopsicker not only added information to what was known about military training, he established that some of the hijackers associated with wealthy Floridians who had both intelligence and Bush family connections. Hopsicker also confirmed that within hours of the attacks, Florida Governor Jeb Bush had a military C 130 Hercules transport fly in to the Venice airport where a hastily loaded rental truck, filled with the records of Huffman Aviation — where Atta, Alshehri, and others had trained — was driven directly into the plane. The C 130 immediately took off for parts unknown.

Experienced military pilots with thousands of hours in all kinds of aircraft, Gary Eitel for example, have told me that the maneuver performed by Flight 77, as described in official reports, was beyond the capabilities of 90 percent of even the best and most experienced pilots in the world. I talked to Eitel on the day of the attacks and he was amazed by the piloting skill used to steer Flight 175 into the second tower. Flight 77 boggled his mind.

I remembered that the BBC had contributed some interesting material to the stories that some hijackers received military training.

> One of the most bizarre ironies of all this is that five of the hijackers lived in a motel right outside the gates of the NSA ....
>
> When Osama bin Laden first moved to Afghanistan, the NSA listened in to every phone call he made on his satellite phone. Over the course of two years it is believed they logged more than 2,000 minutes of conversation ....
>
> It all ended when President Clinton ordered the cruise missile strike on his training camp in 1998. Bin Laden narrowly escaped with his life.
>
> He realised that the NSA was listening in and ditched his satellite phone, and ordered his aides never to talk on the phone again about operations.[39]

Early on the morning of 11 September, when Hani Hanjour and his four accomplices left the Valencia Motel on US route 1 on their way to Washington's Dulles airport, they joined the stream of NSA employees heading to work.

Three hours later, they had turned flight 77 around and slammed it into the Pentagon.[40]

Flight 77 again: the miracle plane. The one that nobody actually *saw* hit the Pentagon; the one that left no recognizable debris matching an airliner; the one French author and investigator Thierry Meyssan did a pretty convincing job of proving it never hit the Pentagon because the hole was way too small and the damage pattern (a key forensic technique used by police officers investigating traffic accidents) was totally inconsistent with a mid-sized passenger jet like a 757; the one where the engines melted, disappeared or evaporated, or were transported into space by the Starship Enterprise and never found; the one that flew like a fighter plane or a cruise missile.[41]

Meyssan was crucified in the American press, although his book *L'Effroyable Imposture*, or *The Horrifying Fraud*, became a runaway bestseller in Europe. This was another lesson for me about what happens in America when one tries to make a conspiracy case in the public arena, based solely upon physical evidence. That approach gave rise to verbal attacks and politically empty debates that merely wasted time and energy. I have never believed that Flight 77 hit the Pentagon. I also deliberately chose not to pursue it in my newsletter because I couldn't prove it by the rigorous standards of either the law courts or by peer-reviewed forensic science. Of course, like Meyssan and everyone else, I've been dogged by the big question about the alleged Pentagon plane: where did Flight 77 go, and what happened to the passengers?

I was now absolutely convinced that some valuable and highly trained assets were among the so-called hijackers and that those assets could not have accomplished the flying required on 9/11. Their behavior was more consistent with the creation of a detailed "legend" to make the public believe they had done the deed.

Remotely piloted airliners?

The technology to fly airliners by remote control or, what the air force calls remotely piloted vehicles (RPVs), has been around since the 1960s. The famed CIA Predator drone is just one example of how far the technology has advanced. These unmanned, armed attack aircraft have successfully taken out single vehicles from high altitudes in Afghanistan and Yemen. Remote piloting of airliners was even described in the declassified Northwoods documents from 1962, as the Joint Chiefs planned to shoot down American airliners and blame it on Fidel Castro — so that the US could have a nice war with Cuba. In those days the Joint Chiefs apparently thought it was bad form to kill too many American citizens when you were attacking your own people.[42]

Boeing Aircraft now has an Unmanned Combat Air Vehicle (UCAV) capable of aerial dogfights and killing tanks.[43]

Shortly after 9/11, investigative reporter Joe Vialls reported on some technology that has since been confirmed. While I do not agree with many of Vialls's other conclusions or political beliefs, he was right when he wrote:

> By the mid-seventies, aircraft systems were even more advanced, with computers controlling onboard autopilots, which in turn were capable of controlling all of the onboard hydraulics. In combination these multiple different functions were now known as the 'Flight Control System' or FCS, in turn integrated with sophisticated avionics capable of automatically landing the aircraft in zero visibility conditions. In summary, by the mid-seventies most of the large jets were capable of effectively navigating hundreds of miles and then making automatic landings at a selected airport in zero-zero fog conditions. All of this could be accomplished unaided, but in theory at least, still under the watchful eyes of the flight deck crews.
>
> In order to make Home Run truly effective, it had to be completely integrated with all onboard systems, and this could only be accomplished with a new aircraft design, several of which were on the drawing boards at that time.
>
> Under cover of extreme secrecy, the multinationals and DARPA went ahead on this basis and built 'back doors' into the new computer designs. There were two very obvious hard requirements at this stage, the first a primary control channel for use in taking over the flight control system and flying the aircraft back to an airfield of choice, and secondly a covert audio channel for monitoring flight deck conversations. Once the primary channel was activated, all aircraft functions came under direct ground control, permanently removing the hijackers and pilots from the control loop.
>
> Remember here, this was not a system designed to 'undermine' the authority of the flight crews, but was put in place as a 'doomsday' device in the event the hijackers started to shoot passengers or crewmembers, possibly including the pilots. Using the perfectly reasonable assumption that hijackers only carry a limited number of bullets, and many aircraft nowadays carry in excess of 300 passengers, Home Run could be used to fly all of the survivors to a friendly airport for a safe auto landing. So the system started out in life for the very best of reasons, but finally fell prey to security leaks, and eventually to compromised computer codes. In light of recent high-profile CIA and FBI spying trials, these leaks and compromised codes should come as no great surprise to anyone.[44]

Back doors? Does that sound like yet another application of the ever-evolving PROMIS software? Remember that DARPA (Defense Advanced Projects Research Agency) is the same group of folks who brought us the Total Information Awareness Program that virtually eliminates any expectation of privacy in the US.

One company in particular, Raytheon, had been directly involved in projects related to the remote piloting of aircraft. The AP wrote about it just after 9/11. That story's name-dropping suggested that people in government were aware that this technology was a hot topic. Raytheon was of interest because it was developing technology to remove pilot-control from airliners under hijack or emergency conditions. Companies like Grumman-Northrop had been flying their Global Hawk RPVs for years.

Are Remote Control Jets Worthwhile?

AP — Several companies and government agencies are developing technology to help aircraft controllers land commercial jets from afar, an effort that could avert future disasters or hijackings.

President Bush has suggested further exploration of the technology since the September 11 terrorist hijackings, but some wonder if moving responsibility for landing planes from the cockpit to ground control is a good idea.

The Raytheon Corp. is one of several companies looking to use new satellite technology that would someday allow jets to be landed by people on the ground, in much the same way that hobbyists bring in their model airplanes by remote control.

Raytheon announced on Monday that the company is working on a secure military and civilian system that relies on ground units to improve the precision of satellite navigation.

The company successfully landed a FedEx Corp. 727 without the help of a pilot at a New Mexico Air Base in August.

'There's some pretty overt national security concerns I would think,' said John Carr, president of the National Air Traffic Controllers Association. 'The devil is in the details. *Is this something we would put on all aircraft? Because I'm sure you can imagine if I can control all aircraft you would create a new target.*'

But according to James Coyne, president of the National Air Transportation Association, the technology could be a way to avert disasters like those in the terrorist attacks or even prevent others like the 1996 Valujet crash in Florida and the 1998 SwissAir crash where crews were apparently stymied by fire.

'Perhaps in both of those cases, if people on the ground could have been made aware of the problems, those planes could have been brought back to safety,' said Coyne, who thinks remote control could be a good idea.

> *Military and civilian jets have been landing on autopilot for years, but the Raytheon test used technology that provides the extremely precise navigational instructions that would be required for remote control from a secure location....*
>
> Boeing spokesman John Dern said the company is waiting to hear from task forces assembled by Mineta before trying to integrate such technology into its commercial airliners.
>
> 'Translating that into the commercial world and certifying such a system would pose big challenges," he said. 'For safety and reliability and redundancy, we'd certainly want to be sure that anything we'd do enhances safety.'[45]

Either NORAD had responsibility for tracking domestically hijacked aircraft or it didn't. If it didn't, who did? The Civil Air Patrol? Local police departments? Air National Guard bases are under NORAD control to respond to external threats. Does some other agency control them for domestic threats? The military would never allow such confusing chains of command.

I was approaching one of those moments a detective lives for — when he knows he's caught the suspect in many, many lies, and the whole pathetic construct begins to fall apart. If only a real detective could get these people into an interrogation room, there would be signed confessions or the certainty of a conviction before the day was over.

It got better, and it got worse: as the logical beauty of the investigation grew, so did the ugliness of the reality it revealed.

Then it hit me. The National Command Authority (NCA) in the United States is the president; in his absence, the vice president, the secretary of defense, and the chairman of the Joint Chiefs of Staff. NCA meetings and protocols routinely include the National Security Advisor in the role of the president's top advisor on national security issues. On September 11th the NCA would have extended downward through NORAD commander General Ralph Eberhart and then to General Arnold at Tyndall Air Force Base in Florida. NORAD had just established that, at minimum, Donald Rumsfeld and General Myers were lying about having no conception of such attacks and no preparedness for them. We already know that Condoleezza Rice had been lying all along.

A memorable quotation

> Generally it is impossible to carry out an act of terror on the scenario which was used in the USA yesterday... As soon as something like that happens here, I am reported about that right away and in a minute we are all up.
>
> — General Anatoly Kornukov,
> Commander in Chief of the Russian Air Force[46]

During the 2000 presidential campaign, George W. Bush vowed that he would not tap into the Social Security trust fund except as a result of war, recession, or a national emergency. On September 11, 2001, shortly after the attacks, President Bush turned to his Budget Director, Mitch Daniels, and said: "Lucky me. I hit the trifecta."[47]

The Russians

I kept seeing the words on Mike Vreeland's note, "Let one happen, stop the rest." He had just returned to Toronto from Moscow in December of 2000 with knowledge of the attacks in the pouches he carried with him. Were the Russians in on it? They certainly had specific knowledge. The *Izvestia* story proved that. Putin had said so on MS-NBC days after 9/11.

Russian intelligence has always been surprisingly effective in penetrating US agencies; only those of Great Britain are historically more vulnerable to Russian infiltration. Neither the FBI nor the CIA has fully recovered from the years when Robert Hannsen and Aldrich Ames (respectively) flipped and served as double agents for the KGB. They did it for money and ego gratification. Could al Qaeda pay that kind of cash, offer that kind of support from its non-existent embassy in Washington? Through its spy satellites, diplomatic pouches, and its large cadre of Caucasian agents free to move around Washington unnoticed and throughout the US with diplomatic immunity?

Running a spy ring is expensive, and it takes a lot of things, especially people, which al Qaeda didn't have. Osama bin Laden and his family did own some satellites, and they hobnobbed with George H.W. Bush and former British Prime Minister John Major. They invested in companies benefiting both Bushes. Dick Cheney's company Halliburton had been involved in joint-venture construction projects with the Bin Ladin Group in the Middle East. But this was truly a case where state sponsorship was the only thing that could explain one or more high-ranking American traitors.

It was becoming clearer that the state sponsor was the United States.

What if Vreeland had been wittingly or unwittingly delivering vague documents in which Russian President Vladimir Putin demanded certain slices of the 9/11 pie in exchange for Russian silence and cooperation? - Immediately after 9/11 Putin was one of America's head cheerleaders. He welcomed George W. Bush to Moscow shortly after the attacks. Did Bush get a look at Putin's intelligence files on how the Bush cabal, its financial backers, and US intelligence agencies had set up the attacks, roughly between 1998 and 2001, by assembling pieces of known terrorist plans already on the shelf; by quietly co-opting some terrorist cells which still believed they were following bin Laden; by arranging for other al Qaeda members who had been "flipped" to recruit the unwitting muscle who would die a martyr's death on September 11th?

It was not until Iraq became the Bush administration's *raison d'être* that the Russian relationship went sour. Iraq had 11 percent of the world's oil, and Russia had around $8 billion of contracts to refurbish the oil infrastructure and $4 billion worth of Saddam's unpaid IOUs.

So where could a few key al Qaeda operatives, some of whom had trained at a CIA sponsored training camp in Chechnya, have possibly gotten detailed information about multiple wargame exercises on 9/11 so that they could complete movements that would fill out the legend of their crime? From their handlers perhaps?

Unlike a police detective, I had no badge, no authority, no legal mandate, no ability to compel people to show me records or even talk to me. But one thing was absolutely certain.

It was time to go out and start asking questions.

CHAPTER 20

Q&A: Many Asked, Some Answered — and Golden Moment

U nlike Detective Sipowicz of *NYPD Blue*, I could not yank anyone into an interrogation room at the police station and question them. With no authority — other than reminding people that *From The Wilderness* was read in 40 countries and by 35 members of congress and the intelligence committees of both houses — I had little to intimidate with. I had few illusions that the powers-that-be were anything more than mildly concerned with me. They had come to read our website often, but I had no illusion that this meant that I was making these people shake in their booties at my approach.

Another difference between me and Sipowicz was that I couldn't and wouldn't make any "deals" promising leniency as he might have, hoping for smaller fish to roll on bigger ones.

It was therefore better to ask questions in the style of the best fictional police interrogator of all time, Lieutenant Columbo; the guy who just couldn't quite "get it," but wanted help, clarification, so he wouldn't make unfair mistakes or cause unnecessary trouble.

In the field

All NORAD did when I first asked for clarification on the names of the wargame exercises was to send me a copy of their official press release. It said in part:

> Before September 11th, 2001, NORAD regularly conducted a variety of exercises that included hijack scenarios. These exercises tested track detection and identification; scramble and interception; hijack procedures; internal and external agency coordination and operational security and communications security procedures.
>
> *Numerous types of civilian and military aircraft were used as mock hijacked aircraft.*
>
> *The planning, execution and lessons learned aspects of NORAD exercises were classified. In fact, during the planning stages only so-called*

trusted agents, those directly involved in the planning and execution, knew details of exercises. For operational security reasons, therefore, NORAD cannot discuss details or results of its pre 9/11 hijack exercises....[1] [emphasis added]

Interesting. The exercises were classified and only a very few people knew the details before they took place. The release blatantly contradicted testimony and reports that these kinds of drills — for planes hijacked and flown into buildings — had not been conducted before 9/11. The classification meant that no one in the Air Force or the FAA (subject by law to the same classification procedures) was free to talk about operational details of any of the games. They could not even, as the saying goes, confirm or deny them.

The classification also prevented the exercises from even being acknowledged without permission on the day of the attacks. These restrictions were in place back then. Thus, as the whole world was screaming for information — the official responses would have automatically been pre-approved, tailored, edited, and tightly controlled to avoid opening the can of maniacal worms buried deep in the wargames.

It would also explain why none of the official timelines appearing in the two years following 9/11 — whether from any news agency, NORAD, the FAA, or the White House — ever perfectly matched. Times, especially about what agency had been notified when, had been frequently changed, subtly, to avoid further discussion of inconsistencies that were being noticed and widely discussed. The floor kept moving. These timeline revisions and inconsistencies, continuing until the last day of 9/11 public hearings, produced a lot of "chaff" for those trying to nail anything down.

What had been consistently missing from September 11th was a benchmark — a fixed, immutable standard that could serve to separate the "fake blips" of bad or confusing information from the real stuff. I assumed, incorrectly, that these inconsistencies were all solely a result of trying to camouflage the wargames.

Showing my cards — major-league tree-shaking

I started off by just placing calls and sending brief e-mails. I hoped to get a response from someone who might make a naïve mistake — any mistake — not knowing where I was going or what I was after. I was not playing with rookies. No one bit on that bait but it was worth a try.

It was time to show my cards. My written questions were certain to set off alarm bells in high places. Somewhere, in some way, there was going to be a response. I hoped I would catch it when it came.

I sent a second, long e-mail to NORAD's office of Public Affairs, laying out everything I knew. I intentionally included some questions whose premises were inaccurate, hoping that one of the recipients might correct me and start a dialogue that my Columbo persona might open into broader areas.

From: Mike Ruppert
Sent: Wednesday, May 05, 2004 11:47 AM
To: 'Maria.Quon@northcom.mil'
Subject: Additional urgent journalist questions for NORAD on deadline
Importance: High

Dear Maj. Quon:

We corresponded briefly on questions regarding training exercises being conducted on September 11th, 2001. Additional key information has come to light and I must now, in fairness, send you a more detailed list of questions which are of the utmost importance. To refresh your memory, my publication "From The Wilderness" is read by 35 members of Congress and the intelligence committees of both Houses. Our website averages 15,000 visitors per day. Our subscribers also include professors at more than 30 universities.

Because these questions are so sensitive and involve great detail I have written out a list of known facts as corroborated by NORAD and/or the major press. I request that you ask someone higher up in NORAD command to review the material before commenting. No offense. But a response to these questions is of critical importance to the American people, the world and the US Military.

Your responses will be included in both a news story and a book on September 11th to be released this summer.

Thank you,
Mike Ruppert
Publisher/Editor, "From The Wilderness"
www.fromthewilderness.com
818-(--------) (home office, private)
818-(--------) (main office), 818-(--------) (cell)

Details and questions follow…

These questions are very important.

I am trying to sort out the role/influence of various wargames being played out on 9/11. I have identified four named, and one unnamed, exercises:

1. Vigilant Guardian (multiple press sources including *Aviation News, Newhouse News*)
2. Vigilant Warrior (Richard Clarke, p. 5 of his book *Against All Enemies*)
3. Northern Guardian (*Toronto Star,* Dec. 9, 2001)
4. Northern Vigilance (*Toronto Star*, Dec. 9, 2001)
5. An unnamed plane-into-building TX at NRO in Virginia (Associated Press Aug. 21, 2002; Mr. John Fulton of the CIA)

In addition it is reported that:

1. Radar "injects" were placed on FAA and NEADS radar screens on 9/11 (*Toronto Star*, Dec. 9, 2001);

2. There were previous live-fly exercises where "Numerous types of civilian and military aircraft had been used as mock hijacked aircraft." (*USA Today*, April, 18, 2004);

3. The plane-into-building scenario that was reportedly rejected for the July 2001 TX [Training Exercise] was, according to *USA Today* on April, 19, 2004, "conducted later." The *USA Today* story also stated that planes from airports in Utah and Washington State were "hijacked" and then escorted by NORAD fighters to airfields;

4. The *Boston Globe*, April 14, 2004, reports that in April 2001 NORAD had requested that JCS wargames include a hijacked commercial airliner being flown into the Pentagon. NORAD has authenticated an e-mail discussing this;

5. There are several references to Vigilant Guardian also involving joint participation with Russian strategic bomber forces on 9/11 and indicating that a portion of NORAD's fighter aircraft had been pulled to the northern part of CONUS on 9/11.

6. DCI George Tenet, in his testimony before the Independent 9/11 commission referred to "Red Team" data indicating OPFOR role playing for these exercises.[2]

7. There are confirmed press reports that other TXs were halted immediately after it was understood that a real hijacking had occurred on 9/11 but no indication as to when Vigilant Guardian was terminated and inserts removed from radar screens.

8. There are conflicting press reports at to whether Vigilant Guardian was a strict cold war-type over-the-pole intercept game or whether it involved hijack scenarios. There are stories indicating both. Clearly there were hijack drills being run on 9/11. I suggest a good read of *USA Today's* April,19, story titled "NORAD had drills of jets as weapons". That story also states that one of the previous NORAD scenarios involved a MASCAL (Mass Casualty) exercise with a hijacked airliner into the World Trade Center. The story also states that NORAD was running two mock drills on 9/11. Other stories suggest clearly that at least one of those exercises (including the NRO) involved hijacked airliners.[3]

9. According to the Associated Press, in the calendar year prior to 9/11, NORAD fighters were scrambled 67 times and flying beside commercial or general aviation aircraft within minutes after minor violations such as failure to respond to transponder

"squawk" instructions, off-course violations, missed check-points or failure to respond to radio transmissions.[4] This did not happen on September 11, 2001, even, in some cases, after IFF [Identify, Friend or Foe] hijack alerts had been activated from the airliners and after a known emergency existed.

10. Apparently there was change in FAA/NORAD scramble-inter-cept procedures sometime in the Spring or Summer of 2001. Previously, requests for scramble had been forwarded to the National Hijack Coordinator but on September 11, 2001, another protocol was in effect.

My questions are as follows:

1. How many TXs were being conducted on 9/11 and what were their names?

2. What is Tyndall AFB and CONR's role in relation to the over-all NORAD mission?

3. Was the plane-into-building TX rejected in July "but conduct-ed later" being carried out on 9/11? The NRO exercise would seem to indicate this.

4. Did any part of any TX on September 11, 2001, involve the World Trade Center, The Pentagon, the Capitol or the White House as an intended target?

5. Of the four names referenced above, do any of them repre-sent an Opposition Force pairing, for example, with Vigilant Guardian representing defending forces and Vigilant Warrior representing attacking forces?

6. Into whose radar screens were the radar "inserts" placed on 9/11?

7. Did any TX on 9/11 involve "live-flys" of airliners or any other aircraft posing as hijacked aircraft? If yes, please specify what kinds of aircraft were used and how they were piloted.

8. Were any of those aircraft remotely piloted?

9. At what time was the Vigilant Guardian TX terminated on 9/11?

10. At what time were the inserts removed from the radar screens?

11. What joint participation/awareness was there between NORAD and the NRO for its exercise?

12. When multiple wargames are being conducted across different commands, areas of operation and theaters, who in DoD is responsible for coordination so that games do not overlap or contaminate each other?

13. How much of NORAD's fighter inventory had been pulled north to participate in Vigilant Guardian or any other TX on 9/11?

14. Who at NORAD possessed authority/responsibility for terminating training exercises in the event of an emergency?
15. What was the FAA's joint role in these exercises?
16. What was the exact scramble procedure, the chain of C3 [Command, Control, Communications] in place on September 11, 2001?
17. Does NORAD or DoD believe, suspect or allege that the reported 9/11 hijackers had compromised NORAD or DoD security to take advantage of the wargame exercises?

I will be completing my book within the next ten days to two weeks. I will also prepare a news story based upon your responses. I would appreciate a reply at your earliest possible convenience. It is clear that these questions are of the utmost importance to the American people and the world's understanding of what happened on September 11th.

I will thank you in advance for a quick response.

Mike Ruppert

When NORAD finally responded it was with a "canned" response.

From: Quon Maria J MAJ USA NORAD US NORTHCOM PA [Maria.Quon@northcom.mil]
Sent: Friday, May 14, 2004 10:42 AM
To: mruppert@copvcia.com
Subject: From The Wilderness query

Dear Mr. Ruppert,

In order to preserve the integrity of the 9/11 Commission proceedings, we will not discuss issues with respect to the events surrounding September 11, 2001...

Additional information about NORAD can be found at our website, http://www.norad.mil/index.cfm?fuseaction=home.who_we_are

Thank you for your query.
V/R,
Maria Quon, Major, US Army

CONR-Tyndall

A slightly different but equally detailed request was sent to NORAD/CONR's press officer, Major Don Arias, at Tyndall AFB where many early 9/11 decisions had been made. Arias had appeared at several of the 9/11 commission hearings at the side of NORAD command officers, including the now-retired General Larry Arnold. I didn't hesitate to take full advantage of my father's background.

From: Mike Ruppert
Sent: Wednesday, May 05, 2004 10:48 AM
To: Maj. Don Arias 1st AF
Subject: Journalist Query Re 9/11 and Vigilant Guardian — On deadline

Dear Maj. Arias:

My name is Mike Ruppert. I am the Publisher/Editor of "From The Wilderness," a newsletter read by 35 members of Congress, the Intel committees of both Houses. We have about 15,000 subscribers in 30 countries including professors at more than 30 universities. Our website is www.fromthewilderness.com. Our daily website traffic averages 15,000 visitors per day.

I have a number of questions concerning 9/11 and it is extremely important that I get the facts correct before finishing a book due to be released this summer. It may help you in your responses to know that I am an "AF brat." My father was an EWO/Radar Operator in F89s during the Korean War, and a navigator in SA16s in the MD ANG afterwards. He holds several decorations for his service as a B17 gunner during WWII. I am familiar with many of the technical terms involved in intercept procedures.

These questions are very important.

I am trying to sort out the role/influence of various wargames being played out on 9/11. I have identified four named, and one unnamed exercises: …

After these introductory paragraphs, the questions were the same as those sent to NORAD.

Don Arias

I waited a week to follow up after revealing what I knew. I left additional phone messages at NORAD and CONR for a couple of days after sending the e-mails, and that was it. It was soon obvious that no one, anywhere, wanted to talk to me. After nine days, I turned up the heat.

From: Mike Ruppert [mruppert@copvcia.com]
Sent: Friday, May 14, 2004 10:00 AM
To: 'Maria.Quon@northcom.mil'
Subject: Second Written Request — Journalist Questions for NORAD on 9/11 Wargames

Dear Major Quon:

This e-mail is a second written request for response to questions which I first submitted you on 5 May.

As the publisher of the *FTW* newsletter I have exercised my prerogative to delay publication of the story and provide NORAD with every conceivable opportunity to respond to these very important questions. I will, at some point, be compelled to publish the story and do not wish to state that NORAD was unresponsive. For your convenience I am attaching the questions again and am praying that NORAD will respond quickly. I can extend my deadline no later than 20 May before being compelled to go ahead.

I will follow this with an additional telephone call.

Thank you,
Mike Ruppert
Publisher/Editor, "From The Wilderness"

From: Mike Ruppert [mruppert@copvcia.com]
Sent: Friday, May 14, 2004 10:12 AM
To: Maj. Don Arias 1st AF
Subject: Second request — Query Re 9/11, Vigilant Guardian and other exercises
Importance: High

Dear Major Arias:

This is my second request for an official response regarding wargame exercises being conducted on 9/11. A copy of my initial request is attached at the end of this message.

As the publisher of *FTW* I can and have extended the deadline to complete this essential story. I want to give NORAD every conceivable opportunity to respond to these important questions and do not want to publish that NORAD, CONR or 1st AF was "unresponsive." I will be following this e-mail shortly with a second telephone request. I have extended my deadline to 20 May to provide you with time, and an additional opportunity to respond.

My contact information remains the same as indicated below.

Sincerely,
Michael C. Ruppert
Publisher/Editor

I followed both e-mails with phone messages sounding like the best, hopelessly confused, "Gee I just want to get it straight" Columbo nice-guy I could be.

Just after noon on May 14, my phone rang. It was Major Don Arias, the press officer at Tyndall. He wanted to talk, and it proved to be paydirt. I grabbed a pen, paper, and started taking furious notes. These excerpts from the interview speak for themselves.

DA: General Arnold said, we need to write all this [events of 9/11] down. And we didn't have a historian in 1st Air Force at the time....

We hired a civilian journalist, a lady by the name of Leslie Filson (sp?) and an Air Force historian to try and do some research and try and get the total story of what happened on 9/11....

MR: Great.

DA: Since then we have hired a team of Air Force historians to do some research to make sure that anybody who did anything in response to 9/11, meaning any military organization, any Air Force unit, uh, uh, would go into the annals of AF history....

We gave several cases of the [resulting] book to the 9/11 commission....

MR: I'm sure you can understand how I got confused. I came across so many different exercise names and then after that one e-mail surfaced from POGO, from the former NORAD member who said we did....

DA: Aw gee.

MR: There've been several other stories that showed that there were even live-fly exercises, a shoot-down exercise, and I was very concerned about what was going on, on 9/11 that might have any way interfered with fighter response.

DA: Oh geez. You know, I call it the grassy-knoll crowd. I mean the Monday morning quarterbacks who look back and say, well, this could have been done better and that could have been done better ....
No system is perfect. And on 9/11, as you know, because you've done some research already, hijackings were a law enforcement issue and there was a series of rules that had to be gotten before military systems could be lent to the FAA. Normally, you know a hijacking would be FAA, FBI, and you know if they couldn't handle it, well, then they could ask for military assistance.

You know it happens on occasions, not with hijackings, but it happens occasionally in other ways. Probably most recently before 9/11 ... I don't know if you remember the Payne Stewart incident....

MR: Very well.

DA: We were asked by the FAA to check this airplane out ....

[Arias then recounted the Payne Stewart incident.]

MR: What I've come across, that were occurring on 9/11, were Vigilant Guardian — a multitude of press stories, 3, 4, 5 stories. Richard Clarke refers to Vigilant Warrior as told to him by General Myers, Air

Force Chief of Staff. He might know something about the Air Force I guess.

DA: (laughing) He might.

MR: Then there's Northern Vigilance and Northern Guardian, which I found referred to as occurring on 9/11. Now the NORAD website has Northern Vigilance saying it was a redeployment of fighter resources to northern Canada and Alaska for an old DEW [Distant Early Warning] line, over the pole, Russian Bear bomber attack, which was also going on, on 9/11. But then there were statements by Jane Garvey of the FAA, from a multitude of FAA controllers and Colonel Marr at NEADS, and his deputy, Light Colonel Deskins, I think her name was.

DA: Yeah, Dawne Deskins, I know her well.

MR: ...and a few others going, "Oh My God, is this part of the exercise?" and I said, well wait a minute. Somebody needs to know what this exercise was and why they would even possibly be confused.

DA: Yeah, (stammers for second). I'm going to find out the name of that exercise, but uh, prior to 9/11, when we exercise, we were in our wartime footing. And you know about military exercises, it's to kind of push our 'outside the box thinking,' to exercise well-known scenarios and probably come up with some new ones. Because it was just such an unprecedented incident, you know, and I was working that day, so I was there. There was an unreal quality to what we were hearing and seeing and, for a moment, you talk about the fog and friction of war, 'it can't be part of the exercise' and that was probably more of the sentiment, like *Oh My God, is this part of the exercise, or what?* And General Arnold, of course, readily ascertained it was not, and just discontinued the exercise. Just terminated the exercise right there, and we switched over to real-world operations. (pauses)

Which was fortuitous because we were already on a wartime footing. Had we not been, our response time may have been a little longer so ... We just happened to be at the right place at the right time....

MR: ...I know that had my Dad [during the Korean War] known that his country was being attacked, with or without the proper orders, if there were bogeys and he knew where they were, he would have taken off and shot them down. And I think every commander would have ordered the same thing.

DA: Certainly. Yeah, and I'll tell you the truth, and you can see this. You can go through the 9/11 website and look at General Arnold's testimony, but I think that'll reflect that that's pretty much what he did .... Let's launch the planes and we'll get the approvals later ....

Pre-9/11 we had seven alert sites with two airplanes each....

MR: Really what I want to nail down is any confusion over the names for all these exercises and what role those exercises might have played with either interfering with or confusing responses on 9/11. I had a big question for DoD, which I'm waiting for a response on and you might be able to help me out.

DA: Uh-huh.

MR: It's a hypothetical. Let's say that CONR is running a TX, Pacific Command is running one, NORAD's running one with the Canadians, all of which are slightly related. Does there have to be someone, somewhere, who knows all of the exercises so that they don't cross contaminate each other and we don't start shooting down Canadian airliners?

DA: They would have to be coordinated, yeah. Our exercises are coordinated, and I got to tell you, you know I'm no expert on exercises; I've seen a few. Every command has them. Some are concurrent, some are not. I know it's common practice, when we have exercises, to get as much bang for the buck as we can. So sometimes we'll have different organizations participating in the same exercise for different reasons. And yes, **there is an exercise shop that is the maestro of that exercise.** Who's doing what? And who's trying to learn what from a particular exercise. [emphasis added]

MR: Well, who would be sitting in like a C3 [Command, Control, Communications] chair to look at Northern Guardian, Northern Vigilance, Northern Whatever ....

DA: To be quite honest at this level of command I don't know the answer to that. I could probably root around and find out what the next echelon is from us ....

If there was a maestro, was it a Tyndall maestro; a NORAD maestro, a Pentagon maestro? Or was there a maestro somewhere else even higher? If there were multiple maestros, how did they communicate with each other and who supervised them?

"Thank you Major Arias!" I said aloud. The FBI had enough troubles already, and I just couldn't blame them for the lack of fighter response too. In the case of an airborne aircraft, that responsibility had never belonged to anyone but NORAD. A few minutes later I checked my e-mail and found that the cordial and concerned Arias had also found something useful that he sent as a follow-up. It was confirmation that there had been a live-fly exercise on 9/11, and that it had been conducted by the Joint Chiefs.

From: Arias Donald C Maj 1AF/PA [Donald.Arias@tyndall.af.mil]
Sent: Friday, May 14, 2004 1:26 PM
To: Mike Ruppert
Subject: RE: Second request — Query Re 9/11, Vigilant Guardian and other exercises
Importance: High

Mr. Ruppert,

The [official NORAD published account of 9/11] book is in the mail — hoping you get it by Monday. Please let me know if you don't. Talked to our exercise shop. The NORAD-wide exercise we were in on 9/11 was indeed Vigilant Guardian.

I also learned something that may help you with your research. The terms used for NORAD exercises have specific meanings. *Per NORAD Instruction 33-7:* "Nicknames: A combination of two separate unclassified words which is assigned an unclassified meaning and is employed for unclassified administration, morale or public information. The first word must begin with the combination of letters of the alphabet allocated to the using agency." A nickname is used exclusively to designate a drill, or exercise. Exercise terms are used to prevent confusion between exercise directives with actual operations."

Vigilant or Amalgam means it is a HQ NORAD sponsored exercise. Guardian means it is a multi-command CPX, or command post exercise (no live-fly). So on 9/11 NORAD was conducting a NORAD-wide, multicommand, command post exercise with no live-fly.

Other exercise terms include:

Warrior = JCS/HQ NORAD sponsored FTX, or field training exercise (live-fly) [emphasis added]

Because 1AF CONR is an intermediate level of command I may have to refer your questions to HQ NORAD — but I'll do what I can to answer them. More to come.

— D.A.

JCS signifies the Joint Chiefs of Staff. The JCS Chairman Richard Myers had named Vigilant Warrior over a secure phone line as he talked to Richard Clarke early in the attacks. As Clarke recounted:

"Not a pretty picture, Dick." Dick Myers, himself a fighter pilot, knew that the days when we had scores of fighters on strip alert had ended with the cold war. "We are in the middle of **Vigilant Warrior,** a NORAD exercise, but … Otis has launched two birds toward New York. Langley [Air Force Base] is trying to get two up now....

It was now 9:28 [emphasis added][5]

Taking the statements of Arias and Clarke together, it was now on the record that the Joint Chiefs *and* NORAD *were* running a live-fly hijack drill on September 11th. Since I had never received any denials of any kind, from anywhere in the Department of Defense or anywhere else about these games, the revelation is that much stronger.

It has not been mentioned publicly in any 9/11 inquiry.

The FAA tape

Although partisan factions within the 9/11 commission had been leaking material that was sometimes damaging to the Bush administration, it became clear with regard to the FAA and NORAD that some of those "leaks" were coming very close to making more damaging revelations that would have served neither party. They were just too risky and revealed too much. One example of this was chilling.

On May 6th, the first day after my questions were in the open and I had shown my cards, the Associated Press dropped an anvil into the mix. The timing of the wire story's release suggested a rush effort at damage control.

I had been deliberately vague in all of my communications with the research community about when I was going to release anything hard on the exercises. I would not make any public disclosures until late May when I spoke at a 9/11 conference in Toronto. There had, however, been a lot of Internet chatter that I was on to something big. No one, however, except for the addressees and whoever else was monitoring my e-mail, had any knowledge of what was laid out in those questions or where I might be going with them. That made a May 6th AP story all the more significant.

> Tape of 9/11 Controllers Was Destroyed
> By LESLIE MILLER
> Associated Press Writer
> May 6, 2004, 3:53 PM EDT
>
> WASHINGTON — Air traffic controllers who handled two of the hijacked flights on September 11, 2001, recorded their experiences shortly after the planes crashed, but a supervisor destroyed the tape, the government said Thursday.
>
> A report by Transportation Department Inspector General Kenneth Mead said the manager for the New York air traffic control center asked the controllers to record their experiences a few hours after the crashes, believing they would be important for law enforcement.
>
> *Sometime between December 2001 and February 2002, an unidentified Federal Aviation Administration quality assurance manager crushed the cassette case in his hand, cut the tape into small pieces and threw them away in multiple trashcans, the report said.*

The manager said he destroyed the tape because he felt it violated FAA policy calling for written statements from controllers who have handled a plane involved in an accident or other serious incident. *He also said he felt the controllers weren't in the right frame of mind to have consented to the taping, the report said.*

"We were told that nobody ever listened to, transcribed, or duplicated the tape," Mead said in the report sent to Sen. John McCain, R-Ariz., who asked the inspector general to look into how well the FAA was cooperating with the independent panel investigating the September 11 attacks.

The panel learned of the tape during interviews with New York air traffic control center personnel between September and October.

Mead said his office referred the case to federal prosecutors in New York, but they declined to prosecute because of lack of criminal intent.

The report did not characterize the tape's destruction as an attempted cover-up but said it could have been valuable in providing the public with a full explanation of what happened on September 11.

"What those six controllers recounted in a group setting on September 11, in their own voices, about what transpired that morning, are [sic] no longer available to assist any investigation or inform the public." The letter said. [emphasis added][6]

Does anyone want to wager that the unidentified "FAA Quality Assurance Manager" who crushed, cut, and scattered this criminal evidence has *not* also been promoted since 9/11? We have only the government's word that the tape was destroyed between late 2001 and early 2002. When was it actually destroyed, and in whose custody had it been during the interval between its making and its destruction? Is anyone surprised that there is no mention of these air traffic controllers in the Independent Commission's final report?

Clearly, someone wanted it known that the tape no longer existed.

A coincidence? History responds

It could have been a pure — if utterly incredible — coincidence.

If the timing of the story of the FAA tape's destruction was just a bizarre coincidence, so then (probably) was the 1974 erasure of another tape-recording having to do with impeachable felonies, possibly including murder, and another sitting president.

In 1974 a gymnastic feat performed by Richard Nixon's personal secretary, Rose Mary Woods, "inadvertently" erased a critical 18 1/2 minutes of secret Oval Office recordings in the Watergate scandal. This occurred, conveniently, just as those tapes were about to be turned over to Congress and a special prosecutor.

Here, I can only recite the words of 9/11 activist and researcher John Judge who says, "It's OK if you call me a conspiracy theorist, just as long as you call yourself a coincidence theorist."

In 1972 President Nixon's "Plumbers Unit" committed the notorious burglary at the Democratic Party's campaign headquarters, triggering the two-year investigation that led to his 1974 resignation. Shortly after the burglary, one Alexander Butterfield — the man who had installed recording equipment and maintained tapes of all Oval office conversations — revealed to the world that the tapes existed.

In Watergate, once it was known that there were tapes, something had to be done about it immediately. But what? Had the 9/11 FAA tape remained forever undisclosed it might never have posed a threat. Recall, however, that the AP story said that several people, including the six involved controllers and the manager, knew of the tape. Almost certainly the FBI, NORAD, and the Pentagon knew of it as well. Only one of them needed to talk. The only way to deal with the FAA tape was to take it out of play by destroying it.

The Nixon tapes were quickly subpoenaed by the Senate Watergate Committee under Sam Ervin. After Butterfield's revelation, any claim by the Nixon administration that the tapes were destroyed would have been a virtual confession of evidence tampering and obstruction of justice. That is why the tapes (apart from the lost 18 minutes) survived.

Nixon and his top staff, unable to deny the recordings' existence, used every possible argument to stall and resist handing them over: national security, executive privilege, attorney-client privilege, personal and unrelated, etc. Sound familiar? The Bush-Cheney White House has used these excuses abundantly (almost since its inception), on everything from 9/11, to the Energy Task Force records, to the bad Iraq intelligence, to the White House-sanctioned torture at Abu Ghraib.

Once in the hands of Congress, the contents of the Nixon tapes would have been made public quickly ,and the game would have been over. To the rescue came the diminutive Woods, Nixon's ever-loyal, lifelong personal secretary. While sitting at her desk and (slowly) transcribing the tapes in legal preparation for the congressional and FBI handover, she performed her miracle. No doubt that's what Richard Nixon had hoped it would be.

According to Woods's testimony, while sitting behind her desk, she simultaneously moved in two different directions across about five feet, and activated two switches or buttons (one with her foot, the other with her finger). With that maneuver she "accidentally" erased the precise segment of the one tape which almost everyone — including some like former White House counsel and Watergate whistleblower John Dean (who has added subtle but important insight to our post-9/11 map) — believed would have immediately convicted Nixon and his top staff of a number of exceedingly serious crimes. It would also have opened the biggest can of worms in America's history before September 11th, much bigger than just the end of one presidency.

A photo of Woods recreating her feat still remains available on the Internet. It was the hottest joke material in the US for about six months. Recent stories suggest that it may soon be possible, using new technology, to restore what Woods erased.[7]

The air traffic controllers' tape had been crushed, cut in little pieces, and distributed into a number of trashcans.

It seems a number of lessons were learned from Watergate.

The press reacts not once, but twice

Another "coincidence" appeared in the *New York Times* as I was completing my wargame analysis. I had been sharing some of my findings (via e-mail) with a few other investigators since late March. By late April the wargame "buzz" was strong.

I had not paid much attention to it on May 28th when Barbara Honegger, who (along with Nico Haupt) had given me most of the critical raw data on the wargames, forwarded an astute "grab" by a 9/11 researcher named Angie.

Angie's Internet blog showed that the *New York Times* had just heavily edited and revised an early-edition of a Sunday, April 25th (published on Saturday) page-one story about FAA and NORAD issues soon to be discussed in a public hearing of the 9/11 commission. But when later editions hit the street, the story had been heavily rewritten; so much so, in fact, that *Times* editors felt obliged to comment on it. They acknowledged that they had been contacted by commission officials and asked to make changes. Before looking at the story and the changes, let's look at what the editors said in later editions.

> A front-page article Sunday about the commission investigating the September 11 attacks reported that commission officials said the panel, on the basis of its examination of the Pentagon's domestic air-defense command, would suggest that quicker military action might have prevented the attack on the Pentagon. After early editions had gone to press, the commission's executive director, Philip D. Zelikow, telephoned the Times and said it was wrong to suggest that such a conclusion had been reached. For late editions, the article was revised to reflect his comment and to make it clear that some commission officials, including Mr. Zelikow, who will be instrumental in writing the final report, say it is too early to draw conclusions about what the report might say on the issue.[8]

After discovering that the original version was unavailable on the *Times* website or through Lexis-Nexis (a service used by journalists), Angie had dug up a copy of the original in a Google cache search at the website of Dallas's *Star-Telegram*. She painstakingly compared the two versions. Most of the changes were cosmetic and had to do with style. Two changes, however, were anything but cosmetic.

The first change corrected the initial story by stating that no final conclusions about NORAD and the FAA had been reached or recorded. This meant that the commission was most likely intending to say something less critical on that issue. This was significant because the original story stated that the sources for the story, who gave the *Times* the original information, were a part of the commission. No inside sources of any kind were mentioned in the revised story.

Statements received after publication of the first story, from Chairman Thomas Kean and Executive Director Philip Zelikow (co-author and former colleague of Condoleezza Rice), made it clear that nothing had been decided, and no conclusions had been reached.

The second important change deleted any reference to "interim reports." If such reports existed, destroying them would bring criminal penalties (like the penalties evaded by the destroyer of the FAA tape). They were permanent records. In the new version, any "interim reports" simply ceased to exist. If they don't exist, there's nothing to destroy.

Both versions, excerpted and compared below, remained full of damning revelations in their own right. Here are excerpts of what Angie found when she compared them:

[Note: Bold text indicates additions to the "corrected" version and the strikethrough text shows most deletions.]

> Posted on Sunday, April 25, 2004
> Title: *9/11 **Panel Set to Detail Flaws in*** Air defenses criticized in 9/11 attack on Pentagon
> By Philip Shenon
> The *New York Times*
> **Editors' Note appended**
>
> WASHINGTON — **April 24** - The commission investigating 9/11 is expected to offer sharp criticism of the Pentagon's domestic air-defense command in its ~~the panel's~~ final report, **according to commission officials who said they believed** and will suggest that quicker military action that morning might have prevented a hijacked passenger **plane** ~~jet~~ from crashing into the Pentagon itself, according to commission officials.
>
> **While other officials stressed that the panel had not reached any final conclusions on** the performance of the North American Aerospace Defense Command, or NORAD, **or whether the Pentagon attack could have been prevented, they said that** NORAD ~~and its~~ failure to **defend Washington and New York City on September 11, 2001, would be subjected to intensive scrutiny at the** ~~protect the Pentagon and the World Trade Center will be a focus of the remaining public~~ hearings of the 10-member commission....
>
> NORAD had time to launch jet fighters that could have intercepted and possibly shot down American Airlines Flight 77, **before it**

which crashed into the Pentagon at 9:37 a.m., more than 50 minutes after the first hijacked plane struck the World Trade Center in New York. A total of The Pentagon attack killed 184 people were killed in the Pentagon attack, including the 59 aboard the hijacked plane.

The panel's chairman, Thomas H. Kean, the former Republican governor of New Jersey, said in an interview that there had been no formal deliberations by the commission about how to judge NORAD performance and said that he was waiting to be briefed on the findings of the panel's investigators.

The commission's executive director, Philip D. Zelikow, said in an interview on Saturday that his investigators had reached no conclusion on whether the plane could have been stopped before striking the Pentagon. 'Any inference that the commission is preparing to reach any such conclusion is false and terribly misleading,' he said.

Other commission officials said the timeline presented to them by Norad suggested that there might have been time to launch jet fighters that could have intercepted — and possibly shoot down — Flight 77.

In testimony last May at a preliminary hearing on NORAD performance, Maj. Gen. Larry Arnold, a retired Norad commander, acknowledged that if fighters had been scrambled faster, they could have reached the airliner, a Boeing 757 ....

Norad officers have said previously that they did not learn of the [shoot-down] order until about 10:10 a.m., a few minutes after the last of the four hijacked jets crashed into a field in rural Pennsylvania. But White House officials have suggested that the order was made given earlier in the morning and should have been communicated immediately to pilots ....

[Note: The order was given but not communicated until 10:10. Why?]

In November, the commission issued a subpoena to the Pentagon after learning that a variety of pertinent documents, tapes and other evidence from NORAD had not been turned over to the panel. The only other federal agency subpoenaed by the commission was the Federal Aviation Administration, which is under scrutiny by the panel for air safety lapses related to its communications with NORAD on September 11 ....

[Tapes? Since NORAD supercedes the FAA in military events, might this also have referred to the FAA tape? Were FAA tapes requested also?]

But their defense of NORAD actions became more difficult this month with the disclosure that well before September 11, Norad planners had specifically weighed considered the possibility well before

September 11 that passenger planes might be used as missiles against domestic targets.

The disclosure came in the form of a newly unearthed 2001 memo showing that in April of that year, NORAD considered an exercise in which military commanders would weigh how to respond to an attack in which terrorists flew a hijacked plane into the Pentagon, **precisely what happened five months later** ....

Asked what information has been gathered about NORAD since the subpoena, **he** Kean said he could not comment until he had reviewed the work of the commission's investigators, noting that he has been consumed in recent days with preparations for the panel's scheduled interview **on Thursday** next week with **Mr. Bush** and Vice President Dick Cheney. But he said the evidence of 'NORAD failures' is 'disturbing.'

By the time three F-16 jet fighters **were airborne** had taken off from Langley Air Force Base, Va., about 105 miles from Washington, American Airlines Flight 77 was **only** seven minutes from plunging into the Pentagon.

Jet fighters stationed at Andrews Air Force Base, Md., a few miles outside Washington and the home base of Air Force One, were not scrambled despite urgent telephone pleas that morning from the Secret Service for help in defending the White House.

[Were the Andrews fighters part of the group that had been re-deployed to Canada and Alaska? This was never asked.]

'You have to wonder why, knowing that planes were being hijacked and one had just crashed in New York, NORAD would not take immediate precautions a few hundred miles away in the nation's capital,' said a commission member, speaking on condition of anonymity because of the commission's rules against public statements that predict its findings ....

But **Mr. Ben-Veniste**, ~~he~~ said the commission hasd 'substantial' new information and **would want to question** ~~wants to ask~~ NORAD commanders **about** 'why the nation's air defenses were in an outward cold war posture rather than one that reflected' a new generation of threats, including the use of hijacked passenger planes as missiles ....

[The wargame data prove this assertion to be laughable.]

Norad also **now frequently** routinely scrambles fighter jets to investigate when passenger planes go off course or report other trouble...

[Adding "now frequently" repeats the lie that it wasn't being done before 9/11, another misrepresentation.]

If all this was a result of partisan maneuvering inside the commission, then it was also a dangerous game for reasons those playing it might not have fathomed.

These two stories also validate points I made earlier in this book explaining why the current economic system creates an inextricable interdependence between the major press, whose gigantic parent companies trade on Wall Street, and the government, which serves Wall Street. Corporate media in America is inherently unable to tell some truths, or even contemplate certain issues; it must survive in a diseased political and economic ecosystem, dependent upon its own food chain, and therefore bound to participate in its crimes.

In the mind of an air traffic controller

The easy task on 9/11 was confirming that hijackings were in progress. The impossible task was locating them.

If the September 11th air traffic controllers ever became fully aware of how the wargames had so perfectly neutralized their desperate efforts, the consequences might be unmanageable. The ATCs must have been pulling their hair out that morning in Dantean anguish, screaming, demanding, "We can't find them. We can't ID the hijacks. Somebody please get the exercise crap off our screens! Remove the inserts! Have any live-flys involved in any FTXs squawk now so that we can find the real things!"

These were proud, dedicated professionals, so severely wounded by 9/11 that they might just not give a damn anymore about jobs, pensions, benefits, medical insurance, jail time for breaking secrecy oaths, or even physical retaliation, if they saw a larger picture. People who have been broken beyond a certain spiritual and emotional point can, on occasion, become fearless and immune to any kind of pressure or threat.

As sure as I recall every detail of my two shootings as a police officer, several nasty fights, and some other terrifying moments, I know, as any combat veteran will tell you, that these controllers are frequently and involuntarily reliving every second of that day over and over. They are stuck in a continuous replay loop of a horror film in which they are characters, and — as they try to heal — are desperately seeking the "Stop/Eject" button. But they can't find it.

Self-forgiveness after trauma like this is hard to come by, even if you did nothing wrong — no evil, and no mistake — to trigger it. Any major trauma, earned or not, evokes an instant need to find out why it happened to you; to find your error and correct it so that it never happens again. It would be too frightening to think that there may have been nothing at all you could have done to prevent (or correct) it. The same thing might happen to you again then. Your mind and soul believe that possibility to be an un-survivable experience. All you want is for the damn tape to stop playing.

A story about one ATC's pain says it all.

Ed Ballinger

Would you speak out if you had 44 years as a controller, were close to retirement and in poor health? Was it worth chasing the questions that nagged at you, when you just weren't sure that there wasn't some reasonable explanation? Making waves would, you might think, only keep you stuck in it more; keep you from moving on.

Ed Ballinger was the ATC handling both Flight 93, departing from Newark, and Flight 175 from Boston. So he was obviously aware of multiple hijackings occurring in real time. His story also shows that he was well aware of Flight 11's fate in close to real time. It was he who would have first detected a missed radio transmission, a transponder being turned off, or a sudden and unauthorized course change.

As the "hijackings" were in progress, and on his own initiative, Ed Ballinger gave his "best-possible" warnings to scores of United pilots. He did it on his own initiative and without any direction: as we shall see, even the National Command Authority remained deadly silent for almost 77 minutes after the second hijack and first impact (when everyone knew it was a synchronized attack), until Flight 93 had become the fourth confirmed hijacking.

A story in Chicago's *Daily Herald* about Ballinger's ordeal didn't mention the wargames.[9] Ballinger didn't mention them either. He must have known about them. The whole Northeast Sector where he worked knew about them, and was in one way or another participating in them. No one would ever take the chance of having a wargame exercise and then not brief the affected controllers. Otherwise they would have begun initiating emergency responses and setting off alarms that would have produced unpredictable results that might have spread throughout the system.

Suburban Flight Dispatcher to Recount Worst Day

Today, Ed Ballinger will speak to a roomful of strangers about the one subject he doesn't care to discuss: The first two hours of his shift as a flight dispatcher for United Airlines on the morning of September 11, 2001.

The Arlington Heights resident and former United Airlines employee will meet with a sub-committee of the 9/11 commission in Washington, DC, so panel members can decide whether his testimony warrants his appearance before the full commission.

Ballinger is there because he was in charge of United Flights 175 and 93 when they crashed into the World Trade Center and a field near Shanksville, PA.[10]

Because perhaps, just perhaps, offering his story will calm the whispering thought that troubles him still: If he'd been told the full extent of what was unfolding sooner that morning, he might have saved Flight 93.

"I don't know what [the panel appearance] is going to be," he said Tuesday after arriving in the capital. "They want to know what I did and why. I've been told it's not finger pointing. It's just finding out what happened."

Part of what happened was his 44-year career at United crumbled after September 11. He found it too hard emotionally to go on with his job as before.... "In my judgment, he is a vital part of the story because Ed Ballinger is the last human being to talk to [Flight 93's cockpit]," said the Wilmette Republican, whose district includes much of Arlington Heights.

"And when all is said and done, he was responsible for preventing multiple hijackings," Kirk added. "I think he probably foiled [another] hijacking...."

"When September 11 came along, that morning, I had 16 flights taking off from the East Coast of the US to the West Coast," he said. "When I sat down, these 16 flights were taking off or just getting ready to take off."

Then the first American Airlines planes struck New York and the Pentagon.

[Note: if this is correct, then NORAD and the White House and the Pentagon *all* knew that three hijackings had occurred by this time. Yet they issued no warnings. Ballinger had to do it by himself.]

Ballinger contacted all his flights to warn them. But United Flight 175 "was not acting appropriately."

He asked Flight 175 to respond. The pilot didn't reply and Ballinger was forced to conclude he'd been compromised and that he was rogue.

[This is exactly what long-standing FAA procedure told him to assume. See Chapter 17.]

By now, the situation was terribly different from previous hijackings Ballinger had handled. **In two hours, he sent 122 messages.**

"I was like screaming on the keyboard. I think I talked to two flights visually. The rest was all banging out short messages," he said.

Realizing what was going on, he sent all his airplanes one message: "Beware of cockpit intrusion."

"93 called me back and says, 'Hi, Ed. Confirmed.'"

Ballinger said he didn't wait for orders from his supervisors, or for Transportation Secretary Norman Mineta's decision to ground all flights. He immediately tried to get his pilots down on the nearest Tarmac.

"As soon as I had a grasp of what was going on... I sent it out immediately. It was before Mineta, and even before the airlines told us to alert the crews," he said.

Dispatchers were told by superiors: Don't tell the pilots why we want them to land.

[Question: Why not? To avoid confirming the attacks were in progress to any airline pilot who didn't yet know, thereby risking an uncontrollable and possibly successful intervention? At least one hijack had already struck the WTC, so the dispatchers' superiors need not have worried about terrorists blowing up the planes in mid air; bombs were not the mode of attack this time. Had the pilots been told about the multiple hijackings and the WTC impact of Flight 175, any struggle for control of the plane could only diminish the eventual death toll, not increase it. All over the country, brave "real" Americans were rising to the challenge, doing whatever they could without waiting for anyone to tell them what to do. They knew damn well what to do.]

"One of the things that upset me was that they knew 45 minutes before that American Airlines had a problem. I put the story together myself (from news accounts)," Ballinger said....

"Perhaps if I had the information sooner, I might have gotten the message to 93 to bar the door."

Perhaps, but [Illinois Congressman Mark] Kirk is adamant that Ballinger did save the passengers and crew of United Flight 23, which on September 11 was about to depart from Newark, NJ, to Los Angeles. Kirk believes Flight 23 was going to be commandeered.

Thanks to Ballinger's quick call, the flight crew told passengers it had a mechanical problem and immediately returned to the gate.

Later, Ballinger was told six men initially wouldn't get off the plane. Later, when they did, they disappeared into the crowd, never to return. Later, authorities checked their luggage and found copies of the Qu'ran and al-Qaida instruction sheets.

"I felt good about that one," Ballinger said.

Kirk admits it's speculation, but said he believes "there are 200 people walking around today because of Ed Ballinger."

The suspect passengers were never found, and are probably still at large, Kirk said....

Ballinger said he was never the same after September 11, and was reluctant to return to work.

"That first day, I'm lucky I didn't hit anyone," he said. "I drove through every red light getting home as quickly as possible. I wanted to get home and medicate myself."

At work, he started second-guessing his own decisions and became, in his words, "ultra-ultra conservative."

"I came to a point where nothing was safe enough," he recalled. "[I] couldn't even make a decision. It put you in jeopardy in every respect."

At age 63, he was told to take a medical leave and long-term disability. He said he couldn't do that. He was then asked if he could retire in six hours.

A Social Security Administration psychiatrist put him on total disability.[11]

What if Ed Ballinger had heard the anguished commentary of his brother and sister ATCs on the destroyed FAA tape? What would have happened if they compared notes? They still can.

Most of the ATCs who testified did so behind closed doors or, when in public, were circumspect and not asked any important questions. The testimony we know about never once mentioned details of wargames other than what had already been published (and left equally unexamined) in the press.

As pieces came together I continued the investigation.

The CIA and the NRO

Getting wargame responses from the CIA and the NRO was not at all difficult. Plausible deniability, properly emplaced, always provides layers of comfort and permits gracious behavior for those it shields. After speaking with Arias I called CIA headquarters on May 14th. A CIA press officer listened politely, gave me an e-mail address and promised to quickly evaluate my questions and tell me where to send them. She kept her word.

> **From:** michetk [michetk@ucia.gov]
> **Sent:** Friday, May 14, 2004 11:59 AM
> **To:** Mike Ruppert
> **Subject:** Re: Journalist Questions -- NRO Plane Into Bldg exercise and Dod/NORAD Live-Fly Hijack and Intercept Exercises on September 11 2001
> **Follow Up Flag:** Follow up
> **Flag Status:** Flagged
>
> Mike,
>
> I looked at your questions and I believe the best person for you to talk with is the director of NRO's public affairs-- Rick Osborne [sic] on 703 808 1013.
>   If you need anything else please let me know.
>   M

I called the NRO on May 17 and left a message for Oborn (CIA had misspelled his name). The receptionist gave me his email address. Off flew another e-mail.

I pulled out all my aces and namedropped shamelessly. I mentioned that I was good friends with the widow of famed CIA U2 pilot Francis Gary Powers, shot down over Russia and captured in 1960. Sue Powers and I had become close in 1992 while working as volunteers in the Perot presidential campaign. That was before we both got extremely "disillusioned" with the "short, floppy-eared Texan" (as he has been known to call himself) when he suddenly dropped out of the race in July of that election year.

From that point on Powers would only refer to Perot after that, as "Pee-rot." On the day Perot suddenly quit, ABC's evening news opened with a shot of me crying on Sue's shoulder. I wasn't the only American to cry that day. In 1994 I had been married in Sue Powers' back yard. The marriage did not last, but my friendship with Sue did.

In my e-mail I also dropped another big name, very well known to students of the CIA's role in Iran-Contra.

> As personal background, after leaving the Air Force my father was on the design-concept team for Titan IIIC at Martin-Marietta in the 1960s. I was privileged to meet retired [CIA Deputy Director for Intelligence, CIA's second highest rank] DDI John McMahon at the Smithsonian Air and Space Museum in 1995 at a private reception honoring the 35th anniversary of the last flight of Francis Gary (Frank) Powers. His widow Sue was a close personal friend. I was born into this "soup," so to speak, at Georgetown Hospital.

Oborn had to like me

Along with NRO-exclusive questions, I attached the original full-disclosure message I had sent to Don Arias for Oborn's edification. I wanted people to know how hard I was rattling cages. Just after noon, he returned my call on my main office number. My staff alerted me at my home office, and he took my return call immediately.

The NRO position was exactly as I had expected. Their drill on September 11th had been a command-post exercise and it did not, according to Oborn, involve any live-fly. It did, however, involve some liaison and role-playing with local Fairfax County police, fire, and emergency units. Oborn said that the NRO's drill was "based on the idea of a Lear Jet or a FedEx plane having a flame-out on take-off from nearby Dulles airport and crashing into the building." The NRO is close to the end of one of Dulles' runways. However, Oborn said, since there was no flying involved, there was no need to coordinate with the military or the FAA.

That brought me again to what was becoming the burning question: Who or what was the "maestro" of 9/11, as Arias had put it, who would have coordinated multiple wargame exercises? After an enjoyable digression about my family and life experience, I asked Oborn a hypothetical question about coordination of multiple wargames and solicited his opinion.

He believed that in the post-9/11 world, coordination for such activities would rest with either the Department of Homeland Security or NORTHCOM (Northern Command which, since its activation in October of 2002, encompasses the US, Canada, and Mexico, and their respective militaries). That was interesting because the current commander of both NORAD and NORTHCOM is General Ralph Eberhart who commanded NORAD on 9/11.

After talking to Oborn I chuckled. Conditioned by a quarter-century of first experiencing and subsequently investigating covert operations and operatives, I had a thought. The NRO is probably one of the top ten high-value targets in the country. Nobody wanted it hit, but if the plans went awry it just might be hit. Everyone knows that there are no guarantees when you start something this big. Things get out of hand; someone fails to follow the plan; loyalties change; people screw up their mission, the fog of war. It would be prudent to have the NRO drill underway, with police, fire, paramedics, and everything else there just in case. Good thinking!

The maestro in hiding — Last ditch efforts

I had been wearing myself out trying to get the answer. For a brief moment, I again hoped I might get lucky when a response came to one of my initial queries.

> **From:** Turner, James, CIV, OASD-PA
> **Sent:** Monday, May 10, 2004 12:25 PM
> **To:** 'Mike Ruppert'
> **Subject:** RE: Journalist Query -- on deadline
>
> Sorry we missed your deadline. Are you still interested in a response?
>
> Jim

I responded instantly providing all the same detailed information. I followed up over the course of a week by sending "Jim" two additional e-mails and leaving three more phone messages — almost begging, in my best bewildered Columbo voice. I never heard from that office again. The e-mail address indicated that Jim worked for the Assistant Secretary of Defense for Public Affairs (OPA).

Same action, same results. It was time to try something else. Then something dawned on me. Jim might not have answered my question, but I certainly had answered his: "Has Ruppert found anything out yet? How much has he got?"

I had one last shot when I received an e-mail from my staff on May 17th.

> **From:** Media 2
> **Sent:** Monday, May 17, 2004 11:09 AM
> **To:** Mike Ruppert
> **Subject:** Re: Joint Staff Public Affairs
>
> I noticed today that a message was left Friday afternoon by a Major MARIA CARL at the Joint Staff Public Affairs.
>
> This message came at about 2:00 P.M....
>
> Her message said that she was responding to an e-mail you had sent to DoD Public Affairs, regarding "exercises" (I'm assuming this has to do with the new 9/11 info).
>
> She is on "Government Travel" this week and is informing you to direct your inquiry to J-7, which is a Directorate at the Joint Staff

Public Affairs office. Phone number is 703-695-7678. Her words were "I believe your answer lies HERE at the Joint Staff with our J-7."

I made the call immediately and sent off another e-mail. By this time I was feeling that it was wasted effort, and I was correct. Two follow-up e-mails and three phone calls later: same action, same result.

Every official entity that could have, and should have, answered the question had in effect "taken the Fifth" by exercising their right to remain silent. Meanwhile, others were being denied that very right. What a monstrous inequity it is that John Ashcroft has been wiretapping attorney-client conferences in "terrorist-related" cases since 9/11. This practice has been used (according to many press reports) against what may be thousands of people, held God knows where: from Guantanamo to Afghanistan, to Iraq, to Diego Garcia, since 9/11. Most of these people have not been formally charged or even permitted to consult with counsel. In the wake of Abu Ghraib and the stunning revelations that horrific abuse had been encouraged from above, even by the White House, I wondered how many of these other detainees had been tortured as well.

The phone bridges: nails into solid wood

Ironically, the last major pieces of evidence that would shed new light on the mental states of many of 9/11's key figures — the proof and the record against which guilt could be nailed — did not turn up until June 17th at the final, and expected-to-be-unimportant, hearing of the 9/11 commission. Had it not been for an alert response by investigative journalist Tom Flocco, one key piece — a one-page press release from the FAA — might have gone completely unnoticed.

The FAA release, testimony, and other records from several sources disclosed that comprehensive communications had been established to every location and key decision point fairly early on; much sooner than previously admitted. This new evidence showed exactly when "phone bridges" (continuously open communications links) had been in place providing real-time data and connecting every part of the National Command Authority, from Air Force One, to the White House, to Dick Cheney, to the Pentagon, to NORAD, to the Department of Transportation, to the FBI, to the FAA.

Since this material had been submitted under oath, it constituted direct legal evidence that the key decision makers, especially Dick Cheney, had been lying from the beginning about what they knew and when they knew it.

Every word of the FAA's submission was precious. Follow-up reporting by Flocco that day would reveal even more.

FAA communications with NORAD
On September 11, 2001

Within minutes after the first aircraft hit the World Trade Center, the FAA immediately established several phone bridges that included

FAA field facilities, the FAA Command Center, FAA headquarters, DOD, the Secret Service, and other government agencies. The US Air Force liaison to the FAA immediately joined the FAA headquarters phone bridge and established contact with NORAD on a separate line. The FAA shared real-time information on the phone bridges about the unfolding events, including information about loss of communication with aircraft, loss of transponder signals, unauthorized changes in course, and other actions being taken by all the flights of interest, including Flight 77. Other parties on the phone bridges, in turn, shared information about actions they were taking.

NORAD logs indicate that the FAA made formal notification about American Flight 77 at 9:24 a.m., but information about the flight was conveyed continuously during the phone bridges before the formal notification.[12]

In a story posted later that same day, Flocco wrote:

Laura Brown, Public Affairs Director at the FAA, initially told this writer at the first 9/11 hearing in Washington that the phone bridges started around 8:20 or 8:25 am, which would be a reasonable assertion since American 11 was determined to be hijacked at 8:13, 8:20, or 8:24 a.m....

[According to Nafeez Ahmed's examination of NORAD and Air Force policy, this had been a standard operating procedure for some time before 9/11. See Chapter 18].

After returning to her office and conferring with superiors, Brown sent an e-mail to this writer later that same evening after 7:00 pm, revising her initial assertions for the commencement of Leidig's phone bridges to around 8:45 am, thus shortening the official attack time-line to the government's advantage.

[Yet another time change, but this one did not negate the statement submitted as evidence and under oath. That could only be changed by a sworn affidavit, submitted to and accepted by the commission.]

Brown had originally said that North American Aerospace Defense Command (NORAD), Defense Secretary Donald Rumsfeld, National Security Council (NSC), Secret Service, and FAA were all connected to the NMCC. But Brown did not mention the White House at the time.

It should be noted that by including the NSC — which is in the White House — one could infer that Brown meant that the White

House was connected to the phone bridges at the outset of the attacks,
further raising serious questions about the lack of military response....

[Richard Clarke's account of events in his book *Against All Enemies* does not
place him in the White House Situation Room (with Condi Rice at his side) until
after Flight 175's impact at 9:03. It does, however, confirm that the phone bridges
were up and running before then. Clarke even indicated that at the very start of
his White House teleconference, he could see Donald Rumsfeld seating himself in
a studio at the Pentagon.[13] If Clarke is right then Donald Rumsfeld was in the
loop by 8:45 and he was committing perjury with the Kean Commission by stating that he was not in the loop until he entered the NMCC sometime after 10
a.m. Rumsfeld's testimony for the 9/11 commission stated that he didn't return to
the NMCC until after 10 a.m., thus implying that he was out of the loop. In fact,
this is basically what he said.[14]]

> In May 2003, the Commission was informed that the Pentagon had
> taped the Significant Event/Air Threat conference call during the
> attacks; and after repeated requests, the Pentagon created a classified
> transcript. (*US News*, 9-8-2003)
> On August 6, the White House conducted what was termed an
> "executive privilege" review of the transcript for the phone bridge con-
> ference call in order to censor the document....[15]

I recalled something I had seen earlier. Don Arias had placed a frantic phone
call to his brother, who worked at the twin towers, just after the first impact. If the
phone bridges were operating — according to the FAA's latest submitted time —
within minutes of Flight 11's 8:46 impact, then that was at around 8:50. Arias's
call had taken place at almost exactly the same time. Was there a connection?

Back to Arias — A golden moment

Digging further into press accounts of Don Arias's personal story, I found clues as
to why he might have helped me. It had again been Barbara Honegger who pointed out Arias's call after I shared some of my findings with her.

How much did he know at that moment? If Ed Ballinger had been in torment
by this time, what had Don Arias been thinking as he called his brother? An *ABC
News* broadcast aired on the evening of the attacks recorded Arias's account.

[Time codes refer to placement in the broadcast segment]

> 03:54:23 COLONEL ROBERT MARR, US AIR FORCE
> And the immediate assumption is that that guy that, that we couldn't
> find [Flight 11] probably hit, hit the World Trade Center.

> 03:54:31 CHARLES GIBSON, ABC NEWS
> (VO) [Voice over] But the FAA still lists American Flight 11 as unac-
> counted for.

03:54:35 LT COLONEL DAWNE DESKINS, AIR NATIONAL GUARD

They told us that they showed the American Airlines Flight 11 was still airborne. So now, we're looking at this, well if, if an aircraft hit the World Trade Center, who was that?

03:54:49 CHARLES GIBSON, ABC NEWS

(VO) Whoever it is, Colonel Deskins knows she needs to call NORAD operations in Florida, to inform the Public Affairs Officer, Don Arias.

03:54:57 LT COLONEL DAWNE DESKINS, AIR NATIONAL GUARD

And his reaction to me at that point was, my God, my brother works in the World Trade Center, and I said well, you have to go call your brother.

03:55:08 CHARLES GIBSON, ABC NEWS

(VO) Arias hears the shock in his brother's voice.

03:55:08 DON ARIAS, PUBLIC AFFAIRS OFFICER

So not the typical phone voice I expected, you know. And, he was just like, hey, you know, he says, I heard a lot of background noise. He says, you know, it's lot of stuff going on here now.

03:55:18 CHARLES GIBSON, ABC NEWS

(VO) The Air Force officer is a former New York City firefighter. So he knows what his brother is up against.

03:55:24 DON ARIAS, PUBLIC AFFAIRS OFFICER

He says, he says, you're not gonna believe what I'm looking at here. I said, what? He says, people are at the windows. He says, there's a guy falling out of the building next door. He says, there are people jumping. And I said, you know, I, I think, I just got a call from the Northeast Air Defense Sector. There's a hijacked plane. I think that's the plane.[16]

From ABC's transcript it was clear that Arias had called his brother in the period between the impacts of Flight 11 and Flight 175. All of the official timelines, even where they differed by a few minutes, established that the hijack of Flight 175 had been confirmed (in compliance with NORAD procedures) as of 8:42.

Four minutes later at 8:46, two events occur almost simultaneously: Flight 11 hits, and the transponder of Flight 175 goes silent — a second confirmation of its hijacking. At that moment Arias and all of NORAD knew that a synchronized multi-plane attack was in progress. The completed phone bridges had been up and running since 8:45 at the latest.

Looking deeper I realized that at least several minutes must have elapsed after Flight 11's impact before Arias made the call. People were jumping from the WTC's windows by then. So the call could not have taken place until after they had first tried the exits and concluded that they had no other choice but to jump to their deaths — a few minutes after the first WTC impact at 8:46 and no later than the second at 9:03.

The FAA's statements show that during that interval of approximately 10 or 12 minutes, the decision makers were aware of 175's hijacked status as well as its Manhattan-bound trajectory, but had issued no warnings, not even to those in the North Tower. This would explain why Arias, according to another report, felt it necessary to tell his brother, as stated in other reports, to get out of the building immediately. He must have believed that his brother was facing imminent death.[17]

Don Arias is also a former NYC firefighter. Because police and firefighters share so many similar experiences, we often develop the same attitudes in response to an emergency. I can just imagine the "command presence" in Arias's voice as he got his brother the hell out of there.

If Arias was warning his brother to leave the WTC, why wasn't the Port Authority, or NYPD, of the NY Fire Department or the Pentagon, or the White House warning anyone else to get out? Arias had been a firefighter. Could he not have thought about the danger facing his former colleagues? The White House and the Pentagon cannot successfully argue that their communications systems did not have the immediate and ready ability to contact any state or local emergency response agency with as much ease as they connected to all the rest of the federal players.

This is a test. This is only a test...

That's what the famed emergency broadcast system of the 60s, 70s, and 80s was all about. Remember? The one that always interrupted *Gunsmoke* or *Rocky and Bullwinkle* during the best parts? In 1970 and '71 when I was interning in the chief's office at LAPD we had a system called CLEMARS (California Law Enforcement Mutual Aid Radio System). My boss, Commander Carol Kirby, explained to me then that if the emergency warranted, Chief Ed Davis could talk to President Nixon with ease. Access to the system was extremely limited, and it was only intended for emergency communication between commanders and other agencies'commanders.

That technology is ubiquitous today. It won't allow 50 New York cops to talk to 50 New York FBI agents at the scene. That's an unrelated red herring offered repeatedly since 9/11. But this technology (by whatever name) absolutely enables the chief of the Port Authority police, or the mayor, or the New York FBI office to have an immediate conference with the Pentagon or the White House during a major disaster. Someone in the NMCC could have easily pushed a button and had any of these agencies on the line in a second and said, Look out, *another one's on the way.*

They could even have just used a normal telephone. There was time enough.

According to this record, no one in a senior command position attempted to do that for the people in the South Tower.

Instead, a few minutes after Flight 11 hit the North Tower at 8:46 and before Flight 175 hit the South Tower at 9:03, an All Clear notice was issued to those who had also fled the South Tower. It advised them to go back to work. For many of those who complied it was a death sentence. The third hijacking, Flight 77, had been confirmed for at least 19 minutes before 175 struck. How many lives might have been saved in even 19 minutes? No one even issued a directive to warn every airline pilot in the country then aloft. Why?

Arias wasn't the only one issuing a warning. John O'Neill, the FBI's just-retired top terrorist hunter, didn't like the idea of sending people back inside either. The systematic suppression of O'Neill's relentless pursuit of Osama bin Laden for years before 9/11, by almost every involved US Agency (State, Justice, CIA, the White House through the Attorney General; probably coordinated by the CIA), is (and will remain) one of 9/11's most enduring legends. Just days before the attacks, O'Neill had started his new job as chief of security for the World Trade Center. He perished, along with many others that day, doing his job.

Why wasn't congress being evacuated by 9:30? Flight 77, the third hijack, had turned towards Washington by 8:55. Those on the phone bridges knew it. Even the revised but unofficial "correction" by the FAA emailed to Tom Flocco on June 17th placed all relevant authorities in the loop by 8:45. Yet the Capitol wasn't evacuated for more than an hour. Everyone understood that multiple attacks were in progress against both New York and Washington. Did someone know that the Capitol would not be attacked?

There were three confirmed and connected hijackings in progress by 9:03 when the second tower was struck and televised live by CNN and by every other network that had managed to get a camera trained on the towers. Flight 77 was nearing the Pentagon. Other records indicate that the Secret Service was aware of this, almost from the moment 77 suddenly changed course (see Chapter 17). If the Secret Service knew, how could Cheney and Bush not know? The Secret Service was at their sides.

Another golden moment

A quick comparison of all these new insights proved them to be the soft but precise blows that cracked the evidentiary diamond.

Flocco's gold strike

Tom Flocco's complete story, filed later the same day, revealed even more.

> June 17, 2004 11:45 pm
> Tom Flocco.com
>
> WASHINGTON — According to the personal written statement of Navy Captain Charles J. Leidig Jr., entered into the record during

today's hearings before the National Commission on Terrorist Attacks Upon the United States, Leidig revealed that on September 10 he was asked by Brigadier General Montague Winfield to stand a portion of his duty as Deputy Director for Operations for the National Military Command Center (NMCC), which would require supervision and operation of all necessary communications as watch commander.

Leidig said "On 10 September 2001, Brigadier General Winfield, US Army, asked that I stand a portion of his duty as Deputy Director for Operations, NMCC, on the following day [September 11]. I agreed and relieved Brigadier General Winfield at 0830 on 11 September 2001."

Winfield had requested Leidig to assume his watch at what turned out to be the very outset of the September 11 attacks — but even after American Flight 11 had already been determined to be hijacked just minutes before Winfield handed over his watch to Leidig.

[According to all known timelines, the second hijacking, that of Flight 175, had been confirmed for at least ten minutes by 8:30. Winfield didn't know?]

Captain Leidig's Commission statement was 1.25 typewritten pages, large font, and double-spaced — the shortest written statement provided by any 9/11 Commission deponent as observed by this writer since the commencement of the probe.

[This] calls into question why Winfield handed over control of communications and supervision of the NMCC to Leidig during the attacks when he knew the Captain had just met the supervision qualifications to stand watch some 30 days earlier ....

[Leidig testified] "Further, I qualified in August 2001 to stand watch as the Deputy Director for Operations in the NMCC ...Shortly after assuming duty, I received the first report of a plane's striking the World Trade Center.... In response to these events, I convened a Significant Event Conference, which was subsequently upgraded to an Air Threat Conference." [This statement may indicate that Leidig was assuming the critical NMCC military communications watch position for the very first time — a fact completely lost upon the Commission, as they never thought to broach the subject for verification.]

[Note: If Leidig received accurate and quick reports of Flight 11's demise, is it remotely conceivable that he wasn't also told that Flight 175 was also a confirmed hijack, off course, and headed towards New York for at least 10 minutes?]

WHITE HOUSE CONNECTED TO NMCC

The National Transportation and Safety Board auditorium had been quiet until an individual stood up and repeatedly questioned why the

Commission was not addressing the issue of 9/11 wargames — specifically Operation Vigilant Guardian — wherein fighters were already in the air during the attacks, some just minutes away from New York City. The legitimate questions were ignored, and the petitioner was removed by secret service and FBI agents.

[I have found no public record indicating when all 9/11 wargames were terminated. Don Arias's statements suggested no live-flys on NORAD's part except in conjunction with a Joint Chief's exercise that would have put JCS in command. Other stories reported that Air National Guard planes had been aloft from Andrews AFB but armed only with bombs. It appears that the commission never asked for clarification about any of this. We know that General Arnold claimed to have terminated Vigilant Guardian just after Flight 11 crashed. What was the exact time? There are records. It is a military ritual to keep records. What about Northern Vigilance, Vigilant Warrior, and the rest?]

Commissioner John Lehman offered that while Air Force Generals Richard Meyers, Ralph Eberhart, and Larry Arnold (Ret.) had been questioned, no one had asked any questions of the "only sailor in the group," Captain Leidig. Lehman asked Leidig about the controlled phone bridges or conferences held during the attacks, which the Captain confirmed were classified and secure phone lines while also indicating that "the President can be included" in such teleconferences.

After some discussion about certain difficulties reaching the Federal Aviation Administration (FAA) and compatibility issues in connections, Leidig confirmed that Vice President Cheney and the White House were connected to the phone bridges.

At that point Chairman Kean quickly cut off Lehman's line of questioning and proceeded to Commissioner Timothy Roemer who smartly decided to pick up on Lehman's phone bridge issue. Whereupon Leidig again confirmed that "I was connected to the White House." [during the Significant Event Conference, which became an Air Threat Conference.]

In response to a pointed question, Leidig also confirmed that the NMCC had the capability to connect to Air Force One, but that it did not do so, at least not during Leidig's watch which was during most of the time period of the actual attacks when the President was still at the elementary school.

Leidig was asked, in effect, why the NMCC did not connect directly to Air Force One, to which he answered "I don't recall," and he repeated his "I don't recall" assertion.

This was the one moment in Leidig's testimony where he seemed to lose facial control and composure....

COMMENCEMENT OF THE PHONE BRIDGES

Immediately at the close of testimony by Myers, Eberhart, Arnold, and Leidig, this writer quickly walked to the head table to individually question Leidig before his aides could escort him from the auditorium.[18] The Air Force generals had left quickly.

When asked "Can you tell me the approximate time when you commenced your supervision of the phone bridges," Leidig told TomFlocco.com, "You'll have to look in the records and Commission staff statements. I can't recall the time."

We then offered to Leidig, "It had to be prior to 8:30 a.m., because the President said 'I know what's going on in New York City, and I'll have more to say about it later in the day,' a statement which was confirmed at 8:30 and 8:35 a.m. in two separate news reports just before Mr. Bush stepped into his limousine for the drive to the elementary school."

"You'll have to check the records. I can't remember," said Leidig, gathering up his papers and briefcase and leaning toward the door.

Interestingly, Leidig had also told Lehman and Roemer that Winfield relieved him and reassumed his duties as Deputy Director for Operations for the MCC just before United Flight 93 crashed in Pennsylvania and the attacks were over, which would have been around 10:00 am....

[If Winfield formally resumed command just before Flight 93 crashed, just after 10 am, some serious questions needed answering. The combat emergency was over by then. Winfield had been absent for more than an hour and a half. Where had he been? What had he been doing? Was he incommunicado? No 9/11 Commissioner ever asked.]

President Bush is attended by a round-the-clock Secret Service detail that would have, of necessity, been connected to the secure phone bridge conference lines.

[Yes, and the Secret Service was among the first agencies confirmed to have been connected to the phone bridges. How could anyone believe that if the Secret Service knew, Bush, Cheney, and Rice didn't know?]

In May 2003 Bush nominated Brigadier General Montague Winfield for promotion to the two-star rank of Major General, and Captain Charles Leidig has recently been nominated by the President to the two-star rank of Navy Admiral.

[How perfectly consistent. Like Dave Frasca at the FBI, two more key players in 9/11 were promoted.]

> Incredibly, neither the 9/11 Commission nor the Congressional Joint Intelligence Committee has ever addressed the inconsistent issues and actions surrounding the time-line during the actual two-hour period of the attacks with regard to key government players.... [Emphasis added]

Flocco, who had attended 8 of the commission's 12 public hearings, watching the rest (twice) on C-SPAN, had been at the right place, at the right time. Yet as others were losing hope he refused to quit or ease up.

Almost ready for the DA

Rarely is a criminal investigation ever totally completed. There are always unanswered questions. Detectives have caseloads and supervisors pressuring them for more clearances. DAs have schedules. Jails get full. The Constitution demands charges and trial without undue delay. Law enforcement agencies have only so much money and time. There comes a time when a decision must be made to step up to the plate or let it go; to say "This is about as good as it's going to get" and take your shot in the prosecutor's office or in court.

For me, and for this book, the problems were money, resources, access, time, and above all, a limited amount of emotional energy. One can only live deeply immersed in evil and crime for so long without paying a price. The public window was rapidly closing on 9/11. The latest conceivable time to make it a relevant public issue would be the November 2004 election. After that it would cease to be an open case for the American people. It would become, to use one of a dedicated investigator's least favorite words: history.

In this chapter we finally proved guilt in some crimes according to legal standards. These include the willful and deliberate failure to perform required duties of a public office: specifically the intentional failure to protect the public and the nation from grievous harm, with specific intent (as demonstrated by perjury, dishonest public responses, and falsified records), resulting in the unlawful death of a human being.

By definition, aside from being a violation of federal statutes, this also describes a homicide. And there are several varieties of homicide. At minimum, what we have documented is involuntary manslaughter. At a maximum, it is premeditated murder. The crimes of perjury, obstruction, falsification of records, negligence (hard to believe at this point), etc., are all lesser included or connected offenses.

I threw a final "Hail Mary" out across the Internet by asking anyone who could produce hard documentary evidence about responsibility for coordinating multiple wargames to help me out. And there was to be one last chance to get a direct answer on the wargames from those who would know, as *FTW* was able to place a live reporter, willing to ask tough questions, in the room for the last public hearing on September 11th.

CHAPTER 21

THE LAST HEARING:
FTW CONFRONTS ON THE WARGAMES
NORAD RUNS

There was to be one last opportunity to get an answer. Having kept a promise made to our subscribers since 9/11, I had put almost every available dollar of sales revenue back into the newsletter. We now had seven writers and editors working part- or full-time. One of them, Michael Kane, was a young 25-year-old activist/journalist from Long Island who had shown heart, brains, and the promise of strong leadership skills for the future. I asked him to go down for the last public hearings of the Kean Commission and get in people's faces about the wargames.

That's exactly what he did.

His resulting story (not published until July 9th) was a grand slam home run in the bottom of the 9th inning with two outs, as far as the commission was concerned.

Kane's story, titled *The Final Fraud,* established, among other things, that:

- Both commission members and 9/11-NORAD commander Ralph Eberhart were completely evasive about who would have been controlling all of the wargames on September 11th. It was a simple question.
- Neither the military nor the commissioners ever addressed the wargames directly, and their few questions and responses about the wargames were evasive, inconsistent with known data, and even pitiable for their lack of credibility.
- The Air Force Generals assumed a totally incredible position regarding NORAD's pre-9/11 duties, missions, and training.
- The Kean Commission yet again revised official times to suit their conclusions rather than seek explanations.
- Both commissioners and witnesses were well aware of my ongoing investigation into the war games.
- As a result of consistently offered "canned" answers, it appeared as though both commissioners and the NORAD commander were

shielding the wargame "maestro." In fact, General Ralph Eberhart even felt obliged to deny that possibility in his opening remarks. His comment reminded this writer of a line from Gilbert and Sullivan, "The guilty flee where no one pursueth." In this case, however, *FTW* was, in fact, in hot pursuit.

- A "phantom" radar Flight confused with Flight 11 on 9/11 might prove to be an official confirmation that a radar inject from the Vigilant Guardian exercise had confused early responses as the attacks began.
- None of the wargame questions was even superficially addressed after two spectator outbursts demanding that the commission explore them adequately.

Here is Mike Kane's story.[1]

The editorial comments by our new Assistant Managing Editor Jamey Hecht (who also edited this book) were priceless.

The Final Fraud:
9/11 Commission Closes its Doors to the Public; Cover-Up Complete

By

Michael Kane

[The players of the Warren Commission farce of our day have taken their bow. The crew begins to strike the set, the actors are going home, and soon the house is cold and the stage empty. There will be no encores, and the reviews are not good. Behind the scenes, the director is relieved but a little nervous; the producers may or may not be satisfied with the return on their investment. So many pretty microphones, such fine suits and ties! But will it play in Peoria?

In this eyewitness account, Mike Kane looks at the Commission's performance on the day of the really big show - NORAD/FAA day. He finds a chorus of costumed players mouthing their lines to their uniformed counterparts as the cameras roll. The dangerous issue they pretend to confront is nowhere to be seen, and before the harmless script comes off the press and into the bookstores, we recognize the gist: "a tale told by an idiot, full of sound and fury, signifying nothing." — JAH]

"*First of all, there's no scheme here or plot to spin this story to try to cover or take a bullet for anyone.*"

— General Eberhart, testimony to 9/11 Commission, June 19, 2004

July 9, 2004 1430 PDT (FTW) — When asked who was responsible for coordinating the multiple wargames running on the morning of September 11, 2001, General Ralph E. Eberhart, the man in charge of NORAD on the morning in question replied,"No Comment."

General Eberhart, testimony to 9/11 Commission on June 17, 2004
(left to right) Gen. Richard B. Myers, Admiral Charles Leidig,
General Ralph E. Eberhart, and Larry Arnold (Retired) moments
before being sworn in to the 9/11 Commission.

It is extremely suspect that Eberhart was unable to comment, when we look at his sworn testimony just moments before this question was posed to him on June 17, 2004, in response to Commissioner Roemer's line of questioning.

Tim Roemer was the only Commissioner to pose a question about military exercises running on the morning of 9/11. He opened by making reference to an 8:38 FAA communication to NEADS regarding a hijacked aircraft headed to New York. The response from NEADS was, "Is this real world or an exercise?" FAA response was, "No, this is not an exercise, not a test."

Roemer then asked General Eberhart:

My question is, you were postured for an exercise against the former Soviet Union. Did that help or hurt? Did that help in terms of were more people prepared? Did you have more people ready? Were more fighters fueled with more fuel? Or did this hurt in terms of people thinking, "No, there's no possibility that this is real world; we're engaged in an exercise," and delay things?

Eberhart's response:

Sir, my belief is that it helped because of the manning, because of the focus, because the crews — they have to be airborne in 15 minutes, and that morning, because of the exercise, they were airborne in 6 or 8 minutes. And so I believe that focus helped.

If the wargames helped "because of the focus," why would General Eberhart be reluctant to go on record regarding the issue of just who was the central person coordinating that focus? Was the General himself, the man who headed NORAD that very morning, in charge of coordinating the multiple wargames on 9/11?

No Comment.

From Russia with love

From the moment Generals Myers, Eberhart, and Arnold were sworn in to testify, they continually stated that NORAD's "military posture on 9/11, by law, by policy, and in practice was focused on responding to external threats, threats originating outside of our borders" (a quotation from General Myers's sworn testimony).

But NORAD was not simply running "an exercise against the former Soviet Union" on 9/11, as Commissioner Roemer's question insinuated. That was only one of the multiple wargames running that morning, titled Northern Vigilance, which was simulating an air attack coming out of Russia. To insinuate, as Commissioner Roemer did, that this was the only exercise that morning lends credence to the three Generals' false claim that NORAD's only mission was to protect against external threats.

The multiple war games running on 9/11 also included (but were not limited to) Vigilant Guardian, which involved hijacking scenarios over the continental United States. None of the war games was ever referenced by name at any time during the hearings. The details of these exercises are the Achilles heel of the "external threat" mantra parroted by all three generals, and these details seem to be classified.

There was one other mention of the wargames from Commissioner Lehman, in which he referred to the military exercises as one of the "happy circumstances" on the morning of 9/11.

In response to General Myers's statement regarding NORAD's legal mission, Commissioner Gorelick noted that it includes control of the airspace above the domestic US (the Continental United States, or CONUS). She read the mandate aloud: "Providing surveillance and control of the airspace of Canada and the United States." Myers actually had the nerve to attempt to use Posse Comitatus as a rationale for absolving the Air Force of responsibility for what happened on 9/11. He claimed that the 1878 Posse Comitatus law (which has, ironically, been seriously undermined by the Patriot Act in the aftermath of 9/11) made it illegal for the military to be involved in "domestic law enforcement." Of course, it does. But that has nothing to do with 9/11, since hijack response had been a NORAD responsibility for decades; and for obvious reasons, nobody had ever raised a Posse Comitatus objection to that mandate in the past (because, for instance, the police do not fly F-16s).

Commissioner Ben Veniste asked General Richard Myers if he had been made aware of the arrest of Zacarias Moussaoui on August 17 as a suspected "suicide hijacker." Myers responded, "I think I would've but I don't recall."

Ben Veniste asked Myers the following question:

> Had you received such information tying together the potential reflected in the August 6th PDB memorandum, that was titled Bin Laden Determined to Strike in the United States, together with this additional information (regarding the Moussaoui suicide-hijacking information), **might you have followed up on a training scenario**, at the least, such as the Positive Force training scenario, where a hijacked plane was presumed to fly into the Pentagon, a proposal that was made and rejected in the year 2000? [emphasis added]

Note: We have already documented how NORAD was, in fact, aggressively implementing such drills.

This is skillful deception, the kind to which Ben Veniste has grown accustomed during his time on the 9/11 Commission. To pose such a question when it is a matter of public record that **such drills were running on the morning of 9/11** is a patently misleading line of questioning.

Myers responded:

I can't answer the hypothetical. It's more — it's the way that we were directed to posture, looking outward.

He reverted to the trusty (but absurd) mantra chanted by all three Generals.

While Commissioners Ben Veniste and Gorelick appeared to be asking "hard-hitting" questions, they always stopped short of anything that would get to the heart of the matter. They made no mention of the wargames running on the morning of 9/11, neither in this round of hearings nor during the previous round, in which Defense Secretary Donald Rumsfeld spoke under oath.

<http://globalresearch.ca/articles/KAN403A.html>

Furthermore, not one of the Commissioners brought up the 67 Air Force interceptions successfully executed during the year prior to 9/11 (AP, August 13, 2002). After the hearing Commissioner John Thompson was asked if there had been any discussion by the commissioners regarding the speed at which the fighter jets responded on 9/11. He said that there had not been, but that there would be.

When?

Such concerns were addressed very briefly during the Commission's first hearings focusing on NORAD, back in May 2003, but nothing of importance was explored at that time. <http://www.9/11commission.gov/archive/hearing2/9/11Commission_Hearing_2003-05-23.htm>

"Waste of time"

The Commissioners were asked about the wargames — after the hearings. When Commissioner Ben Veniste was asked why he chose not to ask questions about the war games running on 9/11, he claimed the time allotted was short and that he had done the best he could. When asked if he knew who was in charge of coordinating the multiple war games that morning, he replied, "You'd have to check with staff on that." To this same crucial question, Commissioner Gorelick replied, "we did look at the exercises running on that day. I don't know the answer to that question." When asked why she chose not to question the generals about the war games she replied, "The staff concluded [that the war games] were not an inhibition to the military doing its job, and therefore I wasn't going to waste my time with that."

Apparently some members of the audience did not agree.

Immediately before Commissioner Gorelick began her allotted time for questioning the generals, a member of the audience, 9/11 activist Nicholas Levis, yelled out, "Ask about the war games that were planned for 9/11." Then another audience member followed his lead:

"Tell us about the war games."

These audience member comments were published in the Associated Press transcript of the hearings. <http://wid.ap.org/transcripts/040617commission911_1.html>

At this point, tension filled the room. Shortly into the questioning, one of the audience members who had just bellowed at the commission stood up and shouted; "This is an outrage! My questions are not being answered, and I'm walking out!"

He was carrying an American flag as he was escorted out.

He must have realized the wargames were not going to be addressed in any meaningful fashion. This outburst, though clearly audible, was omitted from the Associated Press transcript. It seems that this outburst may have been what prompted Commissioner Tim Roemer to throw the one and only softball question about the exercises at General Eberhart later in the hearings. It's regrettable that the protester didn't shout one or two of his questions before being escorted out, but his passionate gesture was helpful in its own way.

Kyle Hence of 9/11 CitizensWatch asked Commissioner Gorelick why fighter jets weren't scrambled from Andrews Air Force Base. Mr. Hence stated that, to his knowledge, at least three fighters from Andrews were performing exercises over 200 miles away on that morning. This left Washington DC defenseless on 9/11. When asked how that could possibly be allowed, Commissioner Gorelick would not comment.

When asked if the commission had ever addressed the multiple war games running on 9/11, and who was in charge of coordinating them, Chairman Kean responded, "Yes, we did, it wasn't a coordination, there were a number of them going on as there are periodically but they were not, and they helped in one way because there were people available who wouldn't have been available otherwise."

When following up for clarification on whether there was an individual in charge of coordinating these drills, Chairman Kean replied, "No, I don't think so. You might want to check with staff on that."

Staff Communication director Jonathan Stull, after being asked the same line of questions repeatedly, has stated he is "looking into this." Mr. Stull later stated,

"This is an issue that the Commission is looking into and will address in the final report." We shall see how far into this they look.

New timeline?

The Commission staff report presented new times for some critical events on 9/11. Based upon this new information, the military response time has been shortened, and the FAA is left as the scapegoat. Least believable is the new time for FAA notification to the military that UA 93 was off course. Here are the new times for events on the morning of 9/11 compared to the original official times.

NOTE: 51 minutes had now been added to the time delay in the FAA's notification of Flight 93's confirmed hijacking. This demonstrates concern about the questions raised in the preceding chapter, and contradicts every official and published record published since 9/11.

Event	Original Official timeline	New 9/11 Staff timeline
FAA informs NORAD about AA11	8:40 (NORAD timeline)	8:37:52
UA 175 transponder switches to different signal	8:42	8:47
FAA informs NORAD about UA 175	8:43	9:02
Phone bridge FAA (disputed)	8:46	Some time after 9:03
FAA informs NORAD about UA 93	9:16	10:07 (is this believable?)
FAA informs NORAD about AA77. They claim the old 9:24 scramble order was actually for "Phantom Flight 11"	9:24	9:36
Cheney shoot-down order for UA 93	9:55	10:20 or so
UA 93 'crash' time - still in dispute	10:06	10:03

**Special thanks to Nicholas Levis for assistance with timeline chart analysis.

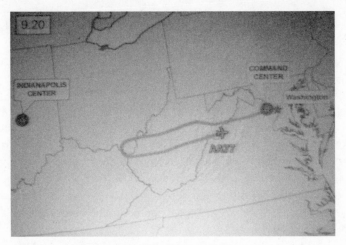

The Commission's visual presentation of Flight 77's path, made
from "radar reconstruction" performed after 9/11

Pentagon "phantom flight"

One of the most shocking claims coming out of the final public hearing was what
the Commission called the "phantom flight." This referred to the plane alleged to
have struck the Pentagon. An FAA communication to NORAD stated it was
Flight 11 — which had already struck 1 WTC — that was off-course and headed
to Washington DC, not Flight 77. The report states it was "unable to identify the
source of this mistaken FAA information."

At 8:54, Flight 77 began deviating from its flight plan, first with a slight turn
toward the south. It then "disappeared completely" at 8:56, according to the 9/11
Commission staff report.

The report continues:

> Shortly after 9:00, Indianapolis Center started notifying other agen-
> cies that American 77 was missing and had possibly crashed .... At 9:09,
> they reported the loss of contact to the FAA regional center, which
> passed this information to FAA headquarters at 9:24 .... Radar recon-
> structions performed after 9/11 reveal that FAA radar equipment
> tracked the flight from the moment its transponder was turned off at
> 8:56 a.m. But for 8 minutes and 13 seconds, between 8:56 a.m. and
> 9:05 a.m., this primary radar information on American 77 was not dis-
> played to controllers at Indianapolis Center. The reasons are technical,
> arising from the way the software processed radar information, as well
> as from poor primary radar coverage where American 77 was flying.
>
> In sum, Indianapolis Center never saw Flight 77 turn around ....
> American 77 traveled undetected for 36 minutes on a course heading
> due east for Washington, DC.

Benedict Sliney, the FAA's National Operations Manager on 9/11 (his *first day* in that position) was questioned by Chairman Kean about the radar & transponder issues of Flight 77. Even after the plane's transponder signal had stopped, Sliney stated, "There are radars that would have seen the target regardless. Would they have known what to be looking for? I do not know."[2]

Orders were issued from the Mission Crew Commander at NEADS at 9:23:

> *"Okay... scramble Langley. Head them towards the Washington area."*

The order to scramble was given to fighters out of Langley Air Force base in Virginia, leaving the fighters scrambled from Otis over New York. However, the Langley fighters were headed east, not north, because they followed a "generic" scramble order. This sent them over the ocean, out of local airspace, because the lead pilot and local FAA controller incorrectly assumed the flight plan instruction to go east was newer guidance that superseded the original scramble order.

Why didn't they follow the scramble order as issued from the Mission Crew Commander at NEADS? A direct order from a Commander most certainly supercedes any "generic" plan.

It is claimed the Langley pilots were never briefed about the reason they were scrambled. As the lead pilot explained, "I reverted to the Russian threat .... I'm thinking cruise missile threat from the sea. You know, you look down and see the Pentagon burning and I thought the bastards snuck one by us."

Seeing how the Langley jets were scrambled out to sea, this "generic" scramble plan must have been assuming an external attack coming from across the Atlantic. But how is it conceivable that well after both Twin Towers are struck, fighter pilots were still thinking of a generic "Russian threat"?

It is claimed the pilots were never made aware that the threat was from hijacked airliners. Wouldn't that information have been included in the NEADS scramble order at 9:23 or shortly thereafter? Two towers are burning and no one tells the fighter jocks?

The Otis jets were scrambled at 8:46 in response to the hijacking of Flight 11. Because the plane's transponder signal had disappeared, NEADS spent the next several minutes searching their radar for the "elusive primary radar return." The Otis jets were airborne by 8:53, well after Flight 11 hit the World Trade Center. But they were sent out off the coast of Long Island because, it is claimed, NEADS did not know where to send the alert fighter aircraft. This allowed Flight 175 to crash into the second World Trade Tower. This is almost exactly what happened to the jets scrambled from Langley, allowing the Pentagon to be struck.

This information is all based on the commission staff report.

<http://www.9/11commission.gov/hearings/hearing12/staff_statement_17.pdf>

NMCC communication

Also under oath beside the three Generals sat Admiral Charles Leidig, the stand-in Deputy Director for Operations of the National Military Command Center

(NMCC) on 9/11 at precisely 0830. This ended up putting him in charge of facilitating the first conference call at the NMCC on 9/11 between multiple agencies including the FAA and NORAD. Throughout the morning there were difficulties getting the FAA into the conference call, which hampered communication flow for some time. Leidig said the FAA was "intermittently" in the call. He said he understood there were compatibility issues between their secure lines and the FAA's, which caused the FAA to "drop out" of the conference call.

NOTE: The FAA had never mentioned these difficulties before. They didn't even mention them in their official statement submitted the same day. In fact, the FAA release, submitted the same day, flatly contradicted the entirely new position taken about Flight 77 by the military:

> "NORAD logs indicate that the FAA made formal notification about American Flight 77 at 9:24 a.m., but information about the flight was conveyed continuously during the phone bridges before the formal notification.

Admiral Leidig stated the NMCC was connected to the White House but not to Air Force One. Why not? "I do not recall." Investigative reporter Tom Flocco has provided a detailed analysis of the strange circumstances surrounding Admiral Leidig's assignment. He was asked by Brigadier General Montague Winfield on September 10th to stand a portion of his duty at 8:30 am on September 11th.

NORAD runs

Mike Kane's questions clearly disturbed General Eberhart and his staff. Not long after we published his account, Kane sent me the following account of how the questioning had gone down.

> June 17, 2004 - The Questioning of Eberhart & Co.
>
> After receiving a statement of No Comment from General Eberhart regarding who coordinated the multiple war games running on the morning of 9/11, a man in military uniform threw his arm in my chest pushing me away from the General.
>
> Another man accompanying the General, wearing a blue suit and glasses, turned to me and said; "You have any questions ask me. You're a reporter?"
>
> I replied, "Yes I am,"
>
> He said, "O.K., I'll be here." He turned and walked out of the conference room quickly. General Eberhart and those accompanying him made their way out to the lobby in front of the conference room. The General spoke, very briefly, to a few individuals as they made their way out.
>
> They headed towards the escalator to head up, instead of heading out of the front exit which was right there. It was obvious this man's

statement that he would be there to answer my questions was not true. I followed them towards the escalator catching this same man and said, "Now could I ask you a few questions?"

Before I could finish this statement he turned abruptly at me and said, "I'll be back in a few seconds."

I asked, "What's your name?"

Just as abruptly, he turned back facing up the escalator and walked briskly up the steps without giving his name. I followed him up as he kicked his step into a higher gear to catch up with the others who were further ahead of him. I had to decide whether to chase after them or head back to the conference room for the start of the next portion of the hearing from the FAA.

I decided not to pursue them any further.

It was made very clear that none of these men had any interest in answering my questions. Plus I was uncertain of how such aggressive reporting tactics would be greeted far away from the conference room. I had no cameraman with me, only an audio recorder that provided less of a "shield" for such tactics.

It was odd to see them exit this way. It would have made more sense for them to have used the exit at the bottom of the escalator where I expected their ride(s) to be waiting. However, this may have left them more susceptible to reporter's questions. The exit route they took cut through the shopping center and food court heading out towards the Metro Station. It is hard to believe these men were leaving to catch the subway. It must be assumed they were going to be picked up on the other side of the building — far away from reporters & cameras.

At the end of the day, Commissioner Kean left through the exit at the bottom of the escalator, where a car was waiting for him. He didn't exit on the other side of the building, but Mr. Kean was not trying to avoid reporters.[3]

By the time *FTW* had published Kane's story, we had learned of another wargame exercise on 9/11. Known as Tripod II, it was, in fact, being set up (and possibly conducted) on September 11 in lower Manhattan.

Another coincidence?

Unlike all the other wargames of September 11, Tripod II did not involve the military. It involved the Justice Department and New York City and State authorities. It had nothing to do with hijackings but was instead an exercise focused on a biowarfare attack that had been set up on New York's Pier 29, about two miles from the World Trade Center.

Tripod II would effectively move the search for the maestro from the Pentagon into the White House.

CHAPTER

GIULIANI AND TRIPOD II

*N*ote: *Before examining the pivotal testimony given by former New York Mayor Rudolph Giuliani on May 19th, 2004 at the Kean Commission hearings, it is important to note that — as of this writing — the Commission's website has not published, or made available, Giuliani's written statement (read into the record) nor any transcript of his testimony during questioning. However, the Commission's final report was released on July 21, 2004. As far as we can tell, his is the only testimony from those or previous hearings not to have been published thus far. There is good reason for this. The substance of his remarks was widely circulated throughout the Internet within hours, but no transcript or evidence of a recording was known or available as I sat down to write this chapter two weeks later. This posed a problem in reporting on what Giuliani actually said.*

According to evidentiary standards practiced by journalists and law enforcement, the only way to quote Giuliani's remarks would have been to produce a tape-recording, a verifiable transcript, or an on-the-record witness who could testify as to what Giuliani actually said. Without that there would have been no "proof" according to our standards. When I discovered this, I immediately sent out an e-mail alert to researchers like Paul Thompson and the "9/11 Truth Alliance" list to which I had belonged for two years. It was a straightforward plea. Someone had to provide a verifiable record.

Within 24 hours that record was available and ironclad. List member Matt Gaines sent an e-mail stating that Berkeley radio station KPFA had a downloadable audio file of Giuliani's testimony on their website. Kyle Hence, co-founder of 9/11 Citizens Watch and Unanswered Questions, responded a few minutes later with a complete transcript that had been immediately typed after watching a video of the hearing made by independent New York videographer and long-time activist Joe Friendly. Paul Thompson, founder of the awe-inspiring 9/11 timeline at www.cooperatriveresearch.org, located a transcript through the (expensive) Lexis-Nexis news service.

That transcript matched perfectly the one provided by Hence and Friendly. We now had evidence.

What Rudolph Giuliani said on May 19th is etched in stone. It cannot be denied. What was also immensely hope-giving was watching how an entire new cadre of dedicated

Americans had taught themselves to investigate, to make records, to protect evidence, and to respond quickly. As a group we had come a long way since September 11ᵗʰ.

Tripod II

Giuliani dropped the bomb about the Tripod II wargame in his opening statement. The implications of his disclosure were to reach far and deep.

> And the reason Pier 92 was selected as the command center was because on the next day, on September 12, Pier 92 was going to have a drill. It had hundreds of people here from FEMA, from the federal government, from the state, from the State Emergency Management Office, and they were getting ready for a drill for a biochemical attack. So that was going to be the place they were going to have the drill.
>
> The equipment was already there. So we were able to establish a command center there within three days that was two and a half to three times bigger than the command center that we had lost at 7 World Trade Center. And it was from there that the rest of the search and rescue effort was completed.[1]

It wasn't until the last commissioner faced Giuliani that any question remotely addressing the crucial issue about notifications and warnings was posed.

> …[Commissioner Fred] Fielding: I think I'm the clean-up hitter here, so there are a couple of things I want to catch on. But first of all, there's some confusion in my mind and others' as to the relationship between OEM [Mayor's Office of Emergency Management] and the Port Authority. **For instance, if the Port Authority at Newark heard that there was a plane headed for Manhattan, could they communicate to the command center of OEM?…** [emphasis added]

Great question!
Giuliani replied:

> Giuliani: **Yes. Port Authority did have, and I'm sure continues to have direct communication with OEM, and frequent communication with OEM. We did exercises and drills with the Port Authority on a fairly frequent basis, including simulating a plane crash for this very reason,** to make sure that the Port Authority, the police department, fire department, the Nassau County people could all respond correctly.
>
> **So they have direct — they have direct communication** with OEM. **And the building, the World Trade Center,** I think you'll have to check with others that know the statistics, I think it was the most responded to building in the city. So they were — they were in — the police, the fire and Port Authority were used to working together in that building. **They do it like seven or eight times a day.**

Why wasn't it done on September 11th? How would the Port Authority hear about missing commercial aircraft? Only from the FAA, NEADS, or NORAD. This implies that the communications ability existed. Telephones existed.

> Fielding: OK. Thank you. One follow-up question — one final question, excuse me. We haven't talked about the aftermath of 9/11, but I know that **FEMA had a major role in this city.** And I guess at one point there must have been some question as to whether there needed to be a federalization of the clean-up effort. And we really could use your comments on what happened because we've had no information on that. [emphasis added]
>
> **Giuliani:** So, you know, that might have been a situation where FEMA would come in, and FEMA would have to help and assist, because the resources aren't there. In New York, or Chicago, or Los Angeles, these police organizations are going to be so big, you have got to kind of work with them instead of try to direct them.

What do we know about Tripod II? *New York* magazine provided more information.

> On the morning of September 12 Richard Sheirer, director of the mayor's Office of Emergency Management, was scheduled to conduct a biological-terrorism drill in a cavernous commercial warehouse on the Hudson. Known as Tripod — short for "trial point of distribution" — the exercise was to test how quickly Sheirer's staff could administer treatments at the kind of ad hoc medical centers that would be set up all over the city in the event of an actual attack. For an audience, **Sheirer had lined up Mayor Rudy Giuliani, the police and fire commissioners, and representatives of the FBI, and the Federal Emergency Management Agency (FEMA)** ....
>
> The night of Tuesday the 11th, Sheirer and his staff never left the Police Academy .... Sheirer knew he needed another building, one big enough to house a command center the size of a football field, but also secure enough to house the mayor. The location was obvious: he commandeered the facility on the Hudson where he had been scheduled to do his Tripod drill the following day. It was a space Sheirer knew well — when he was a rookie in the Fire Department, he had organized quilting and antique fairs there as a side job ....
>
> The new command center is organized just the way the original was: **FEMA and OEM officials sit on a raised platform known as Command and Control.** Surrounding them are ten sections: Health and Medical, Logistics, Transportation, Infrastructure, Law Enforcement, Debris Removal, Aerial Imaging and Mapping, Machinery, Utilities, and Joint Information Center.... [emphasis added][2]

The official website of the Mayor's Office of Emergency Management (OEM) provided still more data. I found two postings relating to Tripod II.

> Press Release — TRIPOD
>
> FOR IMMEDIATE RELEASE Wednesday, May 22, 2002
>
> NEW YORK CITY OFFICE OF EMERGENCY MANAGEMENT
> HOLDS TRIAL POINT-OF-DISPENSING DRILL (TRIPOD)
>
> Drill for Distribution of Medication In the Event of a Biological Attack Had Been Scheduled for September 12, 2001
>
> The New York City Office of Emergency Management (OEM) today held the first-ever Trial Point of Dispensing drill — also known as "Operation TriPOD" — to test OEM's effectiveness in responding to a biological attack (see Event Photos). Tripod is a six-hour, real-time **drill administered by OEM, in cooperation with the United States Department of Justice** (USDoJ), the Weill Medical College of Cornell Medical Center, the New York City Department of Health (DOH), the New York City Fire Department (FDNY), and the New York City Police Department (NYPD), along with the American Red Cross of Greater New York. [emphasis added]
>
> Tripod had originally been scheduled to take place on September 12th, 2001, at Pier 92 — which ironically had served as the temporary home of OEM shortly after the terrorist attacks on 9/11 ....
>
> US DoJ Assistant Attorney General Deborah J. Daniels said, "The Office of Justice Programs, through its **Office for Domestic Preparedness,** is pleased to support the New York City Tripod Exercise. We look forward to strengthening our partnership with the City of New York, through continued strong support of its domestic preparedness activities." [emphasis added][3]

A second press release posted on the same site announced that Tripod II was eventually conducted in May of 2002 at the same location, New York's Pier 92.[4]

When he testified before the Kean Commission, former New York Mayor Rudolph Giuliani provided new information and added even more weight to the evidence showing that the wargames had been used with the intent of delaying response on 9/11. His testimony posed even more contradictions to the official testimonies from our nation's leaders as to who in the National Command Authority became aware and involved on 9/11, and at what times. Importantly, Giuliani also provided still another indirect corroboration that the wargames, either through radar "inserts" or live-fly exercises, had been used to delay and confuse emergency response. There could be no other explanation. Too many people had described confusion and paralysis directly attributable to those exercises.

Any investigation of the wargames by the Kean commission and the major media had been avoided with a discipline and consistency that could have no other purpose by this time except to conceal guilt.

Under oath

Almost nothing in Giuliani's testimony reconciles with what we have presented in the preceding three chapters. We pick up his testimony as he recounts events that took place between 9:03 and 9:38 AM. All of the phone bridges were established before 9:03, and Flight 93 had been a fourth confirmed hijacking since 9:36. As of this writing I have seen no recorded effort by anyone in the National Command Authority to contact New York authorities and issue warnings before the impact of Flight 175. Instead, if Giuliani's testimony is to be believed, he had to call Washington himself. He does not mention any efforts to contact any New York agency by any federal agency. Why?

Records show that a number of communications channels were working and available at this time. Don Arias had — at minimum — been able to call his brother.

> A little below St. Vincent's Hospital, we could see the fire in the Tower. But we saw a big explosion [Flight 175]. And we didn't know what it was. We probably concluded that it was just an after effect of the original attack. But within seconds of seeing it, we received a phone call from the police and were notified that a second plane had hit, and realized at that point that obviously it was a terrorist attack ....
>
> I had already been informed by my chief of staff *that he had reached the White House and by the police commissioner, who I think had reached the Defense Department. I'm not sure exactly.* But both of them had assured me that we had gotten air support, because that's why I wanted to reach the White House. I wanted to make sure that we had air defense for the city ....
>
> And my chief of staff told me that *he was informed by the White House that there were seven planes that were unaccounted for.* And at this point, *I knew of two,* and I had heard reports that the Pentagon had been attacked, that the Sears Tower had been attacked and several other buildings. [emphasis added]

Who had told Giuliani about the two missing planes before this? Such information must have originated with NORAD, NEADS or the FAA. Those communications channels were obviously functioning at that time. But then why no warning? The only likely explanation here is that lower command levels, knowing that the National Command Authority, the White House, and the Pentagon had taken command, assumed that the warnings would come from higher up and thus be more quickly heeded.

So I got through to the White House. Chris Henick was on the phone, who was the, who was then *the deputy political director to President Bush.* And I said to him, "Chris, was the Pentagon attacked?"

And he said, "Confirmed." [Note: the Pentagon was struck at 9:41]

And then I asked him if we had air support. I said, "Have you — do we have air support? Do you have jets out, because I think we're going to get hit again?"

He said, *"The jets were dispatched 12 minutes ago and they should be there very shortly,* and they should be able to defend you against further attack." And then he said, *"We're evacuating the White House and the vice president will call you back very, very shortly."*

[Note: a number of mainstream press accounts fix the White House evacuation order at between 9:41 and 9:45 AM. Thus, there are two events fixing Giuliani's Henick conversation at between 9:41 and 9:45.]

Are we to assume that no one in the White House had Giuliani's number? He was a major player in the Republican Party, a strong supporter of George W. Bush. Why was he talking to a political director and not to the Pentagon or the Situation Room in the White House? Clarke was there. Rice was there. The Situation Room was hooked up to NORAD, the Pentagon, the FAA, the FBI — everybody. He, or someone on his staff, had the numbers.

Not adding up

The problem with the Giuliani-Henick call is that its timing is bounded by three parameters that don't fit together:

- The call starts some time after the Pentagon was hit at 9:41.
- Henick tells Giuliani that fighters "were dispatched 12 minutes ago" to protect "you," i.e., New York City, and we know that the only fighters sent to NYC left from Otis AFB at 8:46 — twelve minutes after that would be *8:58.*
- The end of the Giuliani-Henick call is followed immediately by the start of the Cheney-Giuliani call (see below) and the immediate collapse of the WTC South Tower at *9:59.*

For the sake of argument, let's say that this conversation occurred five minutes after the Pentagon was struck. This would mean that the White House told Giuliani that fighter aircraft had been scrambled and sent to New York seven minutes after 9:37 or 9:41 (depending upon which timeline is used) or between 9:44 and 9:48. The final Kean Commission report released on July 22, 2004, makes no mention of any fighters being sent to New York at this time. The only scramble order even close to Giuliani's account is the scrambling of fighters from Langley Air Force Base to protect Washington at 9:23, which roughly (very roughly) matches the timing of Giuliani's conversation with Henick.

The former mayor's testimony appears to be referring to the Otis fighters that had been directed to establish a Combat Air Patrol (CAP) over New York. But that poses another problem. If this is the case then Giuliani's testimony places the Otis scramble order almost an hour later than official NORAD and NEADS accounts. Were these some other fighter aircraft? If so they have not been mentioned anywhere. And why did Henick not mention the Otis fighters that were — according to NORAD and eyewitness accounts — already in a very visible low-altitude Combat Air Patrol over Manhattan? Giuliani should have been able to see and hear them. Every other New Yorker saw them.

Relying on the testimony of fighter pilots Otis AFB Nash and Duffy, the Kean Commission is quite specific:

> The FAA cleared the airspace. Radar data show that at 9:13, when the Otis fighters were about 115 miles away from the city, the fighters exited their holding pattern and set a course direct for Manhattan. They arrived at 9:25 and set up a combat air patrol (CAP) over the city. (p.24)

Are we to believe that Giuliani somehow remained oblivious to the fighters' presence when every New Yorker was jumping for bitter joy at the arrival of air cover? Are we to believe that no police or fire official told him that the fighters were there? That he couldn't hear them?

The only available benchmarks suggest that the call from Cheney took place much earlier than Giuliani claims. If we reference it to when the scramble order was issued at Otis AFB, the source of New York's fighter cover (8:46), then Giuliani spoke to Henick sometime around 8:58, or about five minutes before 175 struck at 9:03. If Henick knew about other missing planes, he was obviously getting information (at least indirectly) from NORAD and NEADS. From whom? The Secret Service seems the most likely candidate since there are numerous records of their active involvement by this time. At that time it was also known that 175 had been en route to lower Manhattan for 16 minutes. There is no mention of Henick issuing any warning to the New York mayor that a second plane was about to attack.

How could the White House staffer have been certain about "12 minutes" unless there had been a log? He was precise. Where is that log? Why was a political staffer in possession of better data than the Mayor of New York? What does this suggest then about the timing of a call Giuliani then received from Dick Cheney immediately after talking to Henick?

> *And I put down the phone and within seconds got a call in another room from the vice president.* I walked over to that room, picked up the phone. The White House operator was on the phone and said, "Mr. Mayor, the vice president will be on in a moment."
>
> And at that point, I heard a click. The desk started to shake and I heard next Chief Esposito, who was the uniformed head of the police

department. I'm sure it was his voice. I heard him say, "The [South] tower is down. The tower has come down."

The South Tower collapsed at 9:59 AM and was recorded live by a multitude of cameras. This is confirmation that Dick Cheney was making command decisions and in all communications loops at least by this time. But if the White House call took place at 8:58 then — more likely and in conformity with what we already have established — Dick Cheney was actually "hands on" much sooner. As we have seen, Cheney was already in that role between 8:45 (FAA) and no later than about 9:15. The Secret Service, which had snatched Cheney out of his office after Flight 175 had hit at 9:03, was fully informed of all developments, and they never left Cheney's side.

> So the police commissioner and I and the deputy police commissioner, *we jointly decided that we had to try to get everyone out of the building* [North Tower]. So we went downstairs into the basement. We tried two or three exits, could not get out. I don't know if they were locked or blocked or - but we couldn't get out ....

Here is more agonizing confirmation that no evacuation warnings had been issued for either tower prior to 9:02. Yet full knowledge of the danger was available to the National Command Authority that Flight 175 had turned towards New York at 8:42. Twenty silent minutes passed when many of those who died could have been saved.

There is a record of one warning being issued to those in the South Tower. For some reason it did not get through. According to a written statement read into the record the same day that Giuliani testified by Kean Commission staff member John Farmer:

> For example, although the FDNY commanders at the North Tower advised Port Authority police and that tower's building personnel to evacuate the South Tower, shortly before 9:00 a.m., there is no evidence that this advice was communicated effectively to the building personnel in the South Tower. A vital few minutes may have been lost, and when that tower did make its announcement to evacuate at 9:02 a.m., it was the ambiguous advice that everyone may wish to start an orderly evacuation if warranted by conditions on their floor. The Port Authority's Jersey City Police desk was also unaware of the evacuation decisions when, at 9:11 a.m., it advised workers on the 64th floor of the South Tower to stay near the stairwells and wait for assistance.

This was at least ten minutes after Don Arias had placed the call to his brother.

Giuliani's mention of Tripod II, FEMA, and the Department of Justice all rang bells with me. The same grouping of names had appeared in a White House press release placing the vice president in charge (both operationally and from a review standpoint) of a Bush administration plan to protect the nation against terrorist attacks.

CHAPTER 23

DICK CHENEY, FEMA, AND "PERSONS OF INTEREST"

The discovery of the Tripod II exercise in Manhattan being "set up" on September 11th changed the entire dynamic of who, or what, might have been coordinating the war-games of 9/11. Looking for a person or entity inside the Pentagon was pointless now that we had to account for the coordination of an additional exercise involving civilian federal agencies working in concert with state and local agencies. The answer — the White House — seemed obvious, but it needed verification.

The problematic, but enormously useful Barbara Honegger, provided, among her many postings to the 9/11 Truthalliance list, still another crucial piece of evidence in the spring of 2004 when she pointed to a White House press release issued in May 2001. This document placed Dick Cheney in charge of planning, preparing for, and coordinating all US response to a terror attack. Following up, I was able to add other material that placed Cheney in a quiet but unequivocal hands-on management role, before, during, and after 9/11. In that process I came across two powerful, but little-known, men who would soon be among my top "persons-of-interest" in the crimes of 9/11.

> For Immediate Release
> Office of the Press Secretary
> May 8, 2001
>
> Statement by the President
> Domestic Preparedness Against Weapons of Mass Destruction
>
> Protecting America's homeland and citizens from the threat of weapons of mass destruction is one of our Nation's important national security challenges. Today, more nations possess chemical, biological, or nuclear weapons than ever before. Still others seek to join them. Most troubling of all, the list of these countries includes some of the world's least-responsible states — states for whom terror and blackmail are a

way of life. Some non-state terrorist groups have also demonstrated an interest in acquiring weapons of mass destruction.

Against this backdrop, it is clear that the threat of chemical, biological, or nuclear weapons being used against the United States — while not immediate — is very real. That is why our Nation actively seeks to deny chemical, biological, and nuclear weapons to those seeking to acquire them. That is why, together with our allies, we seek to deter anyone who would contemplate their use. And that is also why we must ensure that our Nation is prepared to defend against the harm they can inflict.

Should our efforts to reduce the threat to our country from weapons of mass destruction be less than fully successful, prudence dictates that the United States be fully prepared to deal effectively with the consequences of such a weapon being used here on our soil.

Today, numerous Federal departments and agencies have programs to deal with the consequences of a potential use of a chemical, biological, radiological, or nuclear weapon in the United States. Many of these Federal programs *offer training, planning,* and assistance to state and local governments. *But to maximize their effectiveness, these efforts need to be seamlessly integrated, harmonious, and comprehensive.*

Therefore, I have asked Vice President Cheney to oversee the development of a coordinated national effort so that we may do the very best possible job of protecting our people from catastrophic harm. I have also asked Joe Allbaugh, the Director of the Federal Emergency Management Agency, to create an Office of National Preparedness. This Office will be responsible for implementing the results of those parts of the national effort overseen by Vice President Cheney that deal with consequence management. Specifically it will coordinate all Federal programs dealing with weapons of mass destruction consequence management within the Departments of Defense, Health and Human Services, Justice, and Energy, the Environmental Protection Agency, and other federal agencies. The Office of National Preparedness will work closely with state and local governments to ensure their planning, training, and equipment needs are addressed. FEMA will also work closely with the Department of Justice, in its lead role for crisis management, to ensure that all facets of our response to the threat from weapons of mass destruction are coordinated and cohesive. I will periodically chair a meeting of the National Security Council to review these efforts.

No governmental responsibility is more fundamental than protecting the physical safety of our Nation and its citizens. In today's world, this obligation includes protection against the use of weapons of mass destruction. I look forward to working closely with Congress so that together we can meet this challenge.[1] [emphasis added]

This press release was issued May 8, 2001, about a month prior to the change in NORAD's intercept protocols. While a bit vague in some areas, it does establish certain things. Dick Cheney was charged to oversee the creation of an approach that was "seamlessly integrated and harmonious." He was also placed in a supervisory management role over the activities of the entire effort, which were operational under FEMA's supreme command. "Planning and training" were specifically addressed so this would automatically include war game exercises like Tripod II and all the NORAD/Joint Chiefs wargames of 9/11: Vigilant Guardian, Vigilant Warrior, Northern Vigilance, etc.

Although the announcement focused on weapons of mass destruction, the central issue and rationale for Cheney's management role was "seamless" communication and coordination of responses. The Departments of Defense and Health and Human Services were specifically included in the mandate and placed under Cheney's control. This will become critical for understanding the significance of the roles played by two new names in our 9/11 investigation.

If seamless and coordinated response was the priority, then (by definition) this mandate would create overlap to include all military wargame exercises having to do with terrorism, even if they did not specifically deal with weapons of mass destruction. It would make no sense to have everything integrated except multiple terrorist hijackings or "routine" explosive devices. We have already documented an abundance of warnings on this front (certainly more than on WMD attacks) and shown that concern about multiple hijackings and planes-into-buildings was widespread before 9/11.

The White House left absolutely no doubt as to who was running the show.

> I have also asked Joe Allbaugh, the Director of the Federal Emergency Management Agency, to create an Office of National Preparedness. *This Office will be responsible for implementing the results of those parts of the national effort overseen by Vice President Cheney that deal with consequence management.*[2] [emphasis added]

Implementing means command. FEMA was tasked to do Cheney's bidding.

FEMA

Most Americans think of FEMA as a nice, benevolent agency that comes to help out when there is an earthquake, fire, or flood. It is much, much more than that.

FEMA is an enormously powerful federal agency tasked with, among other things, ensuring the Continuity of Government (COG) in the event of a crisis or "neutralization" of key governmental leaders or institutions. It also maintains dozens of secret governmental command centers, like Pennsylvania's "Site R" to which Dick Cheney was whisked right after 9/11 and where he spent much of his time in the months following 9/11. Collectively, the Continuity of Government operations under FEMA command have come to be known as the "shadow government." In a declared major emergency, arising from events even more devastating than 9/11, FEMA's authority divides the US into ten regions (p. 417) under FEMA control, which then operate semi-autonomously with the full cooperation of the military.

Long a hot topic among many researchers concerned with a "New World Order," FEMA's evolution is the product of three-decades of legislation, executive orders, and Presidential Decision Directives (PDD's). The powers granted to FEMA are astonishing in their breadth and magnitude, and can even include seizure of private vehicles, forced civilian labor on government projects, and appropriation of food and fresh water supplies.

Contrary to spin issued by government and media that FEMA is a favored theme only of right-wing extremists,[3] FEMA and its supra-constitutional authority have been of intense interest to investigators from all over the political spectrum in America for many years. Since 1995 I have read more than a dozen of these executive orders and PDDs and concluded that, in the event that all the stops were pulled and a full emergency declared, only God would have more power.

On July 13, 2004, after it was disclosed that the White House, Homeland Security, and the Department of Justice were investigating procedures for delaying, postponing, or canceling the 2004 presidential election (in the event of a terror attack), Professor Michel Chossudovsky of the University of Ottawa produced a detailed record establishing that the authorities necessary to cancel elections, place the country under martial law and suspend the Constitution were already in place. In spite of spin suggesting that the administration was exploring what needed to be done "in case," the fact was that nothing needed to be done at all. What Secretary Ridge and the White House were doing was only theater.[4] The elections could be cancelled at will, possibly even on the mere "threat" of a terror attack. All it would take would be to raise the threat level to Code Red.

Interestingly, Code Red indicates only a "severe risk of imminent terror attacks." If the elections were postponed under a Code Red, then a mere threat of a terrorist incident would suffice. The threat level is set by the White House through the Department of Homeland Security.

According to Chossudovsky, the steps necessary to suspend and/or nullify the Posse Comitatus Act, which prevents the military from engaging in domestic law enforcement, had been completed over 30 years.

> In other words, the possibility of an impending attack on America by this "outside enemy" has been accepted by the American public; this tacit acceptance has set the stage for the adoption of "the highest threat level": Code Red alert.
>
> What the US public is not aware of is that a Code Red alert suspends civilian government; it triggers a whole series of emergency procedures. It is tantamount to a coup d'etat. (Although in many regards the coup

d'etat has already taken place under the post-9/11 anti-terrorist legislation and the rigging of the 2000 elections that brought George W. Bush into the White House) ....

A Code Red alert, according to the Federal Emergency Management Agency (FEMA), would create conditions for the ("temporary" we are told) suspension of the normal functions of civilian government, implying the cancellation or postponement of federal and state elections.

According to FEMA, Code Red would:

Increase or redirect personnel to address critical emergency needs; Assign emergency response personnel and pre-position and mobilize specially trained teams or resources; Monitor, redirect, or constrain transportation systems; and Close public and government facilities not critical for continuity of essential operations, especially public safety.

(FEMA, <www.fema.gov/pdf/areyouready/security.pdf>)[5]

Truthout columnist William Rivers Pitt agreed substantially with Chossudovsky in a column published one day later:

FEMA was created by Executive Order during the Nixon administration, and became unbelievably powerful during the Reagan years. Ostensibly, FEMA was created to ensure the continuation of government after a nuclear strike. Subsequent Executive Orders over the last thirty years give FEMA, with a Presidential declaration of a national state of emergency, absolute power over all modes of transportation including personal cars, trucks or vehicles of any kind, total control of highways, seaports, airports, aircraft, the national media, all electrical power, gas, petroleum, fuels and minerals, along with all food resources and farms.

In a time of crisis, FEMA would also have absolute power over all health, education and welfare functions, and can develop plans to establish control over the mechanisms of production and distribution, wages, salaries, credit and the flow of money in US financial institutions in any undefined national emergency.

Executive Order 11051 gives FEMA the authority to execute all *Executive Orders granting the above-described powers in the event of a crisis. Executive Order 11310 requires the Justice Department to enforce any and all powers granted to FEMA in a crisis. Executive Order 11921 declares that when a state of emergency is declared by the President, Congress cannot review the action for six months.*

There are some fifteen Executive Orders which outline the powers of FEMA, should the President set them in motion after a disaster or an attack. *Several of them are nebulous enough to encompass the decision to cancel a national election. Whether the legislatures, per Title 3 of the US Code, are allowed to participate in any subsequent election preparations will certainly depend on whether the federal government wants to cut them in on the action.*

Enacting any or all of these Executive Orders would essentially remove the Constitution and the Bill of Rights from the table.

There are a thousand other questions in the mix. What constitutes a state of emergency? What kind of attack would precipitate such a decision? If it is a truck bombing against a building, does that rise to the threshold? Why would an attack in Boston require the balloting in West Virginia or Idaho to be ceased [sic]? Is the threat of an attack enough to precipitate a cancellation?[6] [emphasis added]

FEMA and 9/11

I checked my files for events immediately following September 11th and found the following press release which I had saved on September 11th, 2001:

FEMA Fully Activated in Response to Apparent Terrorist Events
http://www.fema.gov/nwz01/nwz01_92.htm

Washington, DC September 11, 2001 — In response to the apparent terrorist events, FEMA's Washington-based Emergency Response Team (EST) has [been] fully activated and on 24-hour operations. *All 10 of the FEMA regions — headquartered in Boston, New York City, Philadelphia, Atlanta, Chicago, Denton, TX, Denver, San Francisco and Bothell, Wash. — are also fully activated.*

FEMA has activated the Federal Response Plan, which brings together 28 federal agencies and the American Red Cross to assist local and state governments in response to national emergencies and disasters. Already, FEMA has deployed eight Urban Search & Rescue teams (US&R) to New York City to search for victims in the affected buildings. US&R teams are specially trained teams that include engineers and other technical experts as well as specially trained search dogs. Another four teams have been deployed to the Pentagon, for search and rescue efforts there....

FEMA support is working closely with the White House to ensure coordination and management of the consequences of the events....[7] [emphasis added]

So if FEMA was in New York, setting up for a biowarfare exercise the day before the attacks, it is hard to imagine that Dick Cheney was not aware of it. FEMA's head, Joe Allbaugh, was reporting directly to him.

The Kean Commission Final Report also placed FEMA in the communications mix on the day of 9/11.

OEM Initial Response

*By 8:48, officials in OEM headquarters on the 23rd floor of 7 WTC —
just to the north of the North Tower — began to activate the Emergency
Operations* Center by calling such agencies as the FDNY, NYPD,
Department of Health, and the Greater Hospital Association and
instructing them to send their designated representatives to the
OEM. *In addition, the Federal Emergency Management Agency (FEMA)
was called* and asked to send at least five federal Urban Search and
Rescue Teams (such teams are located throughout the United States).
At approximately 8:50, a senior representative from the OEM arrived
in the lobby of the North Tower and began to act as the OEM field
responder to the incident. He soon was joined by several other OEM
officials, including the OEM Director. [emphasis added][8]

Abbot and Hauer

"Stealthy" is perhaps the best word to describe two men who establish Dick
Cheney's "seamless" control over terrorism response before and since 9/11. Both
Admiral Steven Abbot and bioterror expert and creator of New York's Office of
Emergency Management (OEM), Jerome Hauer, now make our detective's list of
"persons of interest" with regard to the attacks. They join the likes of "Rick"
Inderfurth, Dave Frasca, Rudolph Giuliani, Richard Myers, Ralph Eberhart, and
Dick Cheney as persons who have much to explain about 9/11.

Too bad no one asked them.

Admiral Charles S. "Steven" Abbot

Abbot surfaced for the first time with the publication of the Kean Commission's
final report on July 22, 2004, and then only in an obscure footnote to chapter Ten
where the commission addressed immediate 9/11 responses, preparation for terrorist attacks, and organizational responses during the day.

The section that led me to Abbot's name was one of the few places in the 9/11
report that even mentioned Cheney's activities during the day.

> The very process of reviewing these issues underscored the absence of
> an effective government organization dedicated to assessing vulnera-
> bilities and handling problems of protection and preparedness.
> Though a number of agencies had some part of the task, none had
> security as its primary mission. *By September 14, Vice President Cheney
> had decided to recommend, at least as a first step, a new White House
> entity to coordinate all the relevant agencies rather than tackle the chal-
> lenge of combining them in a new department. This new White House
> entity would be a homeland security adviser and Homeland Security*

Council — paralleling the National Security Council system. Vice President Cheney reviewed the proposal with President Bush and other advisers. President Bush announced the new post and its first occupant — Pennsylvania governor Tom Ridge — in his address to a joint session of Congress on September 20. [emphasis added][9]

The footnote from that passage led me to the following:

16. Brill, *After,* pp. 53-55, 89-91. Following interim reports in 1999 and 2000, a congressional commission chaired by former senators Gary Hart and Warren Rudman, and directed by retired general Charles Boyd, had, in January 2001, recommended the creation of a cabinet department dedicated to "homeland security." In May 2001, President Bush named *Vice President Cheney to head a task force on problems of national preparedness.* His recently hired coordinator, *Admiral Steven Abbot, had started work just before the 9/11 attack.* [emphasis added][10]

A look at Abbot's career showed experience with flying, liaison with law enforcement, and anti-terror work. It also disclosed that he had also previously served as the NMCC's Deputy Director of Operations (DDO), the role filled temporarily by Navy Captain Charles Leidig on September 11. Leidig had been in the operational command hot seat (for the first time ever) during the attacks when his boss, General Winfield, asked him to fill in just before the attacks.

The most complete bio I could find of Abbot came from a White House release.

Admiral Steve Abbot
Deputy Director of the Office of Homeland Security

Born in Pensacola, Florida, Admiral Abbot graduated from the United States Naval Academy in June 1966. Admiral Abbot's graduate studies include Oxford University as a Rhodes Scholar and the Program for Senior Officials in National Security at Harvard University. Admiral Abbot also completed US Air Force Test Pilot School and Naval Nuclear Power training.

After being designated a Naval Aviator in 1972, Admiral Abbot completed A-7E training and squadron assignments with VA 27 on board USS *Enterprise* (CVN 65), VA 46 on board USS *John F. Kennedy* (CV 67), and VA 86 as Executive Officer and as Commanding Officer, embarked in USS *Nimitz* (CVN 68). As a test pilot, Admiral Abbot was assigned to the Strike Test Directorate at Naval Air Test Center, Patuxent River, Maryland, and participated in the early flights of the T-34C, TA-7C, and F/A-18.

Shipboard assignments include USS *Henry B. Wilson* (DDG 7) as a newly commissioned Ensign, Executive Officer of USS *Theodore*

Roosevelt (CVN 71), Commanding Officer of USS *Caloosahatchee* (AO 98), and Commanding Officer of USS *Theodore Roosevelt* (CVN 71) from February 1990 until August 1992, a period that included Operation Desert Storm.

Admiral Abbot then served as the *Theodore Roosevelt* Battle Group Commander while assigned as Commander, Carrier Group Eight, and as Commander, Joint Task Force 120.

Admiral Abbot's staff assignments include: Assistant Chief of Staff for Operations for Commander Second Fleet; Director, Aircraft Carrier and Air- Station Programs Division (N885) on the OPNAV Staff; Deputy Director for Operations (Current Operations) on the Joint Staff; and Director of Operations, US European Command.

Admiral Abbot also served as Commander, US Sixth Fleet and Commander, Naval Striking and Support Forces, Southern Europe. During this period he was the Joint Task Force Commander of Operation Silver Wake, the non-combatant evacuation of Albania.

Admiral Abbot's last assignment was Deputy Commander in Chief, US European Command, Stuttgart, Germany. He oversaw the daily activities of a Unified Command with an area of responsibility encompassing 89 countries and more than 13 million square miles...

Abbot is currently serving as Executive Director of the Vice President's National Preparedness Review. Last May, the President asked the Vice President to review and make recommendations to strengthen preparedness against an act of domestic terrorism, particularly one using a weapon of mass destruction. [emphasis added]

Abbot led the staff that supported the Vice President in this effort. The Naval Academy graduate and Rhodes Scholar served in the United States Navy from 1966 until his retirement as a four-star admiral in 2000. His final military assignment was serving as Deputy Commander-in-Chief of the US European Command during the recent conflict in Kosovo. He was a naval aviator, commanding a carrier-based squadron and serving as a test pilot for the F-18 and other aircraft. He commanded the aircraft carrier Theodore Roosevelt from 1990 to 1992, a period that included the Persian Gulf War. He subsequently commanded the Roosevelt Carrier Battle Group."[11]

My first response was to wonder if Leidig and Abbot had ever served together or if Abbot had had any influence in Leidig's placement in the NMCC. I was not able to pursue an answer to that question in time for the publication of this book.

Abbot had been working for Cheney since "just before" the 9/11 attack. In that capacity Abbot served as the Executive Director of Cheney's National Preparedness Review, and thus he would certainly have had a hands-on role in any exercises co-coordinated by Cheney's office.[12] Immediately after 9/11 Abbot was appointed as

Deputy Director of the Office of Homeland Security under Ridge before the office became a cabinet-level department in November of 2002.[13]

In January of 2004 Abbot delivered the keynote address at a disaster response exercise at the University of Missouri's Harry S. Truman School of Public Affairs. The first presentation at that event was a discussion of "Lessons Learned from the [1992] Los Angeles Riots" by a retired Army Lieutenant General.[14]

Abbot's speech that day showed that he also had an overlapping interest in biological warfare with Jerome Hauer (below).

> ...I'll talk about another specific vulnerability we have addressed early on, which is the vulnerability to biological warfare. All of us lived through the anthrax events of last fall, and we recognize that this is not a theoretical issue, this is one in which we need to strengthen the public health and medical systems. We need to enhance our medical communications and surveillance, disease surveillance capabilities, build up the national stockpiles of vaccines and pharmaceuticals and other medical supplies and promote the scientific research and development that will give us a condition in which we are truly prepared, if required...[15]

Filling in the blanks in Abbot's career proved revealing, if challenging.

From the establishment of the Homeland Security Department until June of 2003, Abbot served as "Acting Homeland Security Advisor" to the president.[16] In other words, he stayed in the White House — close to Cheney and Bush. In that capacity he attended White House meetings with Bush, Cheney, and CEO's from the largest defense and communications companies in the country.[17]

Abbot seems to have dropped off the map since the summer of 2003.

Jerome Hauer

In many respects, Jerome Hauer is "A Man for All Seasons" as far as the subject matter of this book is concerned. Not only does he have extensive credentials in governmental and leadership roles, he is also in many respects the embodiment of all the corporate and economic issues discussed in the initial chapters. He was apparently in New York City on 9/11, was a close friend of the recently retired FBI Osama-catcher John O'Neill who was killed that day, and he has many other links which make him of unique interest in any 9/11 investigation.

His most current bio, found at the website of George Washington University, tells only part of the story. The fact that there is no available record of his specific activities on 9/11 is a black hole in what we have been told about government response that day.

Jerome M. Hauer
Director, Response to Emergencies and Disasters Institute
Highlights:

Provost and Vice President for Health Affairs John F. Williams appointed Jerome M. Hauer as the first Director of the Response to Emergencies and Disasters Institute (READI) at The George Washington University in November 2003.

Hauer is working with the Department of Homeland Security to coordinate and deliver first responder, medical, and public health training for the National Capital Region (NCR). READI will *provide cross-discipline training and assist in exercise design and execution in the NCR.* Hauer is also an assistant professor in the School of Public Health & Health Services. Department of Health and Human Services (HHS) Secretary Tommy G. Thompson named Jerome M. Hauer as Acting Assistant Secretary for the Office of Public Health Emergency Preparedness on June 28, 2002. In this role, Hauer was responsible for *coordinating the country's medical and public health preparedness in response to emergencies,* including acts of biological, chemical, and nuclear terrorism. The office oversees over $1 billion dollars per year in bioterrorism preparedness grant funding for state and local governments. Before his appointment as Acting Assistant Secretary in June, Hauer had served as Director of the Office of Public Health Preparedness. *Hauer also served as senior advisor to the Secretary for National Security and Emergency Management during the events of September 11, 2001, and the nation's anthrax crisis.*

Before coming to HHS, Hauer was the first Director of the Mayor's Office of Emergency Management (OEM) for New York City. During his tenure at OEM, Hauer was charged with coordinating the city's planning for and response to natural and man-made events, including acts of terrorism. New York became the first city to develop a bioterrorism response plan and to do large-scale bioterrorism exercises. New York City, under Hauer's leadership, also pioneered surveillance systems for detecting unusual health events. New York has, for years, been recognized as being in the forefront of preparedness for terrorism. A television documentary chronicled the work Hauer and his team did in New York, and has been aired worldwide ....[18] [emphasis added]

Hauer was well-known in New York City where he created New York's Office of Emergency Management (OEM) for Giuliani. He even appeared with Giuliani to testify before the Kean Commission on May 19, 2004, but he was not questioned and submitted only a brief written statement about New York's early preparations for a terror attack. I have been able to find no account of his activities that day. This is unusual since there is reason to believe that Hauer was in New York on that day and he had — at the time — direct responsibilities for crisis management. He also had connections to FEMA. As soon as the crisis began he should have been in the immediate command loop. Was he at Pier 92 with Tripod II?

Remember that Tripod II was a biowarfare exercise and, as we shall see, Hauer's forté is biological warfare.

Apparently Jerome Hauer was wearing two hats on September 11th.

According to HHS, after leaving as head of New York's OEM in the late 1990s, Hauer, by February of 2001, was serving as a "senior advisor to the Secretary for the Department of Health and Human Services, for national security and emergency management."[19] At the same time, however, he was also the Managing Director of Kroll, Inc., one of the nation's most powerful private investigative and security firms, which has long-standing involvement with executive protection of US government officials including the president.[20] This would require close liaison with the Secret Service.[21]

Interestingly, in June 2002, Kroll (formerly named Kroll, O'Gara, Eisenhardt) purchased the German firm Convar, which had been hired after September 11th to recover data from damaged computer hard, drives recovered from the WTC wreckage.[22] Kroll's corporate staff is a Who's Who of high-level retired law enforcement, Secret Service, CIA, FBI, and other intelligence personnel. The company provides substantial services to the Saudi government. Its CEO, Michael G. Cherkasky, is the former chief investigator for the New York County District Attorney's Office where he led the investigation into the first World Trade Center bombing. Part ownership of the firm was acquired by the American International Group (AIG) in the late 1990s, and its board of directors includes Frank G. Wisner Jr., also an AIG board member, who is the son of one of the CIA's creators, Frank Wisner Sr.

Hauer's other corporate affiliations include SAIC, Batelle, DynCorp (Now CSC-DynCorp)[23] and, in his role as a bioterror expert/consultant/US government official, has had a direct hand in making decisions about elevated threat levels from the Department of Homeland Security and the Centers for Disease Control.[24] He serves on the board of Hollis-Eden, a prime beneficiary of the multi-billion dollar Project Bioshield, a 2004 law signed by George W. Bush granting huge vaccine and research contracts to the pharmaceutical industry.[25]

In 2003, according to CNN, in a wargame exercise (TopOff2) conducted simultaneously in Seattle and Chicago, Hauer played the role of the head of FEMA.[26] He has also been the go-to guy for every epidemiological or biowarfare issue since September 11th. These include anthrax, smallpox, West Nile Virus, and SARS. During his time as head of New York's OEM, he had a confrontation with the FBI's chief person-of-interest in the anthrax cases, Steven Hatfill, when Hatfill reportedly disclosed too much information about methods of biological attack. That confrontation was even reported on in the *Washington Post.*[27] My newsletter *FTW* has reported on Hatfill's well-documented (if unmentioned) history of involvement with covert intelligence operations and offensive biological warfare research.[28]

Jerome Hauer, John O'Neill, and September 11th

Jerome Hauer and John O'Neill were very close friends. So close, in fact, that Hauer had drinks with O'Neill on the night of September 10th 2001, at least until well after midnight. He also was asked to identify O'Neill's remains when they were located more than a week after the attacks.

A long article on John O'Neill in the January 14, 2002, issue of the *New Yorker* contained some revealing information about both Hauer and O'Neill.

> On September 10th, O'Neill called Robert Tucker, a friend and security-company executive, and arranged to get together that evening to talk about security issues at the Trade Center. Tucker met O'Neill in the lobby of the North Tower, and the two men rode the elevator up to O'Neill's new office, on the thirty-fourth floor. "He was incredibly proud of what he was doing," Tucker told me. Then they went to a bar at the top of the tower for a drink. Afterward, they headed uptown to Elaine's, where they were joined by their friend Jerry Hauer. Around midnight, the three men dropped in on the China Club, a nightspot in midtown. "John made the statement that he thought something big was going to happen," Hauer recalled.
>
> At 8:46 A.M., when American Airlines Flight 11 crashed into the North Tower, John P. O'Neill Jr., was on a train to New York, to install some computer equipment and visit his father's new office. From the window of the train he saw smoke coming from the Trade Center. He called his father on his cell phone. "He said he was O.K. He was on his way out to assess the damage," John Jr., recalled.
>
> Valerie James was arranging flowers in her office when "the phones started ringing off the hook." A second airliner had just hit the South Tower. "At 9:17, John calls," James remembered. He said, "Honey, I want you to know I'm O.K. My God, Val, it's terrible. There are body parts everywhere. Are you crying?" he asked. She was. Then he said, "Val, I think my employers are dead. I can't lose this job."
>
> "They're going to need you more than ever," she told him.
>
> At 9:25, Anna DiBattista, who was driving to Philadelphia on business, received a call from O'Neill. "The connection was good at the beginning," she recalled. "He was safe and outside. He said he was O.K. I said, 'Are you sure you're out of the building?' He told me he loved me. I knew he was going to go back in."[29]

Thus we know that Hauer was in New York until the early morning hours of September 11th having drinks with O'Neill. If the account is correct, then O'Neill didn't get home until approximately 2:30 yet was able to drop off his girlfriend at 8:17 (How could anyone know the exact time of that?) the next morning. Assuming a reasonable time for what the military calls The Three Ss plus time to pick up James, it is not possible that O'Neill was able to get more than four and half hours sleep. There was likely still alcohol in his bloodstream as the attacks began. O'Neill was born in 1952. How much different would the reactions of a

49-year-old man have been after a long night of drinking and four hours sleep than had he been rested and completely sober?[30]

I ask this question because LAPD personnel used a similar tactic against me during a night of fateful burglaries of my residence and of my car in 1977. I was taken "out of action" in bar by "a friendly officer" of LAPD's METRO Division until last call at 2 a.m. Fortunately, at the time I was only 26, and I recovered fairly quickly. But it was still grueling, and those crimes had been accomplished while it was certain that I could not interrupt them.

O'Neill's remark that "something big was going to happen" could not have been more prophetic. He should have listened to his well-honed "cop" instincts.

More questions: Is it likely that Jerry Hauer hopped on an airplane and went to Washington or someplace else that night? Unlikely, because the Kroll headquarters are in New York. Hauer lived there. Tripod II, a biowarfare exercise involving HHS — where Hauer was acting as an advisor to Secretary Thompson — was "setting up" the next morning.

The *New Yorker* story must be taken seriously. It included (aside from some serious disinformation about terror history and the facts surrounding TWA 800) interviews with Richard Clarke and retired FBI Director Louis Freeh.

Newsday staff writer Laurie Garrett, writing on her personal website 12 days after the attacks added more information about Hauer and O'Neill:

> "There is very little you can do to protect yourselves from bioterrorism," Jerry Hauer told the faculty of Rockefeller University yesterday. "There is very little you can do to protect yourself if a plane crashes into a building. If it happens, it happens. We have to go on."
>
> Hauer, who created New York's emergency response system — which performed remarkably well last week — is now a bioterrorism advisor to Health and Human Services Secretary Tommy Thompson. *With intelligence pouring in that indicated the terrorist network is allied with Saddam Hussein's bioweapons laboratory personnel, as well as missing Russian BW scientists, Hauer said they are scrambling in Washington to get ready.* (See today's *Newsday* website for my article on why we are totally vulnerable to BT and have no solid preparedness policy in place.) As horrific as the deaths of more than 7,000 people in the WTC disaster and two other plane crashes may be, a bioweapon release would be orders of magnitude worse. And we are not ready, in any way, shape, or form, for such an eventuality.
>
> Yesterday Hauer spoke in the famous Buckminster Fuller geodesic dome auditorium on the Rockefeller campus. Security was tight. The scientists, an elite group at Rockefeller that includes several Nobel Prize winners, listened carefully to every word Hauer uttered. He told them what most these laboratory men and women already

knew, if they'd thought about it: That microbes are the ultimate weapon ....

Before the lecture Hauer, who [sic] *I have known for years, confided that he had just been involved that morning in identifying the body of a close friend, John O'Neill, who died in the WTC. Hauer said "body," but from what else he indicated it was obvious O'Neill's remains were nothing the family ought to view.* Hauer hasn't slept in days. He is haggard and jittery. Distraught.

"John O'Neill was head of the FBI's counterterrorism branch in Washington," Hauer told me privately. "He led every important investigation you can name — the USS *Cole*, Tanzania, Kenya bombings. He retired three weeks ago. *I helped him get the job as head of security for the World Trade Center.* And the irony is, the guy he chased for most of his career killed him."[31] [emphasis added]

Hold it! It is now the summer of 2004, and we know that Saddam Hussein had no bioweapons laboratories and that all the intelligence put forth by the White House was cooked. The White House has even admitted the claims were unfounded, and no Iraqi bioweapons or even moderately advanced bioweapon research has been found in post-occupation Iraq.[32]

In a September 22, 2001, *Newsday* story by Garret (published the same day as her missive), Hauer parroted the company line on the threat posed by Saddam:

Friday, Hauer told *Newsday* that in the wake of the events of September 11, there is a new sense of urgency in Washington on the bioterrorism issue. He said there is intelligence information that terrorist Osama "bin Laden wants to acquire these agents, and we know he has links to Saddam. And Saddam Hussein has them," Hauer said.[33]

On reading this I thought of a legendary quotation attributed to one of the CIA's founding leaders, Frank Wisner Sr., who headed the Office of Policy Coordination (an offshoot of World War II's Office of Strategic Services) until it was folded into the agency in the early 1950s. Wisner is reported to have said, "I can play the media like a Mighty Wurlitzer."[34]

Dick Cheney was in the loop on 9/11, much more so than any press account or testimony had revealed. Now, I had found two men — Steve Abbot and Jerome Hauer — who had demonstrable connection to Cheney, FEMA, wargames, and much more.

One question remained: How would Dick Cheney have actually carried out the role of "maestro" on 9/11?

CHAPTER 24

THE SECRET SERVICE AND NATIONAL SPECIAL SECURITY EVENTS

In his book *Against All Enemies,* former Counterterrorism Advisor Richard Clarke made one of the most damning revelations in the 9/11 record. One statement (mysteriously overlooked by the White House censors who held Clarke's book for more than a month) gives the lie to assertions in the final 9/11 report that there were problems with relaying real-time information to Dick Cheney, who was indisputably active in the command loop from the beginning.

It has never been disputed that at all times Cheney was able to communicate with the Pentagon. Nor has it ever been disputed that the Secret Service was always in Cheney's immediate presence. This is where the entire explanation of who knew what and when offered by the Kean Commission irretrievably falls apart. Below, Clarke's description of the unfolding of a key moment on the morning of 9/11 falls between two time-certain events. We can clearly place the time of this moment at approximately 9:40 a.m., or one minute before the impact on the Pentagon.

> During the pause [as people in the White House Situation Room paused to watch President Bush's first televised remarks at 9:30 a.m.], I noticed that Brian *Stafford, Director of the Secret Service,* was now in the room. He pulled me aside ....
>
> *Stafford slipped me a note. "Radar shows aircraft headed this way." Secret Service had a system that allowed them to see what FAA's radar was seeing.* "I'm going to empty out the complex." He was ordering the evacuation of the White House.
>
> Ralph Seigler stuck his head into the room, "There has been an explosion at the Pentagon parking lot, maybe a car bomb."[1] [emphasis added]

"Secret Service had a system that allowed them to see what FAA's radar was seeing"?

Clarke had previously established that while he and other senior managers were operating from the White House Situation Room, Cheney, Rice, and other key personnel were also operating and making decisions in the underground Presidential

Emergency Operations Center (PEOC) which (because of its design to protect the president and provide him with full command, control and communications [C³] in the event of a nuclear attack) had communications abilities either matching or exceeding those in the Situation Room. The PEOC was where the resident was to command in the event of a nuclear (or biological) holocaust. If there was any place that needed to have the ultimate state-of-the-art C³ it was the PEOC.

Only a little analysis is required to establish that two "parallel" command systems were in operation on 9/11. The US Secret Service now emerges as the nexus of essential 9/11 operational control under Cheney's command, and there is an ample body of evidence to confirm that the Secret Service not only had this ability, it also had the statutory and procedural authorities to take command of everything.

Relevant Kean Commission references to Secret Service

> At 9:34, Ronald Reagan Washington National Airport advised the Secret Service of an unknown aircraft heading in the direction of the White House.[2]
>
> [At 9:32] FAA personnel at both Reagan National and Dulles airports notified the Secret Service. The aircraft's identity or type was unknown.[3]

The Kean Commission report then flatly contradicts Clarke's statement above.

> The Secret Service initiated a number of security enhancements around the White House complex. The officials who issued these orders did not know that there were additional hijacked aircraft, or that one such aircraft was en route to Washington. These measures were precautionary steps taken because of the strikes in New York.[4]

The FAA knew. If the Secret Service had the same radar then the Secret Service knew also.

> At 9:33, the tower supervisor at Reagan National Airport picked up a *hotline to the Secret Service and told the Service's operations center* that "an aircraft [is] coming at you and not talking with us." This was the first specific report to the Secret Service of a direct threat to the White House.[5] [emphasis added]

This must be referring to the PEOC. Note that there is a hotline directly to the Secret Service and that the tower supervisor contacted the Secret Service instead of calling NORAD or the NMCC. Therefore, the tower supervisor (presumably following written procedures) must have known that the Secret Service had the fastest command and control capabilities. The system must have been planned to operate that way.

> [At approximately 10:30] General David Wherley — the commander of the 113th Wing — reached out to the Secret Service after hearing

secondhand reports that it wanted fighters airborne. A Secret Service agent had a phone in each ear, one connected to Wherley and the other to a fellow agent at the White House, relaying instructions that the White House agent said he was getting from the Vice President. The guidance for Wherley was to send up the aircraft, with orders to protect the White House and take out any aircraft that threatened the Capitol. General Wherley translated this in military terms to flying "weapons free" — that is, the decision to shoot rests in the cockpit, or in this case in the cockpit of the lead pilot. He passed these instructions to the pilots that launched at 10:42 and afterward.[6]

This is quite revealing. First (if true), it shows that Dick Cheney in the White House had better information on the status of hijacked aircraft than Andrews Air Force Base did. Second, it shows the commanding general at Andrews operating — at least as far as the Kean Commission report is concerned — outside the chain of command and taking scramble orders directly from Cheney without obtaining clearances from the NMCC or NORAD. But was it really outside the chain of command? Or have we been misled about what the real chain of command was?

The commission also dropped another little tidbit about the Secret Service's presence in New York City during the attacks.

OEM Response

After the South Tower was hit, OEM senior leadership decided to remain in its "bunker" and continue conducting operations, even though all civilians had been evacuated from 7 WTC. At approximately 9:30, a senior OEM official ordered the evacuation of the facility, after a Secret Service agent in 7 WTC advised him that additional commercial planes were not accounted for. Prior to its evacuation, no outside agency liaisons had reached OEM. OEM field responders were stationed in each tower's lobby, at the FDNY overall command post, and, at least for some period of time, at the NYPD command post at Church and Vesey.[7] [emphasis added]

According to NORAD's submitted timeline and stories in the *Washington Post* (See Chapter 18), *9:30* was the *exact* time that Flight 93's transponder was turned off. A Secret Service Agent, obviously in direct touch with the PEOC, was in 7 WTC relaying what must have been real-time information. This further corroborates that the Secret Service was getting information as fast as the FAA was and faster than anyone else. Giuliani should have been looped in this also since the OEM was a New York City Agency.

In Chapter 21 we noted that the final Kean Commission report incredibly changed the time when the FAA informed NORAD that Flight 93 was a hijack — from 9:16 a.m. to 10:07 a.m., overruling the initially submitted NORAD timeline and many other records. This added an unbelievable 51 minutes to the time when NORAD would have had any responsibility for responding. However, it is abundantly clear that the Secret Service was responding to Flight 93 for more than a half hour before that. If the Secret Service was able to contact everybody, then why didn't it tell the Pentagon?

Because there was a parallel command system in play.

The Kean Commission report also changed the reported time when Flight 93's transponder was turned off from 9:30 to 9:41.[8]

National Special Security Events (NSSEs)

Clearly, there are events whose significance makes them high-value terrorist targets. These are generally scheduled public events of extreme vulnerability for the president such as inaugurations; major national events such as political conventions; or events where large numbers of dignitaries and a multitude of targets are gathered in one place (the Olympics). Because the time and location of such events is always public knowledge, additional risks are posed.

In anticipating such events (as opposed to terrorists hijacking airliners to use as weapons) both the United States and "terrorists" have certain advantages. While the terrorists know the place and the time, the US government also has the pre-planning ability to approach these events from the standpoint of realizing that there is no other time when the command and control of US response, whether from military or civilian agencies, must be at a higher state of readiness.

Such events are called National Special Security Events. When they occur they are always under the primary control of only one federal agency, the Secret Service. Therefore, it goes without saying that if the Secret Service is the lead agency, its communications, its intelligence systems, and its ability to receive real-time data from any federal agency (including the military) must be the best available. It also must be redundant in many cases with systems operated by the CIA, the FBI, NORAD, the FAA, and especially the involved state and local agencies.

Including the two conventions of the 2004 election season, there have been 16 National Special Security Events. They include:

- The 2000 Republican and Democratic Conventions
- The 2001 Presidential Inauguration
- The 2001 United Nations General Assembly
- The 2002 Winter Olympics in Salt Lake City, Utah
- Super Bowl XXXVI in New Orleans.[9]
- The 2004 G8 Summit at Sea Island, Georgia[10]
- The 2004 Democratic and Republican Conventions[11]

What the Secret Service says about NSSEs

The Secret Service website contains a description of the Secret Service's role in these events.

National Special Security Events

In May of 1998, President Clinton issued Presidential Decision Directive 62. A portion of PDD-62, which is a classified document, deals with the coordination of Federal anti-terrorism and counter-terrorism assets for events of national interest.

In effect, PDD-62 formalized and delineated the roles and responsibilities of federal agencies in the development of security plans for major events. The clarifying of responsibilities serves to focus more clearly the role of each agency and eliminate the duplication of efforts and resources.

When an event is designated a National Special Security Event, the Secret Service assumes its mandated role as the lead agency for the design and implementation of the operational security plan.

The Secret Service has developed a core strategy, the concept of forming partnerships with law enforcement and other security and public safety officials.

The goal of the cooperating federal, state and local agencies is to provide a safe and secure environment for our protectees, other dignitaries, the event participants, and the general public.

Although we cannot discuss the methods and means we utilize to carry out our protective responsibilities, we can say there is a tremendous amount of advance planning and coordination in the areas of venue and motorcade route security, **communications,** credentialing, and training.

Certainly, we emphasize the importance of prevention and deterrence when we are developing an operational security plan, but we are also prepared to respond tactically to a threat if the situation dictates. As a result, we will employ a number of our specialized units during the course of this event.

The skills utilized by our agents and officers to carry out their protective responsibilities are perishable. As a result, our personnel train on a continuing basis so that each individual remains prepared to respond to any eventuality. Their responses must be immediate, well coordinated, and effective. *A variety of training initiatives are conducted to include simulated attacks and medical emergencies, inter-agency tabletop exercises, and field exercises.*[12] [emphasis added]

The Department of Homeland Security offers even more information about how NSSEs work.

National Special Security Events Fact Sheet
For Immediate Release
Office of the Press Secretary
July 9, 2003

The Department of Homeland Security announced that the Republican National Convention to be held in the summer of 2004 in New York City will be designated a National Special Security Event. Previously, the Department announced the designation of the Democratic National Convention site in Boston as a National Special Security Event. When an event is designated a National Special Security Event, the Secret Service assumes its mandated role as the lead federal agency for the design and implementation of the operational security plan and Federal resources are deployed to maintain the level of security needed for the event and the area. The goal of such an operation is to prevent terrorist attacks and criminal acts.

- *Once an event is designated a National Special Security Event, the Secret Service strengthens existing partnerships with federal, state and local law enforcement and public safety officials with the goal of coordinating federal, state and local agencies to provide a safe and secure environment for the event and those in attendance....*

- *The Secret Service is responsible for planning, directing and executing federal security operations at designated NSSE's. The Secret Service also provides federal, state and local law enforcement partners who provide substantial, critical support to the protective mission with the necessary guidance and training regarding their role in the overall operational security plans.*

- *The Secret Service has recently begun sponsoring several training seminars for command-level law enforcement and public safety officials from jurisdictions all over the country to provide fundamental principles for managing security aspects of major events and strategies for reducing vulnerabilities related to terrorism and other criminal acts....*

- To be fully prepared to meet its mission for consequence management within the Department of Homeland Security, *EP&R will pre-position some combination of the following response and recovery assets: the Domestic Emergency Support Team (DEST), Urban Search and Rescue (USAR) teams, national Emergency Response Teams (ERT-N), the Nuclear Incident Response Team (NIRT), the Strategic National Stockpile and Mobile Emergency Response System (MERS).* The specific package will be tailored for each individual event based on *coordination with other federal agencies, state and local jurisdictions, available local resources, mutual aid agreements and other event-specific requirements...*[13] [emphasis added]

One cannot help but wonder about pre-positioning of resources in connection with the Tripod II wargame and the presence of a Secret Service agent in New York's OEM on September 11th. This would have been consistent with Dick Cheney's original mandate. The Secret Service conveniently had offices in WTC7.

Even the US Air Force acknowledges Secret Service supremacy. The Air Force National Security Emergency Preparedness Agency (AFNSEP) "Plans and coordinates Air Force participation in national security emergency preparedness programs as it relates to military support to civil authorities for natural and man-made disasters and emergencies and national security special events."[14]

It also manages a cadre of Air Force Reserve emergency preparedness liaison officers who deploy during or in anticipation of disaster recovery operations or to support national security special events. AFNSEP also works "with *DoD joint staff* [JCS], all services, the *Federal Emergency Management Agency* and other federal agencies to support the national response plan as it relates to incident management.[15] [emphasis added]

Remember that, according to the email from Don Arias, Vigilant Warrior was a Joint Chiefs live-fly hijack drill. All of this would have been coordinated under Dick Cheney's mandate, and the live-fly drill could have been run through the Secret Service's parallel and redundant communications and information systems inside the PEOC, where Dick Cheney was involved and issuing orders shortly after 9 a.m. Some key players — for instance, Myers and the NMCC's DDO and General Winfield — could have been there at the start of the attacks. The JCS wargames, confirmed by Major Arias, had to be run from someplace.

Another air force web-site states that AFNSEP is "the Principle USAF Point of Contact for Homeland Security and is the liaison with other federal agencies …."AFNSEP is also the primary Air Force office tasked with "continuity of government operations which would put it under FEMA's control in the event of a major attack or disaster threatening government operations."[16]

FEMA was placed under Dick Cheney's direct control in May of 2001.

The Kean Commission sinks Rice, points at Secret Service again

Perhaps the most persistently offensive remark made by any government official was the now legendary statement by National Security Advisor Condoleezza Rice that she had "no idea that planes could be used as weapons." One particular passage in the Kean Commission report not only proved Rice's assertion (at best) misleading, it also reinforced the concept that the Secret Service had been preparing for an airplane-as-weapon attack for a long time. Remember, the Secret Service is part of the Treasury Department.

> *Clarke had been concerned about the danger posed by aircraft since at least the 1996 Atlanta Olympics. There he had tried to create an air defense plan using assets from the Treasury Department, after the Defense Department declined to contribute resources. The Secret Service continued to work on the problem of airborne threats to the Washington region. In 1998, Clarke chaired an exercise designed to highlight the inadequacy of the solution. This paper exercise involved a scenario in which a group of*

terrorists commandeered a Learjet on the ground in Atlanta, loaded it
with explosives, and flew it toward a target in Washington, D.C. Clarke
asked officials from the Pentagon, Federal Aviation Administration (FAA),
and Secret Service what they could do about the situation. Officials from
the Pentagon said they could scramble aircraft from Langley Air Force
Base, but they would need to go to the President for rules of engagement, and there was no mechanism to do so. There was no clear
resolution of the problem at the exercise.[17] [emphasis added]

The Secret Service and Bush

A great many questions remain unanswered about President Bush's movements,
statements and actions on September 11th. From a telltale footnote in the Kean
Commission report, it now appears certain that the Secret Service was used by
Cheney that morning to tell the President what to do and when to do it.

> FOOTNOTE 208. USSS memo, interview of Gregory LaDow, Oct.
> 1, 2001, p. 1. *Shortly after the second attack in New York, a senior Secret*
> *Service agent charged with coordinating the President's movements estab-*
> *lished an open line with his counterpart at the FAA, who soon told him*
> *that there were more planes unaccounted for — possibly hijacked — in*
> *addition to the two that had already crashed.* Though the senior agent
> told someone to convey this information to the Secret Service's oper-
> ations center, it either was not passed on or was passed on but not
> disseminated; it failed to reach agents assigned to the Vice President,
> and the Vice President was not evacuated at that time. See Nelson
> Garabito interview (Mar. 11, 2004); USSS memo, interview of
> Nelson Garabito (Oct. 1, 2001); see also Terry Van Steenbergen inter-
> view (Mar. 30, 2004). (p. 464) [emphasis added]

"Counterpart" in this case appears to be another Secret Service Agent, physically present at the FAA headquarters. My hunch is that there is always one there,
and that he or she has the same wonderful communications we already know the
Secret Service has. We have already seen that orders were being issued by Cheney
from a fairly early point and also that the Secret Service seemed to have (understandably) better information than anyone.

In his indispensable 9/11 timeline, investigator Paul Thompson documented
how Bush's Secret Service detail was eager to get him out of the school well before
the now infamous whisper from Chief of Staff Andrew Card between 9:03 and
9:06 a.m. In an essay titled "An Interesting Day" Thompson and Alan Wood
looked further at what appeared to be a case of someone telling the Secret Service
not to evacuate the president.

> Secret Service agents and other security personnel had set up a television
> in a nearby classroom. They turned on the TV just as Flight 175 crashed

into the World Trade Center. According to Sarasota County Sheriff Bill Balkwill, who was in the room, **a Marine responsible for carrying Bush's phone immediately said to Balkwill, "We're out of here. Can you get everyone ready?"** [*Sarasota Herald-Tribune*, 9/10/02] *But he must have been overruled by someone, because Bush did not leave.*

Meanwhile, Secret Service agents burst into Vice President Cheney's White House office. They carried him under his arms — nearly lifting him off the ground — and propelled him down the steps into the White House basement and through a long tunnel toward an underground bunker. Accounts of when this happened vary greatly, from 9:06 [*New York Times*, 9/16/01 (B), *Telegraph*, 12/16/01] **to after 9:30.** [CBS, 9/11/02, *Washington Post*, 1/27/02] **Cheney's own account is vague and contradictory.** [Meet the Press, 9/16/01] The one eyewitness account, by White House photographer David Bohrer, said it happened just after 9:00. [ABC, 9/14/02 (B)] **It's easy to see why the White House would have wanted this event placed at a later time (after Bush's initial statement to the nation rather than after the second crash) to avoid the obvious question: if Cheney was immediately evacuated, why wasn't Bush?**

The Photo-Op Goes On

After Card told Bush about the second plane and quickly left, the classroom was silent for about 30 seconds or so. [*Tampa Tribune*, 9/1/02] The children were about to take turns reading from a story called "The Pet Goat." [AFP, 9/7/02] Bush picked up the book and began to read with the children. [*Tampa Tribune*, 9/1/02] In unison, the children read out loud, "The - Pet - Goat. A - girl - got - a - pet - goat. But - the - goat - did - some - things - that - made - the - girl's - dad - mad." Bush mostly listened, but occasionally asked the children a few questions to encourage them. [*Washington Times*, 10/7/02] At one point he said, "Really good readers, whew! ... These must be sixth-graders!" [*TIME*, 9/12/01]

Who was really in control? Certainly not Bush. In the back of the room, Press Secretary Ari Fleischer caught Bush's eye and held up a pad of paper for him to see, with "DON'T SAY ANYTHING YET" written on it in big block letters. [*Washington Times*, 10/7/02] **Some person or people had overruled the security who wanted Bush evacuated immediately, even as Vice President Cheney was taken from his White House office to a safe location. Bush's security overruled Bush on security matters later in the day on Air Force One, but who overruled them that morning?...** [18]

Once he was out of the classroom, did Bush immediately leave Booker? No. He stayed in the adjacent room with his staff, calling Vice

President Cheney and National Security Advisor Rice, and preparing a speech. [*Telegraph*, 12/16/01, *St. Petersburg Times* 9/8/02] **Incredibly, even as uncertain information began to surface, suggesting that more planes had been hijacked (eventually 11 planes would be suspected)** [CBS, 9/11/02], Bush was allowed to make his remarks at 9:30 — exactly the time and place stated on his advance schedule. [*Federal News Service*, 9/10/01] **Why hasn't Bush's security staff been criticized for their completely inexplicable decision to stay at the school? And why didn't Bush's concern for the children extend to not making them and the rest of the 200 or so people at the school terrorist targets?** [emphasis added]

There is reason to suspect — and many 9/11 investigators suggest — that one reason to keep the President occupied with a perfect alibi was to make certain that he could not issue a shoot-down order. However, looking at the scenario and seeing that Cheney was hauling ass at the same time that Bush was stalled or being stalled, another insight came to me.

Knowing that Cheney was rushing and issuing orders to keep Bush at the school, the "cynical cop" part of me thought, "Well of course! Knowing that the attacks had started, Cheney absolutely had to get to his command center as quickly as possible so that he could make sure everything went "smoothly." He probably passed the Secret Service agents who were supposed to be carrying him. He also had to get there to keep Bush from being put on the spot and take command in front of the cameras.

What would it have meant if Andy Card had whispered to the president something like, "One tower of the World Trade Center has been hit. We have three confirmed hijackings, one of which has turned off its transponder and diverted towards Washington. A major attack is in progress. We await your orders."

Of course we know that the system knew even before Bush entered the classroom. He or his immediate staff was told of multiple hijackings at least four times before he started reading. The key is that while Bush was in the classroom he was in public view and on camera. He could not be accused of knowing and not acting. There he is on tape, doing his elementary school photo op when his Chief of Staff whispers in his ear that the second tower has been hit.

Only one of two things could have happened had he acted based upon what we have every reason to believe he knew. One possibility is that at that second the system would have swung into action and operated the way it was supposed to. Why? Because, starting at the top, people would have been accountable.

Who can imagine how different things might have been.

The other possibility is that George W. Bush could have actually tried to run things, having been officially notified before Cheney could arrive at the PEOC and begin issuing orders. In this latter case, before the end of that tragic day we might all have been radioactive dust; smoldering in the ashes of a global thermonuclear war.

That on-camera delay gave both Cheney and Bush a perfect alibi.

CHAPTER 25

THE COMMISSION'S WILD BLUE YONDER

The Kean Commission final report effectively labeled NORAD as lying in all of its earlier representations and evidentiary submissions by changing many of the most significant timeline entries, exhibits, and testimony NORAD had submitted since 9/11. Then, instead of questioning NORAD, the commission chose to place blame for a lack of timely fighter response squarely on the FAA.

Many independent press organizations and 9/11 researchers paid close attention to these abrupt and unexplained changes. So apparently, did at least one mainstream newspaper and a US Senator from the state of Minnesota (home of the late Senator Paul Wellstone).

The 9/11 activist and investigator Nick Levis described these glaring conflicts in a story for 911Truth.org, an activist/organizing/outreach movement formed in the spring and summer of 2004.[1] Levis had been at the forefront of 9/11 activism from the start, playing a key role in organizing many 9/11Truth events in the US and Germany.

> **Senator Dayton: NORAD Lied About 9/11**
> **Sunday, August 1, 2004**
>
> **Introduction**
> Mark Dayton has become the first US senator to challenge the establishment consensus that "The 9/11 Commission Report" settles the open questions of Sept. 11, 2001.
>
> In Senate hearings last Friday Dayton (D-MN) raised an obvious point: if the timeline of air defense response as promoted in the Kean Commission's best-selling book is correct, then the timeline presented repeatedly by NORAD during the last two years was completely wrong. Yet now no one at NORAD is willing to comment on their own timeline!
>
> When the official story of 9/11 can be changed repeatedly without anyone ever being held accountable, we have no right to ever again expect honest government. Please read the following story and do

your part to support Sen. Dayton for highlighting the contradiction, and to encourage the media to follow up.

Background: Evolution of the Official Story

From the beginning, the 9/11 investigations, official and alternative, have been about timelines: what happened, who knew, and who did what, when, where, and how.

Written by the government's Kean Commission, the just-published "9/11 Commission Report" presents a timeline of air defense response that differs radically from all of the previous official stories.

Since Sept. 11 government representatives have in fact promoted a series of mutually contradictory narratives of how the nation's air defenses responded to the unfolding attacks. Various chronologies were presented at different times by the high military command, the North American Air Defense command (NORAD), the Federal Aviation Administration, and now the Kean Commission.

Little noticed, the original story was delivered by Gen. Richard Myers, the acting Chairman of the Joint Chiefs of Staff on 9/11. Just two days after the events, Myers appeared before the Senate for hearings, scheduled many weeks earlier, to consider his appointment as the nation's supreme military officer. Myers told the Senate that no fighter jets were scrambled to intercept any of the 9/11 flights until after the Pentagon was struck.

The Pentagon attack occurred at 9:38 a.m., a full 1 hour 20 minutes after the first of the 9/11 flights was diverted from its designated flight path.

Myers's statement to the Senate was incredible, given the standard US air defense protocols for dealing with errant instrument flights (including off-course passenger planes). In place many years before Sept. 11, these procedures are automatic and require no special order. Within minutes after a flight ceases to respond to ground control, the FAA is expected to alert NORAD — which scrambles jet fighters to intercept the errant flight for reconnaissance purposes. These are supposed to be airborne within 10 minutes of the problem arising.

This routine was activated on at least 67 occasions in the calendar year prior to June 1, 2001 (when the Joint Chiefs changed the scramble protocols). Exceptional as the events of 9/11 proved to be, the procedures should have also been activated automatically within minutes of each flight diversion on that day.

Before Myers's disturbing admission to the Senate received much notice, NORAD under General Ralph Eberhart effectively put the lie to his statement. A partial timeline of US air defense response published on Sept. 18, 2001 presented the times at which NORAD was alerted about each flight diversion by the FAA. In its statement, NORAD claimed to have responded to the alerts by scrambling two squads of interceptors. These, however, never reached any of their targets in time to intercept, let alone prepare for a possible shoot-down.

As late as May 2003, General Arnold of NORAD, sitting alongside Gen. Myers, presented a slightly revised version of NORAD's Sept. 2001 timeline, in testimony to the Kean Commission.

The NORAD timeline indicated that during the crisis hours of 9/11, the FAA became increasingly slow in delivering alerts to NORAD. This seemed to shift the blame for the failed response to the FAA.

The FAA, however, disputed Gen. Arnold's testimony with a statement of May 21, 2003. The FAA claimed that regardless of the official notification times claimed by NORAD, phone bridges were established immediately after the initial attack (at 8:46). NORAD was informed in real time, throughout, of all developments, including about the plane that ultimately hit the Pentagon, the FAA said.

Thus, for more than a year the FAA has been in open dispute with NORAD on who informed whom and when about the Sept. 11 hijackings; unfortunately, this has never become the major media story it deserves to be.

The Kean Commission itself intervened in June 2004. In a staff statement delivered at its final set of hearings ("Improvising a Homeland Defense"), the Commission outlined a chronology that completely ditched the timeline that NORAD had upheld for two years. It also effectively placed almost all of the blame for delayed air defense response on the FAA.

Generals Arnold and Myers, who testified to the Commission that same morning, were not held to account for having presented an entirely wrong timeline. Instead, they simply thanked the Kean Commission for clearing up the confusion. In return, one commissioner made a point of telling the generals they were not to blame; after all, it was all the FAA's fault!

A group of FAA officials who testified in the subsequent, final session stuck by their old defense that they had in fact provided adequate and timely information to NORAD via the phone bridges. As the hearings concluded, they still disputed both timelines: the old one from NORAD, and the new one from the Kean Commission.

Dayton: Demanding Accountability

Now that the Kean Commission has published the new timeline in its final report, these contradictions must not be simply swept under the rug. Either the Kean Commission is wrong, or else NORAD was pushing a flawed timeline for more than two years. Either way, the FAA story still differs from both.

There can be no excuses. Those responsible for dispensing false information must be held accountable, or else nothing in the behavior of government is likely ever to improve.

Instead of accountability, several of the key figures — Generals Myers and Eberhard, FAA official Ben Sliney — have been promoted since Sept. 11! Yet one or more of them must be wrong about what happened on 9/11.

This is the simple point that Sen. Mark Dayton made yesterday at Senate hearings on the 9/11 Commission Report: now that it has accepted the Kean Commission findings, NORAD must explain its old timeline, and anyone responsible for pushing it, whether intentionally or not, must be held accountable.

To our knowledge the story so far has been reported only by Greg Gordon in the Minneapolis Star-Tribune. An excerpt:

Dayton: FAA, NORAD hid 9/11 failures
By Greg Gordon, Star Tribune Washington Bureau Correspondent
July 31, 2004

WASHINGTON, D.C. — Sen. Mark Dayton, D-Minn., charged Friday that the Federal Aviation Administration (FAA) and the North American Aerospace Defense Command (NORAD) have covered up "catastrophic failures" that left the nation vulnerable during the Sept. 11 hijackings.

"For almost three years now, NORAD officials and FAA officials have been able to hide their critical failures that left this country defenseless during two of the worst hours in our history," Dayton declared during a Senate Governmental Affairs Committee hearing.

[...]

During the hearing, Dayton told leaders of the Sept. 11 commission, that, based on the commission's report, a NORAD chronology made public a week after the attacks was grossly misleading. The chronology said the FAA notified the military's emergency air command of three of the hijackings while those jetliners were still airborne. Dayton cited commission findings that the FAA failed to inform NORAD about three of the planes until after they had crashed.

And, he said, scrambled NORAD fighter planes were sent east over the Atlantic Ocean and was 150 miles from Washington, D.C., when the third plane struck the Pentagon — "farther than they were before they took off."

Dayton said NORAD officials "lied to the American people, they lied to Congress, and they lied to your 9/11 commission to create a false impression of competence, communication and protection of the American people." He told Kean and Hamilton that if the commission's report is correct, President Bush "should fire whoever at FAA, at NORAD ... betrayed their public trust by not telling us the truth."

Asked about Dayton's allegation, a spokesman for Colorado Springs-based NORAD said, "We stand on our testimony to the commission" and declined to discuss the 2001 chronology. Erin Utzinger, a spokeswoman for Dayton, said the senator "assumes the FAA knew of NORAD's cover-up."

In the weeks ahead, we will be presenting a complete treatment of the old NORAD timeline and of "The Emperor's New Timeline" as spelled out in the Kean Commission report. This will be part of a series exposing the many Omissions of the Commission.

(Story: Nicholas Levis)[2]

Kyle Hence, co-founder of 9/11 Citizen's Watch with journalist and investigator John Judge, issued an immediate bulletin calling for a flood of letters to Dayton's office:

> Please read the first 8 pages of Richard Clarke's book [*Against All Enemies*]. His timeline conflicts grossly with that of the Commission's. The Commission has Rumsfeld and Myers out of the loop until well after 10AM. Myers they say was in a car en route to the Pentagon when he saw smoke there. Rumsfeld was in a breakfast meeting through the whole course of the attack. Clarke has them both in a White House-directed videoconference beginning at approximately 9:12 A.M....
>
> Clarke quotes a Deputy Director of the Situation Room in the White House (the Director being in FL with Pres. Bush) saying when Clarke arrives at approximately 9:10 that a "Threat Conference Call" was underway.
>
> The 9/11 Commission has the "Threat conf." starting at 9:37 or 9:39.
>
> These are major discrepancies that beg for answers and explanations. How were they resolved? Is there a cover-up? Why was there been no call for courts martial? How could Rumsfeld, Myers, and the President be left out of the loop over the 109 minutes you mentioned it took for the attacks to be carried out?
>
> Thank you for your diligence in the most critical search for the whole truth about what happened on 9/11.

This brief e-mail has touched on a tip of an iceberg that would throw grave suspicions on the work of the Commission and the supposed cooperation of the Agencies asked to assist in getting to the truth.

Sincerely,
Kyle F. Hence[3]
9/11 Citizens' Watch
<911citizenswatch.org>

With that in mind, let's look for just a second at one analysis covering only a brief part of what the commission had to say about wargames, NORAD, and the FAA. The commission just chose to ignore almost all previously extant testimony and submissions from NORAD and the FAA, especially its statement about the phone bridges. Its treatment of the wargames was insulting.

What did the Commission say about the wargames?

Only one of the wargames being conducted on September 11th was mentioned in the Kean Commission report, and then only superficially in a footnote to the report's first chapter.

Vigilant Guardian

116. On 9/11, NORAD was scheduled to conduct a military exercise, Vigilant Guardian, which postulated a bomber attack from the former Soviet Union. We investigated whether military preparations for the large-scale exercise compromised the military's response to the real-world terrorist attack on 9/11. According to General Eberhart, "it took about 30 seconds" to make the adjustment to the real-world situation. Ralph Eberhart testimony, June 17, 2004. We found that the response was, if anything, expedited by the increased number of staff at the sectors and at NORAD because of the scheduled exercise. See Robert Marr interview (Jan. 23, 2004).[4]

Lies, lies, and more lies

While they are legion, some of the commission's more egregiously false representations are listed below. Compare them with what we have documented thus far. The commission was in effect making the FAA a scapegoat for the lack of fighter response on 9/11.

Prior to 9/11, it was understood that an order to shoot down a commercial aircraft would have to be issued by the National Command Authority (a phrase used to describe the president and secretary of defense). Exercise planners also assumed that the aircraft would originate from outside the United States, allowing time to identify the target and scramble interceptors. The threat of terrorists hijacking commercial airliners within the United States — and using them as guided missiles — was not recognized by NORAD before 9/11.[5]

Radar data show the Otis fighters were airborne at 8:53. Lacking a target, they were vectored toward military-controlled airspace off the Long Island coast. To avoid New York area air traffic and uncertain about what to do, the fighters were brought down to military airspace to "hold as needed." From 9:09 to 9:13, the Otis fighters stayed in this holding pattern.

In summary, NEADS received notice of the hijacking nine minutes before it struck the North Tower. That nine minutes' notice before impact was the most the military would receive of any of the four hijackings.[6]

About a dozen other records indicate the contrary.

Military Notification and Response. The first indication that the NORAD air defenders had of the second hijacked aircraft, United 175, came in a phone call from New York Center to NEADS at 9:03. The notice came at about the time the plane was hitting the South Tower.[7]

Despite the discussions about military assistance, no one from FAA headquarters requested military assistance regarding United 93. Nor did any manager at FAA headquarters pass any of the information it had about United 93 to the military.[8]

Air war over America, NORAD's book on September 11th
More confirmation of the roles of Dick Cheney and the Secret Service

Major Don Arias had been true to his word when he sent me the official account of CONR's (NORAD's) experiences on 9/11. The book, titled *Air War Over America*, was a handsome, four-color, glossy coffee-table book written by Leslie Filson, the special historian hired by the First Air Force. Filson's book documents a version of September 11th that is so different from the Kean Commission report that it seems to be describing a completely different attack.

The contradictions between the Kean Commission report, and the earlier NORAD statements in the air force's published (and publicly available) account, are very unsettling.

All of the following quotations are taken from that book.[9]

Around 8:30 a.m., [*as opposed to 9:03 in the Kean Commission report above*] a Federal Aviation Administration controller in Boston phoned the control tower at Otis with a serious request: American Airlines

Flight 11 had lost its identification signal and appeared headed toward Manhattan. (p. 47)

Normally, the FAA would have contacted officials at the Pentagon's National Military Command Center who would have contacted [NORAD]. The Secretary of Defense would have had to approve the use of military assets to assist in a hijacking .... But nothing was normal on Sept. 11, 2001, and many say the traditional chain of command went by the wayside to get things done....

Military controllers at three air defense sectors — in the northeast, southeast, and west — were monitoring the air picture, only a hot line call away from pilots on immediate alert.... [*This section then continues the misleading assertion that NORAD's radars were all looking outward instead of inward. How could that be if NORAD was running hijack exercises inside the Continental US?*] (pp. 51-52).

Even before Flight 11 had made the first impact, the air force again confirmed, contrary to the commission report, that the FAA had been Johnny-on-the-spot.

"Once we were called by the FAA, we could find split-second hits on what we thought we were looking for," [NEADS Staff Sergeant Larry] Thornton says. "But the area was so congested and it was incredibly difficult to find ...." (p. 56).

[Quoting Major Dawne Deskins at NEADS on events just after Flight 11's impact:] "Our identification section was asking what type of aircraft it was, and Boston Center was reporting American 11 still airborne. So we thought it must have been a weird coincidence." (p. 57)

Could Deskins and her colleagues have been confused by one of the radar injects left in place by the maestro? A subsequent statement by General Arnold suggests that at least some of the exercises continued to run well into the attacks.

United Airlines Flight 175 crashed into the South Tower of the World Trade Center at 9:03 AM with 65 people aboard. Two 767s were gone, and it was anyone's guess what might happen next.

"I thought it might be prudent to pull out of the exercise [Vigilant Guardian] which we did." Arnold says. "We called NORAD, and they were well aware of what had happened obviously. ... As we pulled out of the exercise we were getting calls about United Flight 93 and we were worried about that." (p. 59)

Here Arnold states that Vigilant Guardian was not terminated until about the same time that the first reports of Flight 93's hijacking, which we have already established occurred at around 9:16 or 54 minutes after it had been known that Flight 11 was a hijack. Why did it take so long?

> With little time to grasp what had happened in New York, the FAA
> continued to report more shocking information to the Northeast
> Sector: American Airlines Flight 77 and Delta Airlines Flight 1989,
> both 767s bound for Los Angeles, were possibly hijacked. (p. 63)

Delta Flight 1989 will become critical in our final chapter. But here again, contrary to the Kean commission report, the FAA is communicating in a timely manner with NEADS. It is interesting to note that the NEADS commander Colonel Robert Marr is not mentioned once in the Kean report. In spite of that, almost the entirety of the First Air Force account shows that virtually all the information it was receiving on the status of various possible hijackings was coming directly from the FAA to NEADS and then being sent to the NMCC and NORAD headquarters.

Regarding the possible hijack of Delta Flight 1989, then heading toward Cleveland, the air force account says, "Through the fray, [NEADS Commander Col.] Marr remembers hearing that the FAA was evacuating its Cleveland Center" (p. 73). This too will become important in our final chapter.

The report also describes the confusion as lines of communications collapsed, didn't function properly, or were deliberately confused. In one account of how dedicated airmen rushed to offer assistance, Filson wrote:

> Canadian Forces Capt. Brian Nagel, who was *chief of NEADS live
> exercises,* says, "Guys were getting airborne from a news report and a
> phone call from us."
> "I called up one unit and the guy says, 'Who are you and what do
> you want?'" (p. 74) [emphasis added]

Live exercises? This appears to be another confirmation of live-fly drills in progress. It certainly confirms that operational commands like NEADS did conduct live-fly drills. And like Robert Marr, Nagel is never mentioned in the final Kean Commission report.

As three F 16s flew north towards the Pentagon from Langley Air Force Base at (according to the air force account) "max subsonic speed" — approximately 650 mph, which is less than half of the F 16's top speed — Captain Craig Borgstrom, one of the pilots, described a situation that is anathema to anyone in the military under any condition, let alone in wartime. "We were all three on different frequencies .... *and were getting orders from a lot of different people.*" (p. 66) [emphasis added]

The Air Force and the Secret Service

Who were the different people giving orders to the Langley fighters? At least one of the order givers was Dick Cheney himself, using the Secret Service as his messenger.

Brig. Gen. David Wherley Jr. [Andrews Air Force Base], 113th Wing Commander had just arrived at the operations desk. He would find himself on several phone calls that morning, desperately seeking airborne authorization for his fighters. *"I dial the White House JOC (Joint Operations Center), and the news is showing the White House with people running out the front door,"* Wherley says. *"And the phone rings about eight times before somebody picks it up and ... they have nobody in uniform, it was all Secret Service people and a team communicating with the president."*

A woman at JOC — the Secret Service Command and Control Center — answered the phone. "I'm thinking these are civilians and they don't deal in the language of the military, the rules of engagement, so asked her. 'What do they want me to do?'" he recalls. *"She was standing next to the vice president (Dick Cheney) and she said, 'They want you to put a CAP up.'"*

Everything was happening at once, says Wing Safety Officer Lt. Col. Phil Thompson, who was now the acting SOF [Supervisor of Flying]. *"We were taking calls from the Secret Service and [FAA's] Washington Center,"* he recalls [Again, note that the FAA is actively relaying information]. *"We have a special relationship with these guys by name and face .... They were worried about Flight 93."* (p. 79) [emphasis added]

PART IV

EMPIRE AND DECLINE

CHAPTER 26

THE RECORD

A little guy like me should never have had to write this book.

By the time the Kean Commission's final report was released, a crucial principle of democratic government called "separation of powers" had quietly vanished. Nobody within the government seemed willing or able to defy the executive's mythical narrative of 9/11, even while the executive used the implications of that Big Lie to justify its every move. Massive war appropriations, the Patriot Acts, intelligence "reform," Camp X-Ray at Guantanamo Bay, prison torture abroad, domestic roundups and detentions of Arabs and South Asians, and a hundred tangentially related usurpations of the powers Constitutionally reserved for the legislature and the judiciary — all were driven through by appeals to the official story of 9/11. It seems there are no independent voices of authority remaining outside the Empire's control to challenge, temper or place limits on Imperial crimes and ambitions.

There is only yet another Patrician seeking to replace Caesar on the throne and wear the Imperial purple.

The Kean commission's mandate

The Kean Commission's mandate was laid out in Public Law 107-306, signed by President Bush on November 27, 2002.

> **SEC. 602. PURPOSES.**
>
> The purposes of the Commission are to — (1) examine and report upon the facts and causes relating to the terrorist attacks of September 11, 2001, occurring at the World Trade Center in New York, New York, in Somerset County, Pennsylvania, and at the Pentagon in Virginia; (2) *ascertain, evaluate, and report on the evidence developed by all relevant governmental agencies regarding the facts and circumstances surrounding the attacks;* (3) build upon the investigations of other entities, and avoid unnecessary duplication, by reviewing the findings, conclusions, and recommendations of — (A) the Joint Inquiry of the

Select Committee on Intelligence of the Senate and the Permanent Select Committee on Intelligence of the House of Representatives regarding the terrorist attacks of September 11, 2001, (hereinafter in this title referred to as the "Joint Inquiry"); and (B) other executive branch, congressional, or independent commission investigations into the terrorist attacks of September 11, 2001, other terrorist attacks, and terrorism generally; *(4) make a full and complete accounting of the circumstances surrounding the attacks, and the extent of the United States' preparedness for, and immediate response to, the attacks;* and (5) investigate and report to the President and Congress on its findings, conclusions, and recommendations for corrective measures that can be taken to prevent acts of terrorism. [emphasis added]

SEC. 604. FUNCTIONS OF COMMISSION.

(a) IN GENERAL. — The functions of the Commission are to — (1) conduct an investigation that —

(A) investigates relevant facts and circumstances relating to the terrorist attacks of September 11, 2001, including any relevant legislation, Executive order, regulation, plan, policy, practice, or procedure; and

(B) may include relevant facts and circumstances relating to - (i) intelligence agencies; (ii) law enforcement agencies; (iii) diplomacy; (iv) immigration, nonimmigrant visas, and border control; (v) the flow of assets to terrorist organizations; (vi) commercial aviation; (vii) the role of congressional oversight and resource allocation; and (viii) other areas of the public and private sectors determined relevant by the Commission for its inquiry; 6 USC 101 note.

(2) identify, review, and evaluate the lessons learned from the terrorist attacks of September 11, 2001, regarding the structure, coordination, management policies, and procedures of the Federal Government, and, if appropriate, State and local governments and nongovernmental entities, relative to detecting, preventing, and responding to such terrorist attacks;...

While repeated public statements by commissioners that their mandate was "not to find fault" or "finger point," its legal mandate to make a "complete accounting" appears to have been virtually ignored. Not a single person in the US government has been held accountable for anything. Come to think of it, no one has been held accountable for anything.

This compounds the fact that there has not been a single successful 9/11-realted prosecution anywhere in the world for the 37 months from the day of the attacks to the release of this book.

There's a good reason why no one has even been reprimanded for his or her performance on 9/11. Any reprimand (or more severe sanction) opens the doors to hearings, administrative processes, exculpatory information, discovery, and due legal process that would put these monstrous inconsistencies directly under bright light where they would have to be resolved in order to sustain the punishment. That would be the very last thing the commission would want.

The Empire insists upon the maintenance of its own decorous appearances and its customary credibility, no matter how transparent those appearances, nor how empty that credibility becomes. With regard to the Kean Commission (which was almost, let's remember, a Kissinger Commission) I have said publicly from its inception that the American people should never have expected anything different from what we got. It was designed, planned, constructed, and functioned to achieve one and only one objective: damage control.

The record keepers: A study in conflicts of interest

The Kean Commission has always been riddled with conflicts of interest. In a criminal proceeding these would have resulted in the immediate recusal of most of the Commission's members. For the record, I am hard pressed to think of any human being with prior government service who would not have been excused for cause,[1] given the way the economy and government now operate — as a system of organized crime.

The following is only a partial listing of some of the more obvious conflicts within the Kean Commission. It begins with a look at the Commission's Chairman by economist and historian Michel Chossudovsky, followed by a description of Vice-Chairman Hamilton by independent journalist Jim Rarey.

Thomas Kean (Chairman)

Thomas Kean is a director (and shareholder) of Amerada Hess Corporation, which is involved in the Hess-Delta joint venture with Delta Oil of Saudi Arabia (owned by the Al-Amoudi clans). Delta-Hess "was established in 1998 for the development and exploration of oil fields in the Caspian region.... In Azerbaijan Delta Hess is involved in the Azeri-Chirag-Gunashli PSA [Production Sharing Agreement] (2.72 percent) and the Garabaghli-Kursangi PSA (20 percent). It is also an equity holder in the Baku-Tbilisi-Ceyhan (BTC) oil pipeline": "An air of mystery hangs over Delta-Hess, which... is registered in the Cayman Islands. Hess is in no hurry to reveal the terms of the alliance, which it says are subject to confidentiality clauses. 'There's no reason why this should be public information,' a Hess spokesman says" (*Energy Compass*, 15 Nov. 2002).

Coincidentally, the former Governor of New Jersey is also a member of the Council on Foreign Relations, together with another prominent member of the board of directors of Amerada Hess, former Secretary of the Treasury Nicholas Brady.

It is also worth mentioning that Thomas Kean also sits as co-chairman of the Homeland Security Project (HSP) under the auspices of the Century Foundation.[2] In this capacity, Kean has played a key role in the draft recommendations of the Century Foundation, *which laid the groundwork of the Office of Homeland Security legislation.*

Moreover, it would appear that Delta officials (involved in the UNO-CAL trans-Afghan pipeline consortium) *played a key role in negotiations with the Taliban.* In turn, Enron, the infamous energy giant — whose former CEO, Ken Lay, had close connections to the Bush family — had been contracted in a cozy relationship to undertake feasibility studies for the Unocal-Delta consortium. Enron Corporation had also been entrusted — in liaison with Delta — with pipeline negotiations with the Taliban government.

Wayne Madsen has shown with ample documentation that *George W. Bush also had dealings with Khalid bin Mahfouz, when he was in the Texas oil business.*[3] Both George W. Bush and Khalid bin-Mahfouz were implicated in the Bank of Commerce International (BCCI) scandal.

Other links between Bush and Mahfouz can be found through investments in the Carlyle Group, an American investment firm managed by a board on which former president George Bush himself sat. The younger [George W.] Bush personally held shares in one of the components of the Carlyle group, the Caterair company, between 1990-94. And Carlyle today ranks as a leading contributor to Bush's electoral campaign. On Carlyle's advisory board is found the name of Sami Baarma, director of the Pakistani financial establishment, Prime Commercial Bank, that is based in Lahore and owned by Mahfouz. (See Maggie Mulvihill, Jonathan Wells, and Jack Meyers: Slick deals; the White House connection; Saudi 'agents' close Bush Friends, *Boston Herald*, 11 December 2001).[4] [emphasis added]

Lee Hamilton (Vice Chair)

Commission vice chairman and former congressman Lee Hamilton was appointed [to the Kean Commission] to replace former senate majority leader George Mitchell (CFR), who like [Henry] Kissinger declined to disclose potential conflicts of interest and resigned. Hamilton, a CFR member since at least 1988, was chairman of the House Foreign Affairs Committee and the House Select Intelligence Committee.

In 1987, House Speaker Jim Wright (who later resigned in disgrace) appointed Hamilton to chair a committee investigating the Iran/Contra affair.

When a question was raised about CIA/Contra drug smuggling, the response was release by Hamilton of a cursory review that concluded there was no truth to the charges. The CIA recently released a report [Volume II of the CIA's Inspector General Report on Iran-Contra drug trafficking, released October 8, 1998] (that received almost no publicity) admitting the drug connection.[5]

Barbara Honegger, who played a pivotal role in bringing the information on the wargames into focus, has remained sharply critical of Hamilton. She has some authority on the subject of Hamilton's role in the so-called "October Surprise" of 1980-1981, in which it was charged that George Bush Sr., in concert with future CIA Director Bill Casey, engaged in backdoor negotiations with Iran's new revolutionary government to delay the release of American hostages held since the 1979 seizure of the US embassy in Tehran. Evidence (some of which originated with Honegger) that was serious enough to warrant congressional hearings showed that in exchange for US weapons for use in its pending bloody war with Saddam Hussein's Iraq, the Reagan-Bush team secured a promise from Iran to delay the hostages' release during the 1980 presidential campaign.

President Jimmy Carter had been frantically attempting to secure the hostages' release in an effort to boost his re-election prospects. Instead, however, the hostages were not returned until the very day of Ronald Reagan's first inauguration in January 1981. This was one of history's great "coincidences."

Following her experience as a research assistant at the Hoover Institute, Stanford University, Honegger joined the policy research team of the Reagan-Bush campaign. In 1980, she was part of the Reagan-Bush transition team. In 1981, she worked in the White House Office of Policy Development as a "Research and Policy analyst." Then she resigned, according to some reports because of sex discrimination. Other reports have described her departure from the Reagan administration as a resignation of conscience. Honegger was among the first to go public with allegations of duplicity in the October Surprise. Her 1989 book on the subject, October Surprise (Tudor Press), was well received by the research community, and it remains a useful resource.

Iran-Contra was effectively "managed" by Lee Hamilton in the House and John Kerry (among others) in the Senate throughout the late 1980s to conceal the greatest crimes of the era, crimes committed by a litany of well-known government operatives. At the time, Hamilton was the Chairman of the House Permanent Select Committee on Intelligence.

While many activists regard 2004 Democratic presidential candidate Kerry as something of a hero for bringing many details of Iran-Contra drug activities to light (and into the public record), others, more deeply versed in the evidentiary record, suspect that he also did a masterful job of keeping some of the most damaging Iran-Contra secrets — especially records of CIA proprietary company operations — hidden. I am among the latter group.

Many figures who came under criminal and investigative scrutiny in Iran-Contra, like John Poindexter, Elliot Abrams, Richard Armitage, Dick Cheney, Otto Reich, Colin Powell, and John Negroponte, returned (over little or no congressional opposition) to serve in the current Bush administration after the 2000 (so-called) election.

Honegger's position has consistently been that Hamilton's role was damage control in both the October Surprise and the Iran-Contra hearings. It was obviously a good qualification for his role in 9/11, and Honegger is far from alone in her assessment of the Kean Commission's vice chair.

For more than four decades, veteran Washington journalist Sarah McLendon was the grande dame of the White House Press Corps. Until her January 2003 death (at 92), she was a revered and active journalist known for her feisty confrontations with presidents and the powerful since the Truman administration. In her later years she had a great habit of appearing to be asleep in her wheelchair until the moment when she would wake up and pounce on her prey with incisive questions that revealed she hadn't missed a word of what had been said. Once, on national television and in the middle of a live White House press conference, she even dared to question President Bill Clinton about the abundantly documented record of CIA and Arkansas state government involvement in drug smuggling operations at Arkansas' Mena Regional Intermountain Airport during the 1980s.

In 1994 and 1995, while living in Washington, I was a regular attendee at McLendon's weekly study group at the National Press Club and later at her residence on Connecticut Avenue. After she passed, the National Press Club renamed one of its conference rooms The McLendon Room. In 1992 McLendon offered her observations on Hamilton's behavior as the chief "fact-finder" and chair of the October Surprise and Iran-Contra committees.

> I declined to withdraw the report I made that Congressman Hyde elicited and obtained a promise from Chairman Lee Hamilton, D., Ind. of the House Task Force on October Surprise, that the group would clear President George Bush of going to Paris to cinch a deal of weapons for Iran in exchange for retaining American hostages to be delivered to President Ronald Reagan and not to outgoing President Jimmy Carter. Hyde says he made no such a deal and I must remember that Hamilton is a Democrat. That makes no difference. Hamilton held a press conference to clear Bush before the investigation into the deal between the Reagan-Bush candidates for presidential office and the Iranians had even started. Hamilton then admitted he had not interrogated witnesses or talked with his special attorney hired to investigate the matter.[6]

Sound familiar?

Veteran AP journalist Bob Parry, who broke the first major story linking drug smuggling to Contra support activities, only to later lose his job, offered some additional observations on Lee Hamilton in his independent web newsletter, *Consortium News.*

> One of the key congressional Republicans fighting this rear-guard action was Rep. Dick Cheney of Wyoming, who became the ranking House Republican on the Iran-contra investigation. Cheney already enjoyed a favorable reputation in Washington as a steady conservative hand.
>
> Cheney smartly exploited his relationship with Rep. Lee Hamilton, D-Ind., who was chairman of the Iran-contra panel. Hamilton cared deeply about his reputation for bipartisanship and the Republicans quickly exploited this fact.[7]

Not only did Hamilton fail to find any wrongdoing by top officials in either investigation, he was even "satisfied" with the performance of Marine Lieutenant Colonel Oliver North in the Iran-Contra hearings.

> North appears before the House Select Committee on Intelligence to answer questions about his role in a Contra resupply operation. He lies convincingly: He has "not in any way, at any time violate[d] the principles or legal requirements of the Boland Amendment," which bans federal support for the Nicaraguan counterrevolutionaries. Committee chairman Lee Hamilton, D-Ind., pronounces himself satisfied with North's "good faith." When North's superior, John Poindexter, is told of his successful deception of Congress, Poindexter e-mails Ollie: "Well done."[8]

Philip Zelikow (Executive Director)

Perhaps no more glaring conflict of interest attracted opposition from victim families and 9/11 activists than that of the commission's Executive Director, Philip Zelikow. Concerns were raised when it was disclosed that only two commission members and Zelikow might be allowed to see certain classified presidential records, including the much ballyhooed and publicly debated Presidential Daily Briefing (PDB) of August 6, 2001.

Personally, I viewed the August 6th PDB as a red herring and a hubristic pretext over which the commission could make a show of "battling" the White House for information. The PDB, titled, "Bin Laden Determined to Strike in US" was eventually released in a one and a half page version that was presented to the world as "complete."

Nothing could have been further from the truth. The respected German paper *Die Zeit* published a story in October of 2002, well before the PDB became an issue, stating that the PDB was actually 11.5 pages long.[9] Since I had documented so many other clear, direct, and credible and apparently more detailed warnings, the August 6 PDB was a non-issue for me. But the controversy arising from the public debate forced even the *New York Times* to comment on some of Phil Zelikow's more obvious conflicts of interest.

Advocates for the families said they were alarmed by the commission's disclosure on Thursday that only one of the 10 commissioners would have access to a wide range of the briefings, and that the only person from the commission with similar access would be its staff director, Philip Zelikow, who has close ties to Condoleezza Rice and other senior officials in the Bush administration.

The commission has previously rejected a request from victims' families to limit Mr. Zelikow's responsibilities sharply in light of potential conflict of interests involving the White House.

The families' advocates said the decision to have Mr. Zelikow be one of only two commission officials with wide access to the highly classified documents — the other is Jamie S. Gorelick, a Democratic commission member who was deputy attorney general in the Clinton administration — raised new questions about the investigation's impartiality....

Mr. Zelikow, who wrote a book with Ms. Rice in 1995, was on the Bush administration's transition team for the National Security Council and has acknowledged having contacts earlier this year with Karl Rove, President Bush's chief political adviser, about Mr. Zelikow's scholarly work at the University of Virginia.

"Phil Zelikow has a very large conflict of interest," said Kristen Breitweiser, whose husband, Ronald, was killed at the World Trade Center, and who is a spokeswoman for the Family Steering Committee, an umbrella group that represents several family organizations. "He is very close friends with Condi Rice, he was on the transition team, and some of these documents are going to pertain to that. It's very disturbing."

Mr. Zelikow said in an interview that he frequently dealt in his scholarly work with prominent political figures, Republicans and Democrats alike, and that he had attempted to be even-handed in pursuing the commission's investigation. "I talk to a lot of people in both parties, including highly political people in the Democratic party," he said.[10]

Even while serving on the commission, Zelikow's conduct raised eyebrows. *Newsweek* commented on the fact that Zelikow had sent a fax to the White House about Condoleezza Rice's pending testimony.

The grainy photograph rolled off the fax machine at the White House counsel's office last Monday morning, along with a scribbled note that smacked of blackmail. If the White House didn't allow national-security adviser Condoleezza Rice to testify in public before the 9/11 commission, it read, "This will be all over Washington in 24 hours." The photo, from a Nov. 22, 1945, *New York Times* story, showed Adm. William D. Leahy,

chief of staff to Presidents Franklin Roosevelt and Harry Truman, appearing before a special congressional panel investigating the Japanese attack
on Pearl Harbor. PRESIDENT'S CHIEF OF STAFF TESTIFIES
read the headline over the snapshot of Leahy's very public testimony.
The point was clear: the White House could no longer get away with the
claim that Rice's appearance would be a profound breach of precedent.

> The fax was the work of Philip Zelikow, the commission's execu-
> tive director....[11]

What's more, Zelikow had been serving as a member of President Bush's Foreign
Intelligence Advisory Board (PFIAB) since 2001, and he also made a September
2002 public statement saying that US military action against Iraq would be based
upon a desire to protect Israeli interests rather than any real threat from Iraq.

> Zelikow made his statements about "the unstated threat" during his
> tenure on a highly knowledgeable and well-connected body known as
> the President's Foreign Intelligence Advisory Board (PFIAB), which
> reports directly to the president.
>
> He served on the board between 2001 and 2003.
>
> "Why would Iraq attack America or use nuclear weapons against
> us? I'll tell you what I think the real threat (is) and actually has been
> since 1990 — it's the threat against Israel," Zelikow told a crowd at
> the University of Virginia on Sep. 10, 2002, speaking on a panel of
> foreign policy experts assessing the impact of 9/11 and the future of
> the war on the al-Qaeda terrorist organisation.
>
> "And this is the threat that dare not speak its name, because the
> Europeans don't care deeply about that threat, I will tell you frankly.
> And the American government doesn't want to lean too hard on it
> rhetorically, because it is not a popular sell," said Zelikow.[12]

Perhaps the worst conflict of interest was the fact that Zelikow had advised the
incoming Bush administration on terror-related intelligence matters and had several discussions about bin Laden and al Qaeda in 2000-2001 with Richard Clarke.
By rights, he should have been a witness testifying under oath before the commission instead of its executive director. When many of the victim families learned of
this they were justifiably outraged at an arrangement that would have never been
permitted in a court of law.

> Statement of the Family Steering Committee for
> The 9/11 Independent Commission
> March 20, 2004
>
> From <http://www.911independentcommission.org>
>
> The Family Steering Committee is deeply disturbed to learn about
> Executive Staff Director Phillip Zelikow's participation in urgent

post-election briefings, December 2000, and January 2001, with Sandy Berger and Condoleezza Rice. In this particular meeting the Senior Clinton Administration official clearly warned that al Qaeda posed the worst Security threat facing the nation.

It is apparent that Dr. Zelikow should never have been appointed to be Executive Staff Director of the Commission. As Executive Staff Director his job has been to determine the focus and direction of the Commission's investigation, an investigation whose mandate includes understanding why the Bush administration failed to prioritize the Al Qaeda threat. It is abundantly clear that Dr. Zelikow's conflicts go beyond just the transition period.

It is extremely distressing to learn this information at this late date. This new information clearly calls into question the integrity of this Commission's investigation. The Family Steering Committee repeatedly expressed concerns over all members' conflicts requesting that the commission be forthcoming so as not to taint the validity of the report. The Family Steering Committee was unaware of Dr. Zelikow's participation in this intelligence briefing until today.

As such, the Family Steering Committee is calling for:

1. Dr. Zelikow's immediate resignation.
2. Dr. Zelikow's testimony in public and under oath.
3. Subpoena of Dr. Zelikow's notes from the intelligence briefings he attended with Richard Clarke.
4. The Commission to apologize to the 9/11 families and America for this massive appearance of impropriety.

The Family Steering Committee (FSC) is an independent, nonpartisan group of individuals who lost loved ones on September 11, 2001. The FSC does not receive financial or other support from any outside organizations.

In spite of all the controversy, and calls from many for his resignation, Zelikow remained securely in place at the Kean Commission until this book went to press.

Jamie Gorelick

Freelance journalist Jim Rarey writes:

Considered one of the 50 most powerful women in the country, CFR member Jamie Gorelick is currently vice-chair of the giant mortgage lender and insurer Fannie Mae. From March 1994 until she joined Fannie Mae in May 1997 she was Deputy Attorney General, the number two spot in Janet Reno's Department of Justice.

In May 1995, the Intelligence Community Law Enforcement Policy Board was established to meet quarterly and discuss mutual concerns of the Attorney General and Director of Central Intelligence.

458 CROSSING THE RUBICON

The board was co-chaired by Gorelick and DCI George Tenet. Other members included all of the law enforcement agencies, the Assistant Secretary of State for Intelligence and Research and the Defense Department General Counsel.

This is the same time frame (spring of 1995) in which the Philippine government apprised the FBI, CIA and State Department of "Project Bojinka" an Islamic terrorist plot which included hijacking commercial airlines planes and flying them into the Pentagon, World Trade Center towers, and several other buildings.

The BCCI scandal involved a number of powerful individuals. Clark Clifford and Robert Altman were the top two officers in First American, the new name given Financial General Bankshares when it was taken over by BCCI (known as the Bank of Crooks and Criminals International in the corridors of Washington) with the help of the Jackson Stephens/Lippo Worthen Bank and the Rose Law Firm.

First American is said to have been using the notorious *PROMIS* software.

When BCCI and First American were exposed, the legal defense team for Clifford and Altman attracted a bevy of well-known names including Robert Fiske (later the first "independent counsel" investigating Whitewater and Vince Foster's "suicide"), Robert Bennett (later attorney for Bill Clinton), and *Jamie Gorelick.*

In a somewhat related case in 1978, Financial General Bankshares sued BCCI, two Jackson Stephens' companies (one was Systematics) and a number of individuals. *Two of the attorneys representing Systematics in the controversy over PROMIS software were Webster Hubbell and Hillary Rodham.*

In 1998, while at Fannie Mae, Gorelick served on Clinton's Central Intelligence National Security Advisory Panel as well as the President's Review of Intelligence.[13] [emphasis added]

At one point in the Kean Commission hearings, a brief stir was caused when Republican partisans charged that Gorelick bore some personal blame for the attacks by virtue of having created an "intelligence wall" between the FBI and the CIA.

As we have seen, there was no wall. A 2001 RAND Corporation study offered praise for the working relationships between the FBI and the CIA. It is now also painfully apparent that there is no wall between the Kean Commission and the government it was charged with investigating.

Gorelick also has oil connections. According to 9/11 researcher Bonnie Hayskar who posted the following to the 9/11 TruthAlliance list:

Schlumberger's board members include John M. Deutch, former CIA director from May 1995-Dec. 1996 and Jamie S. Gorelick who, among other things, now serves on the 9/11 Commission and is one of the few allowed access to classified presidential records.

Schlumberger originated in Paris (and is pronounced "slumber-shay"). It moved to Houston, TX in 1940 when the oil business was booming there, but continues to have strong ties to both the UK and France. Today, from the Schlumberger website <http://www.slb.com/> [14]

Schlumberger is the world's premier oil drilling company. As one oil expert told me in Berlin in May of 2004, every time a well is drilled, or oil gets pumped, anywhere Schlumberger is there. According to its website (above), Schlumberger is comprised of two companies: Schlumberger and WesternGeco. Then it notes: "WesternGeco, which is jointly owned with Baker-Hughes, is the world's largest and most advanced surface seismic company."[15] Baker-Hughes was founded and is run by James Baker who is one of the world's foremost petroleum lawyers and the former secretary of state to Bush I. Baker is a Republican. Baker was also a key player in Caspian oil exploration in the 1990s.

Remember, Gorelick is supposed to be a Democrat.

Gorelick was one of four commission members allowed to review presidential intelligence records and make notes before reporting to the commission. It appears that the White House had very little to worry about.

The White House did delay releasing the notes taken by the commissioners,[16] but as Hayskar observed, "Perhaps Jamie's notes were being embargoed by the federal government to be sure she was taking notes only on matters pertaining to 9/11..."[17]

Perhaps it was all just theater.

Jim Rarey fills us in on more of the panel:

Richard Ben-Veniste

Ben-Veniste is a high-visibility Washington attorney and Democrat power broker. He was Democrat counsel to the Senate Whitewater investigation where he blocked inquiries about Webster Hubbell's hiring by the Lippo group and others administered by Truman Arnold.

According to investigative journalist Daniel Hopsicker, Ben-Veniste then turned around and defended Arnold (the man he was supposed to be investigating) before Ken Starr's Whitewater grand jury, for which he was roundly criticized.

Hopsicker also reveals that Arnold had furnished a $2 million airplane to his friend Wally Hilliard for $1. Hilliard, Hopsicker says, owned the Flight school in Venice, Florida, where four of the Islamic terrorist pilots were trained that flew the suicide missions on 9/11.

Another of Ben-Veniste's clients was Barry Seal, the drug running CIA asset of Iran/Contra and Mena, Arkansas notoriety. In fact, Hopsicker relates Ben-Veniste told the Wall Street Journal, "I did my part by launch-

ing him (Seal) into the arms of Vice President Bush who embraced him as an undercover operative."

Fred Fielding

Fielding is another one who has been around the centers of power for a while on the Republican side. *In the Nixon administration he was a deputy counsel working under John Dean. In the Watergate scandal he helped his boss (Dean) handle Howard Hunt's safe full of documents.* They wore rubber gloves so as not to leave fingerprints. Fielding was not one of the 20 or so Nixon associates (including John Dean) that went to jail over their involvement.

Later Fielding served as White House Counsel to President Reagan. More recently he was at least partly responsible for getting George W. Bush's political mentor Karl Rove in hot water over failure to divest his stock in Intel Corporation valued at over $100,000.

Fielding advised Rove, who was planning to divest all of his stock, to hold onto it until a "government certificate of divestiture" could be obtained. The certificate would have allowed deferral of capital gains taxes on stock sold. While he still held the stock, Rove met with Intel executives and Vice President Chaney at which a proposed merger with a Dutch company was discussed. This was a breach of administration ethics rules.

Fielding served on the Bush transition team in early 2001. According to Clay Johnson, Director of Presidential Personnel and Deputy Chief of Staff, "The Vice President asked Fred Fielding, who had been President Reagan's counsel, to come in and he volunteered to — as soon as we had a Cabinet Secretary-to-be, he would sit down with that person and they'd have a nice little chat for an hour or two. And then Fred would tell us whether he was confident that there were no clearance problems or not. If there was something that he thought might be problematic, he would explore it further, and maybe they had to go get some information, whatever." Johnson said the process now takes 60 days.

Jim Thompson

Jim Thompson was the longest-serving governor in Illinois history, completing four terms in office leaving in 1991. He is currently chairman of the large Chicago-based law firm Winston and Strawn....

Thompson got caught in the middle of a messy political battle between outgoing Governor George Ryan and Attorney General Jim Ryan, both Republicans. Governor Ryan was running against Democrat Rod Blagojevich, the victor and incoming governor. At the same time AG Ryan was suing Governor George Ryan over the pardoning of death row inmates. George Ryan hired former governor Jim Thompson to defend against the lawsuit.

Blagojevich had railed in his campaign against the 26 years of Republican corruption and mismanagement. That included 12 of the years when Thompson was governor. To the astonishment of practically everyone, Blagojevich appointed Thompson to lead his transition team.

John Lehman

John Lehman is an investment banker who has served in a number of government positions including as *Secretary of the Navy from 1981 to 1987* under President Reagan. *His first government job was as special counsel and senior staff member to Henry Kissinger on the National Security Council in the Nixon administration.*

Lehman currently serves on several boards of directors including those of Ball Corporation, as chairman of OAO Technology Solutions, Inc. and his own J.F. Lehman & Company. *He is a former chairman of Sperry Marine and investment banker with Paine Webber.* Lehman served 25 years as a naval aviator in the selected reserves.

Slade Gorton

Slade Gorton is a former senator from the State of Washington. After he lost his re-election bid in 2000, he joined the Seattle law firm of Preston, Gates & Ellis, which specializes in environmental issues.

If jury selection rules were being used, Gorton would probably be dismissed from consideration for the commission for cause [a technical term for conflict of interest]. Two days after the 9/11 attacks he told a public-television audience there was nothing government intelligence officials could have done to thwart the attack, according to the *Seattle Times*. The *Times* quotes Gorton as saying, "I doubt we can expect to get too much inside information no matter what we do."

Gorton served two years on the Senate Intelligence Committee. He says that experience and his personal friendship with Trent Lott were responsible for his appointment by Lott.

Tim Roemer

Tim Roemer is a moderate Democrat congressman (at least compared to the Democrat leadership) who is retiring from Congress at the end of this year. He was one of the prime movers in the House championing creation of the Independent Commission. He is credited with bringing the organization representing survivors and families of victims of the 9/11 attacks into the mix of support for the commission. *Roemer is a member of the House Intelligence Committee.* [emphasis added]

Max Cleland

Former Georgia Senator Max Cleland, a triple-amputee from Vietnam, is the exception that proves the rule. But even his kind of courage apparently has its limits. Cleland is a one-term senator from Georgia who lost his reelection bid this year [2004] in a close contest.

> At the age of 28, Cleland was the youngest person and first Vietnam veteran elected to the Georgia State Senate. In 1977, he became the youngest ever head of the Veterans' Administration when appointed by President Jimmy Carter. In 1982 Cleland became the youngest person elected as Georgia Secretary of State. He resigned that position in 1996 to run for the seat being vacated by retiring US Senator Sam Nunn. He was sworn in as a US Senator in 1997.
>
> Barring (intentional) leaks, we will have to wait another 17 months to see what the product of the commission will be. By that time the public's attention will undoubtedly be focused on other things.[18]

Max Cleland was not cut from the same cloth as the rest of the panel. In spite of his all-too-obvious sacrifice he was targeted by the Bush camp and Karl Rove in the 2002 midterm elections as being "soft on defense". He lost his Georgia Senate seat in the same election that saw the feisty Cynthia McKinney lose her House seat. Cleland, however, never rose to McKinney's defense as she was vilified throughout 2002. Perhaps he should have. In July 2004, the phoenix-like McKinney handily defeated five separate opponents to win 51 percent of the vote in the Democratic primary for her old seat. Having done that, her re-election to the House in the 2004 election became a virtual certainty in the Democratic safe seat.

Cleland had also been a sharp critic of the Bush administration's less-than-honest approach to securing an invasion of Iraq. In a fall 2003 interview with *Salon.com*, he pulled very few punches.

> During his six years as a United States senator from the conservative state of Georgia, Max Cleland was known as a moderate Democrat. He drew the wrath of liberals in 2001 when he broke ranks with Democrats and voted for President Bush's tax cuts, and last year he backed the resolution authorizing Bush to wage war with Iraq (though on that vote, at least, he was joined by some liberals)....
>
> Meanwhile, as one of 10 commissioners serving on the independent panel created by Congress to investigate the 9/11 attacks, Cleland bemoans the administration's "Nixonian" love of secrecy and its attempt to "slow walk" the commission into irrelevancy. At the center of the secrecy debate are sensitive presidential daily briefings, or PDBs, that the commission wants to examine as part of its inquiry. Particularly important is the crucial Aug. 6, 2001 PDB, which warned of Osama

bin Laden's desire to hijack commercial planes in the United States. For months the White House resisted, and the commission hinted it might subpoena the document. A deal was finally cut last week, which Cleland opposed, allowing a handpicked subset of commissioners to be briefed on the PDBs.

"We shouldn't be making deals," Cleland complains. "If somebody wants to deal, we issue subpoenas. That's the deal."

It's hard to imagine any recent Democratic senator less soft on national security than Max Cleland, a reflection on the unlikely path he took to the US Senate. In 1967 he volunteered for combat duty. The next year, during the siege of Khe Sahn, Cleland lost both his legs and his right hand to a Viet Cong grenade....

Let's start with the 9/11 commission. What are your concerns about how it's dealing with the White House?

First of all, as someone who co-sponsored legislation creating the 9/11 commission, against great opposition from the White House, this independent commission should be independent and should not be making deals with anybody. I start from there. It's been painfully obvious the administration not only fought the creation of the commission but that their objective was the war in Iraq, and one of the notions that was built on was there was a direct connection between al Qaida and 9/11 and Saddam Hussein. There was not...

What have some of the access problems been?

In May, the commission asked the FAA to give us the documents we're looking for. We've had to subpoena the FAA. We've now had to subpoena documents from NORAD, which they have not given us. I for one think we ought to subpoena the White House for the presidential daily briefings, to know what the president knew, what the administration knew, and when they knew it so we can determine what changes ought to be made in our intelligence infrastructure, our warning system, so that we don't go through this kind of surprise attack again....

So it's not some sort of payback?

And after watching History Channel shows on the Warren Commission last night, the Warren Commission blew it. I'm not going to be part of that. I'm not going to be part of looking at information only partially. I'm not going to be part of just coming to quick conclusions. I'm not going to be part of political pressure to do this or not do that. I'm not going to be part of that. This is serious.

You say you think it should be a national scandal....

It is a national scandal. Here's the deal. The administration made a connection on September 11, and you can read Bob Woodward's book [*Bush at War*]. He's a private citizen. He got access to documents we don't have yet! Just think about that. He's a great reporter and a good guy. Bless his heart. But he got documents over two years ago, handwritten notes from Rumsfeld tying the terrorism attack into Iraq. This administration had a point of view the day that happened. If you look at 9/11 separately you realize it had nothing to do with Saddam Hussein. Except [vice president Dick] Cheney and [Deputy Secretary of Defense Paul] Wolfowitz put a plan together in '92 to try to convince [President] Bush One to invade Iraq, but here's what Bush One said about it, in his book *A World Transformed*, which I think is devastating: "I firmly believed that we should not march into Baghdad. To occupy Iraq would instantly shatter our coalition, turning the whole Arab world against us and make a broken tyrant into a latter day Arab hero. Assigning young soldiers to a fruitless hunt for a secretly entrenched dictator and condemning them to fight what would be an unwinnable urban guerilla war."

Now, this administration bought the Cheney-Wolfowitz plan from '92 hook line and sinker. It was all about using 9/11 as an excuse to go into Baghdad, not as a reason.

What's the significance?
Let's chase this rabbit into the ground here. They had a plan to go to war and when 9/11 happened that's what they did; they went to war....

What's your take on the situation in Iraq?
One word: Disaster. And when the secretary of defense puts out a memo to his top staff and says we don't have the metrics to determine whether we're winning or losing the war on terrorism? If the secretary of defense does not understand that we're losing our rear end in Iraq in order to save our face, he ought to quit being secretary of defense. Because all you have to do is ask any Pfc. out there. They're sitting ducks with targets on their backs; they're getting blown up. The question more and more is, for what? And, when are we coming home?

The president is trying to find a reason, now that there's no weapons of mass destruction, no yellow cake coming from Niger, no connection with al Qaeda and no immediate threat to the United States, we now have a war of choice. I'm telling you we're in a mess. It's a disaster.

If the pattern holds for the rest of the month, we'll have 100 US soldiers killed during November. [Note: As of publication of this book US military deaths in Iraq have exceeded 1,000] We've lost more youngsters killed in Iraq in less than a year than we lost during the first three years of the Vietnam War. And people say there's no Vietnam analogy?[19] [emphasis added]

Cleland resigned from the Kean Commission in November 2003. There was little doubt as to why Cleland left the panel. He had been making too much noise. Whether Max Cleland fully understood what he had been involved in, or whether he fully acknowledged it to himself, remains a mystery. There is no doubt that he had been making big waves.

Scamming America: The Official Guide to the 9/11 Cover-up is a booklet of documents from the activist group NY911Truth; the booklet got its name from a remark made by Cleland after his resignation, when he said, "Bush is scamming America." Here is an excerpt:

> Cleland attacked his own commission after the other members cut a deal to accept highly limited access to CIA reports to the White House that may indicate advance knowledge of the attacks on the part of the Bush administration. "This is a scam," Cleland said. "It's disgusting. America is being cheated."
>
> "As each day goes by," Cleland said, "we learn that this government knew a whole lot more about these terrorists before September 11 than it has ever admitted.... Let's chase this rabbit into the ground. They had a plan to go to war and when 9/11 happened that's what they did; they went to war."[20]

The ostensible reason for Cleland's departure, however, was so that he could accept a nomination from President George W. Bush to serve on the board of directors of the Export-Import Bank.[21]

Cleland was quickly replaced by former Nebraska Senator Bob Kerrey.

Bob Kerrey

One press account neatly summed up Kerrey's own conflicts of interest.

> The selection of Kerrey was made not by Bush, it should be pointed out, but rather by the Senate minority leader, Thomas Daschle (Democrat of South Dakota).
>
> Kerrey's own conflicts of interest are myriad. As vice chairman of the Senate Intelligence Committee, Kerrey is a veteran of political cover-ups. While Kerrey was no longer a senator at the time, the committee on which he had served as the highest-ranking Democrat carried out a whitewash of the government role in 9/11, together with its House counterpart, in their toothless joint investigation of the terrorist attacks last year.
>
> Kerrey was also one of the key figures who approved the nomination of CIA Director Tenet and long remained his defender and

political ally. What the CIA knew before September 11 is one of the key questions facing any legitimate investigation into the events.

The former senator is also complicit in the Bush administration's manipulation of the September 11 events to justify a war, already decided upon, against Iraq. Little more than a year ago, Kerrey surfaced as a leading member of an outfit known as the "Committee for the Liberation of Iraq," formed to promote an unprovoked invasion of the Middle Eastern country.

The group, in which Kerrey was the only prominent Democrat, was essentially an offshoot of the Project for the New American Century (PNAC), a Republican think tank that served as a virtual administration-in-waiting. Its principals included Richard Cheney (now vice president), Donald Rumsfeld (now defense secretary), Paul Wolfowitz (Rumsfeld's deputy secretary), George Bush's younger brother Jeb, the governor of Florida, and Lewis Libby (Cheney's chief of staff). The PNAC elaborated a blueprint for achieving US global hegemony by means of military force, beginning with a war against Iraq.

Kerrey had himself been a proponent of a war against Iraq since 1998, joining right-wing Republicans in sponsoring the "Iraqi Liberation Act" and forging close political ties to the Iraqi National Congress, which is headed by the convicted bank embezzler Ahmed Chalabi.

In September of last year, Kerrey wrote an opinion column for the *Wall Street Journal* entitled "Finish the War: Liberate Iraq," in which he echoed the Bush administration's attempts to justify the war by falsely linking Iraq to the September 11 attacks. He repeated the phony claim that the alleged 9/11 hijackers' ringleader, Mohammed Atta, had met with an Iraqi intelligence agent in Prague five months before the attacks. The allegation has been discredited repeatedly by US and foreign intelligence agencies, which say there is no evidence that Atta was ever in the Czech Republic or left the US during this period.[22]

How does the Kean Commission report stack up against this book?

Many major publications, including the *Los Angeles Times*[23] and the *Washington Post*[24] found a great many deficiencies and unanswered questions in the Kean Commission's final report. Their criticisms, however, focused on less-than-earth shattering but still important omissions.

Let's consider what the Commission had to say about some of the matters I've raised here.

Below is a preliminary review (all that could be completed by press time) of how the Kean Commission report compares to this book in 22 key areas of interest we have thus far examined. The various subjects are laid out in the approximate order in which they have previously appeared.

Oil

Aside from footnotes and cursory discussions of oil as a part of the daily life of the Middle East and its importance to countries like Saudi Arabia, I found only the following references to oil that seemed to suggest it might be related in some way to 9/11.

> In Afghanistan, the State Department tried to end the civil war that had continued since the Soviets' withdrawal. The South Asia bureau [connected to Karl "Rick" Inderfurth] believed it might have a carrot for Afghanistan's warring factions in a project by the Union Oil Company of California (UNOCAL) to build a pipeline across the country. While there was probably never much chance of the pipeline actually being built, the Afghan desk hoped that the prospect of shared pipeline profits might lure faction leaders to a conference table. US diplomats did not favor the Taliban over the rival factions. Despite growing concerns, US diplomats were willing at the time, as one official said, to "give the Taliban a chance." [Kean Report, p.111]
>
> US authorities had continued to try to get cooperation from Pakistan in pressing the Taliban to stop sheltering bin Ladin. President Clinton contacted Sharif again in June 1999, partly to discuss the crisis with India but also to urge Sharif, "in the strongest way I can," to persuade the Taliban to expel bin Ladin. The President suggested that Pakistan use its control over oil supplies to the Taliban and over Afghan imports through Karachi. Sharif suggested instead that Pakistani forces might try to capture bin Ladin themselves. Though no one in Washington thought this was likely to happen, President Clinton gave the idea his blessing. [p. 126]
>
> At the September 17 NSC meeting, there was some further discussion of "phase two" of the war on terrorism. President Bush ordered the Defense Department to be ready to deal with Iraq if Baghdad acted against US interests, with plans to include possibly occupying Iraqi oil fields. [p. 335]

(Oil) Pipelines

Aside from what is above, that's it.

Peak Oil

Is not mentioned once.

National energy policy development group

Is not mentioned once, searching either with the full name, the acronym, or as the "Energy Task Force."

Drugs and opium

Opium is not mentioned once. Drugs are mentioned only in generic descriptions of law enforcement priorities.

Halliburton

Is not mentioned once.

Money laundering

Is mentioned only twice in the body of the report in generic terms related to terrorist financing. There is no mention of money laundering through Wall Street.

Caspian region

The word Caspian does not appear once in the report.

Pakistan

In conjunction with the overwhelming involvement of Pakistan with al Qaeda, the Taliban, and terrorist activities, Pakistan is mentioned 311 times. However, there is no mention of General Mahmud Ahmad, Omar Seed Sheikh, the pre-9/11 wire transfer of $100,000 to Mohammed Atta, or the fact that General Ahmad was in Washington on the day of the attacks. The omission of the Ahmad-Atta wire transfer, in light of the fact that the FBI had confirmed it (See Chapter 8) and that several other wire transactions involving Atta were discussed is incriminating.

The Pakistani ISI is not mentioned once by name.

While the report describes deep and incriminating Pakistani connections to al Qaeda, bin Laden, and the Taliban, there is no discussion of the US government's pressure and aid to those groups except, apparently, in the brief mention above of pipelines.

Karl "Rick" Inderfurth

Is mentioned only twice in the body of the report (17 times total) but there is no mention of his well-documented guidance and approval of Pakistani aid to the Taliban or any direct reference to his continuing negotiations with the Taliban after the so-called 2000 election.

The Carlyle Group

Is not mentioned once.

Khalid bin Mahfouz

Is not mentioned once.

PROMIS software

Is not mentioned once, either by name or indirectly.

Vreeland

Delmart "Mike" Vreeland is not mentioned once.

Dave Frasca

Is not mentioned once.

Sibel Edmonds

Is not mentioned once in the report's body and only twice in the report's footnotes. In the body of the report the commission adopts the FBI's position that it did not have enough translators to process all available intelligence (p. 77).

Coleen Rowley

While the Phoenix memo is mentioned repeatedly, Coleen Rowley is mentioned only once in a footnote. I can find no record in the final report or on the commission's website that Coleen Rowley was even interviewed by the commission.

John O'Neill

Is not mentioned once.

Insider trading

With respect to the massive insider trades that occurred before September 11th, the commission took a position that was deliberately misleading. By saying that al Qaeda did not make the trades the commission brushed off the fact that someone else did. Its statement is flatly contradicted by the reporting on many major press organizations, some of which (e.g., Bloomberg) specialize and are noted for their reliability in financial matters. The commission's explanation is a dog that won't hunt and it flatly contradicts reports from CBS News, Bloomberg, and other respected financial publications.

> 130. Highly publicized allegations of insider trading in advance of 9/11 generally rest on reports of unusual pre-9/11 trading activity in companies whose stock plummeted after the attacks. Some unusual trading did in fact occur, but each such trade proved to have an innocuous explanation. For example, the volume of put options — investments that pay off only when a stock drops in price — surged in the parent companies of United Airlines on September 6 and American Airlines on September 10 — highly suspicious trading on its face. Yet, further investigation has revealed that the trading had no connection with 9/11. A single US-based institutional investor with no conceivable ties to al Qaeda purchased 95 percent of the UAL puts on September 6 as part of a trading strategy that also included buying 115,000 shares of American on September 10. Similarly, much of the seemingly suspicious trading in American on September 10 was traced to a specific US-based options trading newsletter, faxed to its subscribers

on Sunday, September 9, which recommended these trades. These examples typify the evidence examined by the investigation. The SEC and the FBI, aided by other agencies and the securities industry, devoted enormous resources to investigating this issue, including securing the cooperation of many foreign governments. These investigators have found that the apparently suspicious consistently proved innocuous. Joseph Cella interview (Sept. 16, 2003; May 7, 2004; May 10-11, 2004); FBI briefing (Aug. 15, 2003); SEC memo, Division of Enforcement to SEC Chair and Commissioners, "Pre-September 11, 2001 Trading Review, "May 15, 2002; Ken Breen interview (Apr. 23, 2004); Ed G. interview (Feb. 3, 2004) [See also Kean Report footnote, p. 499].

Israel

Although Israel is mentioned some 35 times in the report there is no discussion anywhere of any Israeli intelligence activities (anywhere) prior to 9/11 or the spy ring that had been operating in the US. There is no mention of Amdocs, Comverse, or Odigo.

7WTC

Is not mentioned once.

Enron

Is not mentioned once.

The office of national preparedness

Is not mentioned once.

We have already discussed how the commission reported on NORAD, CONR, the FAA, and the Secret Service. The Kean Report also fails to address the myriad intelligence penetrations achieved, by US intelligence agencies, of al Qaeda and bin Laden, nor does it ask any questions as to why it would not have been possible to stop the attacks based upon these documented penetrations.

In investigating one crime we have stumbled across another. Not only did the Kean commission fail to fulfill it legal mandate, it has criminally misrepresented and hidden key pieces of evidence. This is — in law enforcement parlance — a dead-bang, open-and-shut case. Every commissioner should be headed for jail right now. In a sane world they would be.

But the commission's behavior fits perfectly into our map.

Before concluding this work we must look at how some major developments have played out since 9/11. Not only do those events corroborate our working thesis, they provide further evidence establishing motive, means, and opportunity. They also help answer another question every detective ponders in a tough case: Who benefits?

CHAPTER 27

"WE DON'T NEED NO BADGES"

The plans for the invasion of Afghanistan, the invasion of Iraq, the worldwide deployment of US military forces to control oil reserves, the Patriot Act, Homeland Security, and legislation that sets the stage for biological warfare and complete domestic repression were all in place well before the first plane hit the World Trade Center.[1]

On the day of the attacks themselves, according to University of Illinois Professor of International Law Francis Boyle, two US aircraft carrier battle groups were conveniently "rotating" duty stations off the Pakistani coast. The British had the largest armada since the Falkland Islands war loaded and ready to meet 23,000 British troops already positioned across a short stretch of ocean in Oman, and the US also conveniently had 17,000 troops positioned in Egypt for a joint military exercise called Operation Bright Star.

Two days before 9/11, President Bush was delivered a 27-page top secret document containing a complete battle plan for the invasion of Afghanistan.[2] Other stories soon revealed that the plan had been many months in the making. And as a footnote, the document called for the Pentagon to begin immediate planning options for an invasion of Iraq.[3] With 11 percent of the world's oil, Iraq had been in the crosshairs for a long time.

Journalist Jennifer Van Bergen, writing for *Truthout* (<www.truthout.org>), described in detail how most of the provisions of the Patriot Act had been prepared long before the attacks. She traced many of them back to the 1996 anti-terror legislation enacted after the Oklahoma City bombing. She described how principled lawmakers such as John Conyers of Michigan stood in the breach, even then, to question unconstitutional provisions that were later passed almost without a thought after 9/11/01.[4] Conyers remains one of the last, fearless, clear-headed champions of liberty on Capitol Hill.

Homeland Security can trace its roots backwards to the Hart-Rudman US Commission on National Security (which began its work in 1997 and recommended a cabinet level anti-terrorism department in January of 2001),[5] the Anser Institute for Homeland Security,[6] the previously cited Rand Corporation study from 1999-2000, and early Bush presidential decisions. All are direct and strikingly familiar antecedents showing that the Empire had its track shoes on well before 9/11. More clues.

The foundations of the *National Security Strategy of the United States*, released by Bush on September 17, 2002, have an equally obvious lineage. Most notable among these, in my opinion, was a 1998 Harvard University study, *Catastrophic Terrorism: Elements of a National Policy*, the Foreword of which begins with the concept of "Preventive Defense." The report was authored by Ashton Carter, Phillip D. Zelikow, and former CIA Director John Deutch.[7] Zelikow briefed the incoming Bush administration on al Qaeda threats and has co-authored a book with Condoleezza Rice. These massive conflicts of interest, and his refusal to acknowledge them, have earned him the scorn of many families of 9/11 victims for having assumed the role of executive director of the so-called 9/11 Independent Commission. Additional uproar arose when it was disclosed that he even gave evidence in closed session to the commission he was directing.[8]

These policies and their legal embodiments share a remarkable characteristic — the preponderance of members of the Council on Foreign Relations, the Trilateral Commission, and the Bilderberger Group on the advisory panels and staffs of every commission and every panel that produced them. By my rough calculations, more than 80 percent of the people who first articulated these doctrines and plans belong to one or more of these groups. And behind all of that is the undeniable presence of the corporate, financial, and oil interests supporting globalization and the World Trade Organization. This is the sort of observation that draws the contempt of official (i.e., corporate) media consumers, who tend to regard the group affiliations of policymakers as somehow off-limits to rational analysis. But it turns out that these officials are indeed members of these non-governmental elite groups, and that these groups have stated ideals and historical behavior patterns which are perfectly consistent with the concerns raised here and on the *From The Wilderness* website; concerns about Peak Oil, militarism, and a fascinating but frightening ride down a steep stairway to fascism.

Since we now know that the US government and its intelligence agencies were in possession of enough intelligence to have prevented the attacks of September 11 — and this truth has even been admitted, if obliquely, by the findings of at least one Congressional committee[9] — then what is the justification for the Patriot Act, a law that raped the Constitution, and the subsequent creation of a $40 billion Department of Homeland Security in the largest reorganization of the federal government in 50 years? The claim that these travesties are needed to gather enough knowledge to prevent future terrorist attacks is, clearly, absurd. The system wasn't broken. So why fix it? Just who or what is the enemy?[10]

Perhaps the most offensive post-9/11 statement made by an administration official — even surpassing the outright lie that no one in the administration knew that airplanes could be used as weapons — was made by National Security Advisor

Condoleezza Rice in summer 2002, when she asked a news commentator if it was necessary that the US government have more than 30 percent foreknowledge of a pending attack before taking action to prevent it. The US government had complete foreknowledge of 9/11 and did nothing! In fact, it actively shielded the hijackers from arrest before their crimes occurred, and then stood back and facilitated the attacks as an accomplice. Had the US government not opened the door and then prevented dedicated law enforcement personnel from closing it, the attacks would never have occurred.

Herein lies the true nature of the world since 9/11, consistent with what I wrote in May 2001 when Citigroup purchased Banamex in Mexico. The Empire no longer cares about how it is viewed, whether its actions are legal or not, or whether the world might rise up in political, military, or economic opposition to it. It no longer cares whether the American people rise up and take to the streets by the millions. It doesn't care whether civil disobedience or even a real revolution begins at home. It arrogantly believes it has prepared for every contingency. Among its most elastic mandates for procedural omnipotence is George W. Bush's *National Security Strategy of the United States*.[11] That document enshrines two shocking *de facto* powers of the Empire: to launch, without provocation, pre-emptive strikes anywhere it wishes and against any nation that might someday be a threat; and to create artificial terrorist activity where it wishes to deploy troops, with an avowed policy of lying to the world through unprecedented manipulation of the corporate media with which it colludes. The Empire has thus defined the scope of conflict at the end of the age of oil: a no-holds-barred, no-rules, and no-quarter race for global domination.

Spelling it out

The Proactive Preemptive Operating Group (P2OG) was first revealed when *Los Angeles Times* columnist William Arkin received a 78-page briefing report from the Pentagon in October of 2002. Although initial coverage by the *Times,* warming people up for Arkin's story, did not look deeply into P2OG's darker aspects, even those implied by its name, a deluge of stories from other sources soon confirmed the worst.[12] Arkin's story a day later disclosed the basics, namely that the Pentagon had decided to go out and strike terrorists preemptively: "the largest expansion of covert action by the armed forces since the Vietnam era." Arkin also described how Special Operations troops were going to be sent out on covert missions all over the world to carry out these attacks. P2OG was to be the interface between the CIA and the Pentagon's Joint Special Operations Command to execute the missions.[13]

Included in Arkin's story was an ominous statement buried near the end: "Among other things, this body would launch secret operations aimed at 'stimulating reactions' among terrorists and states possessing weapons of mass destruction — that is, for instance, prodding terrorist cells into action and exposing themselves to 'quick response' attacks by US forces."[14] The implications and real intent were spelled out a few days later by Chris Floyd writing in *CounterPunch* (<www.counterpunch.org>):

> This column stands foursquare with the Honorable Donald H. Rumsfeld, US Secretary of Defense, when he warns that there will be more terrorist attacks against the American people and civilization at large. We know, as does the Honorable Donald H. Rumsfeld, that this statement is an incontrovertible fact, a matter of scientific certainty. And how can we and the Honorable Donald H. Rumsfeld, US Secretary of Defense, be so sure that there will be more terrorist attacks against the American people and civilization at large? Because these attacks will be instigated at the order of the Honorable Donald H. Rumsfeld...
>
> In other words, and let's say this plainly, clearly and soberly, so that no one can mistake the intention of Rumsfeld's plan — the United States government is planning to use "cover and deception," and secret military operations, to provoke murderous terrorist attacks. Let's say it again: Donald Rumsfeld, Dick Cheney, George W. Bush, and the other members of the unelected regime in Washington plan to deliberately foment the murder of innocent people in order to further their geopolitical ambitions...
>
> No, it seems the Pee-Twos have bigger fish to fry. Once they have sparked terrorists into action — by killing their family members? luring them with loot? fueling them with drugs? plying them with jihad propaganda? messing with their mamas? or with agents provocateurs, perhaps, who infiltrate groups then plan and direct the attacks themselves? — they can then take measures against the "states/sub-state actors accountable" for "harboring" the Rumsfeld-roused gangs. What kind of measures exactly? Well, the classified Pentagon program puts it this way: "Their sovereignty will be at risk."
>
> The Pee-Twos will thus come in handy whenever the Regime hankers to add a little oil-laden real estate or a new military base to the Empire's burgeoning portfolio.
>
> Just find a nest of violent malcontents, stir 'em with a stick, and presto: instant "justification" for whatever level of intervention/conquest you might desire. And what if the territory you fancy doesn't actually harbor any convenient marauders to use for fun and profit? Well, surely a God-like "super-Intelligence Support Activity" is capable of creation *ex nihilo*, yes?[15]

Of course, as we have seen consistently since 9/11 and as I not too cheerily predicted in November of 2001, these conflicts, from Afghanistan, to Central Asia, to Iraq, to West Africa, to Indonesia have occurred only in nations that have significant hydrocarbon resources or are critical to their delivery.

A number of stories covering the P2OG also disclosed the rebirth of one of the most corrupt organizations ever to emerge in the history of US covert operations. Called the Intelligence Support Activity (ISA) and reinstituted under the name Gray Fox, it was created by Army General Richard Stillwell in 1981 after the failed hostage rescue mission in Iran, which resulted in the destruction of several US aircraft and many casualties (not to mention the implosion of the Carter administration). The mainstream media paid lip service to the ISA's checkered past, using comments from people like former Defense Secretary Frank Carlucci, who called it "uncoordinated and uncontrolled." But they also left out a great deal: I have written extensively about the ISA and found it connected to organized crime, drug trafficking, money laundering, and assassination.[16] Regular readers of *From The Wilderness* have long been familiar with the names Bo Gritz, Al Carone, Scott Weekly, and Scott Barnes. All were at one time or another ISA operatives (See chapter 10). Throughout Iran-Contra the ISA was up to its nose in drugs, and the heroin-saturated environment in Afghanistan today is as comfortable for the unit now as an old warm blanket.

Journalist Wayne Madsen noted:

> The ISA is working with the Defense Policy Board [formerly] chaired by Richard Perle. US intelligence sources reveal that Perle is actually tasking the ISA with the assistance of former CIA Middle East specialist Reuel Mark Gerecht and former Reagan National Security consultant Michael Ledeen, both veterans of the Iran-Contra affair. Both are officially resident scholars with the right-wing American Enterprise Institute, as is Perle .... Another Iran-Contra alumnus involved with ISA is retired Air Force General Richard Secord, who has established close links with the intelligence services of Azerbaijan, Uzbekistan, Kazakhstan, and the Kurd groups in northern Iraq.[17]

While in Moscow in March 2001, I developed sources who told me, even then, that Uzbekistan was awash in a sea of poppies and that Secord had established fixed-base operations for Evergreen Air and a reincarnated Southern Air Transport at the Tashkent airport. If true, Secord's reported appearance with the ISA as heroin trade in the region exploded after the US occupation of Afghanistan is a replay of the work in which Secord and his cronies engaged in Laos during the Vietnam War and during Iran-Contra. Among his colleagues from that era one finds our current Deputy Secretary of State, Richard Armitage. As I predicted even before the attacks, it was not going to be long before CIA-connected aircraft were flying loads of heroin to markets in Russia, Europe, and maybe even the US itself.

Torture

In this mad scramble for the finish line, the Empire has also sanctioned torture, calling it by the Orwellian name "rendition." In cases where extreme brutality is deemed necessary, the CIA and the Pentagon have resorted to tactics that are well established in covert operations and extremely well described in former CIA case officer Philip Agee's 1975 book, *Inside the Company: CIA Diary.* It gives the people it wants severely tortured to agents from other countries. As one unnamed official put it to the *Washington Post,* "We don't kick the [expletive] out of them. We send them to other countries so they can kick the [expletive] out of them."[18]

Following that, the United States, through another major Iran-Contra player — current UN Ambassador John Negroponte — has demanded immunity from prosecution for war crimes in the International Criminal Court. In a June 2002 bombshell dropped on the UN Security Council, Negroponte said that unless it was granted immunity on peacekeeping missions the US would refuse to participate in any more of them.[19] In the Orwellian Newspeak of today's world, the invasion of Iraq, articulated as an enforcement of UN resolutions, could be described as a peacekeeping mission. And since the US has already stated that it will start conflicts wherever necessary, it has become the extorting arsonist in charge of the fire department.

I was not surprised at all when, in the spring of 2004, the Bush administration nominated Negroponte to become the US Ambassador to the façade of an Iraqi government and congress rolled over without a whimper.

Fortunately, as we will soon see, the Bush regime and the Neocons overplayed their hand to the displeasure of those who put them in power. While it is likely that the regime will be replaced, either electorally or through impeachment, the Empire/Corporation and its ultimate objectives will remain intact.

Deceit

In February 2002 it was disclosed that immediately after the 9/11 attacks the Bush administration had activated the Office of Strategic Influence (OSI) in the Pentagon. The OSI's (not to be confused with the US Air Force's Office of Special Investigations) purpose is to use major media and government-subsidized press organizations to lie to and mislead people around the world (and at home) about US plans and the activities as well as the motivations and beliefs of its enemies. The Pentagon called this a program of "information deception."[20] There was some protest from the media, who were offended at being so publicly exposed in this newly shocking version of what they were already doing. But the general public reacted with genuine outrage, until on February 26 Secretary of Defense Donald Rumsfeld announced that he was disbanding the unit.[21] But the deception did not end there.

On November 18, Rumsfeld told a press briefing that he had given up the name OSI but that he was still seeing to it that the erstwhile office's mission was being fulfilled. He said, "And then there was the Office of Strategic Influence .... You may recall that. And 'oh my goodness gracious isn't that terrible, Henny Penny the sky is going to fall.' I went down that next day and said fine, if you want to savage this thing, fine, I'll give you the corpse. There's the name. You can have the name,

WE DON'T NEED NO BADGES" 477

but I'm gonna keep doing every single thing that needs to be done and I have."[22] By December 19 the *New York Times* and the *Salt Lake Tribune* were reporting that the office's mission was still being carried out. By that time the outrage had subsided.[23]

Nukes

The Bush administration made its global posture clear when it confirmed to the *Los Angeles Times* in March of 2002 that it had prepared contingency plans to use nuclear weapons against seven countries: China, Russia, Iraq, North Korea, Iran, Libya, and Syria.[24] And, according to the *New York Post,* it drove home the point again in December when it hinted in a six-page document that it might use nuclear weapons in a pre-emptive first strike against Iraq if it felt that Iraq might be preparing to use weapons of mass destruction.[25]

TIA

That kind of ruthless resolve has also been focused on the American people, but in a different way. As demonstrated by Total Information Awareness (TIA) — a program created by DARPA — the government is now monitoring almost every activity of all Americans, from bank deposits, to shopping, to web surfing, to academic grades, to divorce records, to spending, to phone calls, to utility usage, to travel.[26] The Empire has placed all of its faith in incredible new technologies, ranging from PROMIS software and its progeny to exotic weapons systems that are now emerging into public view. It not only plans to track everything you do, it plans to employ face recognition software that can be used to prevent you from making a withdrawal at your bank or from boarding a plane.[27] It plans to identify you by your voice,[28] and to recognize you by your unique body odor.[29] It even plans, through the use of "non-invasive neuro-electric sensors," to read your mind.[30] And these developments have been reported in prominent media outlets quoting government sources. There was a time, before the Patriot Act was passed, that a search warrant — a process requiring a judge to review a request to ascertain whether your rights were being violated — would have been required for almost all of this. Those rights don't exist anymore, nor can they return without a popular will to demand them.[31]

Aside from clearly stating that American citizens, having nothing to do with al Qaeda or a foreign organization, might be classified as terrorists,[32] the Bush administration has also stated its intent to explore systems that can "detect whether an individual has been immunized against a threat pathogen or has recently handled threat material."[33] How does one detect a vaccination without elaborate and relatively invasive blood sample processing? Implant an electronic *record* of vaccination under the skin. In its plan for Homeland Security, the Bush White House stated that it wanted all persons entering the country to be prepared to submit "biometric identifiers."[34]

Does the microchip technology exist? Absolutely. It is already being sold to the public. A recent full-page ad from Hitachi describes the new *Mu* chip, which can be attached to passports and banknotes and easily implanted into human beings by subdermal injection. It is 0.4 mm by 0.4 mm, or about the size of a small grain of sand, only flat. It's an RFID (Radio Frequency ID) chip, meaning that when scanned with a device like the ones used to check you out at your local supermarket, it will instantly register your own personal bar code, which will then plug into the master database of your life down at Total Information Awareness.

A much larger chip (the size of a grain of rice) is already on the market and being sold for human implantation. Unlike Hitachi's passive chip, the VeriChip is capable of *sending* radio signals, even of locating your position via satellite-based Global Positioning Systems (GPS). And it is being touted as a way of controlling access to restricted areas, or automatically charging your bank account for purchases, and even interfacing with computer systems.[35] For years now, the public has been conditioned into acceptance of the microchips that are now routinely injected into pets and in some cases, even into small children.

George W. Bush signed the Homeland Security bill into law on November 25, 2002. The first software to implement the TIA program, named *Genoa,* was reported as being delivered to DARPA 23 days later.[36] In praising the software, convicted Iran-Contra felon and former Reagan National security Advisor Admiral John Poindexter — who was to run the program — said that Genoa provides "tools for collaborative reasoning, estimating plausible futures, and creating actionable options for the decision maker."[37] Poindexter's past, however, proved to be too much of liability, especially after he proposed a futures trading market that would speculate on terrorist events.[38] CNN described the financial program, which would have generated profits for those predicting terror attacks thus:

> Under the latest now-canceled program, called the Futures Markets Applied to Prediction (FutureMAP), investors using futures market analysis would have been allowed to predict the likelihood of acts of terrorism or international incidents — such as an attack on Israel or the overthrow of the king of Jordan, both cited as examples on the program's website earlier this week. A correct prediction would yield a profit for the investor.
>
> As news of the program spread through Washington this week, lawmakers — particularly Democrats — reacted with shock and disbelief.[39]

Strangely, as the controversy raged over the terror-futures market, not a single press organ in the US displayed the slightest institutional memory of the insider trading that occurred before September 11th.

TIA and the ill-fated FutureMAP are, of course, nothing more than the enhanced and evolved PROMIS software discussed in Chapter 8. The difference is that what has been previously paid for and procured by illegal covert operations, drug dealing, and theft, was to have been paid for a second time by the American taxpayer as TIA became an appropriations item. Opposition to TIA at the public and congressional level, over its gross violation of privacy in direct violation of the Constitution, led Congress to suspend official funding for the program in 2003. However I knew that TIA was not going away. It was already in place and enormously powerful. I had to wait only until February of 2004 for my confirmation:

> Congress eliminated a Pentagon office developing the terrorist tracking technology because of the outcry over privacy implications. But some of those projects from retired Admiral John Poindexter's Total Information Awareness effort were transferred to US intelligence offices, congressional, federal, and research officials told the Associated Press.
>
> In addition, Congress left undisturbed a separate but similar $64-million research program run by a little-known office called the Advanced Research and Development Activity (ARDA) that has used some of the same researchers as Poindexter's program.
>
> "The whole congressional action looks like a shell game," said Steve Aftergood of the Federation of American Scientists, which tracks work by US intelligence agencies. "There may be enough of a difference for them to claim TIA was terminated while for all practical purposes the identical work is continuing."[40]

Genetically engineered bioweapons

Reporting from Austin, Texas, and Hamburg, Germany, journalist Viviane Lerner said on August 12, 2002 that US Army Special Forces had issued a "brief but explicit" request for US scientists to make proposals to create genetically engineered offensive biological weapons. This was the fourth such US request uncovered by the weapons research watchdog group, *The Sunshine Project,* in 2002 alone. The requests themselves were violations of the US Biological Weapons Anti-Terrorism Act, and clear violations of the Biological and Toxic Weapons Convention. The types of weapons sought were genetically manufactured agents that could do anything from eating metal or concrete to destroying the food crops of an "enemy" country. These weapons, being developed primarily by the military and the National Academy of Sciences, aside from being particularly nasty, are also considerable threats to the ecosystem because of uncertainties as to how they will interact with the environment once outside a closed system.[41]

Real terror

One of the greatest military commanders of all time, Genghis Khan, fully understood terror as a weapon of war. As he set out to conquer the known world and as his armies raced westward across Asia, he would often send scouts ahead to infiltrate and study the culture of his next target. When ready to attack he would then dress up a few of his select warriors in the clothing of the targeted people. He would bloody a few, wound them, and send them well ahead of his armies. His warriors hysterically warned the target audience of the power and might of the great tyrant, described the millions of fierce and invincible troops, and implored the hapless victims to flee for their lives or surrender and ask for mercy. It worked.

By completing a decades-long subjugation of congress to financial interests, the administration has put into place the requisite structures for control of the Empire at home including the control of all law enforcement agencies in an emergency.

I also believe that Senator Paul Wellstone was murdered just before the November 2002 elections (through the mid-flight disablement of his aircraft, possibly with an electromagnetic pulse weapon), as the *coup de grace* in this final destruction of Constitutional government. Following the Patriot Act's statutory removal of constitutional protections, there will soon be few lower court judges in place to question the Emperor's decisions, and the few brave members remaining in Congress to ask the necessary questions, such as Congressmen Ron Paul of Texas, Dennis Kucinich, and John Conyers, will have been rendered little more than ornamental window-dressing for the propaganda machine's sales pitch that debate is still alive.

Congress was not allowed even to read the Patriot Act or the Homeland Security bills before being compelled to vote on them. Congressman Ron Paul of Texas confirmed this in an interview for my video "The Truth and Lies of 9/11," produced after I lectured at Portland State University in November of 2001. This was not the first time this has happened. It happened also with the huge anti-crime legislation enacted in 1994. Other members of Congress with whom I spoke in 2001 expressed the same complaint.

This mindset of the Empire reminds me of the classic line from the 1948 movie *The Treasure of Sierra Madre,* in which Humphrey Bogart confronts disheveled bandits who claim to be policemen. When Bogart asks to see their badges, their leader replies, "Badges? We ain't got no badges! We don't need no badges. I don't have to show you any stinkin' badges!"

Perhaps Bush had been watching that film when he proffered to the American people his remarkable new doctrine of presidential responsibility: "I do not need to explain why I say things. That's the interesting thing about being the president. Maybe somebody needs to explain to me why they say something, but I don't feel like I owe anybody an explanation."

This attitude was perfectly mirrored by America's reaction to the partially successful global campaign against the Iraqi invasion of March 2003. Regardless of the costs and regardless of international law, UN pressure, public opinion, or the inevitably disastrous consequences, the Bush administration proceeded, and the bloody toll is still being paid today even as the financial and environmental costs will remain to be paid by future generations.

On January 10, 2003, Richard Perle, then Chairman of the Defense Department's Policy Board, told the world that no matter what the UN or other nations in the world did or said, the United States was going to attack Iraq when it was ready. Nothing would prevent it.[42] Donald Rumsfeld later added that the Department of Defense didn't have to show the world evidence it had that Iraq possessed weapons of mass destruction.[43]

As if things weren't frightening enough, it was briefly announced in June 2002 that Israel and the United States were in discussions to establish a joint anti-terrorism office in which Israel would assist the United States in monitoring all global instant communications and linking its security network to the Department of Homeland Security. One observer called the move an "Israelization" of American politics.[44]

Following this development, UPI terrorism correspondent Richard Sale disclosed in January 2003 that that Israel's Mossad would be engaging in a more proactive anti-terror policy which would include targeted killings and assassinations *inside* the United States. Although the Israeli embassy denied the report, Sale secured a number of confirmations from Israeli military and intelligence sources and oblique confirmations from official US sources. Sale's story also described a massive expansion of Mossad fueled by a sizeable budget increase.[45]

Meaningful solidarity with the good people of Israel and the United States is impossible without a vigorous condemnation of the evil committed in their names. A consortium of interests including banking, narco-traffic, arms, and key multinational corporations has reached a new level of aggression. While Israel and the US behave with an ever more open and frank contempt for international law and for human life, it would be a mistake to attribute the actions of their elites to nationalism. No, the players in the great game — whose moves include 9/11, the Iraq war, and the approaching global storm — are not motivated by any loyalty to country, nor to ethnicity, nor religion, family, firm, alliance, or friendship. It's just money, and the meaning of money: power.

28

CONQUERING THE AMERICAN PEOPLE

T he post 9/11 erosion of civil liberties and the economic devastation that is being felt here at home are opposite sides of the same coin.

Part I: American liberty

"We're likely to experience more restrictions on our personal freedom than has ever been the case in our country."

US Supreme Court Justice Sandra Day O'Connor, September 30, 2001

Some of the fundamental changes to Americans' legal rights by the Bush Administration and the U.S.A. Patriot Act following the terror attacks:

- *FREEDOM OF ASSOCIATION: The government may monitor religious and political institutions without suspecting criminal activity to assist in terror investigation.*
- *FREEDOM OF INFORMATION: Government has closed once-public immigration hearings, has secretly detained hundreds of people without charges, and has encouraged bureaucrats to resist public records requests.*
- *FREEDOM OF SPEECH: Government may prosecute librarians or keepers of any other records if they tell anyone that the government subpoenaed information related to a terrorism investigation.*
- *RIGHT TO LEGAL REPRESENTATION: Government may monitor federal prison jailhouse conversations between attorneys and clients, and deny lawyers to Americans accused of crimes.*
- *FREEDOM FROM UNREASONABLE SEARCHES: Government may search and seize Americans' papers and effects without probable cause to assist terror investigation.*
- *RIGHT TO A SPEEDY AND PUBLIC TRIAL: Government may jail Americans indefinitely without a trial.*
- *RIGHT TO LIBERTY: Americans may be jailed without being charged or being able to confront witnesses against them.*

Associated Press, September 5, 2002

Thousands of times per day, in the discourse of public officials and candidates, in the media and on the street, America is exalted as the land of the free. While the truth of the matter was never quite as simple as that, the decades when this sentiment had a real basis in fact and in law are long gone. But as that legendary freedom disappears, the beneficiaries of its destruction are shouting about our glorious Freedom ever more loudly.[1]

If you understand nothing else about the map that I have been trying to draw for you, understand that the post 9/11 erosion of civil liberties and the economic devastation that is being felt here at home are opposite sides of the same coin. One begets and demands the other, whether the Empire consciously considers it or not. And the currents of behavior depicted on the map dictate, as surely as gravity pulls things down and not up, that what has already started can only get worse. Until now, in the Empire's domestic ham and eggs breakfast, the American people were playing the role of the chicken rather than the pig.

The Patriot Act

I wrote the following essay for the November 2001 issue of *FTW*:

> The "F" Word
> Fascism: 1. Totalitarianism marked by right-wing dictatorship and bellicose nationalism. 2. Oppressive, dictatorial control.
> *American Heritage Dictionary*
>
> My fellow Americans:
> "On what legal meat does this our Caesar feed?"[2] wrote *New York Times* Columnist William Safire as he blasted President Bush's November 13 [2001] emergency order permitting non-citizens the government has "reason to believe" are terrorists to be tried inside the US by military tribunals. These trials may be held in secret and the prosecutors do not have to produce evidence if it is "in the interests of national security." And the condemned may then be executed "even if a third of the officers disagree." Safire categorized this as a "dictatorial power to jail or execute aliens." Bush's proclamation is a nullification of the 6th Amendment to the US Constitution. At the same time that Caesar Bush was announcing this edict, the Justice Department was announcing, as reported in the AP on November 15, that it would not disclose the identities or status of more than 1,100 people arrested or detained since September 11th, nor would it continue to release a running tally of those detained.
>
> As the anxiety level rises in you, you think, "Well, I'm a citizen so I don't have anything to worry about."
>
> Try harder to refocus on your Christmas list, Harry Potter, and your job.

On October 26th — a date that will live in infamy - the President signed the USA/PATRIOT act, officially known as HR 3162. And you should well note that, according to Representative Ron Paul (R) of Texas — as reported on November 9th by Kelly O'Meara of the *Washington Times' Insight Magazine* — the bill had not even been printed and members of the House could not read it before they were compelled to vote on it. O'Meara wrote, "Meanwhile, efforts to obtain copies of the new bill were stonewalled even by the committee that wrote it." Most of its provisions have nothing to do with fighting terrorism. Under this so-called anti-terrorist measure:

- Any federal law enforcement agency may enter your home or business when you are not there, collect evidence, not tell you about it, and then use that evidence to convict you of a crime; (This nullifies the Fourth Amendment to the Constitution). And, says the ACLU, it doesn't even have to be a terrorism investigation, just a criminal investigation. [Section 213 — The Sneak and Peek provision].

- Any federal law enforcement agency may, if they suspect that you are committing a crime, monitor all of your Internet traffic and read your emails. They may also intercept all of your cell phone calls as well. No warrant is required. (This violates the Fourth and Fifth Amendments to the Constitution.) [Section 202 and 216] [See *FTW* on Carnivore, Vol. IV, No.2, April 30, 2001]

- The FBI or any other federal law enforcement agency may come to your business and seize any of your business records — if they claim it is connected with a terrorist investigation — and they can arrest you if you tell anyone that they were there. (This violates the First and the Fourth Amendments to the Constitution.) [Title II, Section 501]

- The CIA can now operate inside the US and spy on American citizens. And, as directed by Attorney General Ashcroft on November 13, it is also permitted to share its intelligence files with local law enforcement agencies (and vice versa). The CIA has spied on Americans for decades, but the fruits of that spying have never been admissible in court. Now law enforcement will have the ability to rewrite the intelligence as a probable cause statement, conduct an investigation, and introduce it as evidence. This, from material that was collected outside the rules of search and seizure. (There goes the Exclusionary Rule of the Fourth Amendment.) [Titles 2 & 9]

- The foundation for an international secret political police agency is laid by allowing the CIA to receive wiretap information from any local agency and then share it with the intelligence services of any foreign country. [Section 203]

So now a darkness begins to sink over your consciousness. You are angry, first at me, and then you are not quite sure of what to be mad at - but you know you're mad. Reaching through a vaguely guilty conscience you check with yourself and beg of your soul the permission to take the position that you never break any laws. None! You're a good citizen of the Homeland, a good German - I mean American. What can you do anyway?

Then I arouse your rage at me even further by telling you that Section 802 of HR 3162 defines domestic terrorism as "activities that — involve acts dangerous to human life that are a violation of the criminal laws of the United States: ... and appear to be intended to intimidate or coerce a civilian population; or to influence the policy of a government by intimidation or coercion ...."

Under this definition the blocking of a driveway at a federal building or defending yourself when attacked by good "Germans" at a protest march — while protesting these violations of the Constitution — could instantly make you a "domestic terrorist" and subject to some of the stiffest penalties ever enacted into law.

Next, as you retreat further, covering your ears and mind, shutting out the crime that is being perpetrated by your government — against you — you will lash out at me and say, "Look Ruppert, I read the Bill. There's a 'Sunset Clause' in it. All this stuff goes away after four years. It's just for the duration of the terrorist emergency."

Not so. Under Section 224 (b) "With respect to any particular foreign intelligence investigation that began before the date on which the provisions referred to in subsection (a) cease to have effect, or with respect to any particular offense or potential offense that began or occurred before the date on which such provisions cease to have effect, such provisions shall continue in effect." In other words, if the government says that their desire to burglarize, or wiretap you or search your files is part of an investigation that started before December 31, 2005, there is no sunset clause. This could be for a "potential" offense. What is a potential offense? Something you thought about? Something you might have thought about?

Now thoroughly uncomfortable you reach for more straw teddy bears. And I, like a hunter smelling victory, will close in on you with words that will both reassure you and make you a grown-up. Upon reviewing HR 3162 Congressman Paul said to reporter O'Meara, "Our forefathers would think it's time for a revolution. This is why they revolted in the first place .... They revolted against much more mild oppression."

Mao once said, "Revolution is not a dinner party." You squirm in your seat.

OK, the Congressman's noble words stirred you for a moment, made you think of Mel Gibson in *The Patriot*. But you realize that you're not Mel Gibson, you're out of shape, you have bills to pay, a vacation coming soon. Reaching again, you realize something. "Wait! This is a law. It was passed. It's proof that there are checks and balances."

I'm coming to get you now.

Beyond The Law [Not a Steven Seagal Movie]

On November 9th, Attorney General Ashcroft announced that he was ordering the Justice Department to begin wiretapping and monitoring attorney-client communications in terrorist cases where the suspect was incarcerated. This was not even discussed in HR 3162. That same day Senator Patrick Leahy (D), Vermont wrote to Ashcroft. He had many questions to ask about what the Justice Department had been doing by violating the trust of Congress and assuming powers that were not authorized by either law or the Constitution. Leahy even quoted a Supreme Court case (US v. Robel):

"[T]his concept of 'national defense' cannot be deemed an end in itself, justifying any exercise of ... power designed to promote such a goal. Implicit in the term 'national defense' is the notion that defending those values and ideas which set this Nation apart .... It would indeed be ironic if, in the name of national defense, we would sanction the subversion of one of those liberties .... which makes the defense of the Nation worthwhile."

Leahy asked Ashcroft by what authority he had decided — on his own and without judicial review — to nullify the Fifth Amendment to the Constitution. He asked for an explanation and some description of the procedural safeguards that Ashcroft would put in place. He asked Ashcroft to appear before the Judiciary committee and to respond in writing by November 13.

His answer came a little late.

On November 16, Patrick Leahy received an anthrax letter. And, as of this press time, Ashcroft has not responded in writing.

I've got you now.

Moving up the ladder we come to the Vice President, Dick Cheney. *The Washington Post* reported on November 9 that all summer a major constitutional clash had been brewing as the former head of oil giant Halliburton refused to surrender to Congress's investigative arm, the GAO, records from his energy task force. The *Post* story said, "Comptroller General David M. Walker described the fight as a direct threat to the GAO's reason for being, a separation-of-powers issue that would determine whether the legislative branch could exercise the oversight role envisioned by the founding fathers." But the September 11th attacks have changed all that. A planned suit by the GAO against Cheney to get the records of his task force on oil has been put on hold. Cheney's violation of the law goes unchallenged in the goose-stepped march of manufactured polls showing support for the administration. Congressman Henry Waxman (D), CA has blasted Cheney on constitutional grounds but there's little else he can do in the current climate.

And now we come to your President, the guy we started with, by asking what "legal meat" he eats. Apparently he eats anything he damned well pleases. On November 1st, after several months of delays, George W. Bush broke the law himself by changing an Executive Order and declaring that in this national emergency he was going to prevent the release of papers from the Reagan presidency, even though release is mandated by the Presidential Records Act of 1978.

Of what use could these papers be to Osama bin Laden?

These papers would probably shed glaring light on the criminality of the Reagan-Bush (the elder) years of Iran-Contra, the savings and loan plundering of American taxpayers, and the hand-over-fist drug dealing by the CIA at the direction of G.H.W. Bush. But now, in violation of the law, you will never see them. Nor will you likely ever see the papers from the '89-'93 Bush Presidency, or the Clinton years — not to mention those of the current administration. What a convenient way to cover up criminal actions.

Representatives Jan Schakowsky (D), Ill, and the ever-brave Henry Waxman rose to the challenge and wrote Bush a letter on November 6th. They said in closing, "These provisions clearly violate the intent of the law .... The Executive Order violates the intent of Congress and keeps the public in the dark. We urge you to rescind this executive order and instead begin a dialogue with Congress and the public to determine the need for clarification of this law."

Any bets as to who gets the next anthrax letter? Have you noticed that only Democrats have been getting them?

So now you retreat, your decision has been made. Do nothing. This will all go away. In a spasm of pretzel-bending logic you think, "Wait! We still have the Supreme Court."

This is the same Supreme Court that illegally handed George W. Bush the 2000 election. This is the court that stopped and delayed hand counting long enough to prevent the final results from being known. Those results — as buried by the major media in horrendously dishonest stories released last week — were written as supporting the Supreme Court's decision to stop the recounts. And based on that decision, the media recount gave Bush the victory. But, as noted by *EXTRA!* Editor Jim Naureckas in a November 15 *Newsday story,* the media found that it was quite possible, by examining reject-ed ballots, to determine the "clear intent of the voter." Yet none of these ballots were included in the media recount and all of the media organizations recognized that, had those ballots been counted, Al Gore would have won.

As constitutional lawyer Mark H. Levine noted in a December 20, 2000, editorial, what the Supreme Court did was to create a one-case only exception where the "clear intent of the voter" — the standard mandated by Florida law — was no longer applicable. By stopping the hand count and overturning the Florida Supreme Court's correct reading of its own law, it delayed the recount long enough to force a crisis where it could overrule Florida and deliver the election to Bush while thousands of ballots went uncounted.

So much for the Supreme Court.

One of the greatest decisions to ever come out the Supreme Court (when it was one) was rendered in 1866 after the Civil War. The case in question was Abraham Lincoln's suspension of the writ of habeas corpus in arresting protesters and rioters. As recently quoted in an eloquent November 15 article by David Dietman, an attorney and PhD candidate from Erie, Pennsylvania, the Court stated:

"The Constitution of the United States is a law for rulers and people equally in war and in peace, and covers with the shield of its protection all classes of men, at all times, and under all circumstances. No doctrine, involving more pernicious consequences, was ever invented by the wit of man than that any of its provisions can be suspended during any of the great exigencies of government." — *Ex parte Milligan,* 71 US 2 (1866).

So all you have left in which to put your faith (or your fear) is the President. You have no faith in yourself, no faith in God, no trust in your fellow citizens and no willingness to experience discomfort. You fail to praise, support and uplift all of the courage that is beginning to reveal itself around you. You draw your blinds and wave your flags hoping for divine intervention before your name or your job comes up on the list. You are a good German, like the Germans who followed Hitler and allowed him to start a war that killed hundreds of millions of people.

And when it is all over, when they come for your job, when they come for you, when they come for me — when history sheds its inevitable light on the criminals that today rule our country — you will say, "I didn't do anything wrong."

Oh yes you did. Oh yes you did.[3]

Since the publication of that essay the Bush administration has released 8,000 out of 68,000 pages of Reagan records. Release of the rest is blocked by a Bush executive order in contravention of the law. We have not seen the records of the NEPDG. The CIA has been given permission to kill American citizens. The administration has ignored dozens of Congressional requests, fought subpoenas, and defied committee chairpersons responsible for oversight of the Executive Branch. And it has been classified top secret as to whether or not the president had been told that hijackers might use airliners as weapons against civilian targets prior to 9/11.

Just 15 months later we learned that The Patriot Act was in a family way. This follow-on story came a month before the Iraqi invasion.

Trial Balloon?
"Five to Ten Times Worse Than the Patriot Act"
Secret Bush Legislation Sent to Cheney, Hastert, Deepens Assault on Constitution
Patriot II[4]
by Michael C. Ruppert

February 25, 2003, 1800 PST (*FTW*)

WHAT'S IN PATRIOT II?

The Center for Public Integrity was not jesting when its representative told Bill Moyers that Patriot II was five or ten times worse than the first Patriot Act.

Its provisions allow for secret arrests of persons in certain terrorist-related cases until indictments have been handed down and there is no time limitation for this process. America has never permitted secret arrests for indefinite time periods. In addition, Patriot II provides that these terrorist arrests may be under "no bail" conditions and that any federal employee who discloses the identity of someone who has been secretly detained may be imprisoned for up to five years. Throwing away decades of progress obtained as a result of litigation in the 1970s and 80s, the new bill specifically overturns dozens of consent decrees prohibiting law enforcement agencies from infiltrating non-violent religious and civic groups exercising protected first amendment rights.

The bill mandates that government authorities are entitled to have meetings *ex parte* (one-on-one, without defense counsel or a public record) and *in camera* (private) with judges without opposing counsel or defendants even being notified to secure rulings on search warrants, admissibility of evidence and investigative procedures. In certain cases where naturalized American citizens are found to be working with foreign governments, or making donations to foreign based charities later found to be supporting terrorist causes, the Attorney General will have the right to revoke US citizenship and extradite those charged to any country in the world, whether there is an extradition treaty in place or not.

There has been some debate, encouraged by inaccurate and extremely irresponsible reporting by some "alternative" journalists and radio talk show hosts indicating that the bill provides the government with the ability to strip native-born US citizens of their citizenship for seemingly trivial offenses. This is not the case. The actual truth is bad enough.

Section 501 of Patriot II amends section 349 of the Immigration and Nationality Act (8 USC. 1481) pertaining to the citizenship status of those who have *acquired* US citizenship. It states that those who have entered into the armed forces of a foreign government (when such forces are engaged in hostilities against the US), or have joined or provided material support "to a terrorist organization ... if the organization is engaged in hostilities against the United States, its people, or its national security interests" will be deemed to have made a *prima facie* (apparent on its face) statement that they intend to relinquish their citizenship.

Lewis and Moyers were correct in their interpretation of this section in that a naturalized American who makes a donation to an Islamic charity later alleged to have been giving money to a terrorist organization could be stripped of their citizenship and deported anywhere without it ever having been established that he or she even knew how the charity was distributing its money.

Section 126 of the act allows the US government to obtain consumer credit reports and to impose criminal penalties on credit reporting agencies if they disclose to individuals the mere fact that the government has obtained copies of their records.

Section 127 of Patriot II allows the Federal government to supercede all local statutes governing autopsies in terrorism investigations, which means literally that if a person died at the hands of an illegal federal investigation, the autopsy results could be commandeered to show a suicide or some other finding favorable to the government.[5] This would also apply in cases of accidental death due to fatalities resulting from compulsory mass vaccinations. In such cases, instead of finding dangerous vaccines as the cause of death the federal government could instead blame terrorists.

Also in the list of list of noxious provisions, chemical and utility companies would be absolved under the act from requirements that they publicly disclose the kinds of dangerous chemicals in use at their

facilities or "worst case scenario" information about what might happen
if there were malfunctions or breakdowns at their facilities. This
equates to an environmental *carte blanche* for polluters.

And in a particularly chilling passage, section 404 of Patriot II
would impose a penalty of up to five years of imprisonment for anyone who used any form of computer encryption to commit anything
defined as domestic or foreign terrorism. Under the liberal definition
of domestic terrorism contained in Patriot I, a possible interpretation
of this section could be that a reporter who uses PGP or other encryption program to correspond with a foreign confidential source could
be imprisoned for five years — just for using the software. It also suggests that no commercial entity that uses encryption to protect its
proprietary data would be permitted to use any encryption program
to which the government did not already possess a key.

I was completely shocked in July of 2003 when, while speaking at an event at
UC Berkeley with Riva Enteen, program director of the National Lawyer's Guild,
to hear that their reading of Patriot II would actually enable the revocation of citizenship from native-born Americans.

Homeland (IN)Security

Employees of the Department of Homeland Security will be enforcers. They will
carry weapons and they will also enforce drug laws.[6] They will take control of and
coordinate all communications, including radio, teletype and telephone communications at state and local levels to maximize efficiency, and they will coordinate
federal grants and provide equipment to upgrade all state and local radio and closed
"intranet" systems which means that they will both control and monitor all state and
local emergency communications. And they will also set up secure communications
for private industry (the corporations who will be selling the equipment), the banking industry and all other corporations deemed to be "critical infrastructure."

The DHS will collect and share intelligence vital for its primary mission, which
is the protection of critical infrastructure. In the process of doing this, it will access
the intelligence of state and local agencies and "coordinate" the dissemination of
that information.[7] This means that local police agencies, if they want to continue
receiving federal subsidies and don't want to look as though they aren't concerned
about their citizens, will effectively become intelligence-gathering units for the federal government. In addition the DHS Secretary and his employees are also given
total access to all information in any federal agency, whether verified or not on a
level of priority equal with the President and the Director of Central Intelligence.[8]
It will also have complete access to all banking and stock transaction records; once
compiled, these records can be shared with any foreign government the government wishes to share them with. It also allows federal agents to serve search
warrants issued by foreign governments inside this country.

In fulfilling its mandate to enhance cyber security the DHS will be given access to all state and local databases and programs and "upon request" to privately owned data bases (e.g., your medical records) to make sure that each system's vulnerabilities have been analyzed and that the "proper technical assistance" has been rendered to upgrade each system as needed.[9] This is where TIA and the PROMIS back door get introduced. Even if Congressional attempts to suspend funding for the Total Information Awareness (TIA) program remain successful, the program will still be in place and operating "off the books" using either funds obtained from the drug trade or stolen from the US Treasury (see below). The government doesn't give up such power easily. In February 2004, the Associated Press confirmed that TIA research and funding was still in place even though congress had voted to *unfund* the office charged with developing TIA. The research was simply moved to other parts of the Pentagon, resulting in what one observer called "a shell game."

Kissinger, PROMIS, and TIA

Not long after Henry Kissinger withdrew his name as a candidate to head the independent commission investigating 9/11 — ostensibly because he didn't want to name his private clients — journalist Jim Rarey ripped the covers off an unnoticed bombshell in Kissinger's background. Henry Kissinger's partner in one of his consulting firms (Kissinger-McLarty Associates), and the Vice Chairman of Kissinger's other firm (Kissinger & Associates), is former Clinton Chief of Staff Mack McLarty. As it turns out McLarty also sits on the board of directors of a company called *Acxiom*.

That name might not ring a bell, but Acxiom is a recent name-change from a company formerly called *Alltel* that was once known as *Systematics*. *Systematics* is the information, communications, data processing firm owned by Arkansas billionaire and kingmaker Jackson Stephens. Stephens also happens to be the man who employed former NATO Commander Wesley Clark until the latter's unsuccessful bid to win the 2004 Democratic Presidential nomination.

Further, *Systematics* has been part and parcel — in paperwork and court records — of the PROMIS software saga almost from day one. It was *Systematics* that reportedly received stolen copies of the software in the 1980s. If Inslaw founder Bill Hamilton ever had any doubt about the fact that the progeny of his creation were at the heart of TIA, he can lay it to rest now. In a December 17, 2002, story investigative journalist Jim Rarey revealed that Acxiom had been selected "the lead" company to provide software and pull together the network to furnish the information to DARPA's "Information Awareness Office" headed by John Poindexter.[8]

A silent takeover

By issuing security clearances to state and local personnel after appropriate training and screening, DHS will guarantee that only those personnel in local agencies loyal to the federal agenda will be given access to key information. Following on that, the DHS will have the authority to go into any local agency and evaluate its methods for control of sensitive and classified information and it will have legal control of all such information in the hands of local agencies including decision-making power as to who sees it and who doesn't.[10] Voila! All local law enforcement agencies are now working for the federal government.

Smallpox and vaccinations

The Act creating DHS has a particular obsession with biological warfare (biowar) and, in particular, smallpox, which is the only disease specifically mentioned throughout Title 3. And in a magnanimous gift to vaccine makers it has made it a law that, in the event of a declared emergency when millions might be ordered to receive untested (for efficacy) and dangerous vaccinations, the vaccine makers and those who administer the vaccinations at government direction will be immune from lawsuits, even if you drop dead or suffer permanent disability as a result.[11]

In the event that the Secretary of DHS declares a health emergency or "a potential health emergency," certain provisions of US public health laws may be activated to not only compel vaccinations, but to give the DHS the power to condemn and seize private property without advance hearings or court procedures. And during such emergencies the FBI and all other US government functions will report to the DHS Secretary at all times.[12]

The Act also allows the DHS to go to universities under government contract to make sure that their research conforms to the government's needs and desires. The DHS will also exercise security control over material that is deemed sensitive. The DHS will have the ability to suspend funding if the universities are not complying with the government program.[13]

Part II: American money

Benito Mussolini is reported to have said that *"Fascism should more properly be called corporatism, since it is the merger of state and corporate power."* This goes to the heart of the map and shows why what follows is only the beginning. Of course, with the reality of Peak Oil, financial disasters are easy to predict; fish in a barrel. Yet within that global reality there lingers in the hearts and minds of many Americans a belief that somehow the Emperor will see to it that they are protected, that they remain comfortable and continue to have more resources than anyone else as the world suffers. Nonsense! Few will be prepared for how far that destruction has already progressed and fewer still will even think of preparing before the disaster becomes apparent.

There are currently 6.6 million people in the United States either in jail, on probation or on parole.[14] Of those, more than two million are incarcerated. And of those two million — half of whom were added in the last ten years — more than sixty per cent are non-violent drug offenders.[15] There has been a trend in America toward employing many of these prisoners as virtual slave labor for multinational corporations. Inmate laborers now do everything from processing your credit card statements to making your airline reservations, to assembling your tennis shoes. The DoJ operates something called Federal Prison Industries, better known as *Unicor*, as a profit-making venture to benefit American corporations. Unicor runs more than 100 factories in prisons in at least 30 states.[16]

According to Unicor's website:

> One example was its [UNICOR's] role as a supplier to the military during the 1990-91 Persian Gulf conflict. UNICOR provided Kevlar helmets, camouflage battle uniforms, lighting systems, sandbags, blankets, and night vision eyewear for the military to use during Operation Desert Shield and Operation Desert Storm. It even manufactured cables for chemical gas detection devices and for the Patriot missile systems that played a key role in defending Allied troops during the Persian Gulf War. Brigadier General John Cusick, commanding officer of the Defense Personnel Support Center, praised UNICOR for the "superb support [it] provided to America's Fighting Forces" and for helping ensure that "we received the supplies the troops needed to win the war."[17]

About 30 percent of the prisons in this country are run by private corporations which trade their stock based upon how many human beings they "house." In pure economic terms, inmates have become inventory. The two largest of these corporations are Wackenhut and Corrections Corporation of America. Both of these corporations, through their boards of directors and executive management have direct ties to US intelligence agencies, including the CIA.

All of this means that the corrupt economy makes money by first selling drugs to people and then by putting them in prison for using drugs.

That model was mirrored in Iraq. When Iraq released its 12,000-page report on its Weapons of Mass Destruction (WMD) programs, the US government promptly censored several thousand pages. Among the withheld pages were those showing that twenty-one major US corporations had made billions of dollars in profits during the 1980s and '90s by selling Iraq all of the technology, equipment, and weapons that it needed to become the threat that the US insisted it was.[18]

This pandemic of corporate fraud in America has, according to a 2002 FOX News report, wiped out $600 billion in shareholder equity (mostly pension funds held in stocks). Look at the list of corporations under investigation for cooking their books,[19] and consider how much money the top executives made through fraud. The *Financial Times* published an excellent series on this issue, entitled *The Barons of Bankruptcy* (within a broader compendium of reports titled *Capitalism in Crisis*). That report disclosed that 61 executives made an estimated $3.3 billion in insider stock trades before the collapse of their respective companies.[20]

These figures describe only a small fraction of the actual share volume dumped after the prices had been fraudulently inflated by these same executives. For every

CEO or CFO that sold shares, there were members of the boards of directors, the audit committees, and the major shareholders who dumped tens and perhaps hundreds of times as many shares.

The big show made by the Bush administration about corporate reform was just that, a show. One day after the Corporate Reform Act was signed into law by President Bush in late-July of 2002, he turned around and gutted it by declaring a White House policy that whistle-blowing protection would not apply to those who exposed fraudulent practices *unless and until* the whistleblowers were sworn in under oath at a Congressional hearing. That means that the whistle blowers, the one group of people essential to making the new law work, are defenseless. They will have no protection when they go to the FBI, the SEC, or even if they go to congressional staff outside of a hearing.[21]

The master chefs of book cooking

The US government is the champion of book cooking. Its achievements in this area make the recent corporate scandals appear pedestrian. By sleight of hand in changing the dates by which corporations had to pay quarterly income taxes, it conjured up $33 billion in paper money needed to finance the Bush tax cut. One news report quoted former Minnesota congressman Bill Frenzel as saying, "If you look at the books of the corporate world, even the fraudulent ones, they are less subject to manipulation than the federal budget is."[22] We have seen how Bush's budget director Mitch Daniels refused to comply with a congressional request to submit the government's books to the same standards that corporations are now supposed to follow.

The ostrich economy

Only twice in its history has *FTW* issued an urgent economic bulletin warning our subscribers of pending economic crashes. In both cases, our warnings were followed within days by major events. Our first alert on September 9th 2001 was followed two days later by the attacks of 9/11. Our second alert in early July of 2002 was followed only days later by a plunge in the Dow Jones Industrial Average, lasting weeks, which took the index down more than 1400 points.

Anyone who thinks that the market fundamentals aren't just as bad as they were a year ago is delusional. In fact, there are many signs showing that they are much worse. Columnist Arianna Huffington, in May of 2002 warned of a coming economic devastation and stated that the signs of collapse were multiplying:

> Here are a few of them: in the last two years, 433 public companies — including Enron, Global Crossing, and Kmart have declared bankruptcy. Two million Americans have lost their jobs. Four trillion dollars in market value has been lost on Wall Street. And each day brings a fresh, stomach-turning revelation of the rampant corruption infecting corporate America...[23]

Pro forma

Huffington was warning about the dismal failure of legislation that would have banned a non-transparent form of accounting called "*pro forma*." The big money in Congress had seen to it that the bill, sponsored by Senator Paul Sarbanes (D - MD) died in committee. To put it simply, *pro-forma* accounting (as opposed to much stricter Generally Accepted Accounting Principles, or GAAP), allows you to cheat, to hide money, to hide debt and to cook the books. A recent article in *CFO Magazine* revealed that 54 percent of 181 US publicly traded corporations responding to their survey used *pro forma* accounting and that most CFO's felt some pressure to hide data and that many felt pressure to resist change.[24]

Where there is *pro forma* accounting, there is a choice of profit over truth-telling. A look at some of the major corporations opting to use *pro forma* and the media outlets they own says quite a bit about the myth of a free press.

> GENERAL ELECTRIC (NBC)
> AOL/TIME-WARNER (CNN, Headline News, *TIME* Magazine, *PEOPLE*, HBO)
> MICROSOFT (MS-NBC, MSN)
> VIACOM (CBS)
> DISNEY (ABC)
> IBM
> INTEL
> CISCO SYSTEMS
> SUN MICRO
> TRIBUNE Co. (*Los Angeles Times, Chicago Tribune*)
> THE WASHINGTON POST (*Washington Post, NEWSWEEK*)
> THE NEW YORK TIMES (*New York Times, Boston Globe*)[25]

Thus, almost all of the major media outlets in the United States are vested in a system that makes profits and competes by destroying things and hiding the truth. A notable (and ironic) exception in this case is FOX News, which is owned by the Australian company NEWSCORP and it does conform, at least in the most recent filing I could find, to Australian GAAP. But they're not quite off the hook. With Saudi Prince Alwaleed bin Talal as its second largest shareholder, and with former Reagan political strategist and Republican Party operative Roger Ailes as the CEO of its news operations, FOX has plenty of other questions to answer.

What's already been stolen

In March of 2000 Department of Housing and Urban Development (HUD) Inspector General Susan Gaffney testified before the House Committee on government reform. She answered questions about the fact that HUD had lost $17 billion in 1998 and $59 billion in 1999. She could not explain what had happened to the money and when she was asked what HUD had done about the missing funds, her explanation, made simple, was that HUD had made an adjustment to its check-book.[26] In September of 1999, it was disclosed that the US Navy had lost $3 billion in equipment.[27] Most of the equipment had probably been channeled to illegal covert operations. Other losses that turned up soon after that are more difficult to explain.

In August of 2001, *INSIGHT Magazine's* Kelly O'Meara disclosed that the Department of Defense could not account for $1.1 trillion for fiscal year 2000. It had been stolen, or it was lost and nobody knew where to find it. Same thing.[28]

Then the bombshell. On January 29, 2002, CBS News reported that the Pentagon could not account for 25 percent of its funds or more than $2.3 trillion. That amount, reported CBS, equaled $8,000 for every man, woman and child in America. In dissecting the case of one missing batch of money, CBS came up with an explanation that was to fit all the rest of the money. "We know they spent it but we don't know what they spent it on."[29]

A skeptic will say, "How can the Pentagon lose trillions of dollars? Its annual budget is currently only $480 billion (which is larger than all the non-American military spending in the world combined[30])." The answer is simple. The Pentagon manages the pension funds for two million service people, not counting its civilian employees. It also manages their medical insurance plans. It owns real estate, collects rents, and operates concessions and businesses on military bases. And when a multi-year weapons program is approved by Congress all of the earmarked funds go into Pentagon accounts but are only disbursed by year.

The great irony here is that most of the financial data processing for US government accounting systems is done by DynCorp and by Lockheed-Martin.

The Plunge Protection Team and Rigged Markets

(*From FTW's July 2002 economic bulletin*)

> The *Washington Post* acknowledged the existence of a select group of four who could and would intervene in markets to prevent massive capital flight and a run on shares that would cause an economic collapse if there weren't enough cash to pay out during a massive sell off. In his February 23, 1997 story titled "Plunge Protection Team," *Post* reporter Brett Fromson identified the Federal Reserve chairman, the Securities and Exchange Commission chairman, the chairman of the Commodities Futures Trading Commission, and the secretary of the Treasury as the team's key players. The intervention of the team in the 1998 crash of Long Term Capital Management, after it became wildly overexposed in the gold market (see below), revealed that private institutions such as Goldman Sachs, JPMorgan Chase, Merrill Lynch and other major banks could be involved as well.
>
> Fromson quoted a former team member as saying, "In a crisis, a lot of deference is paid to the Fed. They are the only ones with any money." Or, I might add, the ability to print it. The Treasury has lots of money too.

Pointing to the 1987 stock market crash, the single largest crash in history, Fromson observed, "The Fed kept the markets going by flooding the banking system with reserves and stating publicly that it was ready to extend loans to important financial institutions, if needed."

On April 5, 2000 *New York Post* reporter John Crudele reported that the stock market had turned back from the abyss. After a 500-point drop that looked like it was leading to a meltdown, "someone started buying large amounts of stock index futures contracts through two major brokerage firms — Goldman Sachs and Merrill Lynch...Unless the brokers tell, there is no way of knowing which of their clients were making the purchases .... Then the market rebounded."

Calling it the PPT, Crudele both referred to the 1997 *Washington Post* story and suggested that private banks were acting as team captains.

Gold activist David Guyatt, relying on information obtained from Gold Anti-Trust Action Committee (GATA) Chairman Bill Murphy, pointed to the PPT in October 2000:

The hand of the Plunge Protection Team (PPT) is clearly visible for the first time. The entire short gold play over the last few years is a technique that has been used to 'prop up key stocks' and 'fund futures' operations. In the simplest form it works like this. Borrow (at negligible interest rates) someone's [America's, Germany's, Britain's, Goldman Sachs'] gold and sell it in the market. This gives a handsome pool of near-interest-free dollar cash. Whenever the stock market looks shaky, or key stocks come under pressure, dive in and buy, buy, buy...

But it is not only necessary to manipulate the stock market to succeed. It is also necessary to manipulate the gold price and keep the price of gold below the price PPT sold the leased gold for...This is a game of double jeopardy...The problem the PPT now have is that there is virtually no more official gold left to borrow.

The causes of this intervention were a pending NASDAQ crash and the imminent downgrading of IBM and Intel stocks.

And the PPT's hand has been noted recently from as far away as Australia. *Progressive Review* Editor Sam Smith recently quoted a story by Richard Bromby of the *Australian Financial Review:*

At 2:32 Wednesday [June 26], New York time, something extraordinary happened at the corner of Wall and Broad streets. The New York Stock Exchange's Dow Jones industrial index — struggling since the opening bell after the WorldCom fraud revelations — threw off its problems. From an intraday low of 8,926.6, the Dow shot skywards to its high of 9,160 at 3:29 p.m... Could it be the work of the much talked about (but never seen) Plunge Protection Team? There is a belief that this team represents a powerful and secretive hand that is ready to act at any time the Dow looks ready to tank big-time ....

London's *Observer* newspaper last October reported it had information the plunge team was preparing to spend 'billions of dollars' to avert a repeat of 1929 and 1987.

The problem is clear: With a strong dollar the PPT has demonstrated that it has enough cash to suppress gold prices or to save the stock market. It may not have enough cash to do both — especially if the dollar were to suddenly lose its value.

As the *International Forecaster* reported on April 26, "All bets are off if the housing and credit bubbles break and that's a distinct possibility... Debtor's prison is drawing nearer. House and Senate conferences are deciding on a new set of rules for Chapter 7 bankruptcy... If the Plunge Protection Team weren't manipulating the market with all these scandals, the Dow would already be at 4,500."

Adding up the losses

Let's take a look at the financial raiding that can be documented and add it up. The Bush administration has taken some of it just to pay the bills but I have no doubt that vast quantities of this stolen money are being used to manipulate financial markets, stimulate investor confidence and encourage small investors to keep putting their money into a failed Ponzi scheme. Bear in mind that the following "thefts" are just what I can document.

Taken From (source)	Amount
Social Security (2001) — (*USA Today/Washington Post*)	$34 Billion
Social Security (2002) —	
(White House Office of Management and Budget)	$ 455 Billion
Fed. Employee Retirement System to meet	
'02 budget deficits (*Wall Street Journal*, June 13, 2002)	$42 Billion
Civil Service Retirement and Disability Fund	
in '02 (WS Journal, above)	$2 Billion
Stolen from the Department of Defense 1999	$1,100 Billion
Stolen from the Department of Defense 2000	$2,300 Billion
Stolen from HUD 1998	$17 Billion
Stolen from HUD 1999	$59 Billion
US government funds paid to companies and individuals	
not entitled to receive it (Reuters)	$20 Billion
Shareholder Equity Lost to Financial Fraud (FOX)	$600 Billion

TOTAL **$4.629 Trillion Dollars**

Estimated pending withdrawals from Social Security to cover deficits by 2010,

(*Washington Post* citing the Congressional Budget Office) **$845 Billion**

This is taxpayer money. This is retirement money. This is money for medical care. This is the wealth of America and it is being stolen.

How much

Leaving Peak Oil aside, let's examine the American economy from some standard measurements.

Employment

We have already seen that two million Americans have lost their jobs in the last two years. This brings the total as of this writing to about 9.5 million unemployed in the US.[31]

In light of this President Bush has taken a "prudent" action to reduce government spending in an effort to stimulate the economy. He has cut off the funding for a Labor Department program that tracks mass layoffs by US companies. The mass-layoffs statistic was widely used by analysts to measure the health of the economy. But a story in the *San Francisco Chronicle* reported that the Bush Administration told the Bureau of Labor Statistics to "look elsewhere for its funding."[32] I guess if you don't see it, it's not there.

Pension funds

In January of 2003 the US Pension Benefit Guaranty Corporation (PBGC) — the entity that serves to guarantee pensions as the FDIC guarantees bank deposits — announced that it was insolvent. In 2001 the PBGC had $22 billion in assets.[33] This is a classic example of the way major corporate bankruptcies are used as weapons to transfer wealth from the poor to the rich. First the books are cooked. Then the pension funds are looted. Then the companies go bankrupt and the assets are sold off to other powerful financial interests for pennies on the dollar.

Bankruptcies

US personal bankruptcy filings are at an all-time high and setting a new record each month. In the 12-month period ending September 30, 2002, 1.55 million Americans filed for bankruptcy as opposed to 1.44 million for the previous year. This was an increase of 7.7 percent. In just the three months from July-September of 2002, bankruptcy filings had gone up 11.6 percent.[34]

The dollar

The dollar has started a precipitous slide against other currencies. This is a frightening development because most of the world's trade is priced in dollars and most nations hold dollars as their reserve currencies. OPEC also prices its oil in dollars. At this writing the euro is near an all-time high of valuation against the dollar at $1.23.

The Empire depends upon several things to retain its power. One of the most important is the strength of the dollar. But now a wide range of experts is predicting a deflationary recession (depression) in which prices and wages could actually fall. This has disastrous implications, not least of which is that the US is the world's largest debtor nation and its economic survival is predicated upon a heavy influx of foreign investment capital (cash flow) to remain solvent, especially since the Empire's financial markets are burdened with hundreds of trillions of dollars in derivatives (see below). If the dollar loses too much value, then other nations will have to switch to other safer and more stable currencies.

Gold

Gold really deserves a much greater discussion than I can give it here. Over the years excellent work has been done by Bill Murphy and the Gold Anti-Trust Action Committee (GATA) documenting in painstaking detail how gold prices have been artificially suppressed to "protect" financial markets and ensure a ready supply for market manipulations and quick profits. This ties in closely with the activities of the Plunge Protection Team (PPT) above.

The price of gold is a sign to investors of the relative stability of other markets. And if gold prices rise too high too quickly, the derivative paper based on borrowed gold becomes a time bomb for major banks like JPMorgan Chase, and Citigroup. Gold has risen in price more than 30 percent in the last two years while the DOW has dropped 20 percent or more. And there is approximately five times more paper gold than there is actual gold out of the ground.

The housing market and home foreclosures

Few things have been as over-promoted as the "hot" housing market in America. The truth is that it's not that hot and it's about to pop like all the other bubbles. In September of 2002, *USA Today* reported that a record percentage of US homeowners were facing foreclosure at a rate of 1.23 percent, which was the highest rate in 30 years.[35] Completed foreclosures in the third quarter of 2002 set a record at 1.15 percent of mortgages according to the Mortgage Bankers Association.[36] These numbers imply two things. First, that the homeowners couldn't pay their mortgages and, secondly, that they couldn't sell the house to get out from under the mortgage. That means there's pressure on prices.

In August of 2002 the *Financial Times* reported that corporate officers and board members of publicly traded US building companies had started dumping their personally owned shares. According to the *Times* it was the largest sell-off by industry insiders since records of such sales were started in 1996.[37] And sales of homes worth more than $1 million fell by ten percent in the third quarter of 2002, with signs of prices softening in many regions of the country.[38]

The budget deficit

What was a budget surplus when George W. Bush took office is now a record budget deficit that topped $374 billion for Fiscal Year 2003.[39] In August of 2004 the deficit had risen to nearly $400 billion. But, as we already know, different accounting procedures come up with different numbers. *New York Post* reporter John Crudele, citing a letter from then Secretary Paul O'Neil he found on the Treasury Department's website, discovered that the actual deficit for 2001 was $515 billion dollars. O'Neil's letter said,

> Accrual-based financial reporting is critical to gaining comprehensive understanding of the US government's operations. For fiscal 2001, our results were an accrual-based deficit of $515 billion in contrast to a $127 billion budget surplus reported last fall.[40]

Derivatives

A derivative is any financial instrument whose value is totally extrinsic; whereas stocks are at least nominally based on the real assets of some company issuing the shares, derivatives are another step removed from any intrinsic value. When leveraged and traded they can serve as hedges against risk or as insanely speculative instruments. Examples of derivatives are futures, options, forwards, swaps and various combinations of these instruments. They can be based on energy, on gold, on stocks, on just about anything and they can also be created out of thin air. The problem is that they can be incredibly risky, especially when used as leverage. Under the right (or wrong) circumstances they could destroy an institution heavily invested in them, because if everything goes south then enormous quantities of cash are required to "service the paper."

When I attended the economic conference in Moscow in March of 2001, I heard a very sharp Russian economist state that the United States as a whole was sitting atop a $300 trillion derivatives bubble.[41] This may be a bit high but not by much. It is certain that banks like JPMorgan Chase and Citigroup are sitting on derivatives easily within the $20-30 trillion range.[42] If the stock market falls too far, or if the price of gold rises too high, this would likely create a liquidity crisis that could wipe out these and many other banks as well.

Debt

Just about everybody and everything in this country is in deep debt. British economist Chris Sanders (<www.sandersresearch.com/>) recently wrote:

> At 280 percent of GDP and rising, America's total debt burden relative to GDP has far outrun the ability of the economy to finance it out of retained earnings. With net foreign investment income negative, financing the debt requires ever-greater investment from foreigners. Although this later point is so obvious that you may well gloss over it, consider: the implication is that the maintenance of American economic growth requires an accelerating rate of net foreign investment. America already pre-empts more than 70 percent of net world savings."[43]

State and local government funding

Some 28 states are facing the most serious budget crises they have ever known. California, with its attendant political circus, is no exception. Many local governments are in the same or worse condition. Discussions are being held about the interruption or scaling back of vital services such as police, fire, sanitation and health care.

Terrifying insurance

In late November of 2002, Congress also passed a Terrorism Insurance Bill.[44] It became a law that, in the event of a major terrorist attack, insurance companies will not have to bear the burden. The US taxpayer will. And these megalithic giants like AIG will have to sustain only five million dollars in losses before the Treasury steps in to carry up to 90 percent of the remaining burden up to $100 billion. Five million dollars is a drop in the bucket for a company like AIG (the world's largest insurance company), which had more than $5 billion in *profits* in 2001.[45] From what we have seen above, that money will have to come out of Social Security, Medicare, Medicaid, your pension, or the money that should have gone to pave the roads in your neighborhood.

If what I have just presented to you is not enough to demonstrate that a serious economic crisis is on its way, then consider recent statements and actions by two major financial players.

George Soros is one of the most powerful men on the planet. He communes regularly with the likes of Zbigniew Brzezinski and roams freely within the circles of the Trilateral Commission, the Council on Foreign Relations, and the Bilderbergers. A billionaire currency speculator who has destabilized entire national economies, Soros is one of the Empire's own ruling class, the class above the Emperor. Right before the last major plunge in the Dow, Soros predicted a major economic collapse, a devaluation of the dollar, and the ruination of the US economy. Within two weeks the bottom fell out of the Dow as Americans saw their mutual fund 401(k) plans wiped out.

On January 26, 2003, Soros granted an interview to the BBC in which he warned that "globalization is at risk" and that the world stood at the brink of deflation. According to Soros, deflation would benefit only one nation, the nation that was capable of making goods for the lowest possible cost: China. For every other nation, deflation would "exacerbate the global economic downturn."[46] I wonder what will happen if Soros ever acknowledges Peak Oil. Soros is now funding a major effort to unseat George Bush who has exposed the game and become bad for business.

The point of this chapter is that a population preoccupied with survival and the basic needs of life is less inclined to revolt. That is, of course, unless and until they perceive that they have nothing left to lose. And the Empire has prepared for that too.

A message from 35 years ago

Robert F. Kennedy evolved through several stages in his short life. When he was a young lawyer he served as the counsel for the House Un-American Activities committee and participated in a shameless witch-hunt that destroyed the lives of many innocent people. As attorney general serving under his brother John, he turned on organized crime alliances that had done business with his father Joseph during Prohibition and helped elect his brother. He ambitiously prosecuted both civil rights cases and Teamsters President Jimmy Hoffa, while furthering his brother's career and protecting the Kennedy political franchise.

RFK was young, brilliant, charismatic, and powerful. But it was not until after his brother was assassinated in 1963 that he became a visionary. After spending what he and his family described as "some years in the wilderness," haunted by his brother's murder, wrestling with the deeper questions with which life had cornered him, Bobby Kennedy returned in 1966 to run for, and win, a US senate seat in New York. That victory, and his triumph in the California presidential primary two years later, placed him squarely as the front-runner for the White House in the 1968 general election.

On March 18, 1968, less than three months before his death, RFK the visionary delivered a speech at the University of Kansas at Lawrence. He said:

> Too much and for too long we seem to have surrendered personal excellence and community values in the mere accumulation of material things. Our gross national product now is over $800 billion a year.
>
> But that gross national product, if we judge the United States of America by that, counts air pollution, and cigarette advertising, and ambulances to clear our highways of carnage. It counts special locks for our doors, and the jails for people who break them. It counts the destruction of redwoods and the loss of our natural wonder in chaotic sprawl. It counts napalm and it counts nuclear warheads, and armored cars for the police to fight the riots in our cities. It counts Whitman's rifle and Speck's knife, and the television programs which glorify violence in order to sell toys to our children.
>
> Yet the gross national product does not allow for the health of our children, the quality of their education, or they joy of their play. It does not include the beauty of our poetry or the strength of our marriages, the intelligence of our public debate or the integrity of our public officials. It measures neither our wit nor our courage, neither our wisdom nor our learning, neither our passion nor our devotion to our country.
>
> It measures everything, in short, except that which makes life worthwhile. And it can tell us everything about America — except why we are proud that we are Americans.

CHAPTER 29

BIOLOGICAL WARFARE

Part I - If this is help, who needs it?

*Sales of vaccines, once considered a commodity market, are booming
with global revenues set to reach nearly $10 billion in 2006 from $5.4
billion in 2001, according to research published Tuesday.
Analysts at Merrill Lynch said the fastest growing section of the market
would be for flu vaccines, sales of which are expected to more than double to $2 billion in the next five years.*

— Reuters, January 7, 2003

There are some reports, for example, that some countries have been
trying to construct something like an Ebola Virus, and that would be
a very dangerous phenomenon, to say the least. Alvin Toeffler has
written about this in terms of some scientists in their laboratories trying to devise certain types of pathogens that would be ethnically
specific so that they could just eliminate certain ethnic groups and
races; and others are designing some sort of engineering, some sort of
insects that can destroy specific crops....

— DoD News Briefing, Secretary of Defense William S. Cohen
Monday, April 28, 1997, 8:45 a.m. EDT [Special Thanks to Russ
Kick for bringing this quotation to light]

Anthrax vaccines

BioPort is a Michigan company with an exclusive Pentagon contract to develop
and produce a vaccine that protects against anthrax. The US government
announced in December of 2001, approximately six weeks after the anthrax
attacks, that it would be offering BioPort vaccine to thousands of people who
might have been exposed to weaponized anthrax, including congressional staff and
postal workers. Vaccines are only supposed to be given *before* exposure to disease,
not after. Yet a *Washington Post* story reported that the unlicensed vaccine was
going to be administered without complete testing and without even a formal protocol being established by the Food and Drug Administration (FDA).[1]

BioPort had a number of problems. It had never manufactured a vaccine before. It had merely purchased a company with a contract to do so in 1998. In the year before the 9/11 attacks, BioPort had been shut down by the FDA for, among other things, failing to follow proper manufacturing processes, vaccine contamination, and falsification of records.[2] BioPort's vaccine was so bad, and its dangers so widely known, that after its use was made mandatory for all service personnel by Secretary of Defense William Cohen in 1998, more than 400 military personnel either resigned or faced disciplinary action for refusing to take it. They had good reason. At least two deaths had been attributed to it as well as thousands of cases of debilitating illness.[3]

But BioPort had an advantage. Its largest shareholder and a member of the board of directors was the retired Chairman of the Joint Chiefs of Staff, Admiral William Crowe (pronounced like brow).[4] After 9/11 the military orders for BioPort's vaccine went up to $60 million and even before that the government had given BioPort $126 million keep its operations going even though only 4 per cent of its existing contract had been fulfilled.[5]

Although the military had (as of March 2002) suspended its mandatory vaccination program, I could find no evidence that any of BioPort's contracts had been cancelled. In fact, one report indicated that BioPort was using its inside track, by virtue of being the only licensed maker of anthrax vaccine, to compete with a dozen other companies for a newer and more effective drug.[6]

Anthrax treatment and smallpox vaccines

BioPort attracted a great deal of attention from independent researchers post-9/11 and then faded from view as larger corporate entities stepped into the picture. With anthrax permeating Washington and smallpox being increasingly promoted as a major new threat, some real corporate giants appeared on the scene.

The administration quickly rushed to promote Cipro, a powerful and expensive antibiotic with very strong side effects, as a treatment for anthrax — though many other, less potentially dangerous drugs were readily available.[7] The drug's maker, Bayer, had been in serious financial difficulty and watching its stock plunge as a result of 52 deaths and possibly thousands of crippled victims connected with its anti-cholesterol drug Baycol.[8] Revelations that the White House staff had begun taking Cipro nearly a month *before* the first anthrax attacks had sparked a dramatically sharp rise in Bayer's stock price.[9] I suspect that the release of information by the White House on Cipro was ultimately a brilliant marketing strategy.[10] Most Americans probably thought, "If that's what they're taking at the White House then I want it too!"

Bayer's good fortune did not end with Cipro. The same *USA Today* story which disclosed that Bayer was going to be making 200 million doses of Cipro also revealed that HHS Secretary Tommy Thompson had just requested, in a "surprise announcement," 300 million doses of smallpox vaccine, enough to treat everyone in the United States.[11] His initial request was for 54 million doses of the vaccine from the British firm Acambis and the US had also entered into negotiations with pharmaceutical giants Baxter and Merck for additional stockpiles.[12]

Harvard-educated medical researcher Len Horowitz, DMD, MA, MPH looked deeper into the corporate biological intrigue:

> Cipro and smallpox vaccine have much in common besides capturing America's urgent attention in recent weeks. The parent companies that produce these favored elixirs for anthrax and smallpox bioterrorism are linked, strangely enough, to an infamous history involving contaminated blood, the Central Intelligence Agency (CIA), and even the Nazi-associations that the FBI doesn't seem anxious to explore.
>
> Cipro is produced by Germany's Bayer AG, while the smallpox vaccine's newly formed producers are Acambis (previously OraVax), partnered with Baxter and Aventis — created in 1999 by parent companies Hoechst and Rhone-Poulenc, all have jaded histories.
>
> The "Big Three" — Bayer, Baxter, and Rhone-Poulenc — are infamous ... for having infected more than 7,000 American hemophiliacs with the AIDS virus during the early 1980s. They admitted foreknowledge in selling HIV-tainted blood-clotting products and settled the class action case for $100,000 per claimant.
>
> Bayer and Hoechst were formed following World War II from the "decartelization" of Germany's leading industrial organization and Nazi economic engine — I.G. Farben. The CIA [OSS] immediately took over their vacated corporate headquarters which had curiously escaped allied bombings. Historians explain that the Farben complex had been protected by officials of John D. Rockefeller's Standard Oil Company — half owner of the Farben cartel. Many believe that Rockefeller lawyer and Standard Oil business manager, Allen Dulles... protected Farben headquarters from allied bombings. In the current age when past CIA Director James Woolsey lectures on "industrial espionage" as a primary function of the modern intelligence organization, this history may have contemporary ramifications....
>
> After "decartelization," the I.G. Farben plants, including all the labor camps involved in the mostly Jewish genocide, were consolidated into three main holding companies: Bayer, Hoechst, and BASF for the benefit of all the stockholders....
>
> Baxter is a subsidiary of American Home Products (AHP)... [and AHP] like Bayer, Hoechst and BASF is a progeny of I.G. Farben." Aventis, he noted, now owned by Bayer, is a subsidiary of Hoechst. [13]

In the corporate rush to produce smallpox vaccines, we see new companies like Aventis emerging among the beneficiaries. In a little-recognized development,

Aventis was purchased by Bayer on September 3, 2001.[14] Bayer now has a piece of almost every US vaccine program. Shortly after the smallpox grants were requested and after HHS had named Cipro, despite all its faults, as the government's sole drug for treating anthrax, Aventis *found* 70-90 million doses of smallpox vaccines that it made instantly available to the US government, thus giving it a leg up on other competitors.

Smallpox

A great deal of near-hysterical attention was focused on smallpox throughout 2002 as the Homeland Security bill was debated and voted on. Much of what was put forth by in the media makers was blatant disinformation. Space prohibits a detailed discussion of the wisdom and merits of mass vaccination programs, to which I am unalterably opposed. However, as far as smallpox goes, one doctor, Sherry Tenpenny, D.O., told the truth a long time before it was acknowledged in the mainstream media.

> Treatment for smallpox should be surveillance and containment, without vaccination. Smallpox is not highly fatal. There are treatments for smallpox. The vaccine will not protect you from getting the infection. The vaccine has high complication rates, is an experimental drug, and there are many contraindications. (Please see article at: <www.mercola.com/2002/jun/12/smallpox_update.htm>)
>
> Addendum: As I was completing this report this morning, I read in the *New York Times* that the CDC plans to increase the number of "first responders" who receive the vaccination to 500,000 from the agreed-to 15,000.[xiv] Preparations are also underway for rapid mass vaccination of the general public. The more extensive vaccination plan is possible because supplies are increasing. As I have stated before, the government spent more than $780 million to develop its arsenal. Now that we have it, we will use it....
>
> We are setting the stage for a health disaster unlike anything we have seen before in America, and it will be our own doing. World health records (England, Germany, Italy, the Philippines, British India, etc.) document that devastating epidemics followed mass vaccination. The worst smallpox disaster occurred in the Philippines after a 10-year compulsory US program administered 25 million vaccinations to its population of 10 million resulting in 170,000 cases and more than 75,000 deaths from 'smallpox', in a country having only scattered cases in rural villages prior to the onslaught of vaccines....[15]

The top of the biowar food chain

Some of the most horrendous biological warfare experiments ever carried out were conducted by the Japanese in occupied territories of China and Manchuria during

World War II. It's well known that American intelligence rescued a large number of Nazi SS war criminals from likely execution in order to fold them into the newly formed CIA. But it's less frequently observed that a similar pattern holds for the Japanese example; the US failed to prosecute the Japanese perpetrators of the "Unit 731" program. It paid them and brought all their research to the US.[16]

Equipped with data and expertise from other intelligence establishments including those of Nazi Germany and militarist Imperial Japan, the CIA and the Pentagon developed their own formidable bioweapons capability. For decades, the CIA oversaw secret US weapons programs that experimented on unwitting Americans. Many of these experiments involved the airborne dispersal of relatively harmless microorganisms selected to mimic important characteristics of a particular pathogen without incurring disease. But other experiments were far more damaging, and involved the deliberate exposure of unknowing human subjects to radiation anthrax, and even cancer.[17]

The *Guardian* reported on October 29, 2002, that the United States was developing a new generation of weapons that would undermine and likely violate several international treaties. To wit:

- CIA efforts to copy a Soviet cluster bomb designed to disperse biological weapons;
- A project by the Pentagon to build a bioweapon plant from commercially available materials to prove that terrorists could do the same thing;
- Research by the Defense Intelligence Agency into the possibility of genetically engineering a new strain of antibiotic-resistant anthrax;
- A program to produce dried and weaponized anthrax spores, officially for testing US bio-defenses — but far more spores were produced than would be necessary for such a purpose, and it is unclear whether they have been destroyed or stored.[18]

Part II — A trail of dead bodies and legislation

By the end of February 2002, a statistically striking number of world-class microbiologists were starting to drop unnaturally dead all over the globe. This began an intense period of investigation that, instead of answering questions, only raised uglier ones. Michael Davidson, a graduate of the Syracuse University School of Journalism, joined the *FTW* team as an unpaid volunteer, and I tasked him with investigating the deaths. We wanted to determine whether they could somehow be related to legislation pushing toward forced vaccination programs.

Davidson's reporting rattled the mainstream media more than any other *FTW* reporting since 9/11. Follow-up stories appeared in several countries and throughout the US. Perhaps the most attention was paid to our work by Canada's prestigious *Globe and Mail* that ran a Saturday front-page story duplicating most of our research.[19] In correspondence with the *Globe and Mail's* news editor, Bob Cox, I later asked why *FTW* had been omitted from his paper's citations since the most of the research had been done by us. On May 7, 2002, Cox wrote back, "It appears that your publication should have received credit in the *Globe and Mail* for work done to compile the list of microbiologists who died. I would be happy to run a notice in a future edition of the paper doing so." I never received a copy of the notice Cox had promised.

The impact of our stories became evident on Sunday, August 11, 2002, when the *New York Times* published a very odd 7,800-word story on the deaths, written by Lisa Belkin.[20] The essence of the 18-page *Times* piece is that any investigative curiosity about the mysterious deaths of so many world-class microbiologists after 9/11 was a psychological defect among naïve people who needed to find meaning in troubled times. Unless officials, experts, and authorities ratify his or her suspicions in advance, the public citizen is surely spurred by some combination of emotional longing and innumeracy. Rationality is an institutional entitlement reserved for the Paper of Record and the centralized news factories upon which it depends. The rest of us are quaint, harmless bunglers.

The *Times* did not rebut any of our findings, nor did it mention *From The Wilderness* by name. The only factual correction came with a revelation that one of the victims, Set Van Nugyen, who died in Australia was not actually a microbiologist but a technician. So the *Times* inadvertently confirmed that Nugyen had been employed at an Australian research laboratory that had just produced a particularly virulent strain of mousepox.

A response like this in the Sunday edition of the *New York Times* (especially such a feeble response) was an indication that we had struck a nerve. Here is what we wrote. Only those portions of our stories which have already been covered elsewhere in this book have been deleted.

A career in microbiology can be harmful to your health (Revised - updated)

DEATH TOLL MOUNTING AS CONNECTIONS TO DYNCORP, HADRON, PROMIS SOFTWARE AND DISEASE RESEARCH EMERGE

by

Michael Davidson, *FTW* staff writer and Michael C. Ruppert

[ED. NOTE: As *FTW* has begun to investigate serious discussions by legitimate scientists and academics on the possible necessity of reducing the world's population by more than 4 billion people, no stranger set of circumstances since September 11 adds credibility to this possibility than the suspicious deaths of what may be as many as 14 world-class microbiologists. Following on the heels of our two-part series on the coming world oil crisis, this story by Michael Davidson, a graduate of the Syracuse University School of Journalism, takes on new significance. In our original story we incorrectly reported the original date of disappearance of Don Wiley and two other microbiologists. These errors have been corrected, and we have updated the story to include new deaths that have occurred since we published an earlier version on February 14. The newest connections to DynCorp, Hadron and PROMIS software, are leads an amateur would not miss. How else would any microbiologists threatening an ultra secret government biological weapons program be identified than by secretly scanning their databases to see what they were working on? — MCR]

February 28, 2002 (*FTW*) — In the four-month period from November 12 through February 11, seven world-class microbiologists in different parts of the world were reported dead. Six died of "unnatural" causes, while the cause of the seventh's death is questionable. Also on November 12, DynCorp, a major government contractor for data processing, military operations, and intelligence work, was awarded a $322 million contract to develop, produce and store vaccines for the Department of Defense. DynCorp and Hadron, both defense contractors connected to classified research programs on communicable diseases, have also been linked to a software program known as PROMIS, which may have helped identify and target the victims.

In the six weeks prior to November 12, two additional foreign microbiologists were reported dead. Some believe there were as many as five more microbiologists killed during the period, bringing the total as high as 14. These two to seven additional deaths, however, are not the focus of this story. This same period also saw the deaths of three persons involved in medical research or public health.

- On November 12, Benito Que, 52, was found comatose in the street near the laboratory where he worked at the University of Miami Medical School. He died on December 6.
- On November 16, Donald C. Wiley, 57, vanished, and his abandoned rental car was found on the Hernando de Soto Bridge outside Memphis, Tennessee. His body was found on December 20.
- On November 23, Vladimir Pasechnik, 64, was found dead in Wiltshire, England, not far from his home.
- On December 10, Robert Schwartz, 57, was found murdered in his rural home in Loudoun County, Virginia.
- On December 11, Set Van Nguyen, 44, was found dead in the airlock entrance to a walk-in refrigerator in the laboratory where he worked in Victoria State, Australia.
- On February 8, Vladimir Korshunov, 56, was found dead on a Moscow street.

- On February 11, Ian Langford, 40, was found dead in his home in Norwich, England.

Oops!

Prior to these deaths, on October 4, a commercial jetliner traveling from Israel to Novosibirsk, Siberia, was shot down over the Black Sea by an "errant" Ukrainian surface-to-air missile, killing all on board. The missile was over 100 miles off-course. Despite early news stories reporting it as a charter, the flight, Air Sibir 1812, was a regularly scheduled flight.

According to several press reports, including a December 5 article by Barry Chamish[21] and another by Jim Rarey[22], the plane is believed by many in Israel to have had as many as five passengers who were microbiologists. Both Israel and Novosibirsk are homes for cutting-edge microbiological research. Novosibirsk is known as the scientific capital of Siberia, and home to over 50 research facilities and 13 full universities for a population of only 2.5 million people.[23]

At the time of the Black Sea crash, Israeli journalists had been sounding the alarm that two Israeli microbiologists had been recently murdered, allegedly by terrorists. On November 24 a Swissair flight from Berlin to Zurich crashed on its landing approach. Of the 33 persons on board, 24 were killed, including the head of the hematology department at Israel's Ichilov Hospital, as well as directors of the Tel Aviv Public Health Department and Hebrew University School of Medicine. They were the only Israelis on the flight. The names of those killed, as reported in a subsequent Israeli news story but not matched to their job titles, were Avishai Berkman, Amiram Eldor, and Yaacov Matzner.

Besides all being microbiologists, six of the seven scientists who died within weeks of each other died from "unnatural" causes. And four of the seven were doing virtually identical research — research that has global, political, and financial significance.

Que pasa?

The public relations office at the University of Miami Medical School said only that Benito Que was a cell biologist, involved in oncology research in the hematology department. This research relies heavily on DNA sequencing studies. The circumstances of his death raise more questions than they answer.

Que had left his job at a research laboratory at the University of Miami Medical School, apparently heading for his Ford Explorer parked on NW 10th Avenue. The *Miami Herald*, referring to the death as an "incident," reported he had no wallet on him, and quoted Miami police as saying his death may have been the result of a mugging. Police made this statement while at the same time saying there was a lack of visible trauma to Que's body. There is firm belief among Que's friends and family that the scientist was attacked by four men, at least one of whom had a baseball bat. Que's death has now been officially ruled "natural," caused by cardiac arrest. Both the Dade County medical examiner and the Miami Police would not comment on the case, saying only that it is closed.

A Memphis Mystery

Donald C. Wiley of the Howard Hughes Medical Institute at Harvard University was one of the most prominent microbiologists in the world. He had won many of the field's most prestigious awards, including the 1995 Albert Lasker Basic Medical Research Award for work that could make anti-viral vaccines a reality. He was heavily involved in research on DNA sequencing. Wiley was last seen around midnight on November 15, leaving the St. Jude's Children's Research Advisory dinner held at the Peabody Hotel in Memphis, Tennessee. Associates attending the dinner said he showed no signs of intoxication, and no one has admitted to drinking with him.

His rented Mitsubishi Galant was found about four hours later, abandoned on a bridge across the Mississippi River, headed towards Arkansas. Keys were in the ignition, the gas tank full, and the hazard flashers had not been turned on. Wiley's body was found on December 20, snagged on a tree along the Mississippi River in Vidalia, La., 300 miles south of Memphis. Until his body was found, Dr. Wiley's death was handled as a missing person case, and police did no forensic examinations.

Early reports about Wiley's disappearance made no mention of paint marks on his car or a missing hubcap, which turned up in subsequent reports. The type of accident needed to knock off the hubcaps (actually a complete wheel cover) used on recent model Galants would have caused noticeable damage to the sheet metal on either side of the wheel, and probably the wheel itself. No damage to the car s body or wheel has been reported.

Wiley's car was found about a five-minute drive from the hotel where he was last seen. There is a four-hour period in his evening that cannot be accounted for. There is also no explanation as to why he would have been headed into Arkansas late at night. Wiley was staying at his father's home in Memphis.

The Hernando de Soto Bridge carries Interstate 40 out of Memphis, across the Mississippi River into Arkansas. The traffic on the bridge was reduced to a single lane in each direction. This would have caused westbound traffic out of Memphis to slow down and travel in one lane. Anything in the other two closed lanes would have been plainly obvious to every passing person. There are no known witnesses to Wiley stopping his car on the bridge.

On January 14, almost two months after his disappearance, Shelby County Medical Examiner O.C. Smith announced that his department had ruled Wiley's death to be "accidental;" the result of massive injuries suffered in a fall from the Hernando de Soto Bridge. Smith said there were paint marks on Wiley's rental car similar to the paint used on construction signs on the bridge, and that the car's right front hubcap was missing. There has been no report as to which construction signs Wiley hit. There is also no explanation as to why this evidence did not move the Memphis police to consider possibilities other than a "missing person."

Smith theorizes that Wiley pulled over to the outermost lane of the bridge (that lane being closed at the time) to inspect the damage to his car. Smith's subsequent explanation for the fall requires several other things to have occurred simultaneously:

- Wiley had to have had one of the two or three seizures he has per year due to a rare disorder known only to family and close friends, that seizure being brought on by use of alcohol earlier that evening;
- A passing truck creating a huge blast of wind and/or roadway bounce due to heavy traffic; and,
- Wiley had to be standing on the curb next to the guardrail which, because of Wiley's 6-foot-3-inch height, would have come only to his mid-thigh.

These conditions would have put Wiley's center of gravity above the rail, and the seizure would have caused him to lose his balance as the truck created the bounce and blast of wind, thus causing him to fall off the bridge.

Science is Mightier than the Sword

Robert M. Schwartz was a founding member of the Virginia Biotechnology Association and the Executive Director of Research and Development at Virginia's Center for Innovative Technology. He was extremely well respected in biophysics, and regarded as an authority on DNA sequencing.

Co-workers became concerned when he didn't show up at his office on December 10. He was later found dead at his home. Loudoun County Sheriff's officials said Schwartz was stabbed on December 8 with a sword, and had an "X" cut into the back of his neck.

Schwartz's daughter Clara, 19, and three others have been charged in the case. The four are said to have a fascination with fantasy worlds, witchcraft, and the occult. Kyle Hulbert, 18, who allegedly committed the murder, has a history of mental illness, and is reported by the *Washington Post* to have killed Schwartz to prevent the murder of Clara. At the request of Clara Schwartz's attorneys, on February 13 Judge Pamela Grizzle ordered all new evidence introduced about her role in the case to be sealed. She also issued a temporary gag order covering the entire case on police, prosecutors, and defense attorneys.

Breathe Deeply and Carry a Big Stick

Set Van Nguyen was found dead on December 11 at the Commonwealth Scientific and Industrial Research Organization's animal diseases facility in Geelong, Australia. He had worked there 15 years. In January 2001 the journal *Nature* reported that two scientists at this facility had engineered an incredibly virulent form of mousepox, a cousin of smallpox. The researchers were extremely concerned that if similar manipulation could be done to smallpox, a terrifying weapon could be unleashed.

According to Victoria Police, Nguyen died after entering a refrigerated storage facility. "He did not know the room was full of deadly gas which had leaked from a liquid nitrogen cooling system. Unable to breathe, Mr. Nguyen collapsed and died," says the official report.

Nitrogen is not a "deadly" gas, and is a part of air. An extreme overabundance of nitrogen in one's immediate atmosphere would cause shortness of breath, lightheadedness, and fatigue — conditions a biologist would certainly recognize. Additionally, a leak sufficient to fill the room with nitrogen would set off alerts, and would be so massive as to cause a complete loss of cooling, causing the temperature to rise, which would also set off alerts these systems are routinely equipped with.

Russian and British Intelligence — And Old Corpses

In 1989, Vladimir Pasechnik defected from the Former Soviet Union (FSU) to Great Britain while on a trip to Paris. He had been the top scientist in the FSU's bioweapons program, which is heavily dependent upon DNA sequencing. Pasechnik's death was reported in the *New York Times* as having occurred on November 23.

The *Times* obituary indicated that the announcement of Pasechnik's death was made in the United States by Dr. Christopher Davis of Virginia, who stated that the cause of death was a stroke. Davis was the member of British intelligence who de-briefed Dr. Pasechnik at the time of his defection. Davis says he left the intelligence service in 1996, but when asked why a former member of British intelligence would be the person announcing the death of Pasechnik to the US media, he replied that it had come about during a conversation with a reporter he had had a long relationship with. The reporter Davis named is not the author of the *Times* obituary, and Davis declined to say which branch of British intelligence he served in. No reports of Pasechnik's death appeared in Britain for more than a month, until December 29, when his obituary appeared in the *London Telegraph,* which did not include a date of death.

Pasechnik spent the 10 years after his defection working at the Centre for Applied Microbiology and Research at the UK Department of Health, Salisbury. On February 20, 2000, it was announced that, along with partner Caisey Harlingten, Pasechnik had formed a company called Regma Biotechnologies Ltd. Regma describes itself as "a new drug company working to provide powerful alternatives to antibiotics." Like three other microbiologists detailed in this article, Pasechnik was heavily involved in DNA sequencing research. During the anthrax panic of this past fall, Pasechnik offered his services to the British government to help in any way possible. Despite Regma having a public relations department that has released many items to the press over the past two years, the company has not announced the death of one of its two founders.

Bloody February

On February 9 *Pravda.ru* reported that Victor Korshunov had been killed. At the time, Korshunov was head of the microbiology sub-facility at the Russian State Medical University. He was found dead in the entrance to his home with a cranial injury. *Pravda* reports that Korshunov had probably invented either a vaccine to protect against biological weapons, or a weapon itself.

On February 12 a newspaper in Norwich, England, reported the previous day's death of Ian Langford, a senior researcher at the University of East Anglia. The story went on to say that police "were not treating the death as suspicious." The next day, Britain's *Times* reported that Langford was found wedged under a chair "at his blood-spattered and apparently ransacked home."

The February 12 story, from the *Eastern Daily Press,* reports that clerks at a store near Langford's home claim he came in on a daily basis to buy "a big bottle of vodka." Two of the store's staff also claimed Langford had come into the store a few days earlier wearing "just a jumper and a pair of shoes." None of the store's staff would give their name.

It is hard to understand how a man can reach the highest levels of achievement in a scientific field while drinking "a big bottle of vodka" on a daily basis, and strolling around his hometown nearly nude. A February 14 follow-up story from the *Eastern Daily Press* says police believe Langford died after suffering "one or more falls." They say this would account for his head injuries and large amount of blood found at the death scene.

The Howard Hughes Medical Institute — Another Link?

There is another intriguing connection between three of the five American scientists that have died. Wiley, Schwartz, and Benito Que worked for medical research facilities that received grants from Howard Hughes Medical Institute (HHMI). HHMI funds a tremendous number of research programs at schools, hospitals and research facilities, and has long been alleged to be conducting "black ops" biomedical research for intelligence organizations, including the CIA.

Long-time biowarfare investigator Patricia Doyle, PhD, reports that there is a history of people connected to HHMI being murdered. In 1994, Jose Trias met with a friend in Houston, Texas and was planning to go public with his personal knowledge of HHMI "front door" grants being diverted to "back door" black ops bioresearch. The next day, Trias and his wife were found dead in their Chevy Chase, Md., home. Chevy Chase is where HHMI is headquartered. Police described the killings as a professional hit. Tsunao Saitoh, who formerly worked at an HHMI-funded lab at Columbia University, was shot to death on May 7, 1996, while sitting in his car outside his home in La Jolla, Calif. Police also described this as a professional hit.

Beyond the Bizarre

Early-October saw reports that British scientists were planning to exhume the bodies of 10 London victims of the 1918 type-A flu epidemic known as the Spanish Flu. An October 7 report in the UK *Independent* said that victims of the Spanish Flu had been victims of "the world's most deadly virus." British scientists, according to the story, hope to uncover the genetic makeup of the virus, making it easier to combat.

Professor John Oxford of London's Queen Mary's School of Medicine, the British government's flu adviser, acknowledges that the exhumations and subsequent studies will have to be done with extreme caution so the virus is not unleashed to cause another epidemic. The uncovering of a pathogen's genetic structure is the exact work Pasechnik was doing at Regma. Pasechnik died six weeks after the planned exhumations were announced. The need to exhume the bodies assumes no Type-A flu virus sample exists in any lab anywhere in the world.

A piece on MSNBC that aired September 6 makes the British exhumation plans seem odd. The story refers to an article that was to be published the following day in the weekly magazine *Science,* reporting the 1918 flu virus had recently been RNA sequenced. Researchers had traced down and obtained virus samples from archived lung tissue of WWI soldiers, and from an Inuit woman who had been buried in the Alaskan permafrost.

Help Wanted, Spies, and a Link to PROMIS

It was announced January 21 that the director of the CDC, Jeffrey Koplan, is resigning effective March 31. Six days earlier it was announced that Surgeon General David Satcher is also resigning. And there is currently no director for the National Institutes of Health — NIH is being run by an acting director. The recent resignations leave the three most significant medical positions in the federal government simultaneously vacant.

After three months of conflicting reports it is now official that the anthrax that has killed several Americans since October 5 is from US military sources connected to CIA research. The FBI has stated that only 10 people could have had access, yet at the same time they are reporting astounding security breaches at the biowarfare facility at Fort Detrick, Maryland — breaches such as unauthorized nighttime experiments and lab specimens gone missing.

The militarized anthrax used by the US was developed by William C. Patrick III, who holds five classified patents on the process. He has worked at both Fort Detrick, and the Dugway Proving Grounds in Utah. Patrick is now a private biowarfare consultant to the military and CIA. Patrick developed the process by which anthrax spores could be concentrated at the level of one trillion spores per gram. No other country has been able to get concentrations above 500 billion per gram. The anthrax that was sent around the eastern US last fall was concentrated at one trillion spores per gram, according to a Jan. 31 report by Barbara Hatch Rosenberg of the Federation of American Scientists.

In recent years Patrick has worked with Kanatjan Alibekov. Now known by the Americanized "Ken Alibek," he defected to the US in 1992. Before defecting, Alibek was the no. 2 man in the FSU's biowarfare program. His boss was Vladimir Pasechnik.

Currently, Ken Alibek is President of Hadron Advanced Biosystems, a subsidiary of Alexandria, Va.-based Hadron, Inc. Hadron describes itself as a company specializing in the development of technical solutions for the intelligence community. As chief scientist at Hadron, Alibek gave extensive testimony to the House Armed Services Committee about biological weapons on October 20, 1999, and again on May 23, 2000. Hadron announced on December 20 that as of that date, the company had received $12 million in funding for medical biodefense research from the Defense Advanced Research Projects Agency, the US Army

Medical Research and Materiel Command, and the NIH. Hadron said it was working in the field of non-specific immunity.

In the 1980s Hadron was founded and headed by Dr. Earl Brian, a medical doctor and crony of Ronald Reagan and an associate of former Attorney General Edwin Meese. Brian was convicted in the 1980s on fraud charges. Both Hadron and Brian have been closely associated in court documents and numerous credible reports, confirmed since September 11, with the theft of enhanced PROMIS software from its owner, the INSLAW Corporation. PROMIS is a highly sophisticated computer program capable of integrating a wide variety of databases. The software has reportedly been mated in recent years with artificial intelligence. PROMIS has long been known to have been modified by intelligence agencies with a back door that allows for surreptitious retrieval of stored data....

Given this unique capability, and Hadron's prior connections to PROMIS, it is a possibility that the software, by tapping into databases used by each of the victims, could have identified any lines of research that threatened to compromise a larger, and as yet unidentified, more sinister covert operation.

A Pattern?

The DNA sequencing work by several of the microbiologists discussed earlier is aimed at developing drugs that will fight pathogens based on the pathogen's genetic profile. The work is also aimed at eventually developing drugs that will work in cooperation with a person's genetic makeup. Theoretically, a drug could be developed for one specific person. That being the case, it's obvious that one could go down the ladder, and a drug could be developed to effectively treat a much broader class of people sharing a genetic marker. The entire process can also be turned around to develop a pathogen that will affect a broad class of people sharing a genetic marker. A broad class of people sharing a genetic marker could be a group such as a race, or people with brown eyes....

We also know that DNA sequencing research can be used to develop pathogens that target specific genetically related groups. One company, DynCorp, handles data processing for many federal agencies, including the CDC, the Department of Agriculture, several branches of the Department of Justice, the Food and Drug Administration (FDA), and the NIH. On November 12 DynCorp announced that its subsidiary, DynPort Vaccine, had been awarded a $322 million contract to develop, produce, test, and store FDA licensed vaccines for use by the Defense Department. It would be incredibly easy for DynCorp to hide information pertaining to the exact make-up, safety, efficacy, and purpose of the drugs and vaccines the US government has contracted for...

DynCorp has also been directly linked to the development and use of PROMIS software by its founder Bill Hamilton of Inslaw. DynCorp's former Chairman, current board member and the lead investor in Capricorn Holdings, is Herbert Pug Winokur. Winokur was, until recently, Chairman of the Enron Finance Committee. He claimed ignorance as to the fraudulent financial activities of Enron s board even though he was charged with their oversight.[24]

Mike Davidson followed up his original story by reporting on more suspicious deaths just two months later.

Microbiologists Continue to Die

Also in February, *FTW* reported on the extremely suspicious deaths of as many as 14 world-class microbiologists. Since that report, three more microbiologists have died.

At about 8:45 p.m. on February 27, Tanya Holzmayer answered the door of her Mountain View, California, home to find a Domino's Pizza deliveryman. While explaining that she had not ordered a pizza, a man jumped out of the shadows firing several point-black shots at Holzmayer, killing her instantly. The shooter ran down the street, jumped into a Ford Explorer, and sped away. Holzmayer's work was centered on using genomics to develop drugs for HIV/AIDS and cancer.

At about 10 o'clock that night, the body of Guyang "Matthew" Huang was found on a jogging path in a park in Foster City, California. He had been shot once in the head, and a .380 semi-automatic pistol was near his body. Quoted about Huang in the *San Francisco Chronicle* on February 28, Mountain View police Captain Craig Courtin said, "[Huang] did make a phone call to his wife and told her he was on the bay, told her he had shot his boss [Holzmayer,] and ... he threatened suicide."

While the pistol found beside Huang was immediately found to have been registered to him, a month after the incident Mountain View police have not confirmed any ballistic evidence that links Huang's gun to Holzmayer's murder.

Both Holzmayer and Huang, like the other dead microbiologists *FTW* reported on in February, were experts at DNA sequencing. Holzmayer had been Huang's superior at PPD, a Menlo Park, California, biotech firm. Holzmayer fired Huang in June, eight months before the shootings. Holzmayer herself left PPD in recent months, possibly to start her own biotech firm. PPD will not comment, other than to say Holzmayer and Huang both worked there.

Quoted in the *Sacramento Bee* on March 2, Maurille Fournier, Huang's doctoral advisor, said Huang was fired because PPD believed he was doing work for another firm on the side, but that Huang insisted PPD knew about this other work. It is clear from several sources that Holzmayer did not initiate Huang's firing, and did not want to fire him, but was ordered to do so by senior management.

Huang should not have been worried about finding employment. His resume included the fact that he was a senior research fellow at the University of Washington's Department of Molecular Biology and a professor at the University of Massachusetts, Amherst. He was also a founder of the Southern China National Human Genome Research Center.

In another bizarre incident, British microbiologist David Wynn-Williams was killed while jogging near his home in Cambridge, England. Wynn-Williams was an acknowledged expert on the microbiology of the Antarctic ecosystem, and how it could serve as a model for life on other planets. And like the others, Wynn-Williams was involved in DNA sequencing.

According to a March 27 report in England's *Telegraph*, Wynn-Williams was caught between two cars that apparently collided. Neither driver was hurt, yet the impact was enough to kill Wynn-Williams.[25]

FTW's coverage of biowarfare issues continued throughout 2002 as the psychological campaign against Americans intensified.

Bush Signs $4.6 Bil Bioterror Bill
Does Little To Protect Americans' Health, Much for Corporations; Courts Uphold Forced Vaccinations

by
Michael Davidson, *FTW* Staff Writer

July 17, 2002, 16:00 PM PDT (*FTW*) — President George W. Bush signed into law June 12 the Public Health Security and Bioterrorism Response Act of 2002. The bill authorizes spending $4.6 billion on producing and stockpiling vaccines, requires more thorough inspection of food entering the country, and provides assistance to help states improve water source security.

The overwhelming bulk of the expenditures authorized by this new bill are going to pharmaceutical companies, construction firms, and purveyors of laboratory, computer, and communications equipment. Only a pittance is going to hiring human beings to conduct work in preventing or handling a bioterrorism attack. This bill is really just another way for George Bush to transfer taxpayer money to businesses, and has little to do with protecting American citizens.

At the signing, Bush said "last fall's anthrax attacks were an incredible tragedy to a lot of people in America, and it sent a warning that we needed and have heeded." It's nice to know that Bush feels the anthrax attacks were needed, but apparently he's not pushing the FBI to arrest the person who committed them.

The new act, which began life as HR 3448, consists of four sections. Title I, "National Preparedness for Bioterrorism and other Public Health Emergencies," authorizes $2.72 billion for national, state, and local efforts to prepare for bioterrorism and other public health emergencies. The money is allocated as follows:

- $1.16 billion for emergency medical stockpiles, of which $509 million is for smallpox vaccines;
- $450 million for the Centers for Disease Control (CDC), $330 million of which is for facility upgrades and expansion;
- $1 billion for state and local preparedness, including $910 million for already authorized programs to develop and implement emergency programs, as well as to train and equip emergency and health care personnel;
- $25 million for anti-microbial research; and
- $90 million for other ongoing programs.

Title II, "Enhancing Controls on Dangerous Biological Agents and Toxins," establishes a mandatory registration system and national database at CDC for all facilities which possess, use or transfer any of 42 specific biological agents and toxins. This provision is enthusiastically endorsed by the American Society for Microbiology, as the previous 1996 law required registration of only those facilities that were transferring the agents.

Title II also requires facilities to submit the names of all persons having access to these biological agents to the attorney general and the Department of Health and Human Services for screening against criminal, immigration, national security, and other databases. The screening will be looking for persons defined as "restricted" by section 175b of the USA-Patriot Act enacted in October. Among those defined by 175b are aliens that are not permanent US residents, and foreign nationals from terrorism-sponsoring nations.

Title III, "Protection of Food and Drug Supply," allocates $100 million for increased food inspection, improved information management systems, development of rapid detection inspection methods and threat assessment techniques for food safety. There are also a myriad of administrative procedures mandated regarding record keeping, notification to various government entities, as well as registration by manufacturers, importers and transporters.

Title IV, "Drinking Water Security and Safety," authorizes $120 million to help communities with water systems serving over 3,300 people conduct vulnerability assessments, and prepare emergency response plans. Title IV also authorizes $15 million to the Environmental Protection Agency (EPA) to review methods to prevent, detect, and respond to the intentional introduction of chemical, biological, or radiological contaminants into community water systems and review means to prevent supply disruption.

Titles III and IV allocate roughly a quarter billion dollars to solve problems that have not occurred, i.e., tampering with food and water supplies. The nation has suffered through E. coli outbreaks within the food supply chain, but the Bush administration did nothing about them. Under the guise of "anti-terrorism," the administration now sees the need to protect our food and water. It's all just a way to give money to businesses.

In another massive giveaway, this one to the pharmaceutical industry, the Food and Drug Administration (FDA) recently decided to approve drugs used to treat biological, chemical, and nuclear terrorism without their being tested on affected humans. According to a May 31 article in the *New York Times,* the agency said eliminating the requirement for human testing could spur development of anti-terrorism drugs by eliminating the stumbling block of ethical concerns over exposing human volunteers to substances like smallpox or nerve gas.

The new rule will still require any new drug to be tested on humans for safety and side effects. There will be no testing for efficacy in humans of the new drugs. While researchers may be able to make pretty reasonable assumptions from tests on monkeys, there is no certainty that a drug will work identically on the human species....

In March the Federal Appeals Court for the Eighth Circuit ruled that a defendant can be forcibly drugged even though he has not been convicted of a crime and poses no danger to himself or others. The case, United States of America vs. C.T. Sell, involved a St. Louis dentist who has been charged with Medicaid fraud. He has been in jail for over four years, and has never been brought to trial. In a 2-1 decision, the court acknowledged that "the evidence does not support a finding that Sell posed a danger to himself or others" but established government authority to forcibly medicate a person with mind altering drugs on the basis that "charges of fraud" alone are "serious" enough to justify forced medication. The Court further found that there are no limits on the quantities or types of drugs the government can administer.

The American Association of Physicians and Surgeons (AAPS) joined the American Civil Liberties Union (ACLU) in petitioning the Eighth Circuit Court of Appeals for a rehearing in the Sell case. In the Motion for Rehearing, AAPS said "The Decision holds merely that by alleging fraud, the State may inject mind-altering drugs into a prisoner against his will, based on government testimony." The ACLU argued, "The Panel's opinion fails to determine if the government's interest is compelling before applying its balancing test, and fails to acknowledge the fundamental liberty status that the Supreme Court has granted non-dangerous people to be free from involuntary medication by the government."

In early-May, the Eighth Circuit Court issued a 5-4 oral decision not to rehear the case. Americans are now in a situation where:

- The FDA is allowing drugs to be marketed as treatments for biological, chemical or radiological attacks without testing them for efficacy in humans;
- Under federal and state laws, states may arrest, charge and jail people for refusing to take a specific course of treatment for a biological, chemical or radiological attack; and
- A Court of Appeals has ruled that it is perfectly legal for an individual to be forcibly drugged while in government custody.[26]

Other ominous developments suggesting the Empire's darker agenda were reported by investigative journalist and radio public affairs producer Kellia Ramares. She gave us permission to reprint the following story that appeared on the website of Michel Chossudovsky's Institute for Research on Globalization. Ramares' website is at <www.rise4news.net>.

As Bush threatens Iraq with nukes, US ramps up its own biowarfare research (excerpted)

By
Kellia Ramares,
Reprinted with Permission

Jan. 15, 2003, (*FTW*) — When I booted up my AOL account on the morning of December 11th, I was greeted by the picture of someone in a gas mask and the headline: "You gas us; We'll nuke you!" Bad as that was, the headline on *West County Times* was worse: "Pre-emptive nuke strike a possibility." The *San Francisco Chronicle* banner headline was even pithier: "Bush Doctrine: Hit First."

But while George W. Bush threatens Iraq, the United States is expanding its own biowarfare research programs. The government plans to increase the number of biohazard safety level (BSL) 3 and 4 labs around the United States. BSL 3 labs handle live anthrax, botulism, and bubonic plague, among many other things. BSL 4 labs conduct research on an array of even deadlier organisms, including smallpox and Ebola virus.

Steve Erickson, director of the Citizens' Education Project <http://www.citizensedproject.org> in Salt Lake City, Utah said, "This expansion of laboratory capacity within the Defense Department and other departments of government has been in the works for a number of years, probably dating to about 1995. Certainly, the intensity and speed of these developments has picked up since 9/11/2001. The last count we had was about 14 [labs] that were being proposed in various locations by any one of four Cabinet level departments within the US Government. There are some indications now that the National Institutes of Health will be backing off in terms of the numbers of Biological Safety Level Four laboratories, but intends instead to renovate and perhaps build additional Biological Level Three laboratories."

The Department of Energy wants to build a BSL-3 facility at its Los Alamos lab in New Mexico. On December 16th, the DOE released the final Environmental Assessment of plans to build a BSL-3 lab at Lawrence Livermore National Lab (<http://www.llnl.gov>), in the San Francisco suburbs. DOE issued a "Finding of No Significant Impact" for construction of this new facility. Additionally, Lawrence Livermore (LLNL) plans to be a partner in developing The Western National Center for Biodefense and Emerging Diseases, a BSL-4 facility slated for the University of California — Davis.

Why put high containment microbiology labs at nuclear facilities, such as Los Alamos and LLNL?

One might think the ready answer is that at the nuclear weapons lab security measures were already in place that would safeguard the community against accidents or terrorist attacks. But when I posed the question to John Bellardo, director of the Office of Public Affairs of the US Department of Energy's National Nuclear Security Administration, he did not offer even that much substance. Instead, he said, after a long pause, "There is no apparent problem with locating the biosafety level three facility at the Lawrence Livermore National Laboratory. All of the potential ramifications were examined in the environmental assessment, and it was determined that it does not pose any undue harm or potential threat to the human health or the environment."

Bellardo also said that a contract had been let for the construction of a prefabricated building to house the new facility. Construction should be completed by late summer or early fall of 2003.

The real reason for putting a high containment microbiology lab in a nuclear research facility may be to duck oversight protocols.

Professor Barbara Hatch Rosenberg, Chair of the Working Group on Biological Weapons of the Federation of American Scientists, (<http://www.fas.org>) said "when various types of weapons are being researched at the same place, it means that if there is any kind of oversight or investigation or inspection of one type, it puts at risk classified information about the others. And this is a reason why this government frequently objects to any kind of oversight. And this is also, in my view, a reason why different kinds of weapons research should be conducted at different locations, rather than piling them all in the same place."...

While George W. Bush compels the Iraqis to bare all in connection with its weapons programs, what biological horrors is the American government cooking up in the secrecy of its own labs?[27]

Three other recent developments are noteworthy. On June 19, 2002, MSN reported that scientists were preparing for a worldwide flu epidemic, which might kill millions, that would possibly originate in China. Citing a report from the National Academy of Sciences, MSN warned that rare and lethal strains of flu were appearing more frequently and that they had genetically mutated — apparently by themselves — making them far more deadly. "We don't want this in humans or the world will be in deep, deep trouble," wrote MSN quoting researcher Robert G. Webster, PhD.[28] Less than a month later the BBC reported that scientists had actually assembled a virus from scratch in a laboratory resulting in the "first synthetic virus." The story also reported that researchers had used the gene sequence for polio to make it.[29] Why? And just two days later Reuters reported that more than 900 Chinese schoolchildren had been rushed to hospitals with serious side effects after being vaccinated for encephalitis.[30]

Both hopeful and frightening developments were to appear on the biowarfare front in 2003 with an official repudiation of the smallpox vaccination program and the appearance of SARS. Both were tied to what was then emerging as the decline of the Bush dynasty, a regime change intended to facilitate the preservation of the Empire.

CHAPTER 30

THE ORDER OF BATTLE

This war, should it come, is intended to mark the official emergence of the United States as a full-fledged global empire, seizing the sole responsibility and authority as a planetary policeman. It would be the culmination of a plan 10 years or more in the making, carried out by those who believe the United States must seize the opportunity for global domination, even if it means becoming the 'American imperialists' that our enemies have always claimed we were.

Once that is understood, other mysteries solve themselves. For example, why does the administration seem unconcerned about an exit strategy once Saddam is toppled?

Because we won't be leaving...

— Jay Bookman, *Atlanta Journal Constitution*, September 29, 2002

A month after the attacks on the World Trade Center, I was telling my readers, and saying in radio interviews around the country, that the war which had begun that day — a war which Dick Cheney told us would not end in our lifetimes — was a sequential campaign to control the last remaining reserves of oil and gas on the planet. That assessment has been more than validated.

You can see the whole story at a glance. Just look at a map of the world that marks the areas with the greatest oil and gas deposits. Then take a look at where the US military has been most active since 9/11. With this pattern right in front of you, think back on the various pretexts offered by the American government for the sequential wars it has fought or begun to create during this same period. An emotionally interesting exercise, isn't it?

Massive worldwide protests against the US invasion of Iraq might have delayed its March 2003 start, but they could never have stopped it. Behind the Iraqi invasion are the pressures of all the campaigns which the Empire has planned to conduct *after* Iraq, and which will be carried out either under the Bush Neocons or under the more pleasant theme music of a neo-liberal Democratic president using the IMF, the World Bank, NATO, and the UN. Behind that is the reality of Peak Oil.

The short-term prospects are, in my opinion, a lose-lose scenario for mankind. This is especially true as nations realize that the game of petroleum musical chairs has just had several seats removed, and the song is about to end.

Before the invasion of Iraq, information began to leak out concerning not only the motive of securing Iraqi oil, but its urgency as well. I could not have asked for a better confirmation of the real impetus behind the Empire's infinite war than statements made by Britain's Foreign Secretary, Jack Straw, when he addressed a group of British ambassadors in early January 2003. In that speech Straw admitted that oil was a key motivator in Britain's willingness to participate in the US conquest of Iraq. Speaking at a two-day London conference, Straw said that one strategic priority was to:

> bolster the security of British and global energy supplies. A news story reporting on the event also cited a story from Britain's *Guardian* indicating that "some ministers and officials in Whitehall say privately that oil is more important in the calculation than weapons of mass destruction. These ministers have pointed to the instability of current oil sources — the Middle East, Caspian region and Algeria — and the need for secure alternatives."

A *World Socialist Website* story reporting these confirmed details went on to state:

> With UK North Sea oil production in decline, British policy makers have been sounding alarm bells as to future supplies. Analysts estimate that the UK could be totally dependent on imports for its energy requirements within 50 years. The problem is not confined to the UK alone — it is anticipated that more than 92 percent of Europe's oil, and 81 percent of its gas, will have to be imported from overseas within 30 years....
>
> The country, or countries, able to establish control over this vital resource will secure a major advantage over their international rivals. This is a prime factor motivating US policy in the Middle East. By occupying Iraq and seizing its oil resources, the US hopes to establish its undisputed hegemony as against Europe and Japan....
>
> The Blair government has similarly resolved that the issue of oil supplies must be settled by force of arms. In 1998 it commissioned a *Future Strategic Context for Defence* review, aimed at identifying the main challenges facing Britain over the next decades and targeting military resources accordingly. The official British report also stated that offshore energy resources "are likely to become a growing source of international dispute and potential conflict."[1]

A day after that story was published, British Prime Minister Tony Blair was reported on CNN as saying that anyone who suggested that the war was about oil was a "conspiracy theorist."

The struggle for global dominance is not just about possessing the grand prize of the Middle East. It is as much about access to oil, infrastructure, distance to markets, diversification of supply, and maintaining uninterrupted supply. There are smaller, relatively short-lived reserves of oil — some even untapped — in West Africa, Colombia, the South China Sea, Central Asia, and Venezuela. It is imperative to note that these deposits will only delay the onset of Peak Oil and what it means for human civilization. They have already been figured into calculations by oil scientists Campbell, Duncan, and Youngquist, as discussed in previous chapters. Duncan and Youngquist wrote:

> The headline of this section asked, "Can we delay the world peak?" Our response is, Yes, new production brought on-stream well before the 2006 base-line peak can delay it, but only by a few days per Gb [billion barrels] of new production. However, even large increments of new production brought onstream after the peak are not likely to have any effect whatsoever on delaying the base-line world oil peak.
>
> Although we can't precisely predict when the peak will occur, we are assured that it is not a "moving target." In fact the world peak is probably fixed by the most recent production trends of the top 42 oil-producing nations included in this study.[2]

In the short run, any nation that controls these smaller deposits can subsidize its own economy and bring supply onstream while building necessary infrastructure elsewhere (i.e., Iraq). The horrific quagmire into which Iraq has disintegrated, with its escalating death tolls and open resistance against the US occupation, has, as perhaps its only silver lining, proven that the Neocons are fallible.

Our "map" had shown us the road, and we shared it. Our stories were sometimes months ahead of actual events and gave our readers tools to understand what was happening in real time. I have deleted only those portions of the stories that have been described in greater detail elsewhere in this book.

Bush Advisers Planned Iraq War Since 1990s

by
Joe Taglieri, *FTW* Staff

Oct.1, 2002, 17:00 PDT (*FTW*) — The George W. Bush administration's intentions of removing Saddam Hussein from power are not a recent development by any stretch of the imagination. Top White House officials affiliated with conservative think tanks and past administrations have been developing strategies for removing the Iraqi leader since the 1990s.

One such think tank, the Project for the New American Century (PNAC), published a report in September 2000 recommending policies

for preserving and expanding US dominance in world affairs, including an aggressive policy for deposing Saddam Hussein. Members of this
group include Vice President Dick Cheney, Defense Secretary Donald
Rumsfeld, convicted Iran-Contra perjurer and current National
Security Council (NSC) staffer Elliot Abrams, Deputy Defense Secretary
Paul Wolfowitz, and I. Lewis Libby, Cheney's Chief of Staff and Assistant
for National Security Affairs.

Referring to the Persian Gulf region the report states, 'Indeed, the
United States has for decades sought to play a more permanent role in
Gulf regional security. While the unresolved conflict with Iraq pro-
vides the immediate justification, the need for a substantial American
force presence in the Gulf transcends the issue of the regime of Saddam
Hussein.'

The crux of the report advocates bulking up America's military so
it can be "able to rapidly deploy and win multiple simultaneous large-
scale wars." It lists southern Europe, the Middle East, Central and
East Asia as targets for increased military deployments.

Gary Schmitt, one of the report's project co-chairmen and a former
Reagan policy adviser, told *FTW* that a US invasion of Iraq is
inevitable. "We will definitely be involved in Iraq for two reasons," said
Schmitt. "One is because of issues myself [sic], the administration, and
others have laid out for a number of years, and two, there isn't a snow-
ball's chance in hell Saddam will allow inspections that matter."

All The Vice President's Men

US military action against Iraq to oust Saddam Hussein has long been
a goal of members of the present Bush administration. The PNAC
report was based upon a 1992 draft of the Pentagon's *Defense Planning
Guidance,* which was prepared for then-Defense Secretary Cheney,
Wolfowitz, and Libby. At the time Libby and Wolfowitz were part of
Cheney's policy staff.

Libby has an extensive background in international relations and
defense policy. He joined President Reagan's State Department in 1981
as a member of the Policy Planning Staff and then became the director of special projects in the department's Bureau of East Asian and
Pacific Affairs.

Libby was a deputy undersecretary for policy in President George
H. W. Bush's Defense Department headed by Cheney....

Wolfowitz has worked for the government as a defense policy strategist since 1973. He was head of the State Department's Policy Planning
Staff from 1981 to 1982 and was Deputy Assistant Secretary Of Defense
for Regional Programs from 1977 to 1980.

During his time with Regional Programs, Wolfowitz helped establish the force that would become the United States Central Command. He also contributed to the creation of the Navy's Maritime Pre-positioning Ships, which his Defense Department bio describes as the supply ships program that provided "the backbone of the initial US deployment twelve years later in Operation Desert Shield...."

Along with five fellow signatories of PNAC's 1997 statement of principles, Wolfowitz is affiliated with Johns Hopkins University. He was the Dean and Professor of International Relations at the university's Paul H. Nitze School of Advanced International Studies (SAIS)....

SAIS is also home to foreign policy behemoth Zbigniew Brzezinski, the author of a 1997 book foretelling current US conflicts with Iraq and terrorists called *The Grand Chessboard*.

PNAC member Elliot Abrams is a former Assistant Secretary of State who was a major player in the Iran-Contra scandal of the 1980s. He was convicted of several felony offenses including lying to Congress but was later pardoned by President George H. W. Bush....

'RICHARD'S STRING OF PERLES'

Richard Perle is another key Bush policy maker at the center of the administration's push toward war with Iraq. He is the chairman of the Defense Policy Board, which reports policy recommendations to Rumsfeld and Wolfowitz.

Perle was Assistant Secretary of Defense for International Security Policy during both terms of the Reagan administration. He has been a frequent contributor to national media publications and television programs.

He is also a resident fellow of the American Enterprise Institute, a think tank which has a member list that reads like a who's who of conservative politicians, academics, and policy makers....

"It is a badge of honor among the Warrior Class to be identified as one of Richard's String of Perles," Wanniski wrote in a memo posted on his Polycomomics, Inc. website.

Two PNAC men cited by Wanniski as faithful Perlites are William Kristol and Frank Gaffney.

Gaffney is a *Washington Times* columnist and a contributor to Defense News and Investor's Business Daily. During the Reagan Administration he was an Assistant Secretary of Defense under Perle.

Gaffney, who holds a Masters Degree from Johns Hopkins' SAIS, is the founder and president of yet another think tank known as the Center for Security Policy.

Conservative commentator Kristol is the editor of the *Weekly Standard* magazine and a frequent pundit on TV news programs. He is also the PNAC chairman and, according to Wanniski, part of a network of opinion makers who answer to Perle. Kristol's network consists of many editorial page writers and journalists for national publications and television programs...

Tim Barker, *FTW* Staff, contributed to this report. [3]

The months leading up to the March 2003 invasion of Iraq were extremely tense as American supremacy was challenged in the eyes of the world. Massive worldwide demonstrations built unprecedented popular opposition to the US war on Iraq. The formation of a Paris-Berlin-Moscow alliance threatened NATO. And China, swelling with a robust economy and about to launch its first manned space mission, polished its image as the Americans tarnished their own. There is no doubt that the Bush administration had initially hoped for an invasion as early as September 2002; it brazenly showed its hand with large-scale forward deployments of military personnel even inside Northern Iraq itself, and in several countries throughout the region including Jordan. A failed coup attempt in Qatar — denied by the Pentagon — and repeated attacks on vulnerably positioned troops suggested that the Empire was getting into trouble.[4]

As opposition to the blatantly unjustified invasion mounted, the US was seriously delayed in its plans. Hans Blix's UN weapons inspectors found no weapons of mass destruction. *Nobody* found any weapons of mass destruction. The UN opposed unilateral action. Tens of millions of people took to the streets, but to no avail. The attitude of Donald Rumsfeld and his neo-con cohorts never faltered; their implicit message, *we're going to do whatever we want to do, whenever we want to do it,* was never far from the surface.

Richard Perle, then chairman of the Defense Policy Board, had voiced concern about delaying the invasion as early as August of 2002. This was a full seven months before the invasion actually occurred.

> Timing is everything when you do this. If you launched [a public campaign] too far in advance and nothing followed, that would raise questions and fuel a debate that would not be helpful to the administration.... If you join the debate now, but don't act for months, you pay a worse price.[5]

Many, including this writer, hoped and believed for a time that the invasion might be prevented. Although the experienced student of the post-9/11 world would have realized that perhaps an equally dangerous world would have resulted if US momentum had faltered, there was a belief and hope that within that world something other than brute force would be used as a modus operandi.

As the run-up to the Iraqi invasion continued, it was widely assumed throughout the world that Iraq was capable of quick oil production increases. The Bush administration fostered this belief as an incentive for "irrationally exuberant" market movements.

As *FTW* wrote shortly after the invasion:

> Quoting an analyst at the Washington-based Petroleum Finance Co, the AP reported that an investment of $3-6 billion and two years would be required to permit Iraqi production to reach 3 Mbpd. That issue is further compounded by the fact that title to Iraqi oil is presently uncertain and the only way to resolve the issue might be through the recently roughed-up UN.
>
> Just a day later, CBS News' *Market Watch* labeled post-war Iraqi oil as a "wild card," reaffirming evaluations of current Iraqi infrastructure and quoting oil industry expert Kevin Kerr as stating that it would take three years and $7 billion in new investment to bring Iraqi oil production to the 1990 peak of 3.5 Mbpd, $20 billion to reach 5.5 Mbpd, and more than 10 years to double production from current levels if 'everything goes smoothly.'
>
> Everything is not going smoothly. Little noticed by the American press is the fact that saboteurs are ravaging northern Iraqi oil fields. An April 14 AP story quoted Shad, an electrical engineer who would not give his last name, as saying, "It's the worst destruction I have seen in my life. It will set Iraq back many years." Shad should know. He works for the Northern Oil Company, which administers all of the oil fields in northern Iraq.
>
> There is no immediate promise or even a remote possibility that Iraqi production will increase rapidly. US military, economic planners, and experts in the financial markets know this. In his *FTW* interview Campbell stressed that even the loss of seismic charts or the hands-on expertise of people who know how to work each unique oil field could set reconstruction back years. [6]

This sabotage has continued unabated since the occupation and has increased in 2004. Most of the main pipelines leading out of the country are jerry-rigged at best and frequently inoperative.[7] As of this writing, Iraqi oil production stands at a paltry 1.6 Mbpd, well below Iraq's all-time peak of 3 Mbpd in 1990 and about .4 Mbpd below where it was when the US invaded.[8] It's going to be a long time before Iraqi oil comes online, and the US may actually have planned for that. It is, after all, oil in the bank. Meanwhile, the delay in production has made the reserves and infrastructure in Saudi Arabia, Africa, Latin America, and elsewhere all the more important.

The order of battle after 9/11

Canada - NORTHCOM

Canada had been subjugated long before 9/11. It only became visible to many Canadians after that. *FTW's* October 2000 story on PROMIS software left no doubt about it (See Chapter 10).

On October 1, 2002, the military forces of Mexico, Canada, and the Continental US (CONUS) were placed under a joint military command called Northern Command or NORTHCOM. NORTHCOM is headed by American four-star-general Ralph Eberhart, who is also the commander of NORAD that coordinated all US fighter response on 9/11. It makes sense. Canada is currently the single largest foreign supplier of both oil and natural gas to the US, and Mexico is ranked at number four.[9]

I was not totally surprised while I was traveling on my lecture tour in the summer of 2002 to pick up a copy of Canada's *National Post* and read a story on plans for a US military occupation of Canada that was actually being discussed in the Canadian parliament as a "protective" measure:

> Canada's military impotence threatens Canadian sovereignty because it invites the US to take steps to defend itself against terrorist attacks, even to the point of sending troops onto Canadian soil.... [The head of a commission on Canadian security] said it is even possible, if Canada does not cooperate with Washington's continental security plans — that the Americans could seal the Canada-US border and deploy their armed forces in our territory if they felt it necessary.[10]

My Canadian friends are amazed at their new semi-colonial status. Since 9/11 many of their liberties have been stripped, they are obligated to sell their resources to the US without recourse, and now they may find themselves an occupied nation.

Canada has virtually no future petroleum significance for the US. Its much-vaunted tar sands projects in Alberta have proven to be both an ecological and an economic nightmare requiring heavy cash investments; they require huge amounts of natural gas to produce the steam required to separate the oil, and they destroy vast expanses of pristine land with strip mining and highly toxic waste products. There will be no salvation for either Canada or the US in the form of Canadian oil. In fact, one recent analysis dubbed Canadian tar sands as an actual threat to US energy security.[11]

What Canada has that the US must have is natural gas. And under NAFTA and WTO agreements Canada must make its natural gas available to US markets on a first-priority basis. As Canada's gas supplies run out, American demand continues to soar. At this writing a huge natural gas crisis looms for all of North America in the fall and winter of 2004.[12]

Central Asia and the Caspian

By occupying Afghanistan and resurrecting the opium trade, the Empire accomplished several major tasks. First it protected cash flows to its teetering financial markets. Through first-ever deployments in Uzbekistan, Pakistan, Kyrgyzstan, Jordan, Georgia, later followed by major deployments to Qatar and Oman, it quickly surrounded the Middle East. With increased deployments in Turkey, Egypt, Saudi Arabia, and Kuwait, it presented the world with a *fait accompli* for the next step of its plan. And even though Caspian oil proved to be a bust, the final agreement between Pakistan, Afghanistan, and Turkmenistan to begin construction of the trans-Afghan gas pipeline to supply India was signed on December 27, 2002.[13] Time will tell if Afghanistan will ever be pacified enough to see that job finished. Transfer of military operations from US to NATO command on August 11, 2003, may prove an important step in that direction.

Iraq

The basic plan was to capture 11 percent of the world's oil and put it in a bank while Halliburton, DynCorp, and a dozen other corporations get billions of US taxpayer dollars to rebuild the infrastructure for a time when the US will be able to use it, parcel it out to starving allies, or simply withhold it from foes.

As we have already seen, Cheney's Halliburton emerged as the hungry Alpha Dog in Iraq to the point where competitors like Bechtel had to complain publicly of an unfair playing field.[14] This not surprising, since the US Army Corps of Engineers under the control of Donald Rumsfeld has awarded up to $7 billion in no-bid, sole-source contracts to Halliburton. Other favored companies like DynCorp have also received no-bid contracts. Many were surprised at the openness of the corruption when it was announced that Halliburton would also have control over the pumping and distribution of Iraqi oil. These questionable practices have not escaped the notice of Congressman Henry Waxman and his Government Reform Committee.[15]

The Bush administration has even gone so far as to issue a highly controversial Executive Order (13303) handing US oil companies near-blanket immunity from lawsuits and criminal prosecution in their "management" of Iraqi oil.[16]

Saudi Arabia and Iran

While some experts like Michel Chossudovsky disagree with me about the order in which they will be targeted, there is no doubt that these two countries are on the list. I agree with former UN weapons inspector Scott Ritter and Professor Peter Dale Scott that Saudi Arabia will be first. That is primarily because it has the largest reserves; it is the most unstable; and it already has a sizeable American corporate presence.

Iran, with the fifth-largest oil reserves, has a fairly stable government, and will remain surrounded and cut off. It's not going anywhere. Besides, it has already passed its peak of production while Saudi Arabia, with all its instability, appears to be just arriving at peak now. The priority on Saudi Arabia is also a political one, since the power of OPEC can only be broken by direct American control over the Kingdom. Events following the Iraqi occupation have confirmed my assessment.

We wrote in May 2003 that:

The three bombings of expatriate compounds [belonging to the Vinnell security firm] which took place in the Saudi Capital on Monday, May 12, signal more than a "resurgent" al Qaeda. That the CIA, the Bush family, and Osama bin Laden have been cooperating and doing business for decades is now extremely well documented and part of the "9/11 cover-up" being alluded to by Bob Graham, the former chair of the Senate intelligence committee, in his public remarks. As the *Financial Times* reported in separate stories on May 13, the attacks signal the possible start of a campaign to overthrow the feeble Saudi monarchy and represent a serious challenge to the royal family. Quoting a senior Western diplomat in the Saudi capital the *FT* reported, "This is a serious challenge to the al-Sauds. It is on the scale of the 1979 takeover of the Grand Mosque in Mecca...."

A *Times of London* story on May 14, headlined "Firm 'Was Cover for CIA'" discussed Vinnell's spooky past, its longstanding military presence in the region, and noted that the current attack was the second bombing Vinnell had suffered in eight years. It was actually the third bombing of Vinnell operations since 1991. The *Times* did not mention the fact that a Vinnell joint venture with Halliburton's Brown and Root (Vinnell, Brown and Root) had its Ankara office bombed shortly after the Gulf War by a Kurdish separatist group. Brown and Root and the Kurds have been repeatedly connected to heroin smuggling controlled by the CIA from as far back as 1977. (To learn more about the Vinnell Corp. please visit: <www.fromthewilderness.com/free/ciadrugs/bush-cheney-drugs.html.>)

Motives for these bombings might have varied as in the case of the 1991 bombing where Kurdish separatists — feeling betrayed (again) by the CIA — were seeking revenge after being left exposed and vulnerable at the end of the Gulf War.

What is interesting about the bombings is that they targeted the compound occupied by Vinnell employees at a time when most of them weren't there. An AP story on May 13, 2003, stated, "The seven Americans killed lived in a four-story building that was heavily damaged. Seventy Americans employed by the Vinnell Corp., a Virginia company with a contract to train Saudi military and civilian officials, lived in the building. By chance, 50 were away on a training exercise."[17]

The uproar caused by the Bush administration's failure to declassify portions of the Congressional 9/11 intelligence report, released in late July 2003, further underscore this point. This was a clear-cut case of the neo-cons having their cake (hiding their business and financial relationships with Saudis connected to 9/11) and eating it too. I thought it highly amusing that convenient portions of the report — damaging only to the Saudis — were almost immediately leaked to major publications around the country. The names of Omar Al Bayoumi and Osama Basnan, heretofore unmentioned benefactors of hijackers Alhazmi and Almidhar, became household words as Saudi prestige suffered another blow on the world scene.

I wrote to a former member of the House International Relations Committee about it. While the Bush administration, politically weakened by the Watergate-like scandal unfolding over its distorted Iraqi intelligence and a deepening guerilla quagmire in Iraq, could not proceed with a move against the Saudis, an incoming Democratic President certainly could. This would explain why major figures at the Council on Foreign Relations had grown sharply and publicly critical of Bush's misdirection in the war on terror.[18] It has also been a matter of record for some time that major Democratic Party hopefuls have staked out ground by saying that Iraq should never been on the plate in the war on terror and Saudi Arabia should have.[19]

It is obvious that the people of America and the world are being prepared for a move to seize the Saudi oilfields, most likely under the auspices of the UN or NATO and in a pre-manufactured crisis that will make it appear as if the US is merely responding to events.

The House veteran wrote back on condition of anonymity, "A blind man could see this coming." And, as if to fulfill our prophecy, on August 12, 2003, five persons were reported killed in a second day of violent clashes between police and radical fundamentalists.[20]

By the spring of 2004 the Saudi political situation was deteriorating rapidly. Open attacks on government installations and foreign interests resulted in the assassination of a fourth Saudi prince;[21] a December 17, 2003, State Department advisory instructed US citizens to leave the country; open gun battles with Saudi security forces occurred throughout April;[22] in the same month, non-essential US diplomatic staff were evacuated from the capital after the discovery of truck and pipe bombs;[23] a massive truck bomb exploded on April 21st;[24] and open attacks on Saudi oil field workers at a Red Sea facility killed at least two Americans on May 1st.[25]

This rapid disintegration of Saudi control was exactly what *FTW* had been advising its readers to expect for more than 18 months. It was dramatically worsened when allegations surfaced in early 2004 indicating that Saudi oil production has quite possibly already peaked, a condition which — if true — would spell certain doom for a regime that couldn't pay its bills and would most certainly no longer be able to keep a restive population quiet with government handouts. We will look at that development more closely in a later chapter.

Africa

As I had predicted for almost a year before the Iraqi invasion, West Africa moved to center stage immediately after the occupation of Iraq. I reaffirmed these predictions with my readers in the spring of 2003:

Before discussing developments in equatorial Africa it is essential to understand the oil picture there. There are no oil reserves anywhere which rival those of Saudi Arabia with approximately 250 billion barrels (Gb), or Iraq which has approximately 112 Gb. Current world consumption is approximately 1 Gb every eleven days and demand is increasing rapidly. The two critical factors are the accessibility of oil (both geologically and geographically) and how long it takes to get it to market. It takes about six weeks for oil from the Persian Gulf to reach an American gas tank yet it takes only about two weeks for oil from West Africa to make the same journey. Equally important, oil installations in West Africa are in direct and immediate reach of US naval forces from the Atlantic Ocean. There are no political or international coalitions which need to be massaged if intervention becomes necessary.

Nigeria, the world's sixth-largest oil producer, passed its peak of production in 1979 and has estimated reserves of approximately 24 Gb. What makes Nigeria critical is the fact that it can function, with minimal investment, as a so-called "swing" producer. In the event of oil shortages there are wells, pipelines, and refineries already in place and easily accessible which could accommodate a short-term increase in production to control prices or offset shortages. Shell, ChevronTexaco, and TotalFinaElf have heavy investments in the country and until recently, maintained sizeable workforces there.

Recently the US has been exerting tremendous pressure on Nigeria to withdraw from OPEC and its strict production quotas by dangling the prospect of Imperially-funded prosperity in front of it. The appeal of African oil has drawn serious US government attention, even to the point of it sponsoring a January, 2002, Washington conference titled, "African Oil — A Priority for US National Security and African Development." This was reported in *Petroleum Supply Monthly* in December of 2002 and on the World Socialist Web Site in August of the same year.

Aside from Nigeria, the five biggest oil producers in Africa — in descending order are Algeria, Libya, Egypt, and Angola. Angola alone is the ninth largest oil supplier to the US. The US currently imports more oil from these six countries than it does from Saudi Arabia. Recent projections by the US National Intelligence Council as reported in *Petroleum Supply Monthly* estimate that the proportion of US oil imports from sub-Saharan Africa will reach 25 percent by 2015.

I have not been surprised, therefore, as I have seen stories that revolts are brewing in the Central African Republic or that al Qaeda has been linked to weapons shipments in West Africa where it has been reportedly seeking to relocate training bases. One report issued by the *Voice of America* (VOA), a CIA-connected international radio network, in November 2002, has indicated that al Qaeda is quietly supporting nationalist and tribal insurgencies throughout West Africa.

I have previously reported that a reliable CIA source has been insisting that Osama bin Laden is comfortably living in Freetown, the capital of nearby Sierra Leone, for more than a year.

Elsewhere in the region there are signs of small to mid-sized discoveries which, while not affecting Peak Oil, are certainly keys to how Peak Oil politics and economics will be played out. As reported by Wayne Madsen in the Online Journal on January 16, 2003, Western Sahara — illegally occupied by Morocco in 1975 — is now reporting significant finds, and US oil companies like Kerr-McGhee, fronted by former Bush I Secretary of State and consummate oil man James Baker, are signing offshore exploration agreements with the Moroccan government. Baker and his law firm Baker-Potts turn up in every major oil development from Kazakhstan to the Balkans to Africa.

Clearly West Africa is vital to the Empire. The *Times of London* acknowledged this in a July 29, 2002, story headlined, "US Presses Africa to turn on the tap of crude oil." Quoting Walter Kansteiner, US Under Secretary of State for African Affairs, the *Times* reported, "African oil is of national strategic interest to us, and it will increase and become more important as we go forward." ...

In the meantime, strong support for al Qaeda and Osama bin Laden remains unaffected and generally unnoticed throughout the northern half of the African continent. And although there have been no press reports (other than Stratfor) describing the Nigerian rebels as being al Qaeda connected, I wouldn't want to bet that such a "discovery" will not be conveniently made when it comes time for the empire to take the oil.

The map of Peak Oil doesn't always tell us when the empire will make its moves. But since 9/11 it has certainly told us where.[26]

In December 2002, *Stratfor* declared that Africa's next "World War" would occur in the Central African Republic, which had seen major rebel uprisings.[27] In May of 2003 the CIA-connected *Voice of America* reported that NATO would be shifting its focus to West Africa.[28] On May 17, 2003, four large bomb blasts killed 20 people in the Moroccan capital of Casablanca. The blasts were quickly connected to al Qaeda.[29] Throughout 2003 rebel uprisings in Nigeria saw oil platforms shut down, Western oil workers held hostage, pipelines sabotaged, and the sale of six US Navy ships to the Nigerian Navy.[30] In mid-July Chad began pumping oil from a small (900 Mb) reserve westward to the African coast through Cameroon.[31] On July 16th, coups d'etat toppled the governments of the tiny West

African island nations of Sao Tome and Principe.[32] And by August of 2003 the United States Navy was safely parked off the coast of Liberia and US Marines patrolled the capital in a peacekeeping mission to supervise the removal of Liberian strongman Charles Taylor.[33]

These developments were disturbing, but not surprising. I had been watching deployments of US Special Operations personnel throughout Africa since right after 9/11.[34] "War without end, Amen."

Colombia and Peru

All the money to build the new pipelines, wells, and refineries has to come from someplace. The beautiful and decimated nation of Colombia deserves much more space than I can give it in this book. For a year and half prior to 9/11 I had been writing extensively about how Colombia's possession of oil — and its unique role in the drug trade, supplying almost all of the world's cocaine and 60 percent of the heroin entering the US — was making it a cauldron of poisonous regional conflict. The dynamics in Colombia included a massive US military aid program, the presence of large numbers of official and unofficial US military advisors, mercenary armies, and widespread "privatized" air operations. The similarities to the Vietnam War were hard to miss.

Colombia has been ravaged by an internal conflict for more than 40 years. Currently two rebel groups, The Revolutionary Armed Forces of Colombia (FARC) and the National Liberation Army (ELN), control more than a third of the southern part of the country in a semi-autonomous region and have widespread support groups reaching into the urban areas. Both the FARC and the ELN derive most of their income from "taxing" the coca and opium trade in their regions, and they are very well equipped. However they have never shown the slightest interest in politics outside of their country and thus don't fall within the generally accepted definition of terrorist organizations. Neither has launched attacks outside of Colombia, but both have attacked and bombed pipelines owned by US and multinational oil companies inside the country and have engaged in kidnappings of foreign oil executives.

Colombia is important because, according to the US Energy Information Administration (EIA), it is the eighth-largest supplier of petroleum products to the United States.[35] In addition there are significant untapped oil deposits estimated to be in the 3-8 Gb range located in territories occupied by the rebels. The rights to these deposits have been purchased by major oil companies, including Occidental Petroleum. Occidental currently operates one pipeline in Colombia, the Cano-Limon, which was bombed more than 170 times in 2001.[36] The locals now call it "The Flute."

Prior to 9/11 the Bush administration had renamed the already brutal, multibillion military aid package known as Plan Colombia and transformed it from a unilateral anti-narcotics effort into a regional anti-insurgency program known as

The Andean Initiative. On September 6, 2001, the *Washington Post* reported major attacks by the Colombian government against the rebels in an escalation that had caught the attention of Washington's policy makers.[37] Of course, it was the policy makers and their "aid" money that had made the escalation inevitable.

By October 25 — just 44 days after 9/11 — Colin Powell told reporters that, compared with al Qaeda, the FARC and the ELN "probably meet a similar standard" for being classified as terrorist organizations.[38] This was followed in early November by a CNN report that groups sympathetic to al Qaeda were meeting with indigenous rebel and organized crime groups in the South American tri-border region of Argentina, Brazil, and Paraguay.[39]

By February of 2002, the US government was announcing plans to provide direct military assistance to Colombia to help it protect the Cano-Limon pipeline with an additional $98 million in aid.[40] All pretense that US military involvement was an anti-drug operation was dropped, and in September it was announced that detachments of Special Forces troops were going to be sent to Colombia as "advisors."[41] Just days later, veteran reporter Peter Gorman based in Iquitos, Peru, reported that US Marine Jungle Expeditionary Forces had received deployment orders for insertion into Colombia in February of 2003.[42] This is a region where DynCorp aircraft are flying the eradication missions, ferrying Colombian troops into battle, and even occasionally engaging in firefights with rebels on the ground.

Peru is critical. Thick triple-canopy jungle, rugged mountains, and largely inaccessible terrain dominate the region and make it a vastly different military battlefield, much more like Vietnam than Iraq. Without large cities or major infrastructure to protect, the FARC and the ELN are a highly fluid, mobile force hardened by more than 30 years of bitter warfare. They cross borders routinely in their operations and the area around Iquitos is certain to be hotly contested, much as the eastern portions of Cambodia were 40 years ago. In the summer of 2003, as the US teetered on the brink of a devastating natural gas shortage, a story in Britain's *Independent* revealed that President Bush was seeking funds to develop a controversial natural gas pipeline from Peru's Amazon to the coast. The prime contractors were to be Kellogg Brown and Root and Hunt Oil.[43]

All has not been going perfectly for the US and Alvaro Uribe, the President of Colombia. In early December Colombian journalist Ignacio Gomez, speaking in New York, told a group of America's most influential journalists including Tom Brokaw, Dan Rather, and Walter Isaacson, that Uribe was directly connected to drug traffickers and that the US military had helped to organize massacres by right-wing paramilitary groups in Colombia's countryside.[44] At the same time, the Colombian government had announced a total war against the rebels and started it, as all such wars are started, not by attacking the rebels but by attacking peasant villages, bombing and spraying them with defoliant.

By January 17, 2003, Reuters was reporting that 60 additional US Special Forces troops had arrived in Colombia (in addition to those already allotted under the Andean Initiative) to begin the work of protecting the pipeline by training and "advising" Colombian troops.[45]

As soon as Dick Cheney and George W. Bush announced that the war on terrorism would go around the world, wherever terrorism lived, for as long as it took, I knew of a certainty that Colombia and the neighboring countries of Peru, Venezuela, Ecuador, Panama, and Brazil were on the plate of "the war which will not end in our lifetimes".

Venezuela and a coup in Haiti

Venezuela is unique among all the countries where the Empire will fight. It's America's third — or fourth-largest oil supplier (depending upon monthly production figures through September of 2003), and while a drop of Persian Gulf oil takes about six weeks to reach an American gas tank, Venezuelan oil gets here in about four days.

Venezuela is a founding member of OPEC. Worse yet, it is an undeniably democratic nation. Its president Hugo Chavez has won seven elections in five years. That's seven more than George W. Bush has. However Chavez is a charismatic non-aligned leader in Latin America who has open relations with Fidel Castro, North Korea, Iran, and a host of countries the US doesn't like. Prior to 9/11, seeing that US intervention in neighboring Colombia was imminent, President Chavez made it clear that he would not allow US military planes to overfly his country en route to a battle zone. This prompted US military base expansions in Ecuador and the quiet establishment of covert paramilitary and CIA operations in Peru.[46]

The Empire cannot live without Venezuela's oil, and it cannot live with Hugo Chavez. The catch is that, in spite of the Empire's twisted propaganda to paint him as unpopular, he not only survives but he triumphs over every move the Empire makes against him. He made a mockery of what the US government called a 2002 oil-field strike against his "poor" leadership and exposed it for what it was, a well-financed protest by the richest pro-American factions in the country who were outraged that the Chavez government had aggressively protected the oil revenue share retained by his country.

The American intention was to create chaos and economic upheaval that would cause a popular revolt. Throughout 2002 and 2003 abundant evidence surfaced showing that the strings for the strike and an April 2002 short-lived, abortive coup were pulled directly by US intelligence agencies.[47]

At the end of 2002 Press Secretary Ari Fleischer called for a Venezuelan referendum on Chavez even though no election was required by the Venezuelan constitution. After being reminded of the Venezuelan law and receiving a slap on the wrist from the Organization of American States on December 17, 2002, Fleischer backtracked and licked his wounds.[48]

Venezuela is in a position to bring down the Empire as the effects of Peak Oil become apparent. Remember that the key is not just who has oil but who can produce it quickly. These are different things. Only where there are wells, refineries, pipelines, ports, tankers, and existing infrastructure can oil production be rapidly increased — or suddenly diminished. And if even 15 percent of the Empire's oil supply goes away, it must be immediately replaced with 15 percent from someplace or else prices will skyrocket and markets will collapse.

By January of 2003 US oil stocks had evaporated to 27-year lows.[49] This meant that, aside from the Strategic Petroleum Reserve intended for use in war or major economic crises, the US was running on empty. Reports quietly circulating through the oil industry were warning that supplies might soon be interrupted and prices might soar to historic new highs. The Venezuelan "strike," led by pro-Wall Street supporters, succeeded in drastically reducing Venezuela's oil exports but ultimately failed to stir up the coup against Chavez. The US reached a point where it could not start the invasion of Iraq and risk a simultaneous loss of Venezuelan oil.[50] Chavez backed the US into a corner and bought some time. Again, the key to understanding the importance of Venezuelan oil is the fact that while it takes about six weeks for oil from the Persian Gulf to reach your gas tank, Venezuelan oil gets there in about four days.

In March of 2003 elected Haitian President Jean Bertrand Aristide was driven out of his country by what he and many others called a US-sponsored coup d'etat.[51] Many press accounts soon appeared supporting Aristide's allegation.[52]

The reasons for the US overthrow of Aristide are complex and simple at the same time. As global oil shortages and production shortfalls became impossible to conceal in 2004, and as oil prices neared $40 per barrel, Venezuela's importance to US supply was multiplied. This was especially true as Iraqi production lagged due to infrastructure damage and revolt and as Saudi production numbers sank under recent OPEC statements advocating production cuts.

Strategically, in preparation for continued covert, and eventual overt, US military intervention in Venezuela, Haiti represented a prime piece of geography. A look at a map reveals that Haiti (which divides the island of Hispaniola with the Dominican Republic) lies at a virtual midpoint between Florida's southern tip and the coastlines of Venezuela and Colombia. From a military standpoint it is a strategic staging area for future moves onto the South American continent. While the US might logistically be able to mount an invasion or major operations from the Dominican Republic, it would never allow an independent regime allied with Hugo Chavez to remain in power in what would effectively become its rear area.

More than that, Haiti was an Afro-Caribbean nation, successfully led by a charismatic Afro-Caribbean; it was becoming allied with a regionally powerful Venezuela led by its first president of partly African and Indian ancestry. Aristide and Chavez were each democratically elected and were each beginning to respond to the impoverished majorities who put them in power. All this was an unbearable thorn in the side of United States, the hegemon whose permanent public relations problem is its ideological addiction: the same old white supremacy that's shaped the hemisphere for 500 years. Former West Point instructor and Special Forces veteran Stan Goff wrote a breathtaking analysis of the situation for *FTW* just after the coup.[53]

Hugo Chavez wasted no time in declaring to the world that he knew what the Empire's game was. Just after the coup he announced, "Venezuela is not Haiti, and Chavez is not Aristide." In the February 29 speech, even before the dust had settled in Haiti, Chavez also labeled George W. Bush "an asshole." Most importantly, in the same speech, Chavez vowed to cut off Venezuelan oil supplies to the US if it attempted military intervention or to impose trade sanctions.[54]

Chavez was not bluffing, and his remarks were not lost on the world's second-largest oil importer, China. On March 19, 2004, the Venezuelan news agency reported that top-level Chinese diplomats were in Venezuela offering to buy all of Venezuela's US production if the US made any move to further destabilize the country.[55]

The following section demonstrates the gravity of this move by the Chinese government and confirms again that Peak Oil issues are the canvas upon which world history is being painted.

The Far East

Indonesia makes the list of the 18 largest oil reserves. It is situated on the most heavily traveled shipping lanes in the world, the South China Sea, and it also has the largest Muslim population of any country. That is why almost immediately after 9/11 the US deployed large numbers of military personnel to the neighboring Philippines. In spite of quick victories against indigenous Philippine Muslim rebels, suggesting that the Empire might withdraw, it has instead begun building permanent military bases.

It is via the South China Sea, which runs past the Philippines, that both Japan and China receive most of their oil. Whoever controls these shipping lanes will be in a position to determine who survives and who doesn't, who lives and who dies.

Indonesia also possesses one of the world's largest natural gas deposits, of critical interest to Japan and Australia - staunch US allies in the invasions of Iraq. I thought it an ironic twist when, just a day after the *Jakarta Post* reported that Indonesia had natural gas reserves to last for 50 years,[56] a huge car bomb, attributed to the al Qaeda-linked group Jemaah Islamiyah exploded outside the American-favored Marriott Hotel in Jakarta.[57] Coincidentally, the US Embassy cancelled bookings for 10-20 rooms at the hotel just hours before the deadly explosion.[58]

China — The endgame

China and the United States are conjoined twins, and it is not certain that the two can be surgically separated without killing one or both. The reason is that the Empire's economy, its finances, and its future are inextricably tied to the Chinese markets of 1.3 billion eager consumers. One recent story paints the picture best. On January 20, 2003, Reuters reported that General Motors' Chinese sales jumped more than 300 percent in 2002,[59] and China's overall auto sales jumped an amazing 100 percent in 2002.[60]

The future of globalized capitalism rests in China. As I wrote for my subscribers in the fall of 2001:

> According to the US-China Business Council (USCBC) (<www.uschina.org>), new foreign direct investment in China in 2000 alone equaled some $62.66 billion US. This represented a 50.8 percent increase over 1999. Major US corporations with active investments in China include Federal Express, Honeywell, Corning, Ford, Coca-Cola, Pepsi, Halliburton, AIG, Nortel, Microsoft, FMC, Cargill, Xerox (which, according to the Wall Street Journal, is moving its manufacturing operations to China), Chubb, and Emerson Electric.
>
> In the first quarter of 2001 alone, according to the USCBC, selected US exports to China rose by the following percentages: power generation equipment (48 percent); electrical machinery and equipment (17.3 percent); air and spacecraft (113.7 percent); iron and steel (88.5 percent). Total US trade with China is expected to top $107 billion in 2001.
>
> American International Group (AIG), which manages the second-largest pool of investment capital in the world, has approximately 40 percent of its business operations centered in, or around, China. AIG began its history as an American-owned Chinese insurance company, the C.V. Starr Company. (See *FTW*, Vol. IV, No. 5 - August 14, 2001).[61]

Here is an excerpt of the story we published in *From The Wilderness* in September 2002, when I asked our Energy Editor, Dale Allen Pfeiffer, what was going to happen with China as the world came to grips with Peak Oil.

Sizing Up the Competition — Is China The Endgame?

by

Dale Allen Pfeiffer, *FTW* Contributing Editor for Energy

September 25, 2002, 16:00 PDT (*FTW*) — In the last 50 years of the United States' quest for hegemony, it has viewed its chief antagonists either ideologically (the Soviet Union and Red China), or economically (Germany and Japan). These antagonists were either overcome or co-opted. In the last decade of the 20th century, the US occupied the unparalleled position of being the world's only superpower. Now, as we enter the 21st century, this unopposed superpower — at the peak of its military supremacy — may have an Achilles heel. It is running out of energy and so is the planet as a whole.

The 20th century was an era of technological, industrial, and economic progress predicated upon the virtually unrestricted consumption of resources. But the rampant consumption of the 20th century cannot last, not on a finite planet where such consumption is dependent upon nonrenewable resources. The coming century will be an era of resource depletion, as the greed of the last century takes its toll upon the planet.

Be this as it may, the world public does not yet recognize this change. Consumer demand is ever increasing. In fact, the capitalist economy is dependent upon ever increasing consumption — without it, the economic base will stagnate and collapse. And while consumer demand for the key item of energy is expected to increase over the next couple of decades, energy production has reached a plateau and will begin an unalterable decline within the next decade. Very soon there will not be enough.

In the coming years, continued US hegemony will depend upon maintaining control and access to the world's dwindling hydrocarbon reserves, most of which are contained in the Middle East. In achieving this goal, the US will have to find some way to deal with those countries which are expected to take the lead in rising energy demand. Those countries just happen to be the world's most populous countries, and all three are Asian. Ranked by population and projected energy demand, they are China, India, and Indonesia.

China

China is the world's most populous nation, with a current population of 1.3 billion. The GDP, currently $1.27 trillion, is growing at 6.7 percent, down from 7.3 percent last year. Its major trading partners are Japan, the United States, the European Union, South Korea, and Taiwan. China has maintained a trade surplus for some time, which is responsible for a significant portion of the bubbling US trade deficit. While China's trade surplus has been falling in recent years, this is largely due to imports of capital goods needed to refurbish outdated industrial facilities.[62] This is taken to be an investment which could lead to a resurge in the trade surplus.

After the US, China is the second largest energy consumer in the world. The country holds 24 Gb in proven reserves with potential for significant new discoveries both inland and offshore. Oil production amounts to 3.3 million bbl/d. Oil consumption is currently 4.9 million bbl/d and rising. Net oil imports are currently 1.6 million bbl/d, and also rising. China holds 48.3 Tcf of proven natural gas reserves, with production at 0.96 Tcf per year, even with consumption. However, natural gas consumption is also expected to rise. China is 10th on the list of countries ranked by conventional oil endowment. For the past five years, oil production has risen by 1 percent per year, which is well below the rise in demand. To date, China has produced 27 Gb of oil, out of 52 Gb so far discovered. Another 5.2 Gb are estimated to still be awaiting discovery, for a total of 57 Gb. They are expected to reach the midpoint to depletion this year, with the production peak following next year. The depletion rate is currently 3.9 percent per year.

China's primary energy consumption is now equivalent to a fifth of the Organization for Economic Cooperation and Development (OECD) total, and one tenth of the world's total primary energy consumption. The International Energy Agency (IEA) expects that China alone will account for 23 percent of world primary energy demand increase between 1995 and 2020. The OECD will account for another 23 percent, leaving a little more than half for the rest of the world (which will include India and Indonesia).[63]

Currently, China is the world's third-largest oil consumer, behind the United States and Japan. It is expected to surpass Japan within the decade and by 2020 reach a consumption level of 10.5 million bbl/d. China only recently became a net importer of oil, as consumption exceeded production for the first time in 1993. By 2020, China is expected to import 8 million bbl/d, more than the projected net imports

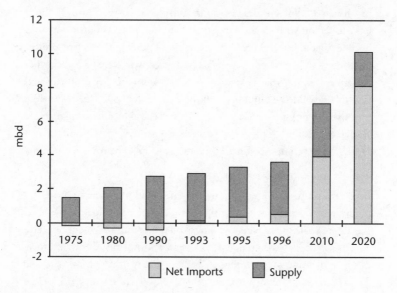

Domestic Supply and Net Imports of Oil

of Japan, Korea, New Zealand, and Australia combined. Oil production in China was virtually nonexistent 50 years ago. Production rose from 0.5 mb/d (thousand barrels per day) in 1970 to 3.2 million bbl/d in 1997. In 1990, China exported five times more crude oil than it imported, yet by 1997 its imports had grown to twice the size of its exports.

TARIM BASIN

China has many other unexplored oil prospects, but the country seems to be pinning its domestic production hopes on the far western Tarim Basin. This is actually three separate basins in the Xinjiang Uygur Autonomous Region. This region, a desert the size of Poland, borders Kazakhstan, Kyrgyzstan, and Tajikistan to the west. Estimates of its potential reserves still vary from a few billion barrels to 80 Gb. Many obstacles impede exploration and development: deep pay zones, high drilling costs, complex geology, high subsurface pressures and temperatures, a harsh climate (temperatures can hit 117 degrees Fahrenheit in summer and -86 degrees in winter[64]), and lack of infrastructure. Xinjiang also suffers from antigovernment violence blamed on its biggest minority group, the Uighurs.

To get the oil out of the distant Tarim Basin and bring it to markets in the east and southwest, China has committed itself to a 2,604-mile pipeline system. However, with construction costs estimated at $5.2 billion and Tarim's output growing more slowly than expected, Chinese officials are struggling to figure out how to make the pipeline pay for itself. The Chinese National Petroleum Corporation (CNPC) has pushed on with smaller investments to build pieces of the network, hoping that these smaller investments will render the entire project unstoppable. The pipeline is so costly that gas will have to be priced at 35 percent above what buyers say they are willing to pay. It is expected that this pipeline will link up with the even larger "Silk Road" pipeline proposed to bring oil and natural gas from Kazakhstan. To finance the Xinjiang pipeline, China has formed a partnership with the Royal Dutch/Shell Group, Exxon-Mobil, and Russia's Gazprom.

The Energy Silk Road

In partnership with Exxon and Mitsubishi, CNPC has submitted a preliminary feasibility study for the world's longest gas pipeline. Dubbed the Energy Silk Road, this pipeline would start in Turkmenistan, and stretch across Uzbekistan and Kazakhstan to Xinjiang's Tarim Basin, a distance of some 4,161 miles. In Xinjiang, it would link up with the Tarim pipeline to continue the journey eastward across China. The estimated cost of $10 billion has stifled investor interest in the project.[65] Similarly, a proposed oil pipeline from Kazakhstan eastward across China has spurred little investor interest due to the high price and the difficult terrain which the pipeline would have to traverse.

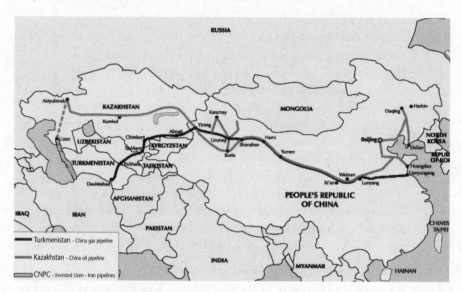

Energy "Silk Route" from Central Asia
Source: IEA and National Pipleine Research Society of Japan

Offshore Oil

While 90 percent of Chinese energy production is located inland, it is beginning to invest more money into offshore production, with significant prospects to be found in Chinese waters. The Chinese National Offshore Oil Corporation (CNOOC) is the company which handles offshore oil production and exploration. Proven offshore reserves are currently 10.7 Gb in 20 offshore oil and gas fields. Offshore production quadrupled between 1994 and 1996, and doubled again by 2000. CNOOC has hopes of major increases in production from fields in the South China Sea. Unconfirmed Chinese reports place potential South China Sea reserves at 213 Gb. However, in 1994 the United States Geological Survey estimated resources at 28 Gb. Exploratory geologists who have worked in the area or who have reviewed studies of the area, say that the results are very disappointing and estimate the South China Sea area could contain as little as a few billion barrels in isolated fields.[66]

Furthermore, the area is troubled by numerous territorial disputes involving China, Vietnam, Chinese Taipei, Malaysia, the Philippines, and Indonesia. These disputes have prevented systematic exploration of the area. There is little indication that the disputing parties will come to an agreement any time soon. There is some likelihood that increased US military involvement in the Philippines is at least partially due to potential or perceived energy resources in the South China Sea.[67]

Imports and Shipping Lanes

Far from relying on inland pipelines for their future natural gas supply, China is planning on building and updating several LNG ports so that it might increase its imports of LNG. In a blow to Indonesia as the top world exporter of LNG, China has recently awarded a coveted natural gas supply contract to Australia.[68] Part of the reason for favoring Australia over Indonesia is probably due to the questionable ability to further crowd traffic in the Strait of Malacca shipping lane. Currently 1,142 ships per day ply the waters through this entrance to the South China Sea. Virtually all Middle Eastern oil shipped to Asian customers must pass through the Strait of Malacca. A trans-shipment pipeline across the Malaysian peninsula has been proposed to ease congestion in the strait.

Energy Trade And Foreign Investment

China currently imports oil from many countries throughout the world, including Iraq, Iran, Saudi Arabia, Sudan, Indonesia, Angola,

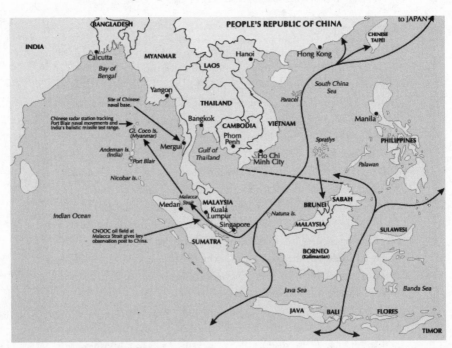

Security of Oil Shipping Routes

Nigeria, Russia, Argentina, Bangladesh, Canada, Colombia, Ecuador, Mexico, Venezuela, and the United States. China has attempted to diversify its energy imports for security reasons. However, like all other oil importers, it must turn to the Middle East for the bulk of its needs.

Likewise, China has had to open itself to foreign investment. This was one of the conditions for admission to the World Trade Organization. Among companies investing in China's domestic energy industry and infrastructure are Saudi Aramco, several Iranian companies, Enron (until their bankruptcy), Chevron, Shell, and Exxon-Mobil.

Energy Infrastructure and Growing Demand

China's energy problems are exacerbated by inadequate infrastructure. As mentioned above Chinese production is still growing at one percent, and production is not expected to peak until next year. However, energy consumption outstripped production in 1993. Even with all the domestic energy projects on the board, China's energy demand will still depend upon imports. Part of the reason for this is that energy reserves are located some distance from industrial centers and urban areas, and the infrastructure between energy sources and centers of demand have not been well developed.

Chinese industrial energy demand will more than double during the next 20 years. China's electricity demand has doubled within the last decade and is likely to quadruple by 2020.

Conclusions

If energy demand in China, India, and Indonesia is allowed to grow as much as analysts say it will, then these three countries may very well crowd the rest of the world out of the energy market. Furthermore, the studies quoted here do not figure in oil production peak and beginning production decline by 2010. These studies are predicated on rising oil production until at least 2020. Even the *Oil and Gas Journal* is now issuing warnings that oil production will not be able to meet demand by the end of the decade. The IEA forecasts that world demand for oil will be at 119 mb/d by 2022. Yet even they offer no word about how this demand will be met.[69]

It is plain that growing energy demands will bring China, India, and Indonesia into conflict with the developed world. The United States in particular, as the top world consumer of oil, will likely either have to curb consumption to make room for other countries or will have to find some way to curb the demands of the emerging energy consumers. Moreover, competition for diminishing oil resources could threaten the US dollar hegemony over world oil transactions.

As competitors for diminishing oil exports, Indonesia and India might not present major problems. Being so energy-poor, India may have no choice but to take what they can get. In August Pakistani President Gen. Pervez Musharaf broke from his nation's recent political course of exchanging nuclear threats with neighboring India. Musharaf said he did not object to India accessing a proposed Central Asian natural gas pipeline originating in Turkmenistan and running through Pakistan. If the proposal is materialized, Pakistan could get a $400 to $500 million annual royalty, according to the Pakistan's *DAWN* English language newspaper. It is likely that the US will have no serious problems in managing India's energy demands.

As for Indonesia, they are currently in the hands of the IMF and the World Bank. If these institutions stay true to their usual scam, Indonesia should soon be completely impoverished. However, Indonesia does control important shipping routes and valuable energy reserves. Therefore, it is likely that Indonesia will see continuing US intervention for the foreseeable future. US approved political leaders and foreign control of energy resources will keep Indonesia under control for at least a little longer.

As a starving world struggles for the remaining energy scraps, it is foreseeable that India and Indonesia may be left to starve, with much of the Third World. Or it is possible that a nuclear exchange and/or bloody war could be spurred on between India and Pakistan strictly for the purpose of population reduction. Such designs are despicable, but not out of the range of possibility for starving nations.

China, on the other hand, will be our major competition.

China is unlikely to become involved in an open war with the US. The annual Chinese military budget was $32 billion in 1997, or roughly an eighth of the $260 billion US military budget for the same year.[70] The US has military bases throughout Asia, including the Philippines and Japan, and now in Central Asia. In the event of a war, the US could easily cut off Chinese energy imports through the Strait of Malacca and from Central Asia. A direct war between China and the US would be a disaster for both countries, and possibly for the entire world.

Though China will avoid open warfare with the US, they might become sucked into a war in the Middle East. Should the US become involved in a protracted war in the Middle East, it is likely that the opponents would be supplied by China. In a US military conquest of the Middle East, China would have to respond by aligning itself with the Muslim resistance. They would likely do anything short of sending Chinese troops to the Middle East to fight against the US.

This being said, China will have to deal with the US Empire, and it will need to force the US into recognizing China as an equal power. This will most likely be achieved through economic means, and possibly through a series of minor wars in third-party countries. Economically, China is in a very strong position with regard to the US. The Chinese control the US trade deficit, while the US has very little economic control over China. Should the Chinese step up the production and export of consumer goods, the US would have no choice but to swell its trade deficit even farther. And should China supply more goods than the US can consume, the economy will suffer. Likewise, should China move away from the US dollar as the international currency of trade, the results for the United States would be disastrous. Ethnic Chinese control 50 percent of the private capital in the Philippines, 70 percent in Indonesia, 80 percent in Thailand and Malaysia. The countries of the Pacific produce 60 percent of the world GDP. In recent sessions of the Asia-Pacific Economic Cooperation Summit there has been a lot of discussion about a Pacific alternative to the US dollar. The golden Yuan has been the leading contender. [71]

The 2003 GM profit story raises the biggest question perfectly. What happens when America's economic survival depends upon sales of vehicles and other products to China that need to run on hydrocarbons which, if China obtains enough, will mean that there won't be enough hydrocarbons left over for America to sustain its own people or even make the products to begin with? There is no painless answer.

The issue of population reduction is becoming clearly visible as the reality of Peak Oil starts to set in. And who among us cannot picture the war criminal Henry Kissinger — protégé of David Rockefeller — sitting back in his chair and muttering with his German accent, "The problem is not that there is too little oil. The problem is just that there are too many people"?

CHAPTER 31

PEAK OIL REVISITED —
THE BILL COLLECTOR CALLS

I must not fear.
Fear is the mind-killer.
Fear is the little death that brings total obliteration.
I will face my fear.
I will permit it to pass over me and through me.
And when it has gone past, I will turn the inner eye to see it's path.
Where the fear has gone there will be nothing.
Only I will remain.

— Frank Herbert, DUNE

The one thing that every Middle Eastern leader, manager, and planner who dreams of holding his country together fears now, is that there will be a widespread uprising, inspired by the perceived victory against Spain after Madrid, and Spain's withdrawal from Iraq, that it might prompt much of the Muslim world to start attacking oil facilities everywhere. This is the way they see that has worked to defeat the West and to avenge their grievances. May God help us all if that happens. Stability must come to Iraq. But how?

— Anonymous Middle Eastern Participant at the Third Conference of
the Association for the Study of Peak Oil and Gas — Berlin, May 2004

The first chapters of this book were written in the summer of 2002. It was much more difficult then to discuss Peak Oil, what it means or how certain, quick, and defiant was to be its arrival. Denial in many minds was so instant and overwhelming that only a trained eye could see its millisecond appearance before encountering the brick wall of a closed mind.

That was then. This is now.

In this chapter, we will briefly revisit the developments with Peak Oil since I started this book. It is essential to do this to see if our map, the hypothetical construct around which we have organized our evidence, is holding up.

By the spring of 2004 things had changed dramatically. This is both the good news and the bad news. In May of 2004 I attended the third annual conference of the Association for the Study of Peak Oil and Gas (ASPO) in Berlin, Germany. Although I have a great many friends in ASPO, I tend to leave conferences feeling as though I've had a big meal but am still hungry. The 2003 and 2004 conferences — governed by scientific protocols — seemed to occur in vacuums, detached from political and economic developments in the outside world; detached from 9/11; from violence and intrigue in Iraq; in Saudi Arabia; in West Africa; in Venezuela; detached from bloodshed; from economic disintegration, and conflict.

That disconnect was nowhere near as obvious in Paris in May of 2003 as it was in Berlin a year later.

From May 24, 2004, as people arrived for the conference, through the final day on May 26, the hottest conversations were as much about what was going on in the headlines as was what being discussed inside the room. The two didn't converge nearly enough. Peak Oil-Berlin was almost twice as large as Paris had been. Many of the 250-plus attendees arrived on both mornings with papers under their arms containing stories about oil shortages and economic issues connected thereto. They tended to meet outside for drinks or meals asking, "Have you seen the cover of the June 2004 *National Geographic?* It's Peak Oil!"; "Did you see the *International Herald Tribune* today on global production and supply?"; "Do you think the Saudis really can increase production or are they bluffing?"; "Did you see where Shell has downgraded their reserves, again!?"; "Did you notice that someone finally attacked a Saudi oil facility? Now the Saudis won't have to prove that they can increase production, either to their people or the markets. It's the perfect excuse."

This had been no overnight development. For almost the entire year between the Paris and Berlin conferences the icons of the mainstream press — the ones known and employed to mold public and business perception — had been acknowledging Peak Oil's reality, sometimes reluctantly, sometimes less than directly, but also sometimes very boldly. CNN, the BBC, the *New York Times,* the *Economist;* dozens of media giants had begun to respond, as a giant ship turning slowly in the water. The ship had clearly changed course, but was it enough? Was it in time? I had saved close to 200 of these stories and I asked my staff to prepare a list of the headlines for possible inclusion as an appendix to this book. There were too many.

Looking at just a few of them makes the point well enough.

- "The End of Cheap Oil" – *National Geographic* (Cover Story) – June 2004.
- "What to Use When the Oil Runs Out" – BBC – 4/21/04
- "Adios Cheap Oil" – Interpress News Agency – 4/27/04
- "Refining Shortfall Goes Global, Drives Oil Strength" – Reuters – 4/26/04
- "G7: Oil Price Threatens World Economy" – *Moscow Times* – 4/26/04
- "World Oil Crisis Looms" – *Jane's* – 4/21/04
- "US Procuring the World's Oil" – *Foreign Policy in Focus* – January 2004

- "Are We Running Out of Oil? Scientist Warns of Looming Crisis" – ABC News.com – 2/11/04
- "Alarm as US Gas Supplies Hit Low" – *Financial Times* – 6/09/03
- "American Account: Iraqi Crude Won't Flow Fast Enough to Cut Oil Prices" – *The Sunday Times* – 6/29/03
- "Big Oil's Dirty Secrets" – *Economist* – 5/18/03
- "Shell Bosses 'Fooled the Market'" – BBC – 4/19/04
- "Blood, Money, and Oil" – US News – 8/18/03
- "Black Gold is King" – *Asia Times Online* – 4/28/04
- "Not in Oil's Name" – Foreign Affairs – July-Aug 2003
- "Soaring Global Demand for Oil Strains Production Capacity" – *Wall Street Journal* – 3/22/04
- "Check That Oil" – *Washington Post* – 11/14/03
- "War of Wars, China Builds Up Oil Reserves" – AP – 3/11/03
- "Asia: Strapped for Energy Resources, China and India Look for Alternatives" – Radio Free Europe/Radio Liberty – 4/20/04
- "China, Japan Both Eye Russian Oil" – *The Korea Times* – 9/20/03
- "China's Demand for Foreign oil Rises at Breakneck Pace" – Knight Ridder – 1/26/04
- 'World Oil and Gas Running Out' – CNN – 10/02/03
- "GLOBAL OIL SUPPLY: ARE WE RUNNING OUT? Experts to Analyze Saudi Arabia's Energy Future" – The Center for Strategic and International Studies, Media Advisory – 2/19/04
- "Debate Rages on Oil Output by Saudis in Future" – The *New York Times* – 2/25/04
- "Oil Reserves" – The *Economist* – 6/21/03
- "Energy Crisis 'Will Limit Births'" – BBC News – 2/13/04
- "Energy Agency Raises Oil Demand Estimates" – AP – 11/13/03
- "3 At Duke Energy Charged With Fraud" – Reuters – 4/22/04
- "Freeze Strains Northeast Power rid: Cold Kills 5 in Michigan, AP Reports" – CNN – 1/16/04
- "Fossil-Fuel Dependency: Do Oil Reserves Foretell Bleak Future?" – *San Francisco Chronicle* – 4/02/04
- "Fuel Disruption Test Planned [Australia]" – AAP – 3/25/03
- "The End of the Oil Age: Ways to Break the Tyranny of Oil are Coming into View. Governments Need to Promote Them" – The *Economist* – 10/23/03

Berlin

Present in Berlin for the ASPO conference on May 25th and 26th were newcomers, senior representatives from BP, ExxonMobil, and the International Energy Agency. They came as nobles called to a commoner's court: polite, courteous, but waving their flags just the same, unperturbed by the growing mess around them. If nothing else their presence did serve as a reminder that Peak Oil was squarely on the table. And even from their denials came startling revelations.

As the press reports, describing a disintegrating world outside, rolled on, the debate inside still seemed removed from it all.

Let them eat oil!

The big three of ASPO, Colin Campbell, Kjell Aleklett, and Jean Laherrère — accompanied by the de facto star of the event, investment banker Matthew Simmons, had their work cut out for them; not with the audience but with those who had come to deny. Natural gas issues facing Europe took up most of the first day. Two things quickly became clear on that account. First, almost all of Europe, soon even perhaps Ireland, was going to become dependent upon Russian natural gas to stay warm (Britain has just become a net gas importer in the face of North Sea decline). Second, Russia had much less natural gas than the economists and bookkeepers had predicted. Simmons asked rhetorically why anyone would stake their future on four large Russian fields that had been shown to be in permanent decline.

It was a good question, especially in light of the fact that Laherrère, with his renowned calculations concluded that natural gas demand in Europe was going to grow at 6.4 percent per year, announced that the global natural gas cliff would hit by approximately 2030 and that there would be zero reserves left by 2050. He calmly announced that, as far as Russian gas reserves went, there was a 50 percent difference between the technical data on Russian gas and what he called the "political" data.

Simmons pointed out that North America had hit its natural gas peak in 1973 and is now in decline in terms of production. Presentations exploring Liquefied Natural Gas (LNG) imports to the US concluded what *FTW* already knew. The cost is too expensive, the lead time too long, and the capital investment too great to make much of a difference here.

Everybody, even the German giant power companies like RWE, talked about coal. Nuclear was also, at least for some, an option, but there were no other viable near-term solutions presented. Token representatives of hydrogen and alternative energies made presentations, but, for those who had looked at hard numbers, this was more for show than substance.

Saudi Arabia

Saudi Arabia's promise to increase production to meet US and world economic needs was *the* hot topic. Much discussion and hard data was devoted to the fact that Ghawar, the largest field in the world, along with all of Saudi Arabia's other large fields, was old and tired. In recent years both water injection and so-called "bottle-brush" drilling had been employed to maintain production, and both of these techniques tend to accelerate decline and can damage the reservoirs.

In bottle-brush drilling a shaft is drilled horizontally over long distances with a number of brush-like openings. As water is forced under pressure into the reservoir the oil is forced upwards toward the wellheads and extraction is thereby increased.

However, when the water table hits the horizontal shaft, often without warning, the whole field is virtually dead, and production falls dramatically. This comes as a surprise in most cases. As several at the conference noted, this is exactly what had already happened in some fields in Oman, Syria, and Yemen.

As William Kennedy, a UK observer at the conference, noted afterwards, "For the record, Ghawar's ultimate recoverable reserves in 1975 were estimated at 60 billion barrels — by ExxonMobil, Texaco, and Chevron. It had produced 55 billion barrels up to the end of 2003 and is still producing at 1.8 billion per annum. That shows you how close it might be to the end. When Ghawar dies, the world is officially in decline."

No one, not even from the major oil companies or the economic camp, rose to defend Saudi Arabia's claim that it could increase production rapidly. The BBC's Adam Porter nailed the International Energy Agency's chief economist Fatih Birol, over his confident assertion that there was plenty of oil.

> In public, Mr Birol denied that supply would not be able to meet rising demand, especially from the buoyant economies in the USA, China, and India.
>
> But after his speech he seemed to change his tune.
>
> "For the time being there is no spare capacity. But we expect demand to increase by the fourth quarter (of the year) by 3 million barrels a day."
>
> He pinned his hopes for an increase in production squarely on troubled Saudi Arabia. "If Saudi does not increase supply by 3 million barrels a day by the end of the year we will face, how can I say this, it will be very difficult. We will have difficult times. They must invest."
>
> *Can Saudi deliver?*
>
> But even Mr Birol admitted that Saudi production was "about flat".
>
> Three million extra barrels a day would mean a huge 30 percent leap in output in just a few months.
>
> When BBC News Online followed up by asking if this giant increase in production was actually possible rather than simply a desire he refused to answer. "You are from the press? This is not for you. This is not for the press." [1]

Mistakes

In his presentation, Matthew Simmons, CEO of Simmons and Company Inter-national, the world's largest private energy investment bank, reeled off a litany of "mistakes" made by the energy industry over decades. He described some of these mistakes as:

- Demand was never understood properly
- Supply was merely aspiration (not actual reality)
- Decline curves became waterfalls
- We didn't have enough rigs (infrastructure)
- There was little fuel substitution
- There were few technology gains

Simmons used last year's Northeast US blackout to highlight some of the counter-productive reactions that had appeared during its worst moments. These, he suggested, paralleled the global rationale that had been brought to bear on current energy policy. "People were idling their car engines just to charge their cell phones. We couldn't refine or pump gas. You need electricity to do that."

Simmons described these mistakes as cascading and compounding over time and suggested that the underlying cause of all of them was the inherent assumption pushed by the financial markets that growth could possibly be infinite when nothing else in the physical universe is; when no organism or species has ever avoided the cycle of growth, maturity, and decline that governs the natural world. He chided that financial analysts on today's markets remember the false alarms about shortages in the 1980s and said that those crises (which never materialized), where many lost jobs by predicting permanent shortages, had failed to understand that they were describing and reacting to political events rather than geologic ones. Many in the markets, he said, were still saying to themselves, "That's never going to happen to me again."

He likened them to the French Army, which in 1940, having spent hundreds of millions to build the Maginot Line of fortresses, had just become ready to fight World War I on the eve of World War II.

We know how that turned out.

Colin Campbell, the "godfather" of the Peak Oil movement, with a bit of pique, divided the conference presenters into three camps: the Surveyors who were reporting hard data and not abstract modeling; the Economists who were denying reality and asserting that money produces energy and not the other way around; and the Pretenders "who know full-well what the situation is, but pretend otherwise for short-term political objectives.

In the last camp, he placed Fatih Birol, chief economist for the International Energy Agency (IEA), supposedly the world's energy watchdog. Even Birol made his own startling revelations on the second day.

Fatih Birol confirmed that another new trend, new since Paris, had become dominant. Many presenters from German and European industry had begun listing a new priority for future energy planning I had not heard before. They all emphasized "energy security" as the top, or one of their most important, concerns for the future. I checked my notes from Paris. I didn't record it being mentioned once. That sounded military to me, at least in terms of building geostrategic alliances that always have military options included. When confronted directly on that point the presenters retreated to assertions that what they really wanted was treaties and economic agreements. Well, I thought, what enforces those things?

Birol also hit hard on this point. Then he engaged in a kind of irrational presentation in which he put forth four points. There first two were telling.

First, he said that the IEA was absolutely certain that there was enough energy to guarantee economic growth until 2025.

In his very next point he said that (in light of Shell's downward revisions and pending revisions from other major oil companies) there was sufficient uncertainty about the true nature of stated world reserves that a new "transparent" reserve accounting system should be established to provide the needed trust for the financial markets.

In other words, his first point was meaningless.

Colin Campbell, seated on the panel with Birol quipped, "If there were transparency it would be clear that we are at peak now and everything might fall apart.

Again, I thought of the headlines and war and said to myself, "Um, it already is."

BP and ExxonMobil also stepped through the looking glass. After presenting a series of slides, which almost everyone in the audience was quite capable of reading, BP spokesman Francis Harper, addressing the issue of "reserve growth" refused to answer two direct questions about how his charts had just absolutely confirmed an imminent peak and decline. He just didn't answer. He did say that "Reserve estimates are uncertain and can vary widely throughout field life."

Later, ASPO founder Campbell speculated that BP was perhaps the worst book-cooker of all the majors when it came to reserves, and that there might be some large surprises coming as increasing pressure was put on the majors to produce transparent and verifiable calculations.

ExxonMobil's G. Jeffrey Johnson, while saying that supply was sufficient to satisfy growth until 2020, also admitted that current decline was at 4-6 percent per year. Economic growth is not possible without increased energy production. When asked by me where ExxonMobil was working feverishly to find new reserves, Johnson rattled off a list of countries and regions already well familiar to *FTW* readers: West Africa, the Middle East, and South America. None of those regions, already well explored, have anything near the two or three Ghawar fields we need to find immediately to avert a crisis.

Infrastructure and investment

Assuming that sufficient oil was found, how much money would be needed to develop it and bring it to market? ExxonMobil's spokesman indicated that a global *annual* investment of $530 billion would be required. The IEA's Fatih Birol stated that a total of $16 trillion would need to be invested before 2030 to develop oil and gas reserves that — even he admitted — no one was sure existed.

Matt Simmons — One on one

Peak Oil advocates quote Matthew Simmons frequently because his voice is refreshing. They also note that there is a duality to his thinking that leaves them scratching their heads from time to time. Those advocating economic reform or seeking to change the financial system built around oil do not always agree with him on those points. He is still a Republican and a die-hard investment banker. I found myself liking him sincerely on a personal level, disagreeing with him on some economic levels, yet remaining grateful for his candor on reserves.

I had him alone in Berlin for almost an hour. Some of his observations were telling.

He insisted that it was imperative that we (the US) begin to examine every area where we use energy and find ways to become more efficient. As an example he said that using a burner tip in a multitude of industrial practices, or in boiling water, was immensely more efficient than converting gas into electricity. He suggested gong to a "three-shift" economy where everyone would be required to work graveyard shifts about one-third of the time was a way to avoid overloads to the grid. The reason is simple, he said. Power generating stations run all night while very little electricity is drawn. Plants cannot be shut down and restarted. After you turn an electrical generating station off, it takes a week to bring it back on line. That's called "spinning" and it's extremely expensive. "Instead of having everything peak between 4 and 6 PM you can spread it out and still have some growth because you'll be making use of capacity that is not being used during off hours."

I thought about how far ahead Europe, and especially Germany, was in its thinking. All electrical uses in hotel rooms are made possible only when your room key is inserted into a slot. Leave the room, take the key, and everything shuts off automatically. Every gas station I saw in Germany had the option for people to purchase biodiesel, the cheapest grade of fuel, at about 90 cents a liter. (And you think US gas prices are bad! Premium gasoline was selling at just under US$5 per gallon). At those prices it's easy to understand why German drivers, when they come to ubiquitous railroad crossings, automatically shut off their engines until the train passes.

Public Enemy Number One, according to Simmons, is not SUVs but air conditioning. His top priority would be to design and build vastly more efficient air conditioners. Ironically, he believes that when gasoline reaches $7 per gallon (and he does believe it will), there may be a lot of people riding together in SUVs rather than in smaller cars. Let's hope!

As for the price of oil, and where he and I part company, is that not only does he see oil rising to $182 a barrel, he thinks that it might be beneficial, especially when it comes to generating some of that $16 trillion that needs to be invested in new oil and gas infrastructure. At $182 a barrel Simmons predicts the pump price will be $7 a gallon. "But", he added cautiously, "We're not going there overnight."

"Forty-one-dollar oil last week was $18 oil in 1980. A year ago we had $30-oil and now we have $40-oil. Has the economy slowed?" he asked rhetorically

I avoided a long discussion about how the economy is rigged and supported by many hidden incentives like Afghanistan's burgeoning heroin trade.

Where he lost me completely was when he postulated that prosperity for developing oil-producing nations would be neatly financed with oil at $182.

"If they can export 25 million barrels per day for the next ten years at that price then they can finance their prosperity. The shareholders will benefit." Yes, I thought, but only by buying more "things" that need energy to operate or manufacture.

Yes, this was the same Matt Simmons who just as steadfastly argues that this kind of production is not possible; the same Matt Simmons who has given *FTW* quotes before that future economic growth is not possible. Then he came back to a left-handed point I think I have been hearing him make but which he has never fully acknowledged. In his presentation on the floor he had referred to the necessity of reducing demand. I had always understood that to be the by-product of a recession.

He bypassed the question in private but did observe, "I'm very worried about sustainability at any price. But at low prices it's a nightmare."

On the question of Saudi Arabia he was unequivocal. "The Saudis are out of capacity. That's my opinion .... They have no infrastructure or extra pipes or gas, oil, and water separators (very expensive large globes used to separate what comes out of a water-injection well). They have very heavy oil that, through a conventional refinery, produces asphalt. We don't need asphalt. We need gasoline. It takes a complex refinery to make gasoline and it only takes 7-10 years to build one."

After two years of study and two days at the conference, it was obvious that a crash building program begun today by Saudi Arabia would make no difference if most of the Saudi fields (especially the biggest ones) had already gone into, or were near, decline.

Ali Samsam Bakhtiari

Another fixture at ASPO conferences is Ali Samsam Bakhtiari, Vice President of the National Iranian oil Company (NIOC). A suave, genial, well-dressed Persian, on whose tribal land the first oil well in the Middle East was drilled, Bakhtiari was doggedly followed by journalists and documentarians looking for relevant quotes. Frequently in the company of Simmons he remained available throughout the conference.

He is firmly in the camp of the surveyors, warning about Peak Oil and convinced of its certainty. It was he who, in Paris, dropped the first hints to me and others that Saudi Arabia might have peaked in May of 2003. I have come to call him, "The Prophet Ali," a label that makes him quickly blush and wave his hands in embarrassment.

Like others from the region attending the conference, Bakhtiari brought new warnings to Berlin. He cited the data about sudden and unexpected declines as the result of bottle-brush drilling in the region and expressed his strong doubts that Saudi Arabia could increase production under any circumstances. While a bit more reticent to express his fears about growing instability within the region, he was more candid in his assessment of the global energy picture.

In his presentation, Bakhtiari told the conference, 'The crisis is very, very near. World War III has started. It has already affected every single citizen of the Middle East. Soon it will spill over to affect every single citizen of the world. Syria's oil production is in terminal decline. Yemen is following. Major Middle East producers, including Saudi Arabia, will peak soon or have already peaked.'

Off the stage he was even more direct, "The present war cannot be confined to the Middle East. It will soon spill over to the rest of the world. The final implications will upset the global applecart."

Rimini — A start

Colin Campbell has, from a true expert's viewpoint, begun the search for immediate, if incomplete solutions. In his final presentation he submitted a draft of a plan to manage decline ethically. Called the Rimini Protocol (formerly the Uppsala Protocol, available at <www.peakoil.net>), Campbell's simple proposal approached Peak Oil from humanitarian and egalitarian imperatives rather than market forces.

Though simple in concept, the two proposals for future consumption in the Rimini Protocol may ultimately force mankind to make a fundamental choice about what its moral "True North" really is.

> *NOW IT IS PROPOSED THAT*
>
> 1. *A convention of nations shall be called to consider the issue with a view to agreeing an Accord with the following objectives:*
>   a. *to avoid profiteering from shortage, such that oil prices may remain in reasonable relationship with production cost;*
>   b. *to allow poor countries to afford their imports;*
>   c. *to avoid destabilising financial flows arising from excessive oil prices;*
>   d. *to encourage consumers to avoid waste;*
>   e. *to stimulate the development of alternative energies.*
> 2. *Such an Accord shall having the following outline provisions:*
>   a. *No country shall produce oil at above its current Depletion Rate, such being defined as annual production as a percentage of the estimated amount left to produce;*
>   b. *Each importing country shall reduce its imports to match the current World Depletion Rate.*
> 3. *Detailed provisions shall be agreed with respect to the definition of categories of oil, exemptions and qualifications, and scientific procedures for the estimation of future discovery and production.*
> 4. *The signatory countries shall cooperate in providing information on their reserves, allowing full technical audit, such that the Depletion Rate shall be accurately determined.*
> 5. *Countries shall have the right to appeal their assessed.*[2]

Dow Jones watches

The start of the Berlin conference on Peak Oil was oddly marked by the simultaneous release of an incredible Op-Ed from the *Dow Jones Newswires*. As it turns out — in a sign that there was some convergence — the story's author was also covering the conference with a critical eye.

THE SKEPTIC: Politicians Take Notice

By Stella Farrington

A DOW JONES NEWSWIRES COLUMN

LONDON (Dow Jones) —Desperate pleas for OPEC to pump more oil are not only futile, but serve to perpetuate the myth that high prices are a temporary problem the producer's group can easily fix.

The sooner it's recognized that high oil prices are not going to go away overnight, and that the Organization of Petroleum Exporting Countries is largely helpless to alleviate the problem, the sooner politicians and industry can hammer out a different solution.

Certainly there's reason to be alarmed by current prices. At $40 a barrel, the oil price is inflationary and will eventually choke global economic growth.

Consumers are being hit by soaring gasoline prices, which are at all-time highs in the US and fast approaching the record of four years ago in the U.K. — a period marked by fuel riots....

...The only country with sufficient spare capacity is Saudi Arabia, which currently pumps 8 million barrels a day and claims it can hike output sustainably to 10 million barrels a day quickly....

And is suits OPEC to maintain the impression it can open the spigots at the drop of a hat. The last thing it wants is for people to sense an oil shortage looming, even only a temporary one, as that could lead to energy conservation and a longer-term decline in demand....

And there's no point in looking outside of OPEC for a quick fix.[3]

As the conference ended, Campbell and others debated whether to take the conference to Brussels ("Broadway" as he called it) — home of the European Union — in 2005 or to go to Portugal. I couldn't help thinking, "What are you waiting for?"

The world awaits

When I got back from the extended trip to Berlin, Cologne, and Toronto, it was like all the "real-life" things that weren't mentioned in Berlin ganged up on me. My inbox was flooded with Peak Oil stories from all over the world. The stories were coming out daily now, and they seemed like pellets from a massive shotgun blast that people had not yet gathered had been unleashed by only one trigger pull and only one shooter. It had always been inevitable that, sooner or later, people, politicians, and the markets would get it, perhaps all at once. It was the "later" possibility that scared most of us in Berlin.

If one scratched any surface in early June of 2004, as the G-8 nations gathered in Georgia with energy and the Middle East as one of their most pressing concerns;[4] as gasoline prices continued to rise; as a wave of terror attacks forced foreign technical service workers to flee Saudi Arabia; as Saudi Arabia continued to *not* increase production; and as more data streamed in suggesting that they couldn't; one could almost feel panic lurking.

People want to be told why they are afraid instead of looking inside to find out for themselves. On other fronts anxiety also rose as a torrent of stories implicating the highest levels of the Bush administration in sanctioned torture, eroded the self-image of most Americans. The sudden resignations of CIA Director George Tenet and his deputy, for covert operations in early June, marked a watershed in a torrent of high-level and damning criticism of the neo-cons from senior military leaders and former government officials.

Americans were being confronted on a daily basis with gut-wrenching documentation and photographs of widespread and horrendous torture at Iraq's Abu Ghraib prison camp. It had been sanctioned, condoned, and approved by the highest levels of the Bush administration, even the President, the Attorney General and the Secretary of Defense. The torture had happened all throughout occupied Iraq, not just Abu Ghraib.

The result has been cognitive dissonance of the highest order as many Americans retreat in the spring of 2004 into their inner selves and say, "But we don't do that."

On behalf of every American who has tried through great sacrifice to stop it for decades, "Oh yes we do!"

The biggest fear however, subtly acknowledged by global policy makers, and not-so-successfully masked, is about energy.

On June 6, 2004, Peak Oil arrived in the *Washington Post*. In a story titled "After the Oil Runs Out" James Jordan and James Powell wrote:

> If you're wondering about the direction of gasoline prices over the long term, forget for a moment about OPEC quotas and drilling in the Arctic National Wildlife Refuge and consider instead the matter of Hubbert's Peak. That's not a place, it's a concept developed a half-century ago by a geologist named M. King Hubbert, and it explains a lot about what's going on today at the gas pump. Hubbert argued that at a certain point oil production peaks, and thereafter it steadily declines regardless of demand. In 1956 he predicted that US oil production would peak about 1970 and decline thereafter. Skeptics scoffed, but he was right....
>
> It now appears that world oil production, about 80 million barrels a day, will soon peak. In fact, conventional oil production has already peaked and is declining. For every ten barrels of conventional oil

consumed, only four new barrels are discovered. Without the unconventional oil from tar sands, liquefied natural gas and other deposits, world production would have peaked several years ago....

Lost in the debate are three much bigger issues: the impact of declining oil production on society, the ways to minimize its effects and when we should act. Unfortunately, politicians and policymakers have ignored Hubbert's Peak and have no plans to deal with it: If it's beyond the next election, forget it....

To appreciate how vital oil is, imagine it suddenly vanished. Virtually all transport — autos, trucks, airplanes, ships and trains — would stop. Without the fertilizers and insecticide made from oil, food output would plunge. Manufacturing output would also drop. Millions in colder regions would freeze.... [5]

It was a tepid entry from the *Post*, but a start. The story relied on generalities about peak and decline, to the exclusion of all the hard data that had surfaced over the last two years. Simultaneously, it tried to give false comfort without foundation.

A month before, on April 26, the *Moscow Times* had been a bit more direct. "G7: Oil Price Threatens World Economy" was the headline, and the story minced no words. Russians seem to take this kind of news in stride much better than Americans.

In a statement released after talks in Washington, the G7's central bankers and finance ministers singled out energy costs as a risk to global growth. Crude oil prices are up about 37 percent from a year ago and have risen 11 percent to nearly 11-year highs around $37 per barrel since the officials last met in Floridaon Feb. 7.

> "It is obvious that rising oil prices can have a negative effect on world GDP growth," said US Treasury Secretary John Snow. German Finance Minister Hans Eichel said the Organization of Petroleum Exporting Countries must "live up to their responsibility for the global economy." [6]

These stories were followed shortly thereafter by more that edged dangerously close to the panic line. And all the sophistry and misleading data spun forth by pundits who misrepresented data throughout May and June of 2004 with only one real intent, to "protect" the markets, had apparently failed. Some, like Sterling Burnett in a *Houston Chronicle* Op Ed blithely claimed that there was enough oil to last for 500 years.[7] Not even the chief critics of Peak Oil would do that. Others, like Victor Canto of the *National Review*, said it was all a matter of economics; need and price would produce a painless substitution with some new energy source he wasn't quite able to describe or hadn't fully researched.[8] Even the shameless George F. Will, writing in the *New York Post*, while not fully able to say that Peak Oil wasn't real, suggested that everything was a function of price and that throwing money at the problem would soften the blow while — at the same time

—offering an unfounded morsel of hope for the easily frightened by saying, "But, then, Alaska may have three times more reserves than originally estimated."[9]

George, we've been there: Estimated reserves? Probable reserves? Proven reserves? Ultimately recoverable reserves? The kind of reserves that caused Shell to downwardly revise its "booked" reserve figures four times in one year?[10] The kind of reserves that caused the IEA's chief economist, Fatih Birol, to state that a deep new transparency is needed in the reporting of so that we can find out how much there really is? The kind of reserves that BP was forced to defend on June 14th while warning that new calculations might result in downward revisions?[11] The kinds of reserves that serve only to define share values and which exist only in the minds of economists, brokers, and stockbrokers? The kinds of reserves which cannot and will never be pumped into your gas tank, or used to grow and transport your food or get you to work?

The kinds of reserves that prompted *BusinessWeek* to ask on June 21st 2004, "Why Isn't Big Oil Drilling More?"[12] or the *Denver Post* to write on June 13th, "US Faces Reality Check Over Oil."[13] or the *New York Times* to write a story asking, why, for six years, ChevronTexaco's stated oil reserves have risen while their production has steadily fallen.[14] Are we drilling more now and enjoying it less? Where is the money to drill with coming from as oil companies buy back shares, streamline, and build up cash reserves?

Duh!

Big oil isn't drilling more because they know there are no more large finds out there to drill in. More drilling doesn't mean more supply. It means more holes in the ground. This is what people like, M. King Hubbert, Kenneth Deffeyes, Richard Duncan, Walter Youngquist, Colin Campbell, Kjell Aleklett, Jean Laherrère, Richard Heinberg, Julian Darley, Matt Simmons, and all of our colleagues have been warning about for years.

That is why I took such great pains earlier in this book to document how the world's economic system is hopelessly corrupt and absolutely incapable of telling the truth. Yet, even still, as this effort which has taken so much to complete, nears an end, there are signs that the thin veneer between outward confidence and fear; between a half-truth which is really a lie and a whole truth which can lead to real solutions; is fast approaching. Until *that* Rubicon is crossed there will be no real solution other than continued war, bloodshed, and destructive behavior that is blocking us from more peaceful, longer-term, and more humane solutions.

George Bush and Dick Cheney may have meant it when they said that the American way of life is not negotiable. But it most certainly is on life-support and now being sustained by cruelty, brute force, and lies.

The markets just can't hide it anymore.

On April 7th, JPMorgan Chase hosted a two-day private conference call for its analysts and major investors titled "Peak Oil, Fact or Fiction?" *FTW* secured permission and got veteran investigative journalist Suzan Mazur on the line to listen to that conference, and we reported on it to our subscribers. (I listened too.) Although he barely stuck a toe into the water, the mere fact that Morgan had decided the subject was important enough to address, was a watershed moment.[15] This, even as Bloomberg and *Forbes* were advising their more sophisticated readership about profit opportunities and likely consequences of Peak Oil's arrival. That, of course, raised the unholy specter of wild speculation that could cause untold human suffering as prices gouged and crippled.

It reminded me of the recommendation of Matthew Simmons in Berlin that oil futures and speculation insist upon a 50 percent margin requirement for investing in oil derivatives (futures).

Finally, at long last, someone said it all in plain English on June 13, 2004. On that day the *Seattle Times* wrote an editorial titled "Oil and S&P Connection Points to Grim News for Stocks." Finally![16]

Even as this was finally admitted, CBS News *MarketWatch* issued a bulletin saying that US new home sales had fallen sharply in April. That was followed shortly thereafter by another bulletin from another source drawing attention to a sudden and dramatic increase in America's M3, credit-based, money supply.

> The Federal Reserve has confirmed our Stock Market Crash forecast by raising the Money Supply (M-3) by crisis proportions, up another 46.8 billion this past week. What awful calamity do they see? Something is up.
>
> This is unprecedented, unheard-of pre-catastrophe M-3 expansion. M-3 is up an amount that we've never seen before without a crisis — $155 billion over the past 4 weeks, a $2.0 trillion annualized pace, a 22.2 percent annualized rate of growth!!! There must be a crisis of historic proportions coming, and the Federal Reserve Bank of the United States is making sure that there is enough liquidity in place to protect our nation's fragile financial system. The amazing thing is, the Fed's actions mean they know what is about to happen. They are aware of a terrible, horrific imminent event. What could it be?[17]

We have to pay for $100-(or higher) a-barrel oil somehow. Why don't we just print the money? Anyone who has heard of the damage done by inflation and hyperinflation to those least able to cope with it should think back to Germany's Weimar Republic in the 1920s. Perhaps they should also look ahead to future wars, as the US Navy announced on May 31st that it was deploying a US aircraft carrier battle group to the Gulf of Guinea off the West African coast for a joint exercise with our newfound friends; the tiny island nations of Sao Tome and Principe, that had just experienced a US-friendly coup.[18]

I no longer need to defend Peak Oil and Gas. My assistance on that front seems wholly unneeded. It's doing fine all by itself. It is what we are doing in the face of it that presents mankind's greatest challenge and the challenge of my future work.

As if to punctuate this chapter and to remind us of the great fear expressed by one attendee at the Berlin conference, on June 16, CNN reported that the security chief for all oil operations in northern Iraq had been assassinated by ambush as he left for work that morning. This, but a day after another bombing of a major Iraqi pipeline.[19]

CHAPTER 32

SUMMATION:
LADIES AND GENTLEMEN OF THE JURY...

As a police officer, I only acted as the investigating officer (lead detective) on two small drug cases through the course of a trial. One was a jury trial, and one was a court trial where the judge was the finder of fact. In the jury case we got a conviction, and in the court case the defendant copped a plea in mid-trial. For the 26 years since my official career ended, it feels as though I have been working on only one very long case.

In law enforcement parlance, homicide cases are cleared in a number of ways: arrest; insufficient evidence; warrant issued, suspect is a fugitive; confession; suspect deceased; etc. But the preferred way for all detectives to get clearances is to identify the perpetrators and establish guilt beyond a reasonable doubt, make an arrest, and then go to prosecution. Clearance does not mean having perfect knowledge of how each specific act was carried out. It means only a certainty that, within the definition of the crime, the suspect was a perpetrator.

I once asked Mel Kissinger, a legendary LAPD homicide detective, how he knew when it was time to go to the DA and commit to a trial in a tough case. He responded that after you'd looked at everything and you were certain the suspect was guilty, you picked the best case you could make out of all the possible combinations, you took it to the Deputy DA, and if he liked it then you showed him everything else so that there would be no surprises. The DA would have to be made aware of any evidence suggesting that the suspect was innocent. Then, he said, if the case went through trial, and to a jury (or a grand jury), that's when you found out how good a case you really had. The jury had the sole responsibility for establishing and declaring the truth.

As for deciding when to go for it, he said, "When your gut and your heart and your head say 'It's ready,' and when it looks like you may never have a better shot, that's when you roll the dice."

What happens in a jury room (at least in principle) is sacrosanct; it is one of the few places where, within broad limitations, a group of men and women may use whatever logic, inspiration, or judgment they wish. They may choose to ignore

incontrovertible evidence, or they may base their decision upon facts both the prosecution and the defense missed or considered irrelevant. They may convict. They
may acquit. They may also completely nullify (by choosing not to enforce) the
statute under which the defendant was prosecuted.

And no one can ever say a word about it unless they can prove jury tampering
or the case is overturned on appeal for procedural errors by the trial judge.

As I sum up and rest my case here, I place this work in your hands so that you
may judge it in the "jury room" of your own mind, heart, and conscience. If you
are courageous, no one else can tamper with you from this point on. No one else
can tell you that this book is, or is not, "proof." You, and you alone, must decide for
yourself what was proved and what was not. As in a criminal trial, it is a solemn
responsibility; perhaps the most important responsibility a citizen has to his fellow
citizens and to society as a whole.

Some 40 years after the release of the mammoth Warren Commission Report
on the assassination of JFK, scholars are still locating, debating, and commenting
on its inconsistencies. While the research community has achieved a hard-won and
highly compelling picture of that homicide's underlying factual narrative from
myriad evidentiary sources, at this late date the endless research into the idiosyn-
crasies of the Warren Report has nothing to do with "clearing" the case, nor with
expediting justice. Some minutiae matter; most don't. A criminal jury, or a grand
jury, generally does not need to know what color shoelaces a suspect wore when
the crime was committed, or what brand of ammunition the suspect used, or how
he got it, in order to decide whether or not the suspect pulled the trigger (in the
case of the murder of the 35th president of the United States, of course, the nouns
"suspect" and "trigger" are to be understood in the plural). Criminal justice is
based upon society's urgent and essential imperative to identify perpetrators and
bring them to justice. Society must fulfill its obligation to protect the citizenry
from future crimes and validate the integrity of the system by producing justice for
crimes already committed. Criminal justice recognizes that criminals who are not
brought to justice will commit more crimes.

So does the public.

My focus has been on "clearing" this case (by identifying and proving guilt), as opposed
to understanding or attempting to explain every detail. Even as long as this book is,
I am certain that I will be criticized for not having included any of a hundred additional 9/11-related anomalies. I picked the ones that I thought would make the best
case possible. Like any trial lawyer, I evaluated my jury, which consists primarily of
my fellow citizens. I did not write this book for the audience of existing 9/11
activists and skeptics even though they likely number in the millions. Instead I've
chosen to address a larger audience, which meant that I couldn't address some of
the more arcane issues about which 9/11 activists have often focused their investigative energies. I stand by that choice. This is my best case. And if it doesn't win
I will not have the slightest inclination to say, "Well, if I had only…"

Homicide convictions routinely occur where many details regarding specific events are unknown. It is not uncommon for detectives to have lingering questions about how certain events took place or how certain pieces of evidence came into being, even while the convicted murderer is in prison or even awaiting execution. The overriding ethical mandate is the certainty of guilt.

It seems to me that ethics are fundamentally what this book is all about.

What happened on 9/11

At this point I am going to break many rules of legal procedure and ask the reader to remember that I am working within the confines of a book and have neither the time nor the resources to produce thousands of pages of records that you probably wouldn't be able to read anyway. What I have given you, however, are more than 900 footnotes that will amount to those thousands of pages of records if you follow them up. Sometimes the footnotes lead to documents with footnotes of their own; whether directly and immediately or through a further document, each footnote eventuates in a legally admissible source (government or business records, witness testimony, scientific data, public transcripts, et cetera). Pursue them to your own satisfaction. Check them for yourself. In a courtroom trial, these would be your exhibits, and I heartily encourage the reader to look into them thoroughly and decide what weight to give them. That is your right as a juror.

In my summation I will present facts that have not yet been entered into evidence. I will engage in some speculation, which, by itself, is not a bad thing although it will pose risks from critics waiting to pounce and quote me out of context. I ask indulgence from the many lawyers who will read this, and I ask them to recognize that, from a logistical standpoint, I must deviate from standard legal procedures. What lawyers present over the course of months in a major criminal case, I must present in over 600 pages.

I am also aware that many who read this book will have a great hunger to understand more of the "whats" and "whys" of September 11th, and because this is in part a literary effort, I feel obligated to share my best answers and opinions in some of these areas. There are going to be many questions I can't answer. There will be some points where I choose to keep my opinion to myself. But I submit that if this book is solid enough, and the reaction positive enough, then it is up to the readers — acting metaphorically in the role of grand jury — to force a public reexamination of the case in a way that will produce complete answers in a credible forum worthy of their trust.

I am also going to act now as an "expert witness." In essence I have been functioning as one from the start.

The why and the how

It is my belief that sometime during the period between late 1998 and early 2000, as certain elites became aware of the pending calamity of Peak Oil, they looked at the first highly confidential exploration and drilling results from the Caspian Basin and shuddered. The economy had already been milked close to collapse, and the Caspian results could not be kept secret forever. The data would surely come out, and what would happen to the markets then? What if some of the major oil companies had been inflating Caspian numbers and hyping-up hopes of a bonanza in order to pump their stock value? What if all the inflated reserve estimates revealed themselves to be bogus all at once?

A major economic collapse was imminent in the fall of 2001. I issued the first of only two economic bulletins from *FTW*, warning of an imminent market collapse, on September 9th.[1] The only other economic alert I ever issued came just before the massive collapse of the Dow Jones in 2002. Remember that? The one where your 401(k) got wiped out? The one that wiped out trillions of dollars in shareholder equity?

It is likely that some of those early Caspian drilling reports came from companies like ExxonMobil, where Condoleezza Rice sat on the board. She was an expert on Kazakhstan. The elites began to grasp that the hoped-for Caspian reserves would not even offer a short reprieve from the onslaught of Peak Oil. Through declassified CIA reports we know that the CIA was aware that US oil production had peaked in 1970 and that the Agency was tracking Soviet oil production in the hopes of predicting a Russian peak in 1977.[2] The CIA is Wall Street. Even if the oil had been there, it could not be monetized, because there was no safe route or pipeline to get it out. Alarms started going off.

It was time for the major players to cash out, and that's what some 20 giant corporations from Enron to WorldCom, to Merck, to Halliburton did, as those in the know pumped and dumped their stocks, sucking the wealth out of pension funds, small investors, and mutual funds from 2000 to 2002. For the most part only the smaller investors and funds were hurt. The people on top cashed out and moved "their" money elsewhere.

Dick Cheney and the neo-cons stepped up with a plan. That was probably more than Al Gore and the neo-liberals had to offer in light of the emergency now building. Any plan was better than no plan. Obviously, the first objective for Dick Cheney and the neo-cons had been to secure control of the White House in the 2000 election so that the rest of the plan could be implemented if necessary. That is why I noted in a January 2001 *FTW* essay titled "Empire," that the Bush cabinet was a war cabinet and that a major conflict was coming.

Their next task was to find out how much time there was before things started collapsing behind high energy prices and dwindling supply. How bad was it really? Who could say? The oil books were as cooked as the Enron books. How much oil was there really? Where was it? Who owned it? How long before the wheels started coming off? It was time to find all of it out accurately and quickly, but in secret. As the election of 2000 passed, the Caspian results grew continually more disappointing.

This would explain the urgency with which the Bush administration convened the National Energy Policy Development Group — under Dick Cheney — immediately after taking office in January. *What do we do now?* That was the bottom line. I believe that this was where the basic motive for 9/11 was fully articulated, understood, and accepted. Even though preparations for the attacks had been underway for years, the moment of truth about whether to execute them did not arrive until Cheney's group had a hard look at the numbers. This would explain why the administration fought all the way to the US Supreme Court to hide those records, and why Dick Cheney felt it necessary to take Justice Antonin Scalia duck hunting in a desperate effort to keep the records secret.

Scalia and the other "Supremes" delivered for him. On July 2, 2004, in a little-noticed 7-2 ruling, the Supreme Court upheld the right of the administration to keep the NEPDG's records secret from the American people. I was not at all surprised. Nothing surprised me after the Supreme Court's ruling in the 2000 election.

After the NEPDG concluded its work in late April 2001, I think an irrevocable decision had been made to cross the Rubicon, that bloody line between an ailing republic and the empire that irreversibly supervened. In May 2001 President Bush placed Dick Cheney in charge of all planning for a terror attack, effectively giving him complete control over FEMA, the military, everything. In June 2001 the NORAD scramble protocols that had worked efficiently since 1976 were rewritten to take most decision-making power out of the hands of Air Force field commanders. Although minor exceptions in those protocols still allowed commanders to act on their own in certain cases, as General Arnold did, the change itself provided deniability for elements of the confusion that Dick Cheney was going to deliberately engineer and control.

From their perspective, the Republican neo-cons were faced with a choice of massive panic and collapse on the financial markets; a loss of public faith in the political system; and the loss of most of their own power and wealth if the truth were known. To borrow a metaphor from Professor Peter Dale Scott, both the neo-libs and the neo-cons were players at a very lucrative crap game. Though they often played viciously against each other, their prime objective was to keep the game going at all costs. Whenever the game was threatened — as is the case with 9/11 — they quickly closed ranks to protect it while the turf over which they continued to fight among themselves grew smaller and smaller and the contests more heated and bloody.

Within their own mindset and within the parameters of an economic and governmental system that functioned (as it continues to function) in the mode of organized crime — incapable of transparency, riddled with corruption and cooked books, based upon the destruction of life for the sake of net profits and supremacy — these men, led by Dick Cheney, chose what they thought was their only logical option. I believe it seemed to them the "right" thing to do; after all, it was only a few thousand lives. Other rulers have made similar choices in the past. But as all empires learn, once the river is crossed there is no turning back. In front of that decision there lay a continuum of ever more vicious bloodletting, decline, and collapse.

The pie was shrinking, and any political diversity remaining in the system was heading for extinction as rapidly as are thousands of species on this afflicted planet. Perhaps mankind, too, is on nature's endangered species list, as we ironically and half-heartedly lament the white rhino and the California condor, the Bengal tiger and the black bear.

The imminent energy crisis was going to be both apocalyptic and unavoidable, and it was going to arrive sooner than expected. Like any "well-planned" government operation, the planning and initial preparations for what became 9/11 had begun in the Clinton administration as a contingency plan. That's when the 19 so-called hijackers (and/or their handlers) began establishing their legends. But the Caspian news would account for the absolutely unfathomable number of mistakes that were made in both the plan's execution and the subsequent cover-up. It was a rush job. Quickly, any number of classified or once-classified contingency plans for a staged attack on the US — like Operation Northwoods — came down off the shelf. As Brzezinski's *Grand Chessboard* shows, the need for such an event had already been acknowledged in 1997 — conveniently, just as al Qaeda and the Taliban were emerging as world and regional players. Operation Northwoods, declassified in the late 1990s, had been planned in 1962.

Since the end of the cold war there had been plenty of time to put a new potential enemy in place, and September 11th was not a new idea.

As Zbigniew Brzezinski had written in 1997, the "immediate" task was to develop and simultaneously control a "direct external threat" to manufacture an attack "like a new Pearl Harbor." That required a credible (at least in the public mind) and well-developed enemy. The need for the same kind of attack was mentioned by the Project for a New American Century (PNAC) in its September 2000 report *Rebuilding America's Defenses*. Such an attack would then provide a pretext for massive sequential military intervention to secure the energy supplies of the Middle East and the lesser (but terribly important) oil-bearing regions including West Africa, Venezuela, Colombia, certain portions of the Southwest Pacific, and any other region with smaller but more readily accessible reserves. The essential thing would be that terrorists or their "allies" must conveniently turn up in each needed area, on schedule.

No problem! That's what the CIA, Mossad, MI6, and every other major intelligence agency does for a living.

Also of primary importance would be any region that included a geostrategic oil transport route. As an example of the latter I would offer the straits of Malacca and the South China Sea through which oil tankers supplying Japan, China, and Korea must pass. Others would include the former Soviet Republic of Georgia, Turkey, and (for the future) Iran. Hence we have convenient bombings in Bali and outbreaks of Muslim terrorism in the Philippines.

As this book goes to press, the US has just conducted a naval exercise — Operation Summer Pulse 01 — in the Southwest Pacific involving seven aircraft carrier battle groups operating off the Chinese coast. Other powers in the region are moving to exercise and contest dominion of a small group of islands called the Spratlys, which may contain a few billion barrels of oil. Conflict there would endanger all tanker traffic. It is for that reason that China has just announced its intentions to build a pipeline to the coast of Burma on the Indian Ocean so that tankers from the Middle East can offload after a much shorter trip and bypass this zone of imminent conflict, while the oil is pumped into China over the eastern foothills of the Himalayas.[3] These and other currently proliferating moves toward a disastrous global war have been accelerated by America's belligerent new unilateralism, for which 9/11 served as the ideal trigger.

Fortunately for the plotters, parts of the Clinton administration (immune from most political concerns) had been protecting, grooming, and nurturing the Taliban and al Qaeda to make sure that a needed enemy would be in place for several years. It is my belief that plans for the attacks of September 11th were being accelerated during at least the last year of the Clinton administration, with the full knowledge of President Clinton and his top advisors including "Sandy" Berger, Madeline Albright, and Bill Richardson, Clinton's Secretary of Energy. I also suspect NATO Commander Wesley Clark, whose liaison with the Kosovo Liberation Army included relations with al Qaeda that provided it with training and battlefield experience. The actual planning involved extremely powerful but relatively "non-aligned" government figures whose pedigrees included membership in the Council on Foreign Relations, the Trilateral Commission, and/or the Bilderberg Group: the protectors of the game.

Almost every major analysis of the 9/11 attacks suggests that they must have been planned for between three and four years. This accounts for the otherwise illogical and inexplicable support of the Taliban by high-ranking officials like Karl "Rick" Inderfurth in his role as assistant secretary of state, and Inderfurth's subsequent transition to continue "negotiations" with the Taliban after the 2000 election. This need to keep al Qaeda and bin Laden in play would also explain why the Clinton administration overlooked so many opportunities to capture or neutralize bin Laden between 1998 and 2001. Osama bin Laden was going to be needed for a long time.

I believe that bin Laden was, and remains, a CIA/ US government/Wall Street asset. This would explain why he has never been caught. There are still wars to fight. He can't be caught for a variety of other reasons, including his family's enormous and diverse financial connections to the same elites that control the United States financial system, and his close interrelationship with a Saudi ruling class that could pull the plug on the US economy even before Peak Oil does. Osama bin Laden also knows way too much, and without him, the Bush administration would have had no excuse for any of what it has done over the last four years. From a strategic point of view, Osama is Dick Cheney's best friend.

A Saudi assault on the US economy would weaken the United States' mad effort to be the last standing contestant in Peak Oil's deadly game of musical chairs. All we really have left is a beleaguered and overextended military. The military depends upon economic power that is now slipping through the Empire's hands as rapidly as water through a sieve. Although the US military is by far the most powerful in the world, it is not more powerful than the world. But that is the game that Dick Cheney and apparently John Kerry, also, have chosen to play.

Saudi Arabia, beset by a host of intractable social and economic issues, also had to go along. Its reserves were deteriorating rapidly, and acknowledgement of that would lead to internal chaos. Everybody had much to hide, and apart from US support of al Qaeda, Saudi Arabia's intelligence chief, Prince Turki, had been a US conduit to, and even close associate of, bin Laden for many years. The control rods were coming out of the Western-driven creation and sponsorship of Muslim fundamentalism. Each side's blackmail cards were all aces, and some Saudi factions supported the legend of bin Laden while others desperately tried to distance themselves form it. Dick Cheney had them over a barrel. Passports were issued, donations made, a paper trail of Saudi support for the hijackers was laid all the way from Saudi Arabia to the ashes of Lower Manhattan. One of the most misleading spins perpetrated by the US media was to tell the world that 15 of the 19 hijackers were from Saudi Arabia. No! Fifteen of the 19 had Saudi passports. Many were from other places all over the Middle East.

By whatever means necessary, certain foreign governments were forced to become at least partly guilty for September 11th before it ever happened, either wittingly or through deception. As the attacks were unfolding, some governments were deeply involved while others were no doubt screaming, "Those dirty rotten bastards! Issue a press release expressing total solidarity with the Americans, or else they'll expose that favor they asked (forced) us to do and say we were part of it!" It is my belief that Mike Vreeland — among his other duties — was a part of that deceitful and shameful process when he came back from Moscow in December of 2000.

Welcome to Geopolitics 101; hardball at its finest.

The how and the what

I do not know whether the plans for Project Bojinka were actual creations of al Qaeda or whether they were planted. But it is quite likely that those plans, captured in 1995, were recalled early-on, probably sometime in late 1999 or 2000, and a strategy began to take shape around them. The World Trade Center was an obvious choice for many reasons.

It had been attacked before. It housed not only the vast archives of criminal investigative records of agencies like the SEC but also an unknown-sized paper trail of financial crimes, cooked books, inflated profits, and sundry other offenses. There were large amounts of gold and negotiables in a number of vaults, many belonging to foreign central banks, that could be secretly removed and later claimed destroyed.

An attack on the Pentagon was vital for several reasons. First, if sufficient popular support were not garnered from the public over the loss of a financial center, it would certainly galvanize the military and even more of the population with an attack on the Pentagon. It is also quite likely that unknown evidence was also destroyed when whatever it was hit the largely unoccupied navy wing of the Pentagon. That wing was under construction, so loss of life was minimal. Constructing a list of those killed at the Pentagon that day and what their actual jobs were would be a difficult, if not impossible, task, but it is something I sure would like to know.

This was a point that Mike Vreeland kept coming back to again and again as he insisted that a homing device had been placed inside the wing that morning.

A handful of individuals at the highest levels of the major media had to know before 9/11, so that their myriad employees would have a sturdy, prefabricated Lee Harvey Oswald-type story to follow (if left to their own devices, they might do something unfortunate, like investigative reporting). But letting anyone outside the boardroom know would have been impossible to manage. Too many people; too little control. As evidenced by the footnotes in this book a great many mainstream journalists of all stripes did start asking some of the most obvious questions right away. A few continued, even after the herd had made it clear which way everyone was supposed to go. That's why there are so many damning little "dots" and so few editorial decisions or assignments putting them together. We, every 9/11 researcher who has stayed the course, had to do it for ourselves. Millions of private Americans and rapidly growing and increasingly influential independent news organizations have been connecting these big, ugly dots and have done incredible jobs. I have tried to recognize and honor as many of these people as I could in this book.

As the planning continued, the legends of the various hijackers continued to be established. Some of these "terrorists" had been turned by US, British, or Israeli intelligence long before 9/11. Some were probably long-time, deep-cover field agents. Certainly some were just expendable fodder. It seems as if some of them wanted to get noticed. Most likely, a search through intelligence and law enforcement records by the planners disclosed not only ideas but pieces of a "legend" that could be quickly — if imperfectly — woven together around the key players like a patchwork quilt. In the earliest stages the key decision, perhaps the most crucial of all, had to be about whom to recruit or deceive into playing the role of hijacker-in-training.

No intelligence agency had deeper or better penetration in the Middle East and South Asia than Israel's Mossad. It probably became a full partner early on. But the "hijackers" who had received US military training were special cases.

I believe that the so-called hijackers who had received this training were probably part of an ultra-secret US military and intelligence joint operation "Opposition Force," or OPFOR, which routinely played bad guys in hijack exercises around the world and inside the US. I believe that it is possible — even likely — that this hijack OPFOR was a joint US-Israeli operation. Sources have told me that exercises like this were also probably used by US and Israeli intelligence agencies to test airline security around the world and especially in the Middle East. There is no airline in the world with more proactive and comprehensive security than El Al. In my too many long years at this I have met a number of former US Special Operations personnel who performed these kinds of missions, whether driving a pickup truck or a fake utility truck to test defenses at nuclear reactors, or posing as small boaters attempting to penetrate the security at submarine bases.

Thus there might have been two reasons why Israeli intelligence was tracking the "ringleaders" so closely before the attacks: first, to provide deniable surveillance and act as a cutout for Dick Cheney and any US agencies; second, to stay close to their own assets, protect them, and "wrangle" them as they maneuvered precariously and noisily through a law enforcement system where people like John O'Neill, Robert Wright, Colleen Rowley, and Ken Williams in Phoenix were trying to apprehend them. There had to be someone like a Dave Frasca to keep the players on the field until game time.

A word of caution about Colleen Rowley: If one accepts her angry memo at face value, then one accepts that the 19 hijackers pulled off the attacks all by themselves. Her memo enshrines the legend even in its apparently insubordinate dissent. That's how covert operations work. And yet the same can be said for Richard Clarke, whose work does not by any means depart from the official core story, but does provide golden fragments of the truth for those who can sift them.[4] Rowley's courageous but limited memo must be read in a similar way.

If the core of the 19 hijackers were US government OPFOR personnel, it would account for certain details of Mohammed Atta's life, like his penchants for strip clubs, liquor, and women. These are hardly the passions of a devout Muslim about to become a martyr. Special Operations personnel have, however, been known to engage in these vices from time to time. Existing assets, already trusted and tested either by combat or covert operations, probably came to mind quickly for the planners who began putting them in place and creating their required legends well before the 2000 election. Frankly, I am not convinced that any of them were on board any of the hijacked flights on 9/11, although I do think it likely that some were. I also think that a few might have been killed. I do not think that all would have been killed, because intelligence agencies need their covert operatives to trust them. Wiping out all of them might have risked a mutiny from "assets" who suddenly realized that they were not going to be taken care of as promised. I do believe that all of the expendable "muscle" of the hijackers was killed.

Certain key allies — Russia and Germany probably, Britain and Israel certainly — had to be consulted in advance. It is likely that the Russians and the Germans were told less than the full truth.

Given the degree of documented intelligence penetration of al Qaeda; the fact that Osama bin Laden had been a CIA asset during the first Afghan conflict against the Soviets; the fact that a number of the so-called hijackers and/or al Qaeda members had been trained in CIA training camps in Chechnya, had fought in CIA/US sponsored guerilla conflicts (e.g., in Kosovo with the KLA in 2000), or had received military training at US installations; given all that, it is reasonable to assume that one or more top al Qaeda officials were in fact double or triple agents. They worked to further an agenda originating out of Washington, strongly influenced by Tel Aviv, rather than out of some ill-defined Muslim hatred of the US. In this class I would include people like Khalid Sheikh Muhammad (KSM), Ramzi bin al-Shibh, and Mohammed Atta.

This would account for the fact that an impressive number of respected press organizations have reported that as many as 9 of the alleged 19 hijackers are still alive.[5] They include: Mohammed Atta, Ahmed Alnami, Saeed Alghamdi, Salem Alhazmi, Waleed Alshehri, Wail Alshehri, Abdulaziz Alomari, Khalid Almihdhar, and Marwan Alshehhi.

Included here are the three known names of the five hijackers reported to have received military training: Atta, Alomari, and Alghamdi. To my knowledge, the other two who were listed have never been named. I strongly suspect that they are also among the living. This would also account for the fact that several of the hijackers were known to have stayed in a motel very close to the super-secret National Security Agency at Fort Meade Maryland just weeks before the attacks. These are Hani Hanjour, Khalid Almidhar, Nawaf Alhazmi, Salem Alhazmi, and Majed Moqed.[6] They were the hijackers who allegedly performed an aerobatic maneuver of supreme skill before crashing a Boeing 757 into the Pentagon. Not one of them had even an instrument rating, let alone the commercial, multi-engine, or jet ratings required to even contemplate such a feat.

We'll get to that.

In covert operations the best kind of an asset is one that has no idea who is really "running" him. That is not to say that I don't believe there are terrorists out there who would do any kind of damage they possibly could to the United States. Even if there weren't before 9/11 (and there were), the US has gone out of its way to create animosity against this country that is in full flower all over the globe. What is clear is that the government's assertions that 19 hijackers, funded from caves in Afghanistan, were able to execute what happened on September 11th is beyond ludicrous. It is also a case that the government has never proven to anybody by any standard other than that used by Randolph Hearst.

On that point it is interesting to note that the US government has failed to produce — publicly, or for the one failed 9/11 criminal prosecution in Germany of Mounir el Motassadeq — either bin al-Shibh or KSM as material witnesses. No mere mortal has seen either one of them since their reported captures. Credible reports have told us that KSM was killed. Any information alleged to have come from these "captured" suspects has come in the form of "press-release prosecution" by the government. None of it has ever been independently authenticated.

Remote control

Based upon the evidence, we can safely say that two airliners hit the World Trade Center. That part was filmed and/or witnessed by many people. We can also safely say that a number of witnesses saw an airliner make an unprecedented aerobatic maneuver over the Pentagon. There is, however, no footage of Flight 77's famed aerial maneuver just as there is no footage that shows an airliner actually hitting the Pentagon. The only thing ever produced was a film that showed the side of the Pentagon and then a large ball of flame.

Many websites have posted what they purported was slow motion footage revealing an aircraft tailfin approaching the Pentagon and the debate over whether it was an F-16 or a cruise missile or something else grew so intense that threats of violence and some serious name-calling took place between advocates of various theories. Since it was based upon evidence that I could not verify as easily as a statement made by Dick Cheney, Condi Rice, or anyone else, I chose not to waste precious time there. I could not personally verify the chain of custody of those films, or that they had not been tampered with. I lack the technical proficiency to judge such things, and I am not an expert in the area of photographic analysis. Flight 77 remains the greatest unsolved mystery of 9/11 but that does not alter my belief in the guilt of the suspects.

What we have, however, is a feat of airplane driving that far exceeds the skills reportedly possessed by any of the alleged hijackers. In fact, the flying skills required for such a maneuver surpass even those of commercial airline pilots. A 2002 story that originated in Portugal confirms this.

The *Portugal News* is a weekly English-language newspaper read largely by expatriate and touring Americans. On March 8, 2002, in a story headlined "September 11 — US Government Accused" it reported:

> A group of military and civilian US pilots, under the chairmanship of Colonel Don de Grand, after deliberating non-stop for 72 hours, has concluded that the flight crews of the four passenger airliners, involved in the September 11th tragedy, had no control over their aircraft.
>
> In a detailed press communiqué the inquiry stated: "The so-called terrorist attack was in fact a superbly executed military operation carried out against the USA, requiring the utmost professional military skill in command, communications, and control. It was flawless in timing, in the choice of selected aircraft to be used as guided missiles and in the coordinated delivery of those missiles to their pre-selected targets."
>
> The report seriously questions whether or not the suspect hijackers, supposedly trained on Cessna light aircraft, could have located a target dead-on 200 miles from take off point. It further throws into doubt their ability to master the intricacies of the instrument flight

rules (IFR) in the 45 minutes from take off to the point of impact. Colonel de Grand said that it would be impossible for novices to have taken control of the four aircraft and orchestrated such a terrible act requiring military precision of the highest order.

A member of the inquiry team, a US Air Force officer who flew over 100 sorties during the Vietnam war, told the press conference: "Those birds (commercial airliners) either had a crack fighter pilot in the left seat, or they were being maneuvered by remote control."

In evidence given to the enquiry, Captain Kent Hill (retd.) of the US Air Force, and friend of Chic Burlingame, the pilot of the plane that crashed into the Pentagon, stated that the US had on several occasions flown an unmanned aircraft, similar in size to a Boeing 737, across the Pacific from Edwards Air Force base in California to South Australia. According to Hill it had flown on a pre-programmed flight path under the control of a pilot in an outside station.

Hill also quoted Bob Ayling, former British Airways boss, in an interview given to the *London Economist* on September 20th, 2001. Ayling admitted that it was now possible to control an aircraft in flight from either the ground or in the air. This was confirmed by expert witnesses at the inquiry who testified that airliners could be controlled by electro-magnetic pulse or radio frequency instrumentation from command and control platforms based either in the air or at ground level.

All members of the inquiry team agreed that even if guns were held to their heads none of them would fly a plane into a building. Their reaction would be to ditch the plane into a river or a field, thereby safeguarding the lives of those on the ground....

During the press conference Captain Hill maintained that the four airliners must have been choreographed by an Airborne Warning and Control System (AWACS). This system can engage several aircraft simultaneously by knocking out their on-board flight controls. He said that all the evidence points to the fact that the pilots and their crews had not taken any evasive action to resist the supposed hijackers. They had not attempted any sudden changes in flight path or nose-dive procedures — which led him to believe that they had no control over their aircraft.

THE NEWS, in an attempt to further substantiate the potential veracity of these findings, spoke to an Algarve-based airline pilot, who has more than 20 years of experience in flying passenger planes, to seek his views. Captain Colin McHattie, currently flying with Cathay Pacific, agreed with the independent commission's findings. However, he explained that while it is possible to fly a plane from the ground, the installation of the necessary equipment is a time-consuming process, and needs extensive planning.[7]

Which brings us back to the wargames again.

The wargames

The military has been practicing shoot-downs of remotely piloted aircraft since the 1950s. I consider it likely that on September 11th all four aircraft were remotely piloted or taken over by a system that can be activated without the flight crew's ability to intervene. I believe that the apparatus to remotely pilot the two planes that struck in New York was housed and operated from within the New York City Office of Emergency Management (or very close by), where we know that a Secret Service agent was already in place and communicating with Dick Cheney. The Secret Service agent's presence is easily explained by the so-called preparations for the Tripod II exercise.

Since 7 WTC was not struck by anything and it collapsed so perfectly, as if in a controlled demolition, I believe that this was necessary and had been planned in advance with the express intent of destroying the electronic equipment needed to make the precise maneuvers necessary to get the airliners to hit the buildings. In law enforcement parlance, that was a task that required "eyeballs." Leaving that equipment behind was too risky. Attempting to get the equipment out unseen in the middle of that kind of emergency would have been stupid. Someone might have questioned why equipment was being loaded onto trucks as people were running for their lives. A cop might have seen the activity as looting and made a log entry. The equipment might have been seized or photographed. Ergo, the requisite demolition charges would have been in place well before the attacks occurred, and the equipment would have vanished with the building.

In that context I cannot help but mark how convenient it was that John O'Neill was occupied the night before the attacks, having drinks until 2:30 in the morning, well past the time when, given his now-famous sense that "something big" was coming "soon," he might conceivably have dropped by for an unannounced inspection.

Remote control technology for commercial aircraft is fairly common. However, one particular company stands out in this area and is noteworthy for one of its executives, Dov Zakheim. Independent journalist Cheryl Seal, writing in New Zealand's *Scoop Media*, is obviously aware of the interrelationships between economics, covert operations, and geopolitics. What I have read of her analysis is cogent, clear, and in my opinion, pretty much right on the money.

She wrote:

> CONCLUSION: The plane was remotely controlled by a command transmitter system, at least in the final minutes. There was an explosive device on board, which was detonated immediately before impact,

probably remotely controlled as well. The timing, trajectory, etc., may have been generated by a software program of some sort that could work this out to the millisecond. The plane's own transponder would have had to have been turned off so that its operation would not interfere with a second transponder placed aboard by the perpetrators — a transponder designed to pick up the signal of a command system transmitter operated somewhere in the area. Or, of course, the plane's own transponder was not actually off — it was just changed to a new setting. In any case, turning the transponder off would not have helped the hijackers to hide from the battery of sophisticated radars encircling DC, so this motivation (hiding from radars) does not make any sense. Here is a description of an advanced, "fully mobile" CTS built by System Planning Corp., the CEO of which is Bush's undersecretary of defense and long time Texas pal Dov Zakheim.[8]

I could not find any records confirming that Zakheim had been the CEO of System Planning Corporation. However, a bio posted at the website of the office of the undersecretary for defense (comptroller) and chief financial officer says of Zakheim that he came to the Pentagon in May of 2001 just prior to the attacks and, "Most recently, he was corporate vice president of System Planning Corp. (SPC), a technology, research and analysis firm based in Arlington, Va."[9]

A quick trip to the SPC website confirmed that the company is engaged in projects including Homeland Security, Intelligence and Advanced Concepts, Advanced Technology, Signatures and Electronic Warfare Technology, Radar Physics, Counterterrorism, Emergency Management, Biowarfare, and Communications Networks.

The SPC website also contains the following statement:

> SPC and TriData have supported crisis and emergency response planning for all levels of the federal government and for state and local (county and city) fire and police departments. *We developed the Federal Emergency Management Agency (FEMA) family of plans (the Federal Emergency Response Plan and Continuity of Operations (COOP) Plan) used to guide federal responses to national emergencies.* We have developed and conducted exercises to test responses to natural and wartime emergencies, including hurricanes, nuclear power plant accidents, and chemical/biological events. TriData has developed executive training models to address a wide array of threats, including industrial espionage and terrorism.[10] [emphasis added]

SPC also plays a key role in planning and executing wargame exercises.

Exercise Planning and Training
- Federal, state, and local exercise support

- Federal exercise development and planning
- State and local exercise training systems

Since 1980 SPC and TriData have provided comprehensive emergency management support to US federal, state, and local governments; to county and city fire and police departments; to international governments; and to private industry. Our experience spans the range of all-hazards emergencies, large and small, and includes disaster preparedness and response planning, documentation, training, and exercise; mitigation support; and post-disaster analysis and reporting. SPC and TriData have relevant experience and staff who are knowledgeable in exercise support relating to acts of terrorism, including threats at four levels:

- Predictable — bomb threats
- Probable — bombing attempts, computer crime
- Possible — hostage taking
- Catastrophic — *aerial bombing,* chemical agents in water supply or air conditioning[11] [emphasis added]

When it comes to remote control technology for the piloting of commercial aircraft, SPC offers the appropriately named,

Flight Termination System

System Planning Corporation is proud to offer the Flight Termination System (FTS), *a fully redundant turnkey range safety and test system for remote control and flight termination of airborne test vehicles.* The FTS consists of SPC's Command Transmitter System (CTS) and custom control, interface, and monitoring subsystems. *The system is fully programmable* and is flexible enough to meet the changing and challenging requirements of today's modern test ranges.

The FTS is generally deployed in one of two configurations:

Multi-Site System: a network of multiple CTS units spread over a large geographic area

Multi-Control System: multiple operator consoles sharing control of a single CTS unit

Multi-Site System

Because many installations require several remote CTS units that can be controlled from either the remote site or a centralized site, the FTS has been developed to control a fully redundant automated network of transmitters. *The system can be configured to operate as a single local site or with up to eight remote sights over an extended range. Each CTS unit may be controlled locally (manually), or as part of the larger FTS system. The fully redundant central control unit also supports either manual or automated modes of operation....*

One of FTS's major strengths is its flexibility. A fully programmable command library provides a variety of mission-specific command tones in addition to the required Command Destruct sequence.

Multi-Control System

FTS also allows multiple missions to be run simultaneously with a single CTS unit. In this mode, multiple operator stations share control of the transmitter unit. The FTS control software ensures that the multi-tasking of the CTS unit is performed seamlessly and is completely transparent to the operators.[12] (emphasis added)

Dov Zakheim resigned as the DoD's chief financial officer in May of 2004. A current bio on him from the SPC website reveals even more interesting information.

Dov S. Zakheim is Corporate Vice President of System Planning Corporation (SPC), a high-technology, research, analysis, and manufacturing firm based in Arlington, Virginia. He is also Chief Executive Officer of SPC International Corporation, a subsidiary of SPC that *specializes in political, military, and economic consulting, and international sales and analysis. In addition, Dr. Zakheim serves as Consultant to the Secretary of Defense and the Under Secretary of Defense for Policy [Doug Feith]. He is an Adjunct Senior Fellow for Asian Studies of the Council on Foreign Relations, Adjunct Scholar of the Heritage Foundation, and a Senior Advisor at the Center for International and Strategic Studies.*

From 1985 until March 1987, Dr. Zakheim was Deputy Under Secretary of Defense for Planning and Resources. In that capacity, he played an active role in the Department's system acquisition and strategic planning processes and guided Department of Defense policy in a number of international economic fora. He also successfully negotiated numerous arms cooperation agreements with various US allies....

Dr. Zakheim is also a trustee of the Foreign Policy Research Institute; serves on the Board of Directors of Search for Common Ground and of Friends of the Jewish Chapel of the United States Naval Academy; and is a member of the Council on Foreign Relations and other professional organizations. Dr. Zakheim is a member of the advisory boards of the Center for Security Policy, the Initiative for Peace and Cooperation in the Middle East, and the American Jewish Committee.[13] [emphasis added]

A check of the SEC website shows no filing for System Planning Corporation, which suggests that the company is privately owned; and the corporate website, for all the information it offers, does not disclose the identities of the corporation's board of directors.

As you may recall, we talked about Zakheim in Chapter 15; Zakheim has close ties to the Israeli government and, as we saw earlier, was the chief financial officer of a US government entity that has "misplaced" more than $3 trillion of our taxpayer dollars. Unconfirmed reports state that he holds dual American-Israeli citizenship. Although the "loss" of that money did not occur on his watch, the reporting of at least $2 trillion of that missing money occurred while he was there, and he made no accounting of it during his tenure except to acknowledge that it was missing. Zakheim was also a signatory on PNAC's report "Rebuilding America's Defenses."

Choreographing disaster: Cleveland airport

I believe that on the day of September 11th, while FAA and NORAD responses were paralyzed and confused by an unknown number of wargame exercises involving inserted radar blips and live-fly exercises, there were also contained within those drills an unknown number of commercial airliners (possibly surplus) being piloted by remote control. It would have been easy to manipulate the transponder codes. It was a shell game. We can still discern the guilty parties. This raises the possibility that one or more of the actual commercial airliners were taken over electronically, diverted into a wargame exercise, possibly over the ocean, and maybe even shot down by pilots who believed they were destroying empty drones. However, in the cases of Flights 11 and 175, I tend to believe that these were the real airliners.

Excellent research by a German independent journalist using the name Woody Box, however, raised another far more interesting possibility. In looking at what happened to Delta's Flight 1989, believed to have been a fifth hijacking, Box discovered that the Cleveland airport was mysteriously shut down, and that two airliners (instead of the reported one) landed there on the morning of September 11th.

Reporting on the website of INN World Report, Box wrote:

> This article will prove that not one, but two planes made an emergency landing in Cleveland — in close succession. The proof is based on local newspaper and radio reports from September 11th and 12th (mainly from the *Akron Beacon Journal* and the *Cleveland Plain Dealer*), statements of eyewitnesses and Internet postings in the morning of 9/11 (people were listening to the radio and immediately submitted the breaking news to the net). One of the flights was indeed Delta 1989. We don't know the identity of the other one, so we call it "Flight X"....
>
> We start with a short summary of the events in Cleveland. At 10 a.m., the airport was evacuated. Without doubt, this had to do with the rumors that a hijacked plane was going to land. The passengers had to leave the airport but were not allowed to take their cars. They had to walk or get a ride at the highway. Busses were not allowed to leave the airport. People around the airport were told to go home. It was a very tense situation. These facts are undisputed.

Cleveland Mayor Michael White held a televised news conference at 11 a.m., after the emergency landing. According to the *Cleveland Plain Dealer,* he said there was an unconfirmed report that the plane might have been hijacked or was carrying a bomb. But in the middle of the news conference, he reported that it had not been hijacked, and later in the day he said no bomb had been found. This was not the only detail that changed in the course of the day. In the morning, White said that air controllers could hear screaming on the plane. In the afternoon, he didn't mention the screams anymore.

We will now examine several parameters of the emergency landing:

1. The moment of landing;
2. The begin [sic] of the evacuation of the passengers;
3. The number of passengers;
4. The place the passengers were interviewed after the evacuation;
5. The exact location of the grounded plane.

We will see that there are two different data for every parameter, suggesting that we are dealing with two different planes. We will omit the "a.m." because it's clear that everything is happening in the morning.

1. The moment of landing

AP and two Ohio newspapers report a landing at 10:45 (1A). However, Delta Airlines has registered 10:10 as the landing time, and Cleveland firefighters can confirm that the landing took place before 10:30.

(1B). Because Delta Airlines did not loose the track of its plane, the 10:10 plane was surely Delta 1989.

So the 10:45 plane is — by definition — Flight X.

2. The begin [sic] of the evacuation of the passengers

The *Akron Beacon Journal* writes in an extra edition from 9/11 that the passengers were released from the plane at 11:15. This is confirmed by Internet postings describing the events in real-time (2A).

However, a passenger from Delta 1989 relates that she had to stay more than two hours in the plane before the FBI started to search it and took the passengers away for questioning. The *Plain Dealer* has learned about a [sic] evacuation time of 12:30, confirming the witness' statement. (2B). Thanks to the most valuable statement of the passenger, we can conclude that Delta 1989 landed at 10:10 and was evacuated at 12:30. Flight X landed at 10:45 and was evacuated at 11:15.

3. The number of passengers

The first press reports tell us that the plane carried 200 passengers. Mayor White mentioned this number on his 11 o'clock conference (3A). He did not say how he got the number. The passenger of Delta 1989 however, she must know it, made an estimation of "60 or so" passengers.

This is confirmed by later reports — the story changed quickly. Now, 69 passengers have been released from the plane, going well with the "60 or so" (3B).

We can conclude that Delta 1989 landed at 10:10, the 69 passengers being evacuated at 12:30. Flight X landed at 10:45, the 200 passengers being released at 11:15.

4. The place the passengers were interviewed after the evacuation

The [sic] most reports say that the passengers were brought into a nearby NASA facility (4A). This is the NASA Glenn Research Center, located near the west end of the airport. It was already evacuated. The passenger of Delta 1989 however tells us that she was taken into a "secure building at the airport." This is confirmed by a report that the Delta 1989 passengers were interviewed in the FAA headquarters. (4B).

Surely the FAA headquarters is not located in the NASA facility.

We can conclude that Delta 1989 landed at 10:10, and at 12:30 the 69 passengers were taken into the FAA headquarters. Flight X landed at 10:45, and at 11:15 the 200 passengers were taken into the evacuated NASA Center.

5. The exact location of the plane

This is the final proof that we have to do with [i.e., we are dealing with] two different planes. Both planes were sitting on a runway, but miles away from each other. One plane was at the west end of runway 28/10 near the NASA center (point 10 in the map). This is confirmed by Associated Press and an eyewitness (5A). The other plane was sitting at the south end of runway 18/36 near the I-X-Center (point 36), also confirmed by two eyewitnesses (5B). The geographic conditions on the airport suggest that the passengers at the west end were taken to the NASA Center and the passengers at the south end to the FAA headquarters.[14]

The question almost asks itself. Was Plane X Flight 77? Was it Flight 93? There were even reports that Flight 93 was confirmed to have landed at Cleveland's airport, which I did not have time to chase down. (I can't do everything.) I have no doubt that Flight 93 (or an aircraft posing as Flight 93) was shot down however. Engines from a Boeing 757 do not bounce for long distances through the air after the direct impact of a nosedive. Nothing bounced at the Pentagon. There wasn't even any recognizable debris except for a very small piece of metal that happened to be painted with the right colors. No tail section. No cockpit. No seats lying about. No suitcases. There were too many witnesses to the fact that a debris trail from 93 was scattered over miles; something that could only have happened from a mid-air explosion. There were too many witnesses placing both military and "civilian" aircraft close to it. There were too many witnesses who reported that they saw missiles in the air.

Imagine the reaction if cameras had filmed a completely empty airliner landing by itself, without any opportunity for statements from the passengers? The order stands! Shoot it down! These are all speculative questions that do not distract me from the issue of guilt or a world that is exploding around all of us.

With the crash of Flight 93 the Rubicon had been crossed once and for all.

And now, for all of the physical evidence fanatics who have dogged me for two years and who have lacked a courtroom wherein they could battle to their conclusive "proof," I offer this:

For a long time I have not believed that the WTC towers collapsed as a result of the impacts. I said from the first days after 9/11 that I had too much experience with the way physical evidence could be manipulated, even inside a courtroom, to waste my time arguing claims that could not be proven as thoroughly and concretely as the ones I have proven here. While I cannot tell the general public, or you who have made so many excellent cases for your positions, how the buildings were brought down, I can certainly now point you to a likely suspect for the requisite studies of what would be required to do it.

I found it in a footnote to the Kean Commission report.

> 1. For the WTC's layout, see Port Authority diagrams, "World Trade Center Concourse Level," "Concourse Level," and "Plaza Level," undated. For the number of square feet of *office space, see Federal Emergency Management Agency (FEMA) report, World Trade Center Building Performance Study," undated.* For the number of workers and passersby, see Port Authority briefing (May 13, 2004).
>
> For the dimensions, *see FEMA report, "World Trade Center Building Performance Study," undated.* In addition, the outside of each tower was covered by a frame of 14-inch-wide steel columns; the centers of the steel columns were 40 inches apart. These exterior walls bore most of the weight of the building. The interior core of the buildings was a hollow steel shaft, in which elevators and stairwells were grouped. Ibid. For stairwells and elevators, see Port Authority response to Commission interrogatory, May 2004.[15] [emphasis added]

As I close this book and end my arguments to you I want to thank a dedicated and meticulous 9/11 researcher named Mark Robinowitz for giving me an analogy about bank robbers that I will leave you with before you begin your deliberations. I have taken his idea and reworked it for you.

I want you to imagine a city with a lot of major banks. Big banks. A city with a well-funded and competent police department. In fact it is the best-funded police department in the state. Imagine that the city has been aware of a large number of bank robberies being committed by some very vicious robbers who have no hesitation to kill. In fact, their intent is to kill as they commit their crimes. The bank robbers have even said that this particular city is their primary target and number one enemy. Imagine also that some members of this gang had once worked for, and been trained by, that same city and were known by name. Most of their phones are tapped. Imagine that their records are available to the authorities and that the city knows where some of them live.

Imagine that the city actually has them under close surveillance and is fully aware of the gang's plans to hit several banks in the city all at once: fully aware, because the city had captured the plans years ago. The city's largest bank has even been hit by the gang once before. It was bloody, but the gang didn't get away with the loot. The city knows of new plans to take the bank from the inside by tunneling, yet does nothing to look for tunnels and places no seismic detectors to warn of digging.

The banks are not warned. Neither is the city's Department of Water and Power.

Now the city, wanting to show its concern, makes a big show of preparing to protect the increasingly alarmed citizenry, stages drills, and makes known its plans to be prepared. The city is aware of all the damage done by the gang throughout the state and has declared the gang to be its most wanted enemy. The Deputy Mayor is placed in charge of all bank robbery prevention planning. He is given command of the police force, the City Attorney's office, the utility companies and every city agency. He is charged with making sure no bank robberies occur.

Now imagine the city also scheduling a series of drills, practicing for bank robbery scenarios, that effectively take almost all available police cars off the streets and out to the city limits just as the bank robbers begin their deadly raid. The drills are slated to occur during the very week when warnings of the planned bank robberies have reached their fever pitch. Imagine a series of false alarms going off at the precise moment the rampage begins — false alarms that the gang could never have engineered.

Imagine that the city (at the direction of the Deputy Mayor) actually schedules fake bank robberies on the same day, which then lead some of the few police cars available in the wrong direction. Other police cars just stop because they don't know where to go. The Deputy Mayor then orders the last remaining police cars to drive in the wrong directions.

The bank robberies are brutal. People are shot and lying about everywhere in crumpled, violated heaps.

Supposedly all of the bank robbers are killed, but it is widely understood that they could not have acted alone. They planned these heists for years, and large numbers of the gang are still on the loose. Imagine that for three years afterwards, no one who helped the bank robbers, no one who bought them their guns, their transportation, the false IDs necessary to get access to dig their tunnels, nobody — is brought to trial and convicted.

If you lived in that city, how long would you wait to remove the Mayor and Deputy Mayor?

I have absolutely no doubt that on the day of September 11th Richard Cheney was in full and complete control of a properly functioning and parallel command and communications system to fulfill what that Delmart "Mike" Vreeland had warned of in August of 2001. "Let one happen. Stop the rest." I am certain also that he had complete access to every part of America's defense, law enforcement, and intelligence establishments that he wanted. Ladies and gentlemen of the jury, Richard Cheney is the maestro. Richard Cheney spoke to whom he needed to speak to while the nation's defenses foundered.

I also suspected that General Richard Myers and the NMCC's Deputy Director of Operations, General Winfield, were actually in the PEOC running the wargames as the attacks began. Thanks to Major Don Arias, we know that Vigilant Warrior was a Joint Chiefs' live-fly exercise being conducted on the morning of 9/11.

Richard Clarke left so many breadcrumbs in his book. None was more amusing or easily understood than the following passage:

> On one screen I could see the Situation Room. I grabbed Mike Fenzel. "How's it going over here?" I asked.
>
> "It's fine," Major Fenzel whispered, "but I can't hear the crisis conference because Mrs. Cheney keeps turning down the volume on you so she can hear CNN... and the Vice President keeps hanging up the open line to you."[16]

This would explain why, even after Richard Clarke reported that Cheney had complained about the communications in the Presidential bunker, Clarke could say, "I was amazed at the speed of the decisions coming from Cheney and, through him, from Bush."[17] I believe that Dick Cheney also had the ability using evolutions of the PROMIS software, to penetrate and override any other radar computer or communications system in the government.

I have placed before you a number of additional persons of interest who I also believe played a role in this crime. I have identified others who most certainly have a lot of explaining to do. As to the guilt of all of these people, you must decide. It is also up to you to decide whether or not any further investigations will be conducted, whether they will have the force of law, or whether what you decide will be enforced after you decide it.

There is no statute of limitations on murder.

There is another good reason why you should take to heart the case I have made and explore it thoroughly. For six years, since I sent out the first 68 copies of *From The Wilderness,* I and all of the wonderful people who write for *FTW,* have been telling you what was going to happen, long before it did happen.

Dale Allen Pfeiffer told you about Peak Oil, about natural gas shortages, about what Peak Oil and Gas means to our food supply. Today those issues are all over the mainstream print and Internet media, and the facts are pouring in with confirmation of Dale's insights.

Eight months before the Iraqi invasion, retired Special Forces Master Sergeant Stan Goff, a former instructor at West Point, warned the world that an invasion of Iraq would turn out exactly as it has today. His 2002 prediction is uncanny for its description of the current tragedy. As we approach our 1,000th American military death in Iraq; as Iraq is being flooded with arms merchants eager to supply a puppet regime; as heroin is sold on Baghdad's streets; and as endless thousands of Iraqi citizens are killed or maimed, the fulfillment of Stan's prescient warning evokes in me deep-seated grief and horror.

I told you four months before the first presidential primary that John Kerry would be the Democratic nominee in 2004. For more than two years I have predicted accurately where conflict would spread, how, and why. And for more than two years I have described, in several stories, a battle among the factions of the American state and a behind-the-scenes move by the CIA (Wall Street) to remove the neo-cons, which is coming to a head as this book is published. Why? Because the neo-cons are bad for business.

Before it became the subject of a federal grand jury which has resulted in both George W. Bush and Dick Cheney hiring criminal defense attorneys, I said that the administration's outing of a covert CIA officer named Valerie Plame — and the forged documents which the entire administration used to make the American people fear a nuclear-tipped Saddam — would be among the means by which the neo-cons were taken down. It's not Bush they want out as much as it is Cheney. George W. Bush is a mentally ill "empty suit."

There are dozens more instances where I, and all the people who have made *FTW*, have been far ahead of events. Why? Because we have the right map, and we are reading it. I have tried to give it to you. Read it. If not for your own sake, then for the sake of the generations in front of us who face a world of war, with no energy and no food; a world of economic collapse and brutal conflicts; a world which is being governed, quite literally, by madmen. Disregard what I present to you here at your own peril.

Just as the Founders performed a fundamentally personal responsibility as ethical human beings when they contemplated, planned, and organized the American republic, responding to the current crisis is your own personal responsibility. You cannot pass the buck. My greatest fear is that my readers will pass the buck anyway, but there is no one and no thing to take it from you. Fortunately there are many who are not fleeing into denial and they, acting on their own or in small communities, are beginning even now to prepare for what lies ahead. Their numbers are growing faster than I can imagine. We are not alone.

If you decide that you want to change things, I am telling you right now that you will change nothing until you change the way money works.

Looking into the future I see small (but very real) reasons to hope. Four states and more than 340 cities and counties in the US have passed resolutions opposing the Patriot Act. In August 2004 the House of Representatives passed a resolution saying that, no matter what threat or attack takes place, the 2004 presidential election should take place. (Who will count the votes and how they will be counted is another matter). Global awareness and discussion of Peak Oil is accelerating rapidly. And my beloved and much admired friend Cynthia McKinney defeated five challengers in a July 2004 primary with 51 percent of the vote to secure the nomination for her old seat in Congress. She is virtually certain to retake that seat in the 4th District of Georgia while retaining her seniority from five previous terms and she will not be silent.

You are reading this book.

It may not sound like much, but it will hopefully prove to be more than we think. Great things are accomplished from humble beginnings, and unlike oil, courage is a limitless and renewable resource.

You will make your decisions in the deepest places where you live. If there is anything that I want you to understand, it is that as a species and as a planet we have reached a point of self-imposed crisis that can neither be postponed nor evaded. That crisis and the values with which it is addressed are matters of life or death. But they are also even more than that: the crisis and our response will constitute, for good or evil, an open and monumental testament that fully and finally reveals our most fundamental nature. It will be a validation of what humanity's deepest priorities really are. If the best we can do for our tens of thousands of years of cultural evolution is to destroy our planet and then ourselves, then perhaps we do not deserve to survive.

Human beings have explored outward to the limits of this planet in search of resources and understanding and experience. We have peered deep into boundless space by sending probes billions of miles away, even beyond the outer planets of the solar system. We also explore backwards in time, extrapolating the sublime mysteries of Big Bang cosmology and theoretical physics. We spend hundreds of millions of dollars and lifetimes of intellectual passion on archaeological digs to find the earliest ancestors of our bodies and of our human mind.

But that mind is readily seduced toward astonishing feats of domination and cruelty. The combination of bureaucracy, technology, and rationalized quantitative measurement that built the great industrial civilization of the past 200 years, also created the Nazi death camps. There, efficiency and centralized control were as developed and refined as their uses were depraved and vile. The same cold, administrative approach to life that built the vast economies of the modern world is also preparing a terrible solution to the collapse of those economies. In the Empire's vision, love and art and religion and community are invisible; they count for nothing. It is as if the human race existed only in a statistical dimension; a calculus equation in need of a solution.

Distilled, all our pursuits essentially ask just two simple questions: Who are we really? And why are we here? We have been looking in the wrong places for our answers.

Let them that have ears listen. Let them that have eyes see.

Appendix A:
JOINT CHIEFS OF STAFF
"NORTHWOODS" DOCUMENT

THE JOINT CHIEFS OF STAFF
WASHINGTON 25, D.C.

UNCLASSIFIED

13 March 1962

MEMORANDUM FOR THE SECRETARY OF DEFENSE

Subject: Justification for US Military Intervention
in Cuba (TS)

1. The Joint Chiefs of Staff have considered the attached
Memorandum for the Chief of Operations, Cuba Project, which
responds to a request of that office for brief but precise
description of pretexts which would provide justification
for US military intervention in Cuba.

2. The Joint Chiefs of Staff recommend that the
proposed memorandum be forwarded as a preliminary submission
suitable for planning purposes. It is assumed that there
will be similar submissions from other agencies and that
these inputs will be used as a basis for developing a
time-phased plan. Individual projects can then be
considered on a case-by-case basis.

3. Further, it is assumed that a single agency will be
given the primary responsibility for developing military
and para-military aspects of the basic plan. It is
recommended that this responsibility for both overt and
covert military operations be assigned the Joint Chiefs of
Staff.

For the Joint Chiefs of Staff:

SYSTEMATICALLY REVIEWED
BY JCS ON _21 May 84_
CLASSIFICATION CONTINUED

L. L. LEMNITZER
Chairman
Joint Chiefs of Staff

1 Enclosure
Memo for Chief of Operations, Cuba Project

EXCLUDED FROM GDS

EXCLUDED FROM AUTOMATIC
REGRADING; DOD DIR 5200.10
DOES NOT APPLY

NOTE BY THE SECRETARIES

to the

JOINT CHIEFS OF STAFF

on

NORTHWOODS (S)

A report* on the above subject is submitted for consideration by the Joint Chiefs of Staff.

F. J. BLOUIN
M. J. INGELIDO
Joint Secretariat

---

* Not reproduced herewith; on file in Joint Secretariat

EXCLUDED FROM GDS
EXCLUDED FROM AUTOMATIC
REGRADING; DOD DIRECTIVE
5200.10 DOES NOT APPLY

TOP SECRET
JCS 1969/321   2165

9 March 1962

COPY   OF   COPIES
SPECIAL DISTRIBUTION

UNCLASSIFIED

REPORT BY THE DEPARTMENT OF DEFENSE AND
JOINT CHIEFS OF STAFF REPRESENTATIVE ON THE
CARIBBEAN SURVEY GROUP

to the

JOINT CHIEFS OF STAFF

on

CUBA PROJECT (TS)

The Chief of Operations, Cuba Project, has requested
that he be furnished the views of the Joint Chiefs of Staff
on this matter by 13 March 1962.

EXCLUDED FROM GDS

UNCLASSIFIED

TOP SECRET   SPECIAL HANDLING   NOFORN

UNCLASSIFIED

JUSTIFICATION FOR US MILITARY INTERVENTION IN CUBA (TS)

THE PROBLEM

1. As requested* by Chief of Operations, Cuba Project, the
Joint Chiefs of Staff are to indicate brief but precise
description of pretexts which they consider would provide
justification for US military intervention in Cuba.

FACTS BEARING ON THE PROBLEM

2. It is recognized that any action which becomes pretext
for US military intervention in Cuba will lead to a political
decision which then would lead to military action.

3. Cognizance has been taken of a suggested course of
action proposed** by the US Navy relating to generated
instances in the Guantanamo area.

4. For additional facts see Enclosure B.

DISCUSSION

5. The suggested courses of action appended to Enclosure A
are based on the premise that US military intervention will
result from a period of heightened US-Cuban tensions which
place the United States in the position of suffering justif-
iable grievances. World opinion, and the United Nations
forum should be favorably affected by developing the international image of the Cuban government as rash and irresponsible,
and as an alarming and unpredictable threat to the peace of
the Western Hemisphere.

6. While the foregoing premise can be utilized at the
present time it will continue to hold good only as long as
there can be reasonable certainty that US military intervention
in Cuba would not directly involve the Soviet Union. There is

---

* Memorandum for General Craig from Chief of Operations,
  Cuba Project, subject: "Operation MONGOOSE", dated
  5 March 1962, on file in General Craig's office.
** Memorandum for the Chairman, Joint Chiefs of Staff, from
  Chief of Naval Operations, subject: "Instances to
  Provoke Military Actions in Cuba (TS)", dated 8 March 1962,
  on file in General Craig's office.

2

UNCLASSIFIED

TOP SECRET   SPECIAL HANDLING   NOFORN

UNCLASSIFIED

as yet no bilateral mutual support agreement binding the USSR
to the defense of Cuba, Cuba has not yet become a member of the
Warsaw Pact, nor have the Soviets established Soviet bases
in Cuba in the pattern of US bases in Western Europe. Therefore,
since time appears to be an important factor in resolution of
the Cuba problem, all projects are suggested within the time
frame of the next few months.

CONCLUSION

7. The suggested courses of action appended to Enclosure A
satisfactorily respond to the statement of the problem. However,
these suggestions should be forwarded as a preliminary submission
suitable for planning purposes, and together with similar inputs
from other agencies, provide a basis for development of a single,
integrated, time-phased plan to focus all efforts on the
objective of justification for US military intervention in Cuba.

RECOMMENDATIONS

8. It is recommended that:

a. Enclosure A together with its attachments should be
forwarded to the Secretary of Defense for approval and
transmittal to the Chief of Operations, Cuba Project.

b. This paper NOT be forwarded to commanders of unified
or specified commands.

c. This paper NOT be forwarded to US officers assigned
to NATO activities.

d. This paper NOT be forwarded to the Chairman, US
Delegation, United Nations Military Staff Committee.

3

UNCLASSIFIED

SECRET   UNCLASSIFIED

MEMORANDUM FOR THE SECRETARY OF DEFENSE

Subject: Justification for US Military Intervention in Cuba (TS)

1. The Joint Chiefs of Staff have considered the attached Memorandum for the Chief of Operations, Cuba Project, which responds to a request* of that office for brief but precise description of pretexts which would provide justification for US military intervention in Cuba.

2. The Joint Chiefs of Staff recommend that the proposed memorandum be forwarded as a preliminary submission suitable for planning purposes. It is assumed that there will be similar submissions from other agencies and that these inputs will be used as a basis for developing a time-phased plan. Individual projects can then be considered on a case-by-case basis.   D

3. Further, it is assumed that a single agency will be given the primary responsibility for developing military and para-military aspects of the basic plan. It is recommended that this responsibility for both overt and covert military operations be assigned the Joint Chiefs of Staff.

---

* Memorandum for Gen Craig from Chief of Operations, Cuba Project, subject, "Operation MONGOOSE", dated 5 March 1962, on file in Gen Craig's office

4   Enclosure A

UNCLASSIFIED

TOP SECRET SPECIAL HANDLING NOFORN

SECRET SPECIAL HANDLING NOFORN

APPENDIX TO ENCLOSURE A

DRAFT

MEMORANDUM FOR CHIEF OF OPERATIONS, CUBA PROJECT

Subject: Justification for US Military Intervention
in Cuba (TS)

1. Reference is made to memorandum from Chief of Operations,
Cuba Project, for General Craig, subject: "Operation MONGOOSE",
dated 5 March 1962, which requested brief but precise
description of pretexts which the Joint Chiefs of Staff
consider would provide justification for US military intervention in Cuba.

2. The projects listed in the enclosure hereto are forwarded
as a preliminary submission suitable for planning purposes.
It is assumed that there will be similar submissions from
other agencies and that these inputs will be used as a basis
for developing a time-phased plan. The individual projects
can then be considered on a case-by-case basis.

3. This plan, incorporating projects selected from the
attached suggestions, or from other sources, should be
developed to focus all efforts on a specific ultimate
objective which would provide adequate justification for
US military intervention. Such a plan would enable a logical
build-up of incidents to be combined with other seemingly
unrelated events to camouflage the ultimate objective and
create the necessary impression of Cuban rashness and
irresponsibility on a large scale, directed at other
countries as well as the United States. The plan would also
properly integrate and time phase the courses of action to
be pursued. The desired resultant from the execution of
this plan would be to place the United States in the apparent
position of suffering defensible grievances from a rash and
irresponsible government of Cuba and to develop an international image of a Cuban threat to peace in the Western
Hemisphere.

 5 Appendix to
Enclosure A

TOP SECRET SPECIAL HANDLING NOFORN

UNCLASSIFIED

4. Time is an important factor in resolution of the Cuban problem. Therefore, the plan should be so time-phased that projects would be operable within the next few months.

5. Inasmuch as the ultimate objective is overt military intervention, it is recommended that primary responsibility for developing military and para-military aspects of the plan for both overt and covert military operations be assigned the Joint Chiefs of Staff.

Appendix to
Enclosure A

UNCLASSIFIED

TOP SECRET SPECIAL HANDLING NOFORN

SECRET SPECIAL HANDLING NOFORN

ANNEX TO APPENDIX TO ENCLOSURE A

PRETEXTS TO JUSTIFY US MILITARY INTERVENTION IN CUBA

(Note: The courses of action which follow are a preliminary submission suitable only for planning purposes. They are arranged neither chronologically nor in ascending order. Together with similar inputs from other agencies, they are intended to provide a point of departure for the development of a single, integrated, time-phased plan. Such a plan would permit the evaluation of individual projects within the context of cumulative, correlated actions designed to lead inexorably to the objective of adequate justification for US military intervention in Cuba).

1. Since it would seem desirable to use legitimate provocation as the basis for US military intervention in Cuba a cover and deception plan, to include requisite preliminary actions such as has been developed in response to Task 33 c, could be executed as an initial effort to provoke Cuban reactions. Harassment plus deceptive actions to convince the Cubans of imminent invasion would be emphasized. Our military posture throughout execution of the plan will allow a rapid change from exercise to intervention if Cuban response justifies.

2. A series of well coordinated incidents will be planned to take place in and around Guantanamo to give genuine appearance of being done by hostile Cuban forces.

a. Incidents to establish a credible attack (not in chronological order):

(1) Start rumors (many). Use clandestine radio.

(2) Land friendly Cubans in uniform "over-the-fence" to stage attack on base.

(3) Capture Cuban (friendly) saboteurs inside the base.

(4) Start riots near the base main gate (friendly Cubans).

Annex to Appendix
to Enclosure A

UNCLASSIFIED

TOP SECRET SPECIAL HANDLING NOFORN

UNCLASSIFIED NOFORN

(5) Blow up ammunition inside the base; start fires.

(6) Burn aircraft on air base (sabotage).

(7) Lob mortar shells from outside of base into base. Some damage to installations.

(8) Capture assault teams approaching from the sea or vicinity of Guantanamo City.

(9) Capture militia group which storms the base.

(10) Sabotage ship in harbor; large fires -- napthalene.

(11) Sink ship near harbor entrance. Conduct funerals for mock-victims (may be lieu of (10)).

b. United States would respond by executing offensive operations to secure water and power supplies, destroying artillery and mortar emplacements which threaten the base.

c. Commence large scale United States military operations.

3. A "Remember the Maine" incident could be arranged in several forms:

a. We could blow up a US ship in Guantanamo Bay and blame Cuba.

b. We could blow up a drone (unmanned) vessel anywhere in the Cuban waters. We could arrange to cause such incident in the vicinity of Havana or Santiago as a spectacular result of Cuban attack from the air or sea, or both. The presence of Cuban planes or ships merely investigating the intent of the vessel could be fairly compelling evidence that the ship was taken under attack. The nearness to Havana or Santiago would add credibility especially to those people that might have heard the blast or have seen the fire. The US could follow up with an air/sea rescue operation covered by US fighters to "evacuate" remaining members of the non-existent crew. Casualty lists in US newspapers would cause a helpful wave of national indignation.

4. We could develop a Communist Cuban terror campaign in the Miami area, in other Florida cities and even in Washington.

8

Annex to Appendix to Enclosure A

UNCLASSIFIED

TOP SECRET SPECIAL HANDLING NOFORN
UNCLASSIFIED

The terror campaign could be pointed at Cuban refugees seeking haven in the United States. We could sink a boatload of Cubans enroute to Florida (real or simulated). We could foster attempts on lives of Cuban refugees in the United States even to the extent of wounding in instances to be widely publicized. Exploding a few plastic bombs in carefully chosen spots, the arrest of Cuban agents and the release of prepared documents substantiating Cuban involvement also would be helpful in projecting the idea of an irresponsible government.

5. A "Cuban-based, Castro-supported" filibuster could be simulated against a neighboring Caribbean nation (in the vein of the 14th of June invasion of the Dominican Republic). We know that Castro is backing subversive efforts clandestinely against Haiti, Dominican Republic, Guatemala, and Nicaragua at present and possible others. These efforts can be magnified and additional ones contrived for exposure. For example, advantage can be taken of the sensitivity of the Dominican Air Force to intrusions within their national air space. "Cuban" B-26 or C-46 type aircraft could make cane-burning raids at night. Soviet Bloc incendiaries could be found. This could be coupled with "Cuban" messages to the Communist underground in the Dominican Republic and "Cuban" shipments of arms which would be found, or intercepted, on the beach.

6. Use of MIG type aircraft by US pilots could provide additional provocation. Harassment of civil air, attacks on surface shipping and destruction of US military drone aircraft by MIG type planes would be useful as complementary actions. An F-86 properly painted would convince air passengers that they saw a Cuban MIG, especially if the pilot of the transport were to announce such fact. The primary drawback to this suggestion appears to be the security risk inherent in obtaining or modifying an aircraft. However, reasonable copies of the MIG could be produced from US resources in about three months.

<table>
<tr><td>9</td><td>Annex to Appendix
to Enclosure A</td></tr>
</table>

TOP SECRET SPECIAL HANDLING NOFORN

UNCLASSIFIED

7. Hijacking attempts against civil air and surface craft should appear to continue as harassing measures condoned by the government of Cuba. Concurrently, genuine defections of Cuban civil and military air and surface craft should be encouraged.

8. It is possible to create an incident which will demonstrate convincingly that a Cuban aircraft has attacked and shot down a chartered civil airliner enroute from the United States to Jamaica, Guatemala, Panama or Venezuela. The destination would be chosen only to cause the flight plan route to cross Cuba. The passengers could be a group of college students off on a holiday or any grouping of persons with a common interest to support chartering a non-scheduled flight.

   a. An aircraft at Eglin AFB would be painted and numbered as an exact duplicate for a civil registered aircraft belonging to a CIA proprietary organization in the Miami area. At a designated time the duplicate would be substituted for the actual civil aircraft and would be loaded with the selected passengers, all boarded under carefully prepared aliases. The actual registered aircraft would be converted to a drone.

   b. Take off times of the drone aircraft and the actual aircraft will be scheduled to allow a rendezvous south of Florida. From the rendezvous point the passenger-carrying aircraft will descend to minimum altitude and go directly into an auxiliary field at Eglin AFB where arrangements will have been made to evacuate the passengers and return the aircraft to its original status. The drone aircraft meanwhile will continue to fly the filed flight plan. When over Cuba the drone will being transmitting on the international distress frequency a "MAY DAY" message stating he is under attack by Cuban MIG aircraft. The transmission will be interrupted by destruction of the aircraft which will be triggered by radio signal. This will allow ICAO radio

10

stations in the Western Hemisphere to tell the US what
has happened to the aircraft instead of the US trying to
"sell" the incident.

9. It is possible to create an incident which will make it
appear that Communist Cuban MIGs have destroyed a USAF aircraft
over international waters in an unprovoked attack.

    a. Approximately 4 or 5 F-101 aircraft will be dispatched
in trail from Homestead AFB, Florida, to the vicinity of Cuba.
Their mission will be to reverse course and simulate fakir
aircraft for an air defense exercise in southern Florida.
These aircraft would conduct variations of these flights at
frequent intervals. Crews would be briefed to remain at
least 12 miles off the Cuban coast; however, they would be
required to carry live ammunition in the event that hostile
actions were taken by the Cuban MIGs.

    b. On one such flight, a pre-briefed pilot would fly
tail-end Charley at considerable interval between aircraft.
While near the Cuban Island this pilot would broadcast that
he had been jumped by MIGs and was going down. No other
calls would be made. The pilot would then fly directly
west at extremely low altitude and land at a secure base, an
Eglin auxiliary. The aircraft would be met by the proper
people, quickly stored and given a new tail number. The
pilot who had performed the mission under an alias, would
resume his proper identity and return to his normal place
of business. The pilot and aircraft would then have
disappeared.

    c. At precisely the same time that the aircraft was
presumably shot down a submarine or small surface craft
would disburse F-101 parts, parachute, etc., at approximately
15 to 20 miles off the Cuban coast and depart. The pilots
returning to Homestead would have a true story as far as
they knew. Search ships and aircraft could be dispatched
and parts of aircraft found.

ENCLOSURE B

FACTS BEARING ON THE PROBLEM

1. The Joint Chiefs of Staff have previously stated[*]
that US unilateral military intervention in Cuba can be
undertaken in the event that the Cuban regime commits hostile
acts against US forces or property which would serve as an
incident upon which to base overt intervention.

2. The need for positive action in the event that current
covert efforts to foster an internal Cuban rebellion are
unsuccessful was indicated[**] by the Joint Chiefs of Staff
on 7 March 1962, as follows:

" - - - determination that a credible internal
revolt is impossible of attainment during the next
9-10 months will require a decision by the United States
to develop a Cuban "provocation" as justification for
positive US military action."

3. It is understood that the Department of State also is
preparing suggested courses of action to develop justification
for US military intervention in Cuba.

_____
[*] JCS 1969/303
[**] JCS 1969/313

Appendix B:
Vreeland Financial Document Sample

FROM : D VREELAND

FAX NO. : 14163623222

May. 29 2002 07:46PM P1

NET: NYC   FILE: OPEN *.*   CODE: SCC-SUP-14-STA-19
REQ#:5426741   CONTACT: SUP-14   AUTH: 3329997

FIN, p 67   t3.45

890810 / 34 / 52 / 364117 / Five Hundred Million U.S. Dollars
                            [$ 500,000,000.00]
Sender: Coutts Bank / Londond England   ACCT # 2339153
Receiver: Morgan Guaranty Trust / NY NY / ACCT # 72 - 200 - 0011
Credit # 002 - 930274 - 79   Martwell Investments
Transaction # L B N / NICK 0941   Security Code: D B M - 102

2nd WIRE
See 890f

890810 / 36 / 11 / 716881 / Five Hundred Million U. S. Dollars
                            [$ 500,000,000.00]
Sender: Chase Manhattan Bank / NY NY / ACCT# 02 - 38168 - 311
Receiver: Marine Midland Bank / NY NY / ACCT# 06 - 1348 - 212
Credit: Pilgrim Investments Inc.
Reference: 7.5 - 20

7.5% - 20yr PBN

MARTWELL INVESTMENTS

890810 / 36 / 11 / 716882 / One Billion U.S. Dollars
                            [$ 1,000,000,000,.00]
Sender: Chase Manhattan Bank / NY NY / ACCT# 20 - 38168 - 311
Receiver: Arab Bank Corp / Monaco / ACCT# 6 - 1 - 38622
Credit: Pilgrim Investments Inc.
Reference: 7.5 - 20

7.5% - 20yr PBN

890810 / 36 / 11 / 716883 / Five Hundred Million U.S. Dollars
                            [$ 500,000,000.00]
Sender: Chase Manhattan Bank / NY NY / ACCT # 02 - 38168 - 311
Receiver: Bank of America Walnut Creek CA. / ACCT # 04 - 382 - 1
Credit: Francis X. Driscoll Trust
Reference: Prime Bank Note Purchase

MARTWELL INVESTMENT

890811 / 36 / 11 / 918119 / Ten Billion U.S. Dollars
                            [$ 10,000,000,000.00]
Sender: Chase Manhattan Bank / NY NY / ACCT# 02 - 38168 - 311
Receiver: Metropolitian Federal of Tennessee / Nashville Tn /
ACCT# 312
Reference: Trading Account / 09 - 7547 - 881

/11/

890811 / 36 / 1018115 / One Hundred Billion Dollars
                        [$ 100,000,000,000.00]
Sender: Chase Manhattan Bank / NY NY / ACCT # 01 -3081 - 12
Receiver: First Interstate Bank of Denver / Denver Co. / ACCT# 0621884
Credit: Pilgrim Investment Inc.
Reference: D B M - 102

Home

About JW

How You Can Help

Media Center

JW Cases

Contact

Contribute

JW Store

JW Events

Specials

Email this article   Printer friendly page

FOR IMMEDIATE RELEASE

July 17, 2003   Contact: Press Office
                                                        (202) 646-5172

MEDIA ADVISORY

CHENEY ENERGY TASK FORCE DOCUMENTS FEATURE MAP OF IRAQI OILFIELDS

Commerce & State Department Reports to Task Force Detail Oilfield & Gas Projects, Contracts & Exploration

Saudi Arabian & UAE Oil Facilities Profiled As Well

(Washington, DC) Judicial Watch, the public interest group that investigates and prosecutes government corruption and abuse, said today that documents turned over by the Commerce Department, under court order as a result of Judicial Watch's Freedom of Information Act (FOIA) lawsuit concerning the activities of the Cheney Energy Task Force, contain a map of Iraqi oilfields, pipelines, refineries and terminals, as well as 2 charts detailing Iraqi oil and gas projects, and "Foreign Suitors for Iraqi Oilfield Contracts." The documents, which are dated March 2001, are available on the Internet at: www.JudicialWatch.org.

The Saudi Arabian and United Arab Emirates (UAE)

Also in the Media Center

- JW Radio (Saturday)
- JW Radio (Daily)
- JW Television
- News Links
- Print Ads
- Newsletters
- Commentary
- A/V Clips
- Additional Links

Press Release Archives

2002

2001

2000

1999

1998

1997

documents likewise feature a map of each country's oilfields, pipelines, refineries and tanker terminals. There are supporting charts with details of the major oil and gas development projects in each country that provide information on the projects, costs, capacity, oil company and status or completion date.

Judicial Watch has been seeking these documents under FOIA since April 19, 2001. Judicial Watch was forced to file a lawsuit in the U.S. District Court for the District of Columbia (Judicial Watch Inc. v. Department of Energy, et al., Civil Action No. 01-0981) when the government failed to comply with the provisions of the FOIA law. U.S. District Court Judge Paul J. Friedman ordered the government to produce the documents on March 5, 2002.

The documents were produced in response to Judicial Watch's on-going efforts to ensure transparency and accountability in government on behalf of the American people. Judicial Watch aggressively pursues those goals by making FOIA requests and seeking access to public information concerning government operations. When the government fails to abide by these "sunshine laws" Judicial Watch files lawsuits in order to obtain the requested information and to hold responsible government officials accountable.

"These documents show the importance of the Energy Task Force and why its operations should be open to the public," stated Judicial Watch President Tom Fitton.

Click here for: MAPS AND CHARTS OF OILFIELDS: CHENEY ENERGY TASK FORCE

Top of Page

Foreign Suitors for Iraqi Oilfield Contracts
as of 5 March 2001

Country	Firm	Iraqi Oil & Gas Projects	Comments/Status
Algeria	Sonatrach	Tuba	Discussions. PSC.
		Blocks 6 & 7	Collecting data.
Australia	BHP	Halfaya	Discussions. PSC.
		Block 6	Collected data.
Belgium	Petrofina	Ahdab	Technical/economic studies (China's CNPC awarded PSC).
		Block 2	Collected data.
Canada	Ranger	Block 6, other	Signed MOU with Baghdad.
	Bow Canada	Khurmala	Joint proposal w/Czech Republic's Strojexport
		Hamrin	Joint proposal w/Czech Republic's Strojexport
	Alberta Energy	Unidentified	None
	CanOxy	Ratawi	Discussions. PSC.
		Block 5	Collected data.
	Chauvco Res.	Ayn Zalah	Advanced talks by late 1996. Service contract for advanced oil recovery (gas injection project) in this aging field.
	Escondido	Ratawi	Discussions. PSC.
		Block 5	Collecting data.
	Talisman	Hamrin, E. Baghdad	Service contract negotiations October 1999.
	IPC	Hamrin	Discussions. Service contract.
	PanCanadian	Unidentified	None
China	CNPC	Ahdab	Production Sharing Contract (PSC) signed June 1997.
		Halfaya	Bid for $4 bn, 23-year PSC.
		Luhais & Subba	Discussions. Service contract.
		Block 5	Collected data, discussions.
	Norinco	Ahdab	PSC signed June 1997 (CNPC consortium partner).
		Rafidain	Discussions. PSC.
	Sinochem	Rafidain	Discussions. PSC.
Czech Republic	Strojexport	Hamrin	Joint project with Bow Canada. Sent team to Iraq in Sept 1997.
		Khurmala	Joint project with Bow Canada
Finland	Neste Oy	Unidentified	None
France	Total Elf Aquitaine	Majnoon	PSC "agreed in principle" January 1997.
	Forasol SA	Saddam	Feasibility study presented to Baghdad in 1997, updated in 1998.
	IBEX	Hamrin	Technical discussions.
	Perenco	Rafidain	Discussions. PSC.
	Total Elf Aquitaine	Nahr Umr	PSC "agreed in principle" January 1997.
Germany	Deminex	Block 1	Collected data.
	Preussag	Ahdab	Technical/economic studies (China's CNPC later awarded PSC).
		Block 2	Collected data
	Slavneft	N. Rumaylah	Subcontractor to Lukoil consortium.
Greece	Kriti	Gharraf	Discussions. PSC.
Hungary	Hanpetro	Block 3	Collected data.
India	ONGC	Tuba	Advanced contract talks in October 1999 (ONGC drilled at least four wells in Tuba in the 1980s). PSC.
		Halfaya	Discussions. PSC.
		Block 8	Collected data.
	Reliance	Tuba	Discussions.
Indonesia	Pertamina	Tuba	Finalized discussions for a PSC in late 1997.
		Block 3	Collected data
Ireland	Bula	Block 4	Discussions.
Italy	Agip	Nasiriya	PSC initialed Apr 97. $2 bn, 23-year project (w/partner Repsol).
		Iraq-Turkey gas pipeline	Discussions.
		Block 1	Collected data, discussions.
	Snamprogetti	Luhais & Subba	Discussions. Service contract.

35AS0713

Country	Firm	Iraqi Oil & Gas Project	Comments/Status
Japan	Japex	Gharraf	Bid and technical/economic oilfield study submitted to Baghdad. March 1997. PSC.
	Mitsubishi	Luhais & Subba	Discussions. Service contract.
Malaysia	Petronas	Ratawi	Discussions. PSC.
		Tuba	Discussions. PSC.
		Block 2	Collected data, discussions
Mexico	Pemex	Unidentified	None.
Netherlands	Larmag	Subba & Luhais	Discussions. Service contract.
	Dutch Royal Shell	Ratawi	Discussions.
		Block 8	Collected data.
Norway	Statoil	Block 1	Collected data.
Pakistan	Crescent	Ratawi	Discussions. PSC.
		Block 5	Collected data.
Romania	Petrom	Khurmala Dome (Karkuk)	Apparently awarded service contract, project in advanced technical infrastructure design phase (setting equipment & materials specifications for project).
		Luhais & Subba	Discussions. Service contract.
		Block 4	Collected data, discussions.
		Qayyarah	Contract talks. Service contract for well drilling and engineering.
	Mol	Block 3	Discussions.
Russia	Kond Petroleum	Rafidain	Discussions. Russian firm Sidanko a possible partner. PSC.
	Lukoil	W. Qurnah	PSC signed March 1997. Topographic surveys in 1998.
		N. Rumaylah	Service contract negotiations to upgrade water injection facilities, develop additional geologic reservoirs.
	Zarubezneft	W. Qurnah	PSC signed March 1997 (Lukoil consortium partner).
		N. Rumaylah	Service contract negotiations (w/Lukoil consortium).
		Hamrin	Invited to bid in mid-1997. Service contract.
	Mashinoimport	W. Qurnah	PSC signed March 1997 (Lukoil consortium partner).
		Luhais, & Subba	Discussions. Service contract.
		N. Rumaylah	Service contract negotiations (w/Lukoil consortium).
	Tatarneft	N. Rumaylah	Subcontractor to Lukoil consortium.
	Rostneft	N. Rumaylah	Subcontractor to Lukoil consortium.
	Sidanko	N. Rumaylah	Subcontractor to Lukoil consortium.
S. Korea	Sangyong	Halfaya	Bidding for $4 bn, 23-year PSC. Seoul in June 1997 invited Iraq Oil Minister to S. Korea for signing ceremony.
	Samsung	Halfaya	Bidding (part of Korean consortium). PSC.
	Pedco	Halfaya	" " "
	Hambo	Halfaya	" " "
	Yukong	Halfaya	" " "
	Daewoo	Rafidain	Discussions. PSC.
Spain	Repsol	Nasiriya	PSC initialed Apr 97. $2 bn, 23-year project (w/partner Agip).
		Block 4	Collected data.
Taiwan	CPC	Gharraf	Discussions. PSC.
		Rafidain	Discussions. PSC.
		Tuba	Discussions. PSC.
Tunisia	Setcar	Unidentified	None
Turkey	TPAO	Gharraf	Bid for PSC. Oilfield study completed January 1997.
		Mansuriya Gas Field	Service contract signed May 1997 to develop field, purchase gas.
		Block 4	Reprocessed seismic data, conducting laboratory studies.
UK	Branch Energy	Gharraf	Discussions. PSC.
	Pacific Resources	Rafidain	Discussions. PSC.
Vietnam	PetroVietnam	Amara	Service contract. Near signing Oct 1999

Saudi Arabia:
Major Oil and Natural Gas Development Projects

Project	Completion Date	Cost ($ million)	Capacity	Company
Aramco Crude Oil Development Projects[1]				
Haradh Gas-Oil Separation Plant No. 2	March 2003	$320	300,000 b/d	Aramco
Qatif Crude Expansion	2005	N/A	500,000 b/d	Aramco
Haradh Gas-Oil Separation Plant No. 3	N/A	N/A	300,000 b/d	Aramco
Projects Open to Foreign Companies[2]				
South Ghawar Area Development (Core Gas Venture #1)	N/A	N/A	N/A	TotalFinaElf,, ExxonMobil, Shell, BP, Chevron/Texaco, ENI, Phillips
Red Sea Area Development (Core Gas Venture #2)	N/A	N/A	N/A	TotalFinaElf,, ExxonMobil Shell, Conoco, Enron/Occidental, Marathon
Shaybah Area Development (Core Gas Venture #3)	N/A	N/A	N/A	TotalFinaElf,, ExxonMobil, Shell, Conoco, Enron/Occidental, Phillips

[1] These projects are designed to replace declining capacity elsewhere in Saudi Arabia's oil infrastructure, keeping total Saudi oil production capacity at about 10.5 million barrels per day. This list does not include routine expenditures necessary to maintain existing oil production facilities or selected natural gas projects managed exclusively by Aramco.

[2] Total direct investment potential in these projects is projected to range up to $40 billion, according to Foreign Minister Saud al-Faysal.

Source: Middle East Economic Survey, Platt's, and other industry journals.

35AS0713

Selected Oil Facilities in Saudi Arabia (U)

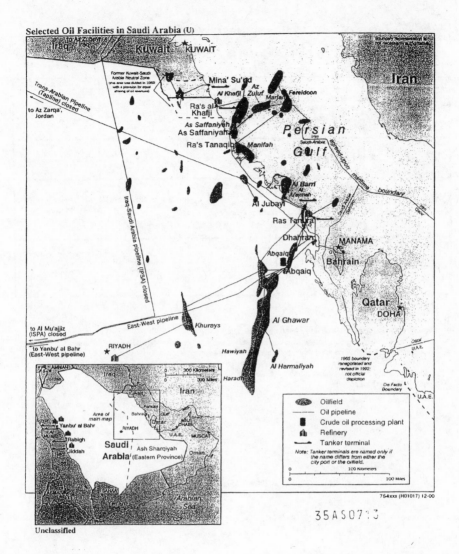

35AS0713

DOC044-0003

United Arab Emirates [1,2,3]

Major Oil and Gas Development Projects

Project	Cost	Capacity	Company/Country	Status
Bab and Bu Hasa expansion including gas reinjection	$2 billion ($1 billion drilling, $600 million field development, $270 million infrastructure)	200,000 b/d	Adco[4]	Proposals due 2nd quarter 2001
Coastal Oilfield development Project at Al-Dhabiya and Rumaitha/Shanayel	$1.5 billion	Early production of 80,000 b/d could be ready by 2007	Adco[4]	Still in Study Phase
Upper Zakum Expansion	Not Available	Acquisition would give Zadco access to new technologies needed to expand production capacity by unspecified amount	Bidders include Shell, ExxonMobil, BP, TotalElfFina	Proposal to acquire equity shares of Zadkum Devel. Co. (ZADCO) due soon--no date specified.
Dolphin Gas Project[3,5]	$8 billion	20 bcm per year	UOG, Qatar, Enron and TotalElfFina	Commercial framework for the project was agreed upon in March 2001.

1) Current UAE oil production capacity is 2.5 million b/d.
2) Capacity expansion plans include adding 600,000 b/d by 2005.
3) Investment opportunities are in downstream projects especially power, desalination and pipeline projects.
4) Adco includes Adnoc, Exxon/Mobil, Shell, BP, TotalElfFina and Partex.
5) The Dolphin Project is a 25 year project that will take Qatar gas to the UAE to stimulate economic growth. Despite the signing of the framework agreement many hurdles remain, including firm sales and purchase deals with customers.

35AS0713

DOC044-0002

Selected Oil Facilities of the United Arab Emirates

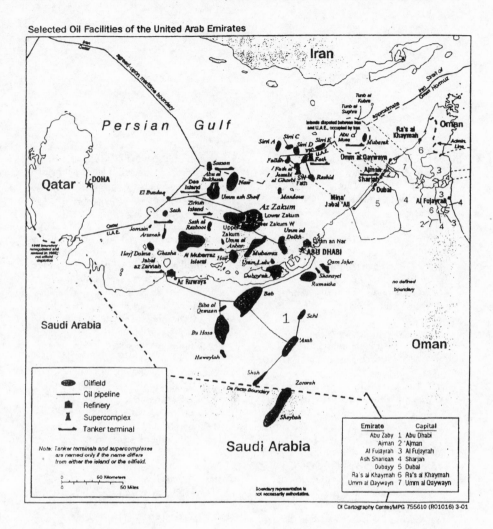

Endnotes

Introduction

1 Richard A. Clarke, *Against All Enemies,* Free Press 2004, p 126.

2 David Rising, "Convicted 9/11 Suspect Leaves Prison," Associated Press, April 7, 2004.

3 Robert B. Stinnett, *Day of Deceit,* Touchstone Books, 2001; John Toland, *Infamy,* Berkeley Publishing Group, 1991.

4 Peter Dale Scott, *The War Conspiracy: The Secret Road to the Second Indochina War,* Bobbs-Merrill, 1972.

5 See Appendix A.

6 <www.mdw.army.mil/news/ Contingency_Planning.html> A PDF archive of this web page has been saved in my files.

7 James Ridgeway, "Bush's 9-11 Secrets, The Government Received Warnings of Bin Laden's Plans to Attack New York and DC," *Village Voice,* July 31, 2003.

8 Eric V. Larson and John E. Peters, Preparing the U.S. Army for Homeland Security, MR-1251/A, ISBN: 0-8330-2919-3, MR-1251/A © 2001, pp. 52, 67, 68. <www.rand.org/publications/ MR/MR1251/>.

9 That adventure saw me featured in the pages of *People* magazine in July of 1992 after volunteers had placed Perot ahead of both Bill Clinton and George H.W. Bush in the polls. I have come to view Perot's sudden withdrawal from that contest as one of the great political betrayals of all time.

10 <http://news.bbc.co.uk/1/hi/world/ americas/1581063.stm>

11 <www.cia.gov/cia/publications/cocaine/ index.html1>. "Central Intelligence Agency Inspector General, Report of Investigation: Allegations of Connections between CIA and the Contras in Cocaine Trafficking to the United States" *(96-0143-IG), October 8, 1998,* <www.cia.gov/cia/publications/cocaine/ index.html> A member of Waters's staff was later fired, presumably for telling of the connection between the impeachment and the release of the report.

12 "Bobby, I didn't know," <www.fromthewilderness.com/free/ pandora/rfk.html.> I say "interested parties and their allies in the dominant political class" because it isn't the entirety of that class that engages in disinformation and cover-up. President and Senator Kennedy were part of the political elite, as was the late Senator Paul Wellstone. But so are several long-lived members of both houses who worked for genuine investigation and disclosure, such as Senator Frank Church, and Congressmen James Traficant, Henry Waxman, and Henry B. Gonzales.

13 Interview with Colin Campbell, *FTW,* October 23, 2002, <www.fromthewilderness.com/free/ ww3/102302_campbell.html>

Chapter 1: Petroleum Man

1 "The world now uses about 26 billion barrels of oil a year, but, in new field discoveries we are finding less than six billion." Walter Youngquist, "The Post Petroleum Paradigm," in *Population and Environment,* Vol. 20, no. 4,(March 1999); Colin Campbell, founder of the Association for the Study of Peak Oil, JPMorgan Chase investor conference call, April 7, 2004. <www.mnforsustain.org/youngquist_w_ post_petroleum_and_population.htm>.

2 Dale Allen Pfeiffer, "Leaping off the Natural Gas Cliff (And a Word Concerning the Foolishness of Ethanol)," in *FTW,* June 21, 2002, <www.fromthewilderness.com/ free/ww3/062102_gascliff.html>.

3 National Energy Policy (NEP), "Chapter 1: Taking Stock: Energy Challenges Facing

the United States," <www.whitehouse.gov/energy/Chapter1.pdf>.

4 Interview with Colin Campbell, *FTW*, October 23, 2002, <www.fromthewilderness.com/free/ww3/102302_campbell.html>; cf. <http://www.istp.murdoch.edu.au/publications/projects/oilfleay/03worldoilgas.html>.

5 Dale Pfeiffer, "The Background is Oil", *FTW*, December 18, 2001, <www.fromthewilderness.com/free/ww3/dec2001_files/background_is_oil.html>

6 Richard C. Duncan, "The Peak of World Oil Production and the Road to the Olduvai Gorge", <www.hubbertpeak.com/Duncan/olduvai2000.htm>

7 National Energy Policy, "Overview", op. cit.

8 Patrick Whitfield, *Permaculture in a Nutshell*, Permanent Publications, 1993, p. 1.

9 Walter Youngquist, "The Post-Petroleum Paradigm — and Population" in *Population and Environment: A Journal of Interdisciplinary Studies,* Vol. 20, no. 4, March 1999, <http://dieoff.org/page171.htm>.

10 National Energy Policy (NEP), "Chapter 8: Strengthening Global Alliances", <www.whitehouse.gov/energy/Chapter8.pdf>.

11 Youngquist, op. cit.

12 See Emmanuel Todd, *After the Empire: The Breakdown of the American Order* ,(European Perspectives: A Series In Social Thought And Cultural Criticism), Columbia University Press, February 2004.

13 Ibid.

14 Ibid.

15 Colin Campbell, "Peak Oil: A Turning Point for Mankind," (lecture at the Technical University of Clausthal, Germany), <www.oilcrisis.com/campbell/>.

16 Katherine Q. Seelye, "White House Joins Fight Against Electric Cars," *New York Times*, October 10, 2002, <http://query.nytimes.com/search/abstract?res=F20F17FE3D5E0C738DDDA90994DA404482>.

17 Duncan, op. cit.

18 Ibid.

19 Mark Clayton, "America's New Coal Rush," *Christian Science Monitor,* February 26, 2004.

20 "Changing All the Rules," Bruce Barcott, *New York Times*, April 4, 2004.

21 National Energy Policy (NEP), "Chapter 1: Taking Stock: Energy Challenges Facing the United States," <www.whitehouse.gov/energy/Chapter1.pdf>.

22 David Pimentel, "Energy and Dollar Costs of Ethanol Production with Corn," *Hubbert Center Newsletter* no. 98/2 (M. King Hubbert Center for Petroleum Supply Studies), <http://hubbert.mines.edu/news/Pimentel_98-2.pdf>.

23 Regarding South America, for example, Pfeiffer writes, "Venezuela also holds what is perhaps the world's greatest deposit of unconventional oil: the Orinoco oil belt, which contains an estimated 1.2 trillion barrels of the sludge known as heavy oil. This is a great resource; however, it is known as heavy sludge because it is highly contaminated by sulfur and heavy metals. The removal and disposal of these elements would have to be attained without destroying the economic viability of the deposits. And, as with the Canadian oil sands, such a project is unlikely to be brought online in time to offset the shock of declining oil production." Cf. Pfeiffer, "What Will Be the Next Target of the Oil Coup?" in *FTW*, January 29, 2002: <www.fromthewilderness.com/free/ww3/01_29_02_what_next.html>.

24 Interview with Colin Campbell, *FTW*, op. cit.

25 IHS Energy News Release, January 12, 2004, IHS Energy Releases its 2003 Annual Supplement — Discoveries and Highlights — Listing all Major E&P Discoveries and Highlighting Key Corporate Activity.

26 "Has global oil production peaked?" The *Christian Science Monitor*, January 29, 2004. Note: Declining discovery rates since the 1960s are abundantly documented and have not been disputed, even by the staunchest critics of Peak Oil. How could they be?

27 See Bruce Thomson, "The Oil Crash and You", <www.geocities.com/davidmdelaney/oil-depletion/convince-sheet-bruce-thompson.pddf> ; and Dale Allen Pfeiffer, "The Background is Oil," *FTW*, Vol. IV no. 9, December 18, 2001,

<www.fromthewilderness.com/free/ww3/dec2001_files/background_is_oil.html>.

28 Richard C. Duncan and Walter Youngquist, "The World Petroleum Life-Cycle," paper presented at the PTTC Workshop, "OPEC Oil Pricing and Independent Oil Producers," Petroleum Technology Transfer Council, Petroleum Engineering Program, University of Southern California, Los Angeles, October 22, 1998: <www.dieoff.com/page133.pdf>.

29 Ibid.

30 Michael C. Ruppert, "Colin Campbell on Oil: Perhaps the World's Foremost Expert on Oil and the Oil Business Confirms the Ever More Apparent Reality of the Post-9-11 World," *FTW*, October 23, 2002: <www.fromthewilderness.com/free/ww3/102302_campbell.html>.

31 Youngquist, op. cit.

32 Michael C. Ruppert, "Paris Peak Oil Conference Reveals Deepening Crisis," , *FTW*, May 30, 2003. <www.fromthewilderness.com/free/ww3/053103_aspo.html.>

33 Jeff Gerth, "Forecast of Rising Demand Challenges Tired Saudi Fields" *New York Times*, February 24, 2004.

34 "Strategic Energy Policy Challenges for the 21st Century: Report of an Independent Task Force Sponsored by the James A. Baker III Institute for Public Policy of Rice University and the Council on Foreign Relations (CFR report), <www.rice.edu/projects/baker/Pubs/workingpapers/cfrbipp_energy/energytf.htm>.

35 Ibid.

36 National Energy Policy: Overview, op. cit., <www.whitehouse.gov/energy/Overview.pdf>.

37 Zbigniew Brzezinski, *The Grand Chessboard: American Primacy and its Geostrategic Imperatives,* Basic Books, 1997, p. 125.

38 Anthony H. Cordesman (with assistance of Sarin Hacatoryan), "The Changing Geopolitics of Energy — Part IV: Regional Developments in the Gulf and Energy Issues Affecting Iran, Iraq and Libya," Strategic Energy Initiative, Center for Strategic and International Studies, August 12, 1998,

<www.csis.org/stratassessment/reports/energyiv81298.pdf>.

39 Interview with Colin Campbell, *FTW*, October 23, 2002: <www.fromthewilderness.com/free/ww3/102302_campbell.html>.

40 Dale Allen Pfeiffer, "Oil Prices and Recession," in *FTW*, April 4, 2002, <www.fromthewilderness.com/free/ww3/04_04_02_oil_recession.html>.

41 Ibid.

42 CFR report, op. cit.

43 National Energy Policy (NEP), "Chapter 1: Taking Stock, op. cit. "

44 "Shell Cuts Oil Reserves Again," MSNBC, March 18, 2004; "Shell Reassesses Reserves Third Time," *Times of London,* April 19,2004.

45 "El Paso Trims Proven Reserves 41%," Reuters, February 18, 2004.

46 James Flanigan, "Increased Scrutiny Could Shrink World Oil Reserves," *Los Angeles Times,* January 18, 2004.

47 Carl Mortished, "North Sea exploration a loser, say oil experts," *Times Online*, January 26, 2004.

48 CFR report, op. cit.

49 Ruppert, "Colin Campbell on Oil," op. cit.

50 Duncan, op. cit. The source of Duncan's figures is BP Amoco: <www.bpamoco.com/worldenergy/>.

51 Dr. John Price, "Oil and Global Recession: A Political Appraisal," May 7, 2001, <www.invisibleuniverse.com/Juice/OilandGlobalRecessionv5.pdf>.

52 Matthew Simmons, "Solving Our Energy Crisis: The Important Role which the Offshore Oil & Gas Industry Must Play," April 30, 2001, <www.simmonsco-intl.com/domino/html/research.nsf/DocID/0FCF6F796370BDC886256B1F004CD4AD/$File/154.pdf>.

53 Charles Galton Darwin, *The Next Million Years,* Doubleday, 1952, p. 210. Cited in Youngquist, "The Post-Petroleum Paradigm," op. cit.

54 J. E. Cohen, *How Many People Can the Earth Support?* W.W. Norton, 1995.

55 D. Pimentel and M. Pimentel, eds. *Food, Energy, And Society* (revised edition), University Press of Colorado, 1996.

56 Jay Hanson, "The 'Longage of Critters' Problem," <http://ww.dieoff.com>.

57 The following are just some of the many news reports that followed this development: "Anthrax Spreads in Washington," *FOX News*, <www.foxnews.com/story/0,2933,37330,00.html>; Steve Moore's "CIA Scientist: A Key Suspect in US Anthrax Attack," Centre for Research on Globalisation, <www.globalresearch.ca/articles/MOO208A.html>; David Ensor, "Official: CIA Uses Anthrax, But No Link to Letters," CNN, <www.cnn.com/2001/US/12/16/cia.anthrax/>; and Matthew L. Wald, "CIA Denies Being Source of Anthrax," *L.A. Times*, December 17, 2001: <www.commondreams.org/headlines01/1217-02.htm>.

58 Space constraints necessitated focusing on oil in this chapter; readers interested in more detail about similar problems with natural gas should consult Dale Allen Pfeiffer, "Leaping Off the Natural Gas Cliff (and a Word Concerning the Foolishness of Ethanol)," in *FTW*, June 21, 2002, op. cit.; and Randy Udall and Steve Andrews, "Methane Madness: A Natural Gas Primer," Aspen, Colorado: Community Office for Resource Efficiency (C.O.R.E.), 2001: <www.hubbertpeak.com/gas/primer/>.

59 "Paris Peak Oil Conference Reveals Deepening Crisis," op. cit.

Chapter 2: Cheney Knew

1 Associated Press, December 15, 2003.

2 Associated Press, January 17, 2004.

3 *Washington Post*, March 2, 2004.

4 See Appendix B.

5 "Japan and China Battle for Russia's Oil and Gas," *New York Times*, January 3, 2004.

6 <www.fromthewilderness.com/free/ww3/index.html#oil>.

7 *San Francisco Chronicle*, April 2, 2004.

8 James Kenneth Galbraith, "The Cost of Empire," *American Prospect*, November 18, 2002.

9 Jeff Gerth, "Forecast of Rising Demand Challenges Tired Saudi Fields," *New York Times*, February 24, 2004.

10 Kjell Aleklett, "Dick Cheney, Peak Oil and the Final Countdown," Association for the Study of Peak Oil, <www.peakoil.net>, May 12 2004.

11 Dick Cheney, Speech to the IP Autumn Lunch, November 15, 1999.

12 Richard Heinberg, "Smoking Gun: The CIA's Interest in Peak Oil," *From The Wilderness*, August 2003, <www.fromthewilderness.com/free/ww3/081503_cia_russ_summary.html>.

Chapter 3: The CIA is Wall Street, and Drug Money is King

1 Bauquis, P-R., "*L'esprit de synthese et la strategie petroliere,*" *Petrole et Techniques*, no. 434, Sept-Oct. 2001.

2 To amortize is to pay off a loan in a long-term series of equal-sized payments.

3 Cf. Jean-Charles Brisard, "The Economic Network of the Bin Laden Family," Appendix VII in Brisard and Dasquié, *Forbidden Truth: U.S.-Taliban Secret Oil Diplomacy and the Failed Hunt for Bin Laden,* Thunder's Mouth Press/Nation Books, 2002, pp. 181-222.

4 Peter Truell and Larry Gurwin, *False Profits: The Inside Story of the World's Most Corrupt Financial Empire,* Houghton Mifflin, 1992.

5 Ibid. See also Alfred McCoy, *The Politics of Heroin: CIA Complicity in the Global Drug Trade,* Lawrence Hill Books, 1991, pp. 445-460.

6 Carl Limbacher, et al., "Enron at the CIA," *NewsMax.com*, July 30, 2002, <www.newsmax.com/showinside.shtml?a=2002/7/30/145747>.

7 Rodney Stich and T.Conan Russel, *Disavow: A CIA Saga of Betrayal,* Diablo Western Press, 1995, pp. 268-269.

8 "While working on the Finding, North had been advised by Stanley Sporkin, the general counsel of the CIA, that a Finding must specifically enumerate each purpose to be accomplished by a particular covert action." "Cf. Final Report of the Independent Council for Iran/Contra Matters," Lawrence E. Walsh, Independent Council, August 4, 1993, Washington, DC, "Volume I: Investigations and Prosecutions, Part III: The Operational Conspiracy: A Legal Analysis", <www.afn.org/~dks/i-c/pIII-legal-analysis.html>.

9 See the articles by Paul Rodriguez and Kelly O'Meara at the solari.com website: <www.solari.com/media/articles%20on%20gideon.htm>.

10 "A former Bank of New York executive and her husband admitted today that they helped launder $7 billion for Russian banks by accessing electronic banking software used by the bank's customers." See Carol Huang, "Bank Exec, Husband Admits Laundering Billions; Moved $7 Billion for Russians through Bank of New York," APBNews.com, February 16, 2000. Cf. also James Petras, "'Dirty Money' Foundation of U.S. Growth and Empire," *FTW*, Vol. IV, no. 3, May 31, 2001, pp. 3 - 5.

11 Ibid.

12 "All Hell Breaks Loose: Citigroup, the Largest Drug Money Laundering Bank in America Buys Mexican Drug Laundering Bank Banamex," *FTW*, Vol. IV, no. 3, May 31, 2001 (cover story).

13 "A CIA investigation earlier this year showed Deutsch, like [Wen Ho] Lee, improperly transferred documents containing national security secrets. But Deutsch was not jailed." Cf. Andrew Chang, "The Next Ordeal: Wen Ho Lee is Free From Jail — but Not Problems," ABCNews.com, September 14, 2000, <http://abcnews.go.com/sections/us/DailyNews/lee000913.html#sidebar>.

14 *U.S. News & World Report*, February 20, 1995, "Washington Whispers," p. 23.

15 Hostages, Part II —A.I.G., *From The Wilderness*, Vol. IV, no. 5, August 14, 2001.

16 Ibid.; see also AIG Financial Report, <www.aigcorporate.com/corpsite/about/content/realfinancial.htm>.

17. Douglas Farrah, "Report Decries Saudi Laxity; US Must Act to Dry Up Al Qaeda Funds, Policy Group Says," *Washington Post*, October 17, 2002, <www.miraserve.com/pressrev/EN17oct02.htm>.

18 Peter Dale Scott, *The War Conspiracy: The Secret Road to the Second Indochina War*, Bobbs-Merrill, 1972, p.193.

19 Catherine Austin Fitts, "The Ultimate New Business Cold Call," *From The Wilderness*, July 1999, <www.fromthewilderness.com/free/economy/nyse_drugs.html>.

20 National Association of State Budget Officers (NASBO), 1999 State Expenditure Report, Washington, DC: NASBO, June 2000, pp. 38, 68. See also "Drug War Facts", <www.drugwarfacts.org/prison.htm>.

21 "New Mafias Go Global," *San Francisco Chronicle*, January 7, 2001.

22 Christian de Brie, "Thick as Thieves," *Le Monde Diplomatique*, April 2000, <http://mondediplo.com/2000/04/05debrie>.

23 "U.N. Estimates Drug Business Equal to 8 Percent of World Trade," Associated Press, June 26, 1997. Cf. Mike Gray, *Drug Crazy*, New York: Random House, 1998.

24 PBS "Frontline",<www.pbs.org/wgbh/pages/frontline/shows/drugs/special/math.html>.

25 "According to the *Interagency Assessment of Cocaine Movement*, an estimated 768 metric tons of cocaine were potentially produced in 2000, of which some 645 metric tons were detected departing South America moving toward the United States. Approximately 87 metric tons were seized en route to the United States and 43 metric tons were seized at US borders, leaving an estimated 515 metric tons potentially smuggled into the country before subtracting domestic federal, state, and local seizures, consumption in the Transit Zone, and transshipment to non-US markets." See also "Cocaine and Crack," National Drug Intelligence Center's National Drug Threat Assessment 2002, December 2001, <www.usdoj.gov/ndic/pubs/716/cocaine.htm>.

26 Michael C. Ruppert, "Cohen receives Drug Abuse Award," *U.S. Journal of Drug and Alcohol Dependence*, Vol. 8, no. 11, November 1984.

27 "Human Rights fears over Colombia aid," BBC News, June 23, 2000, <http://news.bbc.co.uk/1/hi/world/americas/803428.stm>.

28 DEA, <www.usdoj.gov/dea/pubs/intel/intel0901.html>.

29 "Taliban wipe out poppy growing in one season," *New York Times*, reprinted in *The Sydney Morning Herald*, May 21, 2000.

30 DEA, op. cit.

31 "The Supply of Illicit Drugs to the United States," Drug Enforcement Administration, National Narcotics Intelligence Consumers Committee

Report, 1995, August 1996, pp. vii-ix (DEA 96024).

32 "The UN Giveth, And The Drug Trade Prospereth," *High Times*, filed December 15, 1999, <www.hightimes.com/htsite/home/index.php>.

33 "Tobacco Companies Linked To Criminal Organizations In Cigarette Smuggling Trade, Says CPI Investigation," Center for Public Integrity report, March 5, 2001, <www.commondreams.org/news20010/0305-03.htm>.

34 "To constrain massive price spikes, California imposed a cap on the top price electricity could be sold for by producers. Enron found a profitable niche by purchasing California-produced electricity at the cap price, selling it in other states sometimes for as much as five times more, and then purchasing electricity in other states and selling it back into California — a practice investigators suspect led directly to the massive power shortages in California. That crisis cost California consumers and utilities tens of billions of dollars in 2001. But it earned BC Hydro up to $4 billion." Boys Playing a Man's Game," *Republic* (Vancouver), May 16, 2002, <http://1rev.net/archive/38-repub/repub_38_hydro.html>.

35 In "US Wants Caymans to Clamp Down on Firms," *Dallas Morning News*, March 3, 2002, Tom Robberson wrote: "Houston-based Enron Corp. used the Caymans to register 692 offshore corporations as part of a complicated network of subsidiaries that shuffled funds, hid debts and ensured that stockholders would never know that the company was heading for bankruptcy, investigators say," <www.dallasnews.com/latestnews/stories/030302dnintcaymans.bed56.html>.

36 Karen Masterson, "Gramm to work for Swiss bank: UBS Warburg took over much of Enron operation," HoustonChronicle.com, October 7, 2002, <www.chron.com/cs/CDA/story.hts/business/1607686>.

37 "Family Tree: Raul Salinas," PBSOnline, <www.pbs.org/wgbh/pages/frontline/shows/mexico/family/raulsalinas.html>.

38 PBS Special, "Drug Wars," <www.pbs.org/wgbh/pages/frontline/shows/drugs/special/us.html>; <www.pbs.org/wgbh/pages/frontline/shows/drugs/special/math.html>.

39 CPI Report, "Tobacco Companies Linked to Criminal Organizations," op. cit. (note 38).

40 "EU files money-laundering lawsuit against R.J. Reynolds in New York court," Associated Press, October 31, 2002, <http://ca.news.yahoo.com/021031/6/pyb3.html>.

41 Dan Ackerman, "Enron Says Oops," Forbes.com, November 19, 2001.

42 Verne Kopytoff, "Chevron rocked by double whammy; profit falls 81% on Dynergy write-off, gas prices," *San Francisco Chronicle*, July 31, 2002, <www.sfgate.com/cgi-bin/article.cgi?file=/chronicle/archive/2002/07/31/BU142187.DTL&type=business>.

43 CIA proprietary operations are established under law and extremely well documented. Basically the process consists of the Agency, in secret, using its money and personnel to set up what appear to be legitimate companies having nothing whatsoever to do with the agency. As documented by the Church hearings in the 1970s, a great many of them were small air freight operations and proved to be quite profitable. Agency proprietaries can and have operated in any kind of business, including book publishing and news gathering.

44 The Central Intelligence Agency Inspector General, *Report of Investigation* — "Allegations of Connections between CIA and the Contras in Cocaine Trafficking to the United States" (96-0143-IG); Appendices.

45 Michael C. Ruppert, "ONLY THE GODFATHER: CIA and Subsidiaries Exposed in Court Documents As Active Drug Smugglers Using Military Aircraft Washed Through Forest Service," *FTW*, December 1998, <www.fromthewilderness.com/free/pandora/forest_service_c130s.html>.

46 Ibid.

47 Ibid.

48 United States District Court, Northern District of Illinois, Eastern Division — No. 94CR0305; United States of America v. Luis Carlos-Herrera-Lizcano.

49 IG Report (96-0143-IG) Volume II.

50 Ibid.

51 Ibid.

52 Ibid.

53 <www.steamshovelpress.com/offlineillumination4>.

54 "Victorious Warlords Set to Open Opium Floodgates," *Observer*, November 25, 2001, <http://observer.guardian.co.uk/international/story/0,6903,605618,00.html>.

55 "Opium Farmers Rejoice at the Defeat of the Taliban", *Independent*, November 21, 2001.

56 *Asia Times* online, December 4, 2001.

57 "Massive post-war rise in production of Afghan opium," *Independent*, September 26, 2002.

58 "World Bank Chief Issues Opium Alert," by Faisal Islam, *Observer*, March 16, 2003.

59 Afghan Poppy Production Rises Again, Associated Press, April 28, 2003.

60 Michel Chossudovsky, "The Spoils Of War, Afghanistan's Multibillion Dollar Heroin Trade," April 5, 2004, www.globalresearch.ca, citing Congressional testimony of Assistant Secretary of State Robert Charles on April 1, 2004.

61 "US: Afghan Poppy Crop Leaping," Reuters, November 28, 2003.

Chapter 4: Connecting Drugs and Oil

1 "Bush-Cheney White House Obstructs Halliburton Lawsuit: Process Server Threatened With Jail by White House Security; White House Refuses to Allow Complaint to be Lawfully Served On Vice President Cheney," *Judicial Watch*, July 26, 2002, <www.judicialwatch.org/2221.shtml>.

2 "Colombian Judge Orders Cali Drug Lords Freed," Reuters, November 2, 2002.

3 CNN, November 8, 2002.

4 "Halliburton wins contract on Iraq oil firefighting," Reuters, March 6, 2003.

5 "Cost of one contract for aiding US in rebuilding nears $90 million, but little is going to Iraqis," *Los Angeles Times*, May 9, 2003.

6 "A Nation At War: Reconstruction; Details Given On Contract Halliburton Was Awarded," *New York Times*, April 11, 2003.

7 "US says Halliburton deal includes operating Iraq oil fields," Agence France Presse, May 6, 2003.

8. Where the CIA is in control, narcotics flourish — After Afghanistan, Baghdad is flooded with heroin," *Balochistan Post*, May 11 2003.

Chapter 5: A Criminal Meltdown

1 "On December 31, 1999, there will be 1,983,084 adults behind bars in America; by the end of 2004, there will be 1,222,155 non-violent offenders in American jails and prisons. In March of this year, the Justice Policy Institute estimated that at year-end 1999, for the first time, there were more than one million non-violent offenders behind bars; given the current growth rates, the number of Americans incarcerated will reach 2,073,969 by the end of the year 2000. Averaging out the daily prison and jail population growth, the number of Americans incarcerated will reach two million on February 15, 2000" quoted from "The Punishing Decade: Prison and Jail Estimate at the Millennium" (1999), Center on Juvenile and Criminal Justice, 1622 Folsom Street, San Francisco, 94103, <www.cjcj.org/pubs/punishing/punishing.html>.

2 "Correspondent Banking: A Gateway for Money Laundering." See S. Hrg. 107-184, report appears on p. 273 of Volume 1 of Hearing records entitled "Role of US Correspondent Banking in International Money " held on March 1, 2, and 6, 2001, <www.senat.gov/~gov_affairs/020501_psi_minority_report.htm>.

3 Christian De Brie, "Crime — The World's Biggest Free Enterprise. Part I: Thick as Thieves," *Le Monde Diplomatique*, April, 2000, <http://mondediplo.com/2000/04/>.

4 "On May 17, 2001, the chief executive of the largest bank in the United States, Citigroup, appeared at a press conference in Mexico City, to announce Citigroup's $12.5 billion proposed acquisition of Banacci/Banamex, the second largest bank in Mexico. Combined with Citigroup's Confia operation, Citigroup would control 26.4 percent of the Mexican banking

market, and over 21 percent of all Mexican bank accounts. On June 1, Citigroup stated that it had already submitted its required application to the US Federal Reserve Board, and would soon be applying to other agencies." *Inner City Press*, August 20, 2001,<www.innercitypress.org/citimex.html>.

5 "Falló la Mafia," *Por Esto!*, July 24, 2001, <www.poresto.net/especiales/suple11.htm>.

6 Ibid.

7 Tom Flocco, "President Fox guarding narco-hen house?" *World Net Daily*, February 15, 2001,<http://iicas.org/english/Krsten_05_07_01.htm>; Al Giordano, "Mexico: Friends Like These Two Presidents," *Media Awareness Project*, June 3, 1999, <www.mapinc.org/drugnews/v99.n623.a02.html>.

8 Ibid.

9 Flocco, op. cit.

10 Catherine Austin Fitts, "Enron Damage Control by Dyncorp — Harm Assisted at Harvard," *FTW*, Vol. 4, no. 1, March 1, 2002; Kelly Patricia O'Meara, "DynCorp Disgrace," *Insight* magazine, January 14, 2002.

11 "Embattled Director to resign from Harvard Board," Reuters, April 5, 2002.

12 "New Evidence Regarding Improper Financial Maneuvers at Harken Energy During The Bush Era"; a HarvardWatch Memo, October 2002, <www.harvardwatch.org>.

13 *Observer*, April 13, 2003

14 EU Press Release IP/02/1592, Brussels, 31 October 2002. Contact Jonathan Faull: +32-2-295 8658 — Brussels.

15 Ibid.

16 EU Press Release IP/02/1592, op. cit.

17 "Bush anti-corruption chief accused of account fraud," *Telegraph*, August 15, 2002.

18 *CBS Market Watch*, November 5, 2002.

19 <http://hollings.senate.gov/materials/ltr.ombdaniels.pdf>.

Chapter 6: Laying the Foundation

1 Bruce W. Neylan, "The Rush for Caspian Oil," *TIME*, May 4, 1998.

2 Alfred W. McCoy, *The Politics of Heroin: CIA Complicity in the Global Drug Trade*, Lawrence Hill Books, 1992.

3 Ibid, p. 447.

4 John K. Cooley, *Unholy Wars*, Pluto Press, 1999, p. 12.

5 Interview with Vincent Javert in *Le Nouvel Observateur*, Paris, January 15-21, 1998, p. 76, trans. Bill Blum. Special thanks to Jan Rainwater, PhD.

6 Zbigniew Brzezinski, *The Grand Chessboard: American Primacy and its Geostrategic Imperatives*, Basic Books, 1997.

7 Ibid, p. 31.

8 Ibid, p. 125.

9 Ibid, p. 124.

10 Ibid, p. 87.

11 Ibid, p. xiv.

12 Ibid, p.132.

13 Paul Thompson, "The Complete 9/11 Timeline," Center for Cooperative Research, <www.cooperativeresearch.org/completetimeline/index.htm>.

14 "Oil Barons Court Taliban in Texas," the *Telegraph*, December 14, 1997.

15 Brzezinski, p. 53.

16 Ibid., p. 124.

17 Nafeez Ahmed, *The War on Freedom: How and Why America was Attacked September 11, 2001*, Tree of Life Publications, 2002.

18 Bruce W. Nelan,"The Rush for Caspian Oil," *TIME*, May 4, 1998, <www.time.com/time/archive/preview/from_redirect/0,10987,1101980504-139082,00.html>.

19 "Russia's Road to Corruption: How the ClintonAdministration Exported Government Instead of Free Enterprise and Failed the Russian People." Members of the Speaker's Advisory Group on Russia; United States House of Representatives 106th Congress. Hon. Christopher Cox, Chairman; House Policy Committee (Cox Report), September, 2000, <http://policy.house.gov/russia/home.html>

20 "Testimony before the Committee on Banking and Financial Services of the U.S. House of Representatives", presented September 21, 1999.

21 Ibid.

22 Michael C. Ruppert, "The Bank of New York Laundromat," in *FTW*, Vol. II, no. 7, September 1999. Additional corroboration can be found in the *Wall Street Journal, New York Times;* Associated Press, *Washington Post,* and SEC filings at: <www.sec.gov>.

23 Ibid.

24 See Catherine Austin Fitts, "The Money Lords of Harvard: How the Money Works at the World's Richest University," NewsMakingNews.com, 2000, <www.newsmakingnews.com/catharvardmain.htm>.

25 Williamson, op. cit.; Cox Report, op. cit.

26 Williamson, op. cit.

27 Bob Feldman, "Alternative Media Censorship: Sponsored by CIA's Ford Foundation." <www.questionsquestions.net/gatekeepers.html>.

28 Ibid., and James Petras, "The Ford Foundation and the CIA: A documented case of philanthropic collaboration with the Secret Police," December 15, 2001, <www.rebelion.org/petras/english/ford010102.htm>.

29 Williamson, op. cit.

30 Cox Report, op. cit.

31 Williamson, op. cit.

32 Cox Report, op. cit.

33 Cox Report, op. cit.

34 Williamson, op. cit

Chapter 7: Caspian Corruption

1 Brisard and Dasquié, op. cit., p. xxxiii.

2 *Albion Monitor*, February 28, 2002.

3 bid.

4 "Opening the Caspian Oil Tap," *Business Week Online*, December 24, 2001.

5 See "Timeline of Competition between Unocal and Bridas for the Afghanistan Pipeline," *World Press Review*, December 2001, <www.sf.indymedia.org/news/2002/07/136245_comment.php>.

6 Brisard and Dasquié, op. cit., pp. 142-143.

7 "Veep Tried to Aid Firm Key Role in India Debt Row," *New York Daily News*, January 18, 2002; "Cheney, Others Intervened Over Indian Power Plant," the *Washington Post*, January 19, 2002, p. A1.

8 New York Daily News, "Veep..." op. cit.; *Washington Post*,, "Cheney, Others..." op. cit.

9 "As the War Shifts Alliances, Oil Deals Follow," *New York Times*, December 15, 2001.

10 Dan Morgan and David B. Ottaway, "In Iraqi War Scenario, Oil is Key Issue," *Washington Post*, September 15, 2002, <www.washingtonpost.com/ac2/wp-dyn?pagename=article&node=&contentId=A18841-2002Sep14&notFound=true>.

11 *Rebuilding America's Defenses, Strategy, Forces and resources for a New Century*, The Project for a New American Century, September, 2000, p. 14.

12 "Caspian Pipeline System Unveiled," *Pravda*, November 27, 2001, <http://english.pravda.ru/economics/2001/11/27/22172.html>.

13 "Oil Fuels the Iraq Question," *Washington Post* (National Weekly Edition), September 23-29, 2002, p. 15.

14 Ed Vuilliamy, Paul Webster, and Nick Paton, "Scramble to Carve Up Iraqi Oil Reserves Lies behind U.S. Diplomacy," *Guardian Unlimited Observer*, October 6, 2001, <www.observer.co.uk/international/story/0,6903,805530,00.html>.

15 Seymour Hersh, "The Price of Oil," *New Yorker*, July 9, 2001.

16 *FTW*, "The Elephant in the Living Room," March 30, 2002, <http://fromthewilderness.com/free/ww3/04_04_02_elephant.html>.

Chapter 8: Setting Up the War

1 Ahmed, *War on Freedom*, op. cit., p. 27.

2 Peter Dale Scott, "Afghanistan, Turkmenistan Oil and Gas, and the Projected Pipeline," October 21, 2001, <http://socrates.berkeley.edu/~pdscott/q.html>.

3 Ahmed, *War on Freedom*, op. cit.

4 *Guardian*, September 22, 2001; BBC, September 18, 2001; Inter Press Service, November 16, 2001; and *Alexander's Gas and Oil Connections*, February 21, 2002.

5 Brisard and Dasquié, op. cit., p. 33.

6 *Guardian*, September 22, 2001; BBC, September 18, 2001; *Inter Press Service*; November 16, 2001; *Alexander's Gas and Oil Connections*, February 21, 2002; Brisard and Dasquié, op. cit.

7 Brisard and Dasquié, op. cit., p. 35.

8 Ibid., pp. 36-37.

9 Ibid. pp. 40-42.

10 <www.indiareacts.com>, June 26, 2001.

11 "U.S. Tries to Stabilize the Shaky Ground of Central Asia," *Washington Post*, August 27, 2000.

12 *FTW*, Vol. IV, no. 1, March 31, 2001.

13 Thompson timeline, op. cit.

14 <www.cia.gov/cia/public_affairs/speeches/pavitt_04262002.html>.

15 Brisard and Dasquié, op. cit., pp. 40-41.
16 Ibid., pp. 76-77.
17 *Guardian*, September 22, 2001; BBC, September 18, 2001; *Inter Press*.
18 "U.S. 'Planned Attack' on Taleban," BBC, September 18, 2001.
19 Brisard and Dasquié, op. cit., p. 43.
20 Obtained from the website of the Institute for Global Engagement, <www.globalengagement.org/>.
21 See <www.bilderberg.org/roundtable/emchurch.html>.
22 See <www.house.gov>.
23 The Afghanistan Foundation, <http://burningbush.netfirms.com/afghan/congress.htm>.
24 <www.humaneventsonline.com/articles/10-01-01/cover.html>.
25 LAPD investigative records of Special Unit Senator in the author's possession.
26 <www.fromthewilderness.com/free/pandora/rfk.html>.
27 <www.fromthewilderness.com/free/ww3/02_11_02_lucy.html>.
28 *Global Outlook*, no. 2. Summer 2002, Centre for Research on Globalisation (CRG), <www.globalresearch.ca,> June 20, 2002 (revised 27 June).
29 *Times of India*, October 9, 2001
30 Thompson timeline, op. cit.
31 <http://globalresearch.ca/articles/KUP209A.html>.
32 Richard Sale, "Pearl Tracked Al Qaida," UPI, September 30, 2002.
33 Chaim Kupferberg, "9/11 and the Smoking Gun that Turned on its Tracker," Centre for Research on Globalisation (CRG), September 4, 2002, <www.globalresearch.ca/articles/KUP209B.html>.

Chapter 9: Business with the Bin Ladens

1 Brisard and Dasquié, op. cit., p. 103, citing a report in the APS Diplomat Recorder dated March 5, 1994.
2 Ibid., pp. 104-105.
3 "Bin Laden Family has Intricate Ties with Washington," *Wall Street Journal*, September 28-29, 2001.
4 Brisard and Dasquié, op. cit., p. 109, citing "Behind the Veil," *Jerusalem Report*, June 3, 1993.
5 Paul Thompson, "The Complete 9/11 Timeline: Introduction, Credits and Links (Version 1.7)," October 28, 2002, <www.unansweredquestions.net/timeline/>.
6 *FTW*, Vol. I, no. 7, September 19, 1998; "How the U.S. Missed a Chance to Get Bin Laden," *Village Voice*, October 31, 2001; Nafeez Ahmed, *War on Freedom*, p. 203.
7 "Sudan offered to turn over Osama bin Laden," *Washington Post*, October 3, 2001.
8 If this means that OBL is to be "used as a combatant" on the USG side, it strongly suggests that he is a willing participant in such an effort and that his CIA affiliation from the Mujaheddin war of the 1980s has persisted. If the same locution means that OBL is to be "used" as a combatant on the anti-USG terrorist side of the supposed war on terror, it strongly suggests that the USG is engaged in the business of supplying itself with enemies. That practice is called "false flag" operation, and 9/11 is its greatest exemplar in history.
9 Jennifer Gould, "Thanks But No Thanks," *The Village Voice*, November 6, 2001.
10 Brisard and Dasquié, op. cit., p. 104.
11 Ibid, p. 105.
12 See Thompson, "Timeline," op. cit.
13 Ibid.
14 <www.rmfdevelopment.com/political/IridiumSatellite.htm>.
15 Brisard and Dasquié, op. cit., pp. 106-108.
16 Ibid, p. 106.
17 Ibid, p. 107.
18 The Saudi Commercial Bank is the largest in the Kingdom. It is operated by Khalid bin Mahfouz, Saudi Arabia's former treasurer. Mahfouz has been reported in several places to be Osama bin Laden's brother in law. However, he has denied this and brought intense legal pressure to bear demanding retractions of these allegations. He has major partnership investments with the multibillion-dollar Binladin Group of companies, and he is a former director of BCCI, the infamous criminal drug-money laundering bank which performed a number of very useful services for the CIA before its 1991 collapse under criminal investigation by several countries.
19 *Wall Street Journal*, op. cit., September 28-29, 2001.

20 Kurt Eichenwald, "Bin Laden Family Liquidates Holdings with Carlyle Group," *New York Times*, October 26, 2001.

21 Agence France Presse, April 17, 2003, "U.S. Gives Iraqi Rebuilding Contract to Bechtel."

22 *Wall Street Journal*, op. cit., September 28-29, 2001.

23 "The Best Enemies Money Can Buy," *FTW*, Vol. IV, no. 7, October 15, 2001, pp. 13-15.

24 Dan Brody, "Carlyle's Way: Making a Mint Inside 'The Iron Triangle' of Defense, Government, and Industry," *Red Herring*, January 8, 2002, <www.redherring.com/vc/2002/0111/947.html>.

25 Thompson, op. cit.

26 Ibid.

27 Ibid.

28 Michel Chossudovsky, "Osamagate," *Centre for Research on Globalisation*, October 9, 2001, <http://globalresearch.ca/articles/CHO110A.html>.

29 Ibid.

30 Chossudovsky, op. cit.

31 "KLA Rebels Train in Terrorist Camps," *Washington Times*, May 4, 1999.

32 Jared Israel, "Bin Laden, Terrorist Monster: Take Two!" *The Emperor's Clothes* website, October 9, 2001, <www.tenc.net>.

33 Michel Chossudovsky, "Who Is Osama Bin Laden?" Centre for Research on Globalisation (CRG), Montréal; posted September 12, 2001, <www.globalresearch.ca/>.

34 "Startling Revelations by French Intelligence Experts Back David Shayler's Alleged 'Fantasy' about Gadaffi Plot," *Observer*, November 10, 2002.

35 Michael C. Ruppert, "Osama Bin Laden — A CIA Creation and its Blowback," *FTW*, Vol. I, no. 7, September 19, 1998, p. 4.

36 "Conspiracy of Silence by Arnaud de Borchgrave," UPI Commentary, November 18, 2002.

37 Martin Bright, Nick Pelham and Paul Harris, "Britons left in jail amid fears that Saudi Arabia could fall to al-Qaeda," *Guardian /Observer*, Saturday July 27, 2002.

38 Brisard and Dasquié, op. cit., p. 77.

39 Dan Brody, op. cit.; <www.forbes.com/maserati/billionaires2004/LIR0RD0.html?passListId=10&passYear=2004&passListType=Person&uniqueId=0RD0&datatype=Person>.

40 <www.newsmakingnews.com/waterfrontcarneros%209,18,02.htm>.

41 Michael C. Ruppert, "Saudi Arabia: The Sarajevo of the 21st Century," *From The Wilderness*, August 21, 2002, <www.fromthewilderness.com>. New data updating this story has been added to the original, pending upload to the website, for greater clarity within this section. In-text notes within square parentheses were added to the story during the writing of this book.

42 Peter Dale Scott, "FLASH 36: Is U.S. Arms Buildup In Response to Crisis in Saudi Arabia?" August 3, 2002, <http://socrates.berkeley.edu/~pdscott/index.html>.

43 Richard A. Clarke, testimony before the Kean Commission, March 24, 2004.

44 Michael C. Ruppert, "Suppressed Details of Criminal Insider Trading Lead Directly into the CIA's Highest Ranks," *FTW*, Vol. IV, no. 7, October 15, 2001, pp. 6-8; Tom Flocco, "Profits of Death: Insider Trading and 9-11," ed. Michael C. Ruppert, *FTW*, Vol. IV, no. 9, December 27, 2001, pp. 13-16; Tom Flocco and Michael C. Ruppert, "Profits of Death, Part III: All Roads Lead to Deutsche Bank and Harken Energy," *FTW*, Vol. IV, no. 10, January 29, 2002, pp. 11-16; Cf. "The Real Dirt on Bush/Harken Scandal," sf.indymedia.org, July 5, 2002, <www.sf.indymedia.org/news/2002/07/136245_comment.php>.

45 James Ridgeway, "The French Connection," *Village Voice*, January 2-8, 2002.

46 Zbigniew Brzezinski, *The Grand Chessboard*, p. 40.

Chapter 10: PROMIS

1 An impressive cache of online documents on Ari Ben-Menashe can be found at <www.pir.org/main1/Ari_Ben-2Dmenashe.html>.

2 Michael C. Ruppert, "Bin Laden's Magic Carpet — Secret U.S. PROMIS Software", *From The Wilderness*, Vol. IV, No. 8, November 20, 2001.

3 <www.room23.de/room23_view_
detail.php?ID=920>.

4 <http://pr.caltech.edu/media/
lead/102797JP.html>.

Chapter 11: Vreeland I

1 Theodore Shackley, *The Third Option*,
Simon and Schuster, 1981.

2 Rodney Stich and T. Conan Russell,
Disavow, op. cit., p. 239 (See Chapter 5).

3 Ibid, p. 244.

4 Ibid, p 267, citing transcripts of ABC *World
News Tonight*, September 19 & 20, 1984
from a special two-part report on the case.

5 The Intelligence Support Activity (ISA)
was a secret Defense Department
Intelligence Unit closely tied to the
drug trade and deniable covert operations run by the National Security
Council, the Pentagon, and the DCI's
office. The ISA turned up repeatedly
throughout the Iran-Contra scandal and
again in Gary Webb's Dark Alliance.
The ISA was officially disbanded after a
multitude of links to criminal behavior
made it a liability. Yet very few have
noticed a recent (Nov. 2002) decision
by the Bush administration to resurrect
the ISA in its war on terror. Later Gritz
characterizes Barnes as a misguided
author who had accused him of being
part of a plot to assassinate POWs and
also part of a plot to kill President
Ronald Reagan with special .22 caliber
machine guns.

6 James "Bo" Gritz, *Called to Serve*, Lazarus
Publishing, 1991, pp. 547; 423-429.

7 Monika Jensen-Stevenson, *Kiss The Boys
Goodbye*, The Penguin Group, 1990.

8 <www.fromthewilderness.com/
free/pandora/forest_service_c130s.html>.

9 <www.fromthewilderness.com/free/
hall/Mac.html>.

10 "Why Does George W. Bush Fly in Drug
Smuggler Barry Seal's Airplane?" *FTW*,
Vol. II, no. 8, October 31, 1999, pp. 1-7.

11 Terry Reed, *Compromised: Clinton, Bush
and the CIA*, Clandestine Publishing, pp.
473, 502, 506, 516, 529.

12 "Anatomy of a Smear," *TIME*, April 20,
1992.

13 "Military Role in Drug Dealing to be
Discussed in Upcoming A & E Program.
Special Forces Vet Bill Tyree Making

Legal Moves to Upset 1979 Murder
Conviction Based on CIA Ops," *FTW*,
Vol. I, no. 1, March 1998.

14 "Ed Wilson's Revenge," *FTW*, Vol. II, no.
10, January 28, 2000, pp. 3-11.

15 "Ex CIA Agent's Conviction Overturned,"
Associated Press, October 29, 2003; Eric
Lichtblau, "Justice Officials Face Inquiry
in Arms Conviction," *New York Times*,
December 23, 2003; "Case Against Ex
CIA Agent is Dismissed," *Washington
Post*, February 6, 2004.

16 *FTW*, Vol. II, no. 6, August 30, 1999.
<www.fromthewilderness.com/free/hall/
D_D_NY_2.html>.

17 Nick Pron, "Did this man predict September
11th?" *Toronto Star*, October 23, 2001.

18 <www.fromthewilderness.com/
free/ww3/izvestia_story_pic.html>;
Izvestia, September 12, 2001.

19 <www.guerrillanews.com/wildcard/
vreeland_three>.

20 If Mike Vreeland were making up the
story one needs to ask how he could have
obtained an unpublished FBI affidavit
only a month after it was written and
how he would have known where to look
to find it. — MCR

21 The request was repeatedly denied. —
MCR

22 Greta Knutzen, "U.S. and Canadian
Governments' Position Crumbling in the
Case of U.S. Intelligence Officer with
Foreknowledge of 9/11 Attacks," *FTW*,
Vol. IV, no. 11, February 29, 2002,
<www.fromthewilderness.com/free/ww3/
030302_vreeland.html>.

23 <www.fromthewilderness.com/
free/ww3/1252_rev_12802.html>.

Chapter 12: Executing a Conspiracy

1 Greg Palast, "Has Someone Been Sitting
on the FBI?" BBC *Newsnight*, November
11, 2001, <http://news.bbc.co.uk/hi/
english/events/newsnight/newsid_1645000/
1645527.stm.>.

2 Ibid.

3 Jeff Johnson, "Tearful FBI Agent Apologizes
To September 11 Families and Victims,"
Congressional News Service, May 30,
2002, <www.cnsnews.com/nation/
archive/200205/nat20020530d.html>.

4 Ibid.

5 Ibid.

6 Ibid.

7 Ibid.

8 David Schippers, Letter to Thomas J. Kneir, SAC Chicago, May 22, 2002.

9 <http://video.c-span.org:8080/ramgen/idrive/ter053002_judicial.rm>.

10 Rich Connell, "Response to Terror: FBI Brass Accused of Apathy; Investigations: Former agent wrote that Phoenix officials failed to make anti-terrorism a priority," *L.A. Times*, May 25, 2002, <http://pqasb.pqarchiver.com/latimes/index.html?ts=1046042123>; David Johnston, "Pre-Attack Memo Cited bin Laden," *New York Times*, May 14, 2002, <www.nytimes.com/2002/05/15/national/15INQU.html>.

11 Connell, op. cit.

12 Ibid.

13 Anyone familiar with Mr. Specter's role in the Warren Commission will appreciate the irony of his new position: outside the cover-up, shouting to be let in.

14 "FBI's 'Phoenix' Memo Unmasked," Fortune.com, May 22, 2002. Archived at <www.unansweredquestions.net/timeline/2002/fortune052202.html>.

15 Michel Chossudovsky, "Who is Osama bin Laden?" Centre for Research on Globalisation (CRG), Montréal, September 12, 2001, <www.globalresearch.ca/articles/CHO109C.html>.

16 Maria Ressa, "U.S. warned in 1995 of plot to hijack planes, attack buildings," CNN.com, September 18, 2001, <www.cnn.com/2001/U.S./09/18/inv.hijacking.philippines/index.html>.

17 Patrick Martin, "New evidence that U.S. government suppressed September 11 warnings," World Socialist Web Site, May 27, 2002, <www.wsws.org/articles/2002/may2002/sept-m27.shtml>.

18 "The Bombshell Memo: Colleen Rowley's Memo to FBI Director Robert Mueller. An edited version of the agent's 13-page letter." Time.com, May 21, 2002: <www.time.com/time/covers/1101020603/memo.html>.

19 CBS *News*, May 8, 2002, <www.cbsnews.com/stories/2002/05/08/60II/main508362.shtml>.

20 "Chechen warlord reported killed," CNN, April 25, 2002.

21 D. Ian Hopper, "Memo: FBI Destroyed Evidence in Bin Laden Case After Glitch With E-mail Surveillance System," Associated Press, May 28, 2002, <http://sfgate.com/cgi-bin/article.cgi?f=/news/archive/2002/05/28/national1704EDT0711.DTL>.

22 Ibid.

23 Dan Eggen, "Carnivore Glitches Blamed for FBI Woes," *Washington Post*, May 29, 2002, <www.washingtonpost.com/ac2/wp-dyn/A24213-2002May28?language=printer>.

24 "HQ Unit Accused of Quashing Pre-9-11 Probes," ABCNews.com, May 24, 2002, <http://abcnews.go.com/sections/us/DailyNews/warnings020524.html>.

25 Statement for the Record of Dale L. Watson, Executive Assistant Director, Counterterrorism and Counterintelligence, Federal Bureau of Investigation — on Joint Intelligence Committee Inquiry, September 26, 2002, <www.fas.org/irp/congress/2002_hr/092602watson.html>.

26 "Robert M. Blitzer Joins SAIC's Center for Counterterrorism Technology and Analysis as Associate Director", News Release, <www.saic.com/news/dec98/news12-17-98.html>.

27 Brian Ross and Vic Walter, "Called Off the Trail?" ABC *News*, December 19, 2002, <http://abcnews.go.com/sections/primetime/DailyNews/FBI_whistleblowers021219.html>.

28 Letter from Patrick Leahy, Charles Grassley, and Arlen Specter to FBI Director Mueller dated May 24, 2002, <http://leahy.senate.gov/press/200205/05402a.html>.

29 Ibid.

30 Martin, op. cit.

31 Dennis Shipman, "Another Spook Who Sat Behind The Door: A Modern Day Tale," *Black World Today*, <http://athena.tbwt.com/content/article.asp?articleid=854>.

32 CBS *News*, 60 *Minutes*, July 13, 2003, "Lost in Translation"; Gail Sheehy, "Whistelblower Coming In Cold From the FBI," *New York Observer*, April 27, 2004.

33 Ibid.

34 S.D. EDMONDS, Plaintiff, v. FEDERAL BUREAU OF INVESTIGATION,

Defendant., Civil Action No. 02-1294 (ESH), UNITED STATES DISTRICT COURT FOR THE DISTRICT OF COLUMBIA.

35 Op. cit., Sheehy.

36 Letter from Senators Patrick Leahy and Charles Grassley to the Department of Justice Inspector General, June 19, 2002.

37 Andrew Buncombe, "'I saw papers that show U.S. knew al-Qa'ida would attack cities with aeroplanes': Whistleblower the White House wants to silence speaks to the *Independent*," *Independent*, April 2, 2004.

38 Eric Boehlert, "We should have had orange or red-type of alert in June or July in 2001," *Salon*, March 26, 2004.

39 Ibid.

40 <www.fromthewilderness.com/ free/ww3/042604_edmunds_alert.html>. I learned details of Osborne's participation in a telephone conversation with him on April 27.

41 "A copy of Lt. Col. Butler's letter," the *Monterey County Herald*, June 5, 2002, <www.bayarea.com/mld/mcherald/ 3406502.htm>.

42 "Air Force Officer Suspended for Criticizing Bush," Reuters, June 4, 2002, <www.truthout.org/docs_02/ 06.06E.butler.bush.htm>.

43 George Wehrfritz, Catharine Skipp, and John Barry, "Alleged Hijackers May Have Trained at U.S. Bases. The Pentagon has turned over military records on five men to the FBI," *Newsweek*, September 15, 2001, <www.msnbc.com/news/ 629529.asp?cp1=1>.

44 Daniel Hopsicker, "Mohamed Atta and Rudi Dekkers Seen Together in Venice in Weeks Before September 11 Attack," Mad Cow Morning News, February 17, 2003, <www.madcowprod.com>.

45 Jim Stewart, "Ashcroft Flying High," CBS *News*, July 26, 2001, <www.cbsnews.com/stories/2001/07/26/ national/main303601.shtml>.

Chapter 13: Penetration

1 Eric V. Larson and John E. Peters, "Preparing the U.S. Army for Homeland Security," MR-1251/A, ISBN: 0-8330-2919-3, MR-1251/A ©2001, pp. 52, 67, 68, <www.rand.org/publications/MR/ MR1251/>.

2 Duncan Campbell, "They've Got it Tapped," *New Statesman*, August 12, 1988, <www.cooperativeresearch.org/ completetimeline/1990s/ newstatesman081288.html>.

3 Ibid. This has been acknowledged in a multitude of sources.

4 Andrew Bomford, "Echelon Spy Network Revealed," BBC *News*, November 3, 1999, <http://news.bbc.co.uk/1/hi/world/ 503224.stm>.

5 Suzanne Daley, "Europe Accuses U.S. of Economic Spying," *New York Times*, February 24, 2000, <www.sfgate.com/cgi-bin/article.cgi?file=/ chronicle/archive/2000/02/24/ MN101995.DTL>.

6 "The Hi Tech Spy," BBC, April 4, 2001, "Latest advances in listening technology mean that if a bug can be attached to a computer keyboard it is possible to monitor exactly what is being keyed in. Because every key on a computer has a unique sound when depressed, it's simply a case of translating the clicks into words. The threat of this technology has led some internet banks to rely on a degree of mouse movement." <http://news.bbc.co.uk/1/hi/world/ asia-pacific/1259940.stm>.

7 "Q&A: What You Need to Know About Echelon," BBC, May 29, 2001, <http://news.bbc.co.uk/1/hi/sci/tech/135 7513.stm>; "E Mail Users Warned Over Spy Network," BBC, May 29, 2001, <http://news.bbc.co.uk/1/hi/world/ europe/1357264.stm>.

8 Campbell, op. cit.

9 John Diamond, "U.S. Had Agents Inside Al Q'aeda," *U.S.A Today*, June 4, 2002, <www.usatoday.com/news/ sept11/2002/06/03/cia-attacks.htm>.

10 "Terror Intercepts on Eve of Sept 11th Too Vague — NSA," Reuters, October 17, 2002; *U.S.A. Today,* October 18, 2002.

11 Jonathan S. Landay, "NSA didn't share key pre-Sept 11 information, sources say," Knight Ridder Newspapers, January 6, 2002, <www.bayarea.com/mld/bayarea/3416632.htm>.

12 Paul Thompson, "Alhazmi and Almidhar: The 9/11 Hijackers Who Should Have Been Caught," Center for Cooperative Research, <www.cooperativeresearch.org/completetimeline/AAkhalidandnawaf.html>. This excellent 16-page report documents scores of press sources and liberally cites official records and congressional testimony from the fall of 2002. It is one of the most compelling deconstructions of the official position I have seen.

13 Michael Isikoff, "The Informant who lived with the Hijackers," *Newsweek,* September 9, 2002. Archived at <www.truthout.org/docs_02/09.13A.newk.infrmt.htm>; "Hijackers lived with FBI Informant," CBSNews.com, September 9, 2002, <www.cbsnews.com/stories/2002/09/09/attack/main521223.shtml>.

14 Thompson, op. cit.

15 Ibid.

16 Statement for the Record by Lieutenant General Michael V. Hayden, U.S. AF Director, National Security Agency/Chief, Central Security Service Before the Joint Inquiry of the Senate Select Committee on Intelligence and the House Permanent Select Committee on Intelligence, 17 October 2002, <www.fas.org/irp/congress/2002_hr/101702hayden.html>; AP, September 26, 2002.

17 "The 9/11 Terrorists the CIA Should Have Caught," *Newsweek,* June 2, 2002. <www.i-dineout.com/pages2002/newsweek6.2.02.html>; "CIA, FBI, Kept Lips Zipped," CBSNews.com, June 2, 2002, <www.cbsnews.com/stories/2002/06/03/national/printable510870.shtml>.

18 Matthias Gebauer, "Mossad Agents Were On Atta's Tail," *Der Spiegel,* October 1, 2002. Translation archived at <www.cooperativeresearch.org/completetimeline/2002/derspiegel100102.html>; *Die Zeit,* October 1, 2002; Rob Broomby, "Report Details U.S. 'intelligence failures,'" BBC, October 2, 2002, <http://news.bbc.co.uk/1/hi/world/europe/2294487.stm>; *Ha'aretz,* October 3, 2002.

19 Unclassified testimony of George Tenet, June 18, 2002, <www.odci.gov/cia/public_affairs/speeches/dci_testimony_06182002.html>; "The men who brought the world to the brink of war," The *Observer,* September 23, 2001, <www.observer.co.uk/waronterrorism/story/0,1373,556695,00.html>; "Who Did It? FBI Links Names to Terror Attacks," ABC *News,* January 9, 2002, <http://abcnews.go.com/sections/us/DailyNews/WTC_suspects.html>; Terry McDermott, "The Plot," *L.A. Times,* September 1, 2002, <www.latimes.com/news/specials/911/la-na-plot-1sep01.story>.

20 Charles M. Sennott, "Exposing Al Qaeda's European Network," The *Boston Globe,* August 4, 2002. Archived at <www.cooperativeresearch.org/completetimeline/2002/bostonglobe080402.html>.

21 Sebastian Rotella and Josh Meyer, "Wiretaps May Have Foretold Terror Attacks Investigation: Suspected Al Qaeda operatives taped in Italy in 2000 discussed airplanes, airports and strikes 'that will never be forgotten,'" *L.A. Times,* May 29, 2002. Archived at <www.cooperativeresearch.org/completetimeline/2002/latimes052902.html>; "Bugs Recorded Chilling 9/11 Talk," CBSNews.com, May 29, 2002, <www.cbsnews.com/stories/2002/05/29/attack/main510400.shtml>; *Guardian,* May 30, 2002.

22 James Risen and James Dao, "U.S. Believes It Has Recorded Radio Messages From bin Laden," *New York Times,* December 16, 2001, <www.nytimes.com/2001/12/16/international/16CALL.html>; Eric Schmitt with Michael R. Gordon, "A Nation Challenged: New Priorities; Hunt for bin Laden Loses Steam As Winter Grips Afghan Caves," *New York Times,* December 30, 2001, <http://query.nytimes.com/search/article-page.html?res=9D05EED81630F933A05751C1A9679C8B63>.

23 "Italy Tells of Threat at Genoa Summit," *L.A. Times*, September 27, 2001, <www.latimes.com/news/nationworld/nation/la-092701genoa.story>.

24 "Early Warnings," ABC *News*, February 18, 2002, <http://abcnews.go.com/sections/wnt/DailyNews/wnt_missedsignals_1_020218.html>.

25 "The Proof They Did Not Reveal," *Sunday Times*, October 7, 2001. Archived at <www.unansweredquestions.net/timeline/2001/sundaytimes100701.html>.

26 "Call by bin Laden Before Attacks Is Reported," *New York Times*, October 2, 2001, <www.nytimes.com/2001/10/02/national/02INQU.html?ex=1003037250&ei=1&en=d4c8c5c218658dc9>.

27 "Sources dispute reports of bin Laden phone call," CNN, October 2, 2001, <www.cnn.com/2001/U.S./10/02/inv.binladen.mother/>.

28 *Time*, October 5, 2001; Jeff Franks and Jack Redden, "U.S. Spy Satellite to Track Afghans from Space," Reuters, October 6, 2001, <www.intellnet.org/news/2001/10/06/7386-1.html>.

29 "A Big Warning," *ABC News*, June 7, 2002, <http://abcnews.go.com/sections/us/DailyNews/911conversation020607.html>; "September 11's Painful Lessons," CBSNews.com (w/ AP & Reuters), June 19, 2002, <www.cbsnews.com/stories/2002/06/19/attack/main512817.shtml>; Reuters, September 9, 2002.

30 Kevin Hogan, "Will Spyware Work?" *Technology Review*, December, 2001, <www.technologyreview.com/articles/hogan1201.asp>.

31 "Search Seeks Links to Bin Laden," AP, September 12, 2001, <http://the.honoluluadvertiser.com/article/2001/Sep/12/ln/ln28a.html>; ABC *News*, September 12, 2001; Department of Defense News Briefing - Secretary Rumsfeld, September 12, 2001, <www.defenselink.mil/news/Sep2001/t09122001_t0912sd.html>.

32 Ned Stafford, "Newspaper: Echelon Gave Authorities Warning Of Attacks," Yahoo News.co. Archived at <www.fromthewilderness.com/free/ww3/f_a_zeitung_story.html>.

33 "German police confirm Iranian deportee phoned warnings," online.ie, September 14, 2001,<www.online.ie/news/viewer.adp?article=1512332>.

34 *Izvestia*, September 12, 2001. The original Russian *Izvestia* story before the edit can be viewed at <www.fromthewilderness.com/images/izvestia.gif>. An English translation is available at <www.fromthewilderness.com/free/ww3/izvestia_story_pic.html>. I am indebted to former CIA case officer Leutrell Osborne and his son for bringing this to my attention.

35 Jeffrey Robinson, *The Merger: The Conglomeration of International Organized Crime*, Overlook Press, 2000. Excellent overview of the economic and political power of global organized crime syndicates.

36 Richard Sale, "NSA Listens to bin Laden," UPI, February 13, 2001. Archived at, <www.unansweredquestions.org/timeline/2001/upi021301.html>.

37 David Corn, "The September 11 X-Files," The *Nation*, May 31, 2002. Archived at, <www.commondreams.org/views02/0531-03.htm>.

38 Tom Flocco, "The Profits of Death, Part II- Trading with the Enemy," *FTW*, December 11, 2001, <www.fromthewilderness.com/free/ww3/12_11_01_death_profits_pt2.html>.

39 John K. Cooley, "The U.S. Ignored Foreign Warnings," *International Herald Tribune*, May 21, 2002. Currently archived at <www.cooperativeresearch.org/completetimeline/2002/iht052102.html>.

40 Ibid.

41 Ibid.

42 Daniel McGrory, "Moroccan secret agent predicted New York attack," *Times of London*, June 12, 2002, <www.timesonline.co.uk/article/0,,3-324191,00.html>.

43 "There Isn't a Target in Afghanistan Worth a $1M Missile," *Guardian*, October 10, 2001. Archived at, <www.dullesnow.org/missile.html>.

44 "CIA Director Warned Congress About 9/11 Attacks," *The Memory Hole*, <www.thememoryhole.org/tenet-911.htm>. As of this writing, *The Memory Hole* website still had a link to

the NPR story allowing the user to hear the actual report.

Chapter 14: 9/11 Insider Trading

1 "Profiting From Disaster," CBS *News*, September 19, 2001. <www.cbsnews.com/stories/2001/09/19/eveningnews/main311834.shtml>.

2 Judy Mathewson and Michael Nol, "U.S., Germany, Japan Investigate Unusual Trading Before Attack," Bloomberg *Financial News*, September 18, 2001. Archived at <www.themodernreligion.com/terror/wtc-unusualtrading.html>; "Pre-Attack Trading Probed," Bloomberg *Financial News*, September 19, 2001.

3 "Mechanics of Possible Bin Laden Insider Trading Scam," Herzliyya International Policy Institute for CounterTerrorism (ICT), September 22, 2001. Cf. Michael C. Ruppert, "The Case for Bush Administration Advance Knowledge of 9-11 Attacks," *From the Wilderness,* April 22, 2002. Posted at Centre for Research on Globalization <www.globalresearch.ca/articles/RUP204A.html>.

4 ICT, op. cit., citing data from the Chicago Board of Options Exchange (CBOE). Cf. David Roeder, "Terrorists trailed at CBOE," *Chicago Sun-Times*, September 20, 2001. <www.suntimes.com/terror/stories/cst-nws-trade20.html>; David Roeder, "Probe of options trading link to attacks confirmed," *Chicago Sun-Times,* September 21, 2001, <www.suntimes.com/terror/stories/cst-fin-trade21.html>.

5 ICT, op. cit.

6 Judy Mathewson and Vicky Stamas, "Goldman, Lehman Asked for Data," Bloomberg News, September 20, 2001. Archived at <www.thejournalnews.com/newsroom/092001/20suspicious.html>.

7 Bruce Blythe and Judy Mathewson, "Regulators Seek Evidence of Possible Terrorist Insider Trades," Bloomberg News, December 28, 2002. "Bloomberg's News Archive has been discontinued." <http://quote.bloomberg.com/newsarchive/>.

8 Judy Mathewson and Michael Nol, "Securities regulators check out possible terrorist insider trades," Bloomberg News, September 19, 2001. Archived at <http://seattlepi.nwsource.com/business/39439_trade19.shtml>.

9 Agence France Presse, September 22, 2001.

10 Ibid.; Blythe and Mathewson, op.cit.

11 David De Rosa, "The Icing on the Cake May Be the Suspect Puts," Bloomberg News, December 28, 2002. "Bloomberg's *News* Archive has been discontinued." <http://quote.bloomberg.com/newsarchive/>.

12 Lormel, a high-profile FBI manager who is in charge of the FBI's Financial Crimes Section looks to be a replica of David Frasca in the Radical Fundamentalist Unit. A web search shows many instances where Lormel has testified before Congress as an FBI spokesperson. This has implications for the question of who it was that thwarted the Wright investigations in Chicago. While Frasca's behavior bears the marks of conspiratorial behavior more frequently and clearly than does Lorimel's, the latter's position on the insider trading issue is consistent with a member of a secret team protecting CIA's and Wall Street's interests.

13 Kyle F. Hence, "Massive pre-attack 'insider trading' offer authorities hottest trail to accomplices, Part II: Billions in Pre-911 Insider Trading Profits Leaves a Hot Trail: How Bush Administration Naysayers May Have Let it go Cold," The Centre for Research on Globalization, April 21, 2002, <www.globalresearch.ca/articles/HEN204B.html>. Lormel's remarks were given in response to questions. He did not even mention insider trading in his prepared statement before the House Committee on Financial Services.

14 Associated Press, September 20, 2001; From the Office of Public Affairs, September 20, 2001, PO-627, "The U.S. Financial System in the Wake of the Attack on the World Trade Center." Testimony of Paul O'Neill, Secretary of the Treasury Before the Committee on Banking, Housing, and Urban Affairs, United States Senate, September 20, 2001, <www.ustreas.gov/press/releases/po627.htm>

15 Kurt Eichenwald and Edmund L. Andrews "Doubt Over Whether Advance Knowledge of Attacks Was Used for Profit," *New York Times*, September 28, 2001. Archived at <www.mugu.com/pipermail/

upstream-list/2001-September/003492.html>. The *New York Times* story was used effectively and prominently to put out the fires that had been started by earlier reports.

16 Kelly Patricia O'Meara, "Not Much Stock in 'Put' Conspiracy," *Insight* magazine, May 13, 2002, <www.insightmag.com/news/251677.html>.

17 Kathy Fieweger, "Airline stocks may be poised for take off," Reuters, September 10, 2001.

18 Ibid.

19 Christian Berthelsen and Scott Winokur, "Suspicious profits sit uncollected," *San Francisco Chronicle*, September 29, 2001. <www.sfgate.com/cgi-bin/article.cgi?file=/chronicle/archive/2001/09/29/MN186128.DTL>.

20 Teresa Dixon Murray, "LTV Progressive added to the probe of options trading before September 11," *Cleveland Plain Dealer*, October 4, 2001.

21 Scott Winokur, "SEC wants data-sharing system. Network of brokerages would help trace trades by terrorists," *San Francisco Chronicle*, October 19, 2001, <www.sfgate.com/cgi-bin/article.cgi?file=/chronicle/archive/2001/10/19/BU142745.DTL>.

22 Ibid.

23 *Wall Street Journal*, October 2, 2001. Quoted in Barry Grey, "Suspicious trading points to advance knowledge by big investors of September 11 attacks," World Socialist Web Site, October 5, 2001, <www.wsws.org/articles/2001/oct2001/bond-o05.shtml>.

24 Hence, op. cit.; Reuters, December 17, 2001, archived at <www.rediff.com/money/2001/dec/17wtc.htm>.

25 Ibid.

26 I have omitted one section of that original *FTW* story (a detailed discussion of the relationship between the CIA and Wall Street) because we have already covered it in much greater detail in Chapter 3.

27 ICT, op. cit.

28 Michael C. Ruppert, "Suppressed Details of Criminal Insider Trading Lead Directly Into the CIA's Highest Ranks," *From The Wilderness*, Vol. IV. No.7, October 15, 2001, <www.fromthewilderness.com/free/ww3/10_09_01_krongard.html>.

29 O'Meara, op. cit.

30 "Profiting From Disaster," AP, September 19, 2001. Archived at CBSNews.com, September 20, 2001, <www.cbsnews.com/stories/2001/09/19/eveningnews/main311834.shtml>. AP was running a story released in advance of a *60 Minutes* episode scheduled for the following Sunday.

31 ICT, op. cit. The 9/11 insider trading analysis from the Herzliya Institute for Counterterrorism was substantive, at a time when all other such analyses were either superficial or lacking altogether. This has important implications which I explore in the chapter on Israel.

32 Tom Flocco, "Profits of Death, Part I - Insider Trading and 9/11," *From The Wilderness*, Vol. IV, No. 9, December 27, 2001, <www.fromthewilderness.com/free/ww3/12_06_01_death_profits_pt1.html>.

33 Ibid.

34 Ibid.

35 Tom Flocco, "Profits of Death Parts II & III," *From The Wilderness*, Vol. IV, No. 10, January 29, 2002, <www.fromthewilderness.com/free/ww3/12_11_01_death_profits_pt2.html>; Tom Flocco and Michael C. Ruppert, "Part III: All Roads Lead to Deutsche Bank and Harken Energy, W's Own 1991 Insider Trading Scam; The Mother of All Enrons," *From The Wilderness*, January 9, 2002 <www.fromthewilderness.com/free/ww3/01_09_02_death_profits_pt3.html>.

36 Howard Gleckman, "A New Twist in Enron's Can of Worms," *Business Week*, January 17, 2002, <www.businessweek.com/bwdaily/dnflash/jan2002/nf20020117_0563.htm>; Patrick McGeehan, "Enron's Deals Were Marketed to Companies by Wall Street," *New York Times*, February 14, 2002, <www.nytimes.com/2002/02/14/business/14TRU.S..html>.

37 Cf. the following sources regarding Genesis Intermedia and Adnan Khashoggi: "Nasdaq Halts Trading of Genesis Intermedia, Inc. and Requests Additional Information from Company," NasdaqNews.com, September 25, 2001, <www.nasdaqnews.com/news/pr2001/ne_section01_274.html>; Hoover's online, <www.hoovers.com>; Class

Action Securities Lawsuit Filed Against Genesis Intermedia, Inc. by Stull, Stull & Brod,. <www.secfraud.com/filedcases/geni.html>; Michael C. Ruppert, "Saudi Arabia: The Sarajevo of the 21st Century. Is Iraq a Diversion from the Real Invasion or Will Bush Try to Occupy Both Countries at Once? *From The Wilderness*, August 21, 2002. Archived at <www.globalresearch.ca/articles/RUP208A.html>.

38 "Chief Steps Down at Alex. Brown," Bloomberg News, September 14, 2001. Reported in the *New York Times* on September 15, 2001 and archived at <www.unansweredquestions.net/timeline/2001/nyt091501.html>.

39 Bank Loan Report, July 2, 2001.

40 Frank R. Kent (1975). The Story of Alex. Brown & Sons, 1800-1975. (Baltimore, MD: Alex Brown & Sons, 259 p.). Alexander Brown and Sons — History; Banks and banking — Maryland — Baltimore.

41 Edwin J. Perkins (1975). Financing Anglo-American Trade: The House of Brown, 1800-1880. (Cambridge, MA: Harvard University Press, 323 p.). Alex. Brown & Sons; Banks and banking — United States — History — Case studies; International finance.

42 O'Meara, op. cit.

43 Blythe and Mathewson, op. cit.

44 Eichenwald and Andrews, op. cit.

45 "Betting on Terror: An Explosive Idea." *Business Week*, August 8, 2003.

Chapter 15: Israel

1 "Mossad Agents Were on Atta's Tail," *Der Spiegel*, October 1, 2001. Archived at <www.cooperativeresearch.org/completetimeline/2002/derspiegel100102.html>.

2 "Insider notes from United Press International for March 6," UPI, March 6, 2002: <www.upi.com/print.cfm?StoryID=06032002-121706-8744r>.

3 Peter Dale Scott, *Flash* 28, "A U.S. Attack on Iraq Could Create a New Anti-U.S. Coalition," March 18, 2002, <http://socrates.berkeley.edu/~pdscott/qfiraq3.html>.

4 Richard B. Du Boff, "Comparing Violations of UN Resolutions by Iraq and Israel," *Al Jazeerah*, September 23, 2002, <www.aljazeerah.info/Documents/Comparing%20UN%20Resolutions%20for%20Iraq%20and%20Israel.htm>.

5 "Sabra and Shatila 20 years on," BBC *News*, September 14, 2002, <http://news.bbc.co.uk/2/hi/middle_east/2255902.stm>; "Israel/Occupied Territories: Israeli Defence Force war crimes must be investigated," Amnesty International Press Release, November 2, 2002, <http://web.amnesty.org/ai.nsf/Index/MDE151542002?OpenDocument&of=COUNTRIES/ISRAEL/OCCUPIED+TERRITORIES>.

6 "All the 9-11 Airports Serviced By One Israeli Owned Company," Undated, <www.whatreallyhappened.com/ICTS.html>.

7 "The White Van: Were Israelis detained on September 11 Spies?" ABC *News*, June 21, 2002, <http://abcnews.go.com/sections/2020/DailyNews/2020_whitevan_020621.html>.

8 "Palestinians arrest al-Q'aeda 'poseurs,'" *Sydney Morning Herald*, December 8, 2002, <www.smh.com.au/articles/2002/12/07/1038950239070.html>; Danny Rubinstein, "Ibrahim, the Shin bet wants you to join Qaida," *Ha'aretz*, December 15, 2002, <www.haaretzdaily.com/hasen/pages/ShArt.jhtml?itemNo=241042>.

9 "U.S. papers: FBI hunting suspected terrorists with Israeli passports," *Ha'aretz*, June 28, 2002, <www.haaretzdaily.com/hasen/pages/ShArt.jhtml?itemNo=89407&contrassID=2&subContrassID=1&sbSubContrassID=0>.

10 Michael Gillespie, "Israeli Computer Hackers Foiled, Exposed," Washington Report on Middle East Affairs, September 3, 2002. Archived at <www.counterpunch.org/pipermail/counterpunch-list/2002-September/022300.html>.

11 "Israeli Arms Shipment Headed for Iran Seized in Germany," Global Vision News Network, August 29, 2002, <www.gvnews.net/html/DailyNews/alert2070.html>.

12 "Arms Seizure backfires, wounds Israel," *Stratfor*, January 2002, Archived at <www.iansa.org/news/2002/Jan2002/arms_backfire8102.htm>.

13 Michael Gillespie, "Los Angeles Court Hands Down Final Judgment in Anti-Defamation League Illegal Surveillance Case," Washington Report on Middle East Affairs, December 1999, <www.wrmea.com/Washington-Report_org/www/backissues/1299/9912043.html>.

14 Barbara Ferguson, "ADL Found Guilty of Spying by California Court," *The Arab News*, April 25, 2002.

15 This report was originally made public by investigative journalist and former NSA analyst Wayne Madsen in late February and early March of 2002. Madsen obtained the report several months after FOX News stories by Carl Cameron and Brit Hume broke the initial story of the spy ring, but did not mention the DEA connections, which were central to understanding the context of the operation. The undated DEA report, extracted from a larger document, was written sometime in the summer of 2001. It can be found online at <http://cryptome.org/dea-il-spy.htm>.

16 The four-part FOX series by Carl Cameron began on Monday December 17, 2001. Although the story was subsequently removed from the FOX web site and "spiked" as some researchers have called it, transcripts are still available through web searches and through the Federal Document Clearing House. Series archived online at <http://100777.com/nwo/104a.htm>.

17 Cameron, op. cit.; John Mintz, "60 Israelis on Tourist Visas Detained Since September 11," *Washington Post*, November 23, 2001, <www.vanguardnewsnetwork.com/temp/TerrorTimeline/112301_60IsraelisDetainedSinceSept_%2011.htm>.

18 "Instant Messages Warned of WTC Attacks," *Washington Post*, September 28, 2001, <www.fpp.co.uk/online/01/09/WTC_Odigo.html>.

19 "Odigo, Inc., the leading instant messaging provider, secures $15.35 million in private placement," press release, Comverse, Inc., January 9, 2001, <http://216.239.51.100/search?q=cache:CUdFXHT1MHgC:www.comverse.com/press/2001/010109.htm++Press+release++Comverse+Inc.+January+9+2001&hl=en&ie=UTF-8>.

20 Cameron, op. cit. [Part Two, December 18, 2001], <http://100777.com/nwo/104b.htm>.

21 DEA Report, op. cit.

22 5 PM newscast, WJLA TV. The transcript of the story has since been removed from the WJLA web site. However, I was able to recover a copy of the original teleprompter script from the broadcast.

23 "The View from Washington," Poynteronline, September 10, 2002, <http://poynter.org/content/content_print.asp?id=9491>.

24 Elaine Sciolino, "89 Senators Urge Bush Not to Hamper Israel," *New York Times*, November 16, 2001. Archived at <www.ourjerusalem.com/news/story/news20011119a.html>.

25 Jason Keyser, "Israel Urges U.S. to Attack Iraq," Associated Press, August 16, 2002. Archived at <www.firstcoastnews.com/news/2002-08-16/usw_israeliraq.asp>.

26 "Georgia casts votes in bitter house duels," Reuters, August 20, 2002, <www.cynthi-amckinney.net/articles/20020220_bitter_house_duels.htm>; Thomas B. Edsall, "Impact of McKinney Loss Worries Some Democrats; Tension Between Blacks, Jews a Concern," *Washington Post*, August 22, 2002, <www.washingtonpost.com/ac2/wp-dyn?pagename=article&node=&contentId=A47064-2002Aug21&notFound=true>; Jim Burns, "McKinney Contemplating Run For Georgia U.S. Senate Seat," CNS *News*, August 26, 2002: <www.cnsnews.com/ViewPolitics.asp?Page=\Politics\archive\200208\POL20020826d.html>.

27 Jamie Zacharia, "New Congress remains strongly pro-Israel," *Jerusalem Post*, November 6, 2002, <www.jpost.com/servlet/Satellite?pagename=JPost/A/JPArticle/ShowFull&cid=1036619253808>.

28 "U.S. scientist sentenced for selling nuclear trigger devices," Ananova Press Agency, December 29, 2001; "United States II: Nuclear Trigger Smuggler Pleads Guilty," <www.nti.org/d_newswire/issues/newswires/2002_1_2.html>; Cf. Gary Milhollin, Professor Emeritus, University of Wisconsin Law School and Director, Wisconsin Project on Nuclear Arms Control, Testimony

Before the Senate Committee on Governmental Affairs, May 26, 2000, <www.wisconsinproject.org/pubs/testimonies/2000/5-26-00.htm>.

Chapter 16: Silencing Congress

1 Jesse Holland, "Senator Blocks Attempt to Pass Bill," Associated Press, October 10, 2001. Archived at <http://billstclair.com/911timeline/2001/ap101001.html>.

2 "Anthrax Sent to Senate Leader," BBC, October 15, 2001. Archived at <http://news.bbc.co.uk/1/hi/world/americas/1601093.stm>.

3 Andrew Buncombe and Raymond Whittaker, "Anthrax fear grows as 31 Senate staff test positive," *Independent*, October 18, 2001. Archived at <http://news.independent.co.uk/world/americas/story.jsp?story=100130>.

4 "Bush Asks Daschle to Limit Probes," CNN, January 29, 2002 Archived at <www.cnn.com/2002/ALLPOLITICS/01/29/inv.terror.probe/>.

5 <www.ph.ucla.edu/epi/bioter/terroranthraxlinkedus.html>; <www.ph.ucla.edu/epi/bioter/anthraxmatchesarmyspores.html>,

6 Rick Weiss and Joby Warrick, "Army Lost Track of Anthrax Bacteria," *Washington Post*, January 21, 2002. Archived at <www.geocities.com/Ignatius_Ding_2000/Anthrax_Info/WP012102.htm>; "Anthrax attacks," BBC *Newsnight*, March 14, 2002. Archived at <http://news.bbc.co.uk/1/hi/audiovideo/programmes/newsnight/archive/1873368.stm>; William J. Broad and Judith Miller, "Anthrax Inquiry Looks at U.S. Labs," *New York Times,* December 2, 2001. Archived at <www.ph.ucla.edu/epi/bioter/anthraxinquiryuslabs.html>.

7 Jeffrey McMurray, "Rep. Barr Criticizes Bush," Associated Press, November 29, 2001. Archived at <www.counterpunch.org/pipermail/counterpunch-list/2001-November/016673.html>.

8 Transcribed from KPFA archives. Part of text was also included in a subsequent press release from her office.

9 Bob Dart and Stephen Krupin, "McKinney campaign donors named in 9-11 suit," *Atlanta Journal Constitution*, August 17, 2002. Archived at <www.accessatlanta.com/ajc/news/0802/17tersuit.html>.

10 Ibid. Cf. also Bill Torpy, "Some McKinney Donors Probed for Terror Ties: DeKalb Democrat said unaware any donors might support terror," *Atlanta Journal Constitution*, August 3, 2002. Archived at <www.accessatlanta.com/ajc/metro/0802/03mcmoney.html>.

11 Ibid.

12 Dart and Krupin, op. cit.

13 Duncan Campbell, "FBI raids pro-Republicans," *The Guardian*, March 25, 2002, <www.guardian.co.uk/september11/story/0,11209,673543,00.html>.

14 <www.fromthewilderness.com/free/ww3/082202_withercongress.html>.

15 Jennifer Van Bergen, "The U.S.A Patriot Act was Planned Before 9/11," *Truthout*, May 20, 2002, <www.truthout.org/docs_02/05.21B.jvb.usapa.911.htm>.

16 *From The Wilderness*, Vol. 5 No. 7, Nov. 4, 2002.

17 Greg Gordon and Mike Kaszuba, "Co-pilot played minor role in story of Moussaoui," *Minneapolis Star Tribune,* October 26, 2002. Archived at <www.timnews.com/copilot.htm>.

18 <www.fromthewilderness.com/free/ww3/112702_wellstone_update.html>.

Chapter 17: Vreeland II

1 Mishawaka Police Department Supplemental Case Report 00020152, February 8, 2000, signed by Detective Lieutenant Pasqualle Rulli, Jr.

2 Sander Hicks, "Wilcard: Down the rabbit hole with the man who says he tried to warn the world about 9/11," Guerilla News Network: <http://www.guerrillanews.com/wildcard/vreeland_one>.

3 Ibid.

4 "Wanta" has since filed a federal civil suit over the missing trillions and his treatment in US District Court in the Eastern District of Virginia against the United States government, the Attorney General and the Secretary of the Treasury (Case No. 02-363A). Other documents provided by Wanta and confirmed by Vreeland indicate that much of the money is controlled by a firm named AmeriTrust Corporation of Ontario, Canada.

5 After that trip Rahall expressed his basic support for an invasion of Iraq. Solomon was also later to accompany actor-director Sean Penn to Iraq.

6 David Corn, "The September 11 X-Files," The *Nation*, May 30, 2002, <http://www.thenation.com/capitalgames/index.mhtml?bid=3&pid=66>.

7 The current term for the establishment left is "Gatekeeper Left," since its editorial bureaucracy determines which facts and memes are admissible for "progressive" discussion and which are simply too potent and dangerous to admit. If you can't control its implications, stop it at the gate.

8 Navasky had placed himself squarely at odds with the more than 70 per cent of the American people who don't believe that "Oswald acted alone." He also contradicted the findings of the House Select Committee on Assassinations which concluded that JFK had been killed as the result of a "probable conspiracy." Much has been written about the Nation's reprehensible position on the murder, including: Gary L. Aguilar, "Max Holland Rescues the Warren Commission and the *Nation*," *Probe* magazine, September-October 2000 (Vol. 7 No. 6), <http://www.webcom.com/ctka/pr900-holland.html>. Jamey Hecht, "Bad Faith Again: An Open Letter to the *Nation* magazine," Media Monitors Network, May 12, 2003, <http://www.mediamonitors.net/jameyhecht1.html>; E. Martin Schotz, *History Will Not Absolve Us: Orwellian control, Public Denial, and the Murder of President Kennedy* Kurtz, Ulmer and DeLucia, 1996; See also Peter Dale Scott, "Letter to American History Magazine" in response to a hostile review of *Deep Politics and the Death of JFK*, <http://www.webcom.com/ctka/letters/pdscott-on-holland.htm>.

9 Cynthia Cotts, "Laundering The Truth: 'The *Nation*' Defuses a French Bombshell," *Village Voice*, July 24 - 30, 2002, <http://www.villagevoice.com/issues/0230/cotts.php>.

10 Carl Bernstein, "The CIA and the Media - How America's Most Powerful News Media Worked Hand in Glove with the Central Intelligence Agency and Why the Church Committee Covered It Up," *Rolling Stone*, October 20, 1977. Excerpted at: <http://www.realhistoryarchives.com/media/ciamedia.htm>.

11 Ibid.

12 Ibid.

13 Alan Wolper, "The CIA's Copy Desk and the *New York Times*," *Ethics Corner*, January 14, 2003, <http://www.editorandpublisher.com/editorandpublisher/features_columns/article_display.jsp?vnu_content_id=1796082>.

14 "Microwave Radiation of US Embassy in Moscow," <http://www.cheniere.org/briefings/DoDPriore/slides/054.htm>.

15 Associated Press, March 30, 2004, "Russia says its new weapon will make US missile defence useless", as reported by the Canadian Press newswire.

Chapter 18: The Attacks

1 KPFK Listener forum, <http://disc.server.com/discussion.cgi?id=165346&article=10650>. This is just one of hundreds of similar statements from certified instrument-rated pilots that surfaced after 9/11, and it is consistent with interviews I have done with pilots since 9/11.

2 Elaine Scarry, "The Fall of EgyptAir 990," *New York Review of Books*, October 5, 2000, <www.nybooks.com/articles/13830>.

3 Ahmed, op. cit., pp. 145-149.

4 "9/11 and the Public Safety: Seeking Answers and Accountability." <www.unansweredquestions.org/transcript.php>.

5 Robert P. King and Sanjay Bhatt, "Hijackers Had a Tough Time with Flying Lessons," *Cape Cod Times*, Cox News Syndicate, October 21, 2001. Archived at <www.cooperativeresearch.org/completetimeline/2001/coxnews102101.html>.

6 Illarion Bykov and Jared Israel, "Guilty for 9/11: Bush, Rumsfeld, Myers," Emperor's New Clothes, November 14, 2001, <http://emperors-clothes.com/indict/indict-1.htm>.

7 Ibid.

8 "Powerful Evidence that Air Force was made to stand down on 9/11," Emperor's New Clothes, <http://emperors-clothes.com/indict/update630.htm>.

9 Ibid.

10 Bill McAllister, "US capital faces terror on own turf," *Denver Post*, September 11, 2001. Archived at <http://emperors-clothes.com/9/11backups/dp11.htm>; "Tuesday President Bush returns to White House on Marine One," NBC *Nightly News*, September 11, 2001, 6:30 PM (EDT). Archived at <http://emperors-clothes.com/9/11backups/nbc911cover.htm>; *San Diego Union Tribune*, September 12, 2001; David Wastell and Philip Jacobson, "Israeli security issued urgent warning to CIA of large-scale terror attacks," *Sunday Telegraph*, September 16, 2001, http://news.telegraph.co.uk/news/main.jhtml?xml=/news/2001/09/16/wcia16.xml>.

11 Michael Steele, Bloomberg News, December 28, 2001.

12 Tu Thanh Ha, "General Suspects September 11 plot was wider," *Globe and Mail*, June 13, 2002. Archived at <www.unansweredquestions.net/timeline/2002/globeandmail061302.html>.

Attacks Timeline Notes (Chapter 18)

1 *Boston Globe*, Nov. 23, 2001; *New York Times*, Oct. 16, 2001.

2 *Nashua Telegraph*, Sept. 13, 2001.

3 CNN, Sept. 17, 2001; AP August 19, 2002.

4 *Christian Science Monitor*, Sept. 13, 2001.

5 CNN, Sept. 17, 2001.

6 MS-NBC, Sept. 12, 2001.

7 *Newsday*, Sept. 23, 2001; *New York Times*, Sept. 15, 2001.

8 CNN, Sept. 17, 2001; *Washington Post*, Sept. 12, 2001, *Guardian*, Oct. 17, 2001.

9 Staff Report No 17, Kean Commission, undated, posted in June 2004. <www.9-11commission.gov/hearings/hearing12/staff_statement_17.pdf>.

10 *Guardian*, Oct. 17, 2001; *New York Times*, Oct. 16, 2001; *Boston Globe*, Nov. 23, 2001; *Village Voice*, Sept. 13, 2001.

11 *Christian Science Monitor*, Sept. 13, 2001.

12 *Wall Street Journal*, Oct. 15, 2001.

13 *Wahington Post*, Sept. 12, 2001.

14 *Guardian*, Oct. 17, 2001.

15 *Washington Post*, Jan. 27, 2002; BBC Sept. 1, 2002; *Washington Times*, Oct. 7, 2002.

16 *Guardian*, Oct. 17, 2001; *Boston Globe*, Nov. 23, 2001.

17 *Op. cit. Staff report* No. 17

18 ABC *News*, Sept. 11, 2001.

19 *Cape Cod Times*, Aug. 21, 2002.

20 NORAD, Sept. 18, 2001.

21 MS-NBC, Sept. 3, 2002; *Newsweek*, Sept. 22, 2001; AP, Aug. 19, 2001; CNN, Sept. 7, 2001, *Guardian*, Oct. 17, 2001.

22 *Boston Globe*, Now. 23, 2001.

23 *New York Times*, Oct. 16, 2001.

24 *New York Times*, Oct. 16, 2001.

25 *New York Channel 4 News*, Sept. 13, 2001; *Washington Post*, Sept. 15, 2001; NORAD, Sept. 18, 2001; CNN, Sept. 17, 2001.

26 ABC *News*, Sept. 11, 2002.

27 *Confirmation Testimony of Richard Myers Before the Senate Armed Services Committee*, Sept. 13, 2001.

28 *Guardian*, Oct. 17, 2001; *Newsday*, Sept. 10, 2002.

29 *Newsday*, Sept. 10, 2002; *Washington Post*, Sept. 17, 2002.

30 *Washington Post*, Sept. 12, 2001; *Newsday*, Sept. 23, 2001

31 *Aviation Week & Space Technology*, Sept. 9, 2002.

32 NBC, Sept. 16, 2001.

33 *Aviation Week & Space Technology*, Sept. 9, 2002.

34 *Catholic Telegraph*, Dec. 7, 2001; AP, Nov. 26, 2001.

35 CNN, Dec. 4, 2001

36 *Toronto Sun*, Sept. 16, 2001; *Boston Globe*, Nov. 23, 2001; *Washington Post*, July 21, 2001. (Not in Thompson timeline)

37 CNN, Sept. 11, 2001; ABC News, Sept. 11, 2001; All major networks

38 *Guardian*, Oct. 17, 2001; *Boston Globe*, Nov. 23, 2001; *New York Times*, Oct. 16, 2001.

39 NORAD, Sept. 18, 2001; CNN Sept. 17, 2001; *Washington Post* Sept. 15, 2001.

40 *Washington Post*, Sept. 12, 2001; *Newsday*, Sept. 23, 2001.

41 ABC News, Sept. 11, 2002; *New York Times*, Sept. 16, 2001; *Sarasota Herald Tribune*, Sept 10, 2002.

42 *Guardian*, Oct, 17, 2001; *Boston Globe*, Nov. 23, 2001; *Newsday*, Sept. 23, 2001.

43 *New York Times*, Sept. 15, 2001.

44 *Christian Science Monitor*, Sept. 17, 2001.

45 *Telegraph*, Dec. 16, 2001; *New York Times* Sept. 16, 2001

46 *Washington Times*, Oct. 7, 2002; *Daily Mail*, Sept. 8, 2002

47 *Newsweek*, Dec. 31, 2001.

48 CNN, Dec. 4, 2001; *White House Release,* Jan. 5, 2002; *CBS,* Sept. 11, 2002.
49 *USA Today,* Sept. 16, 2001.
50 *New York Observer,* June 17, 2004; *MS-NBC,* Sept. 11, 2002.
51 *Aviation Week & Space Technology,* Sept. 9, 2002.
52 AP, Aug. 19, 2002.
53 *Aviation Week & Space Technology,* Sept. 9, 2002.
54 *Daily Mail,* Sept. 8, 2002; *Washington Times,* Oct. 8, 2002.
55 *Guardian,* Oct. 17, 2001; *Boston Globe,* Nov. 23, 2001; *Telegraph,* Sept. 16, 2001
56 CNN, Oct. 26, 1999; *Tampa Tribune* Sept. 1, 2002.
57 *Newsday,* Sept. 23, 2001; NORAD, Sept. 18, 2001; *Washington Post,* Sept. 12, 2001; *New York Times,* Sept. 12, 2001.
58 *Newsday,* Sept. 23, 2001.
59 *Aviation Week & Space Technology,* June 3, 2002.
60 CNN, Sept. 17, 2001; NORAD, Sept. 18, 2001.
61 *Mirror,* Sept. 13, 2002.
62 NORAD, Sept. 18, 2001; AP, Aug. 19, 2002; CNN, Sept. 17, 2001; *Washington Post,* Sept. 12, 2001.
63 AP, Aug. 19, 2002.
64 *Newsday,* Sept. 23, 2001; NORAD, Sept. 18, 2001; CNN, Sept. 17, 2001.
65 *Telegraph,* Dec. 16, 2001.
66 MS-NBC, Sept. 22, 2001; *Washington Post,* Sept. 12, 2001; CNN, Sept. 12, 2001; *New York Times,* Sept. 12, 2001; *Federal News Service,* Sept. 11, 2001.
67 NORAD, Sept. 18, 2001; *Washington Post,* Sept. 12, 2001.
68 *Guardian,* Oct. 17, 2001; MS-NBC, Sept. 3, 2002; CNN, Sept. 13, 2001.
69 *Newsday,* Sept. 23, 2001; NORAD, Sept. 18, 2001; *Washington Post,* Sept. 12, 2001.
70 *Telegraph,* Dec. 16, 2001.
71 MS-NBC, Sept. 2, 2002; CNN, Sept. 17, 2001.
72 *Aviation Week & Space Technology,* Sept. 9, 2002.
73 Ibid.
74 *Washington Times,* Oct. 8, 2002; *Telegraph,* Dec. 16, 2001.
75 *New York Times,* Sept. 15, 2001; NORAD, Sept 18, 2001; CBS, Sept. 14, 2001; 9/11 Report, June. 17, 2004.
76 *New York Times,* Oct. 16, 2001.
77 *Washington Post,* Jan. 27, 2002; *Pittsburg Post Gazette.*
78 *The Toledo Blade,* Dec. 9, 2001.
79 NORAD, Sept. 18, 2001.
80 *Independent,* Aug. 13, 2002; *CBS News.*
81 AP, Sept. 13, 2001; *Nashua Telegraph,* Sept. 13, 2001.
82 *Philadelphia Daily News,* Nov. 15, 2001.
83 Ibid.
84 *Independent,* Aug. 13, 2002; *CBS,* May 23, 2002; *MS-NBC,* Sept. 22, 2001; NORAD, Sept. 18, 2001; *The Guardian,* Oct. 17, 2001; *Pittsburgh Post Gazette,* Oct. 28, 2001; *Washington Post,* Sept. 12, 2001; CNN, Sept. 12, 2001; AP, Aug. 19, 2002; *New York Times,* Sept. 12, 2001.

Chapter 19: Wargames

1 William B. Scott, "Exercise Jump-Starts Response to Attacks," *Aviation Week and Space Technology,* June 3, 2002; ABC *News,* September 11, 2002.
2 Ibid.
3 Statement of Rep. Christopher Cox in an Associated Press story dated September 16, 2001 reported in the Thompson timeline.
4 "The Defense Technical Information Center (DTIC®) is the central facility for the collection and dissemination of scientific and technical information for the Department of Defense (DoD). As an element of the Defense Information Systems Agency (DISA), DTIC serves as a vital link in the transfer of information among DoD personnel, DoD contractors and potential contractors and other US Government agency personnel and their contractors". <www.dtic.mil>.
5 Op. cit., *Aviation Week.*
6 Hart Seely, "Amid Crisis Simulation, 'We Were Suddenly — No Kidding — Under Attack,'" Newhouse News Service, January 25, 2002.
7 <www.forces.gc.ca/dcds/dir/dpdt/j7Ex/pages/exercises_e.asp>, <www.globalsecurity.org/military/ops/vigilant-guardian.htm> .
8 Op. cit., *Aviation Week.*
9 Mike Kelly, "NORAD confirmed two mock drills on September 11," NJ.com, December 5, 2003.
10 Ibid.

11 Richard A. Clarke, *Against All Enemies,* Free Press 2004, pp 4-5.

12 Scott Simmie, "'Northern Guardian': The Scene at NORAD on September 11," *Toronto Star, Sunday Ontario Edition,* December 9, 2001.

13 Email response from NORAD spokesperson Major Maria Quon dated April 21, 2004. The web site referred to was <www.norad.mil/index.cfm?fuseaction= home.news_rel_09_09_01>.

14 Op. cit., *Toronto Star.*

15 John J. Lumpkin, "Agency Planned Exercise on September 11 built around a plane crashing into a building," Associated Press, August 21, 2002 7:45PM ET.

16 <www.thememoryhole.org/911/ cia-simulation.htm>.

17 ABC *News,* September 11, 2002, Peter Jennings hosts 9/11 interviews. This confirmation referring obliquely to "the exercise" is a quotation taken from statements made by General Arnold to Charles Gibson.

18 Op. cit, *Aviation Week.*

19 Op. cit., Newhouse News Service.

20 Op. cit., NJ.com.

21 <www.norad.mil/index.cfm?fuseaction= home.news_rel_09_09_01>.

22 CNN, June 19, 2002, report by David Ensor.

23 Jonathan S. Landay, "NSA didn't share key pre-September 11 information, sources say," Knight Ridder Newspapers, June 6, 2002.

24 Nicholas Kristoff, "Why Didn't We Stop 9/11?" *New York Times,* April 17, 2004.

25 The email was referenced in a number of news outlets, including the *New York Times* of April 14, 2004. An image of the actual email is available at the Pogo web site <www.pogo.org>.

26 Bryan Bender, "Pentagon crash too unrealistic," *Boston Globe,* April 14, 2001.

27 Steven Komarow and Tom Squitieri, "NORAD had drills of jets as weapons," *USA Today,* April 18, 2004 (updated April 19), >www.usatoday.com/news/ washington/2004-04-18-norad_x.htm>.

28 Barbara Starr, "NORAD exercise had jet crashing into building," CNN, April 19, 2004.

29 Op. cit., Clarke, pp 3-4.

30 Op. cit., *USA Today.*

31 The ambiguous question whether the attacks were to be treated as a crime or as an act of war has been used as an all-purpose tool for neutralizing questions of legality raised by the Bush administration's post 9/11 policies. Detainees at Guantanamo are denied the privileges guaranteed to prisoners of war under the Geneva Conventions, yet the public is continually assured that the nation is at war; America is on a war footing; Bush is a war president; the war on terror will not end in our lifetime.

32 Op. cit., *Aviation Week.*

33 See note 21. "NORAD confirmed it had only eight fighters on the East Coast for emergency scrambles on September 11."

34 Statement of Kristen Breitweiser, Co-Chairperson, September 11th Advocates, Concerning the Joint 9/11 Inquiry, Senate Select Committee on Intelligence, House Permanent Select Committee on Intelligence, September 18, 2002, <http://intelligence.senate.gov/0209hrg/ 020918/breitweiser.pdf>.

35 ABC *News,* <http://abcnews.go.com/ sections/us/DailyNews/WTC_ suspects.html>.

36 George Wehrfritz, Catherine Skipp and John Barry, "Alleged Hijackers may have Trained at Military Bases," *Newsweek,* September 15, 2001.

37 <www.madcowprod.com>; "Mohammed Atta and the Venice Flying Circus," a documentary produced and directed by Daniel Hopsicker.

38 World Socialist Web Site, June 21, 2002 (Citing the Associated Press, Knight Ridder and other sources).

39 The BBC should note how many ways bin Laden and Al Qaeda had been penetrated and by whom, right up to 9/11; especially the 2000 federal New York prosecution that disclosed that the NSA had even broken bin Laden's encrypted communications and was monitoring him in 1999, and possibly even through the first part of 2000. Other stories indicated that bin Laden's communications were monitored right up to 9/11.

40 Tom Carver, "President Bush is pushing for a revamp of security," BBC, June 8, 2002.

41 Thierry Meyssan, "*11* Septembre 2001: L'effroyable imposture," *Editions Carnot,* March 7, 2002.

42 James Bamford, *Body of Secrets,* Anchor Books, 2002; also, <www.fromthewilderness.com/free/ww3/11_20_01_northwoods.pdf>.

43 <www.boeing.com, www.boeing.com/defense-space/military/unmanned/ucav.html>.

44 Joe Vialls, "Home Run: Electronically Hijacking the World Trade Center Attack Aircraft," Copyright Joe Vialls, October 2001.

45 Justin Pope, Associated Press, October 2, 2001.

46 "Sensation: Russia Also Became an Object for Air Terrorists' Attacks," *Pravda,* September 12, 2001, <http://english.pravda.ru/main/2001/09/12/14983.html>.

47 Brad Carlton, "How Bush Hit the 'Trifecta' on 9/11--and the Public Lost Big-Time," *Baltimore Chronicle and Sentinel,* June 12, 2002. See also David Corn, "Capital Games," the *Nation,* June 10, 2002, <www.thenation.com/capitalgames/index.mhtml?bid=3&pid=71>; William Rivers Pitt, "George W. Bush, Political Terrorist," *Truthout,* May 23, 2002, <www.truthout.org/docs_02/05.24A.Political.Terror.htm>.

Chapter 20: Q&A

1 Email from NORAD spokesperson Major Nancy Quon to the author dated April 20, 2004.

2 I was later unable to locate such a reference. It had been mentioned to me by Barbara Honegger in an email as I was rushing to meet the deadline for this book. I included the question and then went to verify it later and was unable to locate any such statement in published records of the hearings. Honegger later advised that she did locate a reference by Tenet to "red teams" on a videotape recording of the hearing and that it had been omitted from the official transcript because Tenet had used the term in an aside to an aide sitting close by as he asked for information.

3 The NRO drill did not involve a hijacked airliner. Seasoned interrogators frequently make mistakes in questioning so that suspects will correct them and start talking. Some suspects are smarter than others.

4 The same technique as in note 3. The "67 times" was in the year prior to June 1, 2001 (rather than September 11, 2001) when the new procedure transferring intercept authority was put in place. I had hopes that NORAD would correct me on this. That way I could have followed with, "Well, how many times were fighters scrambled between June 1, 2001 and September 11th?"

5 Richard A. Clarke, *Against All Enemies,* Free Press 2004, pp 4-5.

6 Leslie Miller, "Tape of 9/11 Controllers Was Destroyed," Associated Press, May 6, 2004.

7 <www.dorsai.org/~walts/rwoods.html>

8 Philip Shenon, "9/11 Panel Set to Detail Flaws in Air Defenses," *New York Times,* Editor's Note Appended, April 25, 2004.

9 In doing the research to source this story, which came to me incomplete over the internet, I found no less than 20 "Daily Herald" newspapers scattered around the US and Canada. Papers of that kind are among the dwindling oases of the media, local and independently owned, which have not been caught up in Wall Street Price/Earnings ratios. As I found them, I offered a silent prayer of thanks for these essential voices crying out from the wilderness, not caring if their stories affront some official version, dutifully telling their readers the truth. Jon Davis' story was exceptionally well written.

10 The Kean Commission actually stated in its final staff report that another ATC had handled both flights 11 and 175. Presumably both airlines and the FAA have ATC contact with pilots or else control was handed off shortly after take-off. Ballinger's role as a flight dispatcher does not conflict with an FAA controller handling the flight.

11 Jon Davis, "Suburban Flight Dispatcher to recount worst day," (Illinois) *Daily Herald,* April 14, 2004.

12 FAA official statement submitted at hearing of the national Commission on Terrorist Attacks Against the United States, June 17, 2004. Reported on and posted by Tom Flocco, <www.tomflocco.com/>.

13 Richard A. Clarke, *Against All Enemies,* Free Press, 2004, p. 3.

14 Testimony of US Secretary of Defense Donald H. Rumsfeld, prepared for delivery to The National Commission on Terrorist Attacks Upon the United States. March 23, 2004.

15 Tom Flocco, "Rookie in the 9/11 Hotseat," June 17, 2004, <www.tomflocco.com>.

16 ABC *News,* September 11th, 2001, interviews by Peter Jennings.

17 FSC Statement Regarding the Hearings on June 16th and 17th, June 14, 2004, Statement of 9/11 Family Steering Committee, <www.911independentcommission.org>.

18 Myers and the top brass reportedly ducked out of the hearings very quickly, limiting his remarks, avoiding questions. Myers claimed he had other pressing duties. Not a single commissioner suggested that Myers' knowledge or testimony might possibly be of essential national interest.

Chapter 21: The Final Hearing

1 Kane, Michael; "The Final Fraud — 9/11 Commission closes its doors to the public; Cover-Up Complete," *From The Wilderness* Publications, July 9, 2004. <www.fromthewilderness.com/ members/071204_final_fraud.shtml>.

2 FAA official statement submitted at hearing of the national Commission on Terrorist Attacks Against the United States, June 17, 2004. Reported on and posted by Tom Flocco at <www.tomflocco.com>.

3 E-mail from Michael Kane to Michael Ruppert, July 23, 2004.

Chapter 22: Giuliani and Tripod

1 Testimony of Rudolph Giuliani before the National Commission on Terrorist Attacks Upon the United States, Eleventh Public Hearing, May 19, 2004; "The 9/11 Commission Report," National Commission on Terrorist Attacks on the United States, released July 22, 2004, <www.9-11commission.gov/>.

2 Griscom, Amanda; "The Man Behind the Mayor," *New York* magazine, October 15, 2001.

3 <www.nyc.gov/html/oem/html/other/ sub_photos_pages/tripod.html>.

4 <www.nyc.gov/html/oem/html/other/ sub_news_pages/tripod05_22_02.html>.

[HHS Release] — "Thompson names director of preparedness office" — Press Release, Department of Health and human Services, May 3, 2002, <www.hhs.gov/news/press/2002pres/ 20020503a.html>.

Chapter 23: Dick Cheney, FEMA, and "Persons of Interest"

1 <www.whitehouse.gov/news/releases/ 2001/05/20010508.html>.

2 Ibid.

3 These would be libertarian (note the lowercase "l") ultra-nationalists, whose obsession with the sovereignty of the United States makes them bitterly oppose international institutions. They tend to regard any infringement of American civil liberties as the work of international forces, which often leads to the strange notion that FEMA is somehow an outgrowth of the United Nations.

4 Of course, this warrants the question why such theater was being tendered to the public in the first place. With the fully developed emergency powers already established in law, an announcement of the need to develop them can only have a political purpose — such as priming the public mind to expect and accept the use of such powers in an eventual emergency.

5 Chossudovsky, Michel, "Coup d'Etat in America," July 13, 2004, <http://globalresearch.ca/articles/ CHO407B.html>.

6 William Rivers Pitt, "Only Cowards Cancel Elections", *Truthout Perspective* July 14, 2004; <www.truthout.org>.

7 This FEMA press announcement had been removed from the FEMA web site as of July 2004.

8 The 9/11 Commission Report; The National Commission on Terrorist Attacks Upon the United States; hereinafter referred to as "The Final Report"; released July 22, 2004; Chapter 9, p. 293.

9 The Final Report; Chapter 10, p 327.

10 The Final report; footnote 16 to Chapter Ten, p. 556.

11 White House Press Release, "Gov. Ridge Names Deputy Director of Homeland Security," Oct 29, 2001.

12 This was documented in a number of locations. I found a good compilation on

him at the Disinfopedia web site, <www.disinfopedia.org/wiki.phtml?title+ Steve_Abbot>. Also, White House Press release dated October 29, 2001. (See footnote 8.)

13 Again confirmed through various sources. Office of the Press Secretary, The White House Press release dated October 29, 2001.

14 The University of Missouri; Media Advisory, MU CAMPUS TO HOST DISASTER RESPONSE POLICY EXERCISE, Jan 5, 2004 <www.missouri.edu/~news/releases/ disasterresponseadvisory.html>.

15 Transcript, "Meeting the Homeland Security Challenge," a conference sponsored by the Fletcher School of Law and Diplomacy, May 25-26, 2002 <http://ifpafletchercambridge.info/ transcripts/abbot.htm>.

16 <www.tenix.com/Main.asp?ID=866>, reported September 2003. Abbot is now listed as a member of the U.S. advisory board for the Micronesia, Southwest Pacific defense conglomerate Tenix.

17 Agenda for the President's National Security Telecommunications Advisory Committee XXVI meeting, April 30, 2003. This conference was held in the Roosevelt Room at the White House and featured some of the most powerful names I have ever come across. President Bush addressed the group which included the top leadership of Lockheed-Martin, Northrop-Grumman, Raytheon, SAIC, AT&T, Boeing and (among others) Microsoft. <www.ncs.gov/nstac/ april2003/nstac_meetings.html>.

18 George Washington University website, <www.homelandsecurity.gwu.edu/dhs/ experts/hauer_bio.html>.

19 DEPARTMENT OF HEALTH AND HUMAN SERVICES NATIONAL COMMITTEE ON VITAL AND HEALTH STATISTICS, transcript, Feb, 26, 2001, <http://ncvhs.hhs.gov/ 020226tr.htm>.

20 Charles Ornstein, "Anthrax Teamwork is a Struggle," *Los Angeles Times,* November 10, 2001.

21 <www.krollworldwide.com>.

22 "Whatever Happened to the WTC Hard Drive Recoveries?" The 7th Fire, <www.the7thfire.com/index2.htm>;

<www.the7thfire.com/ Politics percent20and percent20History/ 9/11/whatever_happened_to_the_wtc_ hard_drives.htm>. This particular citation proved to be a convenient collection of a multitude of references regarding Kroll that proved to be accurate and much easier to use. In addition it provided direct links to original stories, which saved a great deal of time.

23 Various web sites. Information on Hauer's professional life is not difficult to find. The breadth of his overlapping activities and their interrelationships with the issues of this book would make for a remarkable study in its own right.

24 Centers for Disease Control Health Advisory; "National Terrorism Threat Level Increase," February 7, 2003. "Today Jerome Hauer, Acting Assistant Secretary for Public Health and Emergency Preparedness, Department of Health and Human Services (DHHS), briefed the nation's state public health officials about the rationale for increasing the national threat condition for risk of terrorism attack."

25 <www.holliseden.com/content/ ?page_id=310>.

26 "Homeland Security Department to Conduct drills in Seattle, Chicago; CNN, Aired May 11, 2003 - 08:36 ET.

27 Marilyn W. Thompson, "The Pursuit of Steven Hatfill," *Washington Post,* September 14th 2003.

28 Michael C. Ruppert, and Wayne Madsen, "Combining Biological and Economic Warfare," *From The Wilderness,* May 9, 2003, <www.fromthewilderness.com>.

29 Lawrence Wright, "The Counter-Terrorist," *New Yorker,* January 14, 2001.

30 On the evening of November 21st, 1963, several of President Kennedy's Secret Service agents drank until three a.m. in a nightclub owned by Jack Ruby. Their performance the next day was less than exemplary. Palamara, Vincent, *The Strange Actions (and Inaction) of Agent Emory Roberts,* <www.jfklink.com/articles/EmoryRoberts.html>. This refers to events described in Volume 5 of the 26 Volume Warren Commission report.

31 Laurie Garret, "Post 9/11 Daily Journal, Day 12," <www.lauriegarrett.com/ missives_index.html>.

32 Katherine Pfelger, "CIA Boss, Iraq never and Imminent Threat," Associated Press, February 5, 2004. There are dozens of stories and official conformations that could be cited here. Authoritative reports from the UN to British and U.S. agencies have debunked every allegation that any Iraqi weapons research program continued with any force after the first Iraqi war and the imposition of UN sanctions in 1991.

33 Laurie Garret, "U.S. Ill Prepared for Bioterrorism," *Newsday,* September 22, 2001.

34 A web search for "Mighty Wurlitzer" will reveal a multitude of references to this attribution which described the CIA's relationship with the major press. I first heard the phrase used this way in a personal encounter with retired CIA "analyst" Ralph McGehee in 1997. McGehee a former clandestine service case officer was one of the first-ever CIA personnel to go public with criticisms of the agency. He has been a staunch critic of CIA operations and created one of the first publicly available computer data bases (on an early version of DOS no less) shedding light on how the Agency really operated in clandestine operations.

Chapter 24: The Secret Service and National Special Security Events

1 Richard A. Clarke, *Against All Enemies,* Free Press, 2004, pp. 6-7.

2 Kean Commission report, page 9.

3 Ibid, p. 25.

4 Ibid, pp. 35-36.

5 Ibid, p. 39.

6 Ibid, p.44.

7 Ibid, p. 305.

8 Ibid, p. 33.

9 Department of Homeland Security Press Release, July 9, 2003, <www.dhs.gov/dhspublic/display?content=1065>.

10 FAA,National Security Event Flight Advisory, FAA Southern Regional Headquarters (undated), <www.faasafety.gov/notices/2004-Mar/31_G8_Flyer_April_Mtg_final_DRAFT.doc>.

11 Department of Homeland Security web site, <www.dhs.gov>; also the General Services Administration website, <www.gsa.gov/Portal/gsa/ep/contentView.do?pag...-13257&P=1PBB&contentId=15226&contentType=GSA_BASIC>.

12 US Secret Service Advisory, June 10, 2004, <www.ustreas.gov/usss/nsse.shtml>.

13 Department of Homeland Security Press Release, National Special Security Events Fact Sheet, July 9, 2003, <www.dhs.gov/dhspublic/display?content=1065>.

14 <http://c21.maxwell.af.mil/glossary.htm>.

15 <www.afnsep.af.mil/>.

16 <www.globalsecurity.org/military/agency/usaf/afnsep.htm>.

17 op. cit. Kean p. 345.

18 Wood, Allan and Thompson, Paul; "An Interesting Day: President Bush's Movements and Actions on 9/11," May 9, 2003, <www.cooperativeresearch.org>.

Chapter 25: The Commission's Wild Blue Yonder

1 The author served as a board member of <www.911.truth.org> for several months in the spring of 2004 but had to resign due to scheduling conflicts and time issues regarding the completion of this book.

2 Levis, Nicholas; "Senator Dayton: NORAD Lied About 9/11," <www.911Truth.org>, August 1, 2004. Levis had been a principal organizer of a September, 2003 9/11 event at Berlin's Tempodrome amphitheater in which then-former US Congresswoman Cynthia McKinney and the author were the featured speakers.

3 Hence, Kyle, Sample letter for mass mailing to Senator Mark Dayton, posted August 1, 2004 at 911Truth.org; <www.911truth.org/article.php?story=20040731213239607>.

4 Kean Commission report, page 458.

5 Ibid, p. 17.

6 Ibid, p. 21.

7 Ibid, p. 23.

8 Ibid, p. 30.

9 Leslie Filson, *Air War Over America: Sept. 11 Alters the Face of Air Defense Mission;* Headquarters 1st Air Force, Public Affairs Office, Tyndall Air Force Base, FL, 2003. ISBN 0-615-12416-X.

Chapter 26: The Record

1 "The law sets forth a number of reasons why jurors may be excused 'for cause.' For example, a juror who is related to or employed by one of the parties in the

case may be excused for cause." <www.courtinfo.ca.gov/jury/glossary.htm>.

2 <www.homelandsec.org/ABOUTUS/aboutusprojcomm.htm>.

3 <www.globalresearch.ca/articles/MAD202B.html>.

4 Michel Chossudovsky, "New Chairman of 9/11 Commission had business ties with Osama's Brother in Law," Dec 27, 2002, <www.globalrsearch.ca>.

5 Jim Rarey, "9/11 COMMISSION — FORGEDDA BOUDIT" Medium Rare December 29, 2002.

6 Sarah McLendon, "Sarah McLendon's Washington Report," Oct. 20, 1992.

7 Bob Parry, "History on the Ballot," *Covering Up Iran-Contra,* Nov. 5, 2000, <www.consortiumnews.com/2000/110500b.html>.

8 Peter Kornbluh, Oliver Twisted — A day in the life of a would-be Senator, *Mother Jones,* May/June 1994 issue; <www.motherjones.com/news/outfront/1994/05/kornbluh.html>. Korbluh is a senior analyst at the National Security archives where many of the most damaging Iran-Contra records are stored.

9 Oliver Schröm, "Tödliche Fehler," *Die Zeit,* October 2, 2002.

10 Philip Shenon, "Terrorism Panel Subpoenas Tapes from New York," *New York Times,* November 21, 2003.

11 Michael Isikoff, "A New Window on the War Room", *Newsweek,* April 12, 2004 issue.

12 Emad Mekay, "Iraq: War Launched to Protect Israel — Bush Advisor," Interpress Service News Agency (Pakistan), March 29, 2003.

13 Op. cit., Rarey.

14 Bonnie Hayskar, email to 9/11 TruthAlliance list, February 21, 2004 (quoted with permission).

15 <www.slb.com/aboutus/>.

16 Dan Eggen, "White House Holding Notes Taken by 9/11 Commission," *Washington Post,* January 31, 2004.

17 Op. cit., Hayskar.

18 Op. cit., Rarey.

19 Eric Boehlert, "The President Ought to be Ashamed," *Salon,* November 21, 2003.

20 911Truth.org, 9/11 "Commission: The official coverup guide", May 18, 2004,

<www.911truth.org/article.php?story=20040525104145424>.

21 "New Job Takes Cleland off 9/11 Panel," UPI, November 23, 2003.

22 Bill Vann, "War criminal to probe mass murder; Ex-Senator appointed to 9/11 panel," World Socialist Web Site, December 12, 2003.

23 Terry McDermott, "Questions persist despite 9-11 investigations," *Los Angeles Times,* July 26, 2004.

24 William Raspberry, "Failures of the Sept. 11th Commission," *Washington Post,* July 26, 2004.

Chapter 27: "We Don't Need No Badges"

1 HR 3443, The Public Health Security and Bioterrorism Preparedness and Response Act of 2002: <www.fda.gov/oc/bioterrorism/bioact.html>; Model State Emergency Health Powers Act, <www.aapsonline.org/legis/msehpa.pdf>.

2 This was reported by both MS-NBC and NBC as noted by UC professor Peter Dale Scott at <http://ist-socrates.berkeley.edu/~pdscott/qf911.html>. "On Sept. 17, 2001, six days after the attacks on the World Trade Center and the Pentagon, President Bush signed a 2 1/2-page document marked 'TOP SECRET' that outlined the plan for going to war in Afghanistan as part of a global campaign against terrorism. Almost as a footnote, the document also directed the Pentagon to begin planning military options for an invasion of Iraq, senior administration officials said ..." Glenn Kessler, "US Decision On Iraq Has Puzzling Past Opponents of War Wonder When, How Policy Was Set." *Washington Post,* January 12, 2003.

3 Ibid.

4 Jennifer Van Bergen, "The USA Patriot Act Was Planned Before 9/11," May 20, 2002, <www.truthout.org/docs_02/05.21B.jvb.usapa.911.htm>.

5 US Commission on National Security, 21 Century. Hart-Rudman Commission, <www.nssg.gov/>.

6 Cf. Institute for Homeland Security, <www.homelandsecurity.org/>.

7 "Catastrophic Terrorism: Elements of a National Policy, A Project of Visions of

Governance for the Twenty-First Century," A project of the John F. Kennedy School of Government, Harvard University, <www.ksg.harvard.edu/visions/publication/terrorism.htm>.

8 "Two on 9/11 Panel Are Questioned on Earlier Security Roles," Eric Lichtblau and James Risen, *New York Times,* January 15, 2002.

9 Greg Miller, "Hearings Portray Overwhelmed Agencies and Suggest 9/11 Could Have Been Prevented," *Los Angeles Times,* October 19, 2002. Archived at <www.truthout.org/docs_02/10.21C.911.preventable.htm>.

10 And if the enemy is to be "the terrorists," what in the world is supposed to be motivating them? Certainly not some abstract "hatred of freedom"; people commit mayhem because they have an agenda, some demands, a cause. Whether the terrorism is manufactured or genuine, false-flag or foreign, it *must* not have any popularly understood (or even openly stated) motive. If you attribute any actual demands to the bad guys, or allow them to express their own demands in the public arena, then you introduce the risk that those demands might become the subject of rational debate. Worse yet, somebody might find a peaceful resolution to the demands. And then *Presto!* No more terrorist threat.

11 The National Security Strategy of the United States, <www.whitehouse.gov/nsc/print/nssall.html>.

12 Greg Miller, "Wider Pentagon Spy Role Urged," *Los Angeles Times,* October 26, 2002.

13 William Arkin, "The Secret War," *Los Angeles Times,* October 27, 2002. Archived at <www.ratical.org/ratville/CAH/SecretWar.html>.

14 Ibid.

15 Chris Floyd, "Into the Dark," *CounterPunch,* November 1, 2002, <www.counterpunch.org/floyd1101.html>.

16 "Also early in 1982 a new covert unit of the Armed Forces was set up by General Richard Stilwell. Known as the Intelligence Support Activity (ISA), it became a separate entity in the Army's secret world of special operations, with its own commander, a Col. Jerry King. The Army's involvement in secret operations would first become known to the House and Senate intelligence committees in early 1982, when they discovered a project known as Yellow Fruit, which ferried undercover Army operatives to Honduras, where they trained Honduran troops for bloody hit-and-run operations into Nicaragua." — from Daniel Hopsicker and Michael C. Ruppert, "Why Does George W. Bush Fly in Drug Smuggler Barry Seal's Airplane?" *From the Wilderness,* October 1999, <www.fromthewilderness.com/free/politics/W_plane.html>.

17 Wayne Madsen, "Bush Reactivates ISA," *Intelligence Online,* October 24, 2002, <www.intelligenceonline.com>.

18 The Paul Thompson timeline, <www.unansweredquestions.org/timeline/>.

19 "USA. Demands Immunity from Prosecution For War Crimes," *Pravda,* June 23, 2002, <http://english.pravda.ru/main/2002/06/23/30928.html>.

20 "New Pentagon office to spearhead information war," CNN, February 19, 2002, <www.cnn.com/2002/US /02/19/gen.strategic.influence/>.

21 Department of Defense News Briefing, February 26, 2002, excerpts on Office of Strategic Influence, <www.defenselink.mil/today/2002/to20020226.html>.

22 "Secretary Rumsfeld Media Availability En Route to Chile" (Excerpt on DARPA'S Total Information Awareness program), The Federation of American Scientists, <www.fas.org/sgp/news/2002/11/dod111802.html>.

23 Molly Ivins, "Bush Administration Resurrecting Office to Lie to Citizens, Allies," *Salt Lake Tribune,* December 19, 2002, <www.sltrib.com/2002/Dec/12192002/commenta/commenta.asp>; Thom Shanker and Eric Schmidt, "Pentagon Debates Propaganda Push in Allied Nations," the *New York Times,* December 16, 2002. Archived at <www.commondreams.org/headlines02/1216-01.htm>. The *Times* piece is itself disinguous in suggesting that the program was only under consideration for reinstatement. It completely ignored Rumsfeld's admission that he was seeing

to it that OSI operations were carried out.

24 Paul Richter, "US Works up Plan for using Nuclear Arms," *Los Angeles Times,* March 9, 2002. Archived at <www.commondreams.org/headlines02/0309-01.htm>; David G. Savage, "Nuclear Plan Meant to Deter", *Los Angeles Times,* March 11, 2002, <www.latimes.com/news/nationworld/nation/la-031102nukes.story>; Cf. Gyre.org: "Tracking the Next Military and Technological Revolutions." See the keywords "Nuclear War Planning" at <www.gyre.org/news/explore/Nuclear percent20War percent20Planning/0/chrono>.

25 "US Warns Iraq: We'll Nuke You," *New York Post,* December 11, 2002; Marian Wilkerson, "We'll Use Nuclear Arms, US Warns," *Sydney Morning Herald,* December 12, 2002. Archived at <www.newsfrombabylon.com/article.php?sid=2609>.

26 John Markoff, "Pentagon Plans a Computer System that Would Peek at Personal Data of Americans," *New York Times,* November 10, 2002. Archived at <http://cryptome.org/tia-queeg.htm>.

27 "China, Nortel and the Net," *Globe and Mail,* October 19, 2001. Archived at <http://clearwisdom.net/emh/articles/2001/10/24/15005.html>; "Nortel helping China monitor its citizens," *South China Morning Post,* October 19, 2001. Archived at <www.mail-archive.com/uighur-l@taklamakan.org/msg02432.html>. Interestingly, facial recognition software and network modeling software are offshoots of the same relatively recent branch of applied mathematics, called data-mining. The descriptive modeling of a social web of human relationships (say, a terrorist network) uses some of the same techniques as the facial recognition process, because each entails the discovery of otherwise hidden patterns in data sets whose giant size disperses the patterns beyond conventional discovery. Some of the same computational techniques that are used to determine who (among 260 million Americans) is a wanted man, can then be used to determine that the guy standing at the ATM machine (among so many million such machines) is he.

28 Ibid.

29 "Pentagon seeks to detect people by odor," *USA. Today,* December 19, 2002, <www.usatoday.com/news/washington/2002-12-19-pentagon-odor_x.htm>.

30 Frank J. Murray, "NASA Plans to read terrorist's minds at airports," the *Washington Times,* August 17, 2002, <www.washtimes.com/national/20020817-704732.htm>.

31 The gradual introduction of these programs is proceeding quietly, and that stealth is aided by the very spookiness of the technologies. To most of us, the phrase "microchip I.D. implants" sounds too Orwellian, too sci-fi, too paranoid for serious consideration — so the rapid expansion of that technology remains hidden in plain sight. See the "Statement Of Barry Steinhardt, Director, Technology And Liberty Program, American Civil Liberties Union, On Government Data Mining, Before the Technology, Information Policy, Intergovernmental Relations and the Census Subcommittee of the House of Representatives Committee on Government Reform, May 20, 2003", <www.aclu.org/SafeandFree/SafeandFree.cfm?ID=12669&c=206&Type=s&insearch=rfid#_ftn9>. See also see this important report: "Bigger Monster, Weaker Chains: The Growth of an American Surveillance Society," by Jay Stanley and Barry Steinhardt, January 2003, ACLU, Technology and Liberty Program, <www.aclu.org/Privacy/Privacy.cfm?ID=11573&c=39#FileAttach> For a consideration of the implications of implants from the perspective of legal theory, see Elaine M. Ramesh, "Time Enough? Consequences of Human Microchip Implantation," *RISK: Health, Safety & Environment,* Volume 8.373 Franklin Pierce Law Center: 1997, <www.fplc.edu/risk/vol8/fall/ramesh.htm#top>.

32 See the National Strategy for Homeland Security, at <www.whitehouse.gov>. This is also clearly articulated in the Patriot Act under the definition of "Domestic Terrorism."

33 Ibid, p. 38.

34 Homeland Security Strategy, p. 22.

35 Matt Richtel, "Voices in Your Head? Check That Chip in Your Arm," *New York Times,* November 10, 2002. Archived at <www.grailwerk.com/docs/nytimes2.htm>; Kevin Krolicki, "Microchips under the skin offer ID, raise questions," *Los Angeles Times* (Reuters), December 20, 2001.

36 Rowan Scarborough, "Pentagon Delivers First Total Information Software," *Washington Times,* December 18, 2002, www.washtimes.com/national/20021218-37385050.htm.

37 Ibid.

38 Reuters, July 31, 2003.

39 CNN, July 31, 2002, "Poindexter to Resign in Coming Weeks Over Terror Futures Flap."

40 "Anti-terror mining research continues," Associated Press, February 23, 2004. <www.cnn.com/2004/LAW/02/23/terror.privacy.ap/>.

41 Viviane Lerner, "US Special Forces Seek Genetically Engineered Bioweapons," *The Sunshine Project,* August 12, 2002, <www.sunshine-project.org/publications/pr/pr120802.html>.

42 Toby Harnden, "The US Will Attack Iraq Without UN Backing,." *Guardian,* January 10, 2003, <www.dailytelegraph.co.uk/news/main.jhtml?xml=/news/2003/01/10/wirq110.xml&sSheet=/news/2003/01/10/ixnewstop.html>.

43 Roland Watson, "US weapons dossier may remain secret," *Times of London,* January 9, 2003. Archived at <www.prisonplanet.com/news_alert_010903_iraq.html>.

44 "US and Israel discuss joint anti-terror office," *Washington Times,* June 29, 2002, <www.washtimes.com/national/20020629-1359928.htm>.

45 Richard Sale, "Israel to kill in US , allied nations," *Washington Times,* January 15, 2003, <http://washingtontimes.com/upi-breaking/20030115-035849-6156r.htm>.

Chapter 28: Conquering the American People

1 One of the ironies of today's political semantics is the way two synonyms have moved so far apart that they're almost opposites. "Freedom" is a good sturdy propaganda word (since it's an emotional trigger, a common working-class word that's been saturated with sentimental associations). But "liberty," the word the Founding Fathers used so often, has become suspect. "Liberty" is something we only talk about when it's vanishing, using the technical language of "civil liberties." Freedom means the mythical goodness of the USA., without regard to the facts; believing in it is patriotic. Liberty means the actual range of opportunities for the safe execution of one's own decisions; to concern oneself with it is to be a dissident.

2 Paraphrasing Shakespeare, *The Tragedy of Julius Caesar,* Act I, scene ii, "Upon what meat doth this our Caesar feed, that he is grown so great"?

3 Michael C. Ruppert, *From The Wilderness,* Vol. IV, No 8, November 20, 2001.

4 Michael C. Ruppert, *From The Wilderness,* Vol. V, No. 10, February 28, 2003.

5 Readers familiar with the events of November 22, 1963 will recall an apt example of this phenomenon (Federal supersession of state authority in a criminal case, followed by the Federal falsification of autopsy results to the advantage of the Federal government).

6 Homeland Security Act of 2002, hereinafter referred to as "the Act", Title I, Department of Homeland Security, Section 101. Executive Department Mission, <www.whitehouse.gov/deptofhomeland/bill/title1.html#101>; <news.findlaw.com/wp/docs/terrorism/hsa2002.pdf>. The Act, Title 1 Section 102. Secretary functions, <www.whitehouse.gov/deptofhomeland/bill/title1.html#102>; <http://news.findlaw.com/wp/docs/terrorism/hsa2002.pdf>.

7 The Act, Title 2, Section 201. I-Information Analysis and Infrastructure Protection, Sec. 201. Under Secretary for Information Analysis and Infrastructure Protection. www.whitehouse.gov/deptofhomeland/bill/title2.html#201; <news.findlaw.com/wp/docs/terrorism/hsa2002.pdf>.

8 The Act, Title 2, Section 202. Functions Transferred, <www.whitehouse.gov/deptofhomeland/bill/title2.html#202>;

<news.findlaw.com/wp/docs/terrorism/hsa2002.pdf>.

9 The Act, Title 2, Section 223. Enhancement of Non-Federal Cybersecurity, pp. 49-50. <news.findlaw.com/wp/docs/terrorism/hsa2002.pdf>.

10 Ibid, Section 892 [Facilitating Homeland Security Information Sharing Procedures], pp. 299-306, <news.findlaw.com/wp/docs/terrorism/hsa2002.pdf>.

11 The Act, Title 3 [Science and Technology in Support of Homeland Security], section 304 [Conduct of Certain Public Health-Related Activities], pp. 73-82. <news.findlaw.com/wp/docs/terrorism/hsa2002.pdf>.

12 Ibid; The Act, Title 8 [Co-ordination with Non-Federal Entities; Inspector General; United States Secret Service; Coast Guard; General Provisions], section 887 [Coordination with the Department of Health and Human Services under the Public Health Service Act], pp.287-288, <news.findlaw.com/wp/docs/terrorism/hsa2002.pdf>.

13 The Act, Title 3 [Science and Technology in Support of Homeland Security], Section 308 [Conduct of Research, Development, Demonstration, Testing and Evaluation], pp. 87-91, <news.findlaw.com/wp/docs/terrorism/hsa2002.pdf>.

14 "More Than 6 Million People Behind Bars or on Probation or Parole," *Boston Globe,* Associated Press, August 26, 2002, <www.truthout.org/docs_02/08.27F.6M.in.jail.htm>.

15 Jesse Katz, "A Nation of Too Many Prisoners?" *Los Angeles Times,* February 15, 2000, <www.mapinc.org/drugnews/v00/n211/a08.html>.

16 "Of the more than 150,000 men and women currently incarcerated in the federal prison system, 22,000 are employed by Federal Prison Industries, which uses the trade name UNICOR. The wholly owned government corporation was established by Congress in 1934 to provide job skills, training, and employment for prisoners, and now has more than 100 factories operating inside federal prisons nationwide," Silja J.A. Talvi, "Business from behind bars: profitable, or not?" *Christian Science Monitor,* May 14, 2001, <http://csmweb2.emcweb.com/durable/2001/05/14/fp16s1-csm.shtml>. According to Unicor's own literature, "...it should be noted that the average Federal inmate has an 8th grade education, is 37 years old, is serving a 10-year sentence for a drug related offense ..." <www.unicor.gov/history/foreword.htm>.

17 <www.unicor.gov/history/unicor 1980.htm>.

18 Tony Paterson, "Baghdad's uncensored weapons report to UN names Western companies alleged to have developed its weapons of mass destruction," *Independent,* December 18, 2002, <http://archives.econ.utah.edu/archives/marxism/2002w52/msg00008.htm>.

19 As of this writing these include AOL/Time Warner, Enron, WorldCom, Qwest, Tyco, ImClone, Global Crossing, Dynegy, CMS Energy, El Paso, Halliburton, The Williams Co., Clear Channel, Adelphia, Kmart, Reliant (Overstated earnings by $7 billion), Motorola, and Merck (Overstated earnings by $12 billion).

20 Ian Cheng, "Executives in top US collapses made $3.3 bn," *Financial Times,* July 30, 2002. <http://pub97.ezboard.com/fthefinfactsdiscussionforumfrm1.showMessage?topicID=65.topic>; "FT Investigation: The Barons of Bankruptcy," *Financial Times,* August 1, 2002, <http://news.ft.com/servlet/ContentServer?pagename=FT.com/StoryFT/FullStory&c=StoryFT&cid=1028185341976&p=1027953298906>.

21 Kelly Wallace, "Senators: Bush could undercut whistleblowers," (CNN), The Freedom of Information Center, July 31, 2002, http://foi.missouri.edu/whistleblowing/senatorsbush.html; Audrey Hudson, "Security Bill bars blowing whistle," *Washington Times,* June 22, 2002, <www.washtimes.com/national/20020622-42082444.htm>.

22 Martin Crutsinger, "US government is unrivaled champion at cooking the books," *Nation and World,* July 15, 2002, <www.nwaonline.com/pdfarchive/2002/July/15/7-15-02 percent20D1.pdf>.

23 Arianna Huffington, "Why Is Washington Ignoring The Warning Signs of economic Devastation?" May 30, 2002,

<http://senrs.com/why_is_washington_
ignoring_the_warning_signs_of_
economic_devastation.htm>.

24 Ronald Fink, "The Fear of All Sums,"
CFO magazine, August 1, 2002,
<www.elaonline.com/news/
MembersOnly/indnewswkly/
081302.htm#story14>.

25 Special thanks to researcher David Podvin
for compiling this list. The sources he
used to compile it included: "Accounting
for Options," Chetan Perikh; "Earnings
Report Parodies," Comstock Partners,
Inc. October 11, 2001; CNN
MoneyLine — October 25, 2001,
November 30, 2001; Reuters, January
31, 2002; William Fleckenstein,
President Fleckenstein Capital; *Business
Wire,* November 7, 2001; SEC filings
(from the EDGAR data base).

26 Testimony of The Honorable Susan
Gaffney Inspector General, Department
of Housing and Urban Development
before a hearing of the Subcommittee on
Government Management, Information,
and Technology, March 22, 2000, "1999
Audit Results for the Department of
Housing and Urban Development,"
<www.house.gov/reform/gmit/hearings/
2000hearings/000322.hud/000321sg.htm>;
Kelly Patricia O'Meara, "Why Is $59
Billion Missing From HUD?" *Insight*
magazine, November 6, 2000,
<www.insightmag.com/main.cfm?include=
detail&storyid=208636>.

27 "According to the General Accounting
Office, between 1996 and 1998 the
United States Navy 'lost' more than $3
billion worth of goods — tasty items
like guided missile launchers and night
vision equipment. One reason the
diversion of these goodies went
unnoticed, says William J. Lynn III, the
Defense Department's comptroller, is
that the department has been using
more than 330 separate accounting systems to keep track of its possessions. In
April, Lynn told a Senate subcommittee
that he is working hard to reduce that
number to 32," *Bulletin of the Atomic
Scientists,* Vol. 55, No. 5,
September/October 1999, pp. 9-10,
<www.thebulletin.org/issues/
1999/so99/so99briefs.html>.

28 Kelly Patricia O'Meara, "Rumsfeld
Inherits Financial Mess," *Insight* magazine, September 3, 2001.
<www.insightmag.com/main.cfm?include=
detail&storyid=139530>.

29 "The War on Waste," CBS *Evening News,*
January 29, 2002,
<www.cbsnews.com/stories/2002/01/29/
eveningnews/main325985.shtml>.

30 <www.cdi.org/budget/2004/
world-military-spending.cfm>;
.

31 David Turner, "World unemployment
increases to 180m," *Financial Times,*
January 24, 2002, <http://news.ft.com/
servlet/ContentServer?pagename=
FT.com/StoryFT/FullStory&c=
StoryFT&cid=1042491155790>.

32 David Lazarus, "Killing the Messenger:
Layoff-Poll Funds Cut," *San Francisco
Chronicle,* January 2, 2003,
<www.siliconinvestor.com/stocktalk/
msg.gsp?msgid=18395554>.

33 Patrick Martin, "Corporate bankruptcies
exhaust US pension guaranty fund,"
World Socialist Web Site, January 29,
2003, <www.wsws.org/articles/2003/
jan2003/pens-j29.shtml>.

34 "US Bankruptcy Filings Hit Another
Record," Reuters, November 26, 2002,
<www.xtramsn.co.nz/business/
0,,5086-1952222,00.html>.

35 Thomas A. Fogarty, "Home foreclosures at
30-year high," *USA Today,* September 10,
2002, <www.usatoday.com/money/perfi/
housing/2002-09-09-foreclosure_x.htm>.

36 Mark Felsenthal, "Home foreclosures at
record high," Reuters, January 7, 2003,
<www.twincities.com/mld/twincities/
business/4892198.htm>.

37 Peronet Despeignes, "US housing executives offload stock," *Financial Times,* August
28, 2002, <http://news.ft.com/servlet/
ContentServer?pagename=FT.com/StoryFT/
FullStory&c=StoryFT&cid=1028186102
016&p=1012571727088&ft_acl=>.

38 M.A. Nystrom, "Pop Goes the Bubble —
Part II, Sell Your House Now!"
<www.gold-eagle.com/editorials_02/
nystrom122702.html>.

39 <www.digitaleconomist.com/deficit_
2004.html>.

40 John Crudele,"US Treasury Web Site
reveals $1/2 Trillion Deficit for Fiscal

2001," *New York Post,* May 14, 2002. <www.moneyfiles.org/ banking10.html#anchor1248949>.

41 "Moscow Economic Conference Draws 200 From Russia, Germany, Mid East and Asia," *From The Wilderness,* March 31, 2001, <http://fromthewilderness.com/ free/economy/us_econ_threat.html>.

42 Greg Morcroft, "US banks derivatives top $50 trillion," CBS *MarketWatch,* September 6, 2002. <http://cbs.marketwatch.com/news/ story.asp?guid={858881D6-47E0- 42B2-88B7-022F2D352775} &siteid=mktw&dist=&archive=true>.

43 Chris Sanders, "The Unsustainable Nation," October 18, 2001, <www.scoop.co.nz/stories/HL0203/ S00059.htm>.

44 H.R. 3210, (PL 107-297) - The Terrorism Risk Insurance Act, <www.ustreas.gov/ offices/enforcement/ofac/legal/statutes/ statute201.pdf>.

45 Lucy Komisar, "Congress Rips Off Consumers Over Terror Insurance," Pacific News Service, November 20, 2002, <http://news.pacificnews.org/ news/view_article.html?article_id= ea793db419eb4285f06c16c2da956edd>.

46 Todd Zwillich, "Bush Asks Court to Seal MMR Vaccine Records," Reuters *Health,* November 26, 2002, <www.rense.com/ general32/mmr.htm>.

Chapter 29: Biological Warfare

1 Ceci Connolly and Shankar Vedantam, "US Offers Anthrax Vaccine to Thousands," *The Washington Post,* December 19, 2001, Page A01, <www.majorbates.com/ news/19Dec01_WP.htm>.

2 Connolly and Vedantam, op. cit.; Jim Rarey, "Medium Rare, Anthrax — Keystone Cops or Deniability," *FTW,* October 26, 2001, <www.fromthewilderness.com/free/ww3/ 10_26_01_anthraxrarey.html>.

3 Rarey, op. cit.

4 Rarey, op. cit.; Cf. Len Horowitz, <www.tetrahedron.org/>, and many other sources including SEC filings.

5 Ina Gurney, "Vaccine Maker BioPort and bin Laden — A profitable Symbiosis," *Rense.com,* December 19, 2001, <www.rense.com/general18/prp.htm>.

6 Tim Martin, "BioPort working on new vaccine," *Lansing State Journal,* March 11, 2002, <www.lsj.com/news/BioPort/ 020311_BioPort_1a-4a.html>.

7 Cheryl Seal, "The run on Cipro: A Case of 'Corporate Terrorism?'" October 16, 2001, <www.unknownnews.net/ cipro.html>.

8 Rarey, op. cit.

9 Seal, op. cit., "Law of the Land, Feds sued over anthrax documents: Legal group wonders why the White House took Cipro before attacks," *World Net Daily,* June 7, 2002, <www.wnd.com/news/ article.asp?ARTICLE_ID=27888>.

10 "Law of the Land, Feds sued over anthrax documents: Legal group wonders why the White House took Cipro before attacks," *World Net Daily,* June 7, 2002, <www.wnd.com/news/article.asp? ARTICLE_ID=27888>.

11 Julie Appleby, "US Requesting 300 million smallpox vaccines," *USA Today,* October 17, 2001. See also Appleby, op. cit.; Tetrahedron LLC News Release [NO. DITA-90]: "Public Health Expert Says Solving The Anthrax Mailing Mystery May Be Easy: FBI Doesn't Seem Interested," November 12, 2001, <www.tetrahedron.org/news/ NR011112.html>.

12 Appleby, op. cit.

13 Leonard G. Horowitz, "Re: Smallpox Vaccination Concerns," Letter to ACIP-NVAC Smallpox Working Group, CDC, June 6, 2002, <www.geocities.com/ missionstmichael/ SmallpoxHorowitz.html>.

14 Seal, op. cit.; cf. the CorpWatch website: <www.corpwatch.org/>.

15 Sherri Tenpenny, "Smallpox Outbreak: What to Do," the *Sierra Times,* July 15, 2002, <www.sierratimes.com/02/07/15/ arst071502.htm>. Also please visit Tenpenny's website at <www.nmaseminars.com>.

16 Alan Cantwell, Jr., M.D., "Bioterrorism and Armageddon, Separating fact from fantasy in the New World Order," *New Dawn* magazine, November, 2002.

17 Ibid. See also: Leonard Cole, *Clouds of Secrecy: The Army's Germ Warfare Tests Over Populated Areas,* Rowman and

Littlefield, 1988; Michael Uhl and Tod Ensign, *GI Guinea Pigs: How the Pentagon Exposed Our Troops to Dangers More Deadly Than War,* Wideview Books, 1980.

18 Charley Reese, "US Blocks Inspections," King Features Syndicate, December 13, 2002, <http://reese.king-online.com/ Reese_20021213/index.php>; Julian Borger, "US weapons secrets exposed," *Guardian Unlimited,* October 29, 2002, <www.guardian.co.uk/usa/story/ 0,12271,821306,00.html>.

19 Alanna Mitchell, Simon Cooper and Carolyn Abraham, "Scientists Deaths Are Under the Microscope," *Globe and Mail.com,* May 4, 2002, <http://globeandmail.workopolis.com/ servlet/News/fasttrack/20020504/ UMURDN?section=Science>.

20 Lisa Belkin, "The Odds of That," *New York Times,* August 11, 2002, <www.nytimes.com/2002/08/11/ magazine/11COINCIDENCE.html>.

21 <www.barrychamish.com/English/ Newsletter/December percent202001.htm>.

22 <www.worldnewsstand.net/MediumRare/ Archives.htm>.

23 Novosibirsk is also near the location of a deadly outbreak of anthrax, believed to have been created by Soviet bioweapons programs in the 1960s and 70s.

24 <www.fromthewilderness.com/free/ ww3/02_14_02_microbio.html>.

25 <www.fromthewilderness.com/free/ww3/ 04_04_02_new_biowar.html>.

26 <www.fromthewilderness.com/free/ww3/ 071702_bushbiobil.html>.

27 <www.fromthewilderness.com/free/ww3/ 011503_ramp_up_bio.html>.

28 Daniel DeNoon, "Killer Virus Changes its Skin: Ingredients for Worldwide Flu Epidemic Brewing in China," MSN Health, June 17, 2002, <http://content.health.msn.com/ content/article/48/39230.htm>.

29 Dr. David Whitehouse, "First synthetic virus created," BBC *News,* July 11, 2002, <http://news.bbc.co.uk/1/hi/sci/tech/ 2122619.stm>.

30 "Over 900 Ill After China Vaccine," ABCNews.com (Reuters), July 12, 2002, <www.vaccinationnews.com/DailyNews/ July2002/Over900Ill12.htm>.

Chapter 30: Order of Battle

1 Julie Hyland, "Britain: Foreign secretary admits oil central to war vs. Iraq," World Socialist Web Site, January 14, 2003. <www.wsws.org/articles/2003/jan2003/ strw-j14.shtml>.

2 Richard C. Duncan and Walter Youngquist, "The World Petroleum Life-Cycle". Paper presented at the PTTC Workshop "OPEC Pil Pricing and Independent Oil Producers," Petroleum Technology Transfer Council, Petroleum Engineering Program, University of Southern California, Los Angeles, California, October 22, 1999. <http://dieoff.com/page133.htm>.

3 *From The Wilderness,* Vol. 5, No.6, Oct 1, 2002.

4 "Wheels Come off US War Plans for Iraq," *From The Wilderness,* Vol. 5, No. 7, Nov. 4, 2002.

5 *Washington Post,* August 18, 2002.

6 "Crunching numbers," *From The Wilderness,* April 16, 2003, <www.fromthewilderness.com/free/ww3/ 041603_crunching.html>.

7 *Pakistan Tribune,* August 2, 2003.

8 MENAFN.com, April 30, 2004.

9 *Petroleum Supply Monthly,* December, 2002, op. cit.

10 Chris Wattie, "Canada 'all but undefend-ed': study Institute says weakness invites 'anxious' US to violate our border in event of a crisis," *The National Post,* June 11, 2002, <www.ccs21.org/ ccs21nationalpost/ ccs21-npost-5-06-11-02.htm>.

11 "Petro-Canada Reviewing Oilsands Strategy," <www.rigzone.com>, May 2, 2003, <www.rigzone.com/news/ article.asp?a_id=6493>.

12 "When Markets Fail, America Leaps Off the Natural Gas Cliff Without a Parachute," *From The Wilderness,* July 12, 2003, <http://fromthewilderness.com/members/ 071203_no_parachute.html>.

13 "Afghan Pipeline Deal Inked," Rigzone.com, December 27, 2002, <www.rigzone.com/news/article.asp? a_id=5218>.

14 *New York Times,* August 8, 2003.

15 *Government Executive,* April 16, 2003; Associated Press, May 7, 2003.

16 *Los Angeles Times,* August 7, 2003.

17 "Saudi Arabia, West Africa: Next Stops in the Infinite War for Oil," *From The Wilderness,* May 17, 2003, <http://fromthewilderness.com/free/ww3/051503_saudi_africa.html>.

18 "Study: Emergency Responders Unprepared," Associated Press, June 29, 2003.

19 Paul Krugman, "Paths of Glory," New York Times News Service, May 19, 2003.

20 Reuters, August 12, 2003.

21 "Saudi Prince Killed in Ambush," *Pakistan Tribune,* Dec. 2, 2003.

22 "Militant killed in Saudi Shootout," CNN, April 5, 2004; "Gunman, officer killed in Riyadh firefight," CNN April 12, 2004.

23 "Evacuation Is Ordered for Most US Diplomats in Saudi Arabia," *Washington Post,* April 16, 2004.

24 "Saudi Suicide Bomb Toll Revised," CNN, April 21, 2003.

25 "Gunmen Kill Several at Saudi Oil Compound," CNN, May 1, 2004.

26 Op. cit., *From The Wilderness,* Saudi Arabia, West Africa.

27 *Strafor,* December 13, 2002.

28 "US, NATO Allies May Focus on Africa, Predicts NATO Senior Military Commander." Voice of America, May 1, 2003.

29 *Boston Globe,* May 17, 2003.

30 Agence France Presse, April 24, 2003.

31 Associated Press, July 16, 2003.

32 Reuters, July 16, 2003.

33 CNN, August 11, 2003.

34 Reuters, Sept. 18, 2001; BBC, November 27, 2001; confidential sources.

35 *Petroleum Supply Monthly,* December, 2002, Energy Information Administration, Office of Oil and Gas, US Department of Energy, Washington, DC 20585. <http://tonto.eia.doe.gov/FTPROOT/petroleum/psm/01090212.pdf>; "Colombia is our eighth largest supplier of petroleum bi-products," US Congressman Mark Souder (Indiana), "Illegal Drugs" Congressman Souder's Homepage, <www.house.gov/souder/illegal_drugs.html>.

36 Arianna Huffington, "The Bush Oiligarchy's Pipeline Protection Package," Commondreams.org, February 21, 2002, <www.commondreams.org/views02/0225-07.htm>.

37 Scott Wilson, "Wider War in Colombia: As Military Steps Up Attacks on Rebels, Conflict Spreads to Once Stable Areas," *Washington Post,* September 6, 2001, <www.washingtonpost.com/ac2/wp-dyn/A48724-2001Sep5?language=printer>.

38 Jonathan Wright, "Powell sees 'gray areas' in defining terrorism," Reuters, October 25, 2001 <http://colhrnet.igc.org/newitems/oct01/patterson.o25.htm>.

39 Mike Boettcher, "South America's 'tri-border' back on terrorism radar," CNN.com, November 8, 2002, <www.cnn.com/2002/WORLD/americas/11/07/terror.triborder/>.

40 "US Officials Unveil Colombia Plans," Associated Press, February 6, 2002, <www.amazonwatch.org/newsroom/mediaclips02/uwa/020206_uwa_ap.html>.

41 Juan Forero, "New Role for US in Colombia: Protecting Vital Oil Pipeline," *New York Times,* October 4, 2002, <http://query.nytimes.com/gst/abstract.html?res=F20E12F93D5F0C778CDDA90994DA404482>.

42 Peter Gorman, "Marines Ordered Into Colombia," *Narco News Bulletin,* October 25, 2002, <www.narconews.com/article.php3?ArticleID=19>.

43 "Bush, The Rainforest and a Gas Pipeline to Enrich His Friends." Independent, July 30, 2003.

44 Lucy Komisar, "Colombian reporter Tells All — To US Press," *American Reporter,* December 2, 2002, <www.globalexchange.org/colombia/20021211_469.html>.

45 "Quietly US Special Forces Enter Colombia to Train Troops," Ibon Villelabeitia, Reuters, January 17, 2003, <www.truthout.org/docs_02/011903F.ussf.colba.p.htm>.

46 Joe Taglieri, "Turmoil: Miracle In Venezuela: Chavez Dupes US-backed Coup — Democratically Elected Leader Unfriendly to US Foreign Policy Regains Power After Two Days Under Military Arrest," *From The Wilderness,* May 6, 2002, <www.fromthewilderness.com/free/ww3/050702_miracle.html>; Dale Allen Pfeiffer, "Interventions 'r' US," *From the Wilderness,* Vol. V, No. 8,

December 30, 2002,
<http://fromthewilderness.com/free/
ww3/123102_ven_r_us.html>.

47 "Turmoil: Miracle in Venezuela," *From The Wilderness,* May 6, 2002.

48 Al Giordano, "The Day the Empire Died: 32 American Governments Reject DC over Venezuela," December 17, 2002, <www.narconews.com>.

49 Heather Stewart, "US oil stocks evaporate to 27-year low," *Guardian,* January 16, 2003, <www.guardian.co.uk/business/story/0,3604,875662,00.html>.

50 Dale Allen Pfeiffer, "Interventions 'r' US," op. cit.

51 CNN, March 1, 2004, "Aristide: "I call it a coup d'etat".

52 "Aristide's Lawyers Preparing Complaints Against US, France," Associated Press, March 10, 2004; "Role in Haiti Events Backfiring on Washington", Inter Press Service. March 12, 2004; Exclusive Aristide interviews on radio KPFA's "Democracy Now."

53 Stan Goff, "Haiti and Venezuela — Coup and Empire," *From the Wilderness,* March 23, 2004.

54 "Chavez Calls Bush 'Asshole' as Foes Fight Troops." Reuters, February 29, 2004.

55 "Top-level Chinese delegations negotiate crude oil contracts if USA Bush 2 war machine locks on to Venezuela electoral dispute," VHeadline.com, March 19, 2004.

56 "RI Has Enough Gas Reserves for 50 Years," *Jakarta Post,* August 4, 2003.

57 *New York Times,* August 5, 2003.

58 <www.detik.com/peristiwa/2003/08/05/20030805-183447.shtml>.

59 "GM's China Sales Jump Over 300 Percent," Reuters, January 20, 2003, <www.charlotte.com/mld/observer/business/4989471.htm>.

60 "China's Exploding Car Industry," BBC, March 10, 2003.

61 Michael C. Ruppert, "The Chinese Government is not supporting the Taliban with troops: recent stories intended to frighten the right are disinformation and propaganda," *From The Wilderness,* Vol. IV, No. 7, October 24, 2001. <www.fromthewilderness.com/free/ww3/10_24_01_china.html>.

62 China, June 2002, <www.eia.doe.gov/cabs/china.html>.

63 China's Worldwide Quest for Energy Security, 2000, IEA publication, <www.iea.org/public/studies/china.htm>.

64 Joe McDonald, "Politics, security worries drive 2,500-mile pipeline in China," Associated Press. August 14, 2002, <www.bakersfield.com/oil/story/1594068p-1711407c.html>.

65 The Caspian Region, 2002, <www.eia.doe.gov/cabs/caspian.html>.

66 Personal communication with the author.

67 Larry Chin, "The United States in the Philippines: Post 9/11 Imperatives; Oil and Gas in the South China Sea (part 2 of 6)"; *Online Journal;* July 25, 2002, <http://onlinejournal.com/Special_Reports/Chin072502/chin072502.html>.

68 "Australia: Biggest Export Contract Ever;" 2002-08-08, *Pravda.RU.*

69 "World Oil Supplies Running Out Faster than Expected", by OGJ editors, *Oil and Gas Journal,* August 12, 2002.

70 Dr. Norman D. Livergood. "Military Dictatorship USA?" <www.hermes-press.com/militarismindex.htm>.

71 "It is not Euro to make the Dollar Crash, but Yuan," 2001-11-09, <http://english.pravda.ru/economics/2001/11/09/20503.html>.

Chapter 31: Peak Oil Revisited

1 Adam Porter, "Is The World's oil Running Out Fast?, BBC *News,* June 7, 2002.

2 <www.peakoil.net/uhdsg/UppsalaProtocol.html>.

3 Stella Farrington, "THE SKEPTIC: Politicians Take Note: OPEC Can't Cool Oil, The Dow Jones Newswires, May 21, 2004.

4 "G8 offers opportunities for Bush," CNN, Monday, June 7, 2004.

5 James Jordan and James Powell, "After The Oil Runs Out", the *Washington Post,* June 6, 2004, page B07.

6 "G7: Oil Price Threatens World Economy," *The Moscow Times,* April 26, 2004.

7 Op Ed, H. Sterling Burnett, "Enough Oil to Last 500 Years", *The Houston Chronicle,* May 29, 2004.

8 Victor A. Canto, "Hubbert's Holes", the *National Review,* June 4, 2004.

9 George F. Will, "America After Oil", the *New York Post,* June 13, 2004.

10 "Shell Reduces Estimates for Fourth Time This Year", CBC, May 24, 2004.

11 Bruce Stanley, "BP defends oil reserve estimate method", Associated Press Business Wires, June 14, 2004.

12 "Why Isn't Big Oil Drilling More?" *BusinessWeek,* June 21, 2004.

13 Steve Raabe, "US Faces Reality Check Over Oil, *The Denver Post,* June 13, 2002.

14 Alex Berenson, "An Oil Enigma: Production Falls Even as Reserves Rise", the *New York Times,* June 12, 2004.

15 <www.fromthewilderness.com/free/ww3/042204_mazur_morgan_oil.html>

16 Scott Burns, "Oil and S&P connection points to grim news for stocks", the *Seattle* Times, June 13, 2004.

17 <www.safehaven.com/article-1597.htm>.

18 Alex Belida, "US Navy to Deploy Aircraft Carrier Strike Group in the Gulf of Guinea, *Voice of America News*, May 31, 2004.

19 "Oil Security Chief Slain in Iraq", CNN, June 16, 2004, <www.cnn.com/2004/WORLD/meast/06/16/iraq.main/index.html>.

Chapter 32: Summation

1 Michael C. Ruppert, "Global Economic Collapse Likely: Derivatives Bubble About to Burst — Manipulated Gold Prices About to Explode, Can Wall Street Survive?" *From the Wilderness,* Sept 9, 2001, <http://www.fromthewilderness.com/free/ww3/11_09_01_Derivatives.html>.

2 <http://www.fromthewilderness.com/free/ww3/081503_cia_russ_oil.html>.

3 Ching Cheong, "China pipeline plan to secure oil supplies," *Straits Times,* July 31, 2004.

4 Jamey Hecht, "Richard Clarke's Orchestra: Maestro Plays Simple Waltz; Shackled Media Manage to Dance Along," *From The Wilderness,* April 5, 2004, <http://www.fromthewilderness.com/free/ww3/040504_Clarke_orchestra.html>.

5 There are many sources for this. They include: Nick Hopkins, "False identities Mislead FBI," *Guardian,* Sept. 21, 2001; "Dead Saudi Hijacker Resurfaces, Denies Involvement," All Africa.com, Sept. 24, 2001; "At Least Four of the 9/11 Hijackers are Alive and Well," BBC *News,* Sept. 23, 2001; David Bamford, "Hijack 'Suspect' Alive in Morocco," BBC *News,* Sept 22, 2001; Kate Connolly, "Father Insists Alleged Leader is Still Alive," *Guardian,* Sept 2, 2002; "Hijack 'Suspect' Alive and Well," BBC *News,* Sept. 23, 2001; Timothy Maier, "FBI Denies Mix-Up Of 9/11 Terrorists," *Insight* magazine, June 11, 2003.

6 Tom Carver, "President Bush is Pushing for a Revamp of Security," BBC *News,* June 8, 2002. The story refers to Hani Hanjour and his four companions who crashed Flight 77 into the Pentagon.

7 "September 11 — US Government accused," *Portugal News,* March 8, 2002, <http://www.the-news.net/>.

8 Cheryl Seal, "The 9/11 Evidence That May Hang George W. Bush," *Scoop Media,* <http://www.scoop.co.nz, June 12, 2002>.

9 <http://www.dod.mil/comptroller/biozakheim.html>.

10 <http://www.sysplan.com/Homeland_Security>.

11 <http://www.sysplan.com/Homeland_Security>.

12 <http://www.sysplan.com/sysplan/Radar/FTS/index_html>.

13 <http://www.sysplan.com/sysplan/Corporate/Officers/DZakheim>.

14 Woody Box (Nico Haupt), "911: The Cleveland Airport Mystery," INN World Report, May 29, 2004, <http://inn.globalfreepress.com/modules/news/article.php?storyid=323>.

15 Kean Commission report, Footnote 1, Ch. 9 p. 541.

16 Clarke, *Against All Enemies,* p. 8.

17 Richard Clarke, *Against All Enemies,* Free Press, 2004, p. 12

Index

A

Abbot, Charles S. "Steven," 418-421
Abdullah, Prince, 131, 140-142,
Abrams, Elliot, 66
Acxiom, 492
Aero Postale de Mexico, 64-65
Afghanistan
    and drugs, 59-60, 68, 71, 73-74, 75
    occupation, 83, 100, 534
    pipeline, 95-97, 98, 99, 191, 535
Afridi, Ayub, 68
Against All Enemies, 2, 338, 385
Ahmad, Mahmoud, 118-120, 146
Ahmed, Nafeez, 103, 104, 112, 120
Air Force One, 375, 383, 390, 402
airline stock trading, 238-242, 245-
    248
Air National Guard, 354, 386, 390
Alex Brown, 56, 241, 244, 247,
    250-251
    and Bush family, 251
Aleklett, Kjell, 47
Alfa Group of Companies, 72, 73
al-Faisal, Turki, 104, 124, 126, 143, 147
Alhazmi, Nawaf, 229-231
Alghamdi, Saeed, 347, 349, 580
Algiers, The Treaty of, 7
Alhazmi, Nawaf, 229-231, 256, 264,
    319, 349, 580
Allbaugh, Joe, 413, 414, 417
Almidhar, Khalid, 229-231, 256, 264,
    319, 349, 580
Alomari, Abdulaziz, 580

al Qaeda, 10, 85, 126, 136, 185, 208,
    335-336
    in Africa, 538-539
    and BCII, 53
    and Caspian oil, 94, 96, 97, 99, 102,
    and CIA, 107, 115, 117, 579-580
    in Germany, 244
    penetration, 229-237
    in South America, 541
    on September 10, 342-343, 469
Alshehri, Wail, 349, 350, 580
Altman, Robert, 53
Amdocs, 262
American Broadcast Corporation
    (ABC) News, 54, 57, 110, 117,
    177, 217, 235
American Civil Liberties Union
    (ACLU), 484, 524
American Dynasty, 69
American International Group (AIG),
    54, 56, 57, 503, 545
American Israeli Public Affairs
    Committee (AIPAC), 265-266
American Stock Exchange, 50
Andean Initiative, The, 541-542
Andrews Air Force Base, 309, 313, 331-
    332, 398
Annual Energy Outlook 1998, 35
anthrax, 39, 271, 486, 505-509, 516,
    518, 522, 525
Anti-Defamation League of B'nai Brith
    (ADL), 260-261
Arab oil embargo, 28

Arellano Felix Brothers, 65
Arias, Don, 362, 364-369, 385-388,
  390, 408, 411
Aristide, Jean Bertrand, 543-544
Arkansas Development Financial
  Authority (ADFA), 56-57
Armitage, Richard, 73, 91, 115, 119,
  120, 132
Arnold, Larry, 334-335, 341, 354, 365,
  366, 374, 439, 444
Arthur Andersen, 79
Ashcroft, John, 94, 102, 206, 221, 222,
  224, 270
  and Patriot Act, 484, 486
Asia Times, 95, 141,
Associated Press (AP), 12, 71, 95, 209,
  215, 226, 232, 234, 353, 398
  articles, 11, 41, 100, 225, 240,
  271, 305-306, 340-341, 369-370,
  482
Association for the Study of Peak Oil
  and Gas (ASPO), 39, 47, 562
  Berlin conference, 555, 556-557
  Paris conference, 30
Atef, Mohammed, 97-100
Atta, Mohammed, 3, 117-122, 223,
  224, 228, 231, 234, 256, 343, 349,
  350, 466, 468, 579, 580
Austin Chronicle, 70
Australia 167, 227,
Aven, Pyotr, 72
Aviation Week, 334, 337, 341, 347
Ayers, Bradley Earl, 175, 176, 184

B
Bahamas, 73, 74
Baker, James A., 31, 91, 129-131, 539
Bakhtiari, Ali Samsam, 562-563
Balochistan Post, 75
Bamford, James, 9, 228,
Banamex., 56, 78, 473
Banco Nacional de Mexico, *See* Banamex

Bank of America, 77
Bank of New York, 89
bankruptcies, 495, 499, 500
Barnes, Scott, 177-180, 183, 191,
Barr, Bob, 271, 274, 275-278
Bath, James, 131-133
Bayer, 506-508
BBC, 107, 112, 140, 144, 147, 203,
  228, 350
BCCI, 53, 140, 145, 159, 160
ben Laden, Usama, 186
Ben-Veniste, Richard, 459
bin Laden, Abdullah, 147, 148, 203,
  204,
bin Laden, Osama, 3, 10, 12, 53, 80,
  97, 99-100, 103, 108, 116, 118, 355
  as asset, 576, 579-580
  and Bush family, 536
  in Africa, 539
  financing, 123-151
bin Laden, Salem, 124, 132-134,
Bin Laden: The Forbidden Truth, 99
bin Mahfouz, Khaled, 127, 134, 140,
  451, 468
bin Talal, Alwaleed, 145,
BioPort, 505-506
bioterrorism, *See* biowar
biowar, 493, 505-526 *See also* anthrax
Birol, Fatih, 558, 559, 560, 567
Bishop, Baldwin, Rewald,
  Dillingham, and Wong (BBRDW),
  54, 177
Black Tuesday, 246
Blair, Tony, 137, 232,
Body of Secrets, 9
Bolivia, 59
Bosnia, 79, 90, 135, 136
Boston Globe, 344, 360
Bottom of the Barrel, 42
Brewer, Captain Jesse
Brisard, Jean-Charles, 97, 105, 124,
  127, 138, 140

British East India Company, 67
British Gas, 51
British Petroleum-Amoco (BP), 22, 33,
    37, 51, 72, 83, 94, 96, 102, 108,
    144, 560
Brooke, James, 46
Brown and Root, 6, 7, 8, 69-74, 536
Brown Bothers Harriman, 70
Brzezinski, Zbigniew, 32-33, 82-86, 89,
    96-97, 103, 109, 111, 149, 575
Bundy, McGeorge, 90
Bush, George H. W., 82, 88, 98,
    129-133, 170
    and bin Ladens, 130-131
    and CIA, 5
    and Clintons, xv
    as Vice President, 17
Bush, George W., 10, 15, 105, 115,
    134, 139, 185
    administration, 41, 70, 81, 82, 88,
    107, 116, 120, 143, 203, 220, 222,
    227, 254, 451, 456, 462, 471-478
    budget deficit, 501-502
    and financial raiding, 496-500
    and Harken Energy, 79, 160
    and Iraqi invasion, 101, 146
    presidential papers, 487, 489
    as Texas Governor, 79, 133
    2000 election, 487-488
Bush, Jeb, 224, 350, 466
Business Week, 96
Butler, Steve, 222-224

C
CYA , 66
Cabal, Carlos, 65
Calero, Adolfo, 66
Campbell, Colin, 22, 26, 30, 33, 39,
    96, 559, 560, 563
Canada, 162-163, 165, 189, 533-534
Canadian Armed Forces, 334, 336, 345,
    347, 367

Capital Cities, 54
Capitol, the, *See* Pentagon
Carlucci, Frank, 129, 131-133, 475
Carlyle Group, 129-131, 133, 143, 145,
    148, 272, 273, 451, 468
Carone, Albert Vincent, 54
Carter, Jimmy, 83, 452, 462
Casey, Bill, 53, 54, 63, 104, 164, 165,
    170, 181, 452
Caspian Pipeline Consortium (CPC),
    101
CONR, 334, 362, 368
Caspian Sea Basin, 33, 83, 94-102, 573,
    575
Castillo, Celerino, 67
Castro, Fidel, 9
Cavallo, Alfred, 42
Cayman Islands, 61
Central American Task Force (CATF),
    67
Central Asian Republic, 33, 84, 85, 88,
    90, 94, 96-98, 100, 101
Center for Public Integrity (CPI), 69,
    72, 73, 74
CentGas, 97
Central Intelligence Agency (CIA), xv,
    6, 7, 11, 12, 63, 90, 162, 176,
    180-181
    and anthrax, 271, 507, 509, 518
    and Osama bin Laden, 116, 135-
    137, 140, 147, 149
    and drugs, 9, 16, 107, 132, 487
    and hijackers, 229-231
    and insider trading, 132, 245, 247,
    249
    Inspector General Report, xvii, 17
    And ISI, 103-122, 135
    and Israeli spies, 267-268
    and oil companies, 88, 573
    and Patriot Act, 484, 489
    and prisons, 494
    and wargames, 343

Chavez, Hugo, 542, 543-544
Chechnya, 73, 90, 102, 136, 137, 208,
Cheney, Richard (Dick), 24, 36, 41-49,
    69-74, 98, 100, 102, 109, 117, 331,
    333, 337, 388, 412-429, 433-436,
    454, 464, 466, 474, 573, 576
    in charge, 574, 577
    in command on 9/11, 411, 591-592
    and GAO, 486-487
    Guiliani call, 409, 410-411
    and Halliburton, 355
    and phone bridges, 383, 390
    shoot-down order, 399
Chernomyrdin, Victor, 89
Chicago Board Options Exchange
    (CBOE), 50, 238, 240, 251-252, 253
Chin, Larry, 107,
China, 84, 102, 227, 532, 544-551,
    552-553, 558, 576
    and LNG, 550
    offshore oil and gas, 549-550
    and US trade, 545
Chossudovsky, Michel, 104,134-136,
    415, 416
    article, 115-122
Cipro, 506-507, 508
Citigroup, 56, 61, 77, 78
Clarke, Richard, 2, 148, 222, 338, 339,
    343, 365, 368-369, 385, 425, 427,
    428, 433, 456, 579
Clifford, Clark, 53
Clinton, Hillary, xv, 172
Clinton, William Jefferson, 56, 78, 97,
    179, 350, 467
    administration, 15, 73, 74, 79, 88-
    92, 105, 106, 576
    impeachment, xv, 17, 66
CNN, 46, 99, 120, 124, 232
coal, 26-27, 39, 557
Cocaine Politics, 67
cocaine, xv, xvii, 16, 56, 57, 59, 63, 64-
    67, 71

Code Red alert, 415, 416
Cohen, Aaron, 7
Cohen, Dr. Sidney, 59
Coldren, Lee, 105, 108
Colombia, 59, 61, 62, 67, 72, 73, 74,
    540-542, 543
Combat Air Patrol, 410
Community Wizard, xvii
Comverse, 262
Congress, post 9/11, 229, 269-290
Contagion: The Betrayal of Liberty,
    Russia, and the United States in the
    1990s, 88
CONUS (Continental United States),
    342, 360, 396, 534
Convar, 243
Corn, David, 2, 300-303
Corporate Reform Act, 495
Council on Foreign Relations (CFR), 8,
    31-32, 36-38, 57, 83, 86, 90, 91,
    111, 576
Cox, Chris, 92, 112
Cox Report, 91, 92
Crack the CIA, xviii
Crisis Strategy Group (CSG), 338
C3 (Command, Control,
    Communications), 362, 367
Cuba, 9, 53, 228

D

Dabhol, 95, 100
Daniels, Mitch, 81, 495
Dark Alliance Alliance: The CIA, The
    Contras, and the Crack-Cocaine
    Explosion), xvii
Darwin, Sir Charles Galton, 38-39
Daschle, Tom, 269-270, 273, 278
Dasquié, Guillaume, 97, 105, 124, 138,
Davidson, Michael, 509,
    articles, 510-524
Department of Defense (DoD), xv, 12,
    63, 66, 79, 127, 128, 314, 316, 525

Department of Energy (DOE), 33, 44, 84, 525

Department of Homeland Security (DHS), 11, 39, 491-493, 508

Department of Housing and Urban Development (HUD), xiii, xvii-xviii, 55-57, 79, 160, 161, 167, 168, 415, 419-423, 431, 432, 472, 481, 496-497, 499

Department of Justice (DoJ), xv, xvii, 55, 56, 57, 155, 161, 164, 184, 210
on 9/11, 407, 411, 415

Deskins, Dawne, 342, 366, 386

Deutsche Bank, 244, 245, 247, 250-251

Deutsch, John, xviii, 458

DNA research, 512-516, 519-521

D'Orsay, Nordica Theodora, 5-6, 7

Dow Jones, 52, 68, 248, 495, 498, 501, 564

Dresser Industries, 70

Drug Enforcement Administration (DEA), 5, 59, 60, 63, 219
and Israel, 258, 261-265

Drugs, Oil and War: The United States in Afghanistan, Colombia and Indochina, 75

Drug trade, 16, 38, 57, 58, 67, 69, 70, 73, 74, 83, *See also* cocaine

Dubai, 34, 140, 148, 149

Dulles, Allen, 53, 54

Duncan, Richard, 23, 37

DynCorp, 71, 79-80, 161, 497, 511, 519-520, 535

Dynegy, 62

E

Eberhart, Ralph, 334, 348, 354, 381, 390, 438, 442, 534
testimony, 393-396, 402

Echelon, 227-229, 232

Edmonds, Sibel, 220-222, 468

Eitel, Gary, 64, 180, 181, 184, 350

electricity, 27, 28, 32

el Motassadeq, Mounir, 3

El Paso Oil, 36

End of Cheap Oil, The, 30

Energy Information Administration (EIA), 32, 35, 540

Energy Silk Road, 548-549

Enron, 36, 43, 52, 53, 55, 60-62, 75, 79, 94-95, 100, 102, 124, 128, 151, 470

Environmental Protection Agency (EPA), 27, 523

Eurasian Balkans, 85, 86

Export-Import Bank (EXIM), 72

ExxonMobil, 51, 94, 102, 560

F

fascism, 15, 483

Federal Aviation Administration (FAA), 256-257, 282-283, 309, 315
on 9/11, 334-335, 387, 395, 399-402, 410
tape of 9/11, 369-371, 372
and wargames, 336, 343
See also phone bridges

Federal Bureau of Investigation (FBI), 7, 12, 97, 99, 116-121, 147, 163, 170, 185, 204-226, 231-234, 240, 260, and Patriot Act, 484, 493, 495, 518

Federal Emergency Management Agency (FEMA), 405, 406, 411, 412-419, 422, 423, 426, 433, 584

Federal Housing Administration Fund, 56

Federal Prison Industries, *See* UNICOR

Federal Reserve, xv, xvii, 53

Federal Reserve System (FRS), 61

Fielding, Fred, 405-406, 460

Fiers, Alan, 67

"Final Fraud, The," 393-396

Fire Department of New York (FDNY), 407, 411

First American Bancshares, 53

First Union Bank, 77

Fitts, Catherine Austin, xii-xix, 51, 55-57, 79, 160, 161, 193, 317

Fleischer, Ari, 10, 542

Flight 11, 256-257, 334, 335, 341, 385-386, 389, 390, 394, 399, 400, 401, 424, 444, 587

Flight 93, 310, 347, 349, 377-379, 391, 399, 408, 429, 430, 444, 589

Flight 175, 335, 350, 377-379, 385-389, 399, 401, 408, 410, 411, 434, 444, 587

Flight 1989, 587-589

Flight 77, 11, 339, 348-351, 373-375, 384, 388, 399-402, 581

Flight X, 587-589

Flocco, Tom, 234, 249-250, 383-384, 388-389, 391, 392, 402

Food and Drug Administration (FDA), 505, 506, 519, 523, 524

Ford Foundation, 90

Ford Motors, 61

Forbidden Truth, 97, 105, 106, 124, 127, 138, 140

Foster, John, 53

Fox, Vicente, 79

Frasca, Dave, 208, 214-219, 468

Fraud, 494-495, 498, 499, 519, 520, 523-524

Freedom of Information Act (FOIA), 7, 44

Freeh, Louis, 12

French Institute of Petroleum, 31

Fridman, Mikhail, 72

From The Wilderness, articles, 28-29, 33, 139-146, 152-169, 170-173, 193-197, 234, 244-247, 249-256, 275-290, 394-396, 483-491, 497-499, 510-526, 529-533, 545-553

Fuller, Craig, 7

Fulton, John, 11

G

G-8 Summit, 10, 565

Galati, Rocco, 175, 186-190, 194-196, 199

Galbraith, James Kenneth, 47

Garvey, Jane, 339, 343, 348, 366

General Accounting Office (GAO), 41, 43, 486-487

General Electric, 61, 100

General Motors, 25, 60, 61

Ghawar, 557, 558, 560

Giordano, Al, 79

Giuliani, Rudolph, 404-411, 418, 422, 429

"Global Zone of Percolating Violence, The," 86

Globe and Mail, 509

Golden Triangle, 59, 73

Goldman Sachs, 68, 88, 90, 241

Gore, Al, 88, 89, 92

Gorelick, Jamie S., 396, 397, 398, 455, 457-459

Gorton, Slade, 461

Goss, Porter, 119,120, 225

Graham, Bob, 119,120, 225

Graham, Katherine, xiii

Grand Chessboard: America's Primacy and Its Geostrategic Imperatives, The, 32-33, 40, 82, 84, 86, 96, 575

Grantham, Woody, 64

Grasso, Dick, 57

Great Britain,
and al Quaeda, 137-141
as US ally, 528

Great Depression, 92

Greenberg, Maurice "Hank", 56, 57

Grossman, Marc, 118, 120

Gulf of Mexico, 6, 33

Gulf War, 48, 71, 109, 142

H

Hadron Advanced Biosystems, 170, 511, 518, 519

Haiti, 543, 544

Halliburton, 6, 47, 62, 69-75, 102, 191, 467, 535

Hamilton Securities, xvii-xviii, 55-56, 57

Hamilton, William (Bill), 152, 154-159, 161, 162, 164, 166, 168, 171-173

Hanjour, Hani, 351, 580

Hanson, Jay, 39

Harken Energy Corporation, 79, 134, 149, 160,

Harrell, Ronald, 36

Harvard Endowment, 79, 89

Hauer, Jerome (Jerry), 418, 421-426

Haupt, Nico, 335-336, 372

Hekmatyar, Gulbuddin, 104

Hendrix, Dave, 64

Henick, Chris, 410
    Giuliani call, 409, 410-411

heroin trade, 5, 6, 8, 59-60, 69, 72, 75, 132, 134,
    and Afghanistan, 68, 71, 73, 83, 104, 135, 233
    and AIG, 57
    and Laos, 9, 73

Hernandez, Roberto, 78-79

Hersh, Seymour, 102

Herzliya Institute for Counterterrorism, 238, 246, 248, 256

Hewlett Packard, 61

Highfields Capital, 79

High Times, 60

Hijackers, training, 144, 223, 224, 225, 233, 349-350, 576, 578, 580

Hill, The, 43

Hitz, Frederick P., 66-68

Hollings, Fritz, 81

Homeland Security, 11, 39, 280, 419, 433, 471, 477, 478, 491, 508, 584

Honegger, Barbara, 335-336, 343, 372, 385, 452, 453,

Hopsicker, Daniel, 349, 350

Hot Money, 59

House Judiciary Committee, 17

House-Senate Intelligence Review of 9/11, 10

Howard Hughes Medical Institute (HHMI), 513, 517

Hubbert, Dr. M. King, 28-29, 35, 565-566

Huffman Aviation, 350

Hussein, Saddam, 7, 71, 101, 426, 452, 529

hydrocarbon energy, 19-20, 26, 28, 42
    demand for, 29-31,
    and food, 24-25

I

ICTS, 259

Independent news service, 70

Independent, 59, 75, 98

Independent 9/11 Commission, 148, 224, 344, 362, 370, 385, 389-401, 410, 417, 418, 422, 428, 430, 433, 434-443, 445, 448, 450, 456, 461, 466, 470, 472, 536, 590
    and Rudolph Giuliani, 404-409, 411
    timeline, 399

Inderfurth, Karl "Rick", 103, 105, 108-110, 112-114, 467, 576

India, 95, 100, 102, 106, 204, 228, 535, 546, 547, 551, 552, 558

Indonesia, 544, 546, 547, 549, 550-553

Insider trading, 238-253, 468

Insight Magazine, 55, 241, 247, 251

Inter Services Intelligence (ISI), 103-105, 108, 115, 117-122, 135, 137, 138, 228, 234

International Energy Agency (IEA), 37, 547, 551, 558, 559, 560, 567

International Foundation for Privatization and Private Investment (FPI), 90

International Monetary Fund (IMF), 25, 58, 76, 78, 88, 89, 91, 527, 552

Iran, 71, 83, 85
   and oil, 31, 35, 44, 45, 108, 535
Iran-Contra, xv, xvii, 17, 54, 55, 66,
   71, 109, 131-133, 145, 170, 181,
   182, 452-454, 475, 478
Iranian National Oil Company, 31
Iraq, 7, 16, 71
   invasion, xv, 15, 26, 39, 42, 46, 74-
   75, 139-143, 471, 527, 530, 532,
   592-593
   and oil, 31, 35, 44, 45, 96, 100-
   102, 108, 146, 533, 535, 538
   oil fields, Appendix C
   torture in, 565
   and UN resolutions, 258
Iraqi National Congress, 101
Israel, 150, 155, 232, 254-268, 470
   and art students, 261-264, 265
   and Congress, 266
   and UN resolutions, 258-259
   joint US operations, 578-579
Israeli Mossad, 156, 157, 160, 163,
   170, 231, 481, 578-579
Izvetsia, 185-186

J
Jabber, Paul, 7-8
James Baker Institute, 91
Japan, 544, 546, 547, 548, 552
"Japan and China Battle for Russia's Oil
   and Gas," 46
Japan Today, 98
Japan Tobacco, 80
Jellinek, Michael, 334, 335
Jennings, Peter, 54
Jensen-Stevenson, Monika, 178, 179,
   191,
Johnson, Loch K., 110, 153
Johnson, Lyndon B. (LBJ), 70
Joint Chiefs of Staff (JCS), 335, 337-
   339, 351, 354, 360, 367, 368-369,
   390

Joule, James Prescott, 28
JPMorgan Chase, 77, 567-568
Judicial Watch, 42, 43, 44, 45, 129,
   130, 206

K
Kane, Michael, 393-396, 402-403
Karzai, Hamid, 99
Kashagan, 33, 51, 96
Kazakhstan, 51, 68, 88, 94, 95, 475
Kean Commission, *See* Independent
   9/11 Commission
Kean, Thomas, 373, 398, 401, 403
Kellogg, Brown and Root (KBR), 75,
   541
Kennedy, John Franklin (JFK), 17
Kennedy, Robert F. (RFK), 17, 111, 504
Kerrey, Bob, 465, 466
Kerry, John, 90, 182, 452, 593
Khalilzad, Zalmay, 98
Khashoggi, Adnan, 132, 145
Khomeini, Ayatollah, 83
Kissinger, Henry, 83, 95, 492, 553
Klare, Michael, 41, 44, 46, 47
Klayman, Larry, 43, 130, 206
Kosovo, 71, 73, 116, 208, 580
Kosovo Liberation Army (KLA), 71, 73,
   132, 134-137, 576
Kroll Inc., 423, 425
Krongard, A. B. "Buzzy", 56, 244-247,
   250, 251
Kurds, 7, 8, 71, 475, 536
Kuwait, 33, 35, 149

L
Laherrere, Jean H., 30, 557
Langley Air Force Base, 401, 409
Laos, 9, 59, 73, 83, 132, 179
Leach, James, 92
Leahy, Patrick, 269-271, 486
Lehder, Carlos, 57, 74
Lehman, John, 390, 391, 396, 461

Leidig, Charles J. Jr., 384, 388-391, 395, 401, 402
Leonard, George, 66
Leveraged Buyout (LBO), 51, 60
Levin, Carl, 76-77
Lexington Insurance, 57
Libby, I. Lewis, 530
Liquefied Natural Gas (LNG), 28, 33, 95, See also natural gas
Lockheed- Martin, 79, 497
"Longage of Critters" Problem, The, 39
Los Angeles Times, 36, 71, 111, 219

M
Marcello, Carlos, 6
Maresca, John J., 97
Marr, Robert, 334, 341, 366
Massoud, Commander, 113,
Mayor's Office of Emergency Management (OEM), 405, 406, 407, 418, 422, 423, 429
McCarthy, John, 180, 181, 184,
McCoy, Alfred W., 67, 83
McCoy, Bill, 153, 154, 158-160
McDade, Sean, 152, 159, 162, 163, 165, 168,
McKinney, Cynthia, 266-267, 271-279, 301, 594
McLaughlin, John, 184,
McNamara, Joseph, 18
Meacher, Michael, 42
Medellin Cartel, 57, 70, 74
Meese, Ed, 155, 159
Merrill Lynch, 239, 246
Mexico, 44, 64, 65, 78, 169
Meyssan, Thierry, 351
microbiologists, deaths of, 510-524
Middle East, the, 29, 31, 32, 34, 47, 64, 71, 80, 82, 90, 96, 102, and China, 551, 552 and US policy, 528-529, 530, 535, 546, 552, 554, 563, 575

Military District of Washington, 10
Milosevic, Slobodan, 134,
Minerals Management Service (MMS), 35
Mineta, Norman, 338, 348, 354, 378
Monbiot, George, 42
Monde Diplomatique, Le, 58, 77
Morales, Jorge, 67
Morgan Stanley, 239, 246
Moussaouia, Zacarias, 208-214, 218, 230, 231, 290, 344, 396
Mueller, Robert, 12, 205, 207-209, 212, 217, 218, 221, 222
Muhammad, Khalid Shaikh, 122, 129, 343, 580
Musharraf, Pervez, 99, 100, 105, 115,
Muslims, 44, 146, 207, 255, 544, 554
Myers, Richard, 331, 333, 338, 339, 354, 365, 368, 396-397, 592

N
Nabisco, 62
Nafeez, Ahmed, article, 314-316
Naik, Niaz, 107, 108
NASDAQ, 50
National Command Authority (NCA), 346, 354, 377, 383, 407, 408, 411
National Energy Policy (NEP), 24, 32, 35, 41, 467
National Energy Policy Development Group (NEPDG), 24, 32, 35, 36, 37, 42, 574
National Liberation Army (ELN), 540-541
National Military Command Center (NMCC), 384, 385, 387, 389-390, 401-402
National Reconnaissance Office (NRO), 11, and CIA, 340-341
National Security Act of 1947, 53
National Security Agency (NSA), 152, 219, 228-232, 342, 350-351

National Security Council (NSC), xv, 66, 98, 100

National Special Security Events (NSSE), 430-432

National Transportation and Safety Board, 389

Natural gas, 19, 22-24, 27-28, 32, 33, 36, 62, 85, 95, 96, *See also* Liquified Natural Gas

Naylor, R.T., 59

Nazarbayev, Nursultan, 102

Negroponte, John, 453, 476

New York Stock Exchange (NYSE), 56

New York Times, xiii, 31, 46, 75, 101, 129, 130, 144, 148, 206, 223, 343, 510, 515
  articles, 97, 240-241, 253, 372, 373-374, 454-455

Newsweek, 126, 223, 224
  article, 349, 454-456

Nguyen, Set Van, 511, 515

Nicaraguan Humanitarian Assistance Office (NHAO), 66

Nigeria, 26, 31, 46, 538, 539

9/11, covert operations, 259-265
  attacks, 82, 106, 109, 118, 119, 308-332

9/11 timeline, 319-330, 434
  variations, 358

9/11 Truth Movement, xix, 404

Nixon, Richard, 18, 54, 82

Niyazov, 100

Nordex, 90

North American Aerospace Defense Command (NORAD), 310, 315-316, 332, 334-348, 354, 357-375, 378, 383-384, 390, 414, 429, 430, 437-445
  on 9/11, 396, 397, 402, 408
  9/11 timeline, 399

Northern Alliance, 104, 105, 118

NORTHCOM, 534

Northeast Air Defense Sector (NEADS), 310, 334, 341-342, 348
  and FAA, 395
  scramble order, 401, 410

Northern Viligance, 339-340, 342, 359, 366, 367, 390

North, Oliver, xv, 55, 66, 71, 164, 170, 181, 182, 454

North Sea, 33, 36, 528

North Tower, 387, 388, 408, 411

Nugan-Hand, 54

Nunez, Moises, 66

O

Odigo, 262

OEM, *See* Mayor's Office of Emergency Management

Office of Strategic Services (OSS), 53, 54, 57, 67

Oil supply and demand, 22-40, 94-102, 528
  9/11, 467-468

Oil and Global Recession, 37

Oil Crash and You, The, 37

Oil: The Illusion Of Plenty, 42

O'Neill, John, 97, 99, 388, 423-426, 468, 583

1 WTC, 400

Operation Northwoods, 9, 351, 353, 575 Appendix A

Opposition Force (OPFOR), 578-579

Orejuela, Gilberto Rodriguez, 73, 74

Orejuela, Miguel, 74

Organization of Petroleum Exporting Countries (OPEC), 29, 34, 35, 82, 96, 535, 538, 542, 543, 564-566

Organized Crime Intelligence Division (OCID), 5, 6

Osborne, Mike, 291

Otis Air Force Base, 401, 409-410

Overseas Private Investment Corporation (OPIC), 72, 89

P

Pakistan, 59, 71, 75, 83, 95-100, 103-122, 135-137, 204, 228, 467, 534, 535, 552

Pasechnik, Vladimir, 511, 515-516, 517, 518

Pastora, Eden, 67

Patrick, William C. III, 518

Patriot Act (HR3162), 43, 270, 396, 471, 477, 482, 483-489, 522, 593

Patriot Act II, 43, 489-491

Pavitt, James, 108

Peak Oil, 23, 26, 31-33, 47, 49, 82, 96, 98, 467, 472, 539, 554-569

Pearl, Daniel, 121-122

Pentagon, 9, 99, 188, 434
attack, 119, 131, 207, 210, 348, 351, 372, 373-374, 388, 401, 408, 409, 577, 589
funding of, 497-500
as wargame target, 344, 345, 360, 375
See also Flight 77; "phantom flight"

Pentagon Mass Casualty Exercise, 10-11

People's Tribunal, 16, 17

Perle, Richard, 531-532

Perot, Ross, 165, 178-180

Persian Gulf, 31, 44, 530

Peru, 59, 540, 541-542

Petroleum Man, 26, 40

Pfeiffer, Dale Allen, 28-29, 34, 35, 38
article, 545-553

"phantom flight," 394, 400-401

Philip Morris, 60, 61, 80

Phillips, Kevin, 69

Philippines, 46, 544, 549, 550, 552, 553, 575

Phoenix memo, 207-218

phone bridges, 383-385, 386, 388, 390, 391, 399, 402, 408

Pitt, Harvey, 81

Poindexter, John, 453, 454, 478, 479

Policy Analysis Market, 253

Politics of Heroin, The, 67

Por Esto, 79

Port Authority, 387, 405-406, 411

Portuguese News, article, 581-583

Powderburns, 67

Powell, Colin, 119, 120, 132, 142

Powers, Tyrone, 219, 220

Press Enterprise, 64

Preston, Richard, 37

Price, Dr. John, 37-38

Price-To-Earnings Ratio (P/E or "the pop"), 52

pro forma accounting, 60, 496

Project Bojinka, 343, 347, 577

Project for a New American Century (PNAC), 42, 101, 530, 531-532, 575, 587

Project on Government Oversight, 343, 344, 365

PROMIS, 152-173, 234, 242, 245, 249, 250, 268, 458, 468, 477, 478, 492, 510-511, 518-520, 592

Public Health Security and Bioterrorism Response Act (HR3448), 521-523

put options, *See* insider trading

Putin, Vladimir, 136, 185, 222, 233

Q

Qaddafy, Muammar, 137, 138, 183, 237

Que, Benito, 505, 512-513, 517

R

Racketeering Influenced and Corrupt Organizations (RICO), 80

Ramares, Kellia, 524-526

RAND Corporation, 12, 226

Rarey, Jim, 450, 457, 459

Raytheon, 353-354

Reed, Terry, 181-183, 207

remotely piloted vehicles (RPVs), 347, 351-352, 581-586, 587

Reno, Janet, 12, 457
Revolutionary Armed Forces of
    Columbia (FARC), 57, 74, 540-541
Rice, Condoleezza, 10, 11, 12, 51, 94,
    119-121, 222, 433, 455-457, 473,
    573
Richardson, Bill, 112, 114,
Riconosciuto, Michael, 157, 158, 163,
    165
Ridgeway, James, 10, 149
Riyadh, 44
RJReynolds, 62, 80
Rocca, Christina, 99
Rockefeller, David, 32, 83
Roemer, Tim, 395, 396, 398, 461
Rohrabacher, Dana, 111-114
Roosevelt, Franklin, administration, 9
Rowley, Colleen, 208, 209, 214, 219,
    468, 579
Roy, Oliver, 104
Royal Dutch Shell, 35-36, 94
Rubin, Robert, 78
Rumsfeld, Donald, 333, 334-335, 354,
    384, 385, 464, 466, 474, 476, 481,
    535
Russia, 46, 56, 69-73, 77, 79, 82-85, 98,
    101, 105-107, 132, 137, 194, 557
    economy, 87-94,
Russian Mafia, 73, 149
Ryder Scott Co, 36

S
San Francisco Chronicle, 243
San Jose Mercury News, xvii, 17
Saudi Arabia, 85, 99, 104, 123-150,
    565, 576
    and 9/11, 536, 577
    and oil, 31, 44-45, 47, 57, 96, 108,
    535-538, 543, 557-558, 562-564
    oil fields, Appendix C
Saudi Binladen Group (SBG), 104,
    126, 127-129, 143, 355

Scalia, Antonin, and Cheney, 43-44, 574
Schiavo, Mary, 312, 316-318
Schlumberger, 458, 459
Schwartz, Robert M., 511, 514-515,
    517
Scott, Peter Dale, 57, 67, 75, 104, 146,
    154, 233
Secret Service, 1, 43, 375, 384, 388,
    391, 410, 411, 423, 427-436, 583
Securities and Exchange Commission
    (SEC), 54, 81, 239, 242-243, 250,
    253
Security Control of Air Traffic and Air
    Navigation Aids (SCATANA), 347,
    348
SETCO, 66
7 WTC, 583
Seymour, Cheri, 157-159, 162, 163, 168
Shackley, Ted, 73, 83, 132, 176
Shah of Iran, 7
Sharon, Ariel, 259
Shattuck, Mayo, 251
Sheehan, Michael, 113
Sheikh, Omar Saeed, 118, 121, 468
Sheirer, Richard, 406
Shell, See Royal Dutch Shell
Siberia, 46, 72, 73, See also Russia
Sierra Club, 43
Silk Road Energy Strategy, 101-102
Simmons, Matthew, 37-38, 557, 558-
    559, 560-562, 568
Simmons, Tom, 105, 108,
Slansky, Paul, 175, 188-190, 194, 196,
    199, 298
Smallpox, 493, 506-508, 515, 522,
    523, 525, 526
Smith, Walter Bedell, 57
Smith, William French, 63
Solntsevo family, 72
Sony, 61
Soros, George, 503
South China Sea, 529, 544, 549, 550

South Tower, 338, 350, 388, 408, 409, 411

Soviet Union, the former, 34, 73, 84, 87, 93, 94, 135
and Afghanistan, 83, 134

Sporkin, Judge Stanley, xvii, 54-57, 183

Standard Oil, 53

State Department, 12, 99, 101

Stephens, Jackson, 159, 160, 163, 172

Stevens, Ted, 43

Sullivan and Cromwell, 53-54

Summers, Lawrence, 88

Supreme Court, 109, 223, 574

System Planning Corp., 584-585

T

Taglieri, Joe, article, 529-532

Tajikistan, 105, 106

Talbot, Strobe, 105

Taliban, 68, 84, 85, 86, 93-99, 103-115, 125, 576, *See also* al Qaeda

T&G Aviation, 64

Tarim Basin, 548

Tenet, George, 17, 56, 115, 118, 120, 222, 245, 458, 465, 565

Tengiz, 33, 96

Texaco, 94

Thailand, 59, 73

Thompson, Jim, 460, 461

Thompson, Larry, 81

Thompson, Paul, 86, 94, 107, 121, 125-127, 133, 146, 148, 319, 404

Total Information Awareness (TIA), 492

Trans Latin Air, 64-65

transponders, 310-313, 401, 584

Treasury notes, 243

Trilateral Commission, 32, 83, 90, 472, 576

Tripod II, 403, 412, 414, 423, 425, 432, 583
and Guiliani, 404-411

Truthout, 41

Turkmenistan, 33, 88, 95, 96, 97, 99, 100, 191

Twin Towers, 388, 401, 590, *See also* North Tower; South Tower

Tyndall Air Force Base, 334, 354, 362, 364

Tyree, William, 152, 154, 156, 158-160, 162-164, 166-168, 173, 182-184

U

UAL Corp, 238, 246, 248, 250

Unanswered Questions, 317, 404

UNICOR, 494

Union Bank of Switzerland, 61

United Arab Emirates (UAE), 44

United Nations (UN), 58, 105-107, 258-259, 532

United Nations Drug Control Programme (UNDCP), 59

Unocal, 86, 94, 95, 97, 98, 99, 104, 128

Uppsala Protocol, 563

Uribe, Alvaro, 74

US Agency for International Development (USAID), 86, 90

USA Today, 345, 347, 348, 360, 506

US Army Corps of Engineers, 75

US economy, 493-505

US Forest Service, 63

US Geological Survey (USGS), 33, 34, 35

US Supreme Court, 41, 43

US Treasury, 61, 88, 295

Uzbekistan, 105-107, 186, 475

V

Vaccines, 490, 493, 505-508, 513, 516, 519-520, 521-524, 526

Vendrell, Francesc, 105, 108

Venezuela, 31, 35, 46, 542-544

Veniste, Ben, 386-397

Vietnam, 73, 83
Vietnam War, 9, 70, 82, 132, 176, 181
Vigilant Guardian, 335, 337-338, 340-342, 359-361, 363, 364, 365, 390
Vigilant Warrior, 338-340, 359, 361, 365, 368
Village Voice, 10, 125, 149
Vinnell Corporation, 71, 536
Voice of America, 46, 539
Vreeland, Mike, 175-178, 183-191, 193-198, 227, 291-305, 468, 577, 578
    FIN documents, Appendix B

W
Walker, David, 43
Wall Street, 46-47, 50, 53-55, 57, 61, 69, 90
Wall Street Journal, 130-131, 134
Wanta, Leo, 295-296
War on Freedom, 104, 112
Wargames, 11, 310, 333-356, 393-403, 412, 414, 423, 432, 433, 583-585, 587
"War on Terrorism is Bogus, The," 42
Washington Post, xiii, 100, 102, 106, 120,142, 148, 215, 486, 497, 499, 505, 515
    articles, 86, 95, 125, 136, 565-566
Waters, Maxine, 16, 17, 63
Waxman, Henry, 43, 75, 487
Webb, Gary, xvii, 16-17, 62, 67, 219
Weill, Gotschall, and Manges, 55
Wellstone, Paul, 279-290
West Africa, 31, 46, 537-538
Whirlpool, 61
White House Energy Task Force, 41
White, Thomas, 75
Wiley, Donald C., 511, 513-514, 517

Williams, Kenneth, 207, 208, 214, 216, 230
Williamson, Anne, 88-90, 93
Wilson, Edwin (Ed), 132, 158, 177, 183-184, 191
Winfield, Montague, 389, 391, 402, 592
Winokur, Herbert "Pug", 79, 520
Wolfensohn, James, 68
Wolfowitz, Paul, 464,466, 530-531
Wood Mackenzie, 36
Woody Box, 587-589
World Assembly of Muslim Youth (WAMY), 147, 203, 204
World Bank, 25, 68, 78, 88, 89, 527, 552
World Trade Center (WTC), 14, 257, 405, 577
    attacks, 14, 97, 99, 185, 193, 210, 233, 335, 344, 379, 383, 387, 388
    bombing, 207, 216, 235, 343, 423
    as wargames target, 345, 360
    See also Twin Towers; North Tower; South Tower
World Trade Organization, 76, 551
World War II, 9, 38, 40, 53, 57, 67
Wright, Robert Jr., 204-207, 216, 217, 234

Y
Yeltsin, Boris, 88, 89
Youngquist, Walter, 39
Yousef, Ramzi, 343

Z
Zakheim, Dov, 254, 583-584, 586-587
Zelikow, Philip, 372, 373, 374, 454-457, 472

Glossary of Acronyms

ABC American Broadcast Corporation

ACLU American Civil Liberties Union

ADDO Associate Deputy Director of Operations

ADFA Arkansas Development Financial Authority

ADL Anti-Defamation League of B'nai Brith

AFB Air Force Base

AFNSEP The Air Force National Security Emergency Preparedness Agency

AFP Agence France Presse

AI Artificial Intelligence

AIG American International Group

AIPAC American Israeli Public Affairs Committee

AOL America Online

AP Associated Press

ARDA Advanced Research and Development Activity

ASPO Association for the Study of Peak Oil and Gas

BBRDW Bishop, Baldwin, Rewald, Dillingham, and Wong

BCCI Bank of Credit and Commerce International

BND Bundesnachrichtendienst

BP British Petroleum-Amoco

C3 Command, Control, Communications

CATF Central American Task Force

CBOE Chicago Board Options Exchange

CIA Central Intelligence Agency

CSIS Canadian Security and Intelligence Service

CFR Council on Foreign Relations

CLEMARS California Law Enforcement Mutual Aid Radio System

CNN Cable News Network

COG Continuity of Government

CONR CONUS NORAD Region

CONUS Continental United States

CPC Caspian Pipeline Consortium

CPI Center for Public Integrity

CSG Crisis Strategy Group

DA District Attorney

DARPA Defense Advanced Research Projects Agency

DEA Drug Enforcement Administration

DDO Deputy Director of Operations

DHS Department of Homeland Security

DoD Department of Defense

DOE US Department of Energy

DoJ Department of Justice

EIA Energy Information Administration

ELINT electronic intelligence

ELN National Liberation Army

EPA Environmental Protection Agency

EST Emergency Response Team

EU European Union

EXIM Export-Import Bank

FAA Federal Aviation Administration

FARC Revolutionary Armed Forces of Columbia

FAZ Frankfurter Algemeine Zeitung
FBI Federal Bureau of Investigation
FBIHQ Federal Bureau of Investigation headquarters
FDA Food and Drug Administration
FDNY Fire Department of New York
FEMA Federal Emergency Management Agency
FISA Foreign Intelligence Surveillance
FOIA Freedom of Information Act
FPI International Foundation for Privatization and Private Investment
FRS Federal Reserve System
FSB Russian Federal Security Service
FSC Family Steering Committee
FSU Former Soviet Union
FTW From The Wilderness
FutureMAP Futures Markets Applied to Prediction
GAO General Accounting Office
GDP Gross Domestic Product
GID General Intelligence Division
GM General Motors
GNP Gross National Product
GPS Global Positioning Systems
HHMI Howard Hughes Medical Institute
HHS Department of Health and Human Services
HUD Department of Housing and Urban Development
HUMINT human intelligence
ICBM Intercontinental Ballistic and Cruise Missiles
IEA International Energy Agency
IG Inspector General
HIS Institute for Housing and Urban Development Studies
IMF International Monetary Fund
INDG International Network on Disarmament and Globalization

INSNA International Network for Social Network Analysis
ISA Intelligence Support Activity
ISI Inter Services Intelligence
JCS Joint Chiefs of Staff
JFK John Fitzgerald Kennedy
KBR Kellogg, Brown and Root
KGB Committee for State Security
KLA Kosovo Liberation Army
LAPD Los Angeles Police Department
LBJ Lyndon B. Johnson
LBO Leveraged Buyout
LNG Liquefied Natural Gas
MIA Missing in Action
MMS Minerals Management Service
MVD Ministry of Internal Affairs
NAFTA North American Free Trade Agreement
NATO North American Trade Organization
NCA National Command Authority
NCR National Capital Region
NEADS Northeast Air Defense Sector
NEP National Energy Policy
NEPDG National Energy Policy Development Group
NHAO Nicaraguan Humanitarian Assistance Office
NMCC National Military Command Center
NOC non-official cover
NORAD North American Aerospace Defense Command
NPR National Public Radio
NRO National Reconnaissance Office
NSA National Security Agency
NSC National Security Council
NSLU National Security Law Unit
NSSE National Special Security Events
NTSB National Transportation and Safety Board

NYPD New York Police Department
NYSE New York Stock Exchange
OCID Organized Crime Intelligence Division
OECD Organization for Economic Co-operation and Development
OEM Office of Emergency Management
OGI Oil and Gas International
OPEC Organization of Petroleum Exporting Countries
OPIC Overseas Private Investment Corporation
OPR Office of Professional Responsibility
OSS Office of Strategic Services
P2OG Proactive Preemptive Operating Group
PBS Public Broadcasting System
PDB Presidential Daily Briefing
PDD Presidential Decision Directives
P/E or "the pop" price-to-earnings ratio
PEOC Emergency Operations Center
PFIAB President's Foreign Intelligence Advisory Board
PNAC Project for a New American Century
POW Prisoners of War
PROMIS Prosecutor's Management Information System
PSA Production Sharing Agreement
RCMP Royal Canadian Mounted Police
READI Response to Emergencies and Disasters Institute

RFID Radio Frequency ID
RFK Robert F. Kennedy
RFU Radical Fundamentalist Unit
RICO Racketeering Influenced and Corrupt Organizations
RJR RJReynolds
RPVs Remotely piloted vehicles
SAC Special Agent in Charge
SBG Saudi Binladen Group
SCATANA Security Control of Air Traffic and Air Navigation Aids
SEC Securities and Exchange Commission
SIGINT signals intelligence
SMART Self Managing Artificial Reasoning Technology
SSA Supervisory Special Agent
TIA Total Information Awareness
UAE United Arab Emirates
UAE United Arab Emirates
UBL Osama bin Laden
UN United Nations
UNDCP United Nations Drug Control Programme
US&R Urban Search & Rescue teams
USAID US Agency for International Development
USGS US Geological Survey
WAMY World Assembly of Muslim Youth
WSJ Wall Street Journal
WTC World Trade Center

ABOUT THE AUTHOR

MIKE RUPPERT, 53, is the Publisher/Editor of *From the Wilderness* (*FTW*), a newsletter he founded in March 1998 by mailing out 68 copies to friends and researchers. *FTW* is now read by more than 16,000 subscribers in 40 countries, including 40 members of the US Congress, the intelligence committees of both houses, and professors at 30 universities around the world. Through the newsletter and his website, Mike has pioneered innovative analysis and groundbreaking original stories on the impact of the $5-600 billion in drug money that moves through the US economy each year and the illegal covert operations which maintain control of that cash flow for US economic interests.

Since September 11, 2001, he has been the point man in breaking major stories involving government foreknowledge of, and participation in, the attacks and has also pioneered the effort to educate the world about the consequences of Peak Oil — the fact that the world is running out of hydrocarbon energy and what this might mean for human civilization — and its direct connection to September 11. He has given more than 40 lectures in eight countries on the subjects of 9/11, the war on terror, and Peak Oil, his work being recognized by leading political and economic figures in the US, Britain, France and, especially, Germany.

An Honors graduate of UCLA in Political Science, Mike is a former Los Angeles Police Department (LAPD) narcotics investigator who discovered CIA trafficking in drugs in 1977. After attempting to expose this, he was forced out of LAPD in 1978 while earning the highest rating reports possible and having no pending disciplinary actions. Signifying the credibility which Mike has achieved, in August 2004 he was an invited evening speaker at San Francisco's famed Commonwealth Club.

From the Wilderness can be found at: www.fromthewilderness.com

If you have enjoyed *Crossing the Rubicon,* you might enjoy other

BOOKS TO BUILD A NEW SOCIETY

Our books provide positive solutions for people who want
to make a difference. We specialize in:

• **Conscientious Commerce** • **Progressive Leadership**
• **Sustainable Living** • **Ecological Design and Planning**
• **Natural Building & Appropriate Technology** • **New Forestry**
• **Educational and Parenting Resources** • **Environment and Justice**
• **Resistance and Community** • **Nonviolence**

New Society Publishers

ENVIRONMENTAL BENEFITS STATEMENT

New Society Publishers has chosen to produce this book on recycled paper made
with **100% post consumer waste**, processed chlorine free, and old growth free.
For every 5,000 books printed, New Society saves the following resources:[1]

73	Trees
6,587	Pounds of Solid Waste
7,248	Gallons of Water
9,454	Kilowatt Hours of Electricity
11,975	Pounds of Greenhouse Gases
52	Pounds of HAPs, VOCs, and AOX Combined
18	Cubic Yards of Landfill Space

[1]Environmental benefits are calculated based on research done by the Environmental Defense Fund and
other members of the Paper Task Force who study the environmental impacts of the paper industry.
Contact the EDF for more information on this environmental benefits statement, a copy of their report,
and the latest updates on their data.

For a full list of NSP's titles, please call **1-800-567-6772** *or check out our web site at:*

www.newsociety.com

NEW SOCIETY PUBLISHERS